Article 102 TFEU

Article 102 TFEU

Past, Present and Future

Edited by

Assimakis Komninos
Ekaterina Rousseva

Wolters Kluwer

Published by:
Kluwer Law International B.V.
PO Box 316
2400 AH Alphen aan den Rijn
The Netherlands
E-mail: lrs-sales@wolterskluwer.com
Website: www.wolterskluwer.com/en/solutions/kluwerlawinternational

Sold and distributed by:
Wolters Kluwer Legal & Regulatory U.S.
920 Links Avenue
Landisville, PA 17538
United States of America
E-mail: customer.service@wolterskluwer.com

ISBN 978-94-035-0699-9

e-Book: ISBN 978-94-035-0709-5
web-PDF: ISBN 978-94-035-0719-4

Editors

Dr Assimakis Komninos, is a Partner at White & Case LLP, a visiting professor at Panthéon-Assas University Paris II and a Member of the Executive Committee of the Global Competition Law Centre (GCLC) of the College of Europe.

Dr Ekaterina Rousseva, is a Member of the Legal Service of the European Commission, President of the Bulgarian Competition Law Association and a Member of the Executive Committee of the Global Competition Law Centre (GCLC) of the College of Europe.

Contributors

Christian Ahlborn, is a Partner at Covington & Burling LLP in Brussels.

Dr Thomas Buettner, is a case manager at the Chief Economist Team of DG Competition of the European Commission and co-coordinator of the Chief Economist Team's work on antitrust cases and policy.

Fernando Castillo de la Torre, is Principal Legal Adviser, head of the competition and mergers team in the Legal Service of the European Commission.

Clara Chambrey, is an Elève-Avocate specialising in competition and international trade law. She completed her LLM at the College of Europe and obtained a Master's degree from University Paris Panthéon-Assas in European Law.

Dr Magali Eben, is Senior Lecturer in Competition Law at the University of Glasgow, where she directs the programme in International Competition Law and Policy. She is Deputy Director of CREATe, the Centre for Regulation of the Creative Economy, core funded by the AHRC as UK research infrastructure, with a focus on the regulation of creativity, technology and markets.

Dr Liza Lovdahl Gormsen, is a Senior Research Fellow and Director for the Competition Law Forum at the British Institute of International and Comparative Law. She is also a Senior Director at Forward Global and the claimant in *Dr Liza Lovdahl Gormsen v. Meta Platforms, Inc. and Others*.

Luc Gyselen, is Senior counsel at Arnold & Porter LLP, assessor at the Belgian Competition Authority (BMA) and maître de conference at the Law Department of the ULiège.

Massimiliano (Max) Kadar, is Head of Unit A.4 at the Directorate General for Competition (DG COMP) of the European Commission, in charge of coordinating the work of the European Competition Network (ECN) and shaping the Commission's private enforcement policy. An official at the European Commission since 2011, Max is also a visiting lecturer at Freie Universität Berlin and a former visiting lecturer at King's College London.

Krystyna Kowalik-Bańczyk, PhD, LLM (Bruges), DEA (Toulouse), is a Polish judge at the General Court of the European Union since 2016 and has been serving as President of the court's seventh chamber since 2022. Krystyna is also an associate professor of European Law and Competition Law at the Institute of Law Studies, Polish Academy of Sciences, Warsaw.

Sir Philip Lowe, is a former Director-General for Development (1997), Competition (2002-2010) and Energy (2010-2014) at the European Commission and a former non-executive Board Member of the UK Competition and Markets Authority. Currently, he is a Partner at Oxera and a Senior Adviser with Kekst-CNC.

Linsey McCallum, is Deputy Director-General for Antitrust and Regulation of Digital Platforms in the Directorate-General for Competition (DG COMP) of the European Commission.

Giorgio Monti, is Professor of Competition Law at Tilburg University and Research Fellow at the Centre on Regulation in Europe (CERRE).

Dimitrios Nikolaidis, is a Trainee Lawyer at Simpson Thacher & Bartlett LLP, with LLM degrees in European Law from the College of Europe and the University of Athens.

Dr Jorge Padilla, is Chair of Compass Lexecon International. Dr Padilla earned M Phil and D Phil degrees in Economics from the University of Oxford. He is a Founding Fellow of the Royal Economic Society (RES, London), Senior Fellow of George Washington Innovation and Competition Lab (GWU, Washington DC), Research Fellow at the Centro de Estudios Monetarios y Financieros (CEMFI, Madrid), and teaches competition economics at the Toulouse School of Economics (TSE).

Luc Peeperkorn, was Principal Expert Antitrust Policy at DG Competition of the European Commission, a Senior Emile Noël Fellow at the Jean Monnet Center and professor at the College of Europe in Natolin and is currently still teaching at the Brussels School of Competition.

Álvaro Salgado Carranza, is a lawyer in the Antitrust and Competition department of Weil, Gotshal & Manges LLP, in their Brussels office.

Georgia Theodorakopoulou, is an Associate at the Brussels office of Grimaldi Alliance and an Editor at the Journal of European Competition Law & Practice (OUP).

Summary of Contents

Table of Contents

Speech by EVP Margrethe Vestager at the Global Competition Law Centre, College of Europe: Article 102 – The Beating Heart of Antitrust in the EU

Good morning.

It's so nice to be back at the College of Europe!

I am very grateful for your invitation to speak today, on Article 102. Our work against abuses of dominance is constantly evolving and modernizing. And very recently, our work in this area has become oddly controversial.

So I am grateful that we can talk about this topic today, in the setting of the College of Europe. This is a place where we are held to the highest academic standards. This is a place where we can have an honest discussion, grounded in reality and experience. I will open that discussion today with words on the goals of Article 102 enforcement, recent trends, and its future.

Article 102 and the consumer welfare standard

First, let us speak frankly about the goals of Article 102.

In the last few weeks, there has been a very public controversy on the focus of antitrust enforcement. Commentators say that our focus is too limited. The story that is being told is that we focus narrowly on price effects. That we are stuck with an outdated consumer welfare standard. And in contrast, we are told, our US colleagues have endorsed a broader approach, more relevant to the challenges of our times. In the US, they consider the welfare of competitors, workers, the wider society. So there is a divide between our two continents.

If you were a student at the College of Europe, and wrote that thesis, would you get a good grade?

Let's unpack this. First, the theory, then the practice.

Even in theory, the consumer welfare standard does not imply a narrow focus on price. Rather, Article 102 ensures that consumers in the EU get a fair deal out of the competitive process. Yes, the focus of enforcement is on consumers. But this is a very wide goal. From a legal perspective, the Court of Justice has held that Article 102 ensures well-being in the EU by preventing distortions to competition that harm the public interest. As a result, one ensures 'well-being in the EU' by tackling all sorts of anticompetitive effects, may they impact price, choice, diversity, quality or innovation.

We tackle these effects by preventing harm to the competitive process. Preserving a competitive process means protecting all customers. Not just end-consumers, but also industrial consumers that need competitive inputs, or SMEs that need competitive services, or public entities that need to procure equipment at competitive terms. It means focusing on efficiencies and preventing harm to innovation. It means antitrust rules support the entire economy's competitiveness.

Now let's look at the practice.

The *Google Android* case is a good recent example. This is a case where we tackled Google's abusive conduct to protect its position in search. This was not a case on anticompetitive pricing. It was about ensuring that rival search engines are not blocked from accessing the market. And that consumers have a choice as to how they get information on the internet. We found that Google's restrictions to services that give consumers more privacy or different types of searches were abusive. The Court confirmed most of our decision. And when it did, it recognized that protecting consumer choice, privacy and diversity is consistent with both competition and plurality in a democratic society.

Another good example: the *Amazon Marketplace* case. Again, this case was not at all concerned with price effects. The case focused on self-preferencing and consumer choice. We thought that Amazon abused its dominance by using the data of its marketplace sellers for its own benefit. We also thought that it was abusive for Amazon to give preference to its own retail arm for access to the Buy Box. Amazon offered commitments, which we accepted. And as a result, Amazon restored fairness in the way data is used and in the way its competitors market their products on its platform.

A 'narrow focus on price' is not what you take away from those cases. Rather, the consumer welfare standard has given us the possibility of exploring novel non-price effects. And in this regard, I think there is more convergence across the Atlantic now than there has ever been in the history of modern antitrust enforcement.

So how did we get there?

Article 102, in motion

The text of Article 102 itself has remained unchanged since the Rome Treaties. But our approach has evolved.

The recent history of enforcement takes us back to 2008. At the time, the Commission adopted its Guidance on 'enforcement priorities'. The goal was to prioritise conduct that would be most harmful for consumers. But that harm changed over time.

The most transformative change has been digitalisation. Enforcement in the past decade has tackled this head-on. And our interventions have often pushed the boundaries. In 2017, 2018 and 2019 we took three consecutive decisions that concerned Google's anticompetitive practices. We tackled self-preferencing, digital ecosystems and restrictions to protect Google's position in search and exclusive dealing in online search advertising. At times, we have explored and applied new theories of harm. At other times, we have used 'classic' theories of harm, such as tying and exclusivity, but in a new setting.

The strength of Article 102 is that it allows us to address a wide range of conduct, some of which were inconceivable in 1957. The result is that we constantly push the envelope, to be in tune with market evolutions. But we do not work in a vacuum and our effort also needs to be endorsed by the Court. Judicial review plays a crucial role to say whether we get it right. And in this dialogue with our judges, so far we see eye to eye. For the most part, our main decisions in digital markets were confirmed. I don't say this as a boast (all the more that some of these cases continue to be litigated and some of the lawyers are present in this room!). But to show that our judges understand and endorse the need for an evolving approach to unilateral conduct.

This approach is also applicable outside of digital markets. Take some of our investigations in the pharmaceutical sector, such as the ongoing *Teva Copaxone* and *Vifor* cases. In those cases, we are investigating disparagement. We are investigating whether taking advantage of regulatory loopholes to extend patents can be abusive. These are new areas of focus for the Commission under Article 102. Or look at the ongoing Greek electricity case, where we recently issued a statement of objections. In that SO, we tackle predatory pricing, which might have affected competition and deterred investment into alternative and more sustainable energy sources.

There is another trend, often overlooked, in modern antitrust enforcement. 15 years ago, we believed the most harmful cases consisted in exclusionary conduct. This is why we focused our Guidance on such practices. But we now see the resurgence of so-called 'exploitative' cases. And this is because we sometimes see that the exploitation of market power can also lead to significant harm for consumers.

This started with the *Aspen* case. The case concerned excessive pricing and our action led to the company cutting its price for critical cancer drugs. With our more recent action in digital markets, exploitative behaviour remains highly relevant. I would refer you to the ongoing Apple music streaming case. In that case, we are considering whether withholding information to users to avoid that they leave an app store is an abuse of dominance. I am also thinking about the Facebook Marketplace case, which is about Meta's tying its marketplace to its social network and, again, about the use of competitors' data to the benefit of Facebook Marketplace.

If there is a commonality to be found across those cases, it is our capacity to adapt. We place the focus of enforcement on the key factors of the markets we look at, may it be the use of competitors' data, the ability of a platform to self-promote, the implications of ecosystems or the extension of patents. By doing so, our enforcement keeps up with the times.

The future of Article 102

Now, I will finish with a few remarks on the future of Article 102.

First, I would acknowledge how influential Article 102 has been. If ex-ante regulation and Article 102 had a child, it would be the Digital Markets Act. The DMA incorporates many of the lessons learned from Article 102 enforcement. The DMA obligations and prohibitions will start applying on gatekeepers next week. And of course, as parents, we only want the best for our children. So we are determined for the DMA to be a success. But parents don't cease to exist when they have children. Rather, the DMA and antitrust enforcement are complementary. Because every conduct cannot fall into the DMA's neatly defined prohibitions, antitrust enforcement will continue to break new grounds in digital markets.

We also continue adapting the way in which we enforce Article 102. In the past 15 years, the case law on exclusionary abuses has developed substantially. We took stock of all this experience and amended the Guidance Paper in March last year. Doing so, we resolved the divergences between the Guidance Paper and our current enforcement practice.

Last March, we also announced that we would start working on the very first Guidelines on exclusionary abuses of dominance. This is still a work in progress, so I cannot be too specific. But I can say that, in carrying out this work, we apply two broad principles.

The first one is to ensure that our enforcement remains effective. There can be no doubt that an 'effects-based' approach is better tailored to market realities than a formalistic approach. But the effects-based approach does not exclude learning from experience. And if experience tells us that there are certain types of conduct that are particularly harmful for competition, then it should not be necessary to reinvent the wheel over and over again. This means that we will seek to maintain a 'workable' effects-based approach, which is informed by economic thinking and EU case law. I am hopeful that the outcome of this exercise will allow us to provide legal certainty to stakeholders and foster ex-ante compliance.

The second driving principle is that we are trying to tap into the knowledge of other enforcers. In the past 20 years of enforcement of antitrust rules under Regulation 1/2003, the ECN has emerged as a tight and focused enforcement community. In this community, Article 102 is a shared enforcement priority. In fact, most of the decisions taken under Article 102 are now adopted by the NCAs. That is why we are working on the new Guidelines very closely with our colleagues from the NCAs. By doing this, we hope that the Guidelines will lay out a framework that is representative not only of the Commission's enforcement practice, but also of the NCAs.

Conclusion

Let me now close with the idea that, indeed, Article 102 is the beating heart of EU antitrust enforcement. Like any muscle, the heart must exercise to keep in shape. We have been exercising intensely and we will continue to do so.

The Guidelines on exclusionary abuses will set the frame for future enforcement. We need to get them right. An important part of the exercise right now is to listen to the voices of academics and practitioners in the field – I'm pleased to see so many of you here today. Not to mention the students who have been invited to join. Your contribution will ensure that our direction of travel is the right one.

Thank you.

Introduction

Assimakis Komninos & Ekaterina Rousseva[*]

Article 102 TFEU has always inspired curious minds and challenged enforcers. Several decades after its inception, the concepts underlying it continue to trigger debates and inspire legal and economic research. At the same time, Article 102 TFEU is a vital instrument for the functioning of the internal market and for the well-being of the European Union, as acknowledged by the Court of Justice.[1]

Today, the challenges posed by the digitalisation of the economy and the speed with which markets emerge and firms grow, the need to stimulate innovation, the quest for resilience and sustainable development of the European economy, and the changing habits and needs of the European consumers make it even more important to better understand the potential of Article 102 TFEU and to keep it a sharp instrument.[2] This may explain the efforts that the European Commission is currently putting in preparing new guidelines for Article 102 TFEU, that will replace the 2008 Guidance Paper.[3] When the driving wheel needs to take a new turn, past experience is always instructive and inspirational. And the past experience with the application of Article 102 TFEU offers both.

* All views expressed are strictly personal and do not necessarily represent the views of the institutions with which the authors are affiliated.

1. *See* Judgment of the Court of 17 February 2011, *TeliaSonera*, Case C-52/09, ECLI:EU:C:2011:83, para. 22.
2. For a much broader context and perspective, *see* Assimakis Komninos and Alejandra Palacios, 'The "End of Competition Law"?', 20 Competition Law International 147 (2024); Andriani Kalintiri, 'EU Antitrust Law's Resilience: The Good, the Bad, and the Ugly', 43 Yearbook of European Law (13 January 2025) https://doi.org/10.1093/yel/yeae009 (last accessed 31 July 2025).
3. Communication from the Commission – Guidance on the Commission's enforcement priorities in applying Article 82 of the EC Treaty to abusive exclusionary conduct by dominant undertaking, OJ 2009/C 45/02.

After its inception, Article 102 TFEU (then Article 86 of the EEC Treaty) remained a dead letter for almost a decade.[4] The precise reasons for this are debatable but it appears that in view of the prevailing market structure and reviving business in post-war Europe, big firms were desired in order to bring scale and boost the economy.[5] It also appears that the concepts underlying the provision were too abstract to be attractive for application and putting them into operation required boldness.[6] From today's perspective, it is curious that the first cases concerned exploitative abuses,[7] and that the first important debate on Article 102 TFEU was on whether it was supposed to apply only to exploitative conduct or also to be extended to conduct that has an impact on the market structure (i.e., exclusion).[8] Once the dilemma was resolved in the seminal *Continental Can* case,[9] exclusionary abuses became the centre of gravity of the provision, and the debate shifted to how to assess them.

After the clarification of the notion of dominance in *United Brands* in 1978,[10] the next important step was made a year later in another seminal judgment – *Hoffmann-La Roche* – where the Court for the first time defined what exclusionary abuse is.[11] While this definition was later refined,[12] its foundations remained intact and today the assessment of exclusionary abuses still requires proving both recourse to means different from those governing normal competition (competition on the merits) and effects of hindering the maintenance of the degree of competition still existing in the market or the growth of that competition.

---

4. *See* I. Samkalden and Isaac E. Druker, 'Legal Problems Relating to Article 86 of the Treaty of Rome', 3 Common Market Law Review 158 (1965-66) https://doi.org/10.54648/cola1966012 (last accessed 31 July 2025).
5. *See* generally Arved Deringer, *The Competition Law of the European Economic Community: A Commentary on the EEC Rules of Competition (Article 85 to 90) Including the Implementing Regulations and Directives* (Commerce Clearing House: New York, 1968) 156; Corwin D. Edwards, *Controls of Cartels and Monopolies, An International Comparison* (Oceana Publications: Dobbs Ferry, 1967), Ekaterina Rousseva, *Rethinking Exclusionary Abuses in EU Competition Law* (Hart: Oxford/Portland, 2010), 59-60, 177.
6. David J. Gerber, *Law and Competition in Twentieth Century Europe: Protecting Prometheus* (Clarendon Press: Oxford, 1998) 356.
7. *See*, for example, Judgment of the Court of 29 February 1968, *Parke Davis*, Case 24/67, ECLI:EU:C:1968:11; Judgment of the Court of 18 February 1971, *Sirena*, Case 40/70, ECLI:EU:C:1971:18.
8. *See* the seminal book by the late Judge René Joliet, *Monopolization and Abuse of Dominant Position* (Martinus Nijhoff: The Hague, 1970). *See*, generally, Ekaterina Rousseva, *Rethinking Exclusionary Abuses in EU Competition Law* (Hart: Oxford/Portland, 2010); Pinar Akman, *The Concept of Abuse in EU Competition Law, Law and Economic Approaches* (Hart: Oxford/Portland, 2012).
9. Judgment of the Court of 21 February 1973, *Europemballage and Continental Can v. Commission*, Case 6/72, ECLI:EU:C:1973:22.
10. Judgment of the Court of 14 February 1978, *United Brands v. Commission*, Case 27/76, ECLI:EU:C:1978:22.
11. Judgment of the Court of 13 February 1979, *Hoffmann-La Roche v. Commission*, Case 85/76, ECLI:EU:C:1979:36.
12. *See*, for example, Judgment of the Court of 21 December 2023, *European Superleague*, Case C-333/21, ECLI:EU:C:2023:1011, para. 131; Judgment of the Court of 12 May 2022, *Servizio Elettrico Nazionale*, Case C-377/20, ECLI:EU:C:2022:379, para. 69; Judgment of the Court of 27 March 2012, *Post Danmark I*, Case C–209/10, EU:C:2012:172, para. 24.

Shortly after the notion of exclusionary abuse was defined, the concept of special responsibility of dominant undertakings was born in *Michelin I*[13] to become, and remains today, an inseparable part of the reasoning of every abuse case. Along with that, gradually, different tests for the assessment of different types of abuses – predatory pricing, rebates, refusal to deal, tying – emerged. Judgments like *Akzo,*[14] *Michelin I, Hilti*[15] and *Tetra Pak,*[16] *Magill,*[17] and *Bronner*[18] built the foundations.

At the turn of the new century, the so-called modernisation of EU law swept through existing procedural/institutional and substantive structures. On the procedural and institutional side, enforcement was decentralised and the European Commission's exclusive competence to grant exemptions under Article 101(3) TFEU was abolished. On the substantive side, modernisation took the form of the introduction of an effects-based approach that is focused on theories of harm rather than form (i.e., the external characteristics of conduct), no doubt because of the influence of merger control.[19] This meant greater reliance on industrial organisation economics. It started first with a reconsideration of the approach to vertical restraints, then the treatment of horizontal cooperation agreements, followed by a revision of the rules on merger control – to reach the assessment of unilateral conduct. And, indeed, in 2008 the Commission issued a Guidance paper on enforcement priorities for exclusionary abuse, suggesting a reinterpretation of the concept of abuse along the philosophy of the effects-based approach. Although both acclaimed and criticised, the 2008 Guidance Paper, and especially the general framework of assessment of abuse it offered, gave a new impetus to Article 102 TFEU and had undeniably an impact on the development of the case law.

The more recent debates have been centred around the implementation of the effects-based approach, its benefits and drawbacks. Cases like *Intel*[20] and *Google Shopping*[21] have kept the discussion practically oriented. A consensus seems to emerge on the need to preserve the effectiveness of Article 102 TFEU and to strengthen its capability to incentivise innovation. Similarly, there is little doubt that clarity and predictability are desired by all. Where views seem to diverge is on the means and the

13. Judgment of the Court of 9 November 1983, *Nederlandsche Banden Industrie Michelin v. Commission,* Case 322/81, ECLI:EU:C:1983:313.
14. Judgment of the Court of 3 July 1991, *AKZO Chemie v. Commission,* Case C-62/86, ECLI:EU:C:1991:286.
15. Judgment of the Court of 2 March 1994, *Hilti AG v. Commission,* Case C-53/92 P, ECLI:EU:C:1994:77.
16. Judgment of the Court of 14 November 1996, *Tetra Pak International SA v. Commission,* Case C-333/94 P, ECLI:EU:C:1996:436.
17. Judgment of the Court of 6 April 1995, *Radio Telefis Eireann (RTE) and Independent Television Publications Ltd (ITP) v. Commission ('Magill'),* ECLI:EU:C:1995:98.
18. Judgment of the Court of 26 November 1998, *Bronner,* Case C-7/97, ECLI:EU:C:1998:569.
19. On the fundamental role of merger control in influencing the major shift in EU competition law towards an effects-based approach, *see* Carles Esteva Mosso, 'The Contribution of Merger Control to the Definition of Harm to Competition', Speech Made at the 2016 GCLC Conference, 1-2 February 2016, in: http://ec.europa.eu/competition/speeches (last accessed 31 July 2025).
20. Judgment of the Court of 6 September 2017, *Intel v. Commission,* Case C–413/14 P, ECLI:EU:C:2017:632.
21. Judgment of the Court of 10 September 2024, *Google and Alphabet v. Commission (Google Shopping),* Case C-48/22 P, ECLI:EU:C:2024:726.

acceptable trade-offs that need to be made between in-depth assessment and expedient enforcement.

The Commission already took the challenge to work on a solution and its new Guidelines are eagerly awaited towards the end of 2025.

It is in that context that, in March 2024, the Global Competition Law Centre organised the conference entitled 'Article 102 TFEU: past, present, future'. Leading scholars, respected judges, experienced practitioners, influential former and current enforcers and promising young academics gathered together at the College of Europe in Bruges with the task of taking a sober look at the past enforcement of Article 102 TFEU and reflecting on its future.

We are particularly grateful to those who found time in their busy schedules to put their thoughts in writing and produce extremely thoughtful contributions. We believe the present volume will accompany in the best possible way the new Guidelines for Article 102 TFEU, as an important contextual tool.

PART I The Development of Article 102 TFEU

CHAPTER 1

Revisiting the Precedent Value of *Continental Can* and Its Antecedents

Luc Gyselen[*]

1 INTRODUCTION

Before we address the topic selected for today's presentation, we wanted to share an anecdote from our student days here at the College of Europe – the Spaak promotion 1978-1979. We received bi-weekly reading assignments in our EU antitrust law class. Many of us were not used to getting such assignments. Thankfully, Commission decisions and Court of Justice judgments were of manageable length in those days. There were a few exceptions though. The Court's judgment in *United Brands* (1978) held the record. It counted – hold your breath – 309 paragraphs and most students balked at having to plough their way through judgments that long.

Today litigation in cases relating to Article 102 of the Treaty on the Functioning of the European Union (hereafter 'TFEU') leads to Court judgments that can easily be up to four times longer. This raises a 'chicken and egg' question concerning the interaction between the length of a Commission decision that has to meet the required standard of proof and the length of a Court judgment, in particular a General Court judgment, that has to meet the required standard of judicial review. In any event, the two standards are entangled because whatever the Commission has to prove is what the General Court can, and should, verify. However, this discussion is not for our panel – perhaps for the first panel tomorrow morning.

We will focus on just one topic. In section 2, we will briefly restate the precedent value of the Court of Justice's judgment in *Continental Can* (1973).[1] In section 3, we

* The author completed this article on 18 January 2025.

1. Case 6/72, *Europemballage Corp. and Continental Can Company Inc. v. Commission*, EU:C:1973:22.

will examine whether the 1956 *travaux préparatoires* (legal history) of the Treaty instituting the European Economic Community (hereafter 'EEC Treaty' or 'EEC') show traces of a discussion on merger control. The track record appears to be mixed. In section 4, we will review the Commission's early thought process (1959-1966) on what its competition policy should look like. It is clear that the Commission was concerned - generally - about market concentration and - more specifically - about mergers involving dominant companies but that it waited for a good case to show its teeth. In this limited sense, the *travaux préparatoires* of the EEC Treaty and the Commission's brainstorming about its competition policy priorities in the early years after the entry into force of this Treaty constitute antecedents of *Continental Can*.

At the end of this contribution, we will share some high-level thoughts on whether following *Towercast* (2023)[2] and *Illumina Grail* (2024),[3] *Continental Can* might enjoy a second youth.

2 *CONTINENTAL CAN* IN A NUTSHELL

Article 102 TFEU prohibits dominant companies from abusing their market power within the common market. It contains a list of four examples of abusive conduct. Article 102 TFEU prohibits 'in particular (...): (a) directly or indirectly imposing unfair purchase or selling prices or other unfair trading conditions; (b) limiting production, markets or technical development to the prejudice of consumers; (c) applying dissimilar conditions to equivalent transactions with other trading parties, thereby placing them at a competitive disadvantage; (d) making the conclusion of contracts subject to acceptance by the other parties of supplementary obligations which, by their nature or according to commercial usage, have no connection with the subject of such contracts'.

In 1971, the Commission prohibited a merger whereby Continental Can (through its subsidiary Europemballage) had acquired an 80% shareholding in Thomassen & Drijver-Verblifa. According to the Commission, this merger constituted an exclusionary abuse in violation of Article 86 EEC because it had in practice led to the elimination of competition for certain packaging products.[4]

The merging parties obtained the annulment of this decision in the Court of Justice on case-specific grounds (i.e., inadequate definition of the relevant product markets) but the Court upheld the Commission's views on three important, intertwined points of principle. It ruled that: (i) Article 86 EEC (now Article 102 TFEU) not only covered exploitative abuses but also exclusionary abuses; (ii) mergers whereby a dominant company significantly strengthened its market position constituted a subcategory of exclusionary abuse; and (iii) there is no need to prove a causal nexus between the exclusionary abuse and the market power held by the dominant company.

2. Case C-449/21, *Towercast*, EU:C:2023:207.
3. Joined cases C-611/22P and C-625/22P, *Illumina Inc. and Grail LLC v. Commission*, EU:C:2024:677.
4. Decision of 9 December 1971, O.J. L7/25 of 8 January 1972.

We will not spend much time commenting on the third reason. The Court's conclusion that a company may be abusing its dominant position, even if it does not use its market power as an instrument to restrict competition, logically followed from its finding that mergers could be caught by Article 86 EEC because in merger cases, there is no causal nexus between the exclusionary abuse and the market power held by the dominant company. The Court summarized this point as follows: 'the question of the link of causality raised by the applicants which in their opinion has to exist between the dominant position and its abuse, is of no consequence, for the strengthening of the position of an undertaking may be an abuse and prohibited under Article 86 of the Treaty, regardless of the means and procedure by which it is achieved, if it has the effects mentioned above'.[5] That said, the 'no nexus' point subsequently presented important precedent value in some abusive conduct cases. Think of *AstraZeneca* (2005) which concerned – put simply – misconduct in the regulatory process.[6]

We will address the two other reasons in combination. In *Continental Can* (1973), the Court of Justice sided with the Commission's view that Article 86 EEC not only prohibited dominant companies from exploiting customers/consumers but also from engaging in practices aimed at excluding competitors and that mergers involving dominant companies could be a sub-category of such practices.[7]

According to the Court, one had 'to go back to the spirit, general scheme and wording of Article 86 as well as to the system and objectives of the Treaty'.[8]

With regard to 'the spirit', the Court primarily referred to Article 3(f) EEC according to which 'for the purposes set out in Article 2, the Community's activities shall include (...) the institution of a system ensuring that competition in the Common Market is not distorted'.[9]

As for 'the general scheme', the Court observed that 'Articles 85 and 86 seek to achieve the same aim on different levels, *viz.* the maintenance of effective competition within the Common Market' and that it is unthinkable that companies would be able to circumvent the cartel prohibition set forth in Article 85 by merging with each other: 'the restraint of competition which is prohibited if it is the result of behaviour falling under Article 85, cannot become permissible by the fact that such behaviour succeeds under the influence of a dominant undertaking and results in the merger of the undertakings

5. *Supra* n. 1, at para. 27.
6. *See* the Commission's prohibition decision of 15 June 2005 in case AT.37507 (published on 19 July 2006), upheld by the General Court in case T-321/05, *AstraZeneca v. Commission*, EU:T:2010:266, para. 354. In its draft Guidelines on the application of Art. 102 TFEU to abusive exclusionary conduct by dominant undertakings (August 2024), the Commission recalls that 'the assessment of whether a conduct is capable of having exclusionary effects does not require proof that the conduct is enabled by the dominant position' (para. 74).
7. Advocate General Roemer agreed that Art. 86 EEC also covered exclusionary practices but he took a different view on merger control. In his opinion of 21 November 1972, he criticized the Commission for having interpreted Art. 86 EEC 'extensively', in particular by assuming too easily that mergers like the one at stake were causing consumer harm within the meaning of Art. 86(b). *See* Opinion of AG Roemer in case 6/72, *Europemballage Corp. and Continental Can Company Inc. v. Commission*, p. 255.
8. *Supra* n. 1, at para. 22.
9. *Ibid.*, para. 23.

concerned'.[10] According to the Court, 'in the absence of explicit provisions one cannot assume that the Treaty, which prohibits in Article 85 certain decisions of ordinary associations of undertakings restricting competition without eliminating it, permits in Article 86 that undertakings, after merging into an organic unity, should reach such a dominant position that any serious chance of competition is practically rendered impossible', and the Court added that 'if, in order to avoid the prohibitions in Article 85, it sufficed to establish such close connections between the undertakings that they escaped the prohibition of Article 85 without coming within the scope of that of Article 86, then, in contradiction to the basic principles of the Common Market, the partitioning of a substantial part of this market would be allowed'.[11]

With regard to 'the wording', it pointed at Article 86(c), which prohibits discrimination, and Article 86(d), which prohibits tying, as provisions that 'not only aimed at practices which may cause damage to consumers directly, but also at those which are detrimental to them through their impact on an effective competition structure, such as is mentioned in Article 3 (f) of the Treaty'.[12]

The Court did not refer to the *travaux préparatoires* of Article 86 EEC. They were probably not yet available in 1970. Nor did Advocate-General Roemer in his opinion.[13]

In 2016, we spent a summer week in Fiesole reviewing these *travaux préparatoires*. It would take us too far to give the reader a detailed digest of our findings in the

10. *Ibid.*, para. 25.
11. *Ibid.* The Court of Justice concludes that 'Articles 85 and 86 cannot be interpreted in such a way that they contradict each other, because they serve to achieve the same aim'.
12. *Ibid.*, para. 26. In his book *Monopolization and abuse of dominant position – A Comparative Study of the American and European Approaches to the Control of Economic Power* (Vol. 31 in the Collection Scientifique de la Faculté de Droit de l'Université de Liège (1970)), which was largely based on his 1967 S.J.D. dissertation at Northwestern University, prof. Joliet (who would become a judge at the Court of Justice in 1984) relied on the text of Art. 86 EEC to argue that this provision *only* prohibited exploitative abuses. In his view, Art. 86(a) and Art. 86(b) EEC covered the two practices that profit-maximizing monopolists typically engage in to exploit customers and consumers: excessively high 'unfair' prices' (cf. Art. 86(a)) and output restriction in the form of either 'limiting production' or 'limiting technical development' (cf. Art. 86(b)). Joliet further argued that discrimination (Art. 86(c)) and tying (Art. 86(d)) were in the first place other examples of customer exploitation, although they were admittedly also potentially anticompetitive in markets *other than* the one in which the dominant company held its substantial market power. *See* in particular pp. 247-252.
13. In 1996, Advocate-General Fennelly extrajudicually took the view that the CJEU 'cannot rely on the *travaux préparatoires* for the Treaties which are not available to it'. *See* N. Fennelly, *Legal Interpretation at the European Court of Justice,* 20 Fordham International Law Journal, 1996, pp. 656-679, at 666. In the *Inuit* case (2013), Advocate-General Kokott used less categorical language. She noted that the 'drafting history in particular has not played a role thus far in the interpretation of primary law, because the *travaux préparatoires* for the founding Treaties were *largely* not available' (our emphasis). In her view, 'the practice of using conventions to prepare Treaty amendments, like the practice of publishing the mandates of intergovernmental conferences, has led to a fundamental change in this area' and 'the greater transparency in the preparations for Treaty amendments opens up new possibilities for interpreting the Treaties which should be utilized as supplementary means of interpretation if, as in the present case, the meaning of a provision is still unclear having regard to its wording, the regulatory context and the objectives pursued'. *See* AG Kokott's Opinion in case C-583/11 P, *Inuit and others v. European Parliament and Council of the European Union*, EU:C:2013:21, para. 32.

present contribution, even if we limited those to Article 86.[14] However, these *travaux* contain a few remarkable passages regarding merger control.

3 THE *TRAVAUX PRÉPARATOIRES* OF ARTICLE 86 EEC

As we already mentioned in the introduction, the track record of these *travaux* regarding the question of whether or not mergers involving dominant companies should fall within the scope of Article 86 EEC Treaty was mixed. Initially (between April and June 1956), the founding fathers seemed focused on exclusionary practices and even advocated a form of merger control. However, in the course of July 1956, and more clearly in September and October of that year, the thinking had evolved, primarily under the influence of the German delegation at the Common Market Committee (*Groupe du Marché Commun*) and its German chair Hans von der Groeben (who brokered an amended text in October 1956 that came close to the final text of Article 86 EEC, i.e., with its four examples of abuse as we know them today and without any reference to merger control). Let us review this in more detail.

On 21 April 1956, an Intergovernmental Committee consisting of the heads of delegation of the six countries who had signed the Treaty of Paris instituting the European Coal and Steel Community (hereafter the 'ECSC Treaty' or 'ECSC'), chaired by the Belgian Minister of Foreign Affairs Paul-Henri Spaak, presented a report (known as the 'Spaak report') that would serve as the basis for negotiating the EEC and Euratom treaties.[15]

Section 1(b) of Chapter 1 in Title II of Part One of the Report carries the somewhat misleading title 'the problem of monopolies'. In this Section, the Intergovernmental Committee states that 'the Treaty should contain general provisions ensuring that monopoly positions or abusive practices do not lead to the frustration of the common market' and 'in this connection steps should be taken to prevent: (i) a division of markets by *agreement* between enterprises, since this would be tantamount to re-establishing the compartmentalization of the market, (ii) *agreements* to limit production or curb technical progress, because they would run counter to progress in productivity and (iii) the *absorption or domination* of the market for a product by a single enterprise, since this would eliminate one of the essential advantages of a vast

14. For some initial comments on these *travaux préparatoires* with regard to Art. 85 EEC, *see* Luc Gyselen, *What Makes an Agreement Anti-competitive? Lessons from the Past*, in: Written Proceedings of the 2015 Global Competition Law Center Annual conference (Bruylant, 2016), pp. 111-135.
15. The Council of Europe in Strasbourg prepared a full English translation of the Spaak Report (Report by the Heads of Delegations to the Foreign Ministers, provisional English text, restricted SG/A (56) 4, 15 June 1956; CM 3/085). Another English translation can be found in Joseph J.A. Ellis, *Source Material for Article 85 (1) of the EEC Treaty*, 32(2) Fordham Law Review, 1963 pp. 247-278. In our view, the latter translation often reads better. Sometimes, it stays even closer to the original French text than the translation prepared for the Council of Europe.

market, namely that it reconciles the use of mass production techniques with the maintenance of competition' (emphasis added).[16]

At this initial stage, the third example seems to cover unilateral *conduct* whereby a single undertaking would monopolize a market ('absorption' of the market) or at least acquire a dominant position on a market ('domination' of the market) and thereby prevent its rivals from also achieving economies of scale and thereby enhancing their own competitiveness in a wider market.[17] There is no indication that this third example was meant to *also* cover *concentrations* whereby undertakings would absorb or at least dominate the market.[18] However, in a passage immediately following the enumeration of the three examples, the Intergovernmental Committee proposes to empower the Commission 'to adopt regulations (to be approved by the Parliament) in order to work out detailed rules concerning discrimination, *organize control of mergers* and prohibit agreements to partition or exploit markets, limit production or restrict technical progress' (our emphasis).

On 20 June 1956, a 42-page long working document containing the first set of treaty articles drafted 'in accordance with the text of the Report' was issued. The competition rules applicable to undertakings feature in section 1 of Chapter 1 'Competition Rules' of Title III 'Policy of the Common Market'. In line with the Spaak Report, section 1 distinguishes between 'discriminations' (Article 22 and Article 23) and 'monopolies' (Article 24). The latter provision represents the very first version of a treaty article specifically prohibiting anti-competitive company conduct, whether collusive or unilateral.[19]

This draft Article 24 prohibits the three above-mentioned practices featuring in the Spaak Report in almost the exact same terms as those used in that report. It remains unclear whether it prohibits 'absorption or domination' only through exclusionary market conduct or also through mergers. However, in line with what the Intergovernmental Committee had already advocated in the Spaak report, the draft Article 24 explicitly empowers the Commission to adopt implementing regulations (subject to the Parliament's approval), *inter alia,* to organize merger control.[20]

16. This is the Ellis translation which we often found more accurate than the Council of Europe translation. Cf. Ellis, *supra* n. 15, at p. 251. For the original French text, *see* pp. 55-56 of the Spaak Report.
17. There is no reference to, but one might perceive some analogy with, Art. 66(7) ECSC according to which 'the High Authority is empowered to address to public or private enterprises which, in law or in fact, *have or acquire on the market* for one of the products subject to its jurisdiction *a dominant position* which protects them from effective competition in a substantial part of the common market, any recommendations required to prevent the use of such position for purposes contrary to those of the present Treaty'.
18. Pursuant to Art. 66(1) to (6) ECSC, the High Authority could intervene against concentrations that gave the merging parties the power, *inter alia,* 'to influence prices, to control or restrain production or marketing, or to impair the maintenance of effective competition'.
19. Historical Archives of the European Union (HAEU), document CM 3/0099 – MAE 131 f/56 of 20 June 1956.
20. There is no English translation of the forty-two-page long working document. The third sentence of draft Art. 24 in French reads as follows: 'La Commission européenne prend des règlements généraux d'exécution soumis à l'approbation de l'Assemblée qui ont pour objet (a) de déterminer les règles détaillées concernant la discrimination, (b) d'organiser un *contrôle des opérations de concentrations* et (c) de *pratiquer* une interdiction des ententes qui auraient pour

On 26 June 1956, the Intergovernmental Conference on the Common Market and Euratom commences its activities in earnest under Spaak's chairmanship in Brussels (Val Duchesse). The next day, on 27 June 1957, the Common Market Group, as said chaired by Hans von der Groeben, which will report to the Intergovernmental Committee on a rolling basis, circulates a slightly amended version of the draft Article 24.[21]

This draft text now lists *four* practices as being 'incompatible with the common market': (i) market partitioning agreements between companies and agreements between companies that aim to restrict output at the production or distribution level (i.e., the two examples mentioned in the Spaak Report and in the draft version of Article 24 of 20 June 1956); (ii) conduct whereby a company enjoying a monopoly position abuses its market power (but no specific examples given); (iii) customer discrimination (through agreements or abuse); and (iv) mergers that enable the merging companies to acquire a dominant position in the common market.[22]

In other words, whereas the initial draft Article 24 of 20 June 1956 had merely empowered the Commission to adopt a merger control regulation, this new draft Article 24(1) now elevates merger control to the level of a treaty provision.[23]

While another draft text of 4 July 1956 brings no material changes, things dramatically change when new drafts - now renumbered to become Article 42 - are circulated on 6 July and 17 July 1956.

For the purpose of placing *Continental Can* in a historical perspective, two points are noteworthy.

First, the three practices originally mentioned in the Spaak report (i.e., market partitioning agreements between undertakings, agreements between undertakings aimed at limiting production or technical progress and the absorption or domination of the market by a single company) resurface. The drafts of 6 July and 17 July therefore replace the four examples featuring in the draft Article 24 of 27 June 1956 *and* they no longer mention merger control. They do not even empower the Commission to organize merger control via an implementing regulation (contrary to what the draft Article 24 circulated on 20 June 1956 had done).

effet une répartition ou une exploitation des marchés, une limitation de la production ou du progrès technique' (emphasis added).

21. Hans von der Groeben would become the first Commissioner for Competition at the European Commission on 1 January 1958. The Common Market Group further consisted of the following members: Mr Muller-Armack (Germany), Mr Van Tichelen (Belgium), Mr Donnedieu de Vabres (France), Mr Catalano (Italy), Mr Hyzen (Luxembourg) and Mr Linthorst-Homan (Netherlands).
22. HAEC, document CM 3/236 - MAE 139 f/56 of 27 June 1956. The precise wording of this example shows that the notion of monopoly position also includes that of a dominant position ('une entreprise qui ... est en mesure de se soustraire entièrement ou dans une mesure substantielle au jeu de la concurrence').
23. Besides, the draft Art. 24(1) no longer prohibits the listed practices. It merely qualifies them as 'incompatible with the common market'. This probably reflects the lack of consensus among the six negotiating countries - at this early stage - as to whether the EEC Treaty should put in place a prohibition system or rather a more tolerant abuse system (pursuant to which practices are lawful, unless and until they are prohibited by the public enforcer). Let us bear in mind that France already had a prohibition system in place since June 1945 and that Germany was in the process of preparing a statute that would do the same (and was adopted in July 1957) but that the other four negotiating countries where nowhere near adopting a prohibition system.

Second, a footnote concerning the third example, i.e., 'absorption or domination of the market', is added. It reads as follows: 'the question arises whether case (c) should be subject to special scrutiny, given that it does not concern practices but a *situation as such*' (emphasis added). The German delegation added this footnote. It will give rise to discussions between it and the other delegations, in particular the French delegation, in September and October 1956.

At a meeting of the Common Market Group on 3-4 September 1956, Mr Muller-Armack (the German lead delegate) explains that monopolies and oligopolies must be clearly distinguished from cartels because the former are 'not necessarily incompatible with a competition regime' (whereas the latter are). According to him, 'what must be abolished are not the monopolies as such but the abuses that may result from certain monopolistic situations' and he therefore proposes to delete the third example altogether, or at least reformulate it.[24] M. Donnedieu de Vabres (the French lead delegate) declares that he is willing to examine this proposal once Germany has clarified how it defines the notion of abuse.[25]

On 24 September 1956, the Common Market Group's secretariat produces an overview of the draft texts prepared by the experts of each delegation. In line with its position set out earlier that month, the German delegation proposes a separate text for monopolies (no explicit reference to oligopolies) prohibiting companies that face no competition or at least no serious competition from exploiting their market position abusively and listing almost *verbatim* the four examples of abuse that will make it to the final text of Article 86 EEC (in short: excessive pricing, output restriction, discrimination and tying).[26]

On 26 October 1956, Chairman Mr von der Groeben reiterates the point already made by Muller-Armack and circulates separate draft texts for cartels ('ententes') and for monopolies ('monopoles').

Von der Groeben first explains why there should really be two separate provisions - one for agreements and one for monopolies. Agreements that do not generate countervailing efficiencies must be prohibited because they restrict competition between the parties (or between them and their competitors). Monopolies are different,

---

24. *See* document MAE/s. 29/56 of 7 September 1956 ('Memento interne'), at pp. 4-5: 'Les monopoles et les oligopoles ne sont pas nécessairement (...) incompatibles avec un régime de concurrence. Ce qu'il faut supprimer, ce ne sont pas les monopoles en eux-mêmes, mais les abus auxquels certaines situations monopolistiques pourraient aboutir'. *See also* MAE 252 f/56 of 10 September 1956 ('draft minutes of the meeting of the Common Market Group on 3-5 September 1956', Mar. Com. 32), at p. 3: the German delegation opines that monopolies and oligopolies should not be subject to the principle of prohibition ('le principe de l'interdiction pure et simple') but to a control of abuse.
25. *Ibid.*, at p. 5. Mr. Donnedieu de Vabres also argues that not all cartels are necessarily incompatible with the common market. He observes that the French term 'entente' is broader than the German term 'Kartell' and therefore requires a regulation that is more flexible ('plus souple'). Incidentally, it is at this meeting of the Common Market Group that the French delegation proposes a new text for anticompetitive practices. It contains the first seeds of what would ultimately become Art. 85(3) EEC (cf. document MAE 233 f/56 of 4 September 1956).
26. *See* document MAE 325 f/56 of 24 September 1956 ('Tableau synoptique des projets d'articles soumis par les experts des délégations concernant les règles de concurrence applicables aux entreprises', Mar. Com. 52), at pp. 4 and 6.

he says. Competition is already seriously weakened and may even have been eliminated. In these circumstances, he says, it is not the fact of having weakened or eliminated competition that could be prohibited *but only* the abuse of the dominant position (emphasis added).[27]

Von der Groeben then turns to the 'absorption or domination of the market' example which he says requires clarification. Here he is even more explicit. In principle, practices that achieve this do not restrict competition but rather strengthen competition (*'renforcement de la concurrence'*). He seems to take the view that any company has the right to monopolize the market as long as it competes on the merits *and* that a transaction whereby a dominant company acquires one of its competitors in fact constitutes competition on the merits. He adds that such monopolization practices should not be prohibited unless they constitute unfair competition (*'concurrence déloyale'*) but for that, separate treaty provisions must be put in place.[28]

In light of his explanations, von der Groeben proposes a text for the prohibition of abusive exploitation of dominance ('en ce qui concerne l'exploitation abusive') with the four examples that already featured in the German delegation's proposal on 24 September 1956 and will ultimately make it to the final text of Article 86 EEC. No longer any trace of the 'absorption or domination of market' example or, more specifically, merger control. Merger control appears to have left the scene and will not come back on stage – at least not before the signing and entering into force of the EEC Treaty.

However, what happened after the EEC Treaty entered into force on 1 January 1958?

Hans von der Groeben took office as the first Commissioner for Competition on 7 January 1958. He would stay in that position until 2 July 1967. During these nine years,

27. *See* document MAE 468 f/56 of 26 October 1956 'Note sur les règles relatives à la discrimination et aux ententes et monopoles'. The relevant passage at p. 4 reads as follows: 'une des caractéristiques des ententes est qu'elles sont susceptibles d'entraver ou d'empêcher la concurrence, et c'est en considération de cet effet et dans une mesure où cet effet se produit ou est recherché qu'il y a lieu de les interdire. En revanche, en ce qui concerne les monopoles, *la concurrence susceptible d'être compromise ou éliminée existe d'autant moins que le monopole en question est plus parfait*. En conséquence, dans le cas des monopoles, ce n'est pas le fait d'entraver la concurrence, *mais bien seulement l'abus* de la position dominante sur le marché qui pourra faire l'objet d'une interdiction' (emphasis added).
28. If prof. Joliet had had access to the *travaux préparatoires*, he would probably have quoted von de Groeben in support of his thesis that Art. 86 EEC only prohibits exploitative abuses. For the full text of the relevant passage in von der Groeben's memo (*supra* n. 27), *see* p. 5: 'Il a été proposé de stipuler, dans le cadre des dispositions relatives aux ententes et aux monopoles, que: sont notamment incompatibles avec le marché commun, les situations ou les pratiques d'ententes ou de monopole ayant pour objet ou pouvant avoir pour effet d'entraver l'exercice de la concurrence, en *permettant* l'absorption ou la domination du marché d'un produit déterminé par une entreprise ou un groupe d'entreprises. Cette proposition demande encore à être clarifiée. Il semble que cette formule vise les pratiques permettant d'éliminer du marché des entreprises concurrentes. Toutefois, ces pratiques ne consistent pas dans une restriction, mais bien plutôt un *renforcement de la concurrence*; il semble donc qu'elles ne puissent être réprimées que s'il s'agit d'une concurrence déloyale. Or, les dispositions relatives à la concurrence déloyale qui seraient insérées dans le Traité, devraient être séparées, pour des raisons systématiques, de celles qui sont destinées à assurer le maintien de la concurrence' (emphasis added).

Pieter VerLoren van Themaat was Director-General of the Commission's Directorate General for Competition. During von der Groeben's tenure, the topic of merger control came back onto the scene fairly quickly. As we will explain in the next section, the thought process appears to have developed in stages.

4 THE COMMISSION'S THINKING ABOUT MERGER CONTROL IN THE LATE 1950S/EARLY 1960S

As already mentioned, the Court of Justice sided in *Continental Can* with the Commission on the point of principle that mergers are a subcategory of exclusionary abuses prohibited by Article 86 EEC if they enable a dominant company to significantly strengthen its dominant position. In this regard, the Court highlighted, in particular, the complementarity of Article 85 and Article 86 EEC as instruments aimed at 'ensuring that competition in the Common Market is not distorted'. More specifically, if Article 85 EEC prohibits collusive behaviour, a dominant company should not be allowed to circumvent this prohibition via a merger.

It will be recalled that the German delegation took the position during the *travaux préparatoires* that, in contrast with cartels, monopolies and oligopolies were 'not necessarily incompatible with a competition regime' and, as a consequence, it was better to drop the example 'absorption or domination of the market' that had initially raised concerns. However, the Commission and the competition experts representing the six Member States revisited the issue at one of their early 'cartel conferences' (the first of which would take place in November 1958).

At the fourth conference (in June 1959), the notion of an 'economic dominant position' featured on the agenda. It was only discussed in a summary fashion. The Commission had apparently expressed the intention to collect documentation on dominant positions with a view to shaping a 'targeted policy', without, however, clarifying what specific policy it had in mind.[29]

A few months later, it becomes clear that the Commission has concerns about concentrated markets. At the fifth cartel conference (in October 1959), the Commission and Member State representatives agree that a working group will draw up a questionnaire with a view to collecting information from market players in three economic sectors: automobile spark plugs, phosphate fertilizers and newspaper. This emerges from a brief report of the directorate-general for trade and industry of the Dutch Ministry of Foreign Affairs to its State Secretary on 6 January 1960. The authors remind their State Secretary of the fact that Article 86 does not prohibit dominant positions 'as such' but that the conference had considered it more appropriate (*'juister')* to focus the research initially (*'voorlopig'*) on the existence of economic dominant positions in

29. In an internal debriefing note of 27 October 1959 summarizing the discussions of the first four cartel conferences, the Directorate General for trade and industry of the Dutch Ministry of Foreign Affairs talks about a *'gericht beleid'*. We found this note at the National Archives of this Ministry in The Hague (document nr. NA 21826).

order to avoid that one would already have to assess any abuses of dominance at this early stage (*'reeds in het eerste onderzoek'*). This report does not explicitly refer to the three sectors as concentrated markets but subsequent documents confirm that this is the case.[30]

On 28 October 1959, the Commission's DG for competition summarizes the working group's 'conclusions'.[31] The questionnaire (which it would be for the Member State authorities to send out to the relevant companies)[32] covered, on the one hand, general market information (i.e., number of companies, their location, production and consumption volumes in each Member State and import/export volumes within the EU or between the EU and third countries) and, on the other hand, information about the three most important companies (i.e., their production capacity, their actual production, their shares of total production, their share of total import/export, structural links between them in case of shareholdings of at least 30%, any participation in joint sales or purchasing agencies).

At their sixth cartel conference in December 1959, the Member States' representatives approve the questionnaire. Incidentally, in its above-mentioned debriefing report of 6 January 1960, the Directorate General for trade and industry of the Dutch Ministry of Foreign Affairs emphasizes that the Commission had accepted the Dutch proposal to widen the scope of the question regarding the structural links between companies: information would be collected on shareholdings which either amounted to at least 30% or otherwise enabled the company owning the shares to exercise 'decisive influence' over the company in which it had these shares.[33]

In a Communication *'Politique des Ententes'* of 15 February 1960, Commissioner von der Groeben asks his fellow Commissioners to sign off on a number of points, including the adoption of the Directorate General for Competition's work programme for that year.[34] Attached to his Communication is an explanatory memorandum authored by this Directorate General. It contains a brief reference to the sector studies and describes the three sectors covered by the questionnaire as presenting 'a high degree of concentration'. It also adds – cryptically – that while 'the interest of the

30. Internal debriefing note of 6 January 1960 (featuring in document nr. NA 21827), p. 1.
31. Note IV/5076/59-F of 28 October 1959 (also featuring in document nr. NA 21826).
32. It will be recalled that Art. 88 and Art. 89 EEC put in place a system of concurrent jurisdiction between the Member States and the Commission in the field of competition – albeit provisionally, i.e., 'until the entry into force of the provisions adopted in pursuance of Art. 87 EEC' (Art. 88 EEC). On the one hand, the authorities in Member States had the power to 'rule on the admissibility of agreements, decisions and concerted practices and on abuse of a dominant position in the common market in accordance with the law of their country and with the provisions of Art. 85, in particular paragraph 3, and of Article 86' (Art. 88 EEC). On the other hand, and 'without prejudice to Art. 88 EEC', the Commission had the power to 'ensure the application of the principles laid down in Articles 85 and 86' and to 'investigate cases of suspected infringement of these principles' (Art. 89 EEC).
33. *Supra* n. 30, at p. 2.
34. Document IV/(60)17, Vol. 1960/0003. Other points include the strengthening of the Commission's powers under Art. 89 CEE, notably the possibility to start investigations on an ex officio *basis* and to enter into direct contact with companies (with a view to collecting information from them, inviting them to negotiations and addressing cease and desist orders to them).

questionnaires primarily lies in the field of Art. 86 EEC, they might also lead to the detection of prohibited agreements'.[35]

A few months later, in a speech delivered at a competition law conference held in Frankfurt in June 1960, Commissioner von der Groeben repeats the need for monitoring concentrated markets in a more general way. While recalling that the EEC Treaty (in contrast with the ECSC Treaty) does not provide a legal basis for challenging 'industrial concentrations', and even less 'dominant positions in the common market when they already exist', he stresses that 'the success of the common market depends on the well-functioning of the market economy mechanisms' and he announces that the Commission therefore intends to monitor closely any 'trend towards the formation of oligopolistic markets'.[36] He then reiterates the point that the EEC Treaty does not provide a legal basis for stopping concentrations, 'even if they risk changing a market's features' ('même lorsqu'elles risquent de changer l'aspect du marché'), but that his services will not hesitate to apply Article 86 in case they detect abuses of dominance.[37]

The latter statement is somewhat ambiguous but it strikes us as too broad to suggest that von der Groeben already envisaged using Article 86 EEC as an instrument to stop concentrations that would strengthen (or significantly strengthen) an existing dominant position. What he did explicitly envisage was to develop a 'general economic policy' in order to discourage undesirable concentrations from emerging or to limit the margin of manoeuvring of existing oligopolies. In this regard, he refers to the approximation of national legislations (cf. Article 100 EEC) and to a commercial policy which should progressively abolish international trade barriers (cf. Article 110 EEC). Although von der Groeben does not develop this further in his speech, he probably saw the harmonization of national laws as a lever to stimulate cross-border mergers and thus open up too concentrated national markets, while he viewed a commercial policy that would consist in removing barriers of trade between the European Community and third countries as a policy that would open up too concentrated Europe-wide markets.

A year later (1961), in an article in *Wirtschaft und Wettbewerb* on competition policy in the EEC, translated into English and reproduced in a Supplement to the EEC's Bulletin, von der Groeben goes a step further. He advocates a form of merger control under Article 86 EEC and he singles out mergers whereby the merging parties would seek to evade the application of Article 85 EEC.[38] In other words, he expresses the same

35. This is our translation. The original sentence in French reads as follows: 'L' intérêt des renseignements fournis par les Etats membres se situera surtout dans le cadre de l' Art. 86, mais ils pourront peut-être également permettre de déceler des accords interdits'.
36. Speech on 'Le droit des ententes dans la C.E.C. après deux années d'expérience', document X/3237/60-F, BAC 71/1988 222/1960, at pp. 9-10.
37. *Ibid.*, p. 11.
38. Hans von der Groeben, *Wettbewerbspolitik in der Europäischen Wirtschaftsgemeinschaft*, in 11(6) Wirtschaft und Wettbewerb, June 1961, pp. 373-396 and reproduced in the Supplement to the Bulletin of the EEC, 1961 July-August Nos 7-8, pp. 1-30, in particular pp. 20-21 where the relevant passage reads as follows: 'Article 86, then, does not put a brake on any economically justified trend towards the optimal size of enterprises or towards industrial mass production in large units. The intention of this provision is rather to cut out interference with competition even where it does not come from agreements or concerted practices – Article 85 deals with these – but where it stems from a dominant position which may well have developed naturally in the course of competition. Another aim is to *prevent enterprises from using mergers to evade the*

circumvention concern that would be the linchpin of the Court of Justice's reasoning in its *Continental Can* judgment. Besides, in the same article, von der Groeben repeats the less explosive point he already made in Frankfurt, i.e., that the provisions of Article 86 EEC alone are not sufficient to deal with the potentially undesirable consequences of oligopolistic markets and that harmonization of national legislations (Article 100 EEC) or commercial policy measures (Article 110 EEC) might assist in remedying these consequences.[39]

A year later, in October 1962, i.e., close to the end of the first stage of the transitional period provided for the elimination of all customs duties between Member States (cf. Article 14 EEC), the Commission adopts an action programme covering the various fields for which it holds powers, including competition.[40] Both themes in von der Groeben's article, i.e., competition policy as an instrument for merger control and other policies as levers to avoid undesirable mergers, resurface. With regard to the first theme, Article 86 EEC is not explicitly mentioned but the Commission announces that it will present, if necessary ('si cela s'avère necessaire'), draft directives ('des projets de directive') before the end of the second stage of the transitional period (i.e., no later than the end of 1966).

In our view, the Commission delivered on its promise by publishing a study in 1966 on 'Le problème de la concentration dans le marché commun'. Part III of this study contains an opinion ('un avis') concerning the applicability of Articles 85 and 86 EEC to concentrations between companies.[41]

As a matter of fact, a year earlier, von der Groeben spoke clear language in a speech which he delivered at the European Parliament in Strasbourg on 16 June 1965 – so clear that one gets the impression that he must already have been aware of the likely direction of the study's conclusions.[42] He makes the following two points.

First, from a policy point of view, von der Groeben opines that mergers are to be welcomed if they allow the companies involved to grow, that even mergers between large companies are fine as long as there is effective competition between these companies in the market but that mergers by which companies monopolize the market must be stopped.[43]

---

prohibition of cartels laid down in Article 85 and thus to dominate the market to the detriment of competition' (emphasis added).

39. *See* Supplement to the Bulletin, *supra* n. 38, at p. 21: 'For these reasons it is of particular importance that the competition policy of the Community should not encourage economically unjustified concentrations of enterprises and that it should limit the bounds within which existing oligopolies can apply their market strategy. The former aim would be served if for instance tax, company and parent law, were rendered more neutral in their effects on competition, the latter perhaps by a resolute reduction of external customs tariffs applicable to the markets concerned.'
40. Historical Archives of the European Union, COM (62) 275, Vol. 1962/0062, 15 October 1962.
41. Cf. Collection Etudes EEC, Série Concurrence No. 3, Brussels 1966, 26 pages. For Part III, *see* pp. 21-26.
42. H. von der Groeben, *La politique de concurrence, partie intégrante de la politique économique dans le marché commun*, fonds 'BAC' (Brussels Archives of the Commission) No. 144/1992.
43. In French: 'de même que j'ai exprimé clairement une attitude positive à l'égard de la création d'entreprises de dimension européenne et, par conséquent, à l'égard de la grande masse des cas pratiques de fusion, de même, je tiens aussi à dire nettement qu'il y a ici une limite. Croissance des entreprises: oui. Concurrence entre grandes entreprises, si c'est une concurrence efficace:

Second, with regard to the technical legal question of which Treaty provision – Article 85 or Article 86 – could serve as a legal basis to stop such mergers, he explains that the applicability of Article 85 EEC is controversial (for a number of reasons we skip here). As for Article 86 EEC, although he acknowledges once more that this provision only prohibits abuses of dominance, he observes that a dominant company acquiring another company may commit an abuse. He adds that any finding of an abuse requires an examination of the facts at hand in light of the relevant market conditions but that the closer the dominant company gets to a monopoly position by acquiring another company, the more likely it will enter the abuse 'zone' as a result of that acquisition.[44]

Briefly returning to Part III of the Commission's study on 'Le problème de la concentration dans le marché commun' in 1966, we confine our comments to three points.

First, the professors who had assisted the Commission's services in preparing this study proposed to facilitate the application of Article 86 EEC to concentrations by adopting a regulation (on the basis of Article 87 EEC) that would put in place a surveillance system requiring companies to register certain concentrations – in other words, a notification system *avant la lettre* for mergers exceeding certain (undefined) thresholds.[45]

Second, according to the professors, concentrations between a dominant company and another company could – conceptually speaking – best be assimilated into the abuse example featuring in Article 86(b) EEC, i.e., the limitation of production, markets or technical development to the prejudice of consumers.[46]

Third, von der Groeben's observation at the European Parliament in 1965, according to which the closer a dominant company gets to a monopoly position by acquiring another company, the more likely it will enter the abuse 'zone' as a result of that acquisition, features almost *verbatim* in the study.[47]

The 1966 study did not disappear in the Commission's cupboards without any follow-up. In official publications, we read that the Commission had begun to review mergers under Article 86 EEC.

---

oui. Mais monopolisation, c'est-à-dire concentrations qui rendent la concurrence impraticable, qui mettent en questions la liberté de choix et d'action des consommateurs, des fournisseurs et des acheteurs: non'.

44. In French: 'Quant à savoir si l'acquisition d'autres entreprises par une entreprise dominante constitue l'exploitation abusive d'une position dominante au sens de l'article 86, ceci ne peut être déterminé que dans le cas d'espèce à la lumière de la situation de marché. Toutefois, plus une entreprise occupant une position dominante se rapproche d'une situation de monopole par le regroupement avec une autre entreprise, mettant ainsi en question la liberté d'action et de choix des fournisseurs, des acheteurs et des consommateurs, plus il existe une probabilité que cette entreprise entre dans la zone de l'abus du fait de la concentration.'
45. *Supra* n. 41, Part III, para. 4 *in fine,* at p. 22.
46. *Ibid.*, Part III, para. 25 *in fine,* at p. 26.
47. *Ibid.*, Part III, para. 27, at p. 26: 'La limite que l'article 86 impose à une entreprise dominant un marché au regard d'une concentration d'entreprises ne peut être déterminée que dans le cas d'espèce, en fonction de la situation du marché. D'une façon générale, on peut seulement dire que plus une entreprise en position dominante se rapproche du monopole par suite de la concentration avec d'autres entreprises, et met ainsi en cause la possibilité de choix des clients, fournisseurs et consommateurs finals, plus grande est la probabilité qu'elle tombe dans la zone de l'abus.'

For instance, in its second General Report on the activities of the Communities (1968), the Commission notes that 'the increased pressure of competition led to a stronger trend towards industrial combination and cooperation between firms' and that 'in so far as this trend was liable to be relevant to the EEC, it was observed closely from the angle of Art. 86 of the Treaty of Rome' but that 'there has so far been no need to take action under this article'.[48]

In its third General Report (1969), the Commission's message has already evolved. Although 'few of the amalgamations raised problems from the angle of competition policy', it reports that 'the number of cases of combination in respect of which [it] felt a more detailed investigation necessary rose, as it was impossible to establish at the outset that they involved no appreciable restraint of effective competition', and, while 'those investigations already completed showed that in the area controlled by the EEC Treaty there was no need to apply Art. 86, a scheme for an amalgamation in the glass industry which was liable to infringe Article 86 was dropped'.[49]

In April 1970, shortly after the publication of this third General Report, the Commission started ex officio proceedings in *Continental Can*.

5 FINAL THOUGHTS

In light of the Court of Justice's judgments in *Towercast* (2023) and *Illumina – Grail* (2024), one wonders whether its *Continental Can* judgment might enjoy a second youth, in particular with regard to concentrations for which an *ex ante* merger control is not available, be it at the EU level or at that of the EU Member States.

It will be recalled that the three-to-two merger between TDF and Itas in *Towercast* was such a merger. It had no Community dimension and it fell outside the scope of French merger control law. Relying on *Continental Can*, Towercast (the remaining competitor) had asked the French Competition Authority (hereafter 'FCA') to apply Article 102 TFEU. The FCA refused on the ground that Article 21(1) of the EU Council's Regulation No. 139/2004 of 20 January 2004 (hereafter 'EUMR') explicitly excluded the applicability of Regulation No. 1/2003 governing the implementation of Articles 101 and 102 TFEU for all concentrations covered by Article 3 EUMR (including those that did not have a Community dimension). In its view, this rendered the application of Article 102 TFEU to the concentration at stake 'devoid of purpose'.[50] The Paris Court of Appeals was in doubt. It asked the Court of Justice to clarify whether Article 21(1) EUMR precluded a national competition authority from applying Article 102 TFEU to the TDF-Itas merger. The Court ruled that it did not.

The merger in *Illumina – Grail* was another merger that had no Community dimension and fell outside the scope of *ex ante* merger control in France (because it did not meet the relevant thresholds and because the FCA did not have 'call-in' powers to review that merger *ex ante*). This time, unlike in *Towercast*, the FCA had made use of

48. *Ibid.*, para. 22, at p. 40.
49. *Ibid.*, para. 29, at p. 58.
50. *Towercast*, *supra* n. 2, para. 21.

the Article 22 EUMR referral mechanism (with other national competition authorities joining its referral request) and the Commission had accepted these referral requests. The merging parties challenged the relevant Commission's decisions. They argued that the Article 22 EUMR referral mechanism was not available to national competition authorities of Member States when they did not have *ex ante* merger control powers under their national law to review the transaction at stake. They lost their case in the General Court but won it in the Court of Justice.

This closed the door for the Commission to conduct an *ex ante* control of this or similar mergers via the referral mechanism of Article 22 EUMR (unless Member States possessed 'call-in' powers to review mergers below their national thresholds). The Court did not (have to) address the question of whether the Commission could perhaps have relied on *Towercast* (and *Continental Can*) to review this type of merger *ex post* under Article 102 TFEU.

Thus, from a strictly legal point of view, this remains an open question.

Prior to the Court's ruling in *Illumina – Grail*, the Director-General of the Commission's competition department had suggested that *Towercast* (i.e., the Article 102 TFEU enforcement route) could be an alternative to Article 22 EUMR but he had also acknowledged that this approach – as a matter of policy – would be 'messier' and 'more disruptive' than reviewing concentrations *ex ante* through the Article 22 EUMR referral mechanism (because it would give companies 'less legal certainty').[51]

Following the Court's ruling in *Illumina – Grail*, the Commission is still reviewing its options. It seems to be thinking more in the direction of encouraging national competition authorities who do not yet possess 'call-in' powers, to obtain such powers under their national laws to refer 'below-the-thresholds' concentrations in order to preserve the full potential of Article 22 EUMR referral mechanism – at least as a first step.[52] Incidentally, on 31 October 2024, the Commission accepted an Article 22 EUMR referral from the Italian authority, which already holds such 'call-in' powers, for Nvidia's acquisition of Run:AI but it cleared the transaction on 20 December 2024.[53]

That said, it is worth exploring briefly whether, notwithstanding Article 21(1) EUMR, the Commission would have the competence to apply Article 102 TFEU *ex post* to mergers that lack a Community dimension and fall outside the scope of the *ex ante* merger control regimes in the EU Member States.

As we already noted, in *Towercast*, the Court of Justice held that *national* competition authorities have the competence to apply Article 102 TFEU in such cases. Without rehashing its entire reasoning, it is worth mentioning a couple of points.

The Court first quotes recital No. 7 EUMR – a copy-paste version of recital No. 6 of the original Merger Regulation No. 4064/89 of 21 December 1989. Recital No. 7 provides that Articles 101 and 102 TFEU (at the time Articles 81 and 82 EC), '*while applicable*, according to the case law of the Court of Justice, to *certain* concentrations,

51. Cf. GCR report of 10 April 2024 on statements made by O. Guersent.
52. *See* GCR report of 16 October 2024 on statements made by G. Loriot and its report of 26 November 2024 on further statements made by O. Guersent. Amendments to the Merger Regulation (and possibly also Regulation No. 1/2003) would be more time-consuming and certainly also more complex.
53. *See* press release IP/24/6548 in case M. 11766.

were *not sufficient* to control *all* operations which may prove to be incompatible with a system of undistorted competition envisaged in the Treaty' (emphasis added). The Court opines that the original Merger Regulation therefore closed an enforcement gap left by Articles 101 and 102 TFEU and that 'for reasons of legal certainty, the mechanism for the prior control of concentrations as defined in Art. 3 EUMR must be applied as a matter of priority' but that this 'cannot (...) preclude the possibility for *a* competition authority to capture a concentration under Art. 102 TFEU *under certain conditions*' (emphasis added) because 'it is accepted that certain concentrations may both escape an *ex ante* control and be subject to an *ex post* control'.[54] It will be noted that the Court refers to 'a' competition authority. On its face, this reference therefore covers all competition authorities empowered to apply Article 102 TFEU, including the Commission.

The Court then steps up its reasoning by observing, in a more principled way, that the position adopted by the FCA (and some other intervening parties), according to which only the EU Merger Regulation applied, 'ultimately amounts to ruling out the *direct applicability* of a provision of *primary law* by reason of the adoption of a piece of secondary legislation covering certain types of conduct of undertakings on the market' (emphasis added).[55] The Court appears to be saying that Article 102 TFEU - as a provision of primary law - remains applicable for an *ex post* review of mergers that cannot be reviewed *ex ante*, regardless of the enforcement authority - the Commission or a national authority - called upon to apply Article 102 TFEU.

However, the Court then seems to peddle back by making a much narrower point. It observes that the inapplicability of Regulation No. 1/2003, provided for in Article 21(1) EUMR, does not deprive the *national* competition authorities of the power to apply Article 102 TFEU to concentrations that cannot be reviewed *ex ante* because it is 'the procedural law of the Member States that is applicable to concentrations with a non-Community dimension', so these national authorities could have 'recourse to *their own* procedural rules' (emphasis added) to apply Article 102 TFEU to such concentrations.[56] This would seem to imply *a contrario* that the *Commission* cannot apply Article 102 TFEU to such mergers because Regulation No. 1/2003 is the only Regulation that contains *its* 'own procedural rules' for the application of Article 102 TFEU and Article 21(1) EUMR excludes its applicability.

We are struggling a bit with the Court's point. The national competition authorities do not operate in splendid isolation: Regulation No. 1/2003 contains several procedural rules that are binding upon them when they apply Article 101 or 102 TFEU.

The main purpose of Regulation No. 1/2003 was to ensure that these Treaty provisions would 'be applied effectively and uniformly in the Community' (cf. recital No. 1). In order to achieve this, Regulation No. 1 provides that 'the competition authorities of the Member States should be associated more closely with their application' and 'should be empowered to apply Community law' (cf. recital No. 6 announcing Article 5). It is considered 'necessary to *oblige* the competition authorities (...) of the

54. Para. 38, para. 40 and para. 41 *in fine*.
55. Para. 42.
56. *See* respectively para. 48 and para. 50.

Member States to *also* apply Art. 81 and 82 of the Treaty where they apply national competition law to agreements and practices which may affect trade between Member States' (cf. recital No. 8 announcing Article 3(1)) and 'the Commission and the competition authorities of the Member States should form together a network of public authorities applying the Community competition rules in close cooperation' (cf. recital No. 15 announcing Article 11(1)). In order to ensure that the competition rules will be applied 'consistently', it is even considered 'essential to retain the rule that the competition authorities of the Member States are automatically *relieved* of their competence if the Commission initiates its own proceedings' (cf. recital 17 announcing Article 11(6), emphasis added).

It would therefore seem counter-intuitive to conclude that national competition authorities of the EU Member States would have the competence to apply Article 102 TFEU for *ex post* reviews of mergers that fall outside the scope of their national merger control regimes, while the Commission, as guardian of the Treaty who even has the power to 'relieve' them of that competence for the sake of preserving consistency in the application of Article 102 TFEU (or Article 101 TFEU), would not have that competence.

In addition, one could argue that any enforcement gaps work both ways. As the Court of Justice noted in *Towercast* when quoting recital No. 7 EUMR, Article 102 TFEU was not sufficient to control all concentrations.[57] The original Merger regulation narrowed that enforcement gap in 1989 and the amended Merger Regulation (the EUMR) narrowed that gap further in 2004, *inter alia,* by adding an alternative set of notification thresholds and introducing the 'significant impediment of effective competition' test. In our view, it can be argued – the other way round – that Article 102 TFEU can narrow an enforcement gap left by the EU merger control regime and/or the national merger control regimes (e.g., due to the lack of 'call-in' powers at the latter level).

We are by no means suggesting that reactivating Article 102 TFEU as *ex post* merger control tool in the Commission's hands is a great option for mergers that have no Community dimension and fall outside the scope of the Member States' *ex ante* merger control regimes. However, there might be exceptional situations in which it could arguably be a defendable option.

It will be recalled that the Court in *Continental Can* was very much concerned that dominant companies might engage in merger activity in order to circumvent the constraints of Article 101 TFEU regarding collusive conduct (a concern voiced by von der Groeben as early as 1961). In such situations, it could be argued that Regulation No. 1/2003 has *not* become 'devoid of purpose' since the entry into force of Regulation No. 139/2004.

To take a hypothetical example, let us assume that a dominant supplier of goods tries to circumvent the Article 101/102 TFEU case law prohibiting it from entering into exclusive dealing arrangements with large wholesalers by engaging in a string of

57. Para. 38.

acquisitions of these customers and that each of these acquisitions would be too small to be subject to *ex ante* control under EU or even national merger control law.[58]

At first sight, *Zoetis*, an Article 102 TFEU case in which the Commission has opened a formal investigation in March 2024, is interesting. However, conceptually, it is different. In that case, the Commission is not challenging an operation whereby the (allegedly dominant) company acquired a promising pipeline product from a competitor but rather that company's post-acquisition refusal to sell this product to a third party who had obtained the exclusive commercialization rights from that competitor.[59] The press release does not tell us whether the acquisition was a concentration and, if so, whether it was subject to *ex ante* merger control in any of the EU Member States. Even if so, this would remain a case where the Commission has apparently preferred to challenge the company's post-merger conduct (i.e., the refusal to sell) under Article 102 TFEU rather than to rely on *Continental Can* to challenge *ex post* the 'upstream' acquisition of the pipeline product as a killer acquisition.

58. Admittedly, even if these arguments had merit, Art. 21(1)'s explicit exclusion of the applicability of Regulation No. 1 to concentrations as defined in Art. 3 of the Merger Regulation, remains an oddity. That said, while it would require a separate research into the legislative history of Art. 21(1) of Regulation No. 139/2004 (or its predecessor, Art. 22(1) and (2) of Regulation No. 4064/1989), it is worth flagging that Art. 21 (1) accepts the applicability of Regulation No. 1 for cooperative joint ventures. This is, as such, not surprising (cf. Art. 2 (4) of Regulation No. 139/2004 which confirms the applicability of Art. 81(1) EC to joint ventures which would lead to coordination between the companies concerned as well as Art. 3(2) of Regulation No. 4064/1989 according to which these joint ventures are not concentrations). However, we mention this because we wonder whether the rather heated discussions within the Commission on where exactly to draw the line between concentrative and cooperative joint ventures (before and after the introduction of EU merger control in 1989) may have impacted the drafting of Art. 21(1), including the explicit exclusion of Regulation No. 1, with its exception.
59. Case AT.40734, press release IP/24/1687 of 26 March 2024.

CHAPTER 2

Article 102 TFEU: A Christmas Carol

Liza Lovdahl Gormsen

This chapter will focus on the spirit of Article 102 TFEU (Article 102) – past, present and future. Very much like Ebenezer Scrooge in Charles Dicken's A Christmas Carol by taking a journey through the past, present and future, we are hoping to find that spirit. Although Dicken's novel was written in 1843, it was always and always has been a story for an ever-shifting present. The same can be said about Article 102. Studying the past is important to define the future. Like the Ghost of Christmas, who took Ebenezer to the cemetery and showed him his fate if he did not change his ways, the Court of Justice of the European Union (CJEU) will ultimately decide the faith of undertakings if they abuse their dominant position. Initially however, it will be the European Commission (Commission) who will show them the way in its forthcoming guidelines on exclusionary abuses of Article 102. Guidelines – even priority guidelines – can promote change. Although it was Ebenezer's own selfish motive that caused him to change, his redemption nevertheless resulted in acts of good works, charity and kindness towards others.

Looking at the past and present will include a consideration of the various methodologies adopted by the Commission in its enforcement of Article 102 thus far. Looking at the future of Article 102 will entail not only a discussion of the forthcoming exclusionary guidelines but also a consideration of exploitative conduct. Like A Christmas Carol grabbled with the social injustice and exploitation of Victorian society's underclass, so must the Commission grabble with exploitative conduct.

1 THE PAST: DISCUSSION PAPER & ENFORCEMENT PRIORITIES

The enforcement of Article 102 goes back to Continental Can in 1973,[1] but the real need for a change came around 2002-2003 following cases such as British Airways and

1. Case 6/72 *Europemballage Corporation and Continental Can Co. Inc. v. Commission*, EU:C:1973:22.

Michelin II.[2] These cases were considered particularly formalistic and a need to redirect competition policy away from the law in these decisions started emerging. At the 8th annual conference of the European University Institute in Fiesole in June 2003 Mario Monti, then the Competition Commissioner,[3] announced that the Commission had started an internal review of its policy on abuse of a dominant position.[4] The initiation of the policy review came after growing criticism of the application of Article 82 (now Article 102) and the insufficient attention to economic principles and the rigour of the Commission's policy in this area of law.

One of the primary reasons for initiating the review was a greater appreciation of microeconomic theory on the part of the policy-makers and the need to ensure the application of Article 82 was sufficiently responsive to sound economics. It was also Commissioner Monti, who decided to appoint a Chief Economist following the triple defeat in Airtours, Shneider and Tetra Laval.[5] The role of the Chief Economist was to provide an independent economic opinion and methodological guidance on economic policy and general guidance in individual cases. It became imperative for the Commission to ensure all its decisions – not just merger decisions – were well grounded in fact, law and sound economics.

One of the overall conclusions from the annual conference in Fiesole was that the concept of abuse does not lend itself easily to *per se* rules and that a rule of reason approach is normally preferable. Another conclusion was that legal formalism, which focuses on the nature of the behaviour of the dominant firm, should be abandoned in favour of the analysis and evaluation of economic effects.[6] These conclusions led DG COMP to publish its discussion paper on the Application of Article 82 of the Treaty to Exclusionary Abuses in December 2005 (the 'Discussion Paper').[7]

The Discussion Paper highlighted DG COMP's agenda for developing and explaining theories of harm to consumers based on a sound economic assessment of the most frequent types of abusive behaviour.[8] The Discussion Paper focused on four general themes: dominance, general principles, abusive practices, and defences. Through its general framework,[9] DG COMP pinpointed the way in which exclusionary conduct may lead to the foreclosure of rivals and proposed a two-step analysis for

2. Case T-219/99 *British Airways plc v. Commission*, EU:T:2003:343; Case T-203/01 *Manufacture Française des Pneumatiques Michelin v. Commission*, EU:T:2003:250.
3. Mario Monti's tenure as Competition Commissioner was between September 1999 and November 2004.
4. That an internal review was initiated was confirmed in October 2003 by DG Competition Director General Philip Lowe at the annual conference of the Fordham Corporate Law Institute. Philip Lowe, 'DG Competition's Review of the Policy on Abuse of Dominance', in Annual Proceedings of the Fordham Corporate Law Institute 2003 163 (2004).
5. Case T-342/99, *Airtours plc v. Commission*, EU:T:2002:146; Case T-310/01 *Schneider Electric SA v. Commission*, EU:T:2002:254; Case T-5/02 *Tetra-Laval BV v. Commission*, EU:T:2002:264.
6. Claus-Dieter Ehlermann and Isabela Atanasiu (eds), European Competition Law Annual: What is an Abuse of a Dominant Position? (Hart, 2006).
7. Discussion Paper on the Application of Art. 82 of the Treaty to Exclusionary Abuses (December 2005).
8. Commission Discussion Paper on Abuse of Dominance – Frequently Asked Questions, MEMO of 19 December 2005 MEMO/05/486. Available at: http://europa.eu/rapid/pressReleasesAction.do ?reference = MEMO/05/486&format = HTML&aged = 1&language = EN&guiLanguage = en.
9. Discussion Paper, s. 5.

assessing whether a particular conduct is exclusionary. The specific conduct in question must: (i) be capable of foreclosing the market; but (ii) will only be considered abusive where it can be established that the conduct has a market-distorting foreclosure effect.

The Discussion Paper led the Commission to eventually issue its Guidance on enforcement priorities in applying Article 102 (the 'Guidance Paper') in February 2009.[10] Unlike enforcement priority guidelines, only substantive guidelines are binding upon the Commission.[11] While the Commission is allowed to depart from its guidelines, it has to justify such departure.[12]

2 GUIDANCE PAPER

The Guidance Paper was in the form of enforcement priorities rather than substantive guidelines. The CJEU has long recognised the Commission's power to set its administrative priorities within the limits prescribed by the law.[13] The purpose of enforcement priorities is to provide clarity regarding the Commission's general approach in selecting which abuse of dominance cases to pursue as a priority. However, the Guidance Paper is much more than enforcement priorities.

DG Comp was seeking to implement the so-called more economic approach to the enforcement of Article 102 and had prepared draft guidance on exclusionary abuses. The Legal Service opposed their issuance on the grounds that such guidance was inconsistent with the case law.[14] DG Comp accordingly reframed them as enforcement priorities as a compromise enabling DG Comp to practically implement the 'more economic approach' to exclusionary abuses without risking legal inconsistency. This is why the Guidance Paper states: '[t]his document is not intended to constitute a statement of the law and is without prejudice to the interpretation of Article 82 by the Court of Justice or the Court of First Instance of the European Communities'.

The Guidance Paper was seen as the start of a shift away from a formalistic approach to enforcing Article 102, where cases were prioritised by relying on a 'rules-based' approach, to an 'effects-based' approach. This meant that the Commission's priorities were set having regard to the potential effects of the relevant conduct, based on economic analysis. An effects-based approach focuses on the existence of negative effects for competition, which harm consumers, and centres around the economic analysis of each case based on its specific circumstances and facts. The Commission defined harm to consumers as anything that has 'an adverse impact on

10. Communication from the Commission – Guidance on the Commission's enforcement priorities in applying Article 82 of the EC Treaty to abusive exclusionary conduct by dominant undertakings, OJ C 45, 24.2.2009, p. 7. Available at: https://eur-lex.europa.eu/legal-content/EN/TXT/PDF/?uri=CELEX:52009XC0224(01).
11. Cases T-117/07 and T-121/07 *Areva and Others* (T-117/07) *and Alstom* (T-121/07) *v. Commission*, EU:T:2011:69.
12. Case C-376/20 P *Commission v. CK Telecoms UK Investments Ltd.*, EU:C:2023:561, para. 123.
13. Case T-24/90 *Automec Srl v. Commission*, EU:T:1992:97, para. 77.
14. *See* Liza L. Gormsen, 'Why the European Commission's Enforcement Priorities on Article 82 EC Should Be Withdrawn' (2010) E.C.L.R. 45-51.

consumer welfare, whether in the form of higher price levels than would have otherwise prevailed or in some other form such as limiting quality or reducing consumer choice'.[15]

The Guidance Paper proposed an as efficient competitor test (the 'AEC test'), dismissing other possible tests such as the 'profit sacrifice', 'no economic sense' and 'consumer welfare' tests. The merit of the AEC test was seen to be that competition law was about protecting the process of competition rather than protecting competitors, particularly less efficient competitors. The Guidance Paper states that '[t]his may well mean that competitors who deliver less to consumers in terms of price, choice, quality and innovation will leave the market'.[16] This confirmed that the aim of Article 102 is not to protect less efficient competitors. This message was recently reiterated by the CJEU (Grand Chamber) in the Super League case, a preliminary ruling from a request in Spain.[17] While is it easy to say that the aim is not to protect a less efficient competitor, it is harder to actually show it in practice. The AEC test can be used to establish what hypothetical price a competitor as efficient as the dominant undertaking will have to offer to compete and thereby distinguish between an as efficient competitor worthy of protection, and a less efficient competitor not worthy of protection by Article 102.

Three months after the publication of the Guidance Paper, the Commission issued its decision in *Intel*, where it relied on the AEC test.[18] Following an appeal to the General Court and later to the CJEU, Advocate General Wahl's Opinion in *Intel* endorsed the Commission's move away from a rules-based approach to an effects-based approach set forth in the Guidance Paper.[19] Wahl noted that 'EU competition rules seek to capture behaviour that has anticompetitive effects. To date, the form of a particular practice has not been deemed important.'[20] He also noted the Commission's reliance on the AEC test,[21] which 'establishes at what price a competitor as efficient as Intel would have had to offer CPUs in order to compensate an OEM for the loss of an Intel rebate'.[22]

The AEC test lends itself well to price-based abuses. In *Google Shopping*, the General Court stated that 'the use of the as efficient-competitor test is warranted in the case of pricing practices (predatory pricing or a margin squeeze, for example)'.[23] The CJEU reiterated this in *Servizio Elettrico Nazionale* '[r]egarding the first of these two categories of practices, which includes loyalty rebates, low-pricing practices in the

15. Guidance Paper, para. 19.
16. *Ibid.*, para. 6.
17. Case C-333/21 *European Superleague Company, SL v. Fédération internationale de football association (FIFA) and Union of European Football Associations (UEFA)*,EU:C:2023:1011, para. 126.
18. Case COMP/C-3/37.990 – *Intel*, paras 28-31.
19. Opinion of Advocate General Wahl in case C-413/14 P *Intel Corporation Inc. v. Commission*, EU: C:2016:788.
20. *Ibid.*, para. 43.
21. *Ibid.*, para. 27.
22. *Ibid.*, footnote 9.
23. Case T-612/17 *Google LLC and Alphabet, Inc. v. Commission (Google Shopping)*, EU:T:2021:763, para. 538.

form of selective or predatory prices and margin-squeezing practices, it is clear from the case-law that those practices must be assessed, as a general rule, using the "as-efficient competitor" test, which seeks specifically to assess whether such a competitor, considered in abstracto, is capable of reproducing the conduct of the undertaking in a dominant position'.[24]

On the procedural front, the CJEU held in *Unilever Italia*, that where a dominant firm submits evidence 'capable of demonstrating the inability to produce restrictive effects', the relevant competition authority is under an obligation to consider that evidence which, in the case of *Unilever*, entailed the AEC test.[25] However, the court stressed that authorities are not under an obligation to use the AEC test.[26] This message was recently reiterated by the CJEU in *Intel* 'to foreclose a competitor as efficient as the dominant undertaking, which competitor is supposed to meet the same costs as those borne by that undertaking, must be assessed, as a general rule, using the AEC test'.[27] But the 'test is merely one of the ways of assessing whether an undertaking in a dominant position has used means other than those that come within the scope of "normal" competition'.[28]

While the AEC test is a useful tool for certain pricing abuses, it is a time-consuming test and not always an easy test to apply in practice. The Commission started to question whether the more effects-based approach had led to Article 102 being applied less vigorously and effectively than intended.

3 POLICY BRIEF

In March 2023, the Commission decided to revise parts of the Guidance Paper that no longer reflected the Commission's approach in determining whether to pursue as a matter of priority certain cases of exclusionary conduct. The Commission made some amendments to its Guidance Paper with immediate effect (the 'Amending Communication').[29] The Amending Communication marks a certain shift in its approach to abuse of dominance. This shift in approach was explained in the Commission's policy brief titled: A dynamic and workable effects-based approach to Article 102 TFEU (the 'Policy Brief').[30]

The Policy Brief talks about the Commission's 'workable effects-based approach', but assures us that this is not a shift away from an effects-based approach, but merely to avoid some of the pitfalls in the effects-based approach. For example, the

24. Case C-377/20 *Servizio Elettrico Nazionale and Others*, EU:C:2022:379, para. 80.
25. Case C-680/20 *Unilever Italia*, EU:C:2023:33, para. 54.
26. *Ibid.*, para. 58.
27. Case C-240/22 P *Intel Corporation v. Commission*, EU:C:2024:915, para. 181.
28. *Ibid.*
29. Amendments to the Communication from the Commission Guidance on the Commission's enforcement priorities in applying Art. 82 of the EC Treaty to abusive exclusionary conduct by dominant undertakings 27 March 2023, https://competition-policy.ec.europa.eu/document/download/3c8af31c-1bf0-467a-b4a7-a69da6e722bb_en?filename=20230327_amending_communication_art_102_0.pdf.
30. https://competition-policy.ec.europa.eu/document/download/40413680-4eda-4ba0-96b1-e3e9d4e22106_en?filename=kdak23001enn_competition_policy_brief_1_2023_Article102_0.pdf.

digital market's challengers may not be expected to achieve similar cost structures to a dominant incumbent, but could still play a significant role. As such, mandating evidence of foreclosure of as-efficient competitors would have the potential to lead to underenforcement. The Commission therefore sought to avoid an 'unduly strict and dogmatic application' of the AEC standard. According to the Policy Brief, a workable effects-based approach is better tailored to reality, and experience shows that there is no need to do an effects-based approach every time if experience has shown that the conduct is problematic. This has led to arguments being advanced that the Policy Brief presents an intellectually dishonest interpretation of case law. The Commission seems to reinterpret, or at least downplay, some of the key principles now established in the case law and rely on presumptions not supported by case law. Equally, arguments have been advanced that enforcement is too slow, which is a form of underenforcement and would like the law to be applied with less reliance on economics and more reliance on presumptions. In principle, presumptions can speed up enforcement. Either way, it is the Commission's prerogative to extract from a patchwork of sometimes irreconcilable judgments[31] and decide what works best for its enforcement goal. It will ultimately be for the European Courts to decide whether or not to support the Commission's interpretation.

In addition to the Amending Communication, the Commission issued a Call for Evidence consulting on the adoption of guidelines on exclusionary abuses for dominant undertakings (the 'Draft Guidelines').[32]

4 THE PRESENT: DRAFT GUIDELINES ON EXCLUSIONARY ABUSE

Given the complementarity of the Digital Markets Act (the 'DMA') and the fact that DMA is based on the lessons learned from Article 102 enforcement, it may seem natural to discuss this newly enacted regulation. Constraints of time and space however do not allow me to cover the DMA in any detail. However, it is worth mentioning that the enactment of the DMA may reduce the enforcement of Article 102 given digital gatekeepers' potentially abusive practices are now covered by the DMA. An example of this is the Commission's closure of its Article 102 investigation of Apple's app store practices in June 2024.[33] In its press release, the Commission noted that since the initiation of proceedings, Apple had been designated as a 'gatekeeper' in relation to its App Store under the DMA and this covered the scope of the Article 102 investigation, thus was no need to continue its investigation under Article 102.[34] Despite the enormous interest in the DMA, this part of the chapter will focus on the meaning of abuse of dominance set forth in the Draft Guidelines.

31. *See*, for example, conflicting views from the CJEU in *Google Shopping* and *Intel*.
32. https://ec.europa.eu/commission/presscorner/detail/en/IP_23_1911.
33. AT.40716.
34. Press Release, European Comm'n, Commission closes antitrust investigation into Apple's rules for in-app payment system and steering (24 June 2024) https://ec.europa.eu/commission/presscorner/detail/en/mex_24_3444.

According to the Commission, the aim of the Draft Guidelines is three-fold: (i) to systematise the body of case law from the courts on exclusionary conduct; (ii) to draw lessons from the Commission's experience and the case law to promote a workable effects-based approach; (iii) to provide operational guidance to dominant firms and to force compliance.

The Commission has been open about its desire to use its forthcoming guidelines to deal with contradictions and tensions in some of the case law and find a way to systematise case law on exclusionary conduct. This requires a choice on how to interpret conflicting case law. As said, it is for the European Courts to have the final word on the interpretation of the law. A dominant undertaking – under investigation by the Commission – has no other choice but to follow case law if there is a contradiction between the Commission's interpretation and case law. The law of Article 102 is what the Courts say it is.

As seen from the previous section, abuse of dominance is never straightforward. Whish and Bailey say '[i]t is not controversial to say that the meaning of abuse of dominance is controversial'.[35] One part of the controversy is the goals of Article 102, and another is the methodology. In relation to the goals, DG COMP and many NCAs have for some time had a singular fetishism with the objective of consumer welfare. However, former Competition Commissioner and EU Vice President Vestager noted in a speech that EU competition policy can pursue multiple goals such as fairness, level playing field, market integration, preserving the competitive process, consumer welfare, efficiency, innovation and ultimately plurality and democracy.[36] In the *Superleague* case, the CJEU talks about the purpose of Article 102 being to prevent competition from being restricted to the detriment of the public interest, individual undertakings and consumers.[37] This is echoed in the Draft Guidelines, which talk about the public interest, other market players and consumers.[38] Bringing other objectives into the mix is very different from the Guidance Paper, which focused on adverse impact on consumer welfare: 'the aim of the Commission's enforcement activity in relation to exclusionary conduct is [...] to ensure that dominant undertakings do not impair effective competition by foreclosing their competitors in an anti-competitive way, thus having an adverse impact on consumer welfare'.[39] While consumer welfare appears occasionally in the Draft Guidelines, it plays a far less central role in the overall analysis. Economic insights are important in the enforcement of Article 102, but it is apparent from the Draft Guidelines that economics alone cannot provide sufficient guidance on normative goals. Most notably, the Draft Guidelines downplay the

35. Richard Whish and David Bailey, Competition Law (OUP, 2024), Chapter 5.
36. Vestager 'A Principle Based approach to Competition Policy' (Keynote to the Competition Law Tuesdays, 22 October 2022).
37. Case C-333/21, *European Superleague Company, SL v. Fédération internationale de football association (FIFA) and Union of European Football Associations (UEFA)*,EU:C:2023:1011, para. 124.
38. Para. 2.
39. Communication from the Commission – Guidance on the Commission's enforcement priorities in applying Article 82 of the EC Treaty to abusive exclusionary conduct by dominant undertakings, OJ C 45, 24.2.2009, p. 7. Available at: https://eur-lex.europa.eu/legal-content/EN/TXT/PDF/?uri=CELEX:52009XC0224(01), para. 19.

fundamental principle that Article 102 is not intended to protect competitors that are less efficient than the dominant firm.

In relation to methodology, section 3 of the Draft Guidelines proposes a two-stage test for determining whether conduct by a dominant undertaking is liable to constitute an exclusionary abuse. First, does the conduct depart from competition on the merits; and second, is it capable of having exclusionary effects.[40] The Commission sees this two-stage test as cumulative rather than alternative. When a given conduct meets the conditions set out in a specific legal test developed by the Court, such conduct is deemed to be liable to be abusive because it falls outside the scope of competition on the merits and is capable of having exclusionary effects.[41]

The Commission has tried to operationalise the notion of competition on the merits by outlining three scenarios: naked restrictions, conduct with specific legal tests, and other types of conduct. Naked restrictions have no economic interest other than excluding.[42] This conduct always departs from competition on the merits. Conduct where specific legal tests apply, for example, predation, margin squeeze and exclusive dealing.[43] There is no need to show this kind of conduct departs from competition on the merits as it is incorporated in the relevant legal tests. For everything else, the Draft Guidelines outline a list of elements that can be relevant for the analysis, for example, the AEC test.[44]

When deciding whether the conduct is capable of having exclusionary effects, the second limb of the test, the Draft Guidelines propose a more presumption-based approach. This includes identifying a wide range of types of conduct where the capability to produce exclusionary effects may be presumed. The Commission is thereby tipping the balance of the burden of proof away from the Commission towards the allegedly dominant firm.[45] The Draft Guidelines acknowledge that the Courts have not articulated the use of presumptions. Nevertheless, 'the Commission considers that the case-law has developed tools which can be broadly described and conceptualised, for the purpose of these Guidelines, as "presumptions". Therefore, these Guidelines make use of the expression "presumption" (or "presumed") for allocating the evidentiary burdens that result from the application of the specific legal tests set out by the Union Courts'.[46] Section 5 of the Draft Guidelines explicitly preserves the possibility of an efficiency defence and objective necessity defence which allow – at least in theory – a consumer welfare-related analysis. Although the Draft Guidelines do not say it explicitly, it is clear that the Commission does not see it as necessary to engage in any economic analysis for naked restrictions and show exclusionary effects of such conduct.

40. Para. 45.
41. Para. 47.
42. Para. 60(c).
43. Para. 60(b).
44. Para. 55.
45. Footnote 127; para. 60(b).
46. Footnote 131.

5 THE FUTURE: THE DRAGHI REPORT AND EXPLOITATION

Following the publication of the Draft Guidelines, which was discussed in the previous section, Mario Draghi's report on 'The future of European competitiveness'[47] was published. The Draghi report was particularly critical of the Draft Guidelines in relation to a number of issues For example, the Draft Guidelines say that tying can be presumed to have exclusionary effects, but is silent on conditions for that presumption. While the Draft Guidelines cite the case law in a footnote, it does not cite any conditions. The Draghi report mentioned that it would be helpful to know the conditions that trigger the presumptions. The report further emphasised that speed and predictability of decisions need to be improved, noting that '[d]ecade-long cases like the Intel case' *are* 'not isolated episodes'. For Draghi, the Commission's approach to exclusionary abuses under Article 102 is an area that needs to be 'urgently streamlined'. In his view, the Draft Guidelines leave the Commission with 'excessive discretion' which is not conducive to legal certainty for undertakings needing to understand how the Commission will go about enforcing Article 102. In general, guidelines are there to help undertakings self-assess, so if there is ambiguity or uncertainty, the guidelines will not fulfil their purpose. It is difficult to see how the current draft of the guidelines can survive without a number of changes.

6 EXPLOITATIVE ABUSE

As mentioned, exploitative abuses are not covered by the draft guidelines, despite recent expressions of interest by the Commission in bringing enforcement cases in this area. The very first abuse of dominance case *Continental Can*[48] included both exclusionary and exploitative abuses, but as Advocate General Wahl observed that the Commission has been 'extremely reluctant' to use Article 102 to address high prices and has not taken enforcement action for non-price exploitation in over forty years.[49] The cases that have been brought are in particular sectors where typical conditions of competition prevail. There have been a significant number of cases concerning copyright societies (*Latvian Copyright, Tournier, Sabam*), off-patent pharmaceuticals (*Aspen, Hydrocortizone and Lirothyrine*) and, now, in relation to multisided digital platforms (*Apple, Meta*). The German Federal Supreme Court held, in a similar vein, that the fact that Facebook was 'decisive' for some consumers to participate in social life was a relevant factor for determining intervention while simultaneously observing that exploitative abuses are 'not limited to essential products and services'.[50]

47. Mario Draghi, The Future of European Competitiveness, September 2024. Part A available at https://commission.europa.eu/topics/eu-competitiveness/draghi-report_en#paragraph_47059 and Part B here https://commission.europa.eu/document/download/ec1409c1-d4b4-4882-8bdd-3519f86bbb92_en?filename=The%20future%20of%20European%20competitiveness_%20In-depth%20analysis%20and%20recommendations_0.pdf.
48. Case 6/72 *Europemballage Corporation and Continental Can Co. Inc. v. Commission*, EU:C:1973:22.
49. Opinion of AG Wahl in case C-177/16 *Latvian Copyright*, EU:C:2017:286, para. 3.
50. Decision KVR 69/19 Bundesgerichtshof Judgment of 23 June 2020, para. 102.

Most enforcement action has centred around exclusionary conduct rather than exploitative conduct. Traditionally, enforcement against exploitation has mainly been dealt with by the national competition authorities (NCAs) - some more than others. Focusing mainly on exclusionary conduct is not tenable in a digital economy. Data is the pinnacle of the digital economy and those firms born digital - as opposed to analogue - have a greater ability to impose unfair trading conditions due to their data advantage.

Direct exploitation in the form of unfair trading practices and excessive pricing, covered by Article 102(a), was excluded from the scope of the Discussion Paper and the Guidance Paper and will not be part of the forthcoming substantive guidance of Article 102. This is a missed opportunity for two reasons: (i) the data-driven economy - characterised partly by ecosystems - lends itself to possible data exploitation through unfair trading practices and excessive pricing; (ii) there is evidence that markets are becoming more concentrated,[51] which makes exploitation all the more commonplace.

However, if the general aim of guidelines - not just Article 102 guidelines - is to consolidate practice, and ensure consistency and predictability, then the Commission is not in a position to include exploitation in its guidelines as there is very little practice on exploitation to consolidate. That said, guidelines can - whether on exclusionary or exploitative conduct - promote change and they can be drafted with specific policy intentions in mind which may (or may not) come true depending on support from the courts. The Guidance Paper is a great example of how significantly enforcement priorities can shape the evolution of exclusionary abuses as the courts started implementing the thinking behind them. The 'as efficient competitor' test, effects-based approaches to exclusive dealing and tying and the notion of anti-competitive foreclosure all stem from the Guidance Paper that underpins many of its concepts. The Guidance Paper demonstrated how the normative power of an instrument softer than soft law can shape the evolution of exclusionary abuses.[52] While 'real' priority guidelines do nothing more than setting out the Commission's approach as to the choice of cases to pursue as a matter of priority, the Guidance Paper did much more than setting out enforcement priorities.

The Guidance Paper proved itself to be an extremely effective tool at a time when there were very few judicial precedents to use as a basis for developing a comprehensive guidance. There is no need to think that this cannot also be achieved for exploitative conduct. By issuing enforcement priorities, the Commission may be able to set a direction of travel for its own decisional practice and, this way, steer the evolution of EU law on exploitative abuse of dominance. Enforcement priorities' flexibility also means that the Commission can step away from them in the event that experience demonstrates that elements do not correctly calibrate when to enforce against exploitation. In such a situation, the Commission can always resort to issuing a policy brief.

51. IMF Staff Paper, Rising Corporate Market Power: emerging policy issues (March 2021) https://www.imf.org/-/media/Files/Publications/SDN/2021/English/SDNEA2021001.ashx, pp. 16-17.
52. Anne C. Witt, 'The Commission's Guidance Paper on Abusive Exclusionary Conduct: More Radical Than It Appears?' (2010) E. L. Rev. 233-234.

Article 102(a) addresses the 'fairness' of conduct by dominant firms by prohibiting conduct that directly or indirectly 'impose unfair purchase or selling prices or other unfair trading conditions'. Fairness poses, however, a conceptual challenge as it is inherently difficult to decide what is 'fair' in relation to the economic regulation of markets. While 'fairness' features centre stage in wider competition and regulatory policy as one of the two main objectives of the DMA,[53] and underpins exploitative abuses, it remains difficult to translate into a framework for understanding undertakings' rights and obligations. Exploitative abuses have recently assumed greater importance as regulators increasingly investigate such conduct. As mentioned recent cases include the *Aspen* case on excessive pricing of cancer drugs[54] and the *Apple* case on unfair trading terms by withholding information to users.[55] Despite the challenge with the concept of fairness, there is case law such as *United Brands*,[56] which set forth the law on unfair pricing. It becomes somewhat more difficult for non-pricing exploitation such as unfair trading terms. Up until the Commission's recent decision against Apple, the leading case was *BRT v. SABAM*,[57] which the Commission subsequently followed in GEMA statutes.[58] Some authors argue that the 'unifying rationale of these [non-pricing exploitation] cases is not easily stated, but it seems to reflect the consideration that a firm without dominance would not be able to impose such terms on consumers and trading parties, or at least not to the same extent'.[59]

Understanding when it is appropriate to pursue exploitation is of fundamental importance. Firms achieving price and non-price conditions above their marginal cost is an inherent part of competitive markets: it drives incentives to innovate and encourages rivals to enter and expand.[60] Absent careful calibration, intervention to

53. *See* Giorgio Monti and Alexandre de Streel, 'Exploitative Abuses: The Scope and the Limits of Article 102 TFEU' (2023) Robert Schuman Centre for Advanced Studies (working paper), 8. The authors refer in particular to the recent actions taken by competition authorities to address excessive pricing in the pharmaceutical market.
54. https://ec.europa.eu/commission/presscorner/detail/en/ip_21_524.
55. Case AT.40437 – *Apple – App Store Practices* (music streaming).
56. Case 27/76 *United Brands v. Commission*, EU:C:1978:22, para. 252.
57. Case 127/73 *BRT v. SABAM*, EU:C:1974:25, which dealt with the conditions imposed by SABAM (the Belgian association of authors in charge of managing and exploiting copyrights) to its members. In its preliminary ruling, the CJEU found that trading conditions shall be considered abusive inasmuch as they impose obligations which are not absolutely necessary to the attainment of their object (para. 15).
58. Case IV/29.971 – *GEMA statutes*. The Commission inferred two tests from the previous case law (notably from *BRT v. SABAM*): 'indispensability' (whether the conditions exceed the absolutely necessary) and 'equity' (whether they limit the copyright holders' freedom to dispose of their work more than it need be) (para. 36).
59. Robert O'Donoghue and Jorge Padilla, The Law and Economics of Article 102 TFEU (3rd ed., Hart Publishing, 2020), pp. 1023-1024.
60. Electricity prices have undergone significant stress due to the volatility of fuel and gas supply in the uncertain geo-political landscape of the last few years. Against this background, the UK energy regulator (Ofgem) issued open letters addressing electricity price increases during the winter in 2021 (*see* https://www.ofgem.gov.uk/publications/open-letter-trends-balancing-costs-2021), 2022 (*see* https://www.ofgem.gov.uk/publications/open-letter-responding-high-balancing-costs) and 2023 (*see* https://www.ofgem.gov.uk/consultation/price-cap-open-letter-reviewing-additional-wholesale-costs). The Ofgem notes in these letters that occasional high prices in periods with tight margins can allow companies to recover their costs and incentivise investors to bring forward additional generation when there is scarcity of capacity. However,

solve such 'exploitation' may not correct market failures (which is a valid reason for intervention), but instead chill competition and the market forces which would cure it (self-righting markets). It is for these same reasons that regulators have historically exercised significant discretion when seeking to use Article 102 to pursue exploitative conduct. It is, in part, for this reason that the case law and enforcement practice are juxtaposed. The case law articulates no consistent, underlying logic or framework for assessing when enforcement against exploitative conduct is appropriate. Some commentators have suggested that exploitative abuses should be pursued where there is sufficient market failure, i.e., situations that market forces cannot correct by themselves. This has some judicial support. AG Wahl contended in *Latvian Copyright* that excessive pricing was, *inter alia*, unlikely to occur in markets that are not protected by high barriers to entry since the market would otherwise be likely to self-correct.[61] AG Pitruzzella contended in *Sabam* that there may also be 'de facto' monopolies due to factors including 'consumer habits, the absence of alternatives', 'lock-in effects', 'network effects' and 'economies of scale'.[62] The narrower approach is consistent with competition authorities who have almost exclusively brought excessive pricing cases in atypical market conditions.

7 CONCLUSION

As stated from the outset, this chapter does not purport to cover all, or even most, of the Article 102 developments that led the Commission to the process of drafting substantive guidelines on exclusionary conduct; but it has attempted to provide the reasons for why it is happening. Developments in case law since the Guidance Paper in 2009 mark a clear move away from *British Airways* and *Michelin II*, which initiated the review of Article 102 back in 2003. However, the Draft Guidelines do return to a more formalistic approach seen prior to the Guidance Paper for certain kinds of conduct such as naked restrictions. According to the Draft Guidelines, such conduct has no economic interest for an undertaking beyond restricting competition and is deemed to fall outside the scope of competition on the merits and can be presumed to be capable of exclusionary effects. Dominant undertakings will only be able to rebut this presumption in very exceptional circumstances.

The Draft Guidelines also seek to address novel categories of abuse – such as self-preferencing – that are primarily associated with the rise of the digital economy, but without the necessary clarity for undertakings to be able to self-assess compliance. For example, it is clear from case law that the Commission is not obliged to always adopt the AEC test in its analysis and it is clearly the Commission's view that the AEC test lends itself better to pricing cases. This may very well be right, but in summarising the case law, the Draft Guidelines take a somewhat selective approach to the AEC test

consumer protection standards must be respected and certain conducts (persistently high prices, inflexible and expansive offers and intentional exacerbation of tight margins) are disproportionate (and thus exploitative) responses to scarcity.

61. Opinion of AG Wahl in case C-177/16 *Latvian Copyright*, EU:C:2017:286, para. 48.
62. Case C-372/19 *Sabam*, Opinion of AG Pitruzzella, EU:C:2020:598, para. 24.

and it is not clear whether it applies to novel categories of abuse. Trying to pretend that the AEC is not part of enforcement history seems dishonest and may increase uncertainty.

The Commission has decided that the more economic-based approach set out in the Guidance Paper has not worked and has slowed down its enforcement. However, the more economic-based approach did not deter enforcement and economic analysis has not had a negative impact on the Commission's creativity as seen from new theories of harm emerging such as self-preferencing and strategic underinvestment. The Commission's suggested workable effects-based approach appears to acknowledge the importance of economics, but not at the expense of evidence telling a different story.

This chapter has not discussed remedies, but in the Commission Article 102 package, it ought to also consider effective remedies. For Article 102 to be meaningful to society we need to ensure proper remedies, so it would be helpful to have an *ex post* review to assess whether the remedies to date have been effective. The main complaints under Article 102 are coming from competitors, so the Commission is addressing such complaints, rather than providing remedies that are beneficial for consumers. Direct consumer harm to consumers – exploitative abuses – is not covered by the Draft Guidelines, despite recent expressions of interest by the Commission in bringing enforcement cases in this area. For all the reasons explained in this chapter, it would not be realistic to include exploitative abuse in the Draft Guidelines, but it is my hope that the Commission will issue enforcement priorities for exploitative conduct in due course.

CHAPTER 3

The Influence of Economic Regulation in EU Competition Law Assessment and Remedy Design

Dimitrios Nikolaidis

1 INTRODUCTION

The interplay between competition law and economic regulation is a multi-faceted one and a critical point for competition policy. Following the liberalisation initiatives in the mid-1980s, marked by the adoption of sector-specific regulation in network industries - *inter alia,* in the telecommunications and energy sectors - the relationship between competition law and regulatory regimes came to the fore.[1] Even today, a number of modern markets where the European Commission (hereinafter, the 'Commission') and national competition authorities (NCAs) focus their antitrust enforcement actions are subject to sector-specific regulation. It is therefore not uncommon for the Commission and NCAs to apply EU competition law in an environment that is also covered by economic regulation. Similarly, national regulatory authorities (NRAs) apply regulatory principles in areas where competition law is applicable.[2] During the last two decades, the relationship between competition law and sector-specific regulation has grown increasingly prominent due to the exponential growth of data-driven and digital industries, which have become key priorities in regulatory and competition law enforcement efforts.[3]

1. *See* Damien Geradin, *The Opening of State Monopolies to Competition: Main Issues of the Liberalisation Process,* in *The Liberalisation of State Monopolies in the European Union and Beyond* (D. Geradin ed., Kluwer Law International 1999).
2. Robert O'Donoghue and Jorge Padilla, *Law and Economics of Article 102 TFEU,* 60 (2nd ed., Bloomsbury Publishing 2020).
3. *See* Jacques Crémer, Yves-Alexandre de Montjoye and Heike Schweitzer, *Competition Policy for the Digital Era* (European Commission 2019).

The concurrent application of (*ex post*) competition law and (*ex ante*) regulation inevitably entails a degree of overlap,[4] with the same set of activities often falling under the purview of both regimes. The question of whether competition law applies where an issue has already been subject to the relevant regulatory regime has been unequivocally settled by the Court of Justice of the European Union (the 'Court'). In *Deutsche Telekom*,[5] in the context of a margin squeeze case by the German incumbent telecommunications operator, the Court held that the existence of sector-specific regulation does not preclude the application of EU competition law.[6] Even when a regulatory framework governs the behaviour of a dominant undertaking, competition law remains applicable to ensure that the undertaking does not abuse its dominant position. This principle has been reaffirmed in subsequent case law.[7]

The parallel application of competition law and sector-specific regulation, while mutually complementary, raises substantive issues about the extent of their interaction and the influence they exert on each other. The enforcement of competition law in regulated markets must account for the unique characteristics of said markets, which in turn influence the assessment of the anticompetitive conduct and the design of remedies to rectify the infringement and mitigate the anticompetitive effects. Notably, the complexities inherent in such markets often necessitate a thorough evaluation of regulatory impacts and the consideration of more prescriptive, regulatory-like remedies to foster competition in these markets.

This article aims to provide a high-level analysis of the influence of sector-specific regulation on the assessment of dominance and the design and administration of remedies under Article 102 TFEU. It is structured as follows: section 2 examines the impact of regulation on market structure and competitive dynamics, as well as its implications for the assessment of abusive conduct. Section 3 explores the influence of regulation in the design and implementation of remedies.

2 THE ROLE OF REGULATION IN ARTICLE 102 ANALYSIS

The interaction between competition law and sector-specific regulation has become increasingly prominent in EU enforcement practice, particularly under Article 102 TFEU. Regulation plays a significant role in shaping the market structures, competitive

4. For a more analytical discussion on the relationship between temporal and substantive overlap between *ex post* and *ex ante* regimes, *see* Pablo Ibáñez Colomo, *The New EU Competition Law: Innovation, Investment, and Competition in Digital Markets*, Ch. 3 (Hart Publishing 2024).
5. Case C-280/08 P, *Deutsche Telekom AG v. Commission*, EU:C:2010:603.
6. *Ibid.*, para. 80.
7. Case C-295/12, *Telefónica and Telefónica de España v. Commission*, EU:C:2014:2062, para. 135. *See also* Pierre Larouche and Alexandre de Streel, *Interplay Between the New Competition Tool and Sector-Specific Regulation in the EU*, 21 (Publications Office of the European Union 2020), '[t]he reverse situation, where a firm would comply with competition law but not with sectoral regulation, has not yet been explored in the case law. In the 1998 Access Notice, the Commission states that in such a case, compliance with competition law does not prevent liability under sectoral regulation. In practice, such cases are unlikely to arise: since the 2004 reform (Regulation 1/2003), the Commission has ceased to issue non-infringement decisions under Articles 101 or 102 TFEU, and national competition authorities do not have the power to issue such decisions'.

dynamics, and the legal context within which competition law applies. This influence extends both to the definition of the relevant market and the assessment of abusive conduct. In regulated industries, such as telecommunications, energy, transport, and more recently digital markets, regulatory frameworks often pre-establish certain market conditions.[8] This regulatory intervention can both inform and complicate competition law enforcement, as authorities must balance the goals of sector-specific regulation with the fundamental objectives of competition policy.

This chapter examines two dimensions of this relationship. First, it explores how regulation influences the structure and dynamics of the relevant market for competition law purposes. Second, it analyses how regulatory obligations impact the substantive assessment of abuse under Article 102 TFEU, with particular attention to refusal-to-deal cases and the emerging challenges arising from digital regulation, notably the Digital Markets Act (DMA).[9]

2.1 Impact on Market Structure and Competitive Dynamics

It is widely recognised that competition law does not apply in isolation.[10] *Ex ante* regulation, regardless of whether its scope aligns closely with competition law or pursues different policy objectives, is an integral part of the framework within which competition law applies.[11] Most markets are subject to a degree of regulation, which, to a certain extent, prescribes the purview of competition law scrutiny and shapes the structure and dynamics of the market. These regulatory regimes address various concerns and cover a number of sectors, including, *inter alia*, data protection, digital markets, financial services and traditional network industries, such as telecommunications and energy. Both the intrusiveness of regulatory regimes and the room for autonomous conduct left to regulated entities vary, inevitably impacting the scope of competition law enforcement.

Indeed, when designing a regulatory framework to address structural issues within a particular sector, the legislator often defines the market structure in a way that directly impacts competitive dynamics. Where structural market failures are identified, particularly in sectors characterised by high barriers to entry or bottleneck segments, economic regulation may intervene to promote or preserve competition.[12] This regulatory intervention pre-establishes certain key features of the regulated market, including the competitive dynamics and permissible levels of market concentration.[13]

8. Niamh Dunne, *The Role of Regulation in EU Competition Law Assessment*, 44 *World Competition* 287, 294 (2021) https://doi.org/10.54648/woco2021018 (last accessed: 30 October 2024).
9. Regulation (EU) 2022/1925 of the European Parliament and of the Council of 14 September 2022 on contestable and fair markets in the digital sector and amending Directives (EU) 2019/1937 and (EU) 2020/1828 (Digital Markets Act), OJ L 265, 12.10.2022.
10. *See*, for example, Arletta Gorecka, *On the Interplay Between Competition Law and Privacy: The Impact of Meta Platforms Case*, 20 European Competition Journal 555, 569 (2024) https://doi.org/10.1080/17441056.2024.2324586 (last accessed: 30 October 2024).
11. *See* Ibáñez Colomo, *supra* n. 4, p. 73.
12. *Ibid.*, p. 75.
13. Economic regulation intervenes in market decisions such as pricing, competition, market entry, or exit, *see* OECD, *Competition Enforcement and Regulatory Alternatives* 53 (2021).

In this context, economic regulation can be understood as deliberately shaping artificial market structures to achieve specific policy objectives.[14] Consequently, the first point of interaction between regulation and competition law arises in the assessment of market structures where competition law applies. A critical question, therefore, is how these market structures defined by the regulator influence the enforcement of Article 102 TFEU. The question becomes particularly salient in light of the 'more economic approach' to EU competition law, which emphasises the need to consider the economic and legal context for competition assessment.[15]

In this respect, the Court unequivocally held that the competitive conditions set by the applicable regulatory framework determine the parameters for defining the relevant market for the application of Article 102 TFEU. In particular, in *Deutsche Telekom*, the Court affirmed that the relevant telecommunications regulation, as part of the applicable legal framework, 'contributes to the determination of the competitive conditions under which an undertaking [...] carries on its business in the relevant markets, it is [...] a relevant factor in the application of Article [102 TFEU] to the conduct of that undertaking, whether for the purposes of defining the relevant markets, assessing the abusive nature of such conduct or setting the amount of the fines'.[16] According to the Court, the market structures, as shaped by sector-specific regulation, define the context against which competition law analysis is carried out. This approach has been further upheld in ensuing case law, namely in *TeliaSonera*[17] and *Slovak Telekom*.[18] The Court's reasoning demonstrates the recognition of a broader scope for the application of competition law in regulated sectors, recognising that where regulation shapes the competitive dynamics and the market structure, these elements inform the analysis of the relevant markets for the application of Article 102 TFEU.[19]

2.2 Impact on the Assessment of Abuse

As demonstrated above, sector-specific regulation constitutes an integral part of the economic and legal context within which competition law applies. The Court's recognition that the applicable regulatory framework is a relevant factor in assessing the abusive nature of a dominant firm's conduct[20] has significant implications for the application of Article 102 TFEU in regulated industries, as it directly influences the interpretation of the latter. Given its inherently malleable nature, competition law may be adapted to accommodate policy objectives from other regulatory domains, even where these do not fully align with the main goals of competition law, i.e., even in situations where the regulatory regime pursues goals other than consumer welfare and

14. *See* Ibáñez Colomo, *supra* n. 4, Ch. 6, p. 156.
15. *See* Dunne, *supra* n. 8, p. 293.
16. *Deutsche Telekom, supra* n. 5, para. 224.
17. Case C-52/09, *TeliaSonera Sverige AB*, EU:C:2011:83, para. 68.
18. Case T-851/14, *Slovak Telekom, a.s. v. Commission*, EU:T:2018:929, para. 139.
19. *See supra* n. 14.
20. *Deutsche Telekom, supra* n. 5, para. 224.

the protection of the competitive process. This influence may manifest through an alteration of the substantive standards applied in the assessment of abusive conduct or by informing the boundaries of competition on the merits.[21]

Jurisprudence provides several examples where the enforcement of Article 102 TFEU in regulated markets has resulted in the incorporation of regulatory standards into the assessment of abusive conduct. A particularly notable instance of this influence can be observed in case law on refusal to deal, where regulatory considerations have permeated competition law analysis. According to the established framework of Article 102 TFEU, access obligations are imposed only under exceptional circumstances.[22] Under the strict conditions set out in *Bronner*, it needs to be demonstrated that the input is *indispensable* for effective competition in an adjacent market.[23] However, where access is mandated by sector-specific regulation, the indispensability requirement is circumvented, and a less stringent standard applies.

Examples from the enforcement of Article 102 TFU in network industries illustrate this approach. In the telecommunications sector, *Telekomunikacja Polska*[24] and *Slovak Telekom*,[25] demonstrate a deviation from the stringent standard traditionally applied in refusal to deal under Article 102 TFEU. In both cases, the incumbent operators were subject to an *ex ante* obligation to provide wholesale access to their local loops, as mandated by the sectoral regime. The Commission found that the incumbents had engaged in obstructive practices, namely unjustified delays and the imposition of unnecessary conditions on access, which amounted to 'constructive' refusals to deal. Notably, these findings were made without requiring proof of indispensability as established under the *Bronner* doctrine.[26]

This deviation from traditional case law on refusal to deal is justified by the existence of a regulatory regime that has already made the necessary trade-offs between the incumbent firm's incentives to invest in essential facilities - the key rationale underlying the strict indispensability standard - and the imposition of a duty to supply on the dominant undertaking.[27] In this regard, sector-specific regulation predefines access obligations, thereby influencing competition law analysis and lowering the threshold for *ex post* intervention under Article 102 TFEU.

Analogous issues have arisen in the context of the regulatory framework governing access to railway infrastructure. In *Lietuvos geležinkeliai (Lithuanian Railways)*,[28] it was found that the dominant undertaking, as the manager of state-owned infrastructure, was subject to a regulatory obligation to ensure access to the railway network. The deliberate removal of a section of railway tracks, which effectively prevented access, was held to constitute an abuse of dominance under Article 102 TFEU, without

21. *See* Dunne, *supra* n. 8, p. 293.
22. Case C-7/97, *Oscar Bronner*, EU:C:1998:569, paras 39-40.
23. *Ibid.*, para. 38.
24. Commission Decision of 22 June 2011, Case AT.39525, *Telekomunikacja Polska*.
25. Commission Decision of 5 November 2015, Case AT.39523, *Slovak Telekom*.
26. *Oscar Bronner*, *supra* n. 22.
27. *Slovak Telekom*, *supra* n. 18, para. 118.
28. Case T-814/17, *Lietuvos geležinkeliai AB v. Commission*, 18.11.2020, EU:T:2020:545.

the need to satisfy the stringent criteria established in *Bronner*.[29] The Court clarified that where a dominant undertaking operates within a regulatory regime that imposes specific access obligations, *Bronner* criteria do not apply, since the regulatory duty to supply effectively supersedes the need to demonstrate indispensability. Hence, the existence of an *ex ante* regulatory duty to provide access warrants the assessment of whether any failure to do so is capable of having anticompetitive effects.[30]

It follows from the foregoing decisional practice and case law that regulatory obligations arising from sector-specific legislation shape the competitive conditions under which undertakings operate in the relevant markets, thereby informing the application of Article 102 TFEU.[31] This is particularly evident where sector-specific regulation pursues objectives aligned with those of EU competition policy. However, there are instances where it is not entirely clear that the objectives pursued by the *ex ante* regime fully correspond to those of EU competition policy, rendering the influence of the regulatory regime on the analysis under Article 102 TFEU more ambiguous. A prominent example is the preliminary ruling in *Meta Platforms*,[32] where the Court held that a violation of data protection rules, namely the General Data Protection Regulation (GDPR),[33] may be taken into account as part of the assessment under Article 102 TFEU, insofar as it is relevant to determining whether the conduct of a dominant undertaking amounts to an abuse.[34] In other words, compliance with data protection norms forms part of the notion of competition on the merits, and is thus taken into account for the assessment of abusive conduct under Article 102 TFEU.[35]

The integration of regulatory standards extending beyond the traditional objectives of competition law into the application of Article 102 TFEU raises important concerns regarding the proper delineation of such interplay. As discussed above, *ex ante* regulatory regimes undeniably form part of the broader context within which competition law applies, shaping the competitive conditions prevailing in a given

29. *Ibid.*, paras 91-92.
30. *See* Dunne, *supra* n. 8, p. 296.
31. As set out in the Commission's Art. 102 Guidance, para. 82, it may be evident that imposing an obligation to supply is manifestly not capable of negatively affecting the input owner's or other operators' incentives to invest and innovate upstream where regulation, compatible with Community law, already imposes such an obligation on the dominant undertaking. In such cases, it is clear from the considerations underlying the regulatory framework that the necessary balancing of incentives has already been conducted by the public authority when imposing the duty to supply. Similarly, the Commission's Draft Guidelines on Exclusionary Abuses provide that as an example of access restrictions, i.e., where the strict test traditionally applied to refusals to supply does not need to be satisfied, the failure of a dominant undertaking to comply with a regulatory obligation to grant access (para. 116(b)).
32. Case C-252/21, *Meta Platforms Inc and Others*, EU:C:2023:537.
33. Regulation (EU) 2016/679 of the European Parliament and of the Council of 27 April 2016 on the protection of natural persons with regard to the processing of personal data and on the free movement of such data, and repealing Directive 95/46/EC (General Data Protection Regulation), OJ L 119, 4.5.2016.
34. Case C-252/21, *Meta Platforms Inc and Others*, EU:C:2023:537, paras 47-48.
35. Inge Graef, *Meta Platforms: How the CJEU Leaves Competition and Data Protection Authorities with an Assignment*, 30 Maastricht Journal of European and Comparative Law 325, 330-331 (2023) https://doi.org/10.1177/1023263x231205836 (last accessed: 11 November 2024).

market. Although it has been argued that the inclusion of privacy standards as qualitative dimensions of competition, particularly in zero-price digital markets, is not entirely novel,[36] the question remains as to the extent to which the infringement of regulatory standards, especially those pursuing objectives that are difficult to reconcile with the aims of Article 102 TFEU, may impinge its application in such regulated markets.

Similar questions are likely to arise with the advent of digital markets regulation, notably the DMA, which introduces a set of *ex ante* obligations for designated gatekeepers aimed at safeguarding fairness and contestability in digital markets. While these objectives do not appear to depart far from the objectives of competition law[37] and overlap, at least partially, the DMA imposes prescriptive do's and don'ts and intervenes *ex ante*. As a result, a sense of unease may emerge regarding the extent to which compliance with, or infringement of DMA obligations will inform, shape, or even lower the substantive threshold for finding an abuse of dominance. This raises broader concerns about whether the incorporation of regulatory breaches under the DMA into the competition law framework risks distorting the established analytical standards of Article 102 TFEU, potentially blurring the boundary between regulation and competition enforcement. It remains to be seen how enforcement practice and judicial review will determine the extent to which this influence materialises.

3 INFLUENCE OF REGULATION IN THE DESIGN OF REMEDIES

Another area where the influence of economic regulation is observed is in the design and administration of remedies. Remedies in EU competition law, particularly under Article 102 TFEU have traditionally been designed to cease unlawful conduct and prevent its recurrence. In principle, Article 102 TFEU is formulated as a prohibition and not as a tool for actively restructuring markets.[38] A classical cease-and-desist order simply puts an end to the abusive conduct by ordering, for example, the dominant firm to stop an exclusionary or discriminatory practice. Nevertheless, as markets evolve, especially in sectors with entrenched monopoly features, competition authorities have increasingly shifted towards the use of regulatory-like remedies that go beyond mere cessation.[39] These more complex remedies might impose positive duties or structural changes on dominant firms, akin to what a sectoral regulator would do.

36. *See* Renato Nazzini, *Antitrust Enforcement and Privacy Standards* §4, 70 (J. Cannataci, V. Falce and O. Pollicino eds, Edward Elgar Publishing 2020); Gorecka, *supra* n. 10, p. 560
37. Pierre Larouche and Alexandre de Streel, *The European Digital Markets Act: A Revolution Grounded on Traditions*, 12 Journal of European Competition Law & Practice 542, 544 (2021) https://doi.org/10.1093/jeclap/lpab066 (last accessed: 15 November 2024).
38. Pablo Ibáñez Colomo, *Remedies in EU Antitrust Law*, 21 Journal of Competition Law & Economics 1, 3 (2025) https://doi.org/10.1093/joclec/nhae022 (last accessed: 23 January 2025).
39. Pablo Ibáñez Colomo, *'Regulatory' and 'Antitrust' Remedies in EU Competition Law*, 76 (D. Gerard and A. Komninos eds, Kluwer Law International 2020).

3.1 Traditional 'Antitrust' Versus 'Regulatory-Like' Remedies

Under Regulation 1/2003, the baseline remedy for an abuse is to 'bring such infringement to an end'.[40] In other words, the dominant firm must cease the unlawful conduct and not repeat it. This orthodox approach views the Commission's role as simply enforcing a prohibition, preventing it from directly engineering market outcomes. Indeed, it remains contested whether competition authorities may extend their remedial powers to address and reverse the anticompetitive effects of an abusive practice. Some commentators argue that, although not explicitly stated in Regulation 1/2003, the Commission possesses restorative powers, drawing support from judgments in *Commercial Solvents*,[41] *Ufex*[42] and *AKZO*[43] judgments.[44] Other scholars, however, contend that the case law does not unequivocally endorse such an interpretation.[45]

In practice, competition enforcers have found that simply ordering a dominant firm to desist can be insufficient to restore healthy competition in markets with structural issues or in dynamic industries.[46] This has given rise to the design and imposition of regulatory-like remedies, which – compared to the traditional cease-and-desist antitrust remedies – impose more detailed conditions on the firm's conduct or structure, resembling *ex ante* regulation. Such remedies may include mandated access to facilities or platforms,[47] non-discrimination obligations,[48] data-sharing obligations,[49] or even divestitures of assets.[50] Hence, they are more intrusive and prescriptive, effectively requiring the dominant firm to take positive steps to remedy the competitive harm and often require continuous monitoring, akin to regulatory supervision, to ensure that the terms of the remedy are respected.[51]

3.2 The Shift Towards Regulatory-Like Remedies

In recent years, there has been a discernible shift in competition enforcement towards more proactive and prescriptive remedies, both in traditional network industries and in digital markets. This development is closely linked to the increasing prioritisation of

40. Council Regulation (EC) No. 1/2003 of 16 December 2002 on the implementation of the rules on competition laid down in Articles 81 and 82 of the Treaty, OJ L 1, 4.1.2003, Art. 7.
41. Joined Cases 6 and 7/73, *Istituto Chemioterapico Italiano S.p.A. and Commercial Solvents Corporation v. Commission*, EU:C:1974:18.
42. Case C-119/97 P, *Union Française de l'Express (Ufex) v. Commission*, EU:C:1999:116.
43. Case C-62/86, *AKZO Chemie BV v. Commission*, EU:C:1991:286.
44. Friso Bostoen and David van Wamel, *Antitrust Remedies: From Caution to Creativity*, 14 Journal of European Competition Law & Practice 540, 541 (2023) https://doi.org/10.1093/jeclap/lpad051 (last accessed: 23 January 2025).
45. Ibáñez Colomo, *supra* n. 38, p. 7.
46. *Ibid.*, p. 540.
47. Commission Decision of 24 May 2004, Case AT.37792, *Microsoft*.
48. Commission Decision of 27 June 2017, Case AT.39740, *Google Shopping*.
49. Microsoft, concerning interoperability information.
50. Commission Decision of 26 November 2008, Case AT.39388, *German electricity wholesale market (E.ON)*; and Commission Decision of 18 March 2009, Case AT.39402, *RWE*.
51. Ibáñez Colomo, *supra* n. 39, p. 90.

these sectors by competition authorities, including the Commission,[52] and reflects a broader recognition that merely prohibiting specific abusive conduct may be insufficient to restore competitive conditions or to prevent similar issues from recurring in complex and entrenched markets.

Network industries provide early examples of this approach. In liberalised sectors, such as telecommunications and energy, the Commission found that effective enforcement sometimes required it to step into a quasi-regulatory role.[53] As noted above, in the mid-2000s, the Commission addressed margin squeeze abuses by incumbent telecom operators, e.g., in *Deutsche Telekom*[54] and *Telefónica*,[55] where the regulated access pricing still allowed exclusion of competitors. Although not explicitly framed in these terms, the remedies in these cases effectively imposed on the incumbents an obligation to offer wholesale access on reasonable terms or to comply with fair access principles, thereby aligning closely with obligations typically enforced by telecommunications regulators. Even more notably, the Commission accepted commitment decisions under Article 9 of Regulation 1/2003 from energy companies (e.g., *E.ON*[56] and *RWE*)[57] to structurally change their businesses, by divesting transmission networks or gas transmission infrastructure to address foreclosure concerns. Said commitments went beyond mere undertakings to cease unlawful conduct; they constituted regulatory-like restructuring measures aimed at reshaping market conditions.[58] While effectively addressing the structural issues in the regulated markets, these remedies blur the distinction with regulation, as they produce outcomes, such as ownership unbundling, that are traditionally pursued through the sector-specific regulatory framework.

In digital markets, the shift toward proactive, regulatory-like remedies has become increasingly pronounced, particularly in cases against major tech firms. In *Microsoft I*,[59] the Commission imposed both a cease-and-desist obligation to the tying of the media player to Windows, as well as a structural remedy requiring Microsoft to disclose interoperability information on reasonable terms, a duty akin to regulatory licensing obligations. To ensure compliance, a monitoring trustee was appointed, further highlighting the expanding supervisory role undertaken by competition authorities. More recently, in *Google Shopping*,[60] the Commission found that Google abused its dominance by self-preferencing its own comparison shopping service (CSS) in search results. Rather than mandating access to Google's CSS, the remedy required non-discriminatory treatment of rival CSSs, leaving its specification and the redesign of its service to the dominant undertaking. However, the chosen remedy, i.e., a system of

52. Ibáñez Colomo, *supra* n. 38, p. 2.
53. *See* Giorgio Monti, *Managing the Intersection of Utilities Regulation and EC Competition Law*, LSE Law, Society & Economy Working Papers 8/2008, London School of Economics and Political Science (2008).
54. *Deutsche Telekom*, *supra* n. 5.
55. Commission Decision of 4 July 2007, Case AT. 38784, *Telefonica SA (broadband)*.
56. *E.ON*, *supra* n. 50.
57. *RWE*, *supra* n. 50.
58. Ibáñez Colomo, *supra* n. 38, p. 18.
59. *Microsoft*, *supra* n. 47.
60. *Google Shopping*, *supra* n. 48.

auctioning slots in the shopping results box to rival sites, was controversial and, arguably, ineffective at restoring competition.[61] The above underscores the challenges associated with relying on principle-based remedies and self-implementation by dominant firms in digital markets and highlights the growing need for more detailed and prescriptive interventions where appropriate.[62] In such markets, effective enforcement increasingly necessitates a shift towards concrete, regulatory-like solutions to ensure that competition is genuinely restored.

Nonetheless, the evolution toward more regulatory-like remedies under Article 102 TFEU is not without practical challenges. Designing an effective remedy is often as difficult as diagnosing the infringement itself, particularly in digital markets where business models, technical architectures, and market dynamics vary substantially, thereby requiring a case-by-case approach rather than one-size-fits-all solutions.[63] Traditionally, the design of remedies in EU competition law was an afterthought, with enforcement largely confined to imposing negative obligations on undertakings. The centre of gravity is now shifting toward the proactive design and administration of remedies, reflecting broader regulatory influences.[64] This development suggests that certain forms of remedial intervention increasingly extend beyond the traditional boundaries of competition law and draw upon regulatory approaches.

4 CONCLUSION

It follows from the above analysis that the relationship between competition law and sector-specific regulation has become increasingly multifaceted, with the latter significantly influencing the application of the former. As demonstrated, regulation shapes the market structures, competitive dynamics, and the legal context within which competition law applies. Far from being isolated fields, competition enforcement and regulation frequently interact, often blurring the lines between the two. In markets characterised by structural barriers or entrenched dominance, regulatory interventions influence not only the delineation of relevant markets but also the substantive assessment of abusive conduct. The case law of the Court of Justice has consistently confirmed that sector-specific regulation forms part of the broader economic and legal context within which competitive behaviour must be assessed, and that competition law remains applicable even where regulatory obligations exist.

At the same time, the influence of regulation extends beyond market assessment and abuse analysis to the design of remedies. Increasingly, the Commission has moved

61. Filippo Lancieri and Caio Mario S. Pereira Neto, *Designing Remedies for Digital Markets: The Interplay Between Antitrust and Regulation*, 18 Journal of Competition Law & Economics 613, 615 (2021) https://doi.org/10.1093/joclec/nhab022 (last accessed: 22 November 2024).
62. *See* Daniel Mandrescu, *Designing (Restorative) Remedies for Abuses of Dominance by Online Platforms*, 13 Journal of Antitrust Enforcement 1 (2024) https://doi.org/10.1093/jaenfo/jnae 040 (last accessed: 17 January 2025).
63. Anush Ganesh, *Effective Remedies in Digital Market Abuse of Dominance Cases*, 1 European Competition Journal 49 (2024) https://doi.org/10.1080/17441056.2024.2440222 (last accessed: 17 January 2025).
64. Ibáñez Colomo, *supra* n. 38, p. 1.

away from purely cease-and-desist remedies and negative obligations toward more proactive, regulatory-like remedies aimed at addressing the effects of anticompetitive conduct on the market. Especially in digital markets and network industries, remedies now often involve well-defined positive obligations, mirroring regulatory interventions rather than merely prohibiting past conduct.

Finally, the integration of regulatory standards that pursue objectives distinct from competition law's traditional aims, such as data privacy under the GDPR or fairness under the DMA, raises important questions about the proper scope and function of Article 102 TFEU. As competition enforcement focuses on increasingly regulated and dynamic markets, it will be crucial to ensure that competition law maintains its distinct analytical standards while appropriately taking into account the regulatory environment in which it operates. Future enforcement practice and judicial review will play a decisive role in delineating the boundaries of this increasingly complex interplay.

CHAPTER 4

Not Just the Emperor's New Clothes? The Evolving Interpretation of Article 102 TFEU in the Case Law of the EU Court of Justice and EU General Court

Krystyna Kowalik-Bańczyk

Behaviour which may amount to an abuse of a dominant position is forbidden in EU law by Article 102 of the Treaty on the Functioning of the European Union (hereinafter 'TFEU').[1] The text of this provision has remained unchanged since its initial adoption under the Treaty establishing the European Economic Community. Over time, only its numbering has changed as a result of successive Treaty amendments: originally, the prohibition was found under Article 86, then under Article 82 and ultimately, under Article 102 TFEU. But for many years – and still today – the question of what type of conduct may amount to an abuse of a dominant position, and in what circumstances,[2] has remained open.

Article 102 TFEU prohibits abuses of a dominant position by one or more undertakings by providing a non-exhaustive list of potential abuses. To trace the evolution of how the various concepts contained in Article 102 TFEU have been interpreted by the EU courts, namely the EU Court of Justice (hereinafter 'Court of Justice') and the EU General Court (hereinafter 'General Court'), it would be necessary to analyse in detail the use of that provision over seven decades of case law, which is hardly possible within the realm of this chapter. Instead, the focus of this text will be

1. Treaty on the Functioning of the European Union (OJ C 202, 7.6.2016).
2. Nicolas Petit, *Droit européen de la concurrence* (Ed. 3, Paris 2020); Robert O'Donoghue and Jorge Padilla, *The Law and Economics of Article 102 TFEU* (Hart Publishing 2020); Laurence Idot, *L'article 102 TFUE toujours au cœur de l'actualité*, 4 Revue trimestrielle de droit européen 747-754 (2023); Pinar Akman, *The Concept of Abuse in EU Competition Law: Law and Economic Approaches* (Oxford 2012).

confined to the main developments from that seventy-year history; in doing so, it will highlight which analytical concepts have remained constant on the one hand, and which ones are still evolving, on the other.

The predictability of decisions taken by competition authorities in the EU (at both national and EU levels) depends on stable case law emanating from the EU courts. It seems that one concept whose meaning remains open-ended is the very notion of abuse. For many years, the EU courts have tended to follow and accept approaches adopted in particular cases by the European Commission. Subsequently, the calls for a more economic approach and stronger forms of scrutiny resulted in findings of per se abuses becoming increasingly rare.[3] It now appears that demonstrating abuse within the meaning of Article 102 TFEU hinges primarily on demonstrating its anticompetitive effects.

1 REASONS FOR EVOLUTION

As had already been noted, the wording of Article 102 TFEU has remained unchanged since 1957; no secondary legislation has ever been introduced to supplement its application.[4] Consequently, its enforcement and interpretation have been primarily determined by case law and by the decision-making practice of competition authorities in the EU. The list of infringements is open and different passages of Article 102 TFEU have been variously emphasised over time.

Until 2006, the European Commission succeeded in 98% of cases where its decisions were challenged before the EU courts. It was not until 2016 that a Commission decision was completely annulled.[5] The last decade has brought a marked increase in the level of sanctions. For illustrative purposes, in 2018, Google was fined an amount ten times higher than Microsoft's then-record 2008 fine.[6] This phenomenon developed against the backdrop of the market trend towards concentration among large enterprises: enforcement authorities increasingly find themselves dealing with large players who, because of the scale of their activities, face correspondingly high fines. The fact that the Commission imposes such high fines is one of the main reasons why a higher cancellation rate emerged in recent years.[7]

3. It can be called a 'by object restriction', as in the case law or it can be called a 'naked restriction', like in the draft version of European Commission guidelines on the application of Art. 102 TFEU to abusive exclusionary conduct by dominant undertakings.
4. Nicolas Petit, *Droit européen de la concurrence* (Ed. 3, Paris 2020) 363: the definition of dominant position is purely a matter of case law, cf. case 27/76, *United Brands Company and United Brands Continentaal BV v. Commission*, 14.2.1978, EU:C:1978:22, para. 65.
5. *See* these 'stricter' results of the European Commission: Robert O'Donoghue and Jorge Padilla, *The Law and Economics of Article 102 TFEU* (Hart Publishing 2020) 94.
6. Nicolas Petit, *Droit européen de la concurrence* (Ed. 3, Paris 2020) 352.
7. As Pinar Akman observes: 'Strikingly though, this evolution has been not through wins but losses for the Commission', Pinar Akman, *A Critical Inquiry into 'Abuse' in EU Competition Law*, 44 Oxford Journal of Legal Studies 410 (2024) https://doi.org/10.1093/ojls/gqae008. Cf., e.g., cases where the EU courts exercised their unlimited jurisdiction: case T-105/17, *HSBC Holdings and Others v. Commission*, 24.9.2019, EU:T:2019:675; case T-113/17, *Crédit agricole and Crédit agricole Corporate and Investment Bank v. Commission*, 20.12.2023, EU:T:2023:847; case T-106/17, *JPMorgan Chase and Others v. Commission*, 20.12.2023, EU:T:2023:832; case T-671/19,

In parallel, since 2004, Commission decisions are also relatively less numerous given that the application of Article 102 TFEU is now also the responsibility of National Competition Authorities (hereinafter 'NCAs') in the framework of the European Competition Network (hereinafter 'ECN'). The doubts expressed by national courts in their questions referred for a preliminary ruling to the CJ means that the Court of Justice has scrutinised (even if indirectly) the concepts under Article 102 TFEU raised not only by the European Commission's enforcement activity but also that of NCAs.

The European Commission being a major author of competition policy, yet another important consideration is the latter's enforcement priorities. In this regard, the Commission published a Communication on the priorities for the application of Article 102 TFEU to exclusionary practices (dated 5 December 2008 and published in 2009, hereinafter '2008 Communication'), which defined the Commission's priorities as focussing on exclusionary practices and which was amended in 2023.[8] According to the 2023 amended version, a dominant entity may undermine the functioning of the market even if it excludes a less efficient or innovative competitor.[9] A new version of this communication, reflecting the broad shift in case law, is expected to be published soon.[10] In parallel with this initiative, a new notice on the rules for the definition of the relevant market was published in February 2024.[11] A correct definition of the relevant market is essential to the finding of a dominant position[12] and the revised notice reflects new market realities and recent case law. In particular, it recognises the importance of

Qualcomm v. Commission (*Qualcomm* – predatory pricing), 18.9.2024, EU:T:2024:626; case C–176/19 P, *Commission v. Servier and Others*, 27.6.2024, EU:C:2024:549; case T–604/18, *Google and Alphabet v. Commission* (*Google Android*), 14.9.2022, EU:T:2022:541; case T–240/17, *Campine and Campine Recycling v. Commission*, 7.11.2019, EU:T:2019:778; case T–324/17, *SAS Cargo Group and Others v. Commission*, 30.3.2022, EU:T:2022:175; case T–326/17, *Air Canada v. Commission*, 30.3.2022, EU:T:2022:177; joint cases T–386/21 and T–406/21, *Crédit agricole and Others v. Commission*, 6.11.2024, EU:T:2024:776.

8. Communication from the Commission – Amendments to the Commission Communication – Guidance on the Commission's enforcement priorities in applying Article 82 of the EC Treaty to abusive exclusionary conduct by dominant undertakings 2023/C 116/01 JOUE.C.2023.116, *see* https://eur-lex.europa.eu/legal-content/EN/TXT/?uri=uriserv%3AOJ.C_.2023.116.01.0001.01.ENG&toc=OJ%3AC%3A2023%3A116%3ATOC (last accessed 22 July 2025).
9. The new wording of para. 23 of the Priorities Guidance reads as follows: 'In order to avoid anti-competitive foreclosure, the Commission will normally intervene when the measures taken hinder or are likely to hinder competition from competitors considered as efficient as the dominant undertaking.' A footnote to that paragraph states that 'the Court of Justice has held that the concept of "as efficient" competitor refers to efficiency and attractiveness for consumers, in particular in terms of price, choice, quality and innovation, see judgment of 6 September 2017 in Case C-413/14 P, *Intel v. Commission*, EU:C:2017:632, paragraph 134, and judgment of 19 January 2023, Case C-680/20, *Unilever Italia Mkt. Operations*, EU:C:2023:33, paragraph 37'.
10. The Commission led a broad consultation of different versions of this document: https://competition-policy.ec.europa.eu/public-consultations/2024-article-102-guidelines_en.
11. Commission Notice – Commission Notice on the definition of relevant market for the purposes of EU competition law, OJ C 2024.1645.
12. Cf. case T-691/14, *Servier and Others v. Commission*, 12.12.2018, EU:T:2018:922; case C-201/19 P, *Servier and Others v. Commission*, 27.7.2024, EU:C:2024:552. *See*, on the case law practice of assessing market definition: Laurence Idot, *Droit du contentieux de l'UE: Confirmations sur l'article 102 TFUE – l'approche plus économique de l'abus (ex. compression des marges) ne dispense pas de procéder à une délimitation correcte du marché (Trib. UE 12 déc. 2018, aff. T-691/14, Servier, Trib. UE 13 déc. 2018, 2 arrêts, aff. T-827/14, Deutsche Telekom, aff. T-851/14, Slovak Telekom)*, 4 Revue trimestrielle de droit européen 895-858 (2019).

non-price parameters for market definition, including quality, innovation, reliable supply and sustainability. It also gives specific guidance on market definition in the digital context and in innovation-intensive industries.

Since the 2008 Communication and the Commission's stated focus on exclusionary practices, there has been some analogy at the national level in the EU, as the types of practices currently followed by NCAs have also been mainly exclusionary practices. The distinction might be difficult to draw, because, as one of the main authors of competition law points out, 'exclure aujourd'hui, c'est exploiter demain'[13] – that is to say, any exclusionary practice is likely to lead to future exploitation. In this vein, the General Court has examined in recent years different exclusionary practices when controlling the legality of Commission's decisions: exclusivity or exclusive rebates (the *Intel* saga, T-235/18, *Qualcomm,*[14] T-334/19, *Google* AdSense);[15] refusal of access (T-814/17, *Lietuvos;*[16] T-136/19, *Bulgarian Energy Holding,*[17] T-612/17, *Google Shopping*[18] or T-604/18, *Google Android*).[19] A large number of cases examined by the General Court have been subsequently challenged on points of law before the Court of Justice.[20] As regards types of cases, the European Commission has dealt with numerous pharmaceutical (so-called *excessive pricing or pay for delay*), energy and telecommunications cases (mainly in relation to *margin squeeze*), infrastructure access cases

13. Nicolas Petit, *Droit européen de la concurrence* (Ed. 3, Paris 2020) 405.
14. Case T–235/18, *Qualcomm v. Commission* (*Qualcomm* – exclusivity payments), 15.6.2022, EU:T:2022:358.
15. Case T-334/19, *Google and Alphabet v. Commission* (*Google AdSense*), T–334/19, 18.9.2024, EU:T:2024:634.
16. Case T–814/17, *Lietuvos geležinkeliai v. Commission*, 18.11.2020, EU:T:2020:545.
17. Case T–136/19, *Bulgarian Energy Holding and Others v. Commission*, 25.10.2023, EU:T:2023:669. Cf.: Claire Mongouachon, *Refus d'accès: Le Tribunal de l'Union européenne annule la décision de la Commission de sanctionner l'opérateur historique pour refus d'accès à des infrastructures gazières stratégiques en Bulgarie* (*Bulgarian Energy Holding*), 1 Concurrences: Journal des droits de la concurrence 82-86 (2024); Johann Ante, *Neues zum Missbrauch auf Gasinfrastrukturmärkten: Anmerkung zu EuG in Sachen Bulgarian Energy Holding: [T-136/19]*, 12 Neue Zeitschrift für Kartellrecht 660-663 (2023).
18. Case T–612/17, *Google and Alphabet v. Commission* (*Google Shopping*), 10.11.2021, EU:T:2021:763; *see* Marek K. Kolasiński, *Self-preparation in European Union Competition Law after the Google Shopping Judgment: Google LLC v. European Commission (T-612/17)*, 9 European Competition Law Review, 435-440 (2022); Alessia Sophia D'Amico and Baskaran Balasingham, *Super-dominant and Super-problematic? The Scale of Dominance in the Google Shopping Judgment: T-612/17*, 18(3) European Competition Journal 614-630 (2022) https://doi.org/10.1080/17441056.2022.2059962; Michael Tagliavini, *Self-processing and the Concept of Abuse of Dominance: Much Ado About Nothing?*, 5 European Competition Law Review 201-211 (2023); Christian Bergqvist, *Google Shopping and Self-favouring as a Separate Abuse: T-612/17*, 43(4) European Competition Law Review 191-195 (2022); Christian Ahlborn, Gerwin Van Gerven and William Leslie, *Bronner Revisited: Google Shopping and the Resurrection of Discrimination under Article 102 TFEU: Case T-612/17, Google v. Comm*ission, 13(2) Journal of European Competition Law with Practice 87-98 (2022) https://doi.org/10.1093/jeclap/lpac012.
19. Case T–604/18, *Google and Alphabet v. Commission* (*Google Android*), 14.9.2022, EU:T:2022:541.
20. Case C–466/19 P, *Qualcomm and Qualcomm Europe v. Commission*, 28.1.2021, EU:C:2021:76; case C–152/19 P, *Deutsche Telekom v. Commission*, 25.3.2021, EU:C:2021:238; case C–165/19 P, *Slovak Telekom v. Commission*, 25.3.2021, EU:C:2021:239; case C–42/21 P, *Lietuvos geležinkeliai v. Commission*, 12.1.2023, EU:C:2023:12; case C–124/21 P, *International Skating Union v. Commission*, 21.12.2023, EU:C:2023:1012; case C–48/22 P, *Google and Alphabet v. Commission* (*Google Shopping*), 10.9.2024, EU:C:2024:726; case T–136/19, *Bulgarian Energy Holding and*

and digital markets cases. Both pricing practices (*Intel, Qualcomm*)[21] and non-pricing practices (*SEN*, the three *Google* cases) have been of interest to the Commission. There were also cases in which the cumulative application of Articles 101 and 102 TFEU (*Servier, Superleague*)[22] was applicable to oligopolistic markets and Article 102 TFEU to monopoly markets.[23]

This focus on exclusionary practices has not necessarily been followed at the national level. National courts hearing appeals against the decisions of NCAs may of course refer questions for preliminary rulings to the Court of Justice. At present, such references for a preliminary ruling have focussed much less on the decentralisation of competition law enforcement[24] (which was initially the case after 2004) and have looked more at issues of competition law substance.[25] Recently, the Court of Justice, answering a preliminary question from a Spanish court, used this opportunity to deliver a so-called recap judgment, which is easier than in cases based on Article 263 TFEU, involving appeals against European Commission decisions.[26] The preliminary questions on the interpretation of Article 102 TFEU have involved a wide range of market conduct, such as the supply of electricity (C-377/20, *SEN*),[27] the distribution of ice cream (C-680/20, *Unilever*),[28] the activities of online platforms using personal data (C-252/21, *Meta Platforms*)[29] and infringements related to sports governance (Case C-333/21, *Superleague*). Occasionally, Article 102 TFEU cases proceed in parallel before both the European Commission and national authorities: e.g., in the so-called

Others v. Commission, 25.10.2023, EU:T:2023:669; case C–255/22 P, *Orlen v. Commission*, 26.9.2024, EU:C:2024:790; case T-604/18, *Google and Alphabet v. Commission* (*Google Android*), 14.9.2022, EU:T:2022:541.

21. Case C–466/19 P, *Qualcomm and Qualcomm Europe v. Commission*, 28.1.2021, EU:C:2021:76.
22. Case T-691/14, *Servier and Others v. Commission*, 12.12.2018, EU:T:2018:922; case C-201/19 P *Servier and Others v. Commission*, 27.7.2024, EU:C:2024:552.
23. Articles 101 and 102 TFEU are not regarded by Court of Justice as two distinct alternatives: they may be applied cumulatively, Cf. case 85/76, *Hoffmann-La Roche v. Commission*, 13.2.1979, EU:C:1979:36, para. 116; case T-51/89, *Tetra Pak Rausing SA v. Commission*, 10.7.1990,EU: T:1990:41, para. 25; case T-65/98, *Van den Bergh Foods Ltd v. Commission*, 23.10.2003, EU:T: 2003:281; case T-691/14, *Servier and Others v. Commission*, 12.12.2018, EU:T:2018:922.
24. Cf. previous cases, i.e., case C–375/09, *Tele2 Polska*, 3.5.2011, EU:C:2011:270; case C–617/17, *Powszechny Zakład Ubezpieczeń na Zycie*, 3.4.2019, EU:C:2019:283; case C–857/19, *Slovak Telekom*, 25.2.2021, EU:C:2021:139.
25. For instance, *see* recently, for the question of restriction by object, case C-298/22, *Banco BPN/BIC Português and Others*, 29.7.2024, EU:C:2024:638; for the question of ancillary restraints, case C-264/23, *Booking.com and Booking.com (Deutschland)*, 19.9.2024, EU:C:2024: 764; and for refusal to grant access to a platform or digital infrastructure, case C–233/23, *Alphabet and Others*, EU:C:2025:110.
26. Case C–333/21, *European Superleague Company*, 21.12.2023, EU:C:2023:1011.
27. Case C-377/20, *Servizio Elettrico Nazionale and Others*, 12.5.2022, EU:C:2022:379; cf.: Assimakis Komninos, *A Steady Course Towards the Effects-Based Approach: Case C-377/20 Servizio Elettrico Nazionale*, 14(5) Journal of European Competition Law & Practice, 290-292 (2023) https://doi.org/10.1093/jeclap/lpad009; Tom Buytaert, *Arrêt 'Servizio Elettrico Nazionale': abus de position dominante découlant de pratiques d'éviction dans le contexte de la libéralisation du marché électrique*, 294(10) Journal de droit européen 466-470 (2022).
28. Case C–680/20, *Unilever Italia Mkt. Operations*, 19.1.2023, EU:C:2023:33.
29. Case C-252/21, *Meta Platforms and Others*, 4.7.2023, EU:C:2023:537.

pay-for-delay cases.[30] As exemplified by the *Generics* judgment,[31] the answers to preliminary questions sometimes provide the opportunity to state some principles that may seem more diluted in judgments upon direct actions, where the EU courts have to focus on answering the parties' specific pleas.

2 RULES STEMMING FROM THE TRADITIONAL CASE LAW OF THE EU COURTS

Traditionally, the case law of the Court of Justice on Article 102 TFEU was formalistic and detached from contemporary economic rules, as some writers point out.[32] Regardless of the emergence of some distinct 'modes of analysis' under Article 102 TFEU that will be analysed further, certain rules of interpretation remain well established, however. For instance, in the European Union, it is competition rather than the competitors themselves that is protected;[33] competition should not be eliminated as such.[34] Accordingly, a change in the structure of competition by the acquisition of a potential competitor is possible under Article 102 TFEU, as was found for the first time in *Continental Can*[35] and has been confirmed recently in the *Towercast* reply to a request for preliminary ruling from a French court;[36] even if it leads to the establishment (or strengthening) of a dominant position. In order to establish the existence of a dominant position, the EU courts look at both *market share* and *market power*, as established in Cases 27/76 (*United Brands*)[37] and T-51/89 (*Tetra Pak*).[38] A dominant position is characterised by an undertaking's ability to disregard its customers, consumers, and even competitors.[39] Such entities have traditionally been considered to hold a special responsibility[40] given that their market position leads to an economic dependence of consumers and establishes them as 'unavoidable trading partners'.

30. Cf. the '*Servier* saga' and, in parallel, case C-307/18, *Generics (UK) and Others*, 30.1.2020, EU:C:2020:52.
31. Case C-307/18, *Generics (UK) and Others*, 30.1.2020, EU:C:2020:52.
32. Pinar Akman, *A Critical Inquiry into 'Abuse' in EU Competition Law*, 44 Oxford Journal of Legal Studies 410 (2024) https://doi.org/10.1093/ojls/gqae008.
33. Case C-680/20, *Unilever Italia Mkt. Operations*, 19.1.2023, EU:C:2023:33, paras 36 to 39; case C-377/20, *Servizio Elettrico Nazionale and Others*,12.5.2022, EU:C:2022:379, para. 73.
34. Case 6/72, *Europemballage and Continental Can v. Commission*, 21.2.1973, EU:C:1973:22.
35. Case 6/72, *Europemballage and Continental Can v. Commission*, 21.2.1973, EU:C:1973:22.
36. Case C-449/21, *Towercast*, 16.5.2023, EU:C:2023:207. Cf.: Marie Cartapanis, *Seuils de notification: La Cour de justice de l'Union européenne restaure la jurisprudence Continental Can et juge que l'article 102 TFUE est susceptible de s'appliquer à une concentration non notifiable (Towercast)*, 2 Concurrences: revue des droits de la concurrence 78-82 (2023).
37. Case 27/76, *United Brands Company and United Brands Continentaal BV v. Commission*, 14.2.1978, EU:C:1978:22.
38. Case T-51/89, *Tetra Pak Rausing SA v. Commission*, 10.7.1990, EU:T:1990:41.
39. Case 26/76, *Metro SB-Großmärkte v. Commission*, 25.10.1977, EU:C:1977:167; case 85/76, *Hoffmann-La Roche v. Commission*, 13.2.1979, EU:C:1979:36.
40. Case 322/81, *Nederlandsche Banden-Industrie-Michelin v. Commission (Michelin I)*, 9.11.1983, EU:C:1983:313; the concept of special responsibility also appears in: case C-52/09, *TeliaSonera Sverige*, 17.2.2011, EU:C:2011:83, para. 28; case C-280/08, *Deutsche Telekom v. Commission*, 14.10.2010, EU:C:2010:603, para. 83; case C-413/14 P, *Intel v. Commission*, 6.9.2017, EU:C:2017:632, para. 135. On the concept of special responsibility, *see* Ekaterina Rousseva and

Since case 322/81, *Michelin I*,[41] the EU courts have recognised the special responsibility of a dominant entity in the market, taking into account the various indicators of dominance, such as: being the largest player in the market, holding intellectual property rights, considering market position vis-à-vis competitors, barriers to entry, barriers to expansion.[42] The concept of special responsibility might cause some doubts. On the one hand, the abuse cannot be presumed. On the other hand and at the same time, the mere fact of monopolistic or quasi-monopolistic functioning implies that such an entity should pay particular attention to its practices. In traditional case law, it could always have been said that 'big is bad'.[43] When assessing dominance, this could be the very structure of the market when it was so concentrated that it became problematic in itself, or it could be a particular course of conduct on the market – when the dominant entity was able to act in a certain way and no one was able to replicate it. These two scenarios cannot be treated in exactly the same way as they are of a different nature: the first, somewhat more objective; the second subjective.

As indicators of abuse, the EU courts have taken into account various factors, such as the elimination of as-efficient competitors, anti-competitive effects, and anti-competitive intentions[44] (an example of the latter would be Bill Gates' 2008 public speech in which the businessman announced the intention to eliminate Microsoft's competitors).[45] The infringement may involve exclusion or exploitation, may be of a pricing or non-price nature, horizontal (such as predatory pricing or mono-trading) or vertical *(refusal* to sell a licence, etc.). Risks to competition may arise in all markets,[46] including regulated markets,[47] so that not only the practices of technology giants or of the pharmaceutical industry may be of interest to competition authorities applying Article 102 TFEU. The prohibitions in Article 102 TFEU and Article 101 TFEU

Giorgio Monti, The Special Responsibility of Dominant Undertakings in: P. Akman, O. Brook and K. Stylianou (eds), *Research Handbook on Abuse of Dominance and Monopolization* (Edward Elgar 2023).

41. Case 322/81, *Nederlandsche Banden-Industrie-Michelin v. Commission (Michelin I)*, 9.11.1983, EU:C:1983:313.
42. *See*, for example, case C-457/10 P, *AstraZeneca v. Commission*, 6.12.2012, EU:C:2012:770, which concerned the market for medicinal products with innate pathology and the withdrawal of the marketing authorisation – one of the first cases relating to the patent system and conduct aimed at preventing the introduction of a generic version of omeprazole. Cf.: Inge Govaere and Valerie Demedts, *Towards an 'Ex Ante' or Preventive Application of Article 102 TFEU in the Commission's Policy Pursuant to the Astra Zeneca-Case*, in: *Mundi et Europae civis Liber Amicorum Jacques Steenbergen* (Larcier, Brussels 2014) 441 to 452.
43. Case 41/90, *Höfner and Elser*, 23.4.1991, EU:C:1991:161, paras 28 to 34; Nicolas Petit, *Droit européen de la concurrence* (Ed. 3, Paris 2020) 358.
44. Cf. case 62/86, *AKZO v. Commission*, 3.7.1991, EU:C:1991:286 – below cost prices; case C-209/10, *Post Danmark (Post Danmark I)*, 27.3.2012, EU:C:2012:172 – elimination of competitors.
45. Case T-167/08, *Microsoft v. Commission*, 27.6.2012, EU:T:2012:323.
46. Mariateresa Maggiolino, *When an Ice Cream Provides Antitrust Experts with Food for Thought: Unilever Italia*, 60 Common Market Law Review 1433-1452 (2023) https://doi.org/10.54648/cola2023099.
47. Case T-336/07, *Telefónica and Telefónica de España v. Commission*, 29.3.2012, EU:T:2012:172 (such as transport, insurance or sport).

(prohibition of cartels) may also be infringed in parallel.[48] Finally, the principle supported by competition authorities is that competition on the merits is acceptable and positive.[49] It is therefore only the *abuse* of a dominant position in the form primarily of exclusions or exploitation that is to be prohibited.

In the traditional approach to Article 102 TFEU adopted by the EU courts, it was not clear whether proving the *anti-competitive effects* of a certain practice was strictly necessary or if identifying a 'form' of conduct sufficed for Article 102 TFEU to be infringed.[50] This is clearly illustrated by the coexistence of decisions from the same time period, of which some require an assessment of the effects of conduct, while others are limited to assessing the form of the infringement.[51] Some commentators drew analogies between this phenomenon and the dichotomy under Article 101 TFEU, which refers to agreements which, by reason of their object or effect, are liable to give rise to infringements or restrictions of competition. That dichotomy was also picked up on by some after the adoption of the 2008 Guidelines,[52] while others considered that that division was entirely irrelevant since certain practices are prohibited prima facie, irrespectively of their effects.[53] As will be explained in the subsequent sections of this contribution, this position is no longer to be upheld.

In subsequent rulings, such as *Deutsche Telekom I*[54] or *Telia Sonera*,[55] the Court of Justice clarified that, for conduct to constitute an abuse within the meaning of Article 102 TFEU, it must limit or exclude access to the market or the development of as-efficient competitors. *Margin squeeze* cannot therefore constitute an abuse unless

48. Articles 101 and 102 TFEU both seem to be affected by the same conduct, cf. case 85/76, *Hoffmann-La Roche v. Commission*, 13.2.1979, EU:C:1979:36; case T-51/89, *Tetra Pak Rausing SA v. Commission*, 10.7.1990,EU:T:1990:41; case T-480/15, *Agria Polska and Others v. Commission*, 16.5.2017, EU:T:2017:339.
49. *See* case C-413/14 P, *Intel v. Commission*, 6.9.2017, EU:C:2017:632, paras 133 to 134: 'In that regard, it should be borne in mind that Article 102 TFEU is not intended to prevent an undertaking from acquiring, on its own merits, a dominant position on a market. Nor is that provision intended to ensure that competitors less efficient than the dominant undertaking remain on the market (see, inter alia, judgment of 27 March 2012, *Post Danmark*, 209/10, EU:C:2012:172, paragraph 21 and the case-law cited). (134) not every exclusionary effect must necessarily have an adverse effect on competition. Competition on the merits may, by definition, lead to the disappearance from the market or the marginalisation of competitors which are less efficient and therefore less attractive to consumers in terms of, inter alia, price, choice, quality and innovation.'
50. Pinar Akman, *A Critical Inquiry into 'Abuse' in EU Competition Law*, 44 Oxford Journal of Legal Studies 413 (2024) https://doi.org/10.1093/ojls/gqae008.
51. Pablo Ibanez Colomo, *Anticompetitive Effects in EU Competition Law*, 17(2) Journal of Competition Law the Economics 350 (2020) https://doi.org/10.1093/joclec/nhaa031.
52. Bruce Wardhaugh, *Competition, Effects and Predictability: Rule of Law and the Economic Approach to Competition* (Hart 2020) 112; Pablo Ibanez Colomo, *Beyond the 'More Economics-Based Approach': A Legal Perspective on Article 102 TFEU Case Law*, 52 Common Market Law Review 712-713 (2016) https://doi.org/10.54648/cola2016062.
53. Robert O'Donoghue and Jorge Padilla, *The Law and Economics of Article 102 TFEU* (Hart Publishing 2020) 278.
54. Case C-280/08, *Deutsche Telekom v. Commission*, 14.10.2010, EU:C:2010:603.
55. Case C-52/09, *TeliaSonera Sverige*, 17.2.2011, EU:C:2011:83.

those effects are demonstrated.[56] Likewise, in *Bronner,*[57] the Court of Justice held that a refusal to deal would only constitute an infringement if it was shown that the actions of the dominant entity were necessary and the refusal to cooperate eliminated all competition from those seeking access.[58] These statements might suggest that it is always necessary to demonstrate *actual effects* in order to establish an abuse. Yet, in other judgments, the Court of Justice did not require proof of effects. A more formalistic approach sufficed, with no need to assess economic parameters such as price/cost ratios or market coverage.

The as-efficient-competitor test mentioned above requires determining who can be (is) an as-efficient competitor. Since the *AKZO* case in 1991, the Court of Justice has recognised that, in the case of as-efficient competitors, that is to say, competitors capable of supplying similar services/products, below-cost prices may potentially be exclusionary. In subsequent case law, like *Post Danmark I*[59] and *Intel*, this position was supplemented and the Court of Justice added that the as-efficient-competitor test did not only concern prices. On the one hand, the foreclosure of less efficient competitors is the natural result of the competitive process. On the other hand, Article 102 TFEU seeks to ensure that rivals who are able to compete remain on the market despite the presence of the dominant entity on the market. How to show this is extremely important and de facto difficult. Court of Justice requires that the following elements be presented: (1) the causal link between the abuse and the actual or potential effects (*attribution*); (2) certainty and predictability; (3) the role of the competitive process in maintaining the conditions for creating, investing and innovating.[60] In *Post Danmark I*, apart from talking about as-efficient competitors, the Court of Justice considered for the first time that true competition could lead to competitors exiting the market. It stated in paragraph 22 that 'by definition, competition on the merits may lead to the disappearance from the market or the marginalisation of competitors which are less efficient and therefore less attractive to consumers, particularly in terms of price, choice, quality and innovation'.

This adoption of a more economically-informed approach, as encouraged by the Commission itself, has resulted in the increased prominence of an effects-based approach. As mentioned, this has led to a radical increase of successful annulments of Commission decisions which are open to challenge before the EU courts under Article 263 TFEU. Still, this shift has neither been immediate nor coherent. The distinction between cases which could be said to fall within the 'traditional' case law and those which could be said to represent the 'sea change' in the Court's doctrine is fluid and there has not been one specific break-through moment – apart from perhaps the Court of Justice *Intel* decision, which will be discussed below. Importantly, it should not be

56. Case C-280/08, *Deutsche Telekom v. Commission*, 14.10.2010, EU:C:2010:603, para. 234; case C-52/09, *TeliaSonera Sverige*, 17.2.2011, EU:C:2011:83, paras 61 to 63.
57. Case C-7/97, *Bronner*, 26.11.1998, EU:C:1998:569.
58. Case C-7/97, *Bronner*, 26.11.1998, EU:C:1998:569, para. 41.
59. Case C-209/10, *Post Danmark* (*Post Danmark I*), 27.3.2012, EU:C:2012:172.
60. However, in *Servizio Elettrico Nazionale*, the Court of Justice did not answer the question whether the ultimate objective of Art. 102 TFEU was to preserve the appropriate structure of the market or to ensure consumer welfare.

thought that there has been a complete break with previous practice. It seems that the Court of Justice is more likely to follow the economic approach while delivering preliminary rulings, whereas both of the EU courts have shown greater deference to the more traditional, formalistic modes of analysis when they are exercising their judicial review capacity under Article 263 TFEU.[61]

3 CURRENT APPLICATION OF ARTICLE 102 TFEU

Over the last ten years, an increasing number of judgments of the Court of Justice indicate the adoption of an effects-based approach (less formal examination of Article 102 TFEU).[62] This new 'era' started with *Intel* judgment.[63] Pinar Akman qualifies the 'pre-Intel era' as an era of formalism, and the post-Intel era as a modern era or 'the age of effects'. However, as already stated above and prior to the *Intel* case,[64] the Court of Justice already adopted, from *Post Danmark I*, a so-called more economic approach, which no longer protected any particular competitor or market structure.

In several subsequent judgments, the Court of Justice confirmed the need for an analysis of the effects of a possible abuse of a dominant position on *as-efficient* or potential competitors.[65] To qualify as abusive, it must be demonstrated – though not purely hypothetically – that the practice in question has or is likely to have such effects.[66] This concern also gave rise to the 'as-efficient-competitor' test.[67] The *Intel* case, and its second instance judgment in particular, 'hit the European competition law municipality like a bombshell',[68] the Court of Justice contested the Commission's analysis which relied on the assumption that a type of practice can always be abusive.

61. Pinar Akman, *A Critical Inquiry into 'Abuse' in EU Competition Law*, 44 Oxford Journal of Legal Studies 411 (2024) https://doi.org/10.1093/ojls/gqae008, citing as an example of a formal approach the judgment of 19 April 2012, *Tomra Systems and Others v. Commission*, C-549/10 P, EU:C:2012:221.
62. Pinar Akman, *A Critical Inquiry into 'Abuse' in EU Competition Law*, 44 Oxford Journal of Legal Studies 416 (2024) https://doi.org/10.1093/ojls/gqae008, called it a 'Modern Era'.
63. Laurence Idot, *L'article 102 TFUE et les suites de l'arrêt Intel*, 4 Revue trimestrielle de droit européen 766-774 (2022).
64. Case C-209/10, *Post Danmark (Post Danmark I)*, 27.3.2012, EU:C:2012:172.
65. Case C-280/08, *Deutsche Telekom v. Commission*, 14.10.2010, EU:C:2010:603, para. 177; case C-52/09, *TeliaSonera Sverige*, 17.2.2011, EU:C:2011:83, paras 31 to 33, 39 to 40, 43, 63-64, 70 and 73; case C-209/10, *Post Danmark (Post Danmark I)*, 27.3.2012, EU:C:2012:172, paras 21 to 22, 25 and 38.
66. Case C-280/08, *Deutsche Telekom v. Commission*, 14.10.2010, EU:C:2010:603, paras 250, 252 to 254 and 259; case C-52/09, *TeliaSonera Sverige*, 17.2.2011, EU:C:2011:83, para. 64; case C-209/10, *Post Danmark (Post Danmark I)*, 27.3.2012, EU:C:2012:172, paras 25, 40 and 44; case C-23/14, *Post Danmark* (*Post Danmark II*), 6.10.2015, EU:C:2015:651, paras 46 to 49.
67. Ioannis Lianos, *The Price/Non Price Exclusionary Abuses Dichotomy: A Critical Appraisal*, 2 Concurrences: Journal des droits de la concurrence (2009).
68. Anne Witt, *The European Court of Justice and the More Economic Approach to EU Competition Law: Is the Tide Turning?*, 64(2) Antitrust Bulletin 208 (2019) https://doi.org/10.1177/000360 3x19844637. This has been the subject of negative and positive assessments, *see*: Luc Peeperkorn, *Conditional Pricing: Why the General Court Is Wrong in Intel (and What the Court of Justice Can Do to Rebalance the Assessment of Rebates)*, 1 Concurrences: Journal des droits de la concurrence 43-44 (2015); Wouters Wils, *The Judgment of the EU General Court in Intel and the So-called 'More Economic Approach' to 'Abuse of Dominance'*, 37(4) World Competition 405, 418 (2014); Paul Nihoul, *The Ruling of the General Court in Intel: Towards the End of an*

The Grand Chamber of the Court of Justice considered that Article 102 TFEU was not intended to protect less efficient competitors so that they could remain on the market on which the dominant entity operated. It considered instead that it is not just any foreclosing effect that can be considered harmful to competition. The Court set aside the General Court judgment, in which the latter applied the previous, rather formalistic case law; in so doing, the Court of Justice did not limit its pronouncements to specific classes of alleged conduct or practice – thus making it clear that the new approach applies across various categories of alleged abuses.

Intel was also the first judgment in which the Court of Justice had criticised the application of Article 102 TFEU and criticised the European Commission's decision so strongly that it found the latter's decision to be unlawful. *Intel* thus revolutionised the assessment of certain practices (e.g., fidelity exclusivity rebates). In order for an abuse to be proven to the requisite legal standard, the conduct in question must be capable of *restricting competition* and of having *potential exclusionary effects* (here, foreclosure).[69] In its reasoning, the Court of Justice considered that the *Hoffman-La Roche* case law should be clarified (or rather, amended), to the effect that, if an accused party claims its conduct could not have caused foreclosure, the Commission must examine four cumulative elements: (i) the extent of the undertaking's dominant position on the relevant market; (ii) the market share affected by the practice at issue; (iii) the conditions and arrangements for granting rebates, their persistence and their level (or, in other practices, the nature of the practice, its scope and duration); (iv) the Commission must assess the likelihood of a strategy aimed at excluding from the market competitors which are at least as efficient as the dominant entity. The fourth element consists of a 'capacity *to foreclose*' analysis, i.e., an examination of the exclusionary capacity of the perpetrator.[70]

For some time, there were doubts as to whether the move away from the 'formalistic' approach in *Intel* concerned only pricing practices (the *Intel* case involved rebates). However, the Court's reasoning and subsequent rulings indicate that all types of practices can fall within its scope. The second question was whether Intel still mandated the use of the 'as-efficient competitor test' or whether the capacity to foreclose could be examined in different ways under different factual configurations. After several years of the *Intel* case law being applied, it appears that the examination of the capacity to foreclose is a universal requirement and must also be applied when assessing the objective justifications and the positive effects likely to prevail in the assessment of the effects of a practice so that the infringement is not found or the infringement is considered excusable.

After *Intel*, one can indeed see a lasting change in the EU courts' approach to the assessment of the existence of an infringement. Both the Court of Justice and the

Effect-based Approach in European Competition Law, 5(8) Journal of European Competition Law in Practice 521-530 (2014) https://doi.org/10.1093/jeclap/lpu088.

69. Cf. as follow-on to this position: case T-334/19, *Google and Alphabet v. Commission* (*Google AdSense*), T–334/19, 18.9.2024, EU:T:2024:634.
70. Pinar Akman, *A Critical Inquiry into 'Abuse' in EU Competition Law*, 44 Oxford Journal of Legal Studies 418 (2024) https://doi.org/10.1093/ojls/gqae008.

General Court started to apply the principles affirmed in the *Intel* judgment beyond cases concerning pricing practices and did not confine *Intel* to any specific category of factual circumstances.[71] In *MEO,*[72] the Court of Justice even considered that this analysis should be applied to exploitative, rather than solely exclusionary, practices. Another illustrative example is *Generics,*[73] where the Court of Justice stated that, for a practice to be characterised as abusive, it must be capable of restricting competition through foreclosure effects and that this assessment must be carried out taking into account all the relevant facts relating to that conduct.[74] This makes it clear that the Court of Justice takes the same approach irrespective of whether the conduct involves prices or not.[75,76]

The requirement to demonstrate at least potential anticompetitive effects or exclusionary effects on the relevant market was also explicitly set out by the Court of Justice in *Slovak Telekom.*[77] In *ENEL,*[78] the Court of Justice went so far as to reject its previous formalistic approach (i.e., that a particular form of conduct could always constitute an infringement). It stated that it was necessary to demonstrate the effects of an infringement in the form of foreclosure or restrictions of competition (in *ENEL* itself, foreclosure effects) and that the assessment must be based on all the relevant facts.[79] The Court of Justice further confirmed that the as-efficient-competitor test could be applied to any type of conduct.[80] In *Unilever*, the Court of Justice confirmed that the method of analysis in *Intel* also applied to so-called exclusive dealing[81] and thus to non-pricing practices.[82] Court of Justice's subsequent practice therefore dispels any

71. Case T-814/17, *Lietuvos geležinkeliai v. Commission*, 18.11.2020, EU:T:2020:545, para. 76; case T-827/14, *Deutsche Telekom v. Commission*, 13.12.2018, EU:T:2018:930, para. 87. *See also* case C-525/16, *MEO – Serviços de Comunicações e Multimédia*,19.4.2018, EU:C:2018:270-, para. 31.
72. Case C-525/16, *MEO – Serviços de Comunicações e Multimédia*,19.4.2018, EU:C:2018:270.
73. Case C–307/18, *Generics (UK) and Others*, 30.1.2020, EU:C:2020:52. *See*: Lucas Šimas, Marilena Nteve and Georgia Tzifa, *Long-awaited Court of Justice's Say on 'Pay for Delay' Agreements in C-307/18 Generics (UK) Ltd and Others v. Competition and Markets Authority*, 10 European Competition Law Review 521-526 (2020); Niamh Dunne, *Potential competition in EU Law: Generics (UK) Ltd v. Competition and Markets Authority (C-307/18), H Lundbeck A/S v. European Commission (C-591/16 P)*, 12 European Competition Law Review 638-644 (2021); Krystyna Kowalik-Bańczyk, *Commentary on C-307/18 Generics (UK) Ltd v. Competition and Markets Authority: Competition Delayed, Competition Denied?*, 9(3) Journal of antitrust enforcement 592-603 (2021).
74. Case C–307/18, *Generics (UK) and Others*, 30.1.2020, EU:C:2020:52, para. 154, referring to: case C-280/08, *Deutsche Telekom v. Commission*, 14.10.2010, EU:C:2010:603, paras 64 to 66 and 68; and case C-413/14 P, *Intel v. Commission*, 6.9.2017, EU:C:2017:632, para. 138.
75. Such as margin squeeze or rebates.
76. Such as contracts providing for pay for delay.
77. Case C-165/19 P, *Slovak Telekom v. Commission*, 25.3.2021, EU:C:2021:239, para. 51. The effects must be felt by as-efficient competitors, *see* para. 109.
78. Case C-377/20, *Servizio Elettrico Nazionale and Others*, 12.5.2022, EU:C:2022:379.
79. Case C-377/20, *Servizio Elettrico Nazionale and Others*, 12.5.2022, EU:C:2022:379, para. 72.
80. Case C-377/20, *Servizio Elettrico Nazionale and Others*, 12.5.2022, EU:C:2022:379, para. 79.
81. Case C-413/14 P, *Intel v. Commission*, 6.9.2017, EU:C:2017:632.
82. Pinar Akman, *A Critical Inquiry into 'Abuse' in EU Competition Law*, 44 Oxford Journal of Legal Studies 422 (2024) https://doi.org/10.1093/ojls/gqae008; case C-680/20, *Unilever Italia Mkt. Operations*, 19.1.2023, EU:C:2023:33, paras 50, 52 and 59.

doubt as to the scope of the *Intel* analysis – it applies to any exclusionary, price and non-price practices.[83]

The General Court has similarly embraced Intel as part of a comprehensive approach to establishing abuses of dominance. In *Google Shopping*,[84] it held that the Commission was required to demonstrate at least the potential effects of a practice rejecting the idea that certain conduct could constitute an infringement per se.[85] The analysis prescribed by *Intel* is not just a procedural step: it demands a genuine analysis of the effects. Both EU courts – the Court of Justice in *Unilever*[86] and the General Court in *Intel RENV*[87] or *Qualcomm*[88] – have so far confirmed this position, requiring a concrete effects analysis to be undertaken by competition authorities. As Pinar Akman points out, in *Superleague*, the reference to the 'object' of the practice[89] (mirroring the object/effect dichotomy in Article 101 TFEU) does not amount to a direct parallel between Articles 102 and 101 TFEU because, in that case, the 'object' was specifically to bar potential competitors from the market, which the Court of Justice distinguished from actual or potential foreclosure.[90] It seems, therefore, that an infringement can no longer be presumed merely because of the form of the conduct; it is necessary to consider its effects in the overall context of the case.

Since Case C-23/14 (*Post Danmark*), the General Court has adopted a more economic approach,[91] holding that there is no abuse of a dominant position when the conduct amounts to substantive competition, which reflects the approach taken by the Court of Justice in case C-413/14 P, *Intel*. The General Court examines, first of all,

83. Pinar Akman, *A Critical Inquiry into 'Abuse' in EU Competition Law*, 44 Oxford Journal of Legal Studies 425 (2024) https://doi.org/10.1093/ojls/gqae008. According to this author, *Generics*, *Google Shopping*, *ENEL*, *Intel RENV*, *Qualcomm* and *Unilever* introduce an uniform approach to Art. 102 TFEU.
84. Case T–612/17, *Google and Alphabet v. Commission (Google Shopping)*, 10.11.2021, EU:T:2021:763; confirmed by case C-48/22 P, *Google and Alphabet v. Commission (Google Shopping)*, 10.9.2024, EU:C:2024:726.
85. Case T–612/17, *Google and Alphabet v. Commission (Google Shopping)*, 10.11.2021, EU:T:2021:763, para. 441.
86. Case C-680/20, *Unilever Italia Mkt. Operations*,19.1.2023, EU:C:2023:33, paras 52 and 53. *See also* para. 62, which states: 'Article 102 TFEU must be interpreted as meaning that, where there are exclusivity clauses in distribution contracts, a competition authority is required, for the purposes of finding an abuse of a dominant position, to establish, in the light of all the relevant circumstances and taking into account, in particular, the economic analyses produced, as the case may be, by the undertaking in a dominant position as to whether the conduct in question is capable of foreclosing competitors as efficient as that undertaking from the market, that those clauses are capable of restricting competition. The use of an "as efficient competitor test" is optional. However, where the results of such a test are produced by the undertaking concerned during the administrative procedure, the competition authority is required to assess its probative value.'
87. Case T-286/09 RENV, *Intel Corporation v. Commission*, 26.1.2022, EU:T:2022:19, paras 507, 512 and 521. The Commission Decision has been repealed.
88. In the present case, the Commission carried out an impact assessment, but its decision was annulled due to irregularities affecting the rights of the defence with regard to certain pieces of evidence.
89. Case C–333/21, *European Superleague Company*, 21.12.2023, EU:C:2023:1011, para. 131.
90. Pinar Akman, *A Critical Inquiry into 'Abuse' in EU Competition Law*, 44 Oxford Journal of Legal Studies 424 (2024) https://doi.org/10.1093/ojls/gqae008, footnote 104.
91. Case C-23/14, *Post Danmark* (*Post Danmark II*), 6.10.2015, EU:C:2015:651.

whether the practice has a 'capacity to exclude': such an examination gives rise to an assessment of the effects of the practice since it is not looking for an infringement per se. That is well illustrated by the judgment in *Unilever Italia* (C-680/20): in that case, the Court of Justice ruled out the attribution of the actions of its distributors to the producer. The possibility of exclusion is assessed in the light of the evidence provided by both parties. In order to verify the possibility of exclusion, it is important to determine who is excluded – possibly an 'as-efficient competitor' – by reference to the as-efficient-competitor test (AEC). Such a test relates to efficiency and consumer benefits in terms of price, choice, quality or innovation[92] – but it can also serve as a defence to those seeking to demonstrate that they have not infringed competition law and that, therefore, AEC can serve as a shield and not a sword. In the recent case law of the Court of Justice, the court has also confirmed that the purpose of Article 102 TFEU is always to protect the competitive process and not the competitors themselves.[93]

The examination of a specific form of conduct from the point of view of its effects obviously leads to the question of how those effects are to be determined. An objective practice must be examined, but according to the Court of Justice, actual effects can be taken into account in the analysis.[94] As the Court of Justice states, the effects on competition are not sufficient, in themselves, to consider that a practice can restrict competition in a given context: this must be supplemented by an examination of the characteristics of the relevant market, the extent of the practice and the extent of the dominant position. In addition, the potential effects of the conduct should also be taken into account and the very nature of that conduct influences the threshold for establishing an abuse. The threshold is low where the very object of the practice is anti-competitive (or where it is highly likely to substantially eliminate competition); and higher where the practice is ambivalent or (even) lawful or pro-competitive.[95]

4 EVOLUTION OF THE PERSPECTIVE: COMPETITION ON THE MERITS

It is by no means straightforward to determine whether the conduct of the dominant market player constitutes merely competition on the merits. The EU courts aim to safeguard the so-called *Leistungswettbewerb* – that is, competition based on substance – within the EU market. This approach, particularly evident after the Intel judgment, is

92. Case C-413/14 P, *Intel v. Commission*, 6.9.2017, EU:C:2017:632, para. 134; and case C-680/20, *Unilever Italia Mkt. Operations*, 19.1.2023, EU:C:2023:33, para. 37.
93. Case C-680/20, *Unilever Italia Mkt. Operations*, 19.1.2023, EU:C:2023:33, paras 36 to 39; case C-377/20, *Servizio Elettrico Nazionale and Others*, 12.5.2022, EU:C:2022:379, para. 73; *see* Mariateresa Maggiolino, *When an Ice Cream Comes from Antitrust Experts with Food for Thought: Unilever Italia*, 60 Common Market Law Review 1445 (2023) https://doi.org/10.54648/cola2023099.
94. Case C-377/20, *Servizio Elettrico Nazionale and Others*, 12.5.2022, EU:C:2022:379, para. 56.
95. Case C-377/20, *Servizio Elettrico Nazionale and Others*, 12.5.2022, EU:C:2022:379, para. 57.

largely context-specific and closely connected with the analysis of effects (as discussed above).[96]

For more than twenty years, the European Commission relied on the so-called economic approach[97] imposed on it by the General Court judgment in Case T-219/99, *Michelin II* and *British Airways*,[98] which concerned a system of discounts in the airline sector. Prior to that judgment, the Commission could almost rely on a presumption of infringement, illustrated by the *Hoffman-La Roche* case, relating to the market for vitamins and loyalty rebates *(fidelity rebates)*.

In the *ENEL* case,[99] the Court of Justice explicitly invoked the idea which is now the cornerstone for the application of Article 102 TFEU: the concept of competition on the merits. The Court of Justice stated that:

> any practice the implementation of which is of no economic interest to the dominant undertaking, with the exception of the objective of eliminating its competitors in order subsequently to be able to increase its prices by taking advantage of the monopoly situation, must be regarded as a means other than those falling within the scope of competition on the merits.

Here, the Court gave an economic description of the practice and did not refer to the concepts of 'freedom of competition' or freedom of choice. In order for conduct to be anti-competitive, it must lack an independent economic rationale other than foreclosing competitors.

Under the 'economic approach', the Commission avoids penalising *competition on the merits*. The Commission applies this approach to all forms of conduct (exclusionary and exploitative) and seeks to diminish the risk of over-enforcement that would flow from reasoning that, whenever a truly efficient competitor is excluded from the market, an infringement of Article 102 TFEU has occurred. However, effective competition and exclusionary or exploitative measures are not always clearly defined in Commission decisions and case law. As such, in some authors' view, certain forms of pro-competitive behaviour may at times be covered by decisions of Union institutions. This is particularly so given that the line between competition on the merits, and improper conduct is not always clearly demarcated in the decisions.[100] According to

96. Pablo Ibáñez Colomo, *Competition on the Merits*, 61 Common Market Law Review (2024) https://doi.org/10.54648/cola2024026.
97. Anne Witt, *The European Court of Justice and the More Economic Approach to EU Competition Law-Is the Tide Turning?*, 2 Antitrust Bulletin 174-176 (2019) https://doi.org/10.1177/0003603x19844637; Pablo Ibanez Colomo and Andriani Kalintiri, *The Evolution of EU Antitrust Policy: 1966-2017*, 2 Modern Law Review 334-338 (2020) https://doi.org/10.1111/1468-2230.12503.
98. Case T-219/99, *British Airways v. Commission*, 17.12.2023, EU:T:2003:343.
99. Case C-377/20, *Servizio Elettrico Nazionale and Others*, 12.5.2022, EU:C:2022:379, para. 77. That concept is also reflected in case C-680/20, *Unilever Italia Mkt. Operations*, 19.1.2023, EU:C:2023:33, para. 39, which refers to *Servizio Elettrico Nazionale* (paras 71 and 75, 76), which refer to as-efficient competitors to indicate when a practice is not based on competition on the merits.
100. Opinion of Advocate General Rantos in *Servizio Elettrico Nazionale and Others*, C–377/20, EU:C:2021:998, para. 53; Pablo Ibanez Colomo, *The Shaping of EU Competition Law* (Cambridge University Press 2018) 312-313; Nicolas Petit, *Droit européen de la concurrence* (Ed. 3, Paris 2020) 358.

Nicolas Petit, the EU courts have long disregarded economic theories,[101] which explains why the so-called more economic approach – focussing on a practice's impact – initially went unheeded. According to this reasoning, the Court of Justice preferred to rely on certain 'abstract formulas' and treat certain practices as anticompetitive, even if they might not have been so characterised had their effects been fully evaluated. What contributed to this uncertainty was certainly the non-exhaustive nature of the list of abuses under Article 102 TFEU and the resulting breadth of the Commission's discretion relating to enforcement and setting its priorities. There is also no *de minimis rule*, although some commentators have seen it in a case on discriminatory practices under Article 102(c) TFEU, referring to the judgment in Case C-525/16, *MEO*,[102] which addressed a preliminary question on discriminatory downstream prices. In this case, the Court of Justice considered that it was neither necessary nor sensible to examine the threshold below which the practice would be permitted. However, certain circumstances render an assessment of effects and the application of thresholds inevitable. Yet, there is no uniform standard; the estimate is made on a case-by-case basis. The coverage of the practice must also be examined when establishing the existence of an abuse. The aim is to ensure a realistic analysis of the case.

5 EXCLUSIONARY CONDUCT

Since 2008, combating exclusionary conduct has remained a priority for the European Commission. That is why, in the case law of the EU courts, many such practices are assessed when reviewing decisions of the European Commission, while other possible practices may be assessed by the Court of Justice in response to questions referred for a preliminary ruling by national courts. Cases where different exclusionary practices have been reviewed by the EU courts in recent years will be presented below. They all state, on the one hand, that exclusionary practices may occur in very different markets and be of varying nature, but, on the other hand, that the analysis of the effects and possibilities of competitor foreclosure set out above is of universal application.

The first type of exclusionary practice can be 'refusal of access'. It sometimes combines such an access obligation (to preserve competition in the market) with the concepts of 'essential facility' and the doctrine of providing access to essential devices. In recent years, the EU courts have not combined these two issues and recognised that an exclusionary practice in the form of a refusal of access does not mean that access has not been granted to essential facilities and that, consequently, the conceptual framework developed in *Oscar Bronner applies*. In Case T-814/17, *Lietuvos geležinkeliai AB*, in which the General Court's judgment was upheld by the CJ, the General Court concludes the following:

> paragraph 91: 'The requirement to protect the incentive for *a dominant undertaking to* invest in the construction of essential infrastructure does not exist where the

101. Nicolas Petit, *Droit européen de la concurrence* (Ed. 3, Paris 2020) 358.
102. Case C-525/16, *MEO – Serviços de Comunicações e Multimédia*,19.4.2018, EU:C:2018:270, para. 29.

> regulatory framework in force already imposes an obligation to supply on the dominant undertaking or where the dominant position which it has acquired on the market results from a former State monopoly.'
>
> Paragraph 98: '[the removal of the entire track] cannot be analysed in the light of the settled case-law on the refusal to give access to an essential facility, but must be analysed as conduct capable of hindering market entry by making access to that market more difficult and, therefore, of producing an anti-competitive foreclosure effect. It follows that the question whether Article 102 TFEU requires the applicant to repair the track is not relevant in the present case.'

Similarly, in Case T-136/19, *Bulgarian Energy Holding p.*[103] *of the Commission*, concerning the market for the supply of gas in Bulgaria by Transit Pipeline 1, the General Court did not conclude that there had been an infringement of Article 102 TFEU since the entity suspected of abuse of a dominant position had only performed its contractual obligations.

The 'self-referencing' discriminatory practice in Case T-612/17, *Google Shopping* constitutes an unprecedented new form of abuse.[104] In that case, the Commission established that Google favoured its own results on a specialised search site. The conduct involved positioning and showing its own results in a more advantageous fashion and reducing data flows from the general page with Google's results to competing services with specialised search engines in order to increase their own data stream. That new abuse was regarded by the General Court as not being necessary for competition on the merits since it was an improvement in Google's own visibility and a deterioration of its competitors' visibility.[105] Whatever their relevance, results from competing search engines were never treated in the same way as results from Google's comparison shopping service (positioning and visibility were different). The General Court confirmed that this practice reduces competition in the market. It also considered that Google was a gatekeeper by already using the references to the DMA adopted at that time[106] and stating that the Google search engine was a *gateway is the internet* and Google itself is the *gatekeeper*. In its judgment of 10 November 2021, the General Court dismissed Google's action, upholding the Commission's analysis, annulling only the finding of an infringement on the market for general search services, without affecting the amount of the fine imposed. Both the Court of Justice and Advocate General Juliane Kokott also confirmed the Commission's decision upon appeal by Google against the General Court's judgment.[107] In that case, the Court of Justice confirmed that self-referencing constitutes a new and self-standing form of abuse resulting from the

103. Case T-136/19, *Bulgarian Energy Holding and Others v. Commission*, 25.10.2023, EU:T:2023:669.
104. Case T–612/17, *Google and Alphabet v. Commission (Google Shopping)*, 10.11.2021, EU:T:2021:763.
105. Case T-612/17, *Google and Alphabet v. Commission (Google Shopping)*, 10.11.2021, EU:T:2021:763, para. 185.
106. Regulation (EU) 2022/1925 of the European Parliament and of the Council of 14 September 2022 on contestable and fair markets in the digital sector and amending Directives (EU) 2019/1937 and (EU) 2020/1828 (Digital Markets Regulation) (OJ L 265, 12.10.2022, p. 1-66) (hereinafter 'the DMA').
107. Opinion of Advocate General Kokott in *Google and Alphabet v. Commission (Google Shopping)*, C–48/22 P, EU:C:2024:14.

application of unfair conditions of access to competing comparison shopping services when it has at least potential anti-competitive effects (as found by the Commission in the present case, in the form of an exclusion from the market for specialised product search services).

Often, contractual practices where exclusivity clauses are included in a contract are a form of exclusionary practice. In Case T-604/18, *Google Android*, OEMs and MNOs were subject to three types of contractual restrictions: first, mobile app distribution agreements provided for the obligation to pre-install general search apps (Google Search) and browser apps (Chrome). This was a condition for obtaining a licence for the Google app store (Play Store). Second, fragmentation prevention contracts were concluded. On the basis of those provisions, OEMs wishing to install Google apps could not sell devices running versions of Android not approved by Google. Third and last, revenue share agreements were concluded, by which Google granted OEMs and MNOs a proportion of advertising revenues, provided, however, that those OEMs or MNOs agreed not to pre-install competing general search services on any device. All those contractual clauses were regarded by the General Court as exclusionary practices.

In reference to a preliminary ruling made to the Court of Justice in case C-680/20, *Unilever Italia Mkt Operations*, the Court took the view that such exclusivity clauses did not constitute an infringement of Article 102 TFEU per se: their exclusionary effect must be demonstrated. In order to determine what is known as the possibility of exclusion, it is necessary to consider two conditions: first, the competition authority must assess whether there was a strategy of excluding competitors that are at least as efficient. Second, it is necessary to ascertain whether the scheme is objectively justified. In addition, where evidence is produced showing that it is impossible to produce restrictive effects, the competition authority is required to examine it.

Case C-333/21, *European Superleague* is a final example of contractual clauses that constitute exclusionary practices, this time in sport.[108] This case, which was delivered in the context of an answer to the question referred for a preliminary ruling can be viewed as a 'recap judgment', by organising and defining certain concepts and aiming towards a harmonisation of the case law. It was delivered at the same time as other judgments striving to summarise key case law principles, namely in Case C-124/21 P, *International Skating Union*, and in Case C-680/21, *Royal Antwerp Football Club*. In Case C-333/21, the Court of Justice stated that, where an undertaking has exclusive rights conferring on it 'legislative', supervisory and sanctioning powers,[109] that is to say, in a situation where Articles 106 and 102 TFEU apply at the same time, the obligations for gatekeepers are more onerous. The Court of Justice extended the concept of abuse by considering that that concept covers not only a practice capable of excluding equally efficient competitors but also conduct capable of limiting their development[110] and conduct capable of restricting the entry of potential competitors to

108. Case C–333/21, *European Superleague Company*, 21.12.2023, EU:C:2023:1011.
109. As in the following cases: case C-18/88, *GB-Inno-BM*, 13.12.1991, EU:C:1991:474, case C-49/07, *MOTOE*, 1.7.2008, EU:C:2008:376.
110. Case C–333/21, *European Superleague Company*, 21.12.2023, EU:C:2023:1011, para. 129.

the market.[111] As regards proof of abuse, the Court of Justice accepted that different analytical tests are possible depending on the case, but that analysis must always be carried out 'taking into account all the relevant factual circumstances'.[112] That assessment is very innovative in terms of consistency between Articles 101 and 102 TFEU, that is to say, the argument in favour of the admission of certain practices with Article 102 TFEU where they are justified, as is the case under the aegis of Article 101 TFEU. The Court of Justice has accepted three types of 'justifying' circumstances, first, where there is an objective justification for the conduct in question.[113] Second, it authorised *efficiency*, by analogy with paragraph 101. It can be demonstrated that the effects are more pro-competitive than anti-competitive.[114] Third, the Court of Justice accepted the '*Wouters*' exception (C-309/99),[115] referring to the concept of *regulatory restraints*.[116] That entirely new interpretation of Article 102 TFEU could indicate that the analysis of the effects of the conduct in question, imposed since the *Intel* case, may be somewhat mitigated by the extension of the catalogue justifying such a practice.

6 CONCLUSIONS

The declared need for a broader application of the so-called economic approach and effects-based approach, repeated since the beginning of the twenty-first century both by doctrine and in case law, has brought its fruits. It is not like in Hans Christian Andersen's fairy-tale where an adviser had lured an Emperor to wear clothes that did not exist. The Emperor's new clothes are effectively there, even if, sometimes, their exact shape is uncertain.

The change made by the case law of the Court of Justice since the *Intel* judgment to the requirements that the European Commission must demonstrate in order to prove an abuse of a dominant position (through the analysis of the effects of the conduct in question) has led paradoxically to a higher number of European Commission decisions being annulled. The Court has become more demanding of the Commission by introducing more systematic and methodical conditions to demonstrate that a particular form of conduct constitutes an infringement. However, this comes often after many years of burdensome litigation[117] and might put the efficiency of the system in question.

111. Case C-333/21, *European Superleague Company*, 21.12.2023, EU:C:2023:1011, para. 131.
112. Case C-333/21, *European Superleague Company*, 21.12.2023, EU:C:2023:1011, para. 130.
113. Case C-333/21, *European Superleague Company*, 21.12.2023, EU:C:2023:1011, para. 202. Such an argument is not new, *see* case 27/76, *United Brands Company and United Brands Continentaal BV v. Commission*, 14.2.1978, EU:C:1978:22, paras 184 and 188; case C-52/09, *TeliaSonera Sverige*, 17.2.2011, EU:C:2011:83, paras 31 and 75; case C-209/10, *Post Danmark* (*Post Danmark I*), 27.3.2012, EU:C:2012:172, paras 41 to 42.
114. Case C-333/21, *European Superleague Company*, 21.12.2023, EU:C:2023:1011, paras 204 to 220.
115. Case C-309/99, *Wouters and Others*, 19.2.2002, EU:C:2002:98.
116. Case C-333/21, *European Superleague Company*, 21.12.2023, EU:C:2023:1011, paras 183 to 185.
117. Cf. e.g., the *Intel* or the *Servier* saga.

Therefore, this increasing complexity of regulation for businesses and the desire to ensure effective enforcement of competition rules give rise to two trends.

First, since cases under antitrust law tend to be extremely time-consuming and thus not fully effective, new rules such as the DMA have been created. Currently, access to infrastructure can also be subject to non-antitrust procedures, under the form of specific regulation like the DMA,[118] which is also linked to the use of market power (reference is made to large players designated as gatekeepers) .[119] This may raise doubts as to how to deal with a possible situation of double review of the same gatekeeper conduct (since the purpose of the two provisions is different, there is no breach of the ne bis in idem principle).[120] However, the DMA does not require an impact assessment and can thus give the Commission a wider opportunity to act. An additional indication could be a case of commercial practice, C-252/21, *Meta Platforms,*[121] in which the German Cartel Office prohibited Facebook from collecting and processing personal data without users' consent, as this constituted an abuse of a dominant position by Meta. In reply to a question referred for a preliminary ruling by a German court, the Court of Justice stated that the assessment of incompatibility with the GDPR by the national competition authority was permissible in order to establish the existence of an abuse of a dominant position. In addition, the competition authorities are bound by the decisions of other authorities. That 'reciprocal consideration' model is the one to be used for decisions relating to the DMA, ensuring the peaceful coexistence of the two regimes and mutual cooperation between different authorities applying those different regimes.

Second, since Article 102 TFEU must be implemented from the perspective of the analysis of effects, recent years have led to an increase in the burden of proof for competition authorities as they are supposed to clearly demonstrate the existence of an abuse of a dominant position. Article 102 TFEU is used to deal with problems relating to market structure and access to the market. In the case of concentrated markets, the overlap between Article 102 TFEU and merger control can be seen, as in Case 449/21, *Towercast.*[122] However, most of the abuses identified by the Commission concern exclusionary practices and in particular many cases concern access or supply obligations. The catalogue of possible abuses, as indicated in the article, continues to expand. Moreover, the nature of what is considered to concern access[123] sometimes changes.

118. Nicolas Petit, *The Proposed Digital Markets Act (DMA): A Legal and Policy Review,* 12(7) Journal of European Competition Law with Practice 529 (2021) https://doi.org/10.1093/jeclap/lpab062, described that act as sectoral regulation. Some consider that the rules are horizontal in nature: Pinar Akman, *Regulating Competition in Digital Platform Markets: A Critical Assessment of the Framework and Approach of the EU Digital Markets Act,* 47(1) European Law Review 94 (2022).
119. *See* the first judgment, delivered under an expedited procedure – case T-1077/23, *Bytedance v. Commission,* 17.7.2024, EU:T:2024:478.
120. *See* recital 11 in the preamble to the DMA Regulation, which states that the objective is different but complementary to the provisions of antitrust law.
121. Case C-252/21, *Meta Platforms and Others,* 4.7.2023, EU:C:2023:537.
122. Case C-449/21, *Towercast,* 16.3.2023, EU:C:2023:207.
123. *See* case C–233/23, *Alphabet and Others,* EU:C:2025:110, which related to a refusal to provide a service where access was necessary for a more convenient use of a product or service and this was considered as also capable of constituting an abuse prohibited by Art. 102 TFEU.

There is also a new trend appearing – it is permissible to engage with persons suspected of abuse on what may justify its specific conduct (which is very clear from the reasoning given in the *SuperLeague* judgment). Therefore only one thing is certain – the evolution of the interpretation of Article 102 TFEU is far from being complete for the years to come.

CHAPTER 5

Judicial Style and Article 102 TFEU

Giorgio Monti

1 INTRODUCTION

Much effort has been devoted to deciphering the concept of abuse of dominance or criticising the Court of Justice and the General Court for being unable to come up with workable standards.[1] Across the Atlantic, the same kind of criticism is found when it comes to the monopolisation case law.[2] In this chapter, I approach the case law of the EU's apex court (the Court or ECJ) from a different perspective, considering the style that the ECJ uses in its judgments and what this tells us about the concept of abuse of dominance.

Four elements of judicial style are considered. The mechanisms the Court uses in order to depart from previous case law (section 2). The manner by which previous case law is referred to (section 3). The choice of the Court to express the essence of Article 102 TFEU in paragraphs that set out general principles (section 4). The Court's efforts to construct an overarching exclusionary abuse standard (section 5). Space prevents a systematic analysis of these four elements of style across all of the case law, but it is hoped that there are enough exemplars of each to allow for some general conclusions about the role style plays in the development of the law on Article 102 TFEU.

It will become clear in what follows that the manner in which the case law on abuse of dominance has developed reveals that the ECJ frequently strives to keep the law consistent from one case to another, it sometimes engages in practices that distinguish one line of case law from others, and infrequently, it departs from previous

1. Ex multis, *see* Van Bael and Bellis, *Competition Law of the European Union*, 6th ed. (Wolters Kluwer, 2021) Ch. 8 for an admirable mix of summation and critique.
2. Einer Elhague, 'Defining Better Monopolization Standards' (2003) 56 Stanford Law Review 253, Herbert Hovenkamp, 'Exclusion and the Sherman Act' (2005) 72 University of Chicago Law Review 147.

case law. These are all judicial acts consistent with the treatment of prior case law as having the value of a precedent.[3] Moreover, the ECJ's trilogy of judgments delivered in December 2023, of which the most well-known is *European Superleague*, are an attempt by the Grand Chamber to provide a restatement of many aspects of EU competition law.[4] These judgments have the stature of a super-precedent and future developments should pay more heed to what the Court held here than to earlier case law.[5]

The purpose of analysing the Court's style is to discuss what effect this has on the development of the case law on abuse of dominance. A closer look at style can assist the Commission in its efforts to codify the case law in Guidelines, by gaining a more subtle understanding of the case law. It can also reveal how far problems created by judicial style may be resolved.

In what follows I take no view as to the merits of what the Court decides. My focus is on how the Court reasons and the implications of what this inquiry brings. At a high level, it is important to emphasise one point that this chapter reveals: the Court has changed its approach to Article 102 TFEU quite significantly since approximately 2012. The change has been patchy, incremental and perhaps still incomplete. The change aligns, in general terms, with the Commission's position in its Guidance Paper on Article 102 TFEU.[6] The Court's refusal to expressly acknowledge the changes charted in this chapter is the main point that this chapter draws attention to.

2 DEPARTING FROM PREVIOUS CASE LAW

2.1 Overruling

Advocate General La Pergola noted that while the Court 'is not technically bound by its own judgments', 'the cases in which the Court has expressly departed from its earlier case-law are as few as they are celebrated.'[7] There is no competition law judgment which has been deliberately overruled.[8]

3. However, the general view is that 'the Court is not bound by its previous decisions but in practice it does not often depart from them'. Anthony Arnull, 'Opening Up to Fallibility: Precedent and the Court of Justice' (1993) 30 Common Market Law review 247, 248.
4. Case C-333/21 *European Superleague Company v. FIFA and UEFA* EU:C:2023:1011; Case C-680/21 *Royal Antwerp Football Club v. Union royale belge des sociétés de football association ASBL* EU:C:2023:1010; Case C-123/21 P, *International Skating Union v. Commission*, EU:C:2023:1012.
5. Cf. M.J. Gerhardt, *The Power of Precedent* (OUP, 2011) Ch. 6 for a different use of the notion of super-precedent in the US.
6. Communication from the Commission: Guidance on its enforcement priorities in applying Article 82 of the EC Treaty to abusive exclusionary conduct by dominant undertakings [2009] OJ C45/7 (Guidance Paper).
7. Case C-262/96, *Sema Sürül v. Bundesanstalt für Arbeit*, EU:C:1998:55, para. 36 and note 35 respectively.
8. An example of overruling is Case C-10/89, *SA CNL-SUCAL NV v. HAG GF AG* EU:C:1990:359, para. 10: 'the Court believes it necessary to reconsider the interpretation given in that judgment [Case 192/73 *Van Zuylen v HAG*, EU:C:1974:72].' *See*, generally, M. Jacob, *Precedents and Case-Based Reasoning in the European Court of Justice: Unfinished Business* (CUP, 2014) Ch. 6.

The most notable change of direction is the 2017 Grand Chamber judgment *Intel v. Commission* (*Intel 1*).[9] The Court began by recalling the judgment in *Hoffmann-La Roche* where the ECJ had found that a dominant firm that requires its purchasers to buy all or most of the relevant products from the dominant company commits an abuse whether that obligation stems from a contract by which the buyer commits to buy exclusively from the dominant firm or whether a system of discounts is set up by the dominant company such that the buyer has an incentive to remain faithful to the dominant firm.[10] It then held that 'il convient de préciser cette jurisprudence'.[11] This is the first time that the Court has used this form of words to change the law substantially. In the one previous occasion that the Court used this exact phrase,[12] it merely explained in more detail a set of conditions that had been established in an earlier judgment without changing the essence of the previous ruling.[13]

But the delicate phrasing of the Court's intervention in *Intel 1* masks a major transformation to the abuse doctrine carried out by the Grand Chamber. The Court held that while the Commission may be entitled to try and establish an abuse by showing that a dominant firm has put in place a system of loyalty rebates, this cannot suffice when the applicant 'submits, during the administrative procedure, on the basis of supporting evidence, that its conduct was not capable of restricting competition and, in particular, of producing the alleged foreclosure effects.'[14] If this evidence is found to be convincing, the Commission is required to do more to demonstrate that there is an abuse of dominance. In particular, the Court held that the Commission must analyse: '[1] the extent of the undertaking's dominant position on the relevant market ..., [2] the share of the market covered by the challenged practice, [3] ... the conditions and arrangements for granting the rebates in question, [4] their duration and their amount; [5] it is also required to assess the possible existence of a strategy aiming to exclude competitors that are at least as efficient as the dominant undertaking from the market'.[15]

These paragraphs bring two changes to the law on loyalty rebates. The first is in the theory of harm. In *Hoffmann-La Roche* the Court explained that these kinds of contracts harmed competition in three ways. First, they restrict the choices of the buyers and they deny other producers access to the market. Second, the effect of rebates is to apply dissimilar conditions to equivalent transactions because buyers pay different prices depending on whether they accept the rebate. Third, these practices

9. Case C-413/14 P, *Intel v. Commission*, EU:C:2017:632 (*Intel 1*).
10. Case 85/76, *Hoffmann-La Roche v. Commission*, EU:C:1979:36, para. 89.
11. *Intel 1*, *supra* n. 9, para. 138. The English language version is stronger: 'that case-law *must* be further clarified'.
12. This is based on a search for these words on the curia website in English and in French.
13. The issue under consideration was when a trademark owner could object to parallel imports when the parallel importer repackages medicines. The criteria were originally set out in Case 102/77, *Hoffmann-La Roche v. Centrafarm* EU:C:1978:108. The Court held that the criteria should be clarified by adding further specifications to the general statements in the first judgment: Joined cases C-427/93, C-429/93 and C-436/93, *Bristol-Myers Squibb and others v. Paranova A/S*, EU:C:1996:282, para. 51.
14. *Intel 1*, *supra* n. 9, para. 138.
15. *Ibid.*, para. 139.

consolidate the undertaking's dominant position.[16] However, in *Intel 1*, the sole theory of harm left is the foreclosure of rivals. In this way, the Court approved the Commission's stance in the Article 102 Guidance Paper which placed emphasis on anticompetitive foreclosure as the sole rationale for intervening against exclusionary conduct.[17]

The second change is masked behind a procedural twist. The Commission may start a case solely based on the finding of an exclusivity agreement reached through loyalty rebates, but it is likely that nearly all dominant firms will bring economic evidence to cast doubt on whether their exclusivity agreement is capable of restricting competition. De facto, the Commission will almost always have to demonstrate foreclosure by a further economic analysis of the markets.

However, these clarifications required further explanation as the case returned to the General Court so that it could assess whether the Commission had carried out a successful effects analysis in its 2009 decision. In the Renvoi judgment, the General Court sought to clarify the ECJ's new stance in three ways.[18] Dissatisfied with this analysis, the Commission appealed against the Renvoi judgment giving the ECJ a second opportunity to clarify the clarifications made in *Intel 1*.[19] Below, I set out the three points where the two Courts offered sometimes conflicting clarifications of the *Intel 1* judgment.

First, the General Court suggested that when loyalty rebates are discovered, the Commission may take the view that they harm competition but this is 'a mere presumption and not a per se infringement of Article 102 TFEU.'[20] However, on appeal, the ECJ did not use the concept of a presumption to explain the law set in *Intel 1*. Instead, the Court explained the procedural dance that the Commission and dominant undertakings must perform in this way. First, the Commission may submit that loyalty rebates are an abuse of dominance. Second, 'the undertaking in a dominant position submits, during the administrative procedure, on the basis of supporting evidence, that it was not capable of producing the alleged foreclosure effects.'[21] Third, if this evidence is deemed credible by the Commission, it will then have to regroup and, if it finds evidence of likely effects, issue a supplementary statement of objections.[22] This new statement of objections will be based on an effects-based analysis. Conversely, if the Commission dismisses the dominant undertaking's evidence, it may issue a decision based merely on the evidence originally established. As indicated earlier, it is unlikely that the Commission will risk running a case without an effects test for the risk of having its decision quashed and having to restart from scratch. This is reminiscent of

16. *Hoffmann-La Roche, supra* n. 10, para. 90.
17. Guidance Paper, *supra* n. 6, para. 19.
18. Case T-286/09 RENV, *Intel v. Commission*, EU:T:2022:19 (*Intel RENV*).
19. Case C-240/22 P, *Commission v. Intel*, EU:C:2024:915 (*Intel 2*).
20. *Intel RENV, supra* n. 18, para. 124.
21. *Intel 2, supra* n. 19, para. 180.
22. V. Bottka, L. Repa and E. Rousseva 'Ordinary Procedure: From Initiation of Proceedings to the Adoption of a Final Decision' in E. Rousseva (ed.) *EU Antitrust Procedure* (OUP, 2020), paras 6.78-6.82.

the Commission's belts-and-braces approach in Article 101 TFEU where it decides that conduct is restrictive by object and by effect.[23]

Second, the General Court held that if the dominant firm rebuts this presumption then 'as a minimum' the Commission 'is required to examine' the five criteria set out by the Grand Chamber in order to assess the foreclosure capacity of the rebates.[24] This approach by the General Court was criticised by the Commission on appeal as being formalistic.[25] After all, it should not matter how the Commission proves that the conduct is likely to cause anticompetitive foreclosure. For example, there may be no evidence of an exclusionary strategy but the harmful effects may be felt anyway because the duration of the discounts is such as to foreclose rivals. However, the Court in *Intel 2* appears to agree that all five factors matter, even indicating that these are the only five factors to be considered.[26]

Third, the General Court held that the Court in *Intel 1* did not require the carrying out of the as-efficient competitor (AEC) test. Since the test was used by the Commission, it was appropriate for the General Court to review its application.[27] However, in *Intel 2,* the ECJ states that the AEC test is generally an adequate way of working out the capacity of the rebates to foreclose rivals, even if other methods may be selected.[28] This suggests that the Commission would have to offer a good justification for using alternative methods in subsequent cases.

The main point to draw from this extended account of the Intel saga is that the choice of words by the Court is not always a helpful reflection of what the Court does. In *Intel 1* the clarification is de facto a change of approach to the analysis of rebates: an overruling of the effects criteria of yore and a change in the method for assessment. In *Intel 2* the Court offers a quiet overturning of the lower court by not making reference to the notion of presumption which was used by the General Court in the Renvoi judgment and by specifying that the effects of rebates 'must be assessed, as a general rule, using the AEC test'.[29] Having changed course in *Intel 1*, the Court follows through by offering, incrementally, more information about how the new test is to be applied.

2.2 Distinguishing

A more modest way of departing from earlier cases is to distinguish earlier judgments from the one at hand. This approach is more common because it does less violence to

23. Case COMP/D1/38606 – *Groupement des Cartes Bancaires* (17 October 2007), where the Commission finally prevailed nine years later after it was decided that there was no restriction by object but there had been a restriction by effect Case T-491/07 P RENV, *Groupement des cartes bancaires v. Commission*, EU:T:2016:379.
24. *Intel RENV, supra* n. 18, para. 125.
25. *Intel 2, supra* n. 19, paras 110 and 120 (there is some irony here as for decades it was the Commission that was accused of formalism by its critics!).
26. *Intel 2, supra* n. 19, para. 180. It is worth adding that the Court makes reference to paras 47 and 49 of Unilever when the latter is irrelevant to the statement of law here.
27. *Intel RENV, supra* n. 18, para. 126.
28. *Intel 2, supra* n. 19, para. 181.
29. *Ibid.*

the coherence of the legal order. A good illustration of the Court carrying this out both expressly and impliedly is found by surveying the case law on refusals to deal.

Let us start by observing the practice of expressly distinguishing earlier case law. For many years the dominant precedent in this field was *Bronner*. Bolstered by a well-reasoned Opinion by AG Jacobs, the Court held that a refusal to deal with a rival could constitute an abuse only when the goods, services or infrastructure owned by the dominant undertaking were indispensable, when refusal would prevent the rival from entering the market, and when there was no objective justification.[30] However, in a series of cases, the Court narrowed the scope of application of the three *Bronner* criteria. In *Slovak Telecom*, where the abuse constituted various practices by the incumbent telecom operator to hamper rivals by making access to its telecom infrastructure more costly, the Court explained that the *Bronner* criteria applied only when the dominant firm had developed the facility for use in its own business. In this setting, Article 102 TFEU should apply rarely for the following reasons. First, deontologically, the application of Article 102 TFEU to compel access would interfere with the dominant undertaking's property rights and freedom of contract.[31] Second, consequentially, the Court explained that requesting access would reduce incentives for competitors to innovate.[32] However, these two reasons are not relevant in cases when the dominant firm gives access to its facilities to rivals but does so in an unfair manner. In this factual matrix, the *Bronner* conditions 'do not apply'.[33] On the facts of *Slovak Telekom*, the dominant undertaking was under a regulatory obligation to afford access and, as a result, there was no need to establish that the infrastructure to which access was denied was indispensable.

The Court continued to expressly distinguish *Bronner* in *Google Shopping*. Here it held that the criteria established in *Bronner* do not apply 'where a dominant undertaking gives access to its infrastructure but makes that access, provision of services or sale of products subject to unfair conditions'.[34] This is for two reasons. First, that indispensability is not necessary to demonstrate anticompetitive effects when the dominant firm gives access on unfair conditions.[35] Second, that the remedy that follows from a finding of infringement is not an order to give access but a command to provide such access fairly. 'The measures that would be taken in such a context will thus be less detrimental to the freedom of contract of the dominant undertaking and to its right to property than forcing it to give access to its infrastructure where it has reserved that infrastructure for the needs of its own business.'[36]

The refusal to deal line of cases reveals that the Court also distinguishes the case law tacitly. In *Magill*, the Court was confronted with a refusal to license

30. Case C-7/97, *Oscar Bronner v. Mediaprint*, EU:C:1998:569, para. 41.
31. Case C-165/19 P, *Slovak Telekom v. Commission*, EU:C:2021:239, para. 46.
32. *Ibid.*, para. 47.
33. *Ibid.*, para. 50.
34. Case C-48/22 P, *Google LLC and Alphabet Inc v. Commission* (*Google Shopping*), EU:C:2024:726, para. 111.
35. *Ibid.*
36. *Ibid.*, para. 112 (echoing *Slovak Telekom*, *supra* n. 31, para. 51).

copyright-protected material. The Court first explained that a refusal to license would constitute an abuse only in exceptional circumstances. It then went on to explain that the circumstances established by the General Court sufficed to demonstrate that this refusal constituted an abuse on the facts: (i) it prevented the appearance of a new product for which there was potential consumer demand; (ii) there was no justification; (iii) the effect was to reserve the derivative market to the dominant undertaking.[37] When this case was discussed in *Bronner*, the Court expressed some uncertainty as to whether this test applied to a refusal to offer rivals access to the dominant firm's home delivery services as well. The Court's hesitation is found immediately before it set out the threefold test which today we refer to as the *Bronner* criteria: 'even if that case-law on the exercise of an intellectual property right were applicable to the exercise of any property right whatever ...'.[38] Impliedly, the Court established that to determine whether a dominant undertaking's refusal to share its property with others may constitute an abuse, a distinction is drawn between two scenarios. First, cases where the refusal entails the licensing of IP rights, where it is essential that the party requesting access seeks to bring to the market a new product. Second, cases where the refusal does not include reliance on IP rights, in which case mere proof of indispensability is sufficient without requiring the party seeking access to provide a new product or service. By the time the ECJ decided *IMS Health*, this dividing line was so clear as not to require any explanation.[39] AG Tizzano indicated that the additional requirement for the requiring party to offer a new product is important to carry out an appropriate balance between the protection of IP rights and competition.[40]

The takeaway from this line of case law is that when the Court engages with precedent in a forthright manner, it is capable of providing reasons for the distinctions it draws. This makes the application of the law to new facts relatively easy since the criteria for applying the *Bronner* test are now better specified. Conversely, when it fails to do so as in the context of loyalty rebates or refusals to license IP rights, then the approach in subsequent cases becomes more difficult to divine. For example, some have taken the view that the general legal standard in refusals to license is based on whether there are exceptional circumstances, while others have taken the view that the Commission must show that a refusal to license would deny the entry of a new product.[41]

37. Joined cases C-241/91 P and C-242/91 P, *Radio Telefis Eireann (RTE) and Independent Television Publications Ltd (ITP) v. Commission*, EU:C:1995:98, paras 50-56.
38. Bronner, *supra* n. 30, para. 41.
39. Case C-418/01, *IMS Health GmbH & Co. OHG v. NDC Health GmbH & Co. KG*, EU:C:2004:257.
40. Case C-418/01, *IMS Health GmbH & Co. OHG v. NDC Health GmbH & Co. KG*, EU:C:2003:537, Opinion of AG Tizzano, paras 61-66.
41. Compare Steven Anderman, 'Does the Microsoft Case offer a New Paradigm for the Exceptional Circumstances Test and Compulsory Copyright Licenses under EC Competition Law?' (2004) 1(2) Competition Law Review 7 and James Killick, 'IMS and Microsoft Judged in the Cold Light of IMS' (2004) 1(2) Competition Law Review 23.

3 REFERENCES TO EARLIER CASE LAW

In the early years, case law was not cited by the ECJ. Today, case law is cited regularly. When references to earlier case law are made, we find several methods of citation. Sometimes the Court merely cites previous case law, sometimes it prefaces the citation with the word 'see' and sometimes 'see to that effect', and sometimes it asks the reader to 'see by analogy'. These different signals indicate, in descending order, the degree of precision with which previous case law is cited.[42]

By sampling some of the recent case law, we can discern that when the Court writes 'see to that effect', this may be a red arrow to indicate that the Court is departing from the case law and restating the relevant point in a salient manner. Or, as another commentator has put it more delicately, this phrase 'signals a more generous link to an earlier case'.[43] For example, in *Servizio Elettrico Nazionale*, the ECJ writes: 'the purpose of Article 102 TFEU more specifically is, *according to settled case-law*, to prevent conduct of an undertaking in a dominant position that has the effect, *to the detriment of consumers*, of hindering, through recourse to means or resources different from those governing normal competition, maintenance of the degree of competition existing in the market or the growth of that competition'.[44] After making this claim the ECJ asks the reader to see to that effect three judgments which use similar language but only one of the three makes a reference to consumer detriment.[45] The case law is hardly settled!

However, this is not to say that every time the Court asks the reader to 'see to that effect' this indicates a transformation. In the second sentence of the paragraph in *Servizio Elettrico Nazionale* just cited above, for example, the Court states that harm to consumers may be shown directly or indirectly and this is reflected in the two cases cited, even if again the Court asks the reader to see to that effect.[46] And the Court's general reflection on the purposes of competition law in the same judgment reproduces verbatim the analysis in *Telia Sonera*, a case the Court also asks the reader to see to that effect.[47] That the Court uses the same turn of phrase (see to that effect) inconsistently leaves the reader in some doubt as to why this wording is selected. However, there is no doubt that *SEN* is a judgment where the Court exhibited a change of attitude to competition law. The Court concluded its review of the case law by concluding (here without any citation to case law) that 'the well-being of both intermediary and final consumers must be regarded as the ultimate objective warranting the intervention of

42. Jacob, *supra* n. 8, p. 95, footnote 32 referring to the Court's internal drafting guidelines.
43. Jacob, *supra* n. 8, p. 81.
44. Case C-377/20, *Servizio Elettrico Nazionale SpA and others v. Autorità Garante della Concorrenza e del Mercato*, EU:C:2022:379 (*SEN*), para. 44.
45. Chronologically, the Court cites *Hoffmann-La Roche, supra* n. 10, para. 91 where there is no reference to consumer harm, Case C-209/10, *Post Danmark v. Konkurrencerådet*, EU:C:2012:172 (*Post Danmark 1*), para. 24 where there is a reference to consumer detriment, and Case C-307/18, *Generics (UK) Ltd and others v. Competition and Markets Authority*, EU:C:2020:52 (*Generics*), para. 148 where there is no reference to consumer harm.
46. Case C-95/04 P, *British Airways v. Commission*, EU:C:2007:166, paras 106 and 107, and Case C-52/09, *TeliaSonera*, EU:C:2011:83, para. 24.
47. *SEN*, *supra* n. 44, para. 41.

competition law'.[48] To achieve this restatement the Court avoided confronting the fact that not all the judgments prior to this one supported this normative stance. Its method of citation suggests, to an untrained eye, that the conclusion is based on established case law, however.

In one judgment the Court asks the reader to 'see by analogy'. This occurs in *Intel 1* where after listing the five criteria to be used to determine if rebates have anticompetitive effects it refers by analogy to *Post Danmark 1*.[49] However, turning to the paragraph indicated, there is nothing more than a discussion of whether on the facts there was evidence that the dominant firm had pursued an anticompetitive strategy. There is nothing to support the list of factors identified by the ECJ. This is not to call into question the relevance of those factors, but the absence of relevance of the case cited to the proposition of law set out raises doubts as to what the function of citing a prior judgment is. As with *SEN*, the Court creates a new rule suggesting that there is prior case law supporting it when this is far from the case.

The result of this brief survey reveals that the Court masks changes in its approach by a reference to case law that offers no support for the new proposition the Court makes. This occurs both for general propositions (the role of consumer harm in *SEN*) and for specific codifications of a legal test (e.g., the five factors in *Intel 1*). Similar findings about the use of precedent have been made by others in diverse fields of EU Law.[50]

4 GENERAL STATEMENTS

It will not escape the reader of case law that the Court frequently premises specific analysis with restatements of some general propositions from earlier case law. It is not clear what is gained by this exercise. For example, the Court frequently states that 'a dominant undertaking has a special responsibility not to allow its behaviour to impair genuine, undistorted competition on the internal market'.[51] This statement first appeared in *Michelin 1* but in the context of a discussion of the concept of dominance. Only in 2000 did the ECJ use this phrase as a prefatory remark to its analysis of the concept of abuse.[52] Moreover, the statement does not appear in all judgments. This raises the question of why it is found in some judgments and not others.[53]

In some cases, the role of special responsibility is referred to as a way to justify a particular legal standard that allows the dominant firm to carry out a self-assessment of

48. *Ibid.*, para. 46.
49. *Intel 1*, *supra* n. 9, para. 139 referring to *Post Danmark 1*, *supra* n. 45, para. 29.
50. Arnull, *supra* n. 3, pp. 253-258 and Jacob, *supra* n. 8, Ch. 4.
51. Case 322/81, *NV Nederlandsche Banden Industrie Michelin v. Commission*, EU:C:1983:313, para. 57.
52. Joined cases C-395/96 P and C-396/96 P, *Compagnie maritime belge transports SA and others v. Commission*, EU:C:2000:132, para. 85.
53. G. Monti and E. Rousseva 'The Special Responsibility of Dominant Undertakings' in P. Akman, Or Brook and K. Stylianou (eds), *Research Handbook on Abuse of Dominance and Monopolization* (Edward Elgar, 2023).

its conduct. For example, in *Intel 2*, one of the reasons for applying an AEC test to identify the exclusionary capacity of rebates is that this creates legal certainty because it 'enables that undertaking, in light of its special responsibility under Article 102 TFEU, to assess the lawfulness of its own conduct, since it knows its own costs'.[54] However, since every undertaking is expected to self-assess its compliance with EU competition law, the identification of a special responsibility to do so on dominant firms adds nothing to our understanding of Article 102 TFEU.

A more radical reading is possible, but this rests on points that the Court has made only in passing. For example, in *Deutsche Telekom*, the dominant firm had engaged in a margin squeeze, which was proven by showing that the dominant firm would not have been able to offer retail services otherwise than at a loss if it had to pay its own wholesale charges for access to the local loop. One of the applicant's arguments, which was given short shrift, was that the approach of the Commission was incorrect in focusing only on the costs of the dominant undertaking because rivals are 'subject to less onerous legal and material conditions' in the provision of retail services.[55] The reasoning of the applicant was that since rivals have lower operating costs than the dominant firm, this should affect the application of the test for margin squeeze. The Court rejected this line of argument in the following way: 'Even if that assertion were proved, it would not alter either the fact that a dominant undertaking, such as the appellant, cannot adopt pricing practices which are capable of driving equally efficient competitors from the relevant market, or the fact that such an undertaking must, in view of its special responsibility under Article [102 TFEU], be in a position itself to determine whether its pricing practices are compatible with that provision.'[56] One way of interpreting this passage is that even if a price-cost test risks being over-inclusive (risking a Type 1 error) the special responsibility of the dominant undertaking means that this is the best test to use because it allows the dominant firm to self-assess its conduct. It means that in a scenario such as this, one does not need to prove likely exclusionary effects. The special responsibility extends to forbid conduct which may not, in specific circumstances, exclude rivals. Administrability trumps precision. However, this line of argumentation does not seem to have gained traction in subsequent case law.

In contrast, some other general statements appear much less frequently. For example, only in *Tomra* and *Generics* does the Court state that 'it is not the place of a dominant undertaking to dictate how many viable competitors are to be allowed to compete with it'.[57] This is perhaps not surprising because this statement may be inconsistent with some of the Court's more recent case law. For example, if one were

54. *Intel 2*, *supra* n. 19, para. 312. This draws on Case C-280/08 P, *Deutsche Telekom v. Commission* EU:C:2010:603, para. 202.
55. *Deutsche Telekom*, *supra* n. 54, paras 187-191.
56. *Ibid.*, para. 202.
57. *Generics*, *supra* n. 45, para. 161. In Case C-549/10P, *Tomra Systems and Others v. Commission*, EU:C:2012:221, para. 52 the statement is slight different: 'it is not the role of the dominant undertaking to dictate how many viable competitors will be allowed to compete for the remaining contestable portion of demand'.

to apply this general statement to cases of loyalty rebates, it would justify the application of the *Hoffman-La Roche* rule by which any loyalty agreement, irrespective of coverage or duration, is anti-competitive because it forecloses some of the market to rivals. Any foreclosure is an abuse because the dominant form cannot regulate market access. Conversely, the modern approach to rebates embraced in *Intel 1* requires proof of more significant foreclosure effects before a finding of abuse is found and the passage quoted above fits uncomfortably with this line of case law.

A final general statement that is worth discussing is the reference that the Court makes to as efficient competitors. Modern references to this phrase start with the case law on margin squeeze and the concept is also discussed in *Post Danmark 1*, decided in 2012. In the latter case, the Court states this general point by explaining that Article 102 TFEU 'prohibits a dominant undertaking from, among other things, adopting pricing practices that have an exclusionary effect on competitors considered to be as efficient as it is itself and strengthening its dominant position by using methods other than those that are part of competition on the merits'.[58] Before analysing the content of this passage, it is again worth tracing the case law that the Court asks the reader to 'see to that effect' which supports this claim: *AKZO* and *Deutsche Telekom*.

The Court's reference to *AKZO* is vital as it is the first time the phrase as efficient competitors was used. But here the Court's language was much more nuanced than that found in *Post Danmark 1*: it held that prices above AVC but below ATC are abusive part of a plan to eliminate a competitor because they can 'drive from the market undertakings which are *perhaps* as efficient as the dominant undertaking'.[59] Thus this case does not support the view that only as efficient rivals are deserving of protection.

The Court then refers to *Deutsche Telekom*, but reading the relevant passage shows us that this judgment is still based on a fairly traditional reading of competition law which pre-dates the more economic approach found in the recent case law. The Court explains that exclusionary pricing practices can have two effects: first, they exclude 'equally efficient actual or potential competitors', second, they also make 'it more difficult or impossible for its co-contractors to choose between various sources of supply or commercial partners'.[60] Much like in *Hoffmann-La Roche* discussed in section 2, the Court here was still retaining a wider view as to the harm caused by exclusionary practices. As noted there, after *Intel 1*, it appears that the Court takes the view that anticompetitive exclusion is limited to conduct which causes actual or partial foreclosure.

The point to emphasise is that, much like the notion of special responsibility, the manner in which the 'as efficient competitor' phrase comes to be a general element of the notion of abuse is by a transformation of the way the concept was used originally. However, it is clear that the contemporary case law fully embraces the notion that Article 102 TFEU should generally apply when conduct is likely to penalise as-efficient

58. *Post Danmark 1*, *supra* n. 45, para. 25.
59. Case C-62/86, *AKZO Chemie BV v. Commission* EU:C:1991:286, para. 72 (emphasis added).
60. *Deutsche Telekom*, *supra* n. 54, para. 177.

competitors, such that many have said that the Court embraces an as-efficient competitor standard/principle. Scholars are divided as to what this principle is. Professor Akman refers to the work of Richard Posner and puts forward as a definition of the AEC standard the following two elements: 'first, establishing monopoly power, and second, providing the possibility of rebuttal by proof that the practice is, on balance, efficient'.[61] Posner's rationale for this is clear: efficiency being the goal of antitrust law, one cannot tolerate punishing a firm if its conduct is efficient. However, this definition does not help us in any way in characterising what conduct is an abuse of dominance. Others, like Dr Marinova, have taken the view that the as efficient competitor principle is 'a broad conceptual framework for evaluating exclusionary conduct'.[62] More narrowly, Professor Neven reads the case law as stating that when conduct leads to the foreclosure of as-efficient competitors then this is a sufficient condition for finding abuse.[63] But both authors explain that the operationalisation of this principle requires the use of some more specific tests to diagnose the likelihood that an as-efficient competitor is likely to be excluded. From this perspective, the added value of the principle is that it serves as a way of examining if the legal and economic tests used by the Commission are well-aligned with the principle or not. Neven's approach further allows him to conclude that all conduct that is likely to exclude as efficient rivals is necessarily an abuse: a red line may be drawn. Neven's approach tallies with the approach taken by the Court of Justice in *SEN*. In a passage where the Court makes no reference to earlier cases, thereby signalling a new line of thinking, the Court explains:

> The relevance of the material or rational impossibility for a hypothetical competitor, which is as efficient but not in a dominant position, to imitate the practice in question, in order to determine whether that practice is based on means that come within the scope of competition on the merits, is clear from the case-law on practices both related and unrelated to prices.[64]

The Commission condemning a refusal to deal without examining the indispensability of the input, or condemning a discount without a price-cost test to determine if the dominant firm's prices are below cost would likely protect rivals who are not as efficient as the dominant firm because absent indispensability normally a rival should be able to enter and absent below-cost discount an efficient rival should also be able to remain in the market.[65] In sum, the principle serves as a way for the Court to examine whether the decision of the Commission rests on adequate analysis. It applies to both price and non-price abuses.

---

61. Pinar Akman 'A Critical Inquiry into "Abuse" in EU Competition Law' (2024) 44(2) Oxford Journal of Legal Studies 405, 426 https://doi.org/10.1093/ojls/gqae008.
62. Miroslava Marinova, 'The As-Efficient Competitor Test: A Cornerstone of a Controversy in EU Competition Law?' (20 December 2024) Competition Law Insight.
63. Damien J. Neven, 'The As-Efficient Competitor Test and Principle: What Role in the Proposed Guidelines?' (2023) 14 Journal of European Competition Law and Practice 565 https://doi.org/10.1093/jeclap/lpad063.
64. *SEN*, *supra* n. 44, 79.
65. This is a synthesis of *SEN*, *supra* n. 44, paras 80-83.

However, the Court has also said that an abuse may be found even when the conduct risks eliminating rivals who are not as efficient as the dominant undertaking. This is set out explicitly in *Post Danmark 2*. Given the high entry barriers in the relevant market, 'the presence of a less efficient competitor might contribute to intensifying the competitive pressure on that market and, therefore, to exerting a constraint on the conduct of the dominant undertaking'.[66] This calls into question the usefulness of the AEC principle as a general standard by which to assess conduct of dominant undertakings.

5 A GENERAL ABUSE STANDARD?

Over time, the Court of Justice has set out discrete rules and standards in competition law. For example, in *AKZO*, the ECJ set out a rule by which prices below average variable cost constitute an abuse, while the ECJ's *Intel* case law provides a standard by which proof that loyalty rebates are anticompetitive requires a showing of anticompetitive effects by reference to a fixed number of indicators. These two approaches to similar forms of exclusionary conduct are not internally consistent.[67] And it is perhaps because of the Court's preference to articulate discrete approaches for different types of abuse that the ECJ has not, until recently, sought to formulate a general standard to serve as a common denominator for all exclusionary abuse.

The Court however felt compelled to try and generalise its case law as a result of two references for a preliminary ruling coming from the Italian Consiglio di Stato. The Italian court must have sensed that the Grand Chamber's *Intel 1* judgment indicated a major change in the direction of travel for Article 102 TFEU and therefore sent the Court a set of questions that went to the heart of the concept of abuse of dominance. For example, in *Servizio Elettrico Nazionale* the ECJ was asked if conduct is an abuse solely because of potentially restrictive effects or whether there was an additional component relating to the unlawful nature of the conduct. It was also asked about the purpose of the concept of abuse: is it about maximising consumer well-being or about preserving the competitive structure of the market? In *Unilever* the ECJ was asked about the role of the as efficient competitor criterion in cases where the dominant undertaking imposed exclusivity clauses: was *Intel 1* applicable only to the facts of that case, or did it evince a more general standard?

Somewhat surprisingly, the same Chamber, with the same reporting judge, appeared to try and generalise an abuse standard in two different ways. The table below reproduces the text in the two judgments, illustrating the stark differences between the two cases by highlighting certain parts of the text:

66. Case C-23/14, *Post Danmark v. Konkurrencerådet*, EU:C:2015:651 (*Post Danmark 2*), para. 60.
67. Compare Case T-334/19, *Google and Alphabet v. Commission*, EU:T:2024:634 (detailed assessment of effects) and Case T-671/19, *Qualcomm v. Commission* EU:T:2024:626 (price-cost tests appears sufficient). Both judgments have been appealed.

Servizio Elettrico Nazionale	*Unilever*
'in order to establish that an exclusionary practice is abusive, a competition authority must show that, first, that practice was capable, when implemented, of producing such an exclusionary effect, in that it was capable of making it more difficult for competitors to enter or remain on the market in question and, by so doing, that that practice was capable of having an impact on the market structure; *and*, second, that practice relied on the use of means other than those which come within the scope of competition on the merits.'[68]	'Thus, abuse of a dominant position could be established, *inter alia*, where the conduct complained of produced exclusionary effects in respect of competitors that were as efficient as the perpetrator of that conduct in terms of cost structure, capacity to innovate, quality, *or* where that conduct was based on the use of means other than those which come within the scope of 'normal' competition, that is to say, competition on the merits.'[69]

While SEN established a two-step test (which it repeated in the operative part of the judgment),[70] just a year later the ECJ appeared to change its mind and posit that the two steps were alternative conditions (substituting or for and) and did not constitute an exhaustive catalogue of general criteria (suggesting these as options from a longer list: *inter alia*). The Court in *Unilever* also added that exclusionary effects mattered when the conduct was capable of excluding as-efficient competitors, a criterion that is also present in SEN but not in the general formulation of abuse.

It is unsurprising that the Grand Chamber felt it necessary in *European Superleague* to bring some order in the case law. The Court confirms the accuracy of the restatement in *SEN*, takes some points from *Unilever*, and adds something more to the mix:

> In order to find, in a given case, that conduct must be categorised as 'abuse of a dominant position', it is necessary, as a rule, to demonstrate, through the use of methods other than those which are part of competition on the merits between undertakings, that that conduct has the actual or potential effect of restricting that competition by excluding equally efficient competing undertakings from the market(s) concerned, or by hindering their growth on those markets, although the latter may be either the dominated markets or related or neighbouring markets, where that conduct is liable to produce its actual or potential effects.[71]

This indicates a two-stage test: bad acts and anticompetitive effects. The Grand Chamber helpfully adds that anti-competitive effects may manifest themselves in the market where the firm is dominant or in another market when a dominant firm leverages its market power. The Court also clarifies that the effects segment of the test

68. *SEN*, *supra* n. 44, para. 61.
69. Case C-680/20, *Unilever v. Autorità Garante della Concorrenza e del Mercato*, EU:C:2023:33, para. 39. The Court asks the reader to *see*, 'to that effect' paras 69, 71, 75 and 76 of the *SEN* judgment, but not para. 61.
70. *SEN*, *supra* n. 44, point 4 or the operative part.
71. *Superleague*, *supra* n. 4, para. 129.

may be satisfied by showing either total or partial foreclosure and that the legal standard requires a showing that the conduct is capable of foreclosing an as efficient competitor. In addition, the ECJ helps develop the case law in a subsequent passage where it explains that demonstrating an abuse in a specific case 'may entail the use of different analytical templates depending on the type of conduct at issue.'[72] This justifies the Court applying different legal tests for different abuses, but the Grand Chamber insists that whatever test is used, it must demonstrate conduct 'at the very least, is capable of producing exclusionary effects'.[73]

The result of this judgment is to require a systematic review of all the relevant legal tests that have been used to ensure that they are consistent with the analytical framework put forward by the Grand Chamber. For example, in my view, a case of predatory pricing cannot be solely based on prices below average variable cost. In addition, it must be shown that such prices are set for a sufficiently long period of time and set for a sufficient number of customers so that it is likely that conduct can foreclose rivals. In other words, proof of predatory pricing requires reference to an economic theory of harm and an identification of factors that make a finding that predation is likely to harm competition realistic given the theory of harm selected.[74]

In addition to bringing order to Article 102 TFEU however, the Grand Chamber also set out two new approaches to abuse of dominance. First, it suggested that sometimes conduct may be shown to be an abuse 'also where it has been proven to have the actual or potential effect – or even the object – of impeding potentially competing undertakings at an earlier stage.'[75] The Court refers to the *Generics* judgment, where a pay-for-delay scheme was held to be capable of being exclusionary because it blockaded market access. The reference to *Generics* in my view is unhelpful. The Court there explained that based on the documents it had available, it was the CMA and the referring court who considered that the settlement strategy of the dominant firm had as its object to delay entry of generic medicines.[76] The Court did not take a view as to whether there were object restrictions. By this statement, the ECJ is however charting a path towards the identification of conduct that may be treated as abuse without an assessment of likely effects. However, such a general statement begs the question of what conduct falls within this newfound category.

The second innovation the Grand Chamber brings starts with it recalling its earlier case law imposing liability on Member States for anticompetitive regulation based on a joint reading of Articles 102 and 106 TFEU.[77] This case law dealt with a setting where the dominant firm was conferred regulatory powers and was likely to use them to exclude rivals and favour its own services. For example, an entity entrusted

72. *Ibid.*, para. 130.
73. *Ibid.*
74. C. Fumagalli, M. Motta and C. Calcagno, *Exclusionary Practices: The Economics of Monopolisation and Abuse of Dominance* (Cambridge University Press, 2018).
75. *Superleague, supra* n. 4, para. 131.
76. *Generics, supra* n. 45, para. 155.
77. This paragraph summarises the points made in *Superleague, supra* n. 4, paras 132-138. This segment of the judgment arrives without any introduction, following on from t eh identification of object restrictions discussed above.

with regulating access to telephone sets who is also a maker of such products is tempted to exclude rivals to favour its telephones. In this setting, the Court has held that the state acts contrary to Articles 102 and 106 read jointly by simply conferring such regulatory powers because the regulator has a conflict of interest and is likely to exclude rivals and favour itself.[78] The state avoids liability if the firm entrusted with regulating market access is instructed to carry out its regulatory powers by reference to a set of substantive criteria that are transparent, clear and precise and ensure that this power is not exercised in a non-discriminatory manner. In addition, there must be detailed procedural rules governing the application of these substantive standards and there must be a possibility of securing judicial review. Controlling such powers according to the Grand Chamber is 'all the more necessary' when a firm establishes such regulatory powers by itself, without the support of the state.[79] On the facts of the case at hand, regional and global football regulatory bodies like UEFA and FIFA who both control market access for football competition and also organise major sporting competitions must have in place substantive and procedural rules to ensure that anyone seeking to offer a rival football competition may have its application considered impartially by FIFA and UEFA. The absence of such controls entails there is an abuse of a dominant position. This constellation of facts brings up a new type of abuse of dominance whose precise contours will have to be determined in subsequent litigation. Having opened the door to challenging self-regulation via Article 102 TFEU, it is likely that many restrictive practices will be tested in other sporting contexts as well as other instances where professions have restrictive access rules. This litigation will afford the Court of Justice further opportunities to further specify the constituent elements of this abuse of dominance.

6 CONCLUSION

A reader would be excused for concluding that the ECJ is an unreliable court, not least with the way in which the law is re-interpreted and the manner in which cases are cited. This is unfortunate since the Court has sought, since the early days, to exercise intellectual leadership in the development of EU law and competition law in particular.[80] That the Court, in good faith, moves the law forward, however, does not justify the manner in which prior judgments are utilised.

The result of the Court's opacity traced in sections 2 and 3 of this chapter suggests that the student must read all the case law with a keen eye for how the Court modifies previous statements because the Court will not inform the reader that change is afoot. This seems to be the result of a particular judicial style that is not well-suited to signal change. Frequently the ECJ seeks legitimacy in 'consistency and systematicity' rather

78. This example is loosely based on Case C-18/88 *GB-Inno-BM*, EU:C:1991:474.
79. *Superleague*, *supra* n. 4, para. 137.
80. D.J. Gerber, *Law and Competition in Twentieth Century Europe: Protecting Prometheus* (OUP, 1998) 352.

than in 'exhaustive argumentative efforts'.[81] But this source of legitimacy is gone if the references to earlier case law do not reveal the true picture of what is happening.

It would be relatively easy for the Court to avoid this criticism of the use of case law by adopting some relatively straightforward changes to its approach. It appears almost too basic to mention them. First, using quotation marks would erase any trace of doubt that it is citing directly from earlier case law. As a result, the reader would then be aware that if quotation marks are not used the Court is drawing on earlier case law to inspire a new way of expressing its views on how to best interpret the law. Second, a more active engagement with precedent, as we saw in the context of the case law on refusals to deal, allows one to see with greater clarity the rationale for the Court's choices. In that line of case law public reason rather than appeal to precedent allows one to explain the rationale for the different approaches. Presently, it seems that the Court is more concerned about keeping up an appearance that the case law remains constant while everyone sees that standards for assessment are shifting. Greater legitimacy would result in the Court being more transparent about how the case law evolves.

Sections 4 and 5 moved away from precedent to principles: the Court has often tried to formulate general statements to create the foundations for the specific application of Article 102 TFEU to given cases. This is particularly important when the Court responds to questions from national courts where a decision on the facts is for the national judge and so the most the Court can do is provide some high-level principles to assist the national judges. In considering the Court's reasoning generally, Judge Mancini explained why these efforts may come up short: '[t]he case law produced in Luxembourg is rightly criticized for its often stunted reasoning and its frequently oracular tone; but such shortcomings must be attributed ... to the need to render judgments that are acceptable to all the signatories'.[82] That there are divisions in the Court is evident when one looks at the differences that arise from the Opinions of its Advocates General. The dissonance revealed above between *SEN* and *Unilever* may also be down to judges differing as to how to best conceive a general standard for abuse. This aspect of the Court's style is less easy to resolve in a pragmatic manner but it suggests that the role that competition law plays in the EU reflects wider differences among legal and political cultures that are visible in academic writings where believers in the more economic approach premised on predicting likely effects on welfare frequently clash with those pleading for an approach favouring open markets irrespective of precise consequentialist calculations.

Finally, what lessons does this study have for the Commission's efforts to write guidelines? In my view, the main lesson is to refuse to take the Court literally. The notion of abuse by the ECJ 'is approached as if it were meaningful and logically

81. Jacob, *supra* n. 8, p. 189.
82. G.F. Mancini, 'Culture and Politics in the Life of the European Court of Justice' in G.F. Mancini, *Democracy and Constitutionalism in the European Union: Collected Essays* (Hart, 2000) 177, 178. Similarly observing the impact of unanimity, *see* D. Edward, 'How the Court of Justice Works', 20 European Law Review (1995), 539, 556.

complete'.[83] As we have seen, however, the Court does not acknowledge the magnitude of the changes it brings, fails to cite precedent coherently, and advances general standards that have little meaning and are not used systematically. Rather, the case law must be interpreted in the round. It follows that Guidelines are where the Commission can express its informed opinion of how the case law can be read cumulatively and consistently. The Commission can also come to the aid of the Court of Justice itself by providing more elegant rules and standards than the Court is able to provide. Not only because unanimity prevents the Court from being completely clear, but also because judgments react to points of law raised in specific settings, so the Court is never in a position to consider issues afresh in a holistic way. The Commission however can do so in Guidelines.

This approach to writing Guidelines is aided by the super-precedent in *European Superleague*. There is now an overarching standard that serves as a common denominator for all conduct that may be considered an abuse. The Court explains that every discrete test for abuse should be an application of the general legal standard. Thus, rather than trying to go back to the case law to codify it, the time is ripe for the Commission to look forward and chart a path that codifies the abuse doctrine in light of the overall ambition for Article 102 TFEU. This task is perhaps more challenging than merely trying to reconcile and classify the case law for it first requires the Commission to take a stance on the role that Article 102 TFEU should play in regulating dominant undertakings today. It then requires an effort to write up rules and standards that match this overall ambition, which may, at times mean that the Commission jettisons some statements in the case law that no longer fit the new approach to Article 102 TFEU charted by the Court, in the expectation that once the point comes back to the Court, the law will change. Such forward-looking guidelines may, themselves, shape the ECJ's development of the case law by presenting a coherent analytical framework which is appealing to the judiciary.[84]

83. Jacob, *supra* n. 8, p. 148 – he refers to the system of adjudication more widely, but one can legitimately apply this passage to a specific doctrine.
84. As demonstrated in this chapter, the Guidance Paper has influenced the ECJ. I had foreseen this in G. Monti 'Article 82 EC: What Future for the Effects-Based Approach?' (2010) 1(1) Journal of European Competition Law & Practice 2, 8-9 https://doi.org/10.1093/jeclap/lpp005.

CHAPTER 6

The Dwindling Law in Article 102 TFEU

Fernando Castillo de la Torre[*]

1 INTRODUCTION

This contribution discusses whether some (or much) of the 'lawness' in the enforcement of Article 102 TFEU has been lost over recent years. I argue that this is the case, and that this has been mostly the result of the influence of the 'effects based' or 'more economic' approach,[1] and how it has been embraced, at least in part, by the EU judicature.

I do not use 'lawness' as a springboard into a principled enquiry about 'what the law is'.[2] The endeavour is more modest here. I assess rather what is the role of law, *as a practical matter*, in the assessment of cases under Article 102 TFEU. Law has been a core instrument in European integration, in what is sometimes called 'integration through law'. Over seven decades, the Court of Justice has rendered EU law *effectively* enforceable. While competition law enforcement must be based on evidence, and the assessment must rely on a reasonably complete factual enquiry, evidence does not

* I wish to thank the other panellists in the GCLC Annual Conference in Bruges (Belgium), on 1-2 March 2024, and the Vienna Competition Law Days 2024, on 12 September 2024, where many of the ideas reflected in this chapter were presented, for the lively discussions. I would also like to express sincere thanks to Nathan Cambien, Pedro Caro de Sousa, Anthony Dawes, Eric Gippini Fournier, Cristina Sjödin and Wouter Wils, whose comments on previous drafts helped improve this contribution. All errors are mine. This contribution mentions many court cases, and the author has been an agent in a number of them. The views expressed are purely personal and can under no circumstance be attributed to the European Commission.

1. *See*, examining the impact of the 'more economic' approach on the case law, F. Castillo de la Torre, 'Is the Effects-Based Approach Too Cumbersome?: Taking Stock of Recent Practice and Case Law on Article 102 TFEU', in, A. Komninos, A. Claici and D. Waelbroeck (eds), *The Transformation of EU Competition Law: Next Generation Issues*, Kluwer Law International, 2023, 145-198.
2. *See*, in this sense, F. Schauer, 'Lawness', 95 *Wash. U. L. Rev.* 1135 (2018).

deliver verdicts by itself. The assessment of evidence must be guided by the law if EU competition law wants to remain 'law enforcement'.

Infringements of Article 102 TFEU give rise to serious legal consequences, in particular quasi-criminal pecuniary sanctions. Therefore, the determination of legality must be premised on generalised norms which are comprehensible to subjects, to make it possible to adapt their conduct.[3] Moreover, competition law is enshrined in the Treaties and it is therefore part of 'EU constitutional law'. Both the constitutional status of competition law and the quasi-criminal nature of its enforcement should, in my view, influence the normative 'density' of Article 102 TFEU and help strike the right balance between normativity and factuality in its enforcement.

Scholarly appreciation for realising the formal rule of law has not been traditionally part of the mainstream in EU competition enforcement.[4] This can be explained by a near consensus since the early 2000s that effects-based, ad hoc determinations of legality constituted the economically optimal form of market intervention.[5] However, such near consensus has receded and there is increased scholarly interest in competition law as law.[6]

It should not be controversial that economics must influence the interpretation of EU competition law. Economics provides the foundational justifications regarding why competition is valuable in the first place.[7] Articles 101 and 102 TFEU already convey a normative content shaped by economic knowledge. Not only 'prices' are explicitly referred to in Article 101(1) TFEU but also what can be interpreted as output limitations and restrictions on innovation ('limit or control production, markets, technical development, or investment'). Article 101(3) TFEU refers to the contribution to 'improving the production or distribution of goods or to promoting technical or economic progress', benefits of which 'consumers' should get a 'fair share'. However, here the provision refers to some concepts ('progress', 'fairness'), which may not have a clear and unequivocal meaning in the economic literature.

3. R. Stones, *EU Competition Law and the Rule of Law: Justification and Realisation*, PhD thesis, London School of Economics, 2020, 12.
4. However, already in the 2000s the issue of the compatibility of the 'more economic' approach with the rule of law was addressed in the literature, *see*, for example, W-H. Roth, 'The "More Economic Approach" and the Rule of Law', in, D. Schmidtchen, M. Albert and S. Voigt (eds), *The More Economic Approach to European Competition Law*, Mohr Siebeck, 2007, 37-58.
5. R. Stones, 'Why Should Competition Lawyers Care about the Formal Rule of Law', 84(3) *Modern L. Rev.* 608-635, 608 (2021) https://doi.org/10.1111/1468-2230.12625
6. *See* B. Wardhaugh, *Competition, Effects and Predictability: Rule of Law and the Economic Approach to Competition*, Oxford, Hart, 2020. Wardhaugh's overall argument is that an 'effects-based approach' to determining legality is a threat to the rule of law. He ultimately adopts a solution incorporating economic learning into the *ex ante* design of presumptions and structured tests (at 211-222); Stones, *supra* n. 3; J. Lindeboom, 'Formalism in Competition Law', 18(4) *JCLE* (2022) 832-880 https://doi.org/10.1093/joclec/nhac003. *See also*, in the US, M. Stucke, 'Does the Rule of Reason Violate the Rule of Law?', 42(5) *UC Davis L. Rev.* 1375 (2009). Orbach explained how modern antitrust in the US preserves formalism, under a different guise (B. Orbach, 'The Durability of Formalism in Antitrust', 100 *Iowa L. Rev.* 2197 (2015)). The idea that vertical restraints are pro-competitive is formalistic (at 2205), and the application of the 'rule of reason' relies on a dynamic evidentiary process of burden-shifting that is mainly formalistic, since most often courts do not have to 'balance' anything (at 2216-2217).
7. Stones, *supra* n. 3, 22.

While Article 102 TFEU has much of the language of Article 101(1) TFEU, it does not provide for any exception. Some notions in the article, such as 'abuse' or 'dominant position', do not have clear counterpart notions in economics. The authors of the Treaties clearly intended dominant undertakings to be subject to a stricter regime, and the case law has conceptualised this normative intention as the 'special responsibility' of dominant undertakings. Moreover, the Court of Justice has ruled that 'since the structure of competition on the market has already been weakened by the presence of the dominant undertaking, any further weakening of the structure of competition may constitute an abuse of a dominant position'. It would follow 'that fixing an appreciability (*de minimis*) threshold for the purposes of determining whether there is an abuse of a dominant position is not justified' and an abusive practice is 'by its very nature, liable to give rise to not insignificant restrictions of competition'.[8] Yet, since *British Airways*,[9] the case law has shown a willingness to consider possible beneficial effects of prima facie restrictive conduct, as a 'correcting' mechanism comparable to Article 101(3) TFEU.[10] This alignment with Article 101 TFEU may also be seen in the suggestion in recent judgments that there is a category of abuses 'by object'.[11]

This contribution has four main parts. Section 2 provides some explanations about the problem as I see it, and about the relevance of the law versus facts dichotomy as a framework for its analysis. The law has become 'thinner' through different mechanisms, also transforming the nature of the case law in this area. Section 3 takes stock of how facts and normative goals are considered when designing optimal legal tests, how relying only on case-specific evidence, in particular, 'economic evidence', does not provide the required certainty and often leads to inaction, and how competition law is EU constitutional law and should not develop in some sort of legal autarchy. Section 4 zooms in on some uncertainties surrounding the EU case law over the last years, in particular after the judgment of the Court of Justice in *Intel I*.[12] Section 5 deals with the role of evidentiary presumptions, which are increasingly under attack, as they are sometimes seen as a relic of 'formalism' and an obstacle to the application of a full 'effects-based' and 'more economic' approach. I defend their structuring function in the legal analysis and their role in preserving the 'lawness' of competition law. Section 6 discusses the role that the analysis of the conduct, as separate from its effects, still plays today, focusing on the condition that, as a rule, for conduct to be abusive, it must depart from competition on the merits. In my view, the focus on conduct is also a necessary consequence of competition law being law. Section 7 concludes.

---

8. C-23/14, *Post Danmark (II)*, EU:C:2015:651, paras 72-73.
9. C-95/04 P, *British Airways v. Commission*, EU:C:2007:166, para. 86. *See also infra* nn. 138 to 142 and accompanying text.
10. Explicitly making the *rapprochement* between Art. 101(3) TFEU and objective justifications under Art. 102 TFEU, *see* C-333/21, *European Superleague Company*, EU:C:2023:1011, paras 201-209.
11. C-333/21, *European Superleague Company*, EU:C:2023:1011, para. 131; C-48/22 P, *Google and Alphabet v. Commission (Google Shopping)*, EU:C:2024:726, para. 167.
12. C-413/14 P, *Intel v. Commission*, EU:C:2017:632.

2 LAW VERSUS FACTS UNDER THE 'MORE ECONOMIC' APPROACH: IS THE LAW IN COMPETITION LAW BECOMING 'THINNER'?

Regarding exclusionary abuses, which is the focus of this contribution, the main by-product of the 'effects-based' or 'more economic' approach as regards Article 102 TFEU was the 'Guidance on the Commission's enforcement priorities in applying Article [102 TFEU] to abusive exclusionary conduct by dominant undertakings'[13] (in short 'the Guidance' or 'the Guidance on Enforcement Priorities'). The Guidance sought to address what some perceived at the time as a disconnect between the Commission's practice and the state of the law under merger control and Article 101 TFEU on the one hand, and Article 102 TFEU on the other.[14] In particular, the Commission's and the EU Courts' approach towards exclusionary conduct was seen at the time as being largely based on a formalistic[15] framework of assessment and on per se prohibitions, a term imported from the US and often used by the critics, but never previously used, let alone endorsed, by the EU Courts at the time. There were no per se prohibitions as the Court of Justice had recognised in *British Airways* that the disadvantages for competition could be 'counterbalanced, or outweighed, by advantages in terms of efficiency which also benefit the consumer'.[16]

13. OJ 2009 C 45, p. 7. The approach, its evolution, and its consequences, have been the subject of numerous publications. *See* J.H.J. Bourgeois, and D. Waelbroeck. *Ten Years of Effects Based Approach in EU Competition Law*, Bruylant, 2013; A. Witt, *The More Economic Approach to EU Antitrust Law*, Hart Publishing, 2018; P. Ibáñez Colomo, 'Beyond the "More Economics-Based Approach": A Legal Perspective on Article 102 TFEU Case-law', 53 *CML Rev.* 709 (2016) https://doi.org/10.54648/cola2016062; A. Witt, 'The European Court of Justice and the More Economic Approach to EU Competition Law: Is the Tide Turning?', 64(2) *The Antitrust Bulletin* 172-213 (2019) https://doi.org/10.1177/0003603x19844637; L. Peeperkorn, 'The Effects-Based Approach: Still Just as Necessary for an Effective and Coherent EU Competition Policy', in Komninos, Claici and Waelbroeck, *supra* n. 1, 7-32.
14. One of the reasons that appeared to have motivated the changes was the idea that if merger control was based on effects, the enforcement of Arts 101 and 102 TFEU should also be based on effects. It goes without saying that using tools that have proven to be valuable in merger control is to be welcome. However, merger control and antitrust rules (Arts 101 and 102 TFEU) are very different in their nature. Competition rules are prohibition rules that are associated with heavy penalties. They are criminal in the sense of the ECHR, and principles such as the presumption of innocence or a strict application of the principle of legality (whereby the offence must be sufficiently clear in advance) play a prominent role in enforcement. Obviously, merger control does not display those features.
15. The terms 'formalistic' or 'formalism' in the competition law discourse 'appear to derive their meaning almost exclusively from pejorative usage. Hardly anyone would describe themselves as "formalist". Instead, formalism appears to be a concept primarily used to criticize certain approaches to legal reasoning' (Lindeboom, *supra* n. 6, 834).
16. C-95/04 P, *British Airways v. Commission*, EU:C:2007:166, para. 86 and, in first instance, T-219/99, *British Airways v. Commission*, EU:T:2003:343, paras 279-300. It is interesting to trace the use of the expression per se prohibitions in the case law. T-691/14, *Servier and Others v. Commission*, EU:T:2018:922, makes the point that there are no per se infringements in EU law, unlike the situation in US law: 'EU law does not regard any restriction of competition as necessarily and irremediably unlawful, since a restriction of competition by object may, in principle, fall within the exceptions laid down in Article 101(3) TFEU' (para. 294). In other words, the existence of a possibility to economically justify the conduct means that there are no per se prohibitions. The language of per se infringements only appears, in the context of Art. 102

The prevailing view, inspired by developments across the Atlantic, became that EU competition law should be particularly concerned with the 'error cost' of 'false positives', i.e., the costs of mistakenly condemning allegedly pro-competitive behaviour.[17] Taking the so-called consumer welfare standard as its lodestar, the approach focused on 'market outcomes' and proxies for likely harm to consumer welfare. By contrast, the Guidance only briefly mentioned the notion of 'competition on the merits'. Under this approach, if an inefficient competitor is forced to leave the market, the decision-maker should not worry too much about the methods through which this exit came about.

The Guidance on Enforcement Priorities clearly explained that it did not intend to be an expression of substantive law. Therefore, initially, some judgments considered the Guidance irrelevant for examining the lawfulness of decisions.[18] However, the adoption of the Guidance was the catalyst of change and confusion.[19] A few recent judgments appear to give some normative value to the Guidance as a legal benchmark for the legality of Commission decisions,[20] or at least as corroboration or illustration of the findings made by the EU judicature.[21] This prominence is striking. First, the fact that the Commission intended to give priority to certain cases to direct its enforcement practice should not render unlawful its pursuit of other cases. Second, the prominence that has been given to the Guidance has happened after the Commission has spent a decade taking some distance from the Guidance in most cases litigated before the EU courts, *inter alia*, precisely because the case law itself had clearly deviated from that

TFEU, in T-286/09 RENV, *Intel Corporation v. Commission*, EU:T:2022:19, paras 124 and 522, and C-240/22 P, *Commission v. Intel*, EU:C:2024:915, para. 136, precisely to make the point that they do not exist in EU competition law, but with a different reasoning: the inexistence of per se infringements is linked to the need to examine effects, whereas the previous rejection of such category in *Servier* was based on the possibility to justify the conduct. However, the case law has recently hinted at the existence of 'by object' abuses (C-333/21, *European Superleague Company*, EU:C:2023:1011, para. 131; C-48/22 P, *Google and Alphabet v. Commission (Google Shopping)*, EU:C:2024:726, para. 167), what would imply that in some cases there is no analysis of effects. Infringements 'by object' may still be justified, so the lack of analysis of effects cannot mean that there is a per se abuse.

17. Taking over the language of 'error costs' and of 'catching and penalising procompetitive conduct', *see* Opinion of Advocate-general Wahl in C-413/14 P, *Intel v. Commission*, EU:C:2016:788, paras 78 and 119.
18. C-23/14, *Post Danmark (II)*, EU:C:2015:651, paras 52, 57-58, and T-827/14, *Deustche Telekom v. Commission*, EU:T:2018:930, paras 113-114.
19. *See* Castillo de la Torre, *supra* n. 1: 'One could argue that it was the Commission who imposed upon itself certain very demanding constraints. The EU Courts, when annulling certain decisions, may be said to be simply echoing an approach (if not the letter) that the Commission itself initiated' (at 197).
20. *See* T-286/09 RENV, *Intel Corporation v. Commission*, EU:T:2022:19, para. 499; T-671/19, *Qualcomm v. Commission*, EU:T:2024:626, paras 611-622 (appeal pending, C-819/24 P); T-334/19, *Google and Alphabet v. Commission (Google AdSense for Search)*, EU:T:2024:634, para. 712 (appeal pending, C-826/24 P).
21. C-680/20, *Unilever Italia Mkt. Operations*, EU:C:2023:33, para. 51, that refers to the Guidance as 'illustration'.

Guidance on several significant points,[22] and because some elements of the Guidance did not age well when faced with the realities of enforcement. The Guidance was recently amended, to reflect how priorities have changed (as a result of both recent case law and enforcement experience),[23] and the Commission is in the process of adopting interpretative 'Guidelines' which would logically replace the Guidance.[24]

I will often refer to the traditional dichotomy of law versus facts since my impression is that this distinction appeared to have been of no (or at least very limited) interest under the prevailing versions of the 'more economic' approach in the 2000s. In EU competition law, the distinction is crucial notably as some principles, such as the presumption of innocence, apply to the establishment of facts, but not to how to define the offence and to interpret the law.[25] The law, if breaches thereof are to be punished, must be sufficiently clear in advance (principle of legality, *see* below),[26] but the presumption of innocence is not a principle of interpretation of the law: there is no principle requiring that the accused be given the most lenient interpretation of the substantive law defining the offence.

Under the 'more economic' approach, with its focus on effects and some types of outcomes regardless of the conduct and intention of dominant undertakings, the analysis of any given case is likely to turn on certain, often less observable, factors (not even really 'facts' as such), and disagreements in litigation will often be evidential in nature (as the EU judicature will often qualify disagreements on 'economic evidence' as a factual/evidentiary issue), triggering the application of the presumption of innocence.

To be clear: the presumption of innocence is a fundamental principle that must govern competition law enforcement, where heavy fines can be imposed. But competition law provisions are in the Treaty in the expectation that they are applied in practice by public authorities and in private litigation. Therefore, they must be realistically applicable: not only in the laboratories of academia and with comprehensive and perfect information but also in real life, by all judges and authorities. Applying interpretations that move the analysis from (generalised) 'law' to (often case-specific, contextual) 'facts' (in practice to 'effects') has often the opposite consequence. They blur of lines between fact and law, make the former pollute the latter and create a fog on 'what the law really is'. I also have the impression that ad hoc assessments

22. *See* several examples in Communication from the Commission Amendments to the Communication from the Commission – Guidance on the Commission's enforcement priorities in applying Article 82 of the EC Treaty to abusive exclusionary conduct by dominant undertakings (OJ C 116, 31.3.2023, 1-5).
23. *See supra* n. 22 and L. McCallum et al., 'A Dynamic and Workable Effects-Based Approach to Abuse of Dominance', *Competition Policy Brief* (March 2023).
24. A draft set of Guidelines was published on 1 August 2024.
25. *See*, on the principle of presumption of innocence regarding some of the aspects discussed in this article, F. Castillo de la Torre and E. Gippini Fournier, *Evidence, Proof and Judicial Review in EU Competition Law*, Second Edition, Elgar Publishing, 2024, paras 1.054, 1.069, 2.033-2.039, 2.054, 2.088, 2.100-2.101. The presumption of innocence is applicable when it comes to the evaluation of the evidence (i.e., whether a fact has been proven), but not in principle as regards the substantive definition of the infringement to be proven (i.e., whether a fact must be proven).
26. Castillo de la Torre and Gippini Fournier, *supra* n. 25, paras 2.173 and 6.088. *See also* text accompanying *infra* nn. 35 to 42.

compared to generalised rules may tend to favour those who are in a better position to defend themselves.[27] When applicable criteria lead to more factually complex assessments, more resources are necessarily needed, and the asymmetry in fights pitting a small crew of officials against well-resourced corporations (eager to protect their power assisted by generously funded experts) is likely to have a wider impact on the outcome compared to scenarios where such proceedings involve more limited amounts of information and clearer rules. Francis has also very convincingly explained how confusion and indeterminacy in the law tend to favour 'defendants' (i.e., the undertakings accused of abusing their dominant position).[28] It certainly favours unpredictable outcomes and probably inaction as well. When the substance of the law becomes 'thinner', or its scope is blurred, the *effet utile* of Article 102 TFEU is undermined.

The distinction between law and fact is also crucial for distinguishing between what belongs to EU law and what belongs to national law: each national legal system keeps a degree of autonomy, subject to some EU law principles, as regards standards of proof and, in general, how evidence is gathered and assessed (principle of procedural autonomy).[29] However, as we will see, the rather prescriptive language adopted by the Court of Justice in its replies to preliminary references reveals the blurring of this distinction as well.

Lack of interest in this distinction in the 2000s meant that any attempt at structuring the analysis around the categorisation of conduct liable to infringe Article 102 TFEU was seen as formalistic. While much of the fervour has disappeared when faced with the realities of daily enforcement, for some of its more vocal advocates any evidentiary presumption that may structure the analysis based on observable factors is still seen with suspicion.

---

27. As Stones puts it, 'purely effects-based evaluations of lawfulness require the Commission to determine legality through a factually complex, ad hoc analysis that takes a team of economists with information, resources, and expertise months to conduct. Undoubtedly, the richest companies could amass a rival team, scrutinising the potential competitive consequences of every proposed commercial decision, but what of the costs, delay, and likelihood of reasonable disagreement between experts? Furthermore, what about companies that are not able to buy a degree of legal certainty for their envisaged commercial strategy?' (*supra* n. 3, 167-168). The principle that norms ought to be abstract in scope and equally-applicable restraints the state from granting ad hoc privileges to powerful private interests (*supra* n. 3, 144).
28. D. Francis, 'Antitrust Without Competition', 74 *Duke L. J.* 353-439, at 357 and 374 (2024). As Ezrachi puts it 'predictability is further undermined in today's antitrust landscape which has been dominated by technical experts, expert lawyers and skilful economists with the power to advance selective goals. Overall, the fluid nature of the "sponge" and "membrane," and the possibility for them to generate a wide range of outcomes to a given scenario may open the way for opportunism'. (A. Ezrachi, 'Sponge', 5(1) *JAE* 49-75, 67 (2017)). A recent analysis claims to have shown that an application of an effect-based approach increases the rate of acquittals in court (i.e., annulment of Commission decisions), *see* Y. Katsoulacos and G. Makri, 'Economics and Antitrust Enforcement at the EU: An Update', 13(2) JAE (2024) https://doi.org/10.1093/jaenfo/jnae039; Y. Katsoulacos and G. Makri, 'Some Empirical Evidence on the Role of Presumptions and Evidentiary Standards on Antitrust (Under)Enforcement: Is the EC's New Communication on Art. 102 in the Right Direction?', *CPI Antitrust Chronicle* (December 2024)
29. On this, Castillo de la Torre and Gippini Fournier, *supra* n. 25, paras 1.090-1.097. And specifically, recital 5 of reg. 1/2003 ('This Regulation affects neither national rules on the standard of proof nor obligations of competition authorities and courts of the Member States to ascertain the relevant facts of a case, provided that such rules and obligations are compatible with general principles of Community law').

Yet, the Chicago School in its original version was not unpreoccupied by the formal aspects of the law. Rather than advocating an analysis purely based on ad hoc, subject-specific analysis of the actual efficiency consequences of instant conduct, those authors preferred to incorporate economic wisdom into the *ex ante* design of generalised norms: rules, presumptions, and structured tests.[30] For the Chicago School, the limits of knowledge[31] and the belief in the self-correcting features of the market favoured a strong presumption against antitrust intervention, so the rules advocated at the time were limited to prohibiting the most egregious conduct.[32] It was a later reading of the Chicagoan legacy that advocated more context-specific, comprehensive analyses.[33] To be fair, more recently parts of the scholarship have challenged the notion that generalised, predictable norms and economically sophisticated enforcement are mutually exclusive. They advocate the incorporation of economic learning into the design of presumptions and structured tests, thereby aiming to reconcile accurate economic outcomes with approximating the formal rule of law.[34] However, the consumer welfare standard continues to be the focal point of most of those tests, which still tend to rely on large amounts of data.

Beyond the presumption of innocence, a second important principle at stake is that of legality. Article 102 TFEU does not assign responsibility for an undesirable

30. R. Stones, 'The Chicago School and the Formal Rule of Law', 14(4) *JCLE*, 527-567 (2018) https://doi.org/10.1093/joclec/nhz002. Posner's immediate response to the judgment of the US Supreme Court in *Sylvania* was negative: it was 'formless', a 'poor guide to the decision of restricted distribution cases', and did not provide 'usable criteria of illegality'. Rather than case-specific analysis of pro- and anti-competitive consequences, he proposed a more administrable and predictable test comprising three consecutive rules (R. Posner, 'The Rule of Reason and the Economic Approach: Reflections on the Sylvania Decision', 45(1) *U. Chi. L. Rev.* 1, at 15-19 (1977) https://doi.org/10.2307/1599199). Easterbrook was a critic of the ad hoc, subject -specific legal analysis conducted under the rule of reason standard (F.H. Easterbrook 'The Limits of Antitrust' 63(1) *Tex. L. Rev.*, 1-40, at 11-13 (1984)) and favoured the use of presumptions (at 14-15).
31. Bork was clearly concerned about the epistemic limits of any enquiry when he summarised the reasons why a direct economic measurement of welfare effects must fail: 'A statement of what must be done in any direct measurement approach is sufficient to make its impossibility apparent. The Court would have to make a reasonably accurate estimate of efficiency and deadweight loss in an actual situation, and then make the same estimates of those two quantities in a hypothetical situation, in order to determine whether the real or the hypothetical situation is more favourable to consumers … . Passably accurate measurement of the actual situation is not even a theoretical possibility; much less is there any hope of arriving at a correct estimate of the hypothetical situation … . Only by knowing where marginal cost and demand intersect could one know whether there was a restriction of output and what its size was. Nobody knows their curves. Even the companies involved do not … .' (R. Bork, *The Antitrust Paradox*, reprint 1993, 125). Easterbrook famously explained that 'if we assembled twelve economists and gave them all the available data about a business practice, plus an unlimited computer budget, we would not get agreement about whether the practice promoted consumers' welfare or economic efficiency more broadly defined' (*supra* n. 30, at 11).
32. F.H. Easterbrook, 'Workable Antitrust Policy', 84(8) *Mich. L. Rev.* 1696 (1986) https://doi.org/10.2307/1288943.
33. Stones, *supra* n. 30, at 550.
34. *See*, for example, A. Christiansen and W. Kerber, 'Competition Policy with Optimally Differentiated Rules Instead of "Per Se Rules Vs Rule of Reason"' 2 *JCLE* 215 (2006) https://doi.org/10.1093/joclec/nhl009; Y. Katsoulacos and D. Ulph, 'On Optimal Legal Standards for Competition Policy: A General Welfare-Based Analysis' 57 *J. Ind. Econ.* 410 (2009) https://doi.org/10.1111/j.1467-6451.2009.00393.x.

market outcome (harm) that has effectively occurred but regulates conduct through heavy financial penalties if need be. Criminal laws that are too vague to govern conduct are commonly understood to be problematic. The principle of legality is, in my view, a serious objection to excessive reliance on factual elements which may be unknown to the undertaking and on complex economic assessments whose outcome may not be sufficiently foreseeable.

There will always be questions regarding the application of laws at the periphery owing to factual novelty, technological development, and the open-textured vagueness of language.[35] In competition law, changes in our economic understanding of the consequences of business may prompt reappraisal of pre-existing interpretations. The law must recognise this.[36] However, some legal interpretations may be less subject to evolution than others: the potential for evolution hinges on how much the determination of legality depends on the economic analysis of such consequences.

The principle of legality imposes a sufficient degree of clarity on the scope of the offence, and a 'core' normative content thereof, even if a grey area may exist.[37] The case law of both the ECtHR and the Court of Justice allows for clarification through judicial interpretation.[38] The Court of Justice has ruled that the list of practices and types of conduct contained in Article 102 TFEU is not limitative, and does not exhaust the methods of abusing a dominant position prohibited by EU law.[39] This allows for jurisprudential developments where the individual case cannot be readily subsumed

35. F. Schauer, *Playing by the Rules: A Philosophical Examination of Rule-Based Decision-Making in Law and in Life*, Oxford, Clarendon Press, 1991, 35-36; C. Sunstein, 'Problems with Rules' 83 *Cal. L. Rev.* 953, 984-985 (1995) https://doi.org/10.2307/3480896.
36. In the US, the Supreme Court included in *Kimble* a *dictum* about the Court being more willing to overrule antitrust precedents than other precedents ('This Court has viewed *stare decisis* as having less-than-usual force in cases involving the Sherman Act. ... We have therefore felt relatively free to revise our legal analysis as economic understanding evolves and (just as Kimble notes) to reverse antitrust precedents that misperceived a practice's competitive consequences') (*Kimble v. Marvel Entertainment, LLC,* 576 U.S. 446 (2015)). On *stare decisis* in antitrust, *see* B. Orbach, 'Antitrust Stare Decisis', *Antitrust Source* (October 2015), 1.
37. A penumbra of doubt in relation to borderline facts does not in itself make a provision incompatible with Art. 7, provided that it proves to be sufficiently clear in the large majority of cases (*Cantoni v. France*, CE:ECHR:1996:1115JUD001786291, para. 32).
38. The principle that offences and penalties must be defined by law, according to the Court of Justice's case law, requires the law to give a clear definition of offences and the penalties which they attract. That requirement is satisfied where the individual concerned is in a position to ascertain from the wording of the relevant provision and, if need be, with the assistance of the courts' interpretation of it, what acts and omissions will make him criminally liable. This principle cannot be interpreted as precluding the gradual, case-by-case clarification of the rules on criminal liability by judicial interpretation, provided that the result was reasonably foreseeable at the time the offence was committed, especially in the light of the interpretation put on the provision in the case law at the material time (C-201/19 P, *Servier and Others v Commission*, EU:C:2024:552, paras 386-387 with further references). This follows settled case law of the ECtHR (*see, inter alia, Cantoni v. France*, CE:ECHR:1996:1115JUD001786291, para. 35; *Kononov v. Latvia*, CE:ECHR:2010:0517JUD003637604, paras 185, 235). However, the use of overly vague concepts and criteria in interpreting a legislative provision can render the provision itself incompatible with the requirements of clarity and foreseeability as to its effects (*Liivik v. Estonia*, CE:ECHR:2009:0625JUD001215705, paras 96-104).
39. C-52/09, *TeliaSonera Sverige*, EU:C:2011:83, para. 26; C-449/21, *Towercast*, EU:C:2023:207, para. 46.

under existing precedents.[40] In such cases, the novelty, which must concern the factual scenario rather than the general legal criteria as such, may sometimes lead to the non-imposition of a fine.

While the Court of Justice has not developed an overtly rigid interpretation of the constraints inherent in the principle of legality,[41] I am less certain that very vague standards which depend on a fact-intensive examination of the consequences of the conduct as such are compatible with such principle. Foreseeability must be appraised from the angle of the convicted person (possibly after the latter has taken appropriate legal advice) at the time of the commission of the offence. While the principle of legality may not exclude an analysis of 'all relevant circumstances', it does impose, in my view, some predictable limitations on what such circumstances should be. When excessive reliance is put on *ex post* and contextual analysis, the basis for imposing a penalty may be seriously weakened.[42]

To be fair, we will see that part of the indeterminacy comes from how the EU judicature has been recently formulating certain passages of its judgments. While discussing the legal authority and normative nature of judgments is well beyond this article,[43] judgments were interpreted in the past not just as settling a dispute but also as containing normative statements, defining the offence and how to deal with at least

40. Lindeboom, taking as example the *Google Shopping* case, explains this type of reasoning as 'reasoning according to law', where the decision-maker needs to resort to 'merits-based' reasons, and explores the legitimacy of such type of reasoning (J. Lindeboom, 'Rules, Discretion, and Reasoning According to Law: A Dynamic-Positivist Perspective on *Google Shopping*', 13(2) *JECLP* 63-74 (2022) https://doi.org/10.1093/jeclap/lpac008).
41. The Court of Justice has widely understood the circumstances under which a fine can be imposed and had made it quite difficult to rely on lack of awareness of the unlawful nature of the conduct. With regard to whether the offences were committed intentionally or as a result of serious negligence and are therefore liable to be penalised by the imposition of a fine in accordance with Art. 23(2) of Regulation No. 1/2003, it is settled case law that that condition is satisfied where the undertaking concerned cannot be unaware of the anti-competitive nature of its conduct, whether or not it is aware that it is infringing the competition rules of the Treaty (C-280/08 P, *Deutsche Telekom v. Commission* EU:C:2010:603, para. 124; C-295/12 P, *Telefónica and Telefónica de España v. Commission*, EU:C:2014:2062, para. 156; C-591/16 P, *Lundbeck v. Commission*, EU:C:2021:243, paras 156-157).
42. *See*, for a US perspective, G. Werden, 'The Competitive Process Standard', 86(2) *Antitrust Law J.* 579-645, 592-593 (2024), underlining the constitutional difficulties of applying in a criminal case anything which is not a per se rule ('no judge-made presumption can be invoked in a criminal case', at 592).
43. *See* A. Arnull, 'The Normative Status of the Case Law', in A. Arnull (ed.), *The European Union and Its Court of Justice*, 2nd ed., OUP, 2006, and N. MacCormick, *Legal Reasoning and Legal Theory*, OUP, 1978 (2003 reprint), 103-104: 'Legal rulings are normative – they do not report, they set the patterns of behaviour; they do not discover the consequences of given conditions, they ordain what consequences are to follow upon given conditions. They do not present a model of the world, they present a model for it'. The interpretation of EU law that the Court of Justice provides applies *ex tunc*. There is formally no *stare decisis* doctrine in EU law, but logically the EU judicature tends to follow its previous case law. On the different mechanisms at stake, *see* M. Derlén and J. Lindholm, 'Characteristics of Precedent: The Case law of the European Court of Justice and Three Dimensions', 16(6) *Ger. Law J.* 1073 (2015) https://doi.org/10.1017/s2071832200021040; P. Lasok, 'Precedent in EU Law: A Practitioner's View', 13 *JLL* 8-27 (2024).

some factual scenarios.[44] As we will *see* below, over the past few years the Court of Justice has become less prescriptive about substance, where the general nature of the law is kept at a relative 'high level' of abstraction, and more prescriptive about process. Some parts of the judgments are now often formulated as setting out examples of conduct that was prohibited, or at most a presumption or working assumption: in other words, the case law has become more descriptive and less substantively prescriptive.[45] The premise appears to be that embracing an economic-literate competition enforcement needs a certain marginalisation of the value of generalised and predictable legal norms.[46] In parallel, as we will *see* later, the EU judicature often adds rhetorical language, perhaps endeavouring to provide general and principled guidance, that may end up blurring the more operational guidance which is given to decide the case at hand.

The problem I see is that the law on Article 102 TFEU appears to be, to a large extent, still 'work in progress', even after several decades of enforcement of that provision. Much of it is due to the eternal debate about the goals of competition law and ultimately about the very meaning of 'competition' in competition law. Competition law is exceptional in that it is an area where the very purpose of the law and the scope of the prohibitions are subject to a large degree of doctrinal disagreement.[47] This relative indeterminacy, which has had some impact on the case law, is costly[48] and, to some extent, its invocation is probably self-interested.[49] Nothing appears to be written

44. This is what Lindeboom calls the 'rullifiability' of the decision, in the sense that the decision-maker 'has to explain not only why this conduct is anticompetitive or abusive, but on the basis of what general criteria this and similar conduct are anticompetitive or abusive' (*supra* n. 40, at 65).
45. Castillo de la Torre and Gippini Fournier, *supra* n. 25, paras 1.076-1.077. As Stones puts it, 'the EU Courts may have contributed to such significant deviations from the formal rule of law ideal, through operating an unpredictable standard of review, and sometimes failing to prospectively formulate structured, comprehensible tests for determining legality' (*supra* n. 3, 14-15).
46. Stones, *supra* n. 3, 11.
47. There is a wealth of literature on this debate, *see*, for example, D. Zimmer (ed.), *The Goals of Competition Law*, Edward Elgar 2012.
48. From a US perspective, *see* D. Francis, 'Making Sense of Monopolization', 84 *Antitrust L.J.* 779, 790-791 (2022) on the cost of confusion: 'It encourages bad behavior, as confusion and indeterminacy soften the deterrent from practices that would turn out to be unlawful, and it creates an aura of legal risk around practices that might be unpopular but should not be illegal'. *See also* Francis, *supra* n. 28, at 418: 'Almost everyone is worse off as a result. Market participants are left wondering what their rights and obligations really are. Courts and agencies struggle to discern the rules that constrain their work. ... . And – above all during times of deep disagreement about antitrust – the dominance of Rorschachian 'competition' in doctrine makes it tremendously difficult for folks with different views to agree on what the law descriptively is, as a prelude to a fruitful discussion about what changes might be desirable'.
49. In my experience, dominant undertakings tend to have an opportunistic approach to legal certainty: they value such certainty when it positively implies that its conduct is not in breach of Art. 102 TFEU (i.e., 'safe harbours'), but not when it conclusively leads to a finding of abuse (per se). Dominant undertakings tend to favour complex standards, evidential in nature and deeply anchored in the specifics of the case, as it makes it far easier to claim the benefit of the doubt, and escape penalties, as explained by J. Broulík, 'Predictability: A Mistreated Virtue of Competition Law', 12(3) *JAE*, 362-377, at 373-376 (2024) https://doi.org/10.1093/jaenfo/jnad043, talking about strategic considerations as reasons for mistreating predictability. *See also* *infra* n. 82.

in stone and almost everything is 'up for grabs' in every individual abuse case, including much of the law.

The combination of relative indeterminacy of the law and evidentiary complexity of many abuse cases means that, paradoxically, 'competition law without law' does not lead to 'competition law without lawyers'. On the contrary, they have become more necessary and valuable to undertakings than ever (together with consultants), as the number of lawyers dealing with a case tends to increase the more complex the factual matrix and the more uncertain the law.[50] For those making a living as competition policy practitioners the 'business case' for determinacy and predictability is a weak one.

3 SHAPING THE ENFORCEMENT OF ARTICLE 102 TFEU REGARDING EXCLUSIONARY CONDUCT

3.1 Rules, Standards, and Trade-Offs

The open-textured nature of competition rules means that case law has been decisive in their development.[51] I do not think that the Court of Justice had in mind from the outset a great 'rule-design' of how Article 102 TFEU ought to be interpreted which it has followed throughout the years. Instead, the law of Article 102 TFEU is the result of an iterative process of evolution, since competition law applies to a wide variety of business practices.[52] The EU judicature was deciding each case, one by one. However, while settling each dispute, its job could not just stop there. Even if the EU judicature has not developed a doctrine of *stare decisis*, the EU judicature is normally supposed to follow precedent. In each ruling, the EU judicature, while deciding the case at hand, was expected to also provide some normative statement about how to interpret the provision in some factual scenarios, which did not have to be entirely identical to the case at hand.[53]

50. First and Weber Waler noted some ten years ago how the antitrust system was captured by lawyers and economists 'advancing their own self-referential goals, free of political control and economic accountability' (H. First and S. Weber Waller, 'Antitrust's Democratic Deficit', 81 *Fordham L. Rev.* 2543, 2544 (2013)). Lianos has noted 'the emergence of a lucrative global market for technical (mostly economic) expertise in competition law, which has expanded to more than 130 jurisdictions worldwide' (I. Lianos, 'Academic "Capture"? The Hidden Costs of Corporate Funding in Competition Policy Research and Proposed Remedies', *UCL Centre for Law, Economics and Society, Research Paper Series 7/2024*, 6). *See also* J. Broulík, 'Cultural Capture of Competition Policy: Exploring the Risk in the US and the EU', 45(2) *WC* 159-193 (2022) https://doi.org/10.54648/woco2022007.
51. The Court of Justice is widely seen as having a 'rule-making role' meaning 'judge-made law, or the design of general legal standards where black letter law is unclear, ambiguous and/or incomplete' (N. Petit, 'The Future of the Court of Justice in EU Competition Law: New Role and Responsibilities', in, A. Rosas, E. Levits and Y. Bot (eds), *The Court of Justice and the Construction of Europe: Analyses and Perspectives on Sixty Years of Case-Law,* The Hague, T.M.C. Asser Press, 2013).
52. OECD, 'Safe Harbours and Legal Presumptions in Competition Law', Background Note by the Secretariat, DAF/COMP(2017)9, point 9.
53. *See supra* nn. 43 and 44, and accompanying text.

The delineation of impermissible conduct under Article 102 TFEU needs a definition of, among other things, what 'competition', 'abuse' and 'anticompetitive effects' are, and of the relationship that the conduct must have with such effects. It also implies defining an evidential burden-sharing scheme, including the possible use of presumptions or similar evidentiary devices, and the articulation of 'defences' or 'justifications'.

In comparative law, how to provide such delineation for open-textured provisions has been the subject of much scholarly debate.[54] In principle, the various forms for determining the legality of business practices can be sorted from most to least 'generalised' and 'ad hoc', that is from 'per se rules' to 'unstructured ad hoc' assessments.[55] In this context, much literature has been devoted to the pros and cons of 'rules' versus 'standards'. The former relies 'on a limited set of readily available observed factors', whereas the latter depends 'on the fulfilment of some vague normative criterion that should guide the legal assessment, without defining beforehand what set of (or how many) factors or distinctions should be used in that assessment'.[56]

Rules have been often seen as too rigid and leading to 'over-inclusiveness', but in reality, the interaction of rules and standards is a complex one. Both may turn out to be over-inclusive or under-inclusive at one point and corrections, leading to more 'specific' rules or standards, will be made by the judicature (or the legislature) along the way.[57] While the 'effects based' approach is linked to the use of standards, certain documents leading to the Guidance contained proposals for reform that sounded like accepting a limited number of new prescriptions: the purpose of the 'effects based' approach was not necessarily to dispense with all rules but to define *ex ante* rules more informed by economics.[58]

Any decision on the point of designing optimal norms implies some trade-offs regarding, *inter alia,* administrability, predictability, and effectiveness of enforcement, while bearing in mind the presumption of innocence and the purpose of the legal provisions.[59] Trying to avoid perceived 'errors' or overinclusion may shape the more

54. OECD, *supra* n. 52, in particular s. 3 on 'optimal competition rules'. The note assumes that competition law 'seeks to prevent business practices that reduce economic welfare' (points 2 and 5). However, this is not the only purpose of competition law, as set out in OECD (2023), 'The Consumer Welfare Standard: Advantages and Disadvantages Compared to Alterative Standards', *OECD Competition Policy Roundtable Background Note.*
55. Stones, *supra* n. 3, 224.
56. OECD, *supra* n. 52, para. 22. As one author has put it, 'rules exclude considerations which might have been relevant to the decision-maker in the absence of rules, and the rules themselves become reasons for deciding in a particular manner' (Lindeboom, *supra* n. 6, 838).
57. *See*, in this sense, F. Schauer, 'The Convergence of Rules and Standards' *N.Z. L. Rev*. 303 (2003).
58. Lindeboom, *supra* n. 6, 859. *See also supra* n. 30, on the authors at the origin of the Chicago School.
59. As some authors have put it 'the quality of competition law depends not only on the economic accuracy of the rules, but also on the administrability of the enforcement regime, including the provability of the relevant facts at reasonable cost and within a reasonable timeframe' (H. Schweitzer and S. de Ridder, 'How to Fix a Failing Art. 102 TFEU: Substantive Interpretation, Evidentiary Requirements, and the Commission's Future Guidelines on Exclusionary Abuses', 15(4) *JCLP* 21 (2024) https://doi.org/10.1093/jeclap/lpae033).

specific substantive legal standard or rule.[60] However, leaving aside the clear epistemic limitations of any enquiry into 'error costs', discussing errors in individual decisions misses the point that what counts is the effect of the rule as such in all its possible applications.[61] Contrary to common wisdom, there is limited evidence that legal certainty (that rules typically enhance) and decisional errors are correlated.[62] Moreover, the law may be interpreted in ways that may value certain outcomes more than others, or that accept some degree of uncertainty about such outcomes.

The optimal design first involves some normative assumptions, i.e., determining the objective of competition law in that legal system. In principle, standards tend to bring enforcement closer to the direct application to the facts of the underlying objectives of the law. This gives direct normative value to the underlying objectives.[63] Standards assume that the underlying objectives of the law are knowable and amenable to objective assessment.[64] However, the 'direct' application of the purpose of the law is not unproblematic, as a matter of principle. The objective of the law rarely provides operational guidance by itself, and this is more so in competition law due to the vagueness of most statutory provisions. We expect in law enforcement that there is reasoning as to why the facts fit the offence, but we do not expect in any law enforcement action a specific explanation of how the general purpose of the law is enhanced by that action.[65] Applying the objective of the law directly to the facts is not how prohibitions typically work, in particular when they have a quasi-criminal nature.

In competition law, the objectives of the law are often not clearly set out. They are also constantly under discussion. Competition's value is often seen as instrumental: competition is valuable in order to further something which is more important than

60. This is a process of 'optimisation', *see* Stones, *supra* n. 3, 224-256.
61. As Schauer puts it '[f]ollowing ordinary legal rules may produce suboptimal decisions when those decisions are viewed in isolation, but the degree of aggregate suboptimality is commonly thought less than the degree of aggregate suboptimality that would likely exist were decidedly suboptimal decision makers empowered to make their own determinations of the best all-things-considered decision' (F. Schauer, 'The Role of Rules in the Law of Evidence', in, Ch. Dahlman, A. Stein and G. Tuzet (eds), *Philosophical Foundations of Evidence Law*, OUP, 2021, 69-82, 79). *See also* Lindeboom, *supra* n. 6, at 876: 'Looking beyond those immediate effects of the individual case, however, it may be that the general deterrence, predictability, and stability of general rules may, in the longer run, outweigh the negative effects of erroneous decisions in individual cases, in light of the purpose of the rule. In turn, that raises the question of whether an application of the rule to an individual case can be conceived as "erroneous" at all even if the outcome in that individual case is incongruent with the purpose of the rule. The answer may be in the negative if that individual rule-application does contribute to achieving the purpose of the rule by, for instance, increased clarification of the law, or communicating the social meaning of the rule. In other words, even if the purpose of a rule is, say, "maximizing total welfare" and applying that rule to an individual case reduces total welfare, this does not necessarily mean that that application is erroneous, to the extent that having the rule as such may contribute to maximizing total welfare as well'.
62. Lindeboom, *supra* n. 6, 870-877.
63. 'The standard is the way in which the goals, or objectives, of competition policy can be made operational' (OECD (2023), *supra* n. 54, 9).
64. For standards to be fully operational, it is a pre-condition that there is clarity as to what the underlying objective is (*see* J. Broulík, 'Factual Predictability in Competition Law Enforcement: Rules Versus Standards', *Amsterdam Law School Research Paper* No. 2024-10, at 8).
65. *See also* Lindeboom, *supra* n. 6, 841: 'there is a crucial distinction between taking into account purpose in creating the rule and taking into account purpose in applying the rule'.

competition, be it welfare, growth, innovation or market integration. Under a more constitutional view, competition may also be valuable to increase a potentially wider set of principles or values. These objectives which are promoted by competition in turn shape the meaning of competition in the legal system.

Competition is therefore potentially a multidimensional notion. We refer to conduct having an effect on competition, but there is lack of consensus about what competition is as a 'normative measure'.[66] These dimensions may be in conflict sometimes. All this renders any clear definition of prohibited conduct more complex unless the courts settle for a clear and operational notion applicable across the board. However, such uniform notion would risk sacrificing one objective to others.[67]

A second important element in designing optimal norms is how they deal with factual uncertainty. This is also the case in competition law. In practice, how to address factual uncertainties regarding the establishment of the conduct as such (i.e., whether the conduct as such happened: did the agreement contain an exclusivity clause? what was the amount of the rebate given a certain number of sales?) has been less controversial. Those questions can be determined (at least in EU law) in light of the available evidence applying the ordinary standard for a quasi-criminal enquiry arising from the presumption of innocence.

In judicial review and litigation, controversies about factual uncertainties tend to concern the analysis of the *effects* of the conduct. At the time of implementation of the conduct, those effects will happen in the future, and they will be hardly certain, except in some exceptional factual scenarios. Even if we examine what happened after the conduct was implemented, observing market developments may not be enough to decide if those developments may be caused by other factors. Some of the market developments may happen in the longer term, but the authority cannot wait until then before intervening, since otherwise its action may be ineffective. In some cases, the observable market developments may even be absent, due to an intervening action of a third party, and the legal system may still want to prohibit the conduct.

How to deal with these uncertainties is a normative, not an empirical question – and one that is coupled with the ambiguity surrounding the *telos* of competition law. As a result, different legal systems may (and do) provide for different solutions to comparable problems. Some may require certainty leading to acquittal as soon as a reasonable doubt exists. Others may provide for substantive legal standards that

66. Competition may be promoted or hindered, but what is exactly promoted or hindered? The 'competitive process'? Total and/or consumer welfare? Market concentration? Market power? Impact on market participants? Impact on your own efficiency? Impact on rivals' ability/incentive to compete? For a very comprehensive presentation of such possible dimensions, Francis, *supra* n. 28. He explains that economists themselves do not share a consensus regarding the meaning of competition (at 377 and 395). *See also* Ezrachi, *supra* n. 28, 61, explaining that economics is not monolithic or value-free and M. Stucke, 'What Is Competition?', in Zimmer, *supra* n. 47, 27-34.

67. While difficult, I do not think we can just abandon the notion of competition and examine something else. *See*, in favour of abandoning the notion of competition, as an operational concept, since its meaning is 'unliquidated' or 'unelaborated', Francis, *supra* n. 28, in particular at 433-435, suggesting alternative approaches. I would rather work towards a concept of competition that becomes more operational and hopefully puts an end to endless debates. Admittedly not an easy task.

'move' the subject of the proof to elements which the legal system considers more 'provable'. In the case of competition law, this could imply abandoning a focus on 'effects on consumer welfare' (e.g., if it were to be assumed that this is the only goal of competition law) to focus instead on the distortion of the 'competitive process'[68] or the 'capability to restrict competition', to mention but two examples found in EU competition law.

The management of uncertainty often takes the form of evidentiary presumptions,[69] where the subject of the proof is eased as it can be inferred from 'provable elements': if *Fact A* is proven, then *Fact B* is inferred. Presumptions can provide some structure to the analysis and may therefore facilitate enforcement and self-assessment by undertakings. However, since the relevance of those 'provable elements' is based on inferences, their value is instrumental and the other party may provide counterevidence that the 'provable elements' do not actually prove what is actually the subject of the proof in the instant case (*Fact B* is not proven in the instant case, despite proof of *Fact A*). This could be done by trying to disprove *Fact B* directly, or by adducing elements undermining, in the specific case, the existence of *Fact A* or the link between *Facts A and B*. We will further elaborate on presumptions in section 5. What is important to stress at this juncture is that the move from substantive rules to evidentiary presumptions is inevitably a gradual move from law to facts. While the choice of presumptions and their design is a legal one, the application of presumptions engages more directly principles regarding evidence assessment, such as the presumption of innocence.

At the crossroads between the normative and the evidentiary, we find the issue of justifications. Possible justifications or defences must also be considered in the design of optimal rules and standards: it is perfectly acceptable to define a rule or standard that risks being overinclusive while keeping open the possibility for the defendant to justify its conduct (often in view of the objectives of the law). Such exceptions or justifications can coexist with rules: they are, in effect, separate rules which can declare the result of the first rule inapplicable.[70] Logically, defendants have an interest in applying standards where everything (including the absence of any justification) is for the plaintiff (or the authority) to prove. Nevertheless, the legal system may consider that the undertaking is in a better position to explain and justify its conduct and hence that the avoidance of errors is to be achieved by a combination of the application of the legal test that the authority needs to meet and the possible defences or justifications that a company may establish in response.

---

68. *See*, for a presentation of that standard in a US perspective, Werden, *supra* n. 42; T. Wu, 'The "Protection of the Competitive Process" Standard', *Columbia Public Law Research Paper* No. 14-612, and C. Shapiro, 'Antitrust: What Went Wrong and How to Fix it', 35(3) *Antitrust*, 33-45, proposing to replace the term 'consumer welfare standard' with the term 'protecting competition standard'.
69. As Salop puts it 'because legal decisions are made with imperfect information, presumptions play an important role in law' (S. Salop, 'An Enquiry Meet for the Case: Decision Theory, Presumptions, and Evidentiary Burdens in Formulating Antitrust Legal Standards', 2017, https://scholarship.law.georgetown.edu/facpub/2007 (last accessed 22 July 2025)).
70. Lindeboom, *supra* n. 6, 840.

Having examined three main elements that optimal normative design must normally consider, I now turn to whether abandoning rules in favour of standards is necessarily positive. One problematic aspect in the application of most standards is that they are often associated with an analysis of 'the fullness of the defendant's conduct on a case-by-case basis'[71] or, in the language of EU Courts, 'all the relevant factual circumstances'. Ad hoc examinations may be perceived as questioning the very generality of the law.[72] In this connection, it is also generally acknowledged that standards are less administrable than rules.[73] Yet, not all standards are equal. In a recent comparative analysis, it was observed that standards that examine effects on competition and not on welfare appear 'simpler than alternative standards'. This is because 'any "welfare" standard implies that cases should be decided based on a clear understanding of their welfare effects, which are unavoidably complex' and are 'more difficult to administer'.[74] Tests reflecting the effects-based approach often mandate extensive case-by-case assessments instead of allowing one to determine the lawfulness of conduct with relative ease.

It is not the relevance of efficiency or welfare that is problematic as such, but how these elements are considered, and operationally incorporated, in the application of competition rules, and in particular whether each case must turn on a full-blown consumer welfare analysis. And yet, despite its drawbacks, the consumer welfare standard is sometimes presented, still today, as inevitable.[75] I think semantics played a role in its past success.[76] On the one hand, everyone is in favour of 'avoiding errors', but that begs the question of what an error is – or in whose favour we should be most concerned. Moreover, the 'error costs' of individual decisions are in reality

71. D. Crane, 'Rules Versus Standards in Antitrust Adjudication', 64 *Wash. & Lee L. Rev.* 49, at 51 (2007).
72. *See* Stones, *supra* n. 3, 107-108.
73. Broulík, *supra* n. 64, 6. That is one of the reasons why some authors are of the view that standards will, in time, suffer a subtle transformation into rules (Schauer, *supra* n. 57).
74. OECD (2023), *supra* n. 54, 29 and 34. While standards such as 'competitive process' may also give rise to interpretative disagreements, I have the impression that the nature of such controversies are somewhat different. When a standard relies on factors which are less observable, require more information, and possibly modelling, controversies will tend to be perceived as being factual in nature. This applies even if the ultimate objective (consumer harm) is ascertained through 'provable' proxies (market prices and output are commonly used as observable proxies for consumer welfare): since the proxy is an imperfect way to capture the ultimate objective, the accused may always contest the accuracy of the proxy in the specific case. In legal systems applying the presumption of innocence, any doubt about the link of the factual situation, possible proxies and the purpose of the law will be seen under the prism of that principle. I have the impression that controversies around the application of other standards in a specific case, for example, 'competitive process' or 'competition on the merits', are more normative in nature, or at least more 'manageable' and less dependent on complex factual analyses.
75. For the best recent example, N. Petit and L. Radic, 'The Superiority of the Consumer Welfare Standard', EUI Working Paper 2024/20.
76. On the role of semantics in competition law, P. Nihoul, 'Do Words Matter? A Discussion on Words Used to Designate Values Associated with Competition law', in Zimmer, *supra* n. 47, 219-248.

unknowable.[77] On the other hand, we all care about consumers as well. This is what makes a 'consumer-centric' discourse appealing.[78] Such discourse has been embraced by dominant undertakings, but it could be naïve to think that this embrace of a 'consumer welfare' standard is somewhat altruistic, as if large corporations have become the new 'consumer champions'.[79] They embrace it probably to try to counter the argument of capture by one-sided interests: it helps them develop the narrative that they act for the public good. Nonetheless, this approach smells of paternalism.[80] Interestingly, whereas consumer law is based on the vulnerable position of consumers, that can't be protected by market forces, the interest of consumers in competition law is transformed, under the 'effects-based' approach, from a pro-intervention into a self-correcting paradigm, where consumer welfare is mainly applied as a shield from intervention, not as a sword.[81] Do we know what consumers really want? Do they agree to be exclusively considered, under the law, as rational actors only driven by 'welfare' (in fact, price) considerations?

Another objection to the use of standards, or at least those primarily relying on a detailed *ex post* analysis of effects, relates to the quasi-criminal nature of the public enforcement of EU competition law. There is a price to pay in terms of predictability: standards are said to facilitate case-by-case optimisation (error avoidance), but at some cost to the possibility of predicting in advance what the result is likely to be.[82]

Further, regarding the supposed advantages of relying on standards, as we saw above, even the claim that standards lead to case-by-case optimisation is doubtful, in

77. *See* Opinion of Advocate-general Wahl in C-413/14 P, *Intel v. Commission*, EU:C:2016:788, para. 119, where the Advocate-general refers to the 'cost of error' being 'unacceptably high due to over-inclusion'. However, he does not cite any source trying to quantify or estimate such error cost.
78. Petit and Radic, *supra* n. 75, 3: '[A]ttacking consumer welfare means less food on the table for American citizens, the poor, and the workers'.
79. While not all dominant undertaking can be categorised as 'big business', certainly undertakings within the 'big business' category are likely to be dominant in some markets and be the target of an investigation. As one recent editorial puts it, 'monopolists are very good at explaining that the EU's over-regulatory approach is harmful for a trading bloc that wishes to see greater wealth. Brussels-based US lobbies have a lot of traction. Of course one should not trust corporations (whose objective is to make their shareholders richer) to have the EU's general interest at their heart' ('Editorial Comments' 62 *CML Rev* 1, 7 (2025)).
80. *See also infra* n. 283.
81. O. Andriychuk, 'EU Digital Competition Law: The Socio-Legal Foundations', *Cambridge Yearbook of* 25 *European Legal Studies*, 81-104, 90 (2023) https://doi.org/10.1017/cel.2023.12.
82. Schauer, *supra* n. 57, at 309. The use of standards relying on many elements and factual data means that, at least in theory, some undertakings may be deterred from what is considered 'beneficial' conduct, as they may consider it too risky. Such unpredictability affects decisions by undertakings, as they may lack all the necessary factual information and may not always anticipate the outcome of the complex analysis (Broulík, *supra* n. 64, 10). Yet, dominant undertakings abhor per se rules and will typically defend themselves in any proceeding submitting that the authority should apply a complex and demanding standard. Legal certainty only appears to play one way for them, which may lead some to argue that their embrace of complexity may be opportunistic. Complex standards mean less compliance: 'compliance and legal certainty are likely to be greater when there are clear rules regarding which business practices are lawful than if every business practice is potentially subject to a detailed market analysis to determine whether it has anticompetitive effects' (OECD, *supra* n. 52, para. 2).

my view.[83] Crane claims that, in practice, promulgation of law as a standard is more likely to result in adjudicatory error, 'since there are more variables to consider and the relationship between the variables is exponentially more complex'.[84] Advocating a 'more economic' approach in the shape of a case-by-case assessment based on vague standards actually leaves the assessment of complex economic evidence, ultimately, in the hands of adjudicators (judges in EU Courts) having limited experience in either business or economics. It is unclear how the aspiration to achieve fewer errors can really materialise in such context. Besides, times have changed and, as one author puts it, 'the view that it is generally better to risk a bit too much private monopoly rather than a bit too much state action has fractured entirely'.[85]

3.2 Economic 'Facts' as 'Real Life': (The Illusion of) Truth and Accuracy

We all have a sense that there is factual 'truth' out there, that we can discover, whereas law is just a social construct. The move to a 'more economic' approach is conceptually linked to the economic analysis of the law, which was critical of the law as a self-referential system, open to interpretation and adaptable. Instead, the economic analysis of the law favoured the evidence-based impartiality of science.[86] From that perspective, one could argue that the move to 'the facts' from 'the law' is not problematic. As the argument goes, focusing on 'the facts' will surely help take the best decisions. Moreover, since we tend to consider that 'facts' are something objective, focusing on them should avoid discretionary outcomes, and overall, reduce the disagreements in litigation. The 'more economic' approach, and in particular the 'consumer welfare standard', draws from these attractive propositions. They present themselves as more concrete and closer to 'real life': the 'practical need for endowing real-life cases with the weight of empirical evidence.'[87]

This is, of course, very appealing. The language of 'truth' always is. Nobody wants to apply the law in ways that ignore 'market reality' or make untruthful assumptions. Nobody will argue that decisions should not be 'evidence-based' either, to take one of the slogans. By targeting something which is presented as objective and

83. *See supra* nn. 61 and 62 and accompanying text.
84. Crane, *supra* n. 71, at 87. There are those who think that case-by-case, 'all-things-considered' approach creates more risk of errors because of the imperfection of decision-makers and the impossibility to foresee all of the effects of an ad hoc intervention (Christiansen and Kerber, *supra* n. 34). As Ezrachi puts it, 'the disparity between the court's capacity and economic complexity increases the likelihood for mistakes and error costs', (*supra* n. 28, 63). *See also*, for a critical view of the 'error cost' doctrine in antitrust, including the belief in self-correcting markets not being grounded in economic theory and evidence, J.B. Baker, 'Taking the Error out of "Error Cost" Analysis: What's Wrong with Antitrust's Right', 80(1) *Antitrust Law J.* (2015); H. Hovenkamp, 'Antitrust Error Costs', 24 *Univ. Pa. J. Bus. L.* 293 (2022); A. Gavil and S. Salop, 'Probability, Presumptions and Evidentiary Burdens in Antitrust Analysis: Revitalizing the Rule of Reason for Exclusionary Conduct', 168 *U. Pa. L. Rev.* 2107 (2020).
85. Francis, *supra* n. 48, 781.
86. R. Posner, 'The Decline of Law as an Autonomous Discipline: 1962-1987' 100(4) *Harvard L. Rev.* 761 (1987) https://doi.org/10.2307/1341093.
87. Petit and Radic, *supra* n. 75, 1 and 22.

quite specific, i.e., consumer harm, the impression (illusion?) is created that competition enforcement is about the discovery of something concrete and objective.[88]

However, law enforcement is a practical endeavour, not a scientific pursuit. In this promise of 'objective economic truths', the epistemic limitations of competition law enforcement are not always recognised.[89] The point is not whether decisions should be 'evidence-based'. They should be, of course. The point is how much case-specific evidence we really need and which principles or methods are guiding the assessment. Evidence alone will not deliver decisions, and ad hoc examinations may end up questioning the very generality of the law.[90]

Moreover, the sub-text of this 'evidence-based' and 'error cost' approach is not epistemic but normative: when such truth cannot be obtained, the default option should be inaction.[91] As Gavil and Salop put it, referring to the classical 'error cost' analysis, 'it effectively shifts the default presumption from neutral to pro-defense'.[92] Whether articulated in the decision theory language of 'error costs' (even if such costs are often unknowable) or in the language of the fundamental right to the presumption of innocence (when debates are moved from the law to the facts), inaction is the inevitable consequence thus completing the shift to a system superimposing multiple layers of pro-defence defaults.

Consumer welfare is not directly observable. It is an economic abstraction, based on an imaginary consumer, rational of course, who may not really exist. Since consumer welfare is not observable, a determination under that standard needs more 'provable' proxies.[93] The scope of disagreement as to whether the proxy chosen is a good one, whether it is appropriately applied in the instant case, and whether observable proxies are caused by the practice, is likely to be important.[94] As a result,

---

88. Non-price factors (choice, quality, innovation) are not totally excluded, but seen with suspicion, since they are considered 'subjective', and the consumer welfare standard claims to limit discretion. *See* Petit and Radic, *supra* n. 75, at 18-19, 20-21 and 24 ('the CWS narrows the risk of discretionary antitrust standards like protection of competition or the competitive process').
89. On this point, *see* J. Blockx, 'The Limits of the "More Economic" Approach to Antitrust', 42 *World Competition*, 475, 480-487 (2019) https://doi.org/10.54648/woco2019026; J. Lindeboom, 'How Much Economic Analysis in Competition Law and Policy Do We Really Want?', 4 *Concurrences* (2023).
90. *See* Stones, *supra* n. 3, 107-108.
91. Easterbrook, *supra* n. 32 ('skepticism should rule the day'; 'ignorance often leads to inaction', at 1712). In the US, the prevailing view is still that the costs of false convictions in the antitrust context are likely to be significantly larger than the costs of false acquittals, *see infra* n. 102.
92. Gavil and Salop, *supra* n. 84, 2113. *See* D. Melamed, and N. Petit, 'The Misguided Assault on the Consumer Welfare Standard in the Age of Platform Markets', 54(4) *Rev. Ind. Organ.* 741-774 (June 2019) https://doi.org/10.1007/s11151-019-09688-4, referring to 'prudence or pragmatism'. *See also* J.D. Wright, 'Abandoning Antitrust's Chicago Obsession: The Case for Evidence-Based Antitrust', 78 *Antitrust L.J.* 241 (2012), advocating for 'evidence based' antitrust with the clear sub-text that if such evidence does not exist, the authority should not intervene.
93. In actual practice, the 'consumer' means the 'customer' of the dominant undertakings, who is often not the final consumer, and an increase of prices applied to such customers will be considered enough to prove harm (S. Albaek, 'Consumer Welfare in EU Competition Policy', in C. Heide-Jørgensen et al. Poulsen (eds), *Aims and Values in Competition Law*, Copenhagen, DJØF Publishing, 67-88, at 75-76).
94. Wu, *supra* n. 68, 2: 'Decades of practice have shown that the promised scientific certainty of the Chicago method has not materialized, for economics does not yield answers, but arguments'. As

under a consumer welfare standard, the outcome of each case is less predictable than under rules based on a set of more observable factors, while the mantra that errors are avoided is doubtful when those deciding (ultimately, the courts, often not specialised ones) may not have a full understanding of economic and business evidence. The abstract nature of 'welfare' or 'efficiency' means that those notions have not delivered the scientific certitude promised.[95] The need for more administrable or workable approaches is nowadays more widely acknowledged, even by many advocates of some version of the consumer welfare standard.[96]

As for the supposed advantage of limiting discretion claimed to stem from the consumer welfare standard, this is an odd claim since one could argue that the advantage of all rules is that they eliminate that discretion as well. If the aim is limiting discretion, other standards may offer ways to settle disputes in ways that the judges feel more equipped to handle than discussing economic studies. Courts are entitled to carry out a full review of any notion, in particular legal ones, however vague they may sound.[97] They may feel they can better decide if the conduct at issue in a case (which as such must be proven to the required standard) departs from competition on the

Francis puts it: 'The fragile quantifications of economic modelling make a wonderful servant but an indecisive master' (*supra* n. 48, 782); '[...] modeling things like real innovation and nonprice competition with anything like confidence is implausible. This creates room, within 'economics,' for deep disagreement about the implications of evidence and analysis in most real-world cases and for rules intended to help resolve them. It is rare that a professional consensus exists on the decisive questions raised by concrete cases: Is this transaction harmful overall? What would that business do if that practice were prohibited? Can we infer harm or benefit from these documents?' (*supra* n. 48, 822).

95. In order to save the consumer welfare standard, it is sometimes suggested that it is able to accommodate non-price factors. Such accommodation would raise only 'practical' (evidentiary), not conceptual, difficulties (Melamed and Petit, *supra* n. 92: focus on price and output effects is the result of 'prudence or pragmatism'). In other words, if the promise of accuracy fails in such cases, it is the lack of appropriate evidence that is to blame not the underlying legal standard. In my view, these 'theoretical' attempts to interpret the consumer welfare standard more broadly, while acknowledging its limited role in practice for parameters such as choice, quality or innovation (which have been explicitly mentioned by the EU judicature) and 'hoping' that empirical methods will be developed one day, do not really solve the practical problems of law enforcement. The idea that 'one can reasonably expect the development of new tools that will reduce the practical problems' (Melamed and Petit, *supra* n. 92) transpires optimism but leads to inaction. *See also*, in the same vein, Petit and Radic, *supra* n. 75, at 19. In my view, in the choice of standards, effective enforcement should weigh more than the 'conceptual beauty' of the standard, and the 'hopes' that better metrics will magically arrive one day.

96. *See* R. O'Donoghue and J. Padilla, *The Law and Economics of Article 102 TFEU*, 3rd ed., Hart Publishing, 2020, 288.

97. Analysing whether conduct is 'competition on the merits' is about 'classifying the practices at issue in law', *see* C-48/22 P, *Google and Alphabet v. Commission (Google Shopping)*, EU:C:2024:726, para. 171. *See also* T-167/08, *Microsoft v. Commission*, EU:T:2012:323, para. 91: 'the use of imprecise legal concepts within a provision does not prevent liability being established as against a person who contravenes it. As the Commission points out, if it were otherwise, an infringement of Article 101 or 102 TFEU – which are themselves drawn up using imprecise legal concepts, such as distortion of competition or "abuse" of a dominant position – could not give rise to a fine without the prior adoption of a decision establishing the infringement.' In *Towercast*, the Court of Justice has ruled that 'Article 102 TFEU is sufficiently clear, precise and unconditional, with the result that there is no need for a rule of secondary law expressly prescribing or authorising its application by the national authorities and courts' (C-449/21, *Towercast*, EU:C:2023:207, para. 51).

merits (it is an issue of legal qualification of the facts) than assess the soundness of (potentially conflicting) forensic studies.

Moreover, while having a single point of focus (consumer welfare) is attractive, and theoretically tends to create some degree of uniformity across jurisdictions (assuming that facts and economics are the same everywhere), the consumer welfare standard ignores the complexity and variety of goals that competition law may have in each legal system (*see* following section). The 'practical advantage' of such welfare standard, which is that it avoids altogether any legal analysis of the meaning of 'competition' or of 'abuse' (the evidential enquiry is all about the effects on welfare) is at the same time its biggest drawback: it literally voids of any substance all legal notions explicitly mentioned in Article 102 TFEU.

3.3 Competition Law Is Part of the (Wider) Legal System

When someone who practices in other areas observes the enforcement of EU competition law, they may think that competition law has developed in a 'bubble', alien to principles that make law what it is, at least the law as it is understood in continental Europe.[98] Economics may be the same in different countries, but legal systems are different, and competition law is part of a wider legal system.[99] Transplants of legal approaches must be done with care since the institutional setting influences how competition law is understood and enforced. While much of the DNA of competition law may be shared across legal borders, and a sense of 'community' among practitioners and competition officials is likely to emerge, there are differences as well, reflecting both the position of competition law in different legal orders and the different institutional systems of enforcement.

For example, setting a standard based on 'market outcomes' (often understood as 'welfare outcomes'), such as the consumer welfare standard, may be less workable when a heavy financial penalty is involved in systems where a measure of legal certainty is required for the imposition of such sanctions. However, no such penalties traditionally apply in the US, where the consumer welfare standard originated, for monopolisation cases.[100] Because proof of market outcomes attributable to the conduct

98. O. Andriychuk refers to the 'normative autarchy of competition law', *supra* n. 81, 86.
99. *See*, on the influence of each legal system on competition law, Ezrachi, *supra* n. 28. As Gerber has put it, 'goals are discussed without taking into account the ways in which they relate to the institutions that articulate and apply them, the issues are located in an abstract intellectual space that may provide little value for decision-makers', (D. Gerber, 'The Goals of European Competition Law: Some Distortions in the Literature', in Zimmer, *supra* n. 47, 85-94, 89). He also stresses the risk of 'projecting onto the EU institutional scheme assumptions about law that are common at the national level, but that may not be appropriate on the EU level or that may require significant modification on the EU level' (*ibid.*, at 90).
100. Precisely because such standard cannot be a basis for a criminal conviction, *see* Werden, *supra* n. 42. In theory, criminal enforcement is not excluded for section 2 of the Sherman Act. Section 2 violations have been crimes since the Sherman Act's enactment in 1890. The plain language of the statute encompasses three offences: (i) monopolisation, (ii) attempted monopolisation and (iii) conspiracy to monopolise. However, for several decades, the DOJ's criminal enforcement efforts have been limited to the so-called hardcore, or per se, offences under ssection 1. In March 2022 the DOJ signalled that it would criminally prosecute section 2 violations, and

(defendants normally insist that the plaintiff or authority has a duty to prove that any observable market outcome is caused by the conduct) is necessarily very difficult to provide (since typically market outcomes may be explained by more than one factor), if the law-maker (or the courts, in their interpretation) wanted to ensure effective enforcement of the offence, it may shift the delineation of the substantive legal standard towards more 'provable' facts to ensure that the objective of the law is rendered actually operational.[101]

However, it is not just a problem of recognising the interaction between the standard of proof and the substantive legal standard. Constitutional views on the legitimacy of market intervention by public authorities may be markedly different. Different legal systems may weigh differently type 1 and type 2 errors and assess differently enforcement costs.[102] There is no reason to import legal theories corresponding to other constitutional systems, without critically examining to what extent they 'fit' in our own legal system.

In the EU, competition provisions are enshrined in the Treaties and therefore have (and must have), in my opinion, a constitutional dimension.[103] They cannot be just 'downgraded' to 'applied economics', defined and managed by a small group of 'experts' in some discreet branches of economics who know what is right or wrong for us all. They must, as any provision of a constitutional nature, embody some principles or values about how our social and legal order is shaped.[104] This does not mean that

several cases are underway. *See*, for a historical perspective, D. Crane, 'Criminal Enforcement of Section 2 of the Sherman Act: An Empirical Assessment', 84(3) *Antitrust Law J.* 753 (2022) https://doi.org/10.2139/ssrn.4136638.

101. 'Two competition regimes could apply the same standard but result in completely different outcomes if one requires a particularly high standard of proof to assert harm of breaches of the law' (OECD (2023), *supra* n. 54, 5).
102. In the US, the prevailing view is still that the costs of false convictions in the antitrust context are likely to be significantly larger than the costs of false acquittals, *see* Easterbrook, *supra* n. 30, at 4: 'with the presumption that the costs of false convictions in the antitrust context are likely to be significantly larger than the costs of false acquittals, since judicial errors that wrongly excuse an anticompetitive practice may eventually be undone by competitive forces attracted by the presence of monopoly rents. Conversely, judicial errors that wrongly condemn a procompetitive practice are likely to have more significant social costs because such beneficial practices are abandoned by firms and not offset by equilibrating market forces tending to mitigate their impact.' The US Supreme Court later held that: 'Against the slight benefits of antitrust intervention here, we must weigh a realistic assessment of its costs (...) Mistaken inferences and the resulting false condemnations 'are especially costly, because they chill the very conduct the antitrust laws are designed to protect' (*Verizon Communications v. Law Offices of Curtis Trinko* 540 U.S. 398, 414 (2004)).
103. Articles 101 and 102 TFEU are 'vital' or 'fundamental' provisions (C-377/20, *Servizio Elettrico Nazionale and Others*, EU:C:2022:379, paras 42-43; C-124/21 P, *International Skating Union v. Commission*, EU:C:2023:1012, para. 193) which are 'essential for the accomplishment of the tasks entrusted to the European Union' (C-438/22, *Em akaunt BG*, EU:C:2024:71, para. 57) and are part of EU public policy (C-126/97, *Eco Swiss*, EU:C:1999:269, paras 36 and 39; C-124/21 P, *International Skating Union v. Commission*, EU:C:2023:1012, paras 192-193). Although the U.S. Supreme Court has described the Sherman Act as the 'Magna Carta of Free Enterprise' (*United States v. Topco Assocs.*, 405 U.S. 596, 610 (1972)), the U.S. antitrust laws have never been understood as constitutional in any meaningful sense (*see* D. Crane, '"The Magna Carta of Free Enterprise" Really?', 99 *Iowa L. Rev Bull* 17 (2014)).
104. As Andriychuk explains, 'the origins as well as the very legitimacy mandate of competition law are societal, not economic', *supra* n. 81, 88. In the word of Ezrachi, 'by its constitutional nature,

competition law should ignore economic insights, or simply integrate as such a long variety of interests or goals which are different from those of the protection of competition, with the corresponding risk of discretionary decisions based on a balance of interests. This could end up producing results that would be the opposite of the formal function of the law.

Nonetheless, it may be possible to delineate a notion of distortion (or restriction) of competition that, while having a sufficiently clear normative content, may *also* come in support of wider constitutional goals, without ceasing to be competition law. In other words, those other values or principles shape the very notion of competition (and of distortions thereof). Those other values and principles may conceivably also operate in the context of justifications, where the legal order could be more open to considering other interests not considered when defining the initial prohibition. However, such justifications must be defined at the EU level to ensure the uniform application of the law and to avoid the risk of fragmentation.

It is clear from Protocol No. 27 on the internal market and competition, annexed to the Treaty of Lisbon, that the objective of Article 102 TFEU (and of the other EU competition rules) is a system of 'undistorted competition', as part of the internal market established by the EU.[105] Consumers have been also considered in the Treaties: they are explicitly mentioned in Article 101(3) TFEU. These are foundations of competition law from which one cannot depart from in the EU, even if they leave much to further clarification.

The case law has very broadly defined the objectives of Article 102 TFEU: 'the purpose of that provision is to prevent competition from being restricted to the

EU competition Law Is Mandated with Sponge Attributes', *supra* n. 28, 53. *See also* O. Andriychuk, 'Thinking Inside the Box: Why Competition as a Process Is a *Sui Generis* Right: A Methodological Observation', in Zimmer, *supra* n. 47, 95-117, 102 ('the idea of the constitutional significance of competition reflects the common trend of the expansion of constitutional protection of economic values and should be seen in the domain of antitrust as a natural outcome of the development of (European) constitutional law') and J. Baquero Cruz, *Between Competition and Free Movement*, Hart Publishing, 2002, 1 ('[There is a] tendency among competition specialists to treat their topic [...] as distinct from the economic constitutional law of the [... EU]. As the law now stands, however, the competition rules contained in the Treaty have a constitutional status and may be interpreted as shaping a law of economic liberty [...], not only a law of economic efficiency. Thus, an efficiency-oriented approach [...] may not be in tune with the current normative structure'). As Kadar and Holzwarth have explained, an effective enforcement of competition law can function as a protective barrier against excessive concentration and the redistributive effects associated with it (M. Kadar and J. Holzwarth, 'Effects-Based Approach? Effects-Based Approach! The European Commission's "Article 102 Package"' *Neue Zeitschrift für Kartellrecht* 333, 334 (2023)). On competition and democracy, *see* OECD (2024), 'The Interaction Between Competition and Democracy', *OECD Roundtables on Competition Policy Papers*, No. 316, OECD Publishing, Paris; E. Deutscher, *Competition Law and Democracy: Markets as Institutions of Antipower*, Cambridge, Cambridge University Press (Global Competition Law and Economics Policy), 2024.

105. For an analysis of the different Treaty provisions, and their role in interpreting competition law, *see* L. Parret, 'The Multiple Personalities of EU Competition Law: Time for a Comprehensive Debate on Its Objective', in Zimmer, *supra* n. 47, 61-84. *See also*, on market integration, more recently, 'Editorial Comments: Missing in Action? Competition Law as Part of the Internal Market' 60 *CML Rev* 1503 (2023) https://doi.org/10.54648/cola2023114.

detriment of the public interest, individual undertakings and consumers'.[106] While some see the reference to 'consumer well-being' as the 'ultimate objective', mentioned for the first (and only) time in *SEN*,[107] as a recognition of some version of the 'consumer welfare standard', in reality, the sentence refers to 'the ultimate objective warranting the intervention of competition law', which rather explains the reason for having competition rules and not the determinative standard in each individual case.[108] Moreover, the Court of Justice also refers in the very same judgment to the 'public interest', the interest of 'individual undertakings and consumers', and the 'well-being in the European Union'.[109] References to the 'consumer well-being' (or welfare), or more generally the 'interest of consumers', are typically embedded in broader formulas, and *SEN* is clear that harm to consumer welfare (or consumer harm more generally) is not a precondition to finding an abuse.[110]

Other judgments use different language. In several judgments, the Court of Justice has referred to the effect on 'competition and consumer welfare' only in discussing possible justifications and the use of 'and' suggests that 'consumer welfare' (which in the French version of the judgments reads 'les intérêts des consommateurs') is not the only element that can be affected by the conduct.[111] The Court of Justice has been recalling that competition provisions protect 'not only the interests of competitors or of consumers, but also the structure of the market and, in so doing, competition as such',[112] and there are frequent references in recent case law to the 'competitive process'.[113]

106. C-333/21, *European Superleague Company*, EU:C:2023:1011, para. 124, with further references; C-48/22 P, *Google and Alphabet v. Commission (Google Shopping)*, para. 87; C-233/23, *Alphabet and Others*, EU:C:2025:110, para. 37.
107. C-377/20, *Servizio Elettrico Nazionale and Others*, EU:C:2022:379, para. 46. Later judgments, some delivered by the Grand Chamber, have not taken over that language. The judgment in *Google Shopping* does not refer to 'consumer welfare' (or consumer 'well-being') at all, while mentioning the 'detriment' to consumers as relevant, this is in the broader definition of the objectives: 'The purpose of that provision is to prevent competition from being restricted to the detriment of the public interest, individual undertakings and consumers' (C-48/22 P, *Google and Alphabet v. Commission (Google Shopping)*, para. 87).
108. *See*, on this difference, *supra* n. 65.
109. C-377/20, *Servizio Elettrico Nazionale and Others*, EU:C:2022:379, para. 41.
110. *Ibid.*, para. 47. *See also* Schweitzer and De Ridder, *supra* n. 59, 6.
111. C-333/21, *European Superleague Company*, EU:C:2023:1011, para. 204; C-23/14, *Post Danmark (II)*, EU:C:2015:651, para. 49. It is to be noted that other linguistic versions also refer to the 'interest' of consumers, and not to its 'welfare'.
112. C-883/19 P, *HSBC Holdings and Others v. Commission*, EU:C:2023:11, para. 121. *See also* Joined Cases C-501/06 P, C-513/06 P, C-515/06 P and C-519/06 P, *GlaxoSmithKline v. Commission*, para. 63 ('consequently, for a finding that an agreement has an anti-competitive object, it is not necessary that final consumers be deprived of the advantages of effective competition in terms of supply or price'); C-8/08, *T-Mobile Netherlands and Others*, EU:C:2009:343, para. 38.
113. C-457/10 P, *AstraZeneca v. Commission*, EU:C:2012:770, para. 129 ('part of the normal competitive process, provided that the conduct envisaged does not depart from practices coming within the scope of competition on the merits, which is such as to benefit consumers'); C-883/19 P, *HSBC Holdings and Others v. Commission*, EU:C:2023:11, para. 123 ('distortion of the competitive process'); T-604/18, *Google and Alphabet v. Commission (Google Android)*, EU:T:2022:541, para. 574 (appeal pending C-738/22 P); T-201/04, *Microsoft v. Commission*, EU:T:2007:289, para. 1088; T-228/97, *Irish Sugar v. Commission*, EU:T:1999:246: para. 186.

Overall, while the interest of consumers is prominent in the jurisprudential narrative, there is little indication that the interpretation of the EU Courts is exclusively guided by the 'welfare' of consumers in the sense of the neo-classical economic theory. Yet, while the case law does not mandate the authority to verify and assess the impact on welfare, it has taken over the element of 'efficiency' which is connected thereto in ways that, as we will *see*, are controversial. Welfare and efficiency may be the desired consequences of competitive markets, and underpin the existence of competition rules. Assessing the welfare effects of certain practices may contribute to more informed enforcement.[114] However, welfare and efficiency cannot be used as the benchmark to assess the legality of each and every practice.

The 'more economic' approach does not fit well in this constitutional dimension. It epitomises an economic analysis of the law and tends to exclude any internal perspective of the law.[115] Instead, it reflects a prescriptive view of economics, without any basis on the Treaties, under which legal decision-making should exclusively follow the dictates and logic of economics (or rather, of a certain type of economics).[116] It is premised on a single (purely economic) goal,[117] pursued in isolation from other values or principles explicitly provided for in the EU Treaties.[118] It may be stating the obvious, but, even if shaped by economics, competition law is still law. Choosing among the different dimensions of the notion of competition (or abuse) in legal interpretation is not the task of economics, even if economics should also inform that choice.

Moreover, the problem with a utilitarian perception of antitrust is that it assumes that the very process of competition is meaningless unless it delivers some positive outcomes for the economy.[119] However, one could argue that the protection of 'competition' is based on a constitutional presumption that competition will deliver those goods (and maybe others). While the Treaties do open a door for some justifications, a systematic enquiry into whether that is really the case in each individual case becomes unnecessary and, worse, contrary to the competition rules that have been enacted.[120]

---

114. While I do not think that each case must turn on a welfare analysis, or that competition law should only be guided by welfare effects, I do agree that we must take welfare seriously. *See also* Francis, *supra* n. 28, at 436-437.
115. *See* Posner, *supra* n. 86.
116. *See* O. Andriychuk, *The Normative Foundations of European Competition Law*, Elgar Publishing, 2017: 'the role of the lawyers tends to be reduced to their technical expertise: how to communicate the economic truth to the legally (narrow-) minded judges'; Crane, *supra* n. 71, at 50: 'lawyers now play the supporting cast to economists'; Monti, commenting on *Intel*, says: 'law is not to be assessed by what pleases economists' (G. Monti, 'Rebates after the General Court's 2022 Intel Judgment', 60 *CML Rev* 107-140, at 138 (2023) https://doi.org/10.54648/cola2023005).
117. Easterbrook, *supra* n. 32, at 1703, explaining why the pursuit of multiple goals leads to incoherent results.
118. Wardhaugh, *supra* n. 6, 76.
119. Andriychuk, *supra* n. 104, 116, who prefers that competition is considered an independent value. A utilitarian or instrumental view of competition law may be constitutionally problematic in periods of crisis. If competition law does not ostensibly deliver welfare, as promised, the risk is that the enforcement of competition law languishes.
120. This would be the equivalent of a famous *dictum* of the US Supreme Court: 'The Sherman Act reflects a legislative judgment that ultimately competition will produce not only lower prices,

It is telling that some authors dismiss the notions of 'competition on the merits' and the 'special responsibility' as they are 'not economic'. The former is considered an 'irritant'[121] or a 'legacy',[122] and rejected by some because it is 'non-economic' and it 'begs further definition and interpretation'.[123] Economists tend to reject the notion of 'competition on the merits' as they have not developed an economic counterpart for it,[124] and anything which cannot be translated into an economic notion tends to be discarded as irrelevant, in the understanding that competition law must make 'economic sense'. The same criticism has been levelled against the notion of 'special responsibility' (or even 'dominance'!)[125] as it is, again, a 'non-economic' concept,[126] as if normative choices (in this case, constitutional choices in the founding Treaties to subject dominant undertakings to a stricter legal regime) could only be based on notions mentioned in economic handbooks. In other words, the 'more economic approach' takes out of the analysis any element that cannot be translated into an economic concept, thereby reinforcing competition law's inward tendency. Moreover, it excludes an analysis of the 'means' or 'methods' used to compete, something that in principle is of no concern to those exclusively focused on outcomes, not process.

To be clear, as long as the focus is on competition, economic concepts and methods will continue to be fundamental to the substance and enforcement of competition law. Economic assumptions underlying legal doctrine must be supported by economics. The skills of economists will be needed under any standard. As one author has put it 'the relevance of economics for competition law is so obvious that it is hard to believe that ever an interpretation or application of competition law could arise that was not based on economic thinking'.[127] This, however, does not mean

but also better goods and services. The heart of our national economic policy long has been faith in the value of competition .... Even assuming occasional exceptions to the presumed consequences of competition, the statutory policy precludes inquiry into the question whether competition is good or bad' (*Nat'l Soc'y of Prof 'l Eng'rs v. United States*, 435 U.S. 679, 695 (1978)).

121. P. Ibáñez Colomo, 'Competition on the Merits', 61 *CML Rev* 387-416, 202, at 389 (2024) https://doi.org/10.54648/cola2024026.
122. P. Akman, 'A Critical Inquiry into "Abuse" in EU Competition Law', 44(2) *Oxf. J. Leg. Stud.* 405-433, at 412 (2024) https://doi.org/10.1093/ojls/gqae008.
123. *Ibid.*
124. C. Fumagalli, and M. Motta, *Policy Insight 125: Economic Principles for the Enforcement of Abuse of Dominance Provisions*, CEPR Policy Insight No. 125, 2024, https://cepr.org/publications/policy-insight-125-economic-principles-enforcement-abuse-dominance-provisions (last accessed 22 July 2025): 'This premise is to explain why it is not obvious to us how to reconcile the economic notion of abusive conduct with that of 'competition on the merits'. We regard the latter as a perhaps appealing concept, but not one with a clear economic counterpart, at least in the context of abusive practices' (p. 7).
125. It is not uncommon to hear economists complain about the concept of 'dominance', even if Art. 102 TFEU makes it an express pre-condition of the existence of an abuse.
126. Akman, *supra* n. 122, 413. In my view, the fact that 'the concept of special responsibility does not illuminate which practices may constitute an abuse' (at 413) is not determinative, since its purpose is *not* to define which practice is abusive but avoid certain justifications, like 'everyone does it'. In other words, to stress that dominant undertakings may not be entitled to implement conduct that non-dominant undertaking may be actually implementing.
127. W. Wils, 'The Judgment of the EU General Court in *Intel* and the So-Called More Economic Approach to Abuse of Dominance', 37(4) *World Competition* 405-434, at 411 (2014) https://doi.org/10.54648/woco2014042.

outsourcing to economics and to economists the definition of the substance of the law or the outcome of each case.[128] The use of notions, when interpreting and enforcing EU competition law, which cannot be easily translated into economic concepts just shows that there are notions in law which do not have an economic counterpart. That happens in competition law as it happens in any other area of law. There is nothing wrong or odd about it. Competitive law derives its prescriptive force and normative authority from being law.

Beyond the epistemic limitations of forensic economics, it seems to me that it is the plurality of values and dimensions that competition law and its enforcement may have to consider when delineating prohibited conduct that sets a normative limit to what economics may contribute. As explained above, such plurality should not mean indeterminacy of the law, but rather a delineation of prohibited conduct that is sufficiently predictable while integrating the role that competition has in the EU's constitutional setting.

4 THE UNCERTAINTY OF THE LAW TODAY: SUBSTANTIVE LAW AS A (LESS GUIDED) PROCESS?

4.1 Introduction and Some Certainties

While the open-textured nature of Article 102 TFEU partly explains that the law on Article 102 TFEU is and will likely remain 'work in progress', more worrying is that, regarding some types of practices, the case law of EU Courts may not be sending a consistent message nowadays. This inconsistency has increased over the last decade, as the Court of Justice has embraced some elements of the 'more economic' approach.

To be fair, many parts of the analysis in the case law have followed a consistent pattern over the last decades, which largely remains today. There is no appreciability (*de minimis*) threshold for the purposes of determining whether there is an abuse of a dominant position.[129] For some practices, the case law has created what the Court of Justice now calls 'analytical templates'.[130] In this regard, efforts to render the test for predatory pricing more demanding have consistently failed.[131] Attempts to extend the

128. As Francis, puts it (*supra* n. 48, 820), on the temptation to outsource decisions to economists: 'How could it be that courts ought not, ultimately, defer to expert economists in an area like antitrust? The starting point is that "monopolization" – unlike "market power" or "monopoly" – is not an economic concept at all. It is a legal one. There is no "correct economic view" about what monopolization law should be.' He also explains the 'several serious problems prevent us from giving the antitrust keys to the economists and taking the rest of the day off' (at 821-822).
129. C-23/14, *Post Danmark (II)*, EU:C:2015:651, paras 72-73.
130. C-333/21, *European Superleague Company*, EU:C:2023:1011, para. 130. Reference to 'the use of different analytical templates depending on the type of conduct at issue in a given case', is always nuanced by the addition that such use 'must however be made in the light of all the relevant factual circumstances'. *See also*, using the same expression, C-48/22 P, *Google and Alphabet v. Commission (Google Shopping)*, EU:C:2024:726, para. 166; C-240/22 P, *Commission v. Intel*, EU:C:2024:915, para. 179.
131. C-202/07 P, *France Télécom v. Commission*, EU:C:2009:214; T-671/19, *Qualcomm v. Commission*, EU:T:2024:626 (appeal pending, C-819/24 P).

application of *Bronner* to other practices have also failed.[132] It is also quite clear that 'a competition authority discharges its burden of proof if it shows that a practice of an undertaking in a dominant position could impair, by using resources or means other than those governing normal competition, an effective competition structure, without it being necessary for that authority to prove that that practice may also cause direct harm to consumers'.[133] It is sufficient to demonstrate that the practice 'undermin[es] an effective structure of competition',[134] or is capable of having exclusionary effects.[135] *Generics UK* follows a consistent line in recalling that 'it is not the place of a dominant undertaking to dictate how many viable competitors are to be allowed to compete with it',[136] an idea about the role of Article 102 TFEU in disciplining a dominant undertaking's attempts to regulate market access that is echoed in *Superleague*.[137]

The judgments in *SEN* and *Superleague*, in line with settled case law, put primarily and very explicitly in the hands of the dominant undertaking the burden of demonstrating that the practice benefits consumers 'in terms of, specifically, price, choice, quality or innovation'.[138] Yet, even here the case law may convey different nuances in different judgments delivered successively. *Android Auto* sets a somewhat different tone on the burden-shifting mechanism.[139] On the substance, for escaping a finding of abuse, it is for the dominant undertaking to demonstrate, first, that its conduct can allow efficiency gains to be achieved by establishing the actual existence

132. C-42/21 P, *Lietuvos geležinkeliai v. Commission*, EU:C:2023:12; C-152/19 P, *Deutsche Telekom v. Commission*, EU:C:2021:238; C-48/22 P, *Google and Alphabet v. Commission (Google Shopping)*, EU:C:2024:726; C-233/23, *Alphabet and Others*, EU:C:2025:110, paras 40-52.
133. C-377/20, *Servizio Elettrico Nazionale and Others*, EU:C:2022:379, para. 47.
134. *Ibid.*, paras 44 and 47; C-680/20, *Unilever Italia Mkt. Operations*, EU:C:2023:33, para. 36.
135. C-377/20, *Servizio Elettrico Nazionale and Others*, EU:C:2022:379, para. 72.
136. C-307/18, *Generics (UK) and Others*, EU:C:2020:52, para. 161, referring also to C-549/10 P, *Tomra Systems and Others v. Commission*, EU:C:2012:221, para. 42; T-334/19, *Google and Alphabet v. Commission (Google AdSense for Search)*, EU:T:2024:634, para. 596.
137. C-333/21, *European Superleague Company*, EU:C:2023:1011, paras 134-136.
138. C-377/20, *Servizio Elettrico Nazionale and Others*, EU:C:2022:379, paras 46-48 and 84-86. *See also* C-333/21, *European Superleague Company*, EU:C:2023:1011, paras 201-209. Several paragraphs (paras 202, 204, 206, 209) clearly mention that it is the undertaking that must 'demonstrate' the existence of a justification and that it is for the undertaking to discharge its 'burden of proof'. The Court of Justice assimilates this justification to Art. 101(3) TFEU, where the burden of proof is for the undertaking.
139. In that case, the respective burdens of proof were not at all discussed during the proceedings. After referring to existing case law to the effect that the undertaking may 'demonstrate' either that its conduct is objectively necessary, or that the exclusionary effect produced may be counterbalanced or even outweighed by advantages in terms of efficiency which also benefit the consumer (C-233/23, *Alphabet and Others*, EU:C:2025:110, para. 71), the Court of Justice states that it is 'for the concerned undertaking in a dominant position to put forward any objective justification and to submit arguments and evidence in that regard' (*ibid.*, para. 78). There is no reference to the 'demonstration' anymore, and the following paragraph states that 'once the undertaking in a dominant position has satisfied that requirement, it then falls to the competition authority concerned, ..., to *demonstrate* that the arguments and evidence relied on by the undertaking cannot prevail and, consequently, that the justification relied upon cannot be accepted' (*ibid.*, para. 79, emphasis added). The Court of Justice adds that it is for the competent competition authority 'to ascertain whether the refusal by that undertaking in a dominant position to develop a template for the category of apps concerned, which would allow such interoperability, was objectively necessary and to assess whether that refusal was proportionate' (*ibid.*, para. 80).

and extent of those gains; second, that such efficiency gains counteract the likely harmful effects of that conduct on competition and consumer welfare on the market(s) concerned; third, that that conduct is necessary for the achievement of those gains in efficiency; and, fourth, that it does not eliminate effective competition, by removing all or most existing sources of actual or potential competition.[140] The undertaking must provide 'convincing arguments and evidence' to this effect,[141] and 'has to do more than put forward vague, general and theoretical arguments on that point or rely exclusively on its own commercial interests'.[142]

4.2 Hesitations and Uncertainties

While certainties exist, the case law has become hesitant and arguably less coherent on other fronts. Even where a judgment sends a seemingly clear message on a certain point, the message is often embedded in wider narratives and rhetorical language that somehow blur the exact scope of the prohibition or may be interpreted as questioning whether the analysis could be somewhat different in a different set of circumstances. Examples abound and concern different aspects.

First, the case law suggests that there may be no need to analyse the capability to produce exclusionary effects of some types of conduct, but the boundaries of this line of reasoning, while easing enforcement, are not clearly set out. On the one hand, *Superleague* and *Google Shopping* mention in passing for the first time the possibility of having 'by object' infringements of Article 102 TFEU,[143] but case law has not clarified yet what such category would cover. It is certainly narrower than 'conduct departing from competition on the merits' and may arguably cover, *inter alia*, what is often called

140. C-333/21, *European Superleague Company*, EU:C:2023:1011, para. 204. *See* previously, with similar language, C-209/10, *Post Danmark*, EU:C:2012:172, para. 42; C-307/18, *Generics (UK) and Others*, EU:C:2020:52, para. 166; C-377/20, *Servizio Elettrico Nazionale*, EU:C:2022:379, para. 86. The term 'pro-competitive effects' is sometimes, but not often, used in some case law on Art. 101 TFEU (*see* C-264/23, *Booking.com and Booking.com (Deutschland)*, EU:C:2024:764, paras 55, 58; C-331/21, *EDP – Energias de Portugal and Others*, EU:C:2023:812, paras 103-105). Some authors regret the use of the term (*see* F. Wagner-von Papp, 'The Goals of Competition Law: Is "Consumer Welfare" Really Better Defined Than "Competition as Such"?' in R. Tritell, D. Crane and D. Gerard (eds), *Why Antitrust? Voices from the Antitrust Community and Beyond*, Concurrences Books, 2024: '[t]here is an unfortunate tendency in Europe to import the US terminology "pro-competitive" to denote merely efficient conduct'), but I understand that such effects simply mean advantages for consumers, as it is clear in the case law regarding such justification under Art. 102 TFEU.

141. C-333/21, *European Superleague Company*, EU:C:2023:1011, paras 205 and 209. To be clear, this expression does not set any 'standard of proof'. The Court of Justice ruled in *Tetra Laval* that the use of the adjective 'convincing' does not relate to the standard of proof, but 'to the essential function of evidence, which is to establish convincingly the merits of an argument or, as in the present case, of a decision on a merger' (in C-12/03 P, *Commission v. Tetra Laval*, EU:C:2005:87, para. 41).

142. C-307/18, *Generics (UK) and Others*, EU:C:2020:52, para. 166 *in fine*.

143. C-333/21, *European Superleague Company*, EU:C:2023:1011, para. 131. *See also* C-48/22 P, *Google and Alphabet v. Commission (Google Shopping)*, EU:C:2024:726, para. 167. Ibáñez Colomo has been advocating for the recognition of 'by object' infringements of Art. 102 TFEU for quite some time, *see* Ibáñez Colomo, *supra* n. 13.

'naked restrictions'.[144] On the other hand, *Unilever* appeared to say that for finding an abuse it is enough if conduct departs from competition on the merits,[145] whereas *SEN* and *Superleague* consider that this is one of the two conditions, the other one being that conduct must also be capable of restricting competition.[146] This may suggest overall that the Court of Justice is ready to subject some types of conduct to a 'lighter' test of effects (or to legally presume effects altogether), while, of course, the possibility remains open to the dominant undertaking to demonstrate that the conduct is actually justified.

Second, while the case law has settled for a standard of capability to produce exclusionary effects, the different qualifications used to assess that capability do not always send a consistent message. First, the three recent judgments of the Grand Chamber[147] do not refer to the principle that the concept of abuse is an objective one any more.[148] Recalling that there is still some objectivity in the analysis of whether an abuse has been committed is, in my view, particularly important to preserve the formal function of the law, at a time when the scope for disagreement increases in proportion to the factual complexity of cases. Second, the fact that anti-competitive effects failed to materialise is not necessarily conclusive,[149] and *Intel I* qualifies the required capability as 'intrinsic',[150] evoking maybe the idea that context is less relevant.

144. On the notion of 'naked' and 'by object' restrictions, *see* Schweitzer and De Ridder, *supra* n. 59, 18-20. The judgment of the General Court in *Intel I* already hinted at the existence of 'by object' restrictions, regarding which the analysis of capability to produce effects is not necessary: 'showing an anti-competitive object and an anti-competitive effect may, in some cases, be one and the same thing. If it is shown that the object pursued by the conduct of an undertaking in a dominant position is to restrict competition, that conduct will also be liable to have such an effect' (T-286/09, *Intel v. Commission*, EU:T:2014:547, para. 203); 'given that the anti-competitive object is indissociable in the case in point from the potential effect of the so-called "naked restrictions" practices ..., it must be considered that the Commission did not err in relying on their anti-competitive object' (para. 210). The Commission also relied on the anti-competitive object of the three naked restrictions, 'even though reference to such circumstances is not essential in order to characterise them as abusive under Article 82 EC' (para. 211). The findings in this part of the judgment, regarding 'naked restrictions', were taken over in T-286/09 RENV, *Intel v. Commission*, EU:T:2022:19, para. 96.
145. C-680/20, *Unilever Italia Mkt. Operations*, EU:C:2023:33, para. 39.
146. C-377/20, *Servizio Elettrico Nazionale and Others*, EU:C:2022:379, paras 74 and 103; C-333/21, *European Superleague Company*, EU:C:2023:1011, para. 124.
147. C-333/21, *European Superleague Company*, EU:C:2023:1011; C-48/22 P, *Google and Alphabet v. Commission (Google Shopping)*; C-233/23, *Alphabet and Others*, EU:C:2025:110.
148. *See also* C-240/22 P, *Commission v. Intel*, EU:C:2024:915, paras 144, 180, 273, 277, 291 and 331, insisting in the requirement to verify if there is a 'strategy' to exclude competitors. The last judgments where the Court of Justice refers to that principle are C-377/20, *Servizio Elettrico Nazionale and Others*, EU:C:2022:379, para. 60 and C-42/21 P, *Lietuvos geležinkeliai v. Commission*, EU:C:2023:12, para. 77.
149. T-201/04, *Microsoft v. Commission*, EU:T:2007:289, paras 560-564; C-538/18 P and C-539/18 P, *České dráhy v. Commission*, EU:C:2020:53, para. 70; C–377/20, *Servizio Elettrico Nazionale and Others*, EU:C:2022:379, para. 53; C-680/20, *Unilever Italia Mkt. Operations*, EU:C:2023:33, para. 41; C-233/23, *Alphabet and Others*, EU:C:2025:110, paras 55-61. In the latter, the Court of Justice adds that 'first, whether the conduct at issue is abusive cannot depend on the ability of competitors on the market concerned to mitigate such effects and, second, it cannot be ruled out that, in the absence of that conduct, competition on that market could have grown even further' (para. 58).
150. In *Intel I*, the Court of Justice refers to the 'intrinsic capacity' of the conduct to produce effects (C-413/14 P, *Intel v. Commission*, EU:C:2017:632, para. 140). This qualification is again present

However, the case law insists in parallel that the conduct must always be examined in context, often expressed as 'all the relevant factual circumstances'.[151] Moreover, the Court of Justice in *Unilever* uses stricter and somewhat different qualifications: it refers to 'actual' and 'specific' capacity to restrict competition.[152] Third, at the evidential level, *Unilever* also requires 'tangible' evidence of such capacity,[153] adding yet another adjective to the panoply in use to define legal and evidentiary standards in this context.[154] The Court of Justice also considered that any generalisation based on 'economic studies' having examined certain types of conduct in the past is insufficient, as any conclusion must also rely on evidence related to 'factors specific to the circumstances of the case'.[155] The reference in *Unilever* to 'tangible' evidence evokes 'actual' rather than potential effects since it is not obvious how one can have 'tangible' evidence of the potential for consequences which have not happened yet. We will examine further this judgment in section 5.3.

Third, while the notion of competition on the merits is prominent in the legal analysis, sometimes it may be too prominent. Some recent judgments refer to the conduct having the effect of 'hindering competition on the merits and is thus likely to cause direct harm to consumers, or which causes them harm indirectly by hindering or distorting that competition'.[156] If the qualification of 'competition' as 'competition on the merits' simply reflects the 'ideal' that undertakings should more generally compete on the merits, and 'restricting competition on the merits' equals simply 'restricting competition', I do not find it necessarily problematic, but the way this ideal is presented

---

in *Google Android* (T-604/18, *Google and Alphabet v. Commission (Google Android)*, EU:T:2022:541, paras 640-641, appeal pending C-738/22 P). It is unclear whether the Court of Justice, by adding 'intrinsic', intends to add an element of qualification to the 'capability' analysis, in the sense that contextual elements may be less relevant or simply that what happens afterwards (if there are actual effects) is not relevant. In *Google Android* (and also in *SEN*), the Court of Justice has given weight to behavioural studies (paras 320-418, *see also SEN*, *infra* n. 282). Stones rightly points out how behavioural economics represent a challenge to the formal role of law, since legal tests typically rely on economic rationality (*supra* n. 5, at 620). Yet, I think that in recent cases where behavioural biases were at stake, dominant undertakings could have perfectly anticipated them, and in reality, the dominant undertakings were actually knowingly exploiting such biases.

151. *See*, to this effect, C-333/21, *European Superleague Company*, EU:C:2023:1011, para. 130; C-48/22 P, *Google and Alphabet v. Commission (Google Shopping)*, EU:C:2024:726, paras 166 and 168; C-233/23, *Alphabet and Others*, EU:C:2025:110, para. 61. In earlier case law the Court of Justice referred to 'all the relevant facts' (C-307/18, *Generics (UK) and Others*, EU:C:2020:52, para. 154; C–377/20, *Servizio Elettrico Nazionale and Others*, EU:C:2022:379, para. 72).
152. C-680/20, *Unilever Italia Mkt. Operations*, EU:C:2023:33, paras 42, 52 and 53. Recalling the 'actual' capability, C-233/23, *Alphabet and Others*, EU:C:2025:110, para. 57.
153. C-680/20, *Unilever Italia Mkt. Operations*, EU:C:2023:33, para. 42; C-233/23, *Alphabet and Others*, EU:C:2025:110, para. 57.
154. Schauer has referred to the 'tyranny of adjectives' in the evidence discourse (F. Schauer, *The Proof: Uses of Evidence in Law, Politics and Everything Else*, Harvard University Press, 2022, 51).
155. C-680/20, *Unilever Italia Mkt. Operations*, EU:C:2023:33, paras 42-44 or 59.
156. C-333/21, *European Superleague Company*, EU:C:2023:1011, para. 124 (*see also* referring to 'restricting competition on the merits', para. 131); C-48/22 P, *Google and Alphabet v. Commission (Google Shopping)*, EU:C:2024:726, para. 87; C-233/23, *Alphabet and Others*, EU: C:2025:110, paras 37, using the word 'likely', and 51, using the word 'capable', whereas the language is used in French is the same '*susceptible de*'.

in the judgments may lead to confusion. First, the analysis of whether the conduct of the dominant undertaking is abusive does not depend on how rivals compete. Whether other, non-dominant rivals compete 'on the merits' or not is not part of the analysis under Article 102 TFEU.[157] Second, reference to capability to cause harm to consumers does not mean that evidence of such harm is needed.[158] Actually, neither *Superleague* nor *Google Shopping* nor *Android Auto*, where such language is used, require such evidence either. One must probably consider that this language just assumes that a restriction of competition, if demonstrated, *may* cause consumer harm, without shifting the subject of the proof. The presentation of *Superleague*, making a difference between a section on 'the concept' of 'abuse of a dominant position',[159] and a second section on 'the determination of whether there is abuse of a dominant position',[160] suggests that it is only the latter that provides more operational guidance. In the latter, the traditional language referring to the capability to produce exclusionary (actual but also potential) effects remains.[161]

Fourth, while some paragraphs in judgments now refer to effects on 'as-efficient competitors' (AEC) in different contexts, the actual significance of such language is often dubious, and I wonder if the 'AEC principle', as some call it, is more rhetorical than real and operational: it does not appear to be relevant in *SEN* (where efficiency is examined only as part of the analysis of competition on the merits in the context of pricing abuses, and of 'defences');[162] it is irrelevant where the dominant undertaking is protected by high barriers (*Post Danmark II* and *Unilever*);[163] *Google Shopping*, while first ruling that it is 'necessary, as a rule', to demonstrate the actual or potential effect of restricting competition 'by excluding equally efficient competing undertakings from the market(s) concerned', makes it later clear that 'it does not follow that any finding

157. As we will *see* when we discuss the notion of competition on the merits (s. 6.2 below), what may be common practice by non-dominant undertakings is not necessarily relevant for assessing whether the conduct by the dominant undertaking constitutes competition on the merits.
158. C-377/20, *Servizio Elettrico Nazionale and Others*, EU:C:2022:379, para. 47.
159. C-333/21, *European Superleague Company*, EU:C:2023:1011, paras 123-128.
160. *Ibid.*, paras 129-138.
161. *Ibid.*, where the Court of Justice still refers to the conduct being 'liable to produce its actual or potential effects' (para. 129), or being 'at the very least, ... capable of producing exclusionary effects' (para. 130). To complicate further the picture, in *Android Auto*, para. 51 refers to conduct that 'has the actual or potential effect of excluding, obstructing or delaying the development on the market of a product or service which is at least potentially in competition with a product or service supplied or capable of being supplied by the undertaking in a dominant position and constitutes conduct which restricts competition on the merits, and is thereby capable of causing harm to consumers' (C-233/23, *Alphabet and Others*, EU:C:2025:110, para. 51). While the reference to the capability of the product being supplied by the dominant undertaking is an interesting (and very useful) addition, I personally wonder if the last part of this long sentence (after 'and') is not simply referring to the fact that the conduct must depart from competition on the merits (which is different from restricting competition on the merits). Otherwise, it is hard to understand what the role of that final part of the sentence really is.
162. C-377/20, *Servizio Elettrico Nazionale*, EU:C:2022:379, paras 84-86.
163. C-23/14, *Post Danmark (II)*, EU:C:2015:651, para. 60 (*see also*, para. 39, referring to very high market shares and significant economies of scale); C-680/20, *Unilever Italia Mkt. Operations*, EU:C:2023:33, para. 57.

of an infringement under that provision is subject to proof that the conduct concerned is capable of excluding an as-efficient competitor' and concludes that the 'as-efficient' competitor 'test' is 'not mandatory in the context of the application of Article 102 TFEU' and was 'not relevant' in the specific case, a conclusion that leaves one wondering how there can be a rule which is 'not mandatory' and whose 'relevance' must be examined case-by-case;[164] *Superleague* also considers that the level of relative efficiency of new competitors (by reference to the dominant undertaking) is irrelevant to assess conduct that creates obstacles to their entry;[165] and *Android Auto* does not require an examination of whether the excluded competitors were 'as efficient' at all.[166] In addition, as I explain below (section 6.1), the so-called AEC principle is based on a misunderstanding of the case law: less efficient rivals may not be protected against 'competition on the merits', but they may be protected when conduct 'departs from competition on the merits'.

Fifth, the AEC test, as a test that is supposed to operationalise the so-called AEC principle, is presented prominently in *Intel II* for exclusivity rebates,[167] with a tone slightly different from previous judgments, such as *Unilever*, that clearly stresses its merely optional nature in price-based abuses.[168] In the context of a non-price abuse, the Grand Chamber in *Google Shopping* denies its mandatory effect in general and its relevance in the instant case, while leaving open the possibility that it could nonetheless be relevant in other contexts (which remain unspecified, adding a layer of uncertainty).[169] The outcome in *Google Shopping* suggests that the duties to examine an AEC test could in some cases be more procedural than substantive.[170] In this context, the insistence in *Intel II* on the verification of a 'possible existence of a strategy aiming to exclude competitors that are at least as efficient as that undertaking from the market'[171] appears to be at odds with settled case law indicating that, while intent is relevant when present, the notion of abuse is an 'objective' one.[172] If a 'strategy' is not normally needed to prove an infringement,[173] it is unclear why there is an obligation to check its 'possible existence'. The best interpretation seems to be that this requirement is case-specific. It was probably the fact that the Commission considered to have proven that 'strategy' in the *Intel* decision that led the Court of Justice to stress this

164. C-48/22 P, *Google and Alphabet v. Commission (Google Shopping)*, EU:C:2024:726, paras 165, 167, 264 and 269. *See also* text accompanying *infra* nn. 289 to 294.
165. C-333/21, *European Superleague Company*, EU:C:2023:1011, para. 131.
166. C-233/23, *Alphabet and Others*, EU:C:2025:110.
167. C-240/22 P, *Commission v. Intel*, EU:C:2024:915, paras 180-182.
168. C-680/20, *Unilever Italia Mkt. Operations*, EU:C:2023:33, paras 56-58. Also stressing its optional nature, even as regards pricing abuses, C-23/14, *Post Danmark*, EU:C:2015:651, para. 57; C-377/20, *Servizio Elettrico Nazionale*, EU:C:2022:379, para. 81.
169. C-48/22 P, *Google and Alphabet v. Commission (Google Shopping)*, EU:C:2024:726, paras 264-269.
170. *See infra* nn. 290 to 293 and accompanying text.
171. C-240/22 P, *Commission v. Intel*, EU:C:2024:915, in particular para. 291, but also paras 144, 180, 273, 277 and 331.
172. Unless of course such requirement has been abandoned (*see supra* nn. 147 and 148 and accompanying text) what I consider rather doubtful.
173. T-334/19, *Google and Alphabet v. Commission (Google AdSense for Search)*, EU:T:2024:634, paras 678-679, 883 and 981 (appeal pending, C-826/24 P). An exception is predatory pricing below ATC but above AVC.

point in its judgment on appeal in this case, as it is also probably because the Commission actively relied on the AEC test in the *Intel* decision that the test is so prominent in the *Intel* judgments. Such a reading is supported by the fact that the Court of Justice leaves it explicitly open whether the conduct could have been considered abusive for other reasons and recalls the conditions under which the Commission's decision examined the conduct.[174]

Sixth, *Intel I* and *Unilever* have set out a framework of analysis which is mainly procedural in nature. *Unilever* elaborates on *Intel I*, ruling that 'where that undertaking disputes, during the procedure, the specific capacity of those clauses to exclude equally efficient competitors from the market, with supporting evidence', then the authority 'must ensure, at the stage of classifying the infringement, that those clauses were, in the circumstances of the case, actually capable of excluding competitors as efficient as that undertaking from the market'.[175] This duty also applies when 'the undertaking which is under suspicion, without formally arguing that its conduct was incapable of restricting competition, maintains that there are justifications for its conduct'.[176] The Court of Justice adds that '[i]n any event, the submission, in the course of the procedure, of evidence capable of demonstrating the inability to produce restrictive effects gives rise to an obligation for the competition authority to examine that evidence'. This is explicitly based on the right to be heard and the authority must examine 'carefully and impartially all the relevant aspects of the individual case, and, in particular, the evidence submitted by that undertaking'.[177] The rejection of an economic study must be reasoned: 'the competent competition authority cannot exclude the relevance of that study without setting out the reasons why it considers that the study does not contribute to demonstrating that the practices in question were incapable of undermining effective competition on the relevant market'.[178] As we will *see* in section 5.3, *Intel* and *Unilever* leave unanswered critical questions about the evidentiary threshold that the dominant undertaking must meet to trigger the Commission's additional obligations and about what these additional obligations actually are.

4.3 Taking Stock: How Uncertain Is the Law Today?

All the foregoing is concerning: when the case law does not use consistent language and when many passages may have to be understood as being limited to the context of individual cases and may lack clear precedent value for other cases, the clarity and generality of the law suffers. The bottom line, or the common thread, appears to be that over the past few years, the Court of Justice has become less prescriptive about substance, where the general nature of the law is kept at a relative 'high level' of abstraction, and more prescriptive about the process. In other words, the rule of law as a constraining factor in decision-making increasingly takes the shape of procedural

174. C-240/22 P, *Commission v. Intel*, EU:C:2024:915, paras 339-343.
175. C-680/20, *Unilever Italia Mkt. Operations*, EU:C:2023:33, para. 52.
176. *Ibid.* paras 52 and 53.
177. *Ibid.*, para. 54.
178. *Ibid.*, para. 55.

safeguards. The 'clarification' of the case law in *Intel I* is a jurisprudential change that *SEN* and *Unilever* (which extend some of the language in *Intel I* to a wider set of practices)[179] develop into two procedural principles, namely the right to be heard and the principle of good administration or impartial examination of the case.[180]

After *Intel I* and *Unilever*, for some practices, a 'reticulated burden-shifting framework' remains in place,[181] but it appears to be less guided by any 'hard' substantive norm.[182] Ironically, the 'clarification' in *Intel I* did not really render the law more comprehensible, or the delineation of prohibited conduct more predictable. On the contrary, proof of anti-competitive effects is, at least for some types of practices, increasingly taking the form of a dialectic process, where the Commission is, first, required to adduce sufficient proof that the conduct is capable of producing (at least potential) anti-competitive effects, and may in certain cases rely on certain rebuttable presumptions (*see also* section 5.3 below), but the dominant undertaking may adduce evidence to the contrary that must be systematically assessed. The Commission must analyse 'all the relevant factual circumstances', carefully and impartially, and the EU judicature is not always clear about what really guides 'in substance' such dynamic and comprehensive examination. Even if evidence of lack of effects may not be enough to disprove the Commission's case,[183] judgments also require 'tangible' evidence to

179. C-377/20, *Servizio Elettrico Nazionale and Others*, EU:C:2022:379, para. 52; C-680/20, *Unilever Italia Mkt. Operations*, EU:C:2023:33, para. 54.
180. I must confess it is not clear to me why, if there were to be a rule providing that a certain conduct is prohibited, not engaging with certain type of arguments that do not contest that the facts correspond to the rule, but rather tend to question the rule as such, indicates any partiality or any breach of the rights of defence. It is probably because there is no rule (substantive presumption) anymore, but just at most an evidentiary presumption, that those rights become relevant. But those rights cannot as such require the transformation of a rule into an evidentiary presumption.
181. I take this very telling expression from Crane, *supra* n. 71, at 63.
182. As Lindeboom puts it: 'the result of *Intel* of that the Commission is likely to be more constrained by (procedural and evidential) rules after *Intel* than it had been by the (substantive) rule from *Hoffmann-La Roche* ... After *Intel*, the liberating formalism of *Hoffmann-La Roche* has likely been replaced by a more constraining evidential formalism' (*supra* n. 6, 875). He generally considers that a new formalism is thereby crated, based on economic models (*ibid.*, 862-863). As Crane has observed, 'European law is more likely to draw on formal rules to prohibit loyalty rebates, U.S. law is more likely to draw on formal rules to permit them. Europe employs legal formalism, and the United States uses economic formalism' (D. Crane, 'Formalism and Functionalism in the Antitrust Treatment of Loyalty Rebates: A Comparative Perspective' 81 *Antitrust Law J.* 209, 210 (2016)).
183. The fact 'a certain course of conduct has not produced actual anti-competitive effects cannot rule out the possibility that that conduct was in fact capable of doing so when it was implemented, even if a long period of time has passed since that conduct took place' (C-377/20, *Servizio Elettrico Nazionale*, EU:C:2022:379, para. 54). The Court of Justice in *SEN* further holds that, while the evidence produced by a dominant undertaking attesting to the lack of actual effects 'cannot be regarded as sufficient of itself to preclude the application of Article 102 TFEU', this 'may constitute evidence that the conduct in question was not capable of producing the alleged exclusionary effects'. However, the Court adds that this evidence must 'be supplemented, by the undertaking concerned, by items of evidence intended to show that that absence of actual effects was indeed the consequence of the fact that that conduct was unable to produce such effects' (*Ibid.*, para. 56). *See also* C-233/23, *Alphabet and Others*, EU:C:2025:110, paras 55-61, and T-334/19, *Google and Alphabet v. Commission (Google AdSense for Search)*, EU:T:2024:634, para. 674, where the fact that certain of Google's competing intermediaries were able to win a few bids organised by publishers was not such as to rule out that the

support the Commission's case. There is some loss of generality and predictability inherent in every ad hoc assessment that results from this mainly procedural framework favoured in *Intel I* and *Unilever*.

While some judgments hint at the fact that the analysis of effects may be lighter in some circumstances, outside some obvious candidate scenarios it is still unclear when that will be the case. Should the Commission run its case under a 'lighter' standard and risk that the EU Courts will apply a 'stricter' one? Even practices such as exclusivity may end up being subject to a demanding examination of an increasing number of 'relevant' circumstances. Case in point: *Google AdSense*. The General Court first recalled *Unilever* to the effect that 'by reason of their nature, exclusivity clauses give rise to legitimate concerns of competition', while their ability to exclude competitors 'is not automatic'.[184] Yet, these 'legitimate concerns', which could evoke a consistent line of case law on exclusive dealing,[185] do not appear to really 'lighten' the burden of the Commission later in the judgment. The General Court, after confirming one by one almost all the findings of the Commission, annulled the decision solely because the analysis of duration was deemed to be insufficient as it 'failed to take into consideration all the relevant circumstances of the case in the context of the assessment of the duration'.[186]

If the motive behind the change in *Intel I* was to ensure, through more elaborate processes, more economically accurate outcomes, the jury is still out on whether adjudication has become more economically literate as a result, or just more complex in the hope that accuracy will be somehow the end result. In the shorter term, the 'all the relevant factual circumstances' approach could be transforming judicial review into a formalistic exercise if it is interpreted as a review where the EU judicature mainly checks whether all boxes in a long list have been sufficiently ticked, without explaining why an 'unticked' box can *actually* alter the outcome.[187] All this in a context where it

exclusivity clause in GSAs concluded with the thirty-four all sites direct partners was capable of producing a effects contrary to Art. 102 TFEU.

184. T-334/19, *Google and Alphabet v. Commission (Google AdSense for Search)*, EU:T:2024:634, paras 384, 406 and 779 (appeal pending, C-826/24 P).

185. *See infra* n. 234 and accompanying text.

186. T-334/19, *Google and Alphabet v. Commission (Google AdSense for Search)*, EU:T:2024:634, paras 717, 722, 903, 908, 993 and 998. Compare to previous cases where what was relevant was the 'actual duration' of the agreements (T-65/98, *Van den Bergh Foods v. Commission*, EU:T:2003:281, para. 105; on appeal, C-552/03 P *Unilever Bestfoods v. Commission*, EU:C:2006:607, para. 55). In *Langnese-Iglo*, the applicant had claimed that the average duration of the exclusivity clause was 'only about two-and-a-half years' (T-7/93 *Langnese-Iglo v. Commission*, EU:T:1995:98, para. 77) and that 'the managers of sales outlets as a general rule terminate their contracts as early as possible in order to negotiate better conditions' (*ibid*). The GC rejected the claim that this demonstrated the inability to restrict competition of the clause, relying on the 'effective duration' of the agreements, which was 'around two and half years', and not on whether the agreements could be terminated earlier (para. 111). Moreover, the GC considered that an 'effective duration' of 'around two and half years' was sufficient to consider that the clause was 'liable appreciably to affect competition' (*ibid*). *See also infra* n. 243.

187. Castillo de la Torre and Gippini Fournier, *supra* n. 25, para. 6.083. This procedural approach to judicial review is probably the result of complexity, as Ezrachi puts it, 'it is perhaps not surprising that when overwhelmed with economic complexity, some courts have been known to favour a procedural route – resolving a case on a technicality – thus avoiding the pitfalls of complex econometric analysis' (*supra* n. 28, 63).

may not be clear what 'all relevant factual circumstances' means, and applicants will try to expand the notion of relevance as much as possible. While it is undisputed that enhancing the completeness of the evidential enquiry will in turn enhance the confidence in the factual assessment, not everything is relevant,[188] and the case law is starting to recognise that not every error should lead to an annulment if decisions are based on a body of evidence that largely exceeds what would be required to discharge the burden of proof.[189]

188. As Easterbrook explains 'when everything is relevant, nothing is dispositive' (*supra* n. 30, at 12).

189. If the Commission actually examines something out of caution, it runs the risk of having the decision annulled in case an error is found regarding that additional element, since the General Court may decide that evaluating whether the Commission had proven its case after an error was found would imply substituting its assessment for that of the Commission. Some decisions may be based on a body of evidence that largely exceeds what would be required to discharge the burden of proof, and therefore a gap or error should not be fatal. By considering what remains of the case the judges are not substituting their assessment for that of the Commission, but exercising the function of judicial review by determining if the error is relevant for the outcome, as they routinely do in other contexts. Not every error must lead to the annulment of the act, as some judgments are beginning to recall: T-321/05 *AstraZeneca v. Commission*, EU:T:2010:266, paras 182 and 196-197, where one error and one 'lacuna' did not affect the 'soundness' of the conclusions of the Commission; T-312/20, *EVH v. Commission*, EU:T:2023:252, para. 351 (*see*, on appeal, C-464/23 P, C-465/23 P, C-467/23 P, C-468/23 P and C-470/23 P, *EVH and Others v. Commission*, EU:C:2025:478, in particular paras 87, 190, 214-215); T-334/19, *Google and Alphabet v. Commission (Google AdSense for Search)*, EU:T:2024:634, para. 340, where the applicant did not show that a SSNIP test, which was not mandatory anyway, would have resulted in a conclusion different from the one that the Commission drew in the decision; C-240/22 P, *Commission v. Intel*, EU:C:2024:915, para. 204: 'it is not sufficient for the undertaking in a dominant position to call into question the accuracy of one of the calculations made in the AEC test in order to invalidate the Commission's conclusion, based on such a test, relating to the capability of a loyalty rebate scheme to foreclose a competitor as efficient as that undertaking. The deficiency or error identified must also be capable of altering the result of the test, changing it from negative to positive, in such a way as to give rise to reasonable doubt as to the validity of the result adopted by the Commission and, therefore, as to the capability of the rebates concerned to foreclose a competitor as efficient as the undertaking in a dominant position. That type of doubt may arise due to calculation errors or due to selective or incomplete consideration of evidence'. The judgment in *CK Telecoms* ruled that the EU judicature must examine whether a deficiency in the examination by the Commission has, or at least may have, an impact on the outcome (C-376/20 P, *Commission v. CK Telecoms UK Investments*, EU:C:2023:561, paras 269-270). The Court of Justice upheld one of the Commission's grounds of appeal because the General Court failed to carry out an overall examination of whether it could be considered that the Commission had demonstrated to the requisite legal standard the existence of a SIEC, in light of: (i) the outcome of its examination of CK Telecoms' arguments at first instance concerning some of the relevant circumstances; and (ii) the other relevant circumstances that formed part of the Commission's overall analysis and that, since they were not challenged, could therefore be regarded as established. In *Orlen*, the Court of Justice recalled that 'the existence of a manifest error of assessment cannot correspond to the presence of a mere irregularity or omission on the part of the Commission, since a certain degree of seriousness, capable of calling into question the validity of the analysis which the Commission carried out, must be reached' (Case C-255/22 P, *Orlen v. Commission*, EU:C:2024:790, para. 115). When some pieces of evidence have been discarded as inadmissible, it is settled case law that the EU judicature still examines if remaining evidence is enough to prove the relevant point (T-191/98, T-212/98-T-214/98, *Atlantic Container Line and Others v. Commission*, EU:T:2003:245, para. 338; T-379/10 and T-381/10, *Keramag and Others v. Commission*, EU:T:2013:457, para. 264).

While one may perceive a certain effort to put some order in the case law as of the judgment in *Superleague*, with no less than three recent judgments on Article 102 TFEU having been delivered by the Grand Chamber,[190] I am not sure the case law has overall become clearer as a result. Some language has certainly become 'more standard' in very recent judgments, but it remains somewhat vague, and judgments are not always internally consistent on significant nuances. Words matter, and parties will very vigorously debate about the meaning of every word used in every single judgment.[191] In this context, I wonder if consequences must be drawn from the fact that the three Grand Chamber judgments do not recall that the concept of abuse is an objective one,[192] or from the fact that they contain only limited references to the 'burden-shifting' scheme set out in *Intel I* and *Unilever*, described above.[193] All in all, the recent judgments still convey the impression that there may be different visions of how to deal with Article 102 TFEU cases within the EU judicature itself; or that the EU judicature may be trying to please too many people.

Unlike undertakings and their representatives, which may interpret the case law in the way that suits best their case in one instance, and then advance a different interpretation in a different case, the Commission should be consistent in its interpretation throughout its decisional practice, and must therefore make its own call on 'what the law is' (which will then be subject to review by the EU judicature). The problem also arises, with even more force, at the national level, where competition authorities and courts must apply substantive law which, as was argued above, is becoming unclear on some points, and where the asymmetry of means between some 'smaller' authorities and some large undertakings, which in my view typically favours the latter in complex factual and economic settings, is even more acutely felt.[194] Inevitably, in order to ascertain what the legal standards really are, some 'weighing' of the different judgments is necessary. For example, Grand Chamber judgments tend to be given more

190. C-333/21, *European Superleague Company*, EU:C:2023:1011; C-48/22 P, *Google and Alphabet v. Commission (Google Shopping)*; C-233/23, *Alphabet and Others*, EU:C:2025:110.
191. Personally, I also find that the fact that the legal debate often relied on the English version of the judgments does not really help, as other linguistic versions may better capture what the judges actually mean. I have found over the years many instances where the English version of the judgment was not quite accurate.
192. *See supra* nn. 147 and 148 and accompanying text.
193. In *Superleague* there is no reference to such scheme while *Unilever* is mentioned regarding the need for 'tangible points of analysis and evidence' (C-333/21, *European Superleague Company*, EU:C:2023:1011, para. 130). In *Google Shopping* there is no reference to *Unilever* as such, and only a brief one, at the end, to paras 138 and 139 of *Intel* (C-48/22 P, *Google and Alphabet v. Commission (Google Shopping)*, EU:C:2024:726, para. 265). *Android Auto* makes no reference to *Intel I* and refers to *Unilever* to explain that an authority may find that there has been an infringement despite the lack of effect, and the need for 'tangible evidence' of 'actual capability' since the existence of doubt in that regard must benefit the undertaking which engages the practice (C-233/23, *Alphabet and Others*, EU:C:2025:110, paras 56-57). There is nothing in that judgment about the burden-shifting mechanism first mentioned in *Intel I*.
194. The type of evidentiary process which appears to be favoured in the case law has a sophisticated authority in mind (which the Commission can arguably be), rather than the typical litigant in national proceedings. On how different standards may be more suitable depending on the institutional setting, including experience and resources, *see* OECD, *supra* n. 52, paras 36-37.

authority than judgments of a chamber of three judges, and more weight will be given to statements which appear to be more consistently used by the EU Courts.

Leaving aside that this situation is sub-optimal from the point of view of the formal function of the law (and of legal certainty), it is a factor that in my view has also contributed to delays in the enforcement process. Decisions are sometimes drafted covering all possible bases, including, just in case, remotely or even implausibly relevant issues, attempting to provide alternative reasonings for any given conclusion, and replying to every single argument of the parties, even if they are probably prima facie irrelevant. This typically delays the procedure. In turn, engaging with some factual elements in the decision may end up being interpreted as recognition of their relevance (otherwise, why would the Commission deal with them?). The Commission may have to explain why it is relying more on one judgment than on another, in a context where any reading of the case law tends to be contested, as undertakings are increasingly able to find some sentence or paragraph in a judgment that seemingly contradicts the interpretation of the Commission. Likewise, the losing party in the General Court will often find something in the case law of the Court of Justice that may support its case on appeal against the General Court's decision. And the legal debate will go on and on and on, but often without the law becoming clearer as a result, particularly if the judgment putting an end to the litigation just decides the instant case and leaves open whether much of what is said therein applies to the next case.

5 ON PRESUMPTIONS AND OTHER EVIDENTIARY BURDEN-SHIFTING TOOLS

5.1 Presumptions: Sources and Operation

Decision theory, often influenced by Bayesian approaches, has very significantly contributed to the understanding of the use of presumptions.[195] This theory postulates that decision-makers normally approach cases and build their initial analysis based on prior knowledge, i.e., non-case-specific information.[196] Under a (Bayesian) view of 'belief', decision-makers hold beliefs with varying degrees of subjective probability and update them as they encounter new evidence.[197] Some priors may have an impact not

195. Gavil and Salop, *supra* n. 84, 2119: 'decision theory provides a methodology for information-gathering and decision-making when outcomes are uncertain, information is inherently imperfect, and information is costly to obtain'.

196. This is background information that takes often the form of '*non-case-specific* beliefs about how the world works with which a fact-finder approaches the task of adjudication' (D. Nance, *The Burdens of Proof: Discriminatory Power, Weight of Evidence, and Tenacity of Belief*, Cambridge University Press, 2016, 97, emphasis in the original). On evidentiary tools as being primarily based on generalisations of different types *see* Castillo de la Torre and Gippini Fournier, *supra* n. 25, paras 1.025-1.026 and 2.078-2.092, and A. Kalintiri, 'Analytical Shortcuts in EU Competition Enforcement: Proxies, Premises and Presumptions', 16(3) *JCLE* 392-433 https://doi.org/10.1093/joclec/nhaa013.

197. I assume here that what is relevant in this context is an internal conception of probability (as opposed to an external one). To be clear, saying that evidence is probabilistic says nothing about whether those probabilities can or should be reduced to, or expressed in terms of,

just on the belief-building process but may become legally relevant as the basis for some evidentiary burden-shifting, often called 'presumptions'.[198] Absent any evidence running against some observable elements that the burdened party has proven, that party is considered to have discharged its burden. Taking decisions based on probability, inferences and presumptions is consistent with a decision-theoretic approach to the enforcement of competition law.

In some cases, presumptions may be part of the substantive law itself (some call them legal or substantive presumptions). *Fact A* has a likely link with *Fact B*, but the law does not require anything beyond proving *Fact A* for finding an infringement.[199] In other words, demonstrating *Fact A* is enough to consider that the offence has been committed. This may be how the law is drafted, or this may be the interpretation by the courts. This definition of the offence may result from choices related to ease or difficulty of proving certain points (*Fact B*),[200] or from the consideration that additional fact-finding is unlikely to change the outcome in the great majority of cases.[201] In other

numbers. I must also note that the very idea of 'belief' as the basis for factual decisions has generally come under severe attack. For a critical view of 'belief' as basis for a theory of evidence, *see* J. Ferrer, 'Proven Facts, Beliefs and Reasoned Verdicts', in C. Dahlman, A. Stein and G. Tuzet (eds), *Philosophical Foundations of Evidence Law*, Oxford, OUP, 2021, 40-52. The causal factors of our beliefs are partly inaccessible to us. The act of believing may be seen as involuntary, and under no circumstances can the individual in question decide to have a particular belief. Yet, I find that Bayesian approaches explain rather well the assessment of evidence for some aspects of the analysis of competition cases, where the threshold is one of 'capability' (to restrict competition) and therefore, in my view, inherently probabilistic.

198. The word 'presumption' may cover a variety of phenomena, *see infra* nn. 213 and 225. *See also* R. Allen, 'Burden of Proof', 13(3-4) *Law, Probability and Risk*, 195-219, at 208 (2014) https://doi.org/10.1093/lpr/mgu005: 'all the difficulties about presumptions are eliminated once one recognizes that there is no such thing as a "presumption." The word "presumption" is simply a label that has been applied to a widely differing set of decisions concerning the proper mode of trial and the manner in which facts are to be established to resolve legal disputes. .... All the confusion and controversy surrounding presumptions – and I mean that literally, all of it – has been caused by the failure to recognize that the word "presumption" is simply a label applied to a range of evidentiary decisions that are made for the various reasons that inform the structuring of litigation'.
199. OECD, *supra* n. 52, paras 55-60.
200. For example, substantive rules decide whether several individuals, or several acts for that matter, shall be treated as members of a class, and may already delineate the law to avoid the characteristic difficulty in finding evidence (Ch. Engel, *Neglect the Base Rate: It's the Law!* (1 December 2012), MPI Collective Goods Preprint, No. 2012/23, at 8). This is also reflected, in my view, in the case law of EU Courts. *See* Castillo de la Torre and Gippini Fournier, *supra* n. 25, para. 1.046, for examples.
201. From the point of view of decision-making theory, the rationale for per se rules is said to be that it is not justified to engage into a complex enquiry when the likelihood of anticompetitive conduct is so great as to render unjustified the costs of determining whether the particular case involved anticompetitive conduct. *See* F.C. Beckner and S. Salop, 'Decision Theory and Antitrust Rules', 67 *Antitrust L.J.* 41, 41-76, at 63 (1999-2000): 'The rational decision maker will only gather additional information if the expected benefit of the information exceeds the cost of gathering the information'. Beckner and Salop consider that courts require three sources of information: presumptions, logical analysis and factual investigation (at 43). Kaplow explains that 'the cost of information gathering is a first-order consideration in legal system design' (L. Kaplow, 'On the Design of Legal Rules: Balancing Versus Structured Decision Procedures', 132 Harv. L. Rev. 992, 1015 (2019)); 'the value of (additional) information justifies further effort if it exceeds the cost of collecting the information' (1016); 'more information tends to be worth collecting when our uninformed decision is a close call than

cases, the law or the case law still leaves some margin to the decision-maker to decide, when evidence to the contrary is provided, that *Fact B* cannot be implied from *Fact A*. We are mainly concerned by these evidentiary presumptions since the first type of presumption belongs rather to substantive law.

An important reason why presumptions are particularly appropriate in competition law relates to the prospective nature of the assessment. Competition law does not assign responsibility for an undesirable harm that has *effectively* occurred but regulates conduct *ex ante*: the analysis considers the circumstances at the time when the conduct is implemented. Conduct is prohibited because of its link to a certain (possible or probable) outcome, but the analysis is about conduct nonetheless. Any prospective analysis necessarily relies on generalisations and classes.[202] An entirely case-specific, 'all things considered' analysis blurs both the prospective and the prescriptive nature of any rule.

The sources for presumptions may be of a different nature. Most of them convey a strong evidentiary link between *Fact A* (typically a conduct with some observable features) and *Fact B* (e.g., in competition law, the capability or likelihood of a certain effect on competition). In some cases, presumptions overcome the impossibility of proving *Fact B* to a high standard of proof. In some other cases, it may be possible to prove *Fact B* directly, but it is unreasonably costly and time-consuming to gather enough evidence to reach a conclusion (positive or negative) with enough confidence. In this regard, an important element in normative design concerns the decision as to who is going to bear the additional costs associated with the gathering of case-specific information that may allow the decision-maker to deviate from the initial assumption.[203] The use of presumptions allocates costs and benefits of information-gathering.

---

when it seems to be a slam dunk.' (1018). As Stein explains, 'a substantive law policy would never be sound if it were to ignore anticipated enforcement expenses that include the costs of both fact-finding errors and their avoidance' (A. Stein, *Foundations of Evidence Law*, OUP, 2005, 8).

202. *See* C. Engel, 'Uncertain Judges', 176 *JITE* 44-47, 44 (2020) https://doi.org/10.1628/jite-2020-0007: 'rules are meant to be general, which is why a concept of causality is required that establishes whether a cause that is subsumed under some class is frequently associated with an effect that is a member of some other class'. *See also* Engel, *supra* n. 200, 15: 'if the law asks for prognostic evaluation, the base rate of the event is legally relevant'. There is a wealth of literature on the difference between deterministic and probabilistic conceptions of causation. *See*, for example, F. Schauer and B.A. Spellman, 'Probabilistic Causation in Law', 176 *JITE* 4-17 (2020) https://doi.org/10.1628/jite-2020-0003. The authors explain that 'predictive conceptions of causation are typically about types and not about tokens – about classes and not about particulars – and are accordingly probabilistic rather than deterministic' (at 5). What counts is whether the conduct makes the effect more probable, not whether an observed effect is caused by the conduct. Such probabilistic approaches are common for regulations which try to incentivise a certain behaviour (one can safely say that smoking causes cancer, even though not every smoker will develop cancer and not every cancer suffered by a smoker will be caused by smoking). Under this approach, the counterfactual is not about whether the observable market development would happen absent the conduct, but whether absent the conduct, the market development would be less likely.
203. Gavil and Salop, *supra* n. 84, at 2120: 'the optimal evidentiary standard would balance the direction and strength of the presumption with the reliability and cost of the available evidence'. On the importance of evidentiary rules and presumption when designing optimal enforcement, *see* OECD, *supra* n. 52, para. 26.

Who must bear that cost (and risk) can be legally articulated in terms of the burden of proof (legal or evidential).[204]

Evidentiary presumptions need not always be based on the strong evidentiary link between *Facts A and B*. The design of evidentiary presumptions may be also based on parties' relative ease of access to the evidence on specific issues.[205] This encourages completeness by eliciting the submission of additional evidence from the other side. Presumptions may also be explained by deterrence policy or other policy considerations.[206] When a presumption is not only based on experience or technical consensus, it introduces elements which may not make fact-finding more accurate and may be unrelated to the conviction of the decision-maker.[207] The source of the presumption may have a role in assessing when and how it can be 'rebutted'.[208]

Normally, a party may try to curtail the operation of a presumption by presenting evidence undermining the facts underlying the presumption (that *Fact A* is not true), or by showing evidence that weighs against and offsets the effects of the presumption, i.e., adducing case-specific evidence that tend to support the conclusion that *Fact B* is not true, despite showing that *Fact A* is true. In the first case, the presumption will simply not apply if the evidence is conclusive about *Fact A* not being true. In the second the existence of *Fact A* may continue to carry some evidentiary weight:[209] the evidential assessment does not start from an epistemic *tabula rasa*. Presumptions, if based on strong evidentiary links, typically rely on the belief-building process, in the sense that the prior upon which the presumption is based (the link between *Facts A and B* under normal circumstances, based on experience) will represent the background knowledge (the base rate, so to say) against which any new and case-specific evidence will be

204. On the difference between the legal burden of proof and the evidential burden of proof, *see* Castillo de la Torre and Gippini Fournier, *supra* n. 25, paras 1.032-1.037. These notions are known under different names in different legal system: burden of production versus burden of persuasion (in the US) or subjective versus objective burden of proof (in some legal systems in continental Europe).
205. C. Volpin, 'The Ball Is in Your Court: Evidential Burden of Proof and the Proof-Proximity Principle in EU Competition Law' 51 *CML Rev* 1159-86 (2014) https://doi.org/10.54648/cola2014089; Castillo de la Torre and Gippini Fournier, *supra* n. 25, paras 2.112-2.113 (on other, non-evidentiary, basis for presumptions); OECD, *supra* n. 52, s. 4.3.
206. Deterrence in this context is 'the impact on future's participants' choice of conduct in light of the legal standard' (Salop, *supra* n. 69, 18).
207. L. Burkhart, *Kartellrechtliche Vermutungen bei Art. 101 AEUV: Beginn und Ende der Beteiligung an einem Kartell*, Moh Siebeck, 2022, 16 and 42-43. When presumptions are not based on experience, they do not imply that the fact-finder is convinced about the truth about the fact, and such presumption may conceptually relate more to the objective burden of proof. He mentions some typical justifications: proximity to the evidence, that the evidence is in the sphere of the other party, the inability through no fault of his own to produce such proof, avoiding a requirement to prove a negative, effectiveness (35, 48).
208. In practice, because presumptions may serve multiple purposes (judicial efficiency or public policy goals) their evidentiary strength may not always be crucial in their rebuttal. Such wider purposes may also be the basis for their irrebuttable nature in some cases (becoming de facto substantive rules). If the purpose is to elicit evidence-gathering, the presumption will have had the desired effect when the party provides all the evidence that it considers to be in its interest. The presumption may, however, still have a role to play as a decision rule, in case of doubt.
209. Salop, *supra* n. 69, 37-44.

examined.[210] In other words, the presumption does not simply evaporate when there is an attempt at rebutting it. The decision-maker assesses whether the case-specific information allows it to deviate from the prior that the presumption represents. If that is the case, then the presumption is effectively rebutted. The amount of specific information required to depart from that prior must correspond to a level that would allow the decision-maker to deviate significantly from the background information.[211]

5.2 Presumptions in EU Competition Law: A Structuring Tool Often Embedded in the Law

After having examined how presumptions may be part of the optimal normative design in competition law enforcement (*see* section 3.1 above), and their sources and operation generally (*see* section 5.1 above), it is now time to zoom in on the state of the debate in the EU. I will focus here on the second condition to establish an abuse, namely the capability to produce exclusionary effects.[212]

The EU judicature does use the expression 'presumption' (or 'presumed') in some contexts, but there is no general theory of presumptions in EU law.[213] What is

210. Emphasis in obtaining 'case-specific' evidence may end up leading to a sort of 'base rate neglect', a well-documented cognitive bias. If the decision-maker in a competition case examines only the situation at hand, omitting to consider prior guidance, experience, assumptions (you name it), it will tend to underestimate the probability (capability, in our case) of certain effects occurring.

211. Salop, *supra* n. 69, 28: 'where case-specific evidence is less definitive, decision theory would counsel that more evidence should be required for rebuttal to achieve a particular level of reliability'. Moreover, too much evidence of events after the conduct may create a hindsight bias and transform conduct that the dominant undertaking expected to have some effects into innocuous one, just because we have more information than the undertaking had at the time it implemented its conduct.

212. Although it cannot be excluded that some presumptions may be relevant for assessing whether conduct departs from competition of the merits, that appears to be less frequently the case.

213. Burkhart, *supra* n. 207, 15. On the different conceptions of 'presumptions' in different legal systems of the Member States, *see* the Opinion of Advocate General Bobek in C-621/15, *Sanofi*, EU:C:2017:176, paras 28-30. For an attempt at listing and classifying different presumptions applied in EU competition law, *see* C. Ritter, 'Presumptions in EU Competition Law', 6(2) *JAE* 189 (2018) https://doi.org/10.1093/jaenfo/jny008. Regarding semantics, *see also supra* n. 198. One must bear in mind that, in some legal systems, the expression 'presumption' is also used in general when a specific body of evidence is strong enough to shift the evidential burden of proof to the other party (*see*, for example, C-74/14, *Eturas and Others*, EU:C:2016:42, paras 40-41). This phenomenon also exists in EU law, *see* Castillo de la Torre and Gippini Fournier, *supra* n. 25, paras 2.116-2.127. This evidentiary burden-shifting between the Commission and the undertaking under investigation has been accepted as a matter of principle based on the case-specific evidence already adduced (C-204/00 P, C-205/00 P, C-211/00 P, C-213/00 P, C-217/00 P and C-219/00 P, *Aalborg Portland and Others v. Commission*, EU:C:2004:6, para. 79: '[a]lthough according to those principles the legal burden of proof is borne either by the Commission or by the undertaking or association concerned, the factual evidence on which a party relies may be of such a kind as to require the other party to provide an explanation or justification, failing which it is permissible to conclude that the burden of proof has been discharged'; C-609/13 P, *Duravit and Others v. Commission*, EU:C:2017:46, para. 57; C-591/16 P, *Lundbeck v. Commission*, EU:C:2021:243, para. 79) also in Art. 102 TFEU cases (T-612/17, *Google and Alphabet v. Commission (Google Shopping)*, EU:T:2021:763, para. 133). It is not in that sense that I use the word 'presumption' here. Moreover, the opposite may also happen. Without explicitly using the term 'presumption', decision-makers in some systems may assume

clear, in any event, is that evidentiary presumptions are not necessarily contrary to the presumption of innocence.[214] The benefit of the doubt does not mean that we should ignore any general, non-case-specific information the enforcers may have, in particular about the possible or probable effects of some categories of conduct.[215]

The case law of EU Courts has held that some presumptions belong more to the interpretation of the law than to a simple question of fact. For example, it has long been held that the causal link between 'concertation' and 'practice' which the concept of concerted practice requires can be presumed: it is to be expected that participants in an information exchange will make use of the information obtained in determining their course of conduct on the market.[216] The Court of Justice decided in *T-Mobile* that this presumption is an issue of substance (of the interpretation of Article 101 TFEU) and not an issue of evidence or procedure (to be in principle governed by national law).[217] Other presumptions, such as those concerning liability for acts of fully owned subsidiaries[218] or for attendance of meetings without taking distance,[219] also apply at the national level, indicating that they follow from the substantive interpretation of Articles 101 and 102 TFEU.

The tendency of the Court of Justice to provide prescriptive guidance for the enforcement at the national level goes beyond presumptions. The Court of Justice, while formally leaving to the national court the task of assessing the evidence, is increasingly prescriptive regarding the process of submission and assessment of that evidence at the national level.[220] In my view, the general attitude of the Court of Justice

---

some effects based on certain 'standard' observable factors and the evidential burden is then shifted to the other party. Such 'structured' burden-shifting rule may also be considered a type of presumption, in the broader sense.

214. Castillo de la Torre and Gippini Fournier, *supra* n. 25, para. 2.101. The ECtHR accepts that proof 'beyond reasonable doubt' may follow from 'the coexistence of sufficiently strong, clear and concordant inferences or of similar unrebutted presumptions of fact'. *See*, for example, ECtHR, *Jalloh v. Germany*, CE:ECHR:2006:0711JUD005481000, para. 67; ECtHR, *Ramirez Sanchez v. France*, CE:ECHR:2006:0704JUD005945000, para. 117; ECtHR, *Öcalan v. Turkey*, CE:ECHR:2005:0512JUD004622199, para. 180.
215. Opinion of Advocate General Kokott in C-8/08 P, *T-Mobile Netherlands and Others*, EU:C:2009:110, paras 93-94: 'national courts may not ignore the typical characteristics of evidence adduced in determining infringements of the competition rules and must permit reference to be made to common experience when evaluating typical events'. Under Art. 102 TFEU, the doubt is about the effects being more than a 'mere hypothesis', *see* C-233/23, *Alphabet and Others*, EU:C:2025:110, para. 57. One may have a doubt whether the likelihood of something occurring is 60 or 80% but may have no doubt about the fact that the 'threshold' of capability is met.
216. Castillo de la Torre and Gippini Fournier, *supra* n. 25, para. 2.107.
217. C-8/08, *T-Mobile Netherlands and Others*, EU:C:2009:343.
218. C-377/20, *Servizio Elettrico Nazionale and Others*, EU:C:2022:379, paras 109-123.
219. C-74/14, *Eturas and Others*, EU:C:2016:42, paras 46-48.
220. In *SEN*, the Court of Justice gives extensive guidance on how to proceed with the assessment of the evidence in the particular case at hand (C-377/20, *Servizio Elettrico Nazionale and Others*, EU:C:2022:379, paras 87-103). In *Unilever*, the Court of Justice describes the types of evidence that the decision-maker must collect to sufficiently prove a case, and provides some guidance on the evidential 'dynamics' between the undertaking and the authority (C-680/20, *Unilever Italia Mkt. Operations*, EU:C:2023:33, paras 42, 44 and 59). In *EDP* the Court of Justice defines what it calls the 'standard of proof' regarding potential competition (C-331/21, *EDP – Energias de Portugal and Others*, EU:C:2023:812, para. 65).

reveals that it is fully aware that presumptions structure the evidentiary dynamics and provide predictability. It conveys the principle that the recognition of presumptions, even rebuttable ones, is a central question of law, somewhat embedded in the normative fabric of Article 102 TFEU. In practice, the existence of presumptions for the application of competition law should have a common answer throughout the EU.[221] Yet, while being part of such legal fabric, to the extent that they are evidentiary in nature, presumptions engage more directly with the presumption of innocence and other rights typically associated with the assessment of evidence.

5.3 Presumptions of (Capability of Producing) Exclusionary Effects

Some recent judgments (and their follow-ups) could be interpreted as questioning the use of presumptions in the context of the analysis of whether the conduct is capable of producing exclusionary effects.

The first one is *Intel I*. The circumstances of the case are well-known. The General Court considered in *Intel II* that the judgment in *Intel I* acknowledged the existence of a 'presumption' that some types of rebates have exclusionary effects (a 'mere presumption', as put by the General Court)[222] that the undertakings can rebut.[223] The case law moved from a substantive presumption (effectively, a legal rule) that appeared to define what the offence was based on the relevant conduct,[224] to an evidentiary

221. In the US doctrine, Gavil and Salop already point out that higher courts are better positioned to make judgments about presumptions, as lower courts may have less information about the probable categorical effects of conduct, and consider that 'the recognition of a presumption is a question of law' (*supra* n. 84, 2120).
222. T-286/09 RENV, *Intel Corporation v. Commission*, EU:T:2022:19, paras 124, 522. Also considering that *Intel I* provides for a presumption, *see* Opinion of Advocate-general Rantos in C-377/20, C-377/20, *Servizio Elettrico Nazionale and Others*, EU:C:2021:998, note 36. Although Opinion of Advocate-general Wahl in C-413/14 P, *Intel v. Commission*, EU:C:2016:788, refers to a 'presumption', in reality in his view the authority would be obliged to assess 'all the circumstances', *see* paras 73, 80, 119-120. The 'presumption' does not appear to have any operational value. In particular, para. 120 reads: 'to avoid over-inclusion, the assessment of capability as concerns presumptively unlawful behaviour must be understood as seeking to ascertain that, having regard to all circumstances, the behaviour in question does not just have ambivalent effects on the market or only produce ancillary restrictive effects necessary for the performance of something which is pro-competitive, but that *its presumed restrictive effects are in fact confirmed*. Absent such a confirmation, a fully-fledged analysis has to be performed' (emphasis added). Moreover, his view was that the effect must happen 'in all likelihood' (para. 117). It is simply not clear what fully-fledged analysis should be performed in this subsequent stage of the analysis when 'all the circumstances' of the case have already been taken into account in order to determine whether the presumptively anticompetitive effects are confirmed.
223. The judgment on appeal does not correct the language of the General Court on this point, and confirms that the Commission is under an obligation to assess the possible exclusionary effects 'only if that undertaking submits, during the administrative procedure, on the basis of supporting evidence, that its conduct was not capable of restricting competition and, in particular, of producing the alleged foreclosure effects' (C-240/22 P, *Commission v. Intel*, EU:C:2024:915, para. 144).
224. Monti, *supra* n. 116, at 121.

presumption (or a factual inference).[225] Leaving aside whether the different elements mentioned in paragraph 139 of the judgment of the Court of Justice in *Intel I* must be verified in every single case,[226] or whether it really makes sense to check all of them in all cases,[227] *Intel I* means in practice that the circumstances specific to the case will have to be scrutinised if the dominant undertaking tries to rebut the presumption by putting forward arguments and 'supporting evidence' to the effect that the conduct was not capable of restricting competition.[228] Yet, insofar as *Intel I* appears to accept some uses of presumptive reasoning, the practical effects of *Intel I* depend on how this evidential dynamics between the enforcer and the undertaking is understood in practice.[229]

The second judgment is *Unilever*. It is worth having a closer look at this judgment. The Court of Justice recalls the presumption of innocence and requires for the first time 'tangible' evidence of the 'actual capacity' to restrict competition.[230] The Court of Justice further stresses that 'although ... a competition authority may rely on the guidance from economic sciences, confirmed by empirical or behavioural studies, the taking into consideration of that guidance cannot, however, be sufficient'. It adds

225. Preferring to conceptualise *Intel I* and *Unilever* in terms of factual inferences, *see* Schweitzer and De Ridder *supra* n. 59, at 15-16, and note 186: 'Sometimes, these inferences are also referred to as "factual presumptions." To clearly distinguish factual inferences from legal presumptions, we exclusively use the term "factual inferences" ... . Contrary to "factual inferences," legal presumptions do not have a purely empirical, but (also, sometimes primarily) a normative basis (e.g. the goal to elicit information from the defendant or to react to the cost and/or difficulties of access to evidence).'
226. *See* critical, Monti, *supra* n. 116, at 128 and 139: 'from this economic perspective, the list provided by the ECJ is meaningless and the Court should have simply indicated that the Commission's task is to consider factors relevant to explaining the validity of the theory of harm advanced'; 'The stance taken by the GC in Intel appears somewhat rigid in requiring a fulfilment of all factors enumerated by the ECJ for the duration of the abuse. This formalistic approach is precisely the sort of legal translation of economics that leads to mistaken inferences.'
227. Monti, *supra* n. 116, at 138. The judgment of the General Court in *Google AdSense* confirms that it is not necessary to have a 'strategy' to exclude as efficient competitors, referring to settled case law (T-334/19, *Google and Alphabet v. Commission (Google AdSense for Search)*, EU:T:2024:634, paras 678-679, 883 and 981).
228. C-240/22 P, *Commission v. Intel*, EU:C:2024:915, paras 144, 180 and 277.
229. Schweitzer and De Ridder also consider that 'the case law on exclusionary abuses has not outright abandoned a reliance on simplifying rules that implicate an inference of anticompetitive effect, but that these rules have become more differentiated and sensitive to context within a structured proceeding' (*supra* n. 59, 7). The judgment of the Court of Justice in *Intel II*, that was aimed at clarifying the scope of the duty of the Commission in this regard, ended up being anchored on the nature and magnitude of errors found by the General Court. Yet, *Intel II* suggests that the Commission does not have to necessarily carry out additional enquiries, at least in some cases, but can limit itself to assess the evidence provided by the undertaking, *see* C-240/22 P, *Commission v. Intel*, EU:C:2024:915, para. 274: 'the Commission is entitled to base its assessment on the same premises and evidence as those submitted by the undertaking concerned, just as it may carry out its own analyses on the basis of other evidence obtained during its investigation'. *See also* para. 145, which appears to prevent applicants, in the context of an AEC test, from relying on evidence submitted for the first time in court proceedings.
230. C-680/20, *Unilever Italia Mkt. Operations*, EU:C:2023:33, paras 42 and 52 ('is actually capable of producing such effects'). The link in the sentence to 'beyond mere hypothesis' may imply that more than hypothetical effects will suffice to have 'actual capacity'. *See also* C-233/23, *Alphabet and Others*, EU:C:2025:110, para. 57.

that 'factors specific to the circumstances of the case ... must be taken into account when determining whether, in the light of that guidance, the conduct at issue must be regarded as having had, at least during part of the period during which it was implemented, the ability to produce exclusionary effects on the market concerned'.[231] *Unilever* appears to warn against excessive use of generalisations, as the authority must check that the background conditions justifying such tools are met in the specific case.[232] The Court of Justice leaves open the possibility of having unusual circumstances where effects would be hypothetical, and 'actual' and 'specific' capacity may simply mean that such capacity is 'beyond mere hypothesis'.[233] Yet, insofar as the fact that the judgment may suggest that it is for the authority, not for the undertaking, to verify that there are no such exceptional circumstances may shift the evidential dynamics to a considerable extent.

The judgment does not stop there. It explains that 'although, by reason of their nature, exclusivity clauses give rise to legitimate concerns of competition, their ability to exclude competitors is not automatic, as, moreover, is illustrated by [the Guidance]'.[234] This paragraph could be interpreted as establishing a presumption. However, it could also mean that no presumption may exist since the ability to exclude competitors is not 'automatic'. This would be odd. Presumptions are not based on the 'automaticity' of such ability. They may be based on the high likelihood that such ability exists or, in other words, that such ability exists in most cases. If the effect was 'automatically' caused by the conduct, we would logically have a substantive rule, not just a presumption. If exclusivity 'by nature' gives rise to 'legitimate concerns of competition', the legitimacy of such concerns can only be understood as expressing the likelihood of such ability arising, as well as indicating that exclusivity is not competition on the merits since it does not disclose anything about the 'quality' of the product or service in question (*see* section 6 below).

Subsequent paragraphs do not shed much light on the scope of burden-shifting. The Court rules that 'where that undertaking disputes, during the procedure, the specific capacity of those clauses to exclude equally efficient competitors from the market, with supporting evidence', then the authority 'must ensure, at the stage of classifying the infringement, that those clauses were, in the circumstances of the case, actually capable of excluding competitors as efficient as that undertaking from the market'.[235] This paragraph only states that if the Commission's case is contested, the

231. C-680/20, *Unilever Italia Mkt. Operations*, EU:C:2023:33, para. 44. In the same line, in *Superleague*, the Court of Justice recalls that the analysis must be made 'in the light of all the relevant factual circumstances ..., irrespective of whether they concern the conduct itself, the market(s) in question or the functioning of competition on that or those market(s)'. The demonstration that the conduct, at the very least, is capable of producing exclusionary effects must be made 'on the basis of specific, tangible points of analysis and evidence' (C-333/21, *European Superleague Company*, EU:C:2023:1011, para. 130).
232. C-680/20, *Unilever Italia Mkt. Operations*, EU:C:2023:33, para. 43: 'a competition authority cannot rely on the effects that that practice might produce, or might have produced, if certain specific circumstances had arisen, but which were not prevailing on the market at the time when that practice was implemented and which did not, at the time, appear likely to arise'.
233. *See supra* n. 230.
234. C-680/20, *Unilever Italia Mkt. Operations*, EU:C:2023:33, para. 51.
235. *Ibid.*, para. 52.

Commission must provide proof of its case, generally. This general statement stresses that the analysis must be specific ('in the circumstances of the case') but does not specify *how* to prove that capability to exclude competitors.

The Court of Justice considers that the duty also applies when the undertaking, without formally arguing that its conduct was incapable of restricting competition, maintains that there are justifications for its conduct.[236] Surely, in principle, if the undertaking justifies its conduct, the Commission must prove first that there is something to justify. However, this line of argument in *Unilever*, linked to a mere attempt to justify a conduct, appears to deviate from the situation under Article 101 TFEU, where the simple fact that the undertaking submits evidence to the effect that the conduct is covered by Article 101(3) TFEU does not trigger an obligation to examine the effects of the conduct, when the authority has initially qualified the conduct as restrictive by object.[237] I wonder if this part of *Unilever* really applies to all situations, and in particular abuses which may ultimately be considered as 'by object'. Moreover, if the evidence submitted in view of justifying the conduct is really weak, why should such weak evidence trigger any positive obligation to positively prove 'actual' and 'specific' capacity to produce restrictive effects? If the evidence shows no benefits in accordance with the demanding requirements of the case law,[238] why should anticompetitive effects still need to be demonstrated and weighed against non-existent benefits? In such case, it should be enough for the authority to provide an explanation as to why the evidence adduced to justify the conduct does not meet the legal requirements. In my view, an overall interpretation of the law implies that the duty to ascertain if the conduct, 'in the circumstances of the case', is 'actually capable of excluding competitors' only applies when the undertaking has met its own burden to prove such 'efficiencies'.

The Court of Justice adds that '[i]n any event, the submission, in the course of the procedure, of evidence capable of demonstrating the inability to produce restrictive effects gives rise to an obligation for the competition authority to examine that evidence'. This is explicitly based on the right to be heard, which means that the authority must pay due attention to the observations submitted by that undertaking, 'examining carefully and impartially all the relevant aspects of the individual case, and, in particular, the evidence submitted by that undertaking'.[239] Once again, the Commission cannot just dismiss that evidence out of hand, it must 'examine' it, where the approach focuses on the evidentiary process, rather than the substance (*see* section 4.3

236. *Ibid.*, para. 53.
237. *See* Joined Cases C-501/06 P, C-513/06 P, C-515/06 P and C-519/06 P, *GlaxoSmithKline v. Commission*, para. 63: 'for a finding that an agreement has an anti-competitive object, it is not necessary that final consumers be deprived of the advantages of effective competition in terms of supply or price'. In that case there was also an analysis of whether Art. 101(3) TFEU was applicable.
238. *See supra* nn. 138 to 142 and accompanying text.
239. C-680/20, *Unilever Italia Mkt. Operations*, EU:C:2023:33, para. 54.

above). While the rejection of an economic study must be reasoned,[240] nothing in *Unilever* suggests so far that some presumptions, let alone simple inferences that may shift the burden of proof, are now unlawful.

The legal standard for effects is 'capability' to produce effects, i.e., 'beyond mere hypothesis'.[241] It is logical to start the thought process by referring to some working assumptions, which indicate that a certain class of conduct, under some standard conditions, has a high probability of producing some exclusionary effect. To the extent that evidential completeness may help the dominant undertaking, it can be open to it to provide counterevidence to substantiate that the background assumptions for the generalisations on which the prospective analysis is based are not present in the instant case. The background knowledge that an evidentiary presumption typically embodies still constitutes the benchmark against which new specific evidence (both that provided by the undertaking and by the authority) must be assessed. The fact that the undertaking is trying to rebut a presumption does not mean that suddenly the prior probability of the conduct to restrict competition based on proof of *Fact A* has gone down to zero.

I do not think the case law stands in the way of this approach to evidential reasoning. *Unilever* may consider that general 'guidance' may not be 'sufficient', but it does not stand for the proposition that it must be altogether ignored as soon as we engage with case-specific evidence. The judgment makes it clear that the analysis of the specific circumstances of the case must be done 'in the light of that guidance', i.e., 'the guidance from economic sciences, confirmed by empirical or behavioural studies'. *Unilever* is about arguing that the presumption does not apply in the instant case since the background conditions for the application of the generalisation on which the presumption is based are not present ('certain specific circumstances'). *Unilever* is not about having to demonstrate everything as if background knowledge did not exist. Later in the judgment, the Court of Justice does not exclude that the Commission may prove its case after having 'examined' the economic study trying to prove the inability of the conduct to produce exclusionary effects.

Neither does *Intel I* stand in the way of giving weight, in the assessment of whether the conduct is capable of producing exclusionary effects, to the presumption that the conduct has a high exclusionary potential. We discussed before that the most recent case law suggests, by recognising the category of abuses 'by object', that the Court of Justice is ready to subject some type of conduct to a 'lighter' test of effects (or to legally presume effects altogether),[242] which necessarily implies the normative acceptance of some presumptive reasoning. Admittedly, *Intel* and *Unilever* leave unanswered critical questions about the evidentiary threshold that the dominant undertaking must meet to trigger the Commission's additional obligations. It is unclear what kind of supporting evidence is sufficient to challenge the presumption. Under

240. *Ibid.*, para. 55: 'the competent competition authority cannot exclude the relevance of that study without setting out the reasons why it considers that the study does not contribute to demonstrating that the practices in question were incapable of undermining effective competition on the relevant market'.
241. *Ibid.*, para. 42.
242. *See supra* nn. 143 to 146 and accompanying text.

some reading of *Intel I*, the mere fact that the undertaking provides some counterevidence is enough to somehow forget about the presumption and obliges the Commission to prove its case exclusively and entirely through case-specific evidence. I cannot see how that can be the case. The duty of the Commission to prove its case remains, but the amount of evidence necessary depends on the relevance and reliability of the case-specific evidence on which the undertaking is relying.[243] The evidentiary value of a presumption does not magically disappear as soon as any evidence, however weak, is provided in rebuttal.

Presumptions are not contrary to the duty to consider 'all the relevant factual circumstances' either. The decision-maker cannot approach any examination about the potential relevance of an element without having some prior, background knowledge. That non-case-specific knowledge is both clearly 'relevant' and in turn helpful to define what else can be 'relevant'. I find it somewhat contradictory to use the 'decision-theoretic' language of 'error costs' to avoid 'type 1' errors while pleading for an 'all-thing-considered', 'no priors' approach, which is to me the very opposite of decision theory.

The intensity of the duty to consider 'all the relevant factual circumstances' may be different in its practical implementation in each case.[244] There are several examples. The test of predatory pricing is built on a 'presumption' and there is 'no need for the

243. *Google Adsense* provides a precedent where the attempt to question the ability to restrict competition was unsuccessful on some points (T-334/19, *Google and Alphabet v. Commission (Google AdSense for Search)*, EU:T:2024:634). After recalling *Unilever* (*ibid.*, paras 663-664 and 667), the General Court considered that the evidence submitted by the applicant regarding the AEC test was insufficient to question the Commission's findings (*Ibid.*, paras 670-675, the decision was annulled for other reasons). While this suggests that in some cases a mere attempt to question those findings does not trigger a far-reaching obligation to demonstrate the case on the basis of case-specific evidence, and the Commission may simply explain why the supporting evidence submitted by the undertaking is insufficient, the fact that later in the judgment the General Court annulled the decision for insufficient examination of the duration of the exclusivity clauses makes it difficult to draw definitive conclusions on the scope of the duties of the Commission.

244. As we saw in s. 4, not everything can be relevant in every single case. On the contrary, it is settled case law that in the most egregious violations of competition law the analysis of context may be a very light one, and it is also common for such analysis to be part of the burden-shifting mechanism, so that it will be for the undertaking to show that there is something exceptional that would allow the decision-maker to deviate from the presumption. As regards, in particular, particularly serious infringements of the competition rules, such an examination may be limited to what is strictly necessary in order to establish the existence of a restriction of competition 'by object'. *See* C-373/14 P, *Toshiba Corporation v. Commission*, EU:C:2016:26, paras 31-34; C-469/15 P, *FSL and Others v. Commission*, EU:C:2017:308, paras 106-107; T-350/17, *Singapore Airlines and Singapore Airlines Cargo v. Commission*, EU:T:2022:186, paras 415-424 and 481-482; T-172/21, *Valve v. Commission*, EU:T:2023:587, para. 171. In the context of restrictions by object, the Court of Justice has recently ruled that 'the purpose of taking the context into account is thus to ascertain that no particular circumstance surrounding the agreement, decision or concerted practice at issue is such as to rebut the presumption that the form of coordination to which it belongs is harmful to competition' (C-298/22, *Banco BPN v. BIC Português and Others*, EU:C:2024:638, para. 48). The same should logically apply in the context of Art. 102 TFEU, for some types of conduct. The very existence of the possibility for the undertaking to justify its conduct shows that not 'anything' is initially relevant: by definition, the factual elements on which a justification is based are 'relevant' and still, they do not have to examined by the authority of its own motion.

Commission to undertake any analysis other than such a comparison of the prices charged by the dominant undertaking and of some of its costs'.[245] In other words, the rest is 'not relevant'. In *Qualcomm (predation)*, the General Court also held that the Commission was not required, when examining whether an undertaking in a dominant position charged predatory prices, to examine whether the share of the market covered by the contested practice is of sufficient magnitude for that practice to have anticompetitive effects,[246] even if the applicant claimed that such an obligation stemmed from the *Intel I* judgment.[247] The analysis of context was also quite light regarding the 'naked restrictions' in *Intel II*.[248]

While the need for presumptions should be rather uncontroversial, a different issue is whether specific presumptions are appropriate, relevant or strong enough. First, I have the impression that disagreements about the use of specific presumptions rarely turn on their evidentiary value (their aptitude to demonstrate that there is some probability that the conduct will have some specific type of effects), but rather on what the relevant effects are (foreclosure as opposed to milder forms of exclusion, or impact on the competitive process), how likely the effects must be (likely, as opposed to lower estimations of probability) and ultimately about the goals of competition law. The legal test becomes relevant here: proving *Fact A* may be enough to presume a detrimental impact on the competitive process, but not enough to presume harm to consumer welfare. Second, the strength of presumptions operates in a *continuum*: there are presumptions of varying 'strength', and some may be so 'soft' that the term should not be used. More specific presumptions, based on more than one observable or 'provable' element, may carry more weight than broadly delineated ones, as they integrate already some more specific, while still easily observable, factors.

Finally, one could yet wonder about the practical added value of presumptions. *Unilever* and *Intel I* present evidentiary shifts as a 'sequential' burden-shifting phenomenon: first, the Commission tries to rely on the typical effects of a certain type of conduct; second, the undertaking contests that presumption by submitting supporting evidence; third, the Commission reacts to it by relying (and maybe gathering) additional evidence, or if the evidence adduced by the undertaking is too weak, by explaining why this is so. The reality of decision-making does not necessarily follow that pattern. There is no formal ping-pong between the parties.[249] The presumption

245. T-671/19, *Qualcomm v. Commission*, EU:T:2024:626, para. 521.
246. *Ibid.*, para. 522. The *Qualcomm* judgment also recalls that the Commission is not 'required to respond specifically in the contested decision to all the observations of fact and law which it had raised during the administrative procedure' (para. 404).
247. *Ibid.*, para. 517.
248. *See supra* n. 144.
249. Castillo de la Torre and Gippini Fournier, *supra* n. 25, paras 1.035 and 2.053. As explained by Sibony and Barbier de la Serre, the evidential burden of proof does not change formally during the proceedings, the match is typically played as if both players were serving at the same time, and the judge would count the points at the end (A-L. Sibony and E. Barbier de la Serre, 'Charge de la preuve et théorie du contrôle en droit communautaire de la concurrence: pour un changement de perspective', 43(2) *RTD eur.*, 218 (2007)). From a US perspective, Kaplow explains very much the same thing: 'much evidence is expressly comparative; indeed, characterization evidence is relevant precisely to the extent that it bears differentially on competing understandings of the defendant's alleged act. Attempting to separate the two is

tends to act rather as a decision-making rule: at the end the decision-maker assesses whether case-specific evidence is strong enough to deviate from the presumption, weighing the strength of the presumption and the reliability of the additional, case-specific, evidence produced.[250] A strong presumption can only be rebutted by very reliable case-specific evidence.[251] And a weak one may be rebutted by less reliable evidence. The additional evidence may also in part tend to confirm the presumption.

In practice, to avoid delays, and depending on how the undertaking is expected to react, the Commission may not want to wait until the undertaking has been formally presented with a preliminary finding – regardless of whether it takes the form of a presumption or is simply a conclusion supported by sufficient evidence (typically in a statement of objections), to gather additional evidence. Since the Commission may have to rely on additional evidence if the undertaking tries to rebut a presumption (something that may not always be known in advance), the added value of a presumption could be limited in practice at least in some scenarios. However, such presumption, as a 'decision rule', helps the decision-maker to make a finding, where, once the enquiry is completed, and after supporting evidence has been submitted to try to prove that the conduct was not capable of producing exclusionary effects, it must make the call one way or the other.

6 REFOCUSING ON THE CONDUCT

6.1 The Analysis of the Conduct Still Matters

The 'more economic' approach has traditionally objected to the condition regarding the use of means or methods departing from competition on the merits by claiming that it is 'non-economic'.[252] In our 'law v facts' dichotomy, the notion of competition on the merits focuses on the conduct as a conceptually separate notion from its effects, and therefore it appears to be perceived as 'too legal' and (the worst sin of all) 'formalistic', if one considers that it implies some sort of value judgment of conduct based on categories or on the nature of the practice, which is conceptually independent of the analysis of the effect of the conduct.

However, the Court of Justice appears to remain unconvinced by the approach whereby the existence of an abuse depends exclusively on its effects. In practical terms, the analysis of the conduct may constitute the first filter of the analysis. It may reveal

artificial and fraught' (*supra* n. 201, at 995); that there is no actual shift in the evidentiary process during civil court proceedings: 'the factfinder, whether a judge or a jury, does not at any point during the trial announce that the plaintiff has won (or even has the lead) on step 1' (*ibid.*, at 1039).

250. As Salop puts it, 'the evidentiary rebuttal burden should be set at a level where the prediction of the outcome based on the case-specific evidence alone on balance is more reliable (i.e., more accurate) than the prediction based on the presumption alone' (n. 69, at 23).

251. Salop, *supra* n. 69, at 4. The strength may depend not only on the likelihood, but also the magnitude, of the effects. An effect that is likely but limited may not weigh the same as an effect that is less likely but it is significant. And the evidence that may rebut such presumption may also be different.

252. *See supra* nn. 121 to 126 and accompanying text.

whether the dominant undertaking is not competing 'on the merits', something that should lead to further, probably more detailed, examination of its potential effects. Nonetheless, the relevance of this condition does not mean that it is systematically examined in detail in each case. In some cases, there will be little debate about it, or the assessment is more implicit.[253] In some other cases absence of capability to produce effects will render unnecessary any examination of this issue. Some of the elements of the analysis may be relevant for both conditions, i.e., also when examining the capability to restrict competition.[254]

When the Court of Justice ruled in *SEN* that 'the abusive nature of a practice does not depend on the form it takes or took, but presupposes that the practice is or was capable of restricting competition and, more specifically, of producing, on implementation, the alleged exclusionary effects',[255] it was literally just saying that: that 'form' is not enough, and that the conduct must also be capable of restricting competition. Identifying 'form' as not a sufficient condition of a finding of abuse obviously does not transform 'form' into something irrelevant. Just a few paragraphs later, the Court of Justice itself refers to different 'forms' of conduct, in its analysis.[256] The case law also refers to some practices constituting autonomous or independent 'forms of abuse',[257] and the fact that they may have effects similar to a refusal to supply is irrelevant, showing once again that the type of conduct at stake (the 'form' so to speak) matters.

Although the 'more economic' approach advocates doing away with formalism, this is so only up to a point. When 'exclusivity rebates' are treated as 'pricing abuses' (and somewhat equated to lower prices),[258] and not as exclusive dealing, it means that the 'form' to achieve exclusivity (a contractual obligation as opposed to a rebate system which is conditional upon exclusivity) becomes crucial for the analysis. This formalism, undoubtedly favourable to dominant undertakings, can be said to be the opposite of an effects-based approach.[259]

253. In the same way as the fact that case law in the 1970s and 1980s did not always contain an elaborate discussion on effects did not mean that effects were irrelevant at the time. Form as such was never a reason to find an infringement of Art. 102 TFEU.
254. Moreover, when the case law has developed specific legal tests for some types of conduct, the test is supposed to already integrate and give shape to the general conditions for finding an abuse, i.e., absence of competition on the merits and capability to produce exclusionary effects.
255. C-377/20, *Servizio Elettrico Nazionale and Others*, EU:C:2022:379, para. 72.
256. *Ibid.*, para. 80.
257. C-52/09, *TeliaSonera Sverige*, EU:C:2011:83, paras 55-58; C-295/12 P, *Telefónica and Telefónica de España v. Commission*, EU:C:2014:2062, para. 75; C-42/21 P, *Lietuvos geležinkeliai v. Commission*, EU:C:2023:12, para. 91; C-48/22 P, *Google and Alphabet v. Commission (Google Shopping)*, EU:C:2024:726, para. 85.
258. *See*, Opinion of Advocate-general Wahl in C-413/14 P, *Intel v. Commission*, EU:C:2016:788, including rebates in the category of 'price based exclusion' (together with margin squeeze and predatory pricing) (para. 102).
259. Many authors have explained why this conceptual *rapprochement* between predation and exclusivity rebates is incorrect, since exclusionary rebates have little to do with other pricing abuses, such as predatory pricing (*see* Wils, *supra* n. 127, at 422-424; Fumagalli and Motta, *supra* n. 124, considering that exclusive dealing and practice that reference rivals (such as exclusivity rebates) should be presumed unlawful). The application of the AEC test 'as a rule' would be also formalistic as it prevents decision-makers from deciding based on other considerations (Lindeboom, *supra* n. 6, 866). *See* C-240/22 P, *Commission v. Intel*, EU:C:2024:915, para. 343, where the Court of Justice states that, since the AEC test is a

For some authors, the Court of Justice had shown over the last years a general 'indifference' to the exclusion or marginalisation of competitors which are less efficient.[260] The claim that the notion of conduct departing from competition on the merits had been abandoned was grounded on the case law according to which it is not the role of Article 102 TFEU to 'seek to ensure that competitors less efficient than the undertaking with the dominant position should remain on the market'.[261]

However, that view was always based on an obviously truncated quotation of the case law. The Court of Justice generally observed in *Post Danmark I*, *Intel I* and *SEN* that Article 102 TFEU cannot be relied on by less efficient undertakings as a shelter from 'competition on the merits' by the dominant undertaking. It does not follow that every finding of abuse is contingent on demonstrating that the conduct is capable of foreclosing an equally efficient competitor.[262] The general principle is simply that 'competition on the merits may, by definition, lead to the departure from the market or the marginalisation of competitors that are less efficient and so less attractive to consumers from the point of view of, among other things, price, choice, quality or

hypothetical exercise, whether the rivals are actually foreclosed is irrelevant. The AEC test may 'demonstrate that the contested rebates were, in breach of Article 102 TFEU, capable of foreclosing a competitor presumed to be as efficient as Intel in terms of costs, choice, quality and innovation, even if AMD had not itself been foreclosed, just as it may reveal the lack of such capability, despite the fact that one or other of the dominant undertaking's competitors left the market or was marginalised'.

260. Akman, *supra* n. 122, at 417, who proposes an interpretation of the notion of competition on the merits in terms of 'as-efficient competitor' principle. *See also* D. Neven, 'The As-Efficient Competitor Test and Principle. What Role in the Proposed Guidelines?', 14(8) *JECLP* 565-581 (2023) https://doi.org/10.1093/jeclap/lpad063. While Neven captures the essence of the case law ('when the conduct of the dominant firm does not lead to the marginalization of as efficient competitors but to the marginalization of less efficient ones, the criteria to identify a conduct as abusive is competition on the merit') he suggests that since the notion is not 'operational', the Commission should follow the notions as suggested by Advocate-General Rantos in *SEN* (p. 572), which in essence equates competition on the merits to anti-competitive effects. However, the judgment in *SEN* clearly deviates from that approach effectively refusing the approach suggested by the Advocate-General. Much of the economic literature tends to be relatively unpreoccupied by the fate of less efficient competitors, and rarely discuss the notion of competition on the merits, *see, inter alia*, A. Barbera, N. Fajardo Acosta, T. Klein, 'The Role of the AEC Principle and Tests in a Dynamic and Workable Effects-Based Approach to Abuse of Dominance', 14(8) *JECLP* 582-594 (2023) https://doi.org/10.1093/jeclap/lpad057.

261. C-209/10, *Post Danmark*, EU:C:2012:172, para. 21.

262. The few judgments in the 2010s (*Post Danmark I and II or Intel*) where the AEC test was invoked concerned pricing practices, where logically a level of price is not indicative of anything in isolation. Accordingly, the two conditions for finding an abuse 'collapse', since excluding an AEC is indication of the conduct departing from competition on the merits. But the fact that, for pricing abuses, the two conditions may somehow collapse does not mean that they do for any other type of conduct. Those judgments still mention prominently the notion of 'competition on the merits' (C-209/10, *Post Danmark*, EU:C:2012:172, para. 22; C-413/14 P, *Intel v. Commission*, EU:C:2017:632, paras 134 and 136). Moreover, while excluding a competitor that is 'as efficient' as the dominant undertaking is certainly a good indicator that the dominant undertaking is not competing on the merits, this does not mean that a dominant undertaking is competing on the merits when implementing any other conduct: it's not because 'when A then B' that 'B = A'.

innovation'.[263] This is totally uncontroversial. EU competition law has never been understood in any other way. The fallacy is the extrapolation of that *dictum* to draw a normative prescription that conduct (any conduct) cannot constitute an abuse *unless* it forecloses an equally efficient competitor. Declaring that something is *not* the purpose of Article 102 TFEU does not transform this 'irrelevant purpose' into the normative benchmark to examine every conduct or to delineate those who may rely on Article 102 TFEU.[264]

How this alleged 'AEC principle' has found its way into 'the mainstream', after the 'AEC test' appeared (very legitimately) first in certain types of price abuses,[265] still remains a mystery to me personally.[266] First, the reason for adopting the AEC test for certain pricing abuses was that it is more in line with legal certainty, as the dominant undertaking can conduct the test itself, given that the 'competitor' that can be excluded from the market is a hypothetical one. That advantage is not present for any other type of abuse. Second, who is 'as-efficient' today says little about the longer-term developments in the market, and we should be undoubtedly concerned about potential entrants that, by definition, cannot be said to be as efficient (or not) as the dominant undertaking. Third, efficiency also covers 'choice, quality or innovation', which cannot be captured by any AEC test. Competition decision-making and adjudication cannot be reduced to a discussion about how efficient the dominant undertaking and its competitors are, with the result that, if competitors are less efficient, we do not really care about the conduct, i.e., what the dominant undertaking actually did. Competition law regulates conduct. It is not aimed at deciding which rivals deserve to stay in the market. Yet, the expression 'as-efficient competitor' populates many paragraphs in recent judgments where, awkwardly, the expression does not appear to actually play any operational role, other than the application of the price-cost test for some types of abuse and, procedurally, the Commission's obligation to engage with the arguments to this effect submitted by the undertaking (*see* sections 4.2 and 4.3 above).

263. C-209/10, *Post Danmark*, EU:C:2012:172, para. 22; C-413/14 P, *Intel v. Commission*, EU:C: 2017:632, para. 134; C-377/20, *Servizio Elettrico Nazionale and Others*, EU:C:2022:379, para. 73.
264. In those very judgments, the Court of Justice also states that 'it is not the purpose of Article 102 TFEU to prevent an undertaking from acquiring, on its own merits, on account of its skills and abilities in particular, a dominant position on a market' (C-377/20, *Servizio Elettrico Nazionale and Others*, EU:C:2022:379, para. 73; C-680/20, *Unilever Italia Mkt. Operations*, EU:C:2023:33, para. 37) (adding 'or to ensure that competitors less efficient than an undertaking in such a position should remain on the market'). This 'non-objective' is, however, not the benchmark to assess the legality of the conduct.
265. The language of 'as efficient' competitor is used for the first time in cases relating to margin squeeze, *see* C-280/08 P, *Deutsche Telekom v. Commission* EU:C:2010:603; C-52/09, *TeliaSonera Sverige*, EU:C:2011:83.
266. Fumagalli and Motta, *supra* n. 124, 2: '[w]e also note that in some quarters the economic approach to abuse of dominance cases has been equated to the use of the (misleadingly named) "as efficient competitor test." We strongly disagree: the now vast body of economic knowledge on exclusionary practices clearly indicates that price-cost tests are useful when dealing with certain practices, but irrelevant or misleading with others'.

6.2 'Conduct Departing from Competition on the Merits' Is Not a Narrow Concept

It is of course always easier to dismiss a notion when it is first misinterpreted so that it becomes a strawman. On the basis of a very narrow interpretation of the concept of conduct departing from competition on the merits (which would only cover conduct that amounts to a 'mischief or a wrongful act', or something 'improper'), some academics dismiss the notion as they see the danger that the notion of competition on the merits may lead to a narrow definition of the concept of abuse.[267] I do not think that risk exists, because that narrow interpretation has never been the one adopted by the EU judicature. Indeed, while some dominant undertakings have pleaded for 'narrowing' the notion, these attempts have been unsuccessful so far.

The fear that the notion of competition on the merits would lead to a narrow interpretation of the concept of abuse is, in my view, often based on a very common error, namely the conflation between the notion of 'normal competition' and of conduct that non-dominant undertakings can implement. In the context of the analysis of whether the conduct departs from competition on the merits, the notion of 'normal competition' does not refer to conduct that is often implemented in the market at issue by undertakings that do not hold a dominant position.[268] On the contrary, dominant undertakings may have to refrain from engaging in certain practices that are unobjectionable for undertakings that do not hold a dominant position.[269] Such conduct is unobjectionable when implemented by non-dominant undertakings not because it is competition on the merits, but simply because the undertaking is not dominant. This is the central consequence of the special responsibility of dominant undertakings, which limits the means to compete that dominant undertakings have at their disposal.[270]

---

267. P. Ibáñez Colomo, 'Competition on the Merits', 61 *CML Rev.* 387-416, at 389, 390, 392, 393, 398 (2024) https://doi.org/10.54648/cola2024026. At 388, he refers to conduct which is not 'inherently sinister'.
268. *See* Opinion of Advocate-general Rantos in C-377/20, *Servizio Elettrico Nazionale and Others*, EU:C:2021:998: 'Indeed, a practice that is generally followed or business conduct which normally contributes to an improvement in the production or distribution of goods and which has a beneficial effect on competition may restrict such competition where it is engaged in by a dominant undertaking.' (para. 59); 'The expression "*normal* competition" is potentially confusing because practices which, usually, are lawful, ordinary and consistent with fair market practice and which could therefore be described as "normal" can, when adopted by an undertaking in a dominant position, nevertheless infringe Art. 102 TFEU as a result of the dominant undertaking's "special responsibility"' (note 33). Dominant undertakings are not handicapped by being prevented from using some practices, since Art. 102 TFEU assumes that such practices have a higher exclusionary potential when implemented by dominant undertakings. Typically, dominant undertakings draw large advantages from their dominant positions. That is why they are subject to a stricter legal regime under the Treaties (*see supra* s. 1).
269. *See, inter alia*, T-111/96, *ITT Promedia v. Commission*, EU:T:2010:266, para. 139; T-65/98, *Van den Bergh Foods v. Commission*, para. 159; C-42/21 P, *Lietuvos geležinkeliai v. Commission*, EU:C:2023:12, para. 107.
270. Recalling that special responsibility, *see* C-333/21, *European Superleague Company*, EU:C:2023:1011, para. 128; C-48/22 P, *Google and Alphabet v. Commission (Google Shopping)*, EU:C:2024:726, para. 163.

Therefore, whether the conduct departs from competition on the merits is not primarily about the 'purpose' of that conduct or about whether the conduct is also 'available to rivals' or 'replicable' by rivals,[271] even if, in my view, the 'purpose' and whether the conduct is not available to rivals may be indicative of conduct departing from competition on the merits.[272] For instance, tying was repeatedly described as conduct departing from competition on the merits in *Microsoft*,[273] without the General Court requiring the conduct to be 'improper', 'wrongful', 'abnormal' or 'sinister'. Freezer exclusivity was not considered 'improper' in *Van den Bergh Foods* and still was considered conduct departing from competition on the merits when implemented by a dominant undertaking.[274]

One may wonder if the condition is redundant since, once it is proven that a conduct by a dominant company causes harm to consumers, why is an additional condition necessary to find an abuse? Leaving aside that if there is proof that the conduct actually causes consumer harm, my intuition is that it is most likely not going to constitute competition on the merits,[275] the narrative is tempting but flawed. Those who consider the notion unnecessary for this reason also advocate for a very demanding test for effects, which is not about 'capability' to produce effects, but about 'likely' consumer harm. If one is very demanding for the condition regarding the effects, which is interpreted narrowly, it may be logical to advocate for the irrelevance of additional conditions. Under such an interpretation only a very limited number of cases could be pursued anyway, so no further limiting criterion would be needed. However, the threshold for effects is less demanding in EU law and therefore other factors must come into play to act as a 'filter' and differentiate anti-competitive exclusionary effect from exclusion which is the outcome of legitimate competitive conduct.

271. Ibáñez Colomo, *supra* n. 267, 393.
272. *See*, on the latter, C-377/20, *Servizio Elettrico Nazionale and Others*, EU:C:2022:379, paras 77-78, where the Court of Justice takes the non-replicability of the dominant undertaking's conduct as an indication that such conduct falls outside the scope of competition on the merits. By contrast, the Court (rightly) does not draw the opposite conclusion from the replicability of the dominant undertaking's conduct (*see*, in detail, Castillo de la Torre, *supra* n. 1, 187). The Court of Justice did not take over the language of the referring court, that mentioned conduct 'characterised by a specific "unlawful" component' (*see* para. 27).
273. T-201/04, *Microsoft v. Commission*, EU:T:2007:289, paras 407, 1046, 1048, 1069-1070.
274. T-65/98, *Van den Bergh Foods v. Commission*, EU:T:2003:281, paras 157-159.
275. One could imagine a scenario where, due the exercice of an entitlement (a property right, for example), a dominant undertaking causes consumer harm, but existing law would not consider such action abusive (as the exercice of a property right is only abusive under the *Bronner* criteria). In such case, the case law takes the long term into account, *see* referring to the *Bronner* test, C-233/23, *Alphabet and Others*, EU:C:2025:110, para. 42: 'in the long term, it is generally favourable to the development of competition and in the interest of consumers'. There will be limiting principles that exceptionally encroach upon that right to ensure the effectiveness of competition law. Such limiting principles will inform, in that context, what is an acceptable way to compete 'on the merits', when the means to exclude competition is the exercise of a legal entitlement. Such exceptional scenario shows that whether conduct consists in the exercise of some legal entitlements (the 'form' so to speak) is a relevant element in the analysis, even if economists may favour other approaches.

6.3 Competition on the Merits after *Google Shopping*

Several judgments link 'normal competition' to competition based on 'performance' and 'quality'.[276] The Court of Justice ruled in *SEN* that 'conduct which has the effect of broadening consumer choice by putting new goods on the market or by increasing the quantity or quality of the goods already on offer must, inter alia, be considered to come within the scope of competition on the merits'.[277] If the dominant undertaking's product or service is objectively better or has a lower price (absent predatory conduct), it is entirely normal that competitors are excluded, at least until they develop a better product or make their product available under more attractive conditions such as a lower price. By contrast, if the dominant undertaking uses some business strategies (often contractual, but not always) which are '*capable* of making it *more difficult* for competitors to enter or remain on the market in question',[278] beyond what would be the result of the quality of the dominant undertaking's product, that may be a problem.

Having an allegedly better product does not exonerate from liability, if the business practice at issue is unrelated to that quality and can have exclusionary effects.[279] Less efficient competitors may exit the market because of a practice that is in itself a reflection of the superior efficiency of the dominant undertaking, but the case law does not confer a right on the dominant undertaking to exclude competitors, by any means, just because it is more efficient than them.[280] While the effort to protect cost

276. C-62/86, *Akzo v. Commission*, EU:C:1991:286, para. 70; C-202/07 P, *France Telecom v. Commission*, EU:T:2009:214, para. 106; C-377/20, *Servizio Elettrico Nazionale and Others*, EU:C:2022:379, para. 75 (*see also* 'skills and abilities' at para. 73); C-209/10, *Post Danmark*, EU:C:2012:172, para. 24; C-42/21 P, *Lietuvos geležinkeliai v. Commission*, EU:C:2023:12, para. 107; T-111/96, *ITT Promedia v. Commission*, EU:T:1998:183, para. 138.
277. C-377/20, *Servizio Elettrico Nazionale and Others*, EU:C:2022:379, para. 85.
278. *Ibid.*, para. 61 (emphasis added); C-23/14, *Post Danmark (II)*, EU:C:2015:651, para. 31.
279. As the General Court held in T-155/06 *Tomra v. Commission*, EU:T:2010:370, para. 37: 'if that technology was really so markedly superior to that of their competitors that customers would never have purchased the latter's products anyway, it becomes even more difficult to explain the use of exclusivity agreements, quantity commitments and other individualised rebate schemes'. *Google Android* provides another good illustration, also stressing how important consumer choice is. The General Court held that 'even assuming that Google Search and Chrome are superior in terms of quality to the services offered by rivals' (a point on which the General Court did not take a definitive view), 'that would not be decisive since it is not claimed that the various services offered by the rivals are not technically capable of meeting consumer needs' (T-604/18, *Google and Alphabet v. Commission (Google Android)*, EU:T:2022:541, para. 577; appeal pending C-738/22 P). The General Court added that 'the needs of consumers are not necessarily met by what is qualitatively the best solution, assuming that Google might claim that its services represent such a solution, given that variables other than technical quality, such as the protection of privacy or the account taken of specific linguistic features of search queries, also play a role.' (para. 578). The General Court considered that 'in a situation such as' the one at hand, 'the Commission was not required to determine precisely whether those usage shares could be explained not only by pre-installation – as it believes – but also, or rather, by the superior quality claimed by Google' (para. 575, *see also* para. 583).
280. The simple fact that in the longer term a less efficient rival may exit the market as a result of inferior performance (what is not normally known at the time of the conduct) does not provide a justification for a dominant undertaking to 'push' it (artificially) out of the market, anticipating in time that possible exit through conduct of the dominant undertaking that as such does not reveal any superior performance.

reduction and successful innovation of the dominant undertaking is understandable,[281] this does not mean that we should not care about less efficient rivals if the impugned conduct is unrelated to such cost reduction or innovation.

Beyond pricing abuses where efficiency has a role to play in the analysis, the decision-maker's role should not be to examine the relative efficiency of the dominant undertaking and its competitors, in all relevant dimensions that efficiency may have. Even if the competitor is less efficient, the enquiry cannot stop there and ignore what the dominant undertaking actually did. Causation is not excluded when competitors are less efficient.[282] The focus on the efficiency of competitors has the somewhat perverse effect of redirecting the enquiry to those competitors as if they were the 'bad guys' in the story.[283] While an analysis of efficiency may be relevant for some types of abuses, the case law cannot have generally transformed the legal test into one of ascertaining who is the 'fittest' competitor and should therefore 'survive'.

In my view, the *Google Shopping* judgment of the Court of Justice confirms this approach. The Court of Justice rejects a narrow concept of competition on the merits, advanced by Google. The relevant factual circumstances to examine if conduct departs from competition on the merits 'include not only those that concern the conduct itself, but also those that concern the market or markets in question or the functioning of

281. Barbera et al., *supra* n. 260, referring to the 'appropriability' of dynamic competition (at 583-584).

282. *See*, for the view that causal link does not exist when competitor is less efficient, Ibáñez Colomo, *supra* n. 267, 403. However, the analysis of efficiency is not the necessary consequence of the requirement of the existence of a causal link. Arguing that the dominant product was better anyway, has never been accepted as an argument to exclude causation (*see supra* n. 279). In *SEN*, in examining causation, the Court of Justice did not require or suggest conducting a counterfactual analysis, as the conduct made it 'impossible' to ascertain the 'objective causes' for the differences in the lists. The existence of a bias, proven through behavioural studies, was enough (C-377/20, *Servizio Elettrico Nazionale and Others*, EU:C:2022:379, paras 98-99). Moreover, the Court of Justice considered that its conclusion could not be put into question by 'the actions that competitor undertakings potentially took or could have taken, such as purchasing files from third parties containing information on customers in the protected market, in order to limit the harmful consequences of that practice' (para. 102). *See also*, to the same effect, C-233/23, *Alphabet and Others*, EU:C:2025:110, para. 58: 'whether the conduct at issue is abusive cannot depend on the ability of competitors on the market concerned to mitigate such effects'. The Court of Justice ruled in *Google Shopping* that a counterfactual analysis is *not* the only way to prove causation (C-48/22 P, *Google and Alphabet v. Commission (Google Shopping)*, EU:C:2024:726, paras 228-229). In *AstraZeneca*, the General Court also found, in another part of the judgment, that conduct remains an abuse even if the dominant undertaking could hypothetically have engaged in other conduct (even lawful one) that would also have been capable of restricting competition. The mere existence of such hypothetical alternative conduct does not mean that the conduct actually implemented by the dominant undertaking was incapable of restricting competition (T-321/05, *AstraZeneca v. Commission*, EU:T:2010:266, para. 836).

283. It is not for rivals to defend themselves against accusation of inefficiency. As W. Wils has put it: 'Like the Gosplan in the Soviet Union, competition authorities thus decide which producers are deemed efficient enough to be allowed onto the market. This is fundamentally at odds with the philosophy underlying the EU Treaties.' (n. 127, at 432). *See also* M. Adam and F. Maier-Rigaud, 'The Law and Economics of Article 82 EC and the Commission Guidance Paper on Exclusionary Conduct' *Zeitschrift für Wettbewerbsrecht*, 131 (2009) https://doi.org/10.15375/zwer-2009-0108: 'Following an equally efficient competitor test ... would amount to the paternalistic assumption that consumers are wrongly buying from less efficient competitors and that dominant firms therefore need to be called in to restore market efficiency' (at 139).

competition on that or those market(s). Thus, circumstances relating to the context in which the conduct of the undertaking in a dominant position is implemented, such as the characteristics of the sector concerned, must be regarded as relevant'.[284] This contextual approach is not unproblematic in some cases. While it appears that the notion of conduct departing from competition on the merits does not consist of a list of practices that dominant undertakings must not use, one could argue that a purely contextual, case-by-case approach provides less guidance on what constitutes competition on the merits. However, one must interpret this part of the judgment as a reply to Google's argument, according to which only the 'nature' (or the form) of the conduct mattered for the examination. This is certainly not the case, as it is clear when abuses are related to prices or product design since price or design as such are not indicative of anything in isolation. In other words, the notion of conduct departing from competition on the merits does not depend on its form alone.[285]

Moreover, the Court of Justice does not stop there. It later explains that the circumstances relied upon in the instant case were relevant for the purpose of classifying the practices at issue in law 'since they enabled those practices to be placed in the context of the two relevant markets and the functioning of competition on those markets and were thus capable of demonstrating that potential exclusionary effects on the downstream market, namely, that of specialised comparison shopping search services, and the success of Google's comparison shopping service on that market since the implementation of those practices, referred to in the decision at issue, were due not to the merits of that service but to those practices combined with the specific circumstances identified'.[286] It is to be noted here how the Court of Justice examines the effects through the prism of whether the potential effects (in the instant case, the success of Google's comparison shopping service) were due to the 'merits of the service' or to the conduct, in its context. The expression 'merits of the service' evokes the idea of competition based on quality and performance, as opposed to one based on business practices unrelated to the quality of the product or service.[287]

Therefore, while the analysis is contextual, *Google Shopping* also provides guidance on the criteria to use. The lack of a general definition of 'conduct departing from competition on the merits' did not appear to be a major obstacle to deciding the case. The enquiry must not be about examining in the abstract if a product or service is better (whether it is cheaper is a more objective feature). The authority should not assess who is the most efficient competitor, or who has the best product. It should focus on whether the conduct reflects such efficiency or quality, which is a different matter. Admittedly, such analysis may not always be straightforward, when the

284. C-48/22 P, *Google and Alphabet v. Commission (Google Shopping)*, EU:C:2024:726, para. 168.
285. '[D]epending on the circumstances of a case, almost any type of otherwise normal commercial conduct can be turned into an instrument of anticompetitive exclusion by a dominant undertaking, including price competition, product design, or innovation' (Schweitzer and De Ridder, *supra* n. 59, 11).
286. C-48/22 P, *Google and Alphabet v. Commission (Google Shopping)*, EU:C:2024:726, para. 171.
287. Or arguably to an increase in output, to the extent that *SEN* also refers to an increase in 'quantity' as coming 'within the scope of competition on the merits' (C-377/20, *Servizio Elettrico Nazionale and Others*, EU:C:2022:379, para. 85).

conduct may also be interpreted as providing a product or service under better conditions for the customers. As some authors have rightly put it, competition on the merits 'stands for the general idea that, first, dominant undertakings shall compete on account of their skills, abilities, and superior performance, striving to offer consumers the best value for money or most attractive product or deal instead of competing by obstructing their competitors' effective access to markets, resources, data, or customers or by otherwise creating competitive disadvantages for actual or potential rivals'.[288]

The *Google Shopping* judgment has also helped to put an end to some misunderstandings on the 'as efficient' competitor approach (both the 'principle' and the 'test') described above. The Court of Justice, repeating language in *Superleague*, first considers that effects refer 'as a rule' to 'the actual or potential effect of restricting that competition by excluding equally efficient competing undertakings from the market or markets concerned, or by hindering their growth on those markets', while adding immediately that the effects also cover 'impeding potentially competing undertakings at an earlier stage, through the placing of obstacles to entry or the use of other blocking measures or other means different from those which govern competition on the merits, from even entering that or those market(s) and, in so doing, preventing the growth of competition therein to the detriment of consumers, by limiting production, product or alternative service development or innovation'.[289] However, one cannot infer from this that 'existing not-as-efficient' competitors are fair game for the dominant undertaking. On the contrary, the Court explains that 'it does not follow' from the fact that the objective of Article 102 TFEU 'is not to ensure that competitors less efficient than the dominant undertaking remain on the market', that 'any finding of an infringement under that provision is subject to proof that the conduct concerned is capable of excluding an as-efficient competitor'.[290]

The assessment of the capability of the conduct at issue to foreclose an as-efficient competitor is relevant 'where the dominant undertaking submitted, during the administrative procedure, on the basis of supporting evidence, that its conduct was not capable of restricting competition and, in particular, of producing the alleged foreclosure effects'.[291] However, such 'relevance' appears to be more procedural than substantive in the sense that the authority must assess the submissions, but it does not mean that it is bound to accept the arguments of the undertaking. One possible

288. Schweitzer and De Ridder, *supra* n. 59, 11. 'If the antitrust law serves to eliminate distortions in competition, then, in theory, the firms with better quality goods and cheaper prices will win out' (Wu, *supra* n. 68, 10).

289. C-48/22 P, *Google and Alphabet v. Commission (Google Shopping)*, EU:C:2024:726, paras 165 and 167. *See also* C-333/21, *European Superleague Company*, EU:C:2023:1011, paras 129 and 131; C-233/23, *Alphabet and Others*, EU:C:2025:110, para. 54.

290. C-48/22 P, *Google and Alphabet v. Commission (Google Shopping)*, EU:C:2024:726, paras 263-264. *SEN* is also quite clear on this point. Nowhere in its reply to the third question, concerning the capability of producing effects, does the Court refer in *SEN* to the efficiency of competitors affected by the exclusionary effects. The Court's answer to the first question suggests that the efficiency of hypothetical competitors is, at least for certain types of conduct, an issue that pertains to the condition for a finding of abuse regarding the use of means not based on competition on the merits rather than to the condition regarding the capability of exclusionary effects (C-377/20, *Servizio Elettrico Nazionale*, EU:C:2022:379, paras 78-82).

291. C-48/22 P, *Google and Alphabet v. Commission (Google Shopping)*, EU:C:2024:726, para. 265.

criterion may be, *inter alia*, 'the as-efficient competitor test, where that test is relevant, its assessment of the relevance of such a test being, where appropriate, subject to review by the EU judicature'.[292] The Court of Justice does not explain further when such test is relevant. The judgment just decides the case at hand. Despite Google having submitted during the administrative procedure that its conduct was not capable of restricting competition and submitting that the 'AEC principle' should be applied, the Court of Justice concludes that the Commission was not obliged to provide proof of exclusion of an as-efficient competitor or to apply the AEC test.[293] In other words, while the Commission must engage with any argument to the effect that the conduct does not foreclose as-efficient competitors, and provide reasons in its decision on that point, that does not mean that it is bound to prove that the conduct can exclude as-efficient competitors. The mere allegation is not enough to render the standard or the test relevant. Ultimately the Court of Justice agrees with the General Court that the AEC test was neither 'mandatory in the context of the application of Article 102 TFEU' nor relevant 'in the circumstances of the present case'.[294] In actual practice, the Court of Justice has not found so far that the 'test' would be relevant beyond pricing practices and appears to be irrelevant regarding new entrants. So, the initial 'rule' is devoid of much content, to the point that the observer may wonder if there is a 'rule' at all, since it does not appear to create any 'mandatory' test, and its relevance is decided on the basis of a case-by-case examination.

7 SOME FINAL THOUGHTS

Recent jurisprudential trends in the enforcement of Article 102 TFEU have created some uncertainty and indeterminacy about what Article 102 TFEU really prohibits, and how to prove it. The 'clarification' in *Intel I* did not really render the law more comprehensible, or the delineation of prohibited conduct more predictable. Admittedly, many elements in the interpretation of Article 102 TFEU have resisted the pressure for change. Nonetheless, the lack of clear distinction between the rhetorical language of goals, efficiency and merits and operational guidance on legal tests to find an infringement, on the one hand, and the use of standards that foster evidentiary and procedural complexity, on the other, make enforcement increasingly difficult and unpredictable, at least for some types of practices.

The current emphasis on the completeness of the enquiry and the 'all things considered' assessment, clothed in the language of fundamental rights, assumes a background of systemic epistemological doubt about the ability of decision-makers to distinguish between conduct that undermines competition and conduct that promotes it. It also undermines the generality of the law in favour of more ad hoc adjudication, with greater scope for disagreements about the assessment of 'all the relevant factual circumstances' and accordingly with less predictable outcomes. It is questionable whether this ad hoc 'all the relevant factual circumstances' assessment really reduces

292. *Ibid.*, para. 266.
293. *Ibid.*, paras 267-268.
294. *Ibid.*, para. 269.

'error costs', optimises the normative design, and brings about more economically literate outcomes, because the disputes of an economic nature are ultimately decided by generalist judges, and 'error costs' tend to be actually unknowable. While it is understandable that the case law increasingly required a somewhat more explicit and explainable story linking the conduct to its possible effects (a 'theory of harm', but where harm is not necessarily equated to 'consumer harm'), the related loss of 'substance' or 'density' in the law is problematic to me.

It is not just that process may be prevailing over substance. The creeping language of 'efficiency', theoretically providing some objective benchmark, is also puzzling. Turning adjudication into an analysis of the relative efficiency of the dominant undertaking and its competitors, where the conduct does not really matter if competitors are less efficient, is not only overtly complex but, in my personal view, also not warranted, outside some pricing abuses, under any reasonable interpretation of the law. While this approach has logically not been generally accepted so far by the EU judicature, as it would transform decision-makers into arbiters of who deserves to stay in the market, the case law contains language about efficiency whose operational value remains uncertain.

Competition law must remain recognisable 'as law'.[295] While it is ultimately for the Court of Justice to provide a final and authoritative interpretation of the law, the Commission ought to play an important role in preserving core elements of 'lawness' in this area, through its decision-making and, if need be, by adopting general documents, guided by the *effet utile* of the enforcement of EU competition law. By identifying core principles and systematising the case law, without being distracted by the language of every paragraph of every judgment, it must be possible to separate operational principles, both substantive and evidentiary, from context-specific findings or statements, and rhetorical language.

Such efforts ought to build on the finding that there is no contradiction between 'evidence-based' decision-making and using presumptions or inferences that structure the debate under some scenarios. Evidence alone does not deliver legal decisions. It is the production and assessment of evidence, guided by clear substantive laws and fair processes, that leads to legal outcomes. And considering 'all the relevant factual circumstances' in the abstract, without having a clear understanding of how the law guides the determination of 'relevance', is a recipe for 'lawless' competition enforcement. Abandoning legal rules in favour of 'facts' is not neutral.

We saw above that in the optimal normative design, the existence of burden-shifting schemes and justifications is important. To the extent that the case law has accepted, departing from the text of Article 102 TFEU, the existence of possible justifications for the restrictive conduct, and the hesitations in applying presumptions in the assessment of the capability to restrict competition are misplaced. In EU competition law, by stressing that capability to produce at least potential effects is

295. In my view, striking the right balance must start by giving due weight to the fact that EU competition law is law, and therefore it must deploy features (yes, sometimes 'formal' features) that law typically, if not always, displays. As Lindeboom has put it 'legal language has an inherent commitment to form' (*supra* n. 6, 836).

sufficient to prove the infringement, the case law reflects the view that some uncertainty is *normatively acceptable* and that such effects may not actually happen. The risk of 'false positives' or overinclusiveness that some may see embedded in the notion of competition on the merits or in the use of presumptions is compensated by the possibility both to prove that the presumption does not apply in the specific case (with enough case-specific evidence to confidently deviate from the prior that the presumption represents) and to justify the conduct by demonstrating that it *actually* benefits consumers and it is necessary to achieve those benefits.[296] When the alleged benefits can be obtained in less restrictive ways, the reasons not to prohibit the conduct decline, even if the restrictive effect is not particularly pronounced or probable. A reasonably inclusive interpretation of the capacity to produce effects and the application of burden-sharing schemes between the authority and the dominant undertaking strikes the right balance, whereas a demanding approach to such capacity would lead to underinclusiveness, without any compensating mechanism.[297]

Fundamental rights are not an obstacle to this restructuring effort. I do not see why the presumption of innocence, the right to be heard or the right to an impartial examination should prevent the development of rules, 'analytical templates', and strong or soft presumptions, where appropriate. Such principles are not incompatible with clarity and predictability.

The efforts that I mention are not easy. They imply evaluative assessments and interpretative choices. Any interpretation is likely to be contested by dominant undertakings and their advocates which may well find some language in one judgment that may suggest that a different interpretation is possible. Any hint that the public enforcer may be able to rely on a lighter test for effects or on presumptions, even soft ones, is at risk of being dismissed by critics as the last relic of 'formalism' or as the enforcer taking short-cuts. Some may reiterate that the correct legal approach is for each case to be assessed from an epistemic *tabula rasa*, adjudicating on the basis of 'case-specific' evidence and taking into account a long, open-ended list of 'all the relevant factual circumstances'.

In practice, this is even more challenging because dominant undertakings have nowadays a large influence in shaping the public debate. The financial means of those who are today the possible targets of investigations in some economic sectors are manifold those under suspicion of committing abuses two or three decades ago. Such financial means are not only used to look for the best representation and defence in

296. *See also*, in similar sense, Schweitzer and De Ridder, *supra* n. 59, 20; Castillo de la Torre and Gippini Fournier, *supra* n. 25, para. 1.089; C-377/20, *Servizio Elettrico Nazionale and Others*, EU:C:2022:379, paras 84-86. Admittedly, the way in which the case law has sometimes formulated the test regarding benefits for consumers as connected to the notion of competition on the merits creates some degree of circularity that future case law should address.

297. On the risk of adopting the wrong decision if the standards regarding harm are too high, in situation where benefits may be lower than the harm anyway, *see* Kaplow, *supra* n. 201, at 1000 and 1044. Going back to the exclusivity rebates, it is clear that the same benefit for consumers, by way of lower prices, may be obtained by rebates that would have less potential for exclusionary effects (i.e., of the type that is normally considered uncontroversial). Declaring conditional rebates abusive unless objectively justified may be more efficient that allowing conditional rebates without even examining if there is an objective justification.

cases (those undertakings are also better prepared to engage in the most complex evidentiary scenarios, their preferred battling ground)[298] but also to shape the public debate outside the courts (but with a view to influence judicial interpretations), rarely by the undertakings directly of course.[299]

At present, the case law gives rise to questions regarding what 'standards' to apply in Article 102 TFEU, what the Commission must prove, how to engage with arguments raised by the dominant undertakings in their defence, and what the analysis of 'all the relevant factual circumstances' means in actual practice. As market power has increased across the economy, the clarity of rules – and hence compliance with the rules and enforcement by all sorts of authorities – may be nosediving. The result could be an increase in anticompetitive behaviour exactly when we would want to push for this behaviour to be constrained and controlled.

298. *See*, on how complex standards and ad hoc adjudication favour those with deeper pockets, *supra* n. 27.

299. *See* Lianos, *supra* n. 50, 34 and 36 ('the development and defence of particular theoretical positions in academic forums becomes an integral component of establishing legitimacy for courtroom arguments'; 'Large digital platforms occupy a uniquely influential position in competition economics through their dual role as major consumers of forensic services and significant funders of academic research. … This dual market presence enables these platforms to effectively orchestrate substantial resources and shape the production of knowledge and discourse in competition economics. … The ability to simultaneously influence both academic research directions and forensic economic analysis creates risks for the independent development of competition theory and practice'); Ezrachi explains that capture that is not case or industry specific but rather concerns the regulatory framework is 'often inconspicuous' and, when successful, it is perfect: 'the subjects of this capture will operate within what they perceive to be a clearly defined framework. They would often do so with a sense of purity and with little awareness of the sophistication with which the trusted framework in which they operate has been affected by interested parties' (*supra* n. 28, 71); AAG Jonathan Kanter's Remarks for the Fordham Competition Law Institute's 51st Annual Conference on International Antitrust Law and Policy (https://www.justice.gov/archives/opa/speech/assistant-attorney-general-jonathan-kanter-delivers-remarks-fordham-competition-law-0 (last accessed 22 July 2025)): 'All over the world, money earmarked specifically to discourage antitrust and competition law enforcement is finding its way into the expert community upon which we all depend'; Broulík, *supra* n. 50; Editorial in *CML Rev*, *supra* n. 79; T. Valletti, '"Doubt is Their Product": The Difference Between Research and Academic Lobbying', https://www.promarket.org/2020/09/28/difference-between-research-academic-lobbying-hidden-funding/ (last accessed 22 July 2025). Literature by economic consultants is sometimes mentioned in opinions of Advocates-general. For example, in the Opinion in *Intel I*, only one article is mentioned as representative of 'contemporary economic literature', and the article is written by a professor and consultant in one of the most well-known economic consulting firms (*see* Opinion of Advocate-general Wahl in C-413/14 P, *Intel v. Commission*, EU:C:2016:788, para. 94 and footnotes 64 and 70).

PART II Market Definition and Dominance

CHAPTER 7

Revisiting Market Definition While Revisiting Abuse of Dominance: Power and Methods in the Twenty-First Century

Magali Eben[*]

1 INTRODUCTION

It is safe to say that 2024 has been a watershed year for guidance on abuse of dominance. The European Commission proposed draft Guide*lines* on exclusionary abuses of dominance under Article 102 TFEU, after its initial amendment to its Guid*ance* on enforcement priorities and its adoption of a policy brief in 2023. But the Guidelines were not the only treat the Commission gave the competition law community: earlier in the year, the Commission also published the long-awaited final text of the revised Market Definition Notice. These documents are portrayed as consolidations and interpretations of the decisional practice and case law,[1] yet they cannot entirely be divorced from the broader context of debate about the relevance of competition law for society. These new guidance documents come at a time of significant re-thinking of the value of competition policy, and a broader concern about the need to fight economic power, in Europe and beyond. The conceptualisations of economic power – and what

* Thank you to the participants in the Global Competition Law Centre (GCLC)'s 19th annual conference for their comments. All errors are my own. In accordance with the ASCOLA Declaration of Transparency and Disclosure, I confirm that I have no conflicts to declare.

1. Draft Communication from the Commission, Guidelines on the application of Article 102 of the Treaty on the Functioning of the European Union to abusive exclusionary conduct by dominance undertakings (2024) (hereafter 'Draft Guidelines') para. 9; Commission Notice on the definition of the relevant market for the purposes of Union competition law OJ C, C/2024/1645, 22.2.2024 (hereafter 'Revised Notice') para. 3.

the concerns are which lead policymakers to want to control the exercise of that power in the first place – may be changing. If competition policy cares about more than market power and consumer welfare, this may call for a parallel reconsideration of the approach to drawing the boundaries of relevant markets. It is not clear yet how exactly the relationship between competition policy and economic power will evolve in the years to come. Yet, even though these discussions did not provide the explicit rationale for guidance (nor lead to visible material changes), they provide the backdrop against which to assess any policy documents. This chapter takes this context as the backdrop for its analysis, raising a few questions about the relationship between (market) power and market definition. As this chapter argues, the concept of power used to enforce the law represents a particular understanding of the harm the law ought to address. Market definition is intrinsically related to this power and thus these harms, which are also expressed in the tools and methodologies used to define relevant markets. If the concept of exercise of power changes, market definition might need a rethink.

First, the chapter reviews the Revised Market Definition Notice to consider its changes within the broader debate about the enduring relevance of market definition and its various purposes. Second, the chapter sets out the relationship between market definition and various understandings of power and the concerns about the exercise of power. Third, the chapter contextualises the draft guidelines against these ways of thinking about power, and thus its implications for how market definition can develop further.

This chapter is structured as follows. Section 2 examines the enduring relevance of market definition, exploring its legal sources, its purposes, and ongoing critiques. It considers that market definition serves not merely as a tool for establishing market power, but as a broader framing device within which to understand the analysis of the conduct and theory of harm. Section 3 investigates the relationship between market definition and economic power, reflecting that different conceptions of the exercise of power – and the associated harms – might influence the approach taken to market definition, and vice versa. Methodologies adopted to define relevant markets are not content-neutral, they shape and are shaped by the theories of harm in the analysis. Market definition cannot be evaluated properly unless the concerns about economic power at the heart of the law are fully understood. Therefore, section 4 attempts to provide a start to exploration, contextualising these discussions on market definition within the framework of abuse of dominance. It reflects on the notion of dominance in the European Union, tracing the evolution of the European Commission's approach and assessing its latest draft Guidelines. Finally, section 5 reflects on the future trajectory of market definition in light of contemporary shifts in competition policy, particularly as more varied concerns about economic power take centre stage (again). This chapter intends to shine a light on an area where there is currently too much obscurity: the relationship between the exercise of power and the chosen approach to market definition. It asks readers to consider that, if the perspectives on abuse of dominance were to change, it may be necessary to (re)consider market definition in more depth too.

2 THE ENDURING RELEVANCE OF MARKET DEFINITION

2.1 Market Definition in EU Competition Law

Article 102 TFEU, the provision on abuse of dominance in the European Union (EU), does not explicitly require market definition, nor describe its methodology. The law on market definition can be found in the jurisprudence of the General Court (which hears appeals against Commission decisions) and, to a more limited extent, the Court of Justice. Given the wide margin of discretion afforded to the Commission by the Courts, most of the guidance on market definition can be found in the decisional practice of the European Commission, and in its Notice on Market Definition, which applies to all competition law provisions.[2] While the identification of markets has long been a feature of competition law cases, how strictly the boundaries of a market have been identified has varied over time.[3] As will be shown in section 3, the methodology adopted has evolved historically, being shaped not only by the prevailing understandings of injurious use of power but also by the import of US thinking into EU enforcement.

The conceptual economic frameworks adopted for market definition mostly find their origin in the tests developed for merger control in the United States of America ('US' hereafter) (as discussed in section 3 of this chapter). Unsurprisingly, therefore, the quantitative methodologies used share commonalities across the Atlantic. Market definition existed in some capacity, however, before the introduction of such frameworks as the 'Hypothetical Monopolist Test' and before the introduction of econometric tests. Even now, the Commission often relies on 'qualitative' market definition, referring to product characteristics, intended usage or customer preferences, without reliance on econometric or statistical tools.[4] The conceptual frameworks and methods used to define relevant markets cannot be divorced from the purposes of market definition and, ultimately, from the goals of the competition law provisions.

There is increasing reflection in scholarship on the purpose of market definition. The most widely accepted rationale for market definition is that it provides a basis for establishing market power. At the same time, a few scholars question the narrative which focuses on markets as tools solely for the findings of market power.[5] In many

2. In the EU, the guidance on market definition can be found in a single document applicable to all provisions, as opposed to other jurisdictions such as the US where market definition may be discussed in a specific context, such as merger control. The Commission's Notice on Market Definition applies to both Arts 101 and 102 TFEU, as well as merger control.
3. For an insightful overview of the arrival of modern market definition in EU competition law, *see* Miguel Sousa Ferro, *Market Definition in EU Competition Law* (Edward Elgar 2019) 2-8.
4. Revised Notice, *supra* n. 1, para. 31, paras 48-50. Indeed, both the Notice and the jurisprudence of the Court of Justice of the EU confirms that the SSNIP test, in its particular expression of the Hypothetical Monopolist Test, is only one approach the Commission can take to market definition. *See* Case T-70/10, *Feralpi Holding v. Commission* EU:T:2014:1031, para. 188.
5. David Glasner and Sean Sullivan, *The Logic of Market Definition*, 83 Antitrust Law Journal 293 (2020); Magali Eben, *The Antitrust Market Does Not Exist: Pursuit of Objectivity in a Purposive Process*, 17(3) Journal of Competition Law & Economics 586 (2021) https://doi.org/10.1093/joclec/nhab001; Viktoria Robertson, *A New Era for Antitrust Market Definition*, 1 Concurrences

cases, a finding of market power is a legal requirement.[6] When market shares are used as proxies for market power, market definition may seem unavoidable, since market shares cannot be calculated without reference to a market.[7] This wrongly conflates the requirement of market power with a requirement of market definition, however. Market definition is only central to market power if enforcers rely on market shares to calculate it.[8] There has been considerable scepticism that market power could be measured directly in a legally meaningful way,[9] yet many stakeholders have argued for direct measurements of market power instead of indirect measurements through market shares.[10] If market power could be established directly, market definition could be avoided for this purpose.

Yet direct calculations of market power would not render market definition obsolete. Even where market power could be established directly, market definition still has a role to play in competition law. Market definition endures because of its value as a narrative tool.[11] Relevant markets have an important framing function: market definition provides a tool to draw the boundaries within which to assess and collect evidence, to provide a better understanding of the economic context of the conduct and its impact.[12] Market definition can indeed enable the calculation of market shares, but it has merit beyond this purpose: it provides a tool to draw the boundaries within which to assess the feasibility of the alleged conduct, theory of harm and anti-competitive effects alleged.[13] Crucially, this need not be a binary choice between the market power function of market definition and its framing function.[14] After all, the harms addressed

84 (2021); Rupprecht Podszun, *The Arbitrariness of Market Definition and an Evolutionary Concept of Markets*, 61(1) The Antitrust Bulletin 121 https://doi.org/10.1177/0003603x15625109.

6. Findings of market power are required to a different extent under all provisions. *See* Revised Notice, *supra* n. 1 above, para. 9.
7. Case C-439/11 P, *Ziegler v. Commission* ECLI:EU:C:2013:513, para. 63.
8. Magali Eben, 'Product Market Definition' in Maggiolino et al. eds, *Elgar Encyclopaedia of Competition Law* (Edward Elgar forthcoming).
9. Werden even goes so far as to state that '[t]he problem is that direct proof of dominance is just an urban legend'. He adds that 'courts hold out the possibility of direct proof, but they never find proffered proof sufficient'. (Greg Werden, 'Market Delineation under the New Merger Guidelines: Gerrymandering Redux' in Sean Sullivan ed., *The 2023 U.S. Merger Guidelines: A Review* (Concurrences 2024) 186-187, paras 556-557). Kirkwood argued that market definition endured because of 'the weight of precedent' (John B. Kirkwood, *Market Power and Antitrust Enforcement*, 98 Boston University Law Review 1207 (2018)).
10. Louis Kaplow, *Why (Ever) Define Markets?*, 124(2) Harvard Law Review 437 (2010); Greg Werden, *Why (Ever) Define Markets? An Answer to Professor Kaplow*, 78(3) Antitrust Law Journal 729 (2013); Richard S. Markovits, *On the Inevitable Arbitrariness of Market Definitions*, 47(4) The Antitrust Bulletin 571 (2002) https://doi.org/10.1177/0003603x0204700402; Ian Ayres, *A Private Revolution: Markovits and Markets*, 64 Chicago-Kent Law Review 861 (1988).
11. Werden, *supra* n. 10, 741, Podszun, *supra* n. 5, 129; Kirkwood, *supra* n. 9, 1207 (who does note, however, that '[t]his narrative force does not justify the market definition/market share paradigm. If the market definition is incorrect, it is no help to have it' (1209), a point also made by Lemley and Mckenna, to which Kirkwood also refers in his footnote 237 (Mark Lemley and Mark McKenna, *Is Pepsi Really a Substitute for Coke? Market Definition in Antitrust and IP*, 100 Georgetown Law Journal 2098 (2012) https://doi.org/10.31235/osf.io/fqp9v).
12. Eben, *supra* n. 8.
13. Described as the 'purposive approach' to market definition in Eben, *supra* n. 5.
14. It may, however, be the case that the approaches to market definition will vary depending on its use, whether to establish market shares or to characterise the economic context within which to

by the law are intrinsically connected to the exercise of power. This chapter returns to this point below in section 4.

2.2 The Debate and the Revised Notice

The purposes of market definition need to be re-iterated because they often get overlooked in a more encompassing urge to make the enforcement of competition law more productive and efficient. In a laudable quest for improvements in enforcement, market definition has at times been dismissed as a pointless and, even worse, counter-productive exercise.[15] And yet, market definition has made a bit of a comeback in 2024, although it never truly disappeared. Most readers will be familiar with the debate around market definition, which assumes various forms. The most well-known critique of market definition focuses on its utility in establishing market power. Prominent thinkers contend that market definition is a flawed way to establish market power, which should instead be established directly.[16] Indeed, as highlighted above, it is market power which is required, and market definition need not be the only accepted method to establish it. Yet, as indicated, even if we set aside market definition as a means to establish market power, we must still consider the other reasons for defining markets.

More recently, the focus has been on methodological and procedural challenges in defining markets. In most jurisdictions, antitrust authorities are grappling with the challenges of digital markets, often dealing with the very same digital players. From zero prices and multi-sidedness to ecosystems and innovation, market definition needs to grapple with increasing complexity.[17] These methodological challenges may be more pressing where market definition is used to achieve an accurate representation of market power, but remain critical under its other functions too. In addition, stakeholders expressed concerns about the burdensome and lengthy process of market definition, particularly when it is applied in a very formalistic manner.[18] Market definition has been described as 'a playground for economists'[19] which creates an inordinate amount of (sometimes conflicting) evidence for competition authorities to consider, and may increase the length of the procedure. Arguably the answers to methodological

assess the conduct, as suggested by Robertson in Viktoria Robertson, 'Current issues in Defining Relevant Antitrust Markets: Data, Digitalization and Innovation' in Pier L. Parcu, Giorgio Monti and Marco Botta (eds) *Economic Analysis in EU Competition policy: Recent Trends at the National and EU Level* (Edward Elgar 2021). This chapter focuses on variations in methodologies based on the interpretation of exercise of power, rather than the distinction with market characterisation.

15. Louis Kaplow, *Market Definition: Impossible and Counterproductive*, 79(1) Antitrust Law Journal 361 (2013).
16. Kaplow, *supra* n. 10; Markovits, *supra* n. 10.
17. Magali Eben and Viktoria Robertson, *Digital Market Definition in the European Union, United States, and Brazil: Past, Present, and Future*, 18(2) Journal of Competition Law and Economics 41 (2022) https://doi.org/10.1093/joclec/nhab018.
18. Competition and Markets Authority (United Kingdom) 'A New Pro-Competition Regime for Digital Markets' Consultation document (July 2020) paras 54-55, available at https://www.gov.uk/government/consultations/a-new-pro-competition-regime-for-digital-markets.
19. A description heard in several venues.

questions are less 'fundamental' than those questioning how formal market definition ought to be. Yet there is in fact a link between the methods chosen, the level of formalism required, and the purpose for which market definition is used. Having clear boundaries may be less pressing where market definition is used to characterise economic relationships than when it is a prerequisite to establish market power. The burdens associated with formal market definition explain, to some extent, why market definition was abandoned in the European regulations on digital markets, including the Digital Markets Act (DMA).[20] Instead of an ex-post assessment of power and conduct, the DMA focuses on *ex ante* prohibitions imposed on designated gatekeepers. This can be seen as a reduction of the burden involved in market definition, but can also be justified substantively if the regulations pursue different goals, with different understandings of power and harm.[21]

Although market definition lost the battle in the regulation of digital markets, it has not ceded significant ground in EU competition law. If one thing is clear from the adoption of the revised Notice, it is that market definition is here to stay, at least for now. In addition to its attempt to take up the challenges of market definition in the contexts of digital markets, ecosystems, and innovation and uncertainty, the Commission appears to have taken the revision of the Notice as an opportunity to be more explicit about the purposive nature of market definition, acknowledging its purposes beyond market power. The revised Notice expands on the role of market definition, in comparison to the 1997 version. The revised Notice still, understandably, puts market power at the centre of the exercise, referring to it as 'the most notabl[e]' use of market definition.[22] However, the revised Notice also presents market definition as an exercise 'closely related to the objectives' of the different competition law provisions.[23] It also acknowledges that 'the outcome of market definition can differ' with the different competitive concerns under consideration.[24] The revised Notice covers a greater variety of issues and more clearly illustrates the complexity of market definition. Still, it does not stray very far from the market power nexus of competition law, nor does it reflect on the connection between concepts of power and market definition. This is understandable, as the aim of the Notice was not to overhaul existing practice. However, market definition cannot be divorced from the broader context in which competition law operates. If the notions of power and harm evolve in abuse of dominance, then market definition should likely follow suit. In fact, what may appear to be methodological or procedural challenges can be more than technical hurdles. Where methodologies are used which were designed at a time when the harmful exercise of market power was understood primarily in terms of price and output, these approaches to market definition are likely to reflect these concerns. If competition

20. Regulation (EU) 2022/1925 of the European Parliament and of the Council of 14 September 2022 on contestable and fair markets in the digital sector and amending Directives (EU) 2019/1937 and (EU) 2020/1828 (Digital Markets Act) OJ L 265, 12.10.2022, Recital 23.
21. Magali Eben, *A Renewed Vision of Market Definition's Importance: Competition Law in the Collective Interest*, CREATe Working Paper 2024/9 (2024).
22. Revised Notice, *supra* n. 1, para. 7.
23. Revised Notice, *supra* n. 1, para. 9.
24. Revised Notice, *supra* n. 1, para. 18.

policy expands beyond (or retracts away from) such harm and power, this calls into question whether the approach to market definition actually captures these concerns. The next section will contemplate this relationship between power and the relevant market.

3 ECONOMIC POWER AND MARKET DEFINITION

3.1 Linking Power to Market Definition

Competition law mainly addresses conduct which reflects the exercise of power and/or which is harmful because the entity engaging in it has power. The exercise of power can create a variety of concerns. Various forms of conduct, causing various forms of harm (be it exclusion or exploitation), are brought as abuse of dominance cases, and mergers can be challenged under different theories of harm.

Competition law does not operate in a vacuum. The way power is defined has always been influenced by broader societal concerns about economic power. Although most people discussing competition law will refer specifically to 'market power', it is not inevitable that market power (in a narrow economic sense) is the only form of power considered problematic, nor that, when market power *is* the focus, it will be exercised in the same manner in every case. Indeed, economic power can take on different forms, arise from different sources, and therefore generate different types of harm.[25]

These different understandings of power and the harm it causes cannot be divorced from market definition. As Nachbar aptly stated, 'market definition is necessarily normative'.[26] It represents an understanding of competition and the harmful effects of the exercise of power. This is the case not merely for market definition as a general enterprise, but more specifically for the methods chosen to engage in it. The methods and baselines chosen in market definition are based on (explicit and implicit)[27] assumptions on what kind of exercise of power is problematic. The methods which are routinely discussed as the standards for market definition – such as the 'Hypothetical Monopolist Test' (HMT) and 'Small but Significant Non-Transitory Increase in Price' (SSNIP) test – are not devoid of normative substance, but themselves reflect (policy) choices about the type of concerns the law ought to address. To understand this point, it is worth briefly harking back to the context in which these tests – and their predecessors – were adopted.

25. Sean Sullivan, 'The Evolution (and Devolution) of Market Structure Reasoning' in Sean Sullivan ed., *The 2023 U.S. Merger Guidelines: A Review* (Concurrences 2024) 152, paras 437-438; Or Brook and Magali Eben, 'Abuse Without Dominance and Monopolization Without Monopoly' in Pinar Akman, Or Brook and Konstantinos Stylianou (eds), *Research Handbook on Abuse of Dominance and Monopolization* (Edward Elgar 2023).
26. Thomas Nachbar, *Qualitative Market Definition*, 109 Virginia Law Review 373 (2023).
27. As well articulated by Kauper: Thomas E. Kauper, *The Problem of Market Definition under EC Competition Law*, 20(5) Fordham International Law Journal 1694 (1996).

3.2 Methods Prior to the HMT

Although the market played roles of increasing importance in early antitrust cases in the United States,[28] early US market definition did not formally rely on frameworks such as the HMT nor use empirical tests based on it (which started being developed mainly after the introduction of the HMT in the 1980s).[29] Instead, they engaged in a variety of thought exercises focused on substitution (including rudimentary discussions of cross-elasticity of demand).[30] Qualitative market definition, based on product characteristics and uses, was affirmed by the Courts[31] and even led to the definition of sub-markets under the infamous *Brown Shoe* practical indicia standard.[32] These approaches prevailed especially during the 1960s-1970s. Qualitative analysis was also the main approach in the EU's early cases, at least once relevant markets started being defined with more than a perfunctory statement of their existence.[33] The EU's early regulations, guidance documents, and cases engaged primarily in qualitative exercises. Regulations and notices referred to 'competing products' as those which were identical

28. Werden explains that '[t]he notion of a relevant market is at least implicit in the early monopolization cases', referring to the shares in various alternative markets considered in 1945 in *United States v. Aluminum Co. of Am.* (148 F.2d 416, 424 (2d Cir. 1945)) and that 'earliest usage of the term "relevant market" in a reported federal antitrust decision was in a merger case, the Supreme Court's 1948 decision United States v. Columbia Steel Co' (334 U.S. 495, 508 (1948)). He explains that it is the Celler-Kefauver Act's introduction of the wording 'any line of commerce in any section of the country' which officially introduces market definition, however. (Greg Werden, *The History of Antitrust Market Delineation*, 76 Marquette Law Review 128-130 (1992)).
29. Werden, *supra* n. 28, 209.
30. Werden discusses the introduction of cross-elasticity of demand and substitution in the early 1950s cases *Times-Picayune Publishing Co. v. United States* (345 U.S. 594 (1953)) and *Cellophane* (*United States v. E.L du Pont de Nemours & Co* 351 U.S. 377 (1956)) (in Werden, *supra* n. 28, 130-139).
31. *United States v. Bethlehem Steel Corp.*, 168 F. Supp. 576 (S.D.N.Y. 1958) 592, referring to *United States v. E.I. du Pont de Nemours Co.*, 1957, 353 U.S. 586, 77 S.Ct. 872, 1 L.Ed.2d 1057. *See* Werden, *supra* n. 28, 144-152.
32. *Brown Shoe Co. v. United States* 370 U.S. 294, 325 (1962).
33. In the 50s-70s, cases referred to 'products under consideration' or 'products covered by the contract' or the conduct. These included some brand-specific submarkets, such as in Joined cases 56 and 58-64, *Établissements Consten S.à.R.L.* and *Grundig-Verkaufs-GmbH v. Commission of the European Economic Community* ECLI:EU:C:1966:41. Early judgments referred to markets for the relevant products, without much guidance as to how they should be defined (e.g., preliminary ruling in Case 56-65, *Société Technique Minière (L.T.M.) v. Maschinenbau Ulm GmbH* (M.B.U.). ECLI:EU:C:1966:38.) From the 1970s there was a start at explanation of which products to include. The Court referred, sparingly but increasingly, to substitution in a few cases under the EEC Treaty. Case 40-70, *Sirena S.r.l. v. Eda S.r.l. and others* ECLI:EU:C:1971:18, para. 16. Arguably *Sirena v. Eda* is when the Court refers explicitly to 'substitution' between products for the first time, or at least one of the first times, when establishing that a company had 'power to impede the maintenance of effective competition over a considerable part of the relevant market', i.e., a dominant position. The first time, according to Focsaneanu: Lazar Focsaneanu, *La jurisprudence de la Cour de Justice des C.E. en matière de concurrence: marché des produits en considération*, 191 Revue du Marché Commun 589 (1975). 'Substitutes' also make appearances in the cases on the Dyestuffs cartel: Case 48-69, *Imperial Chemical Industries Ltd. v. Commission of the European Communities* ECLI:EU:C:1972:70, para. 54; Case 49-69, *Badische Anilin & Soda-Fabrik AG v. Commission of the European Communities* ECLI:EU:C:1972:71, para. 20; Case 54-69, SA *française des matières colorantes (Francolor) v. Commission of the European Communities* ECLI:EU:C:1972:75, para. 42, *see also* references to elasticity of demand in para. 61.

or similar, mainly from the point of view of customers, based on characteristics, intended usage, or price.[34] Court judgments referred to similar products or comparable services, making up relevant markets.[35] Products to be included in the relevant market could be identified by reference to their characteristics, which made them 'particularly apt to satisfy an inelastic need' and 'only to a limited extent interchangeable with other products'.[36] Two pivotal moments occurred in the 1970s: First, the Court held in 1973 in *Continental Can* that market definition is necessary to establish a dominant position, referring to the interchangeability of products.[37] Second, the Commission included a stand-alone section on market definition in its decision in the seminal *United Brands* case, holding that bananas could not be substituted by other fruits based on their nature, price, or use.[38] The Court followed the Commission's reasoning in this case, (controversially) referring, *inter alia*, to the 'special features' of bananas which mean they satisfy a very distinct customer demand compared to other fruit.[39]

The approaches taken to market definition in these early cases cannot be divorced from the concerns of the day in competition policy. Although it is not straightforward to draw a one-per-one relationship between the methods of market definition and the goals of the law in the 1960s-1970s (as opposed to after the introduction of the HMT discussed next), there have been attempts in the literature to reflect on their implications for the scope of the law. It has been argued that the *Brown Shoe* practical indicia and submarkets in early US cases reflected a concern not for efficiency or consumer welfare but for the protection and independence of small enterprises and the fairness in transactions between smaller and bigger, more powerful, firms.[40] Werden contends that the indicia based on industry or public recognition, which were used in some cases, had 'little, if anything to do with the potential for market power',[41] while indicia based on distinct customers' special demand had 'not

34. Focsaneanu, *supra* n. 33, 582, helpfully reviewed several regulations and notices which referred to competing products in some way, including Regulation No. 19/65/EEC of 2 March of the Council on application of Art. 85(3) of the Treaty to certain categories of agreements and concerted practices; Commission Notice of 27 May 1970 concerning agreements, decisions and concerted practices of minor importance which do not fall under Art. 85(1) of the Treaty establishing the European Economic Community; Regulation (EEC) No. 2779/72 of the Commission of 21 December 1972 on the application of Art. 85(3) of the Treaty to categories of specialisation agreements; Regulation (EEC) No. 2822/71 of the Council of 20 December 1971 supplementing the provisions of Regulation No. 17 implementing Arts 85 and 86 of the Treaty.
35. E.g., Case 78-70, *Deutsche Gramophon Gesellschaft mbH v. Metro-SB-Großmärkte GmbH & Co. KG.* ECLI:EU:C:1971:59, paras 17-18 (abuse of dominance).
36. Case 6-72, *Europemballage Corporation and Continental Can Company Inc. v. Commission of the European Communities* ECLI:EU:C:1973:22, para. 32.
37. Case 6-72, *Europemballage Corporation and Continental Can Company Inc. v. Commission of the European Communities* ECLI:EU:C:1973:22, para. 32.
38. Commission Decision of 17 December 1975, IV/26699 – *Chiquita*, II.A.2.
39. Case 27/76, *United Brands Company and United Brands Continentaal BV v. Commission of the European Communities. – Chiquita Bananas* ECLI:EU:C:1978:22, para. 22, para. 31's wording in particular has been subject to quite some debate: 'The banana has certain characteristics, appearance, taste, softness, seedlessness, easy handling, a constant level of production which enable it to satisfy the constant needs of an important section of the population consisting of the very young, the old and the sick.'
40. Kauper, *supra* n. 27, 1683-1684; Sullivan, *supra* n. 25,155-157 (paras 448-452).
41. Werden, *supra* n. 28, 174.

necessarily a great deal' to do with market power unless these customers could be discriminated against.[42] Instead of widespread price or output effects, the grounds for a market definition based on distinct customers was the 'unique impact' of a merger on 'that class of purchasers'.[43]

It is worth noting here that early communications by the European Commission, which engaged in qualitative market definition by defining competing products by reference to their characteristics or usage, also referred to the protection of SMEs as an important consideration. The Commission Notice of 27 May 1970 established that agreements of minor importance did not have to be notified. An agreement was of minor importance if the products concerned by the agreement amounted to 5% or less of the group of similar products, in addition to turnover thresholds below 15 or 20 million units.[44] One of the main objectives in establishing such *de minimis* rules was, according to the Notice, to facilitate cooperation between SMEs.[45] The Notice does not explicitly link the qualitative approach chosen to identify competing products to this objective – and it may be less easy to connect the protection of SMEs to the approach to market definition here than to the turnover thresholds[46] – yet it is a noticeable context, which perhaps raises similar questions as those which were raised in the US. In the *Grundig* case, where the Commission's focus on competition between (the distributors of) products of the same brand was approved by the Court, the Court referred to 'various stages and manifestations of competition' as being relevant to 'freedom of competition'.[47] Instead of identifying 'relevant markets' (although without this wording) around similar products of different manufacturers, they were defined by identifying products of the same manufacturer. Although this case is significantly influenced by the single market imperative, the reference to freedom of competition as an objective is noteworthy when considering how much the intended aim matters when defining markets.[48]

Both US and EU scholars criticised some of the brand-specific (after-) market definitions by the European Commission in specific cases, which were allegedly concerned with power imbalances in bilateral relationships, with one company being considered dominant because its customer or supplier was dependent on it, rather than an exercise of power to the direct detriment of consumer welfare. Some US scholars considered that the market definitions were artificially constructed to fit a narrative

42. Werden, *supra* n. 28, 176.
43. Blue Bell, Inc., 395 F. Supp. at 542-43.
44. Commission Notice of 27 May 1970 concerning agreements, decisions and concerted practices of minor importance which do not fall under Article 85(1) of the Treaty establishing the European Economic Community, OJ C 64, 2.6.1970, p. 1-2, II.
45. *Supra* s. 1 'Introduction'.
46. As done by Focsaneanu, *supra* n. 33, 583, for example.
47. Joined cases 56 and 58-64, *Établissements Consten S.à.R.L. and Grundig-Verkaufs-GmbH v. Commission of the European Economic Community* ECLI:EU:C:1966:41, 342.
48. In this judgment, the applicants claimed that the Commission had made an error in restricting its examination solely to products of a specific make, arguing that this indicated an incorrect understanding of competition, and it should have instead considered competition between 'similar products of different makes'. The Court disagreed, arguing that there are 'various stages and manifestations of competition' which are relevant to the 'principle of freedom of competition'.

which was actually about dependence of (and harm to) other companies when dependence ought not to be relevant to dominance to begin with.[49] The criticism by some EU scholars, on the other hand, seemed to be more open to decisions based on dependence: while some argued that a delineation of relevant markets should be abandoned, and others argued that they should be defined more explicitly based on this dependence,[50] they did not critique the relevance of dependence as such.[51] Fishwick acutely diagnoses the root cause of the disagreement: an 'ambivalence about the objectives of competition policy' in the 1970s-1980s.[52]

3.3 The Scope of the HMT

The US approach to the identification of relevant markets changed with the adoption of the HMT, which was officially put forward for the first time in the US' 1982 Merger Guidelines.[53] The 1984 Merger Guidelines, revised from the 1982 version, provide some insights on the rationale behind market definition: the adopted standards were designed to enable the Department of Justice to analyse 'the likely competitive impact of a merger within economically meaningful markets – i.e., markets that could be subject to the exercise of market power'. Thus, the Guidelines put forward that a market would need to be defined 'in which firms could effectively exercise market

49. Eleanor Fox, *Abuse of a Dominant Position Under the Treaty of Rome: A Comparison with US Law*, Annual Proceedings of the Fordham Corporate Law Institute (1983), as cited in Francis Fishwick, *Definition of the Relevant Market in Community Competition Policy: A Report for the Commission of the European Communities* (1986) 11, https://dspace.lib.cranfield.ac.uk/items/a0a63666-7429-4362-8593-894c096bec8b (last accessed 21 July 2025).
50. *See* these sources cited in Fishwick, *supra* n. 49, 11: Michel Waelbroeck, *Rapport Général: La Notion d'Entreprise(s) en Position Dominante et les Méthodes de Contrôle en Droit Comparé* (1977); Michel Glais and Philippe Laurent, *Traité D'économie et de Droit de la Concurrence* (PUL 1983).
51. Kauper refers, for example, to the *Hugin/Liptons* decision which he wrote 'is best understood as a decision not based on economic concerns, but on concerns over fairness to buyers dependent on a supply that the Commission and the Court of Justice wished to preserve in the market place. The market definition was carefully tailored to this end.' (Kauper, *supra* n. 27, 1698).
52. Fishwick, *supra* n. 49, 13.
53. U.S. Department of Justice, Merger Guidelines (14 June 1982) (hereinafter '1982 Merger Guidelines'). The antecedents of the HMT and SSNIP test are varied and to some extent disputed, but it is generally acknowledged that one of the first articulations for a legal audience a SSNIP test for substitution under a HMT was put forward by a Professor of economics in Morris A. Adelman, *Economic Aspects of the Bethlehem Opinion,* 45(5) Virginia Law Review 688-690 (1959) https://doi.org/10.2307/1070847. In this article, Adelman criticised the *Bethlehem* approach of identifying markets based on the characteristics and uses of products, and suggested instead a test based on price increases. (Note, in particular: 'The definition of the market and the definition of monopoly are interdependent: a market is a slice of the economy which is monopolized if it Is under unified control; conversely, monopoly is control of a market. No matter how the boundaries may be drawn in terms of products or areas, there is a single test: if, within this purported market, prices were appreciably raised or volume curtailed, would supply enter in such amounts as to restore approximately the old price and output?'). Incidentally, Adelman also expressed concerns about the theories of harm in this decision, since he did not agree that the harm to customers put forward by the court was convincing, particularly as the court did not link it to the existence of market power (e.g., 694-696). It is conceivable that his incentive to put forward a SSNIP-like test was motivated in part by his scepticism about the theories of harm in the case.

power if they were able to coordinate their actions'. This would be done as follows: 'Formally, a market is defined as a product or group of products and a geographic area in which it is sold such that a hypothetical, profit-maximizing firm, not subject to price regulation, that was the only present and future seller of those products in that area would impose a "small but significant and non-transitory" increase in price above prevailing or likely future levels.'[54] The HMT, and particularly the derived SSNIP 'test' subsequently found their way into EU discourse too, being incorporated in the 1997 Market Definition Notice.[55] But the HMT was adopted against the background of specific concerns. The merger guidelines were concerned that mergers may enable tacit collusion between competitors – thus its focus was on coordinated effects as a theory of harm.[56] The HMT was introduced to reflect this specific concern: it 'scoped relevant markets around the identification of potential exercises of market power through coordinated conduct'.[57] As Werden explains, the 'HMT rationalized market delineation by linking it to the market power concern presented by a case.'[58] This concern was particularly linked to price. It is easy to see the parallels with the question posed by the 1978 Areeda-Turner Treatise about what 'quantum of market power is an appropriate subject of concern', a concern which they suggested was a price increase of between 5 and 10%.[59] The HMT defines the market from the lens of a concern that the merger will enable firms to join forces and thus acquire (or enhance) market power, enabling them to increase prices post-merger. It reflected the risk that a merger would 'bring about a cartel acting like the hypothetical monopolist.'[60] Thus, the HMT focuses on the identification of a group of products which could be monopolised, particularly on price, enabling a comparison of the current price with a potential post-merger monopoly price.[61]

3.4 Methods for Different Concerns

The 1984 Merger Guidelines' focus on coordinated effects had a profound impact on the method for market definition, scoping it around this particular exercise of power (and not reflecting on the approach to market definition in the context of different

54. U.S. Department of Justice Merger Guidelines, (14 June 984) (hereafter '1984 Merger Guidelines') §2.0.
55. Commission Notice on the definition of the relevant market for the purposes of Union competition law OJ C 372/6, 9.12.1997 (hereafter '1997 Notice') paras 15-19. Although both the Notice and the jurisprudence of the Court of Justice of the EU confirms that the SSNIP test, in its particular expression of the Hypothetical Monopolist Test, is only one approach the Commission can take to market defintion. *See* Case T-70/10, *Feralpi Holding v. Commission* EU:T:2014:1031, para. 188.
56. Sullivan, *supra* n. 25, 157, para. 452.
57. Sullivan, *supra* n. 25, 157, para. 454.
58. Werden, *supra* n. 9, 190, para. 574.
59. Phillip Areeda and Donald F. Turner, *Anti Trust Law* 2 (Aspen 1978) 347, 398-400, cited in Werden, *supra* n. 28, 187-188.
60. Timothy Brennan, *The Kinetic Rise and Potential Fall of Market Definition,* in Pier L. Parcu, Giorgio Monti and Marco Botta (eds) *Economic Analysis in EU Competition Policy: Recent Trends at the National and EU Level* (Edward Elgar 2021) 78.
61. Werden, *supra* n. 9,190, para. 573.

exercises of power). It has been argued that where cases involve different concerns, the HMT may not be appropriate.[62]

This was a criticism levelled against subsequent versions of the merger guidelines in the US, which expanded theories of harm in merger cases but did not correspondingly expand market definition methods. Sullivan recently lamented that the 1992 and 1997 revisions 'introduced new theories of competitive harm without making the corresponding revisions to market definition or market concentration thresholds to adjust structural reasoning to the distinct competitive mechanisms underlying each type of harm. The HMT, designed to identify potential collusive groups, was put to off-label use scoping markets for differentiated-products unilateral effects theories.'[63]

This criticism applies beyond mergers, in unilateral conduct cases, since the type of (exercise of) power which motivates abuse of dominance cases (or 'monopolization' in the US) is not equivalent to coordinated effects concerns in mergers.[64] Indeed, Posner is said to have argued as early as 1976 that the criteria for the relevant market should be different in monopolisation and merger cases, given the different concerns in these cases.[65] The HMT is most appropriate where the concern is the future power to increase price (as a result of the merger/conduct), less so where the concern is the ability of an undertaking to impede rivals – and thus maintain prices beyond the competitive level, or negatively influence other parameters of competition – or to damage trading partners. The 'Cellophane Fallacy' when using the SSNIP test[66] is only an expression of this more foundational point about using HMT approaches to market definition for different concerns than coordinated price effects in mergers.

Modified HMT tests have been suggested for unilateral conduct cases, such as the SSNDP ('small but significant non-transitory *decrease* in price') test, which is meant to be tailored to the particular concern that the powerful company is able to maintain its higher prices because of its exclusionary conduct.[67] Other scholars, such as Sullivan, have proposed a variety of methods tailored to specific theories of harm'[68] or have suggested methods which combine the market power and characterisation functions of

62. Sullivan, *supra* n. 25, 158-159, paras 458-459; Kirkwood, *supra* n. 9, 1210; Brennan, *supra* n. 60, 68-69.
63. Sullivan, *supra* n. 25, 162, para. 469.
64. Brennan, *supra* n. 60, 68-69, 78-79.
65. Richard A. Posner, *Antitrust Law: An Economic Perspective* (1976) 130, 128-129, cited in Werden, *supra* n. 28, 186.
66. This fallacy arises because it is not evident whether (and by how much) prevailing prices are already higher because of market power. If the price charged is already at supra-competitive level and is taken as the baseline for the SSNIP test, increasing the price at this level, even by a small amount, will inevitably mean customers stop purchasing the product, even where there are no substitutes. Named after the US judgment *US v. Du Pont de Nemours & Co* [1956] 351 US 377. Brennan, *supra* n. 60, 78.
67. Lawrence White, 'Market Power and Market Definition in Monopolization Cases: A Paradigm is Missing', in Wayne D. Collins ed., *Issues in Competition Law and Policy* (ABA 2008), available at https://www.justice.gov/archives/atr/market-power-and-market-definition-monopolization-cases-paradigm-missing-0.
68. Sean Sullivan, *Modular Market Definition*, 55 University of California Davis Law Review, 1091 (2021) https://doi.org/10.2139/ssrn.3738364.

market definition.[69] Some have suggested the calculation of direct effects, from which relevant markets can be deduced; others have queried the feasibility of incorporating non-price dimensions in a form of market delineation. There have been suggestions that, where the aim of a policy is to protect smaller or less powerful companies, and theories of harm are constructed around dependent suppliers or customers, the approach to market definition could reflect that.[70]

This chapter does not intend to explore the feasibility of different methods and their appropriateness for a variety of concerns. What these proposals illustrate is that the approach one adopts to define relevant markets reflects specific theories of harm, and particular concerns about the exercise of power.

US scholars have noted their scepticism around the 2023 merger guidelines, which have a wide variety of theories of harm and multiple approaches to market definition but have not clearly connected the approaches to market definition to the way (market) power is exercised in each of them.[71] This chapter does not intend to review the US' current approaches and hurdles when it comes to market definition. Rather, it wishes to focus on the EU, to make the point that the way dominance is understood in Europe should have a profound impact on how we approach market definition. This is not a new issue. Early on in the European attempt at establishing an approach to market definition, cautionary calls went out reminding the European community to be conscious of the specific US views on power and aims of competition policy which formed the context for their methods of market definition. In 1986, Fishwick wrote that '[t]o those involved in the European discussion of the dominance concept, US economists' use of perfect competition as a basis for analysis may seem barely credible'.[72] In Europe, at the time, dominance was less consistently understood by reference to a departure from perfect competition, and it was argued it could be established on the basis of relationships of dependence with rivals, buyers, and suppliers. Thus, Fishwick emphasised that the context in which the US approach to market definition was developed differed from that of the EU, and he cautioned that 'the more specific definition of dominance in the USA [had to be] borne in mind' when using US analysis to 'develop the relevant market concept for the benefit of EEC jurisprudence'.[73] Fishwick's consideration that dominance meant something else in the EU than in the US is crucial – and one which ought to be tested. The point stands to this

69. Jhun and Panhans, for example, 'propose implied market shares as a framework that stays true to the original motivation of traditional market definition but can also accommodate, in a fairly nuanced way, the kind of market demand information that is used in competitive effects analysis. ... Including a set of firms that are relevant for analysis without necessarily implying that they should all be included to the same degree in the denominator of a share calculation can be a way to reconcile some of the tensions that have been noted since the onset of tests like the HMT'. *See* Jennifer S. Jhun and Matthew T. Panhans, *Implied Market Shares and Antitrust Markets as Fuzzy Sets*, 69(2-4) The Antitrust Bulletin 117 (2024).
70. Kauper, *supra* n. 27, 1683-1684; Sullivan, *supra* n. 68, 1142.
71. Sullivan, *supra* n. 25, 167, para. 491; Werden, *supra* n. 9, 187-190, paras 560, 574.
72. Fishwick, *supra* n. 49, 16.
73. Fishwick, *supra* n. 49, 17. Wording in brackets changed merely for grammatical time consistency.

day, however, and is perhaps most pertinent now as the Commission embarks on its rethinking of abuse of dominance.

As with most aspects of competition law, to truly gauge the effectiveness of market definition, it is important to understand the economic, social, and policy context surrounding it. Where market definition is used in abuse of dominance cases, the guidelines on Article 102 form a crucial part of this context. It is therefore important to understand: what are the concerns underpinning Article 102 cases, and what assumptions are made about their causes? As early as 1997, Kauper wrote that 'the manner in which markets are defined is often relevant to assessing the policies, not all of which are economic, underlying the development in any given system of competition policy standards'.[74] This chapter wishes to highlight this idea for the twenty-first century, and reflect that it also holds in the opposite direction: the manner in which the (harmful) exercise of power is understood in competition policy indicates how appropriate the chosen approach to market definition is. To make this point, the next section will reflect on the understanding of abuse of dominance in the EU up to this point, and the questions raised by the new Guidelines. It is only against that backdrop that we can determine whether the approach to market definition makes sense. This is no easy feat – and this chapter can only be the start of the reflection.

4 POWER AND ABUSE OF DOMINANCE

This chapter queries whether any evolution of abuse of dominance should prompt a reconsideration of market definition. If dominance is understood not (only) as the ability to raise prices, but may also refer to the ability to exclude rivals and trading partners, control ecosystems, or entrench economic dependencies, then market definition frameworks that focus solely on price-based substitutability may be ill-equipped to address modern competition concerns. It is not possible to evaluate the appropriateness of approaches to market definition without knowing first what kind of economic power, and what type of exercise of such power, is of concern to the enforcement of the law. If the concerns about the exercise of power diverge – either between jurisdictions or over time – it is not self-evident that the same methodology to market definition remains appropriate throughout. Thus, it is important to unpack how dominance is understood under Article 102 TFEU.

4.1 Understanding Dominance

As Petit accurately notes, different concepts of power 'shape conflicting views about what antitrust laws can achieve'.[75] They reflect different concerns and different theories of harm. The type of exercise of power covered by competition policy can diverge over time as well as between jurisdictions. Differences between the EU and the

74. Kauper, *supra* n. 27,1682.
75. Nicolas Petit, 'Understanding Market Power: An Economics Perspective' in Pinar Akman, Or Brook and Konstantinos Stylianou (eds), *Research Handbook on Abuse of Dominance and Monopolization* (Edward Elgar 2023) 26.

US are notoriously difficult to capture, since comparing one jurisdiction with another at the same point in time may overlook that international dialogue between enforcers may lead one jurisdiction to adapt to another gradually rather than instantaneously. Moreover, the intricacies of the different institutional and cultural contexts may make a one-to-one comparison challenging. Yet it cannot be denied that, at least on the surface, there are differences between the way the exercise of power is portrayed in the US and EU. Melamed argued that US antitrust law 'embodies the simple idea that we will endure the costs of market power when they are the result of efficient conduct but not when they are the result of anticompetitive conduct, which is conduct that tends to cause an increase in market power for reasons other than competition on the merits'.[76] One can query to what extent abuse of dominance in the EU expresses a similar attitude to market power. The EU appears to historically have expressed disapproval of the injurious use of market power (rather than its unlawful acquisition or extension, as in the US) and considering that special responsibility is the corollary of power.

Divergences can also take place over time. The philosophical and doctrinal foundations on which competition policy is based are not set in stone. Over time, there may be different visions of competitive markets, and of the role competition law should play in rectifying market failures. The neoclassical view of the market as the vehicle for an efficient allocation of resources between rational actors has had a profound impact on modern-day competition policy. With it came a belief that competition law should be used to address the market failures associated with market power, and a view that intervention is justified where it would make these markets more efficient.

It is not the only view of competition (law) propounded over the years. Markets, and the process of competition, have been put forward as vehicles of liberty – and competition law as a means of ensuring that markets remain undominated and that economic actors can operate free from the restraints imposed by private[77] power.[78] Until a few years ago, these discussions might have seemed merely quaint anecdotes from history. Yet recently the narrative of competition as freedom has made a comeback, both implicitly and explicitly, in the scholarly debate.[79]

76. A. Douglas Melamed, *Response Antitrust Law Is Not That Complicated*, 130 Harvard Law Review 167 (2017).
77. And, in a different context and to lesser extent, public power.
78. Amartya Sen, *Markets and Freedoms: Achievements and Limitations of the Market Mechanism in Promoting Individual Freedoms*, 45 Oxford Economic Papers 519 (1993) https://doi.org/10.1093/oxfordjournals.oep.a042106; Giuliano Amato, *Antitrust and the Bounds of Power: The Dilemma of Liberal Democracy in the History of the Market* (Hart Publishing 1997) 2; David J. Gerber, *Law and Competition in the Twentieth Century: Protecting Prometheus* (Clarendon Press Oxford 2001).
79. E.g., Anna Gerbrandy and Pauline Phoa, *The Power of Big Tech Corporations as Modern Bigness and a Vocabulary for Shaping Competition Law as Counter-Power* (Routledge 2022); Elias Deutscher, *The Competition-Democracy Nexus Unpacked: Competition Law, Republican Liberty, and Democracy*, 41 Yearbook of European Law 197 (2022) https://doi.org/10.1093/yel/yeac003; Ioannis Lianos, *Competition Law as a Form of Social Regulation*, 65(1) The Antitrust Bulletin 3 (2020) https://doi.org/10.1177/0003603x19898626; Dina Waked, *Competition Law and Policy in the Global South: Power, Coercion and Distribution*, Current Legal Problems 1 (2023); Lina Khan, *Amazon's Antitrust Paradox*, 126(10) Yale Law Journal 710 (2017); Rupprecht Podszun, *Politics of Antitrust Law*, 47 International Review of Intellectual Property and Competition Law 383 (2016) https://doi.org/10.1007/s40319-016-0480-y.

The extent to which freedom from domination features in the actual enforcement of EU competition law can be debated,[80] though it is not far-fetched to claim that recent Commission decisions would have fit rather comfortably in a policy aimed at economic freedom rather than consumer welfare if such a policy were to exist. Makris has argued that decisions such as *Google Android* and *Amazon Marketplace commitments* could be read as illustrations that the 'analysis should be sensitive not only to consumer welfare stricto sensu … but also to economic power understood as the ability to create dependencies and curtail opportunities to compete'.[81] This view of economic power is distinct from that of market power, at least insofar as market power is defined narrowly as the ability to reduce output or sustain prices above competitive levels.[82]

In theory, different concepts of *power* may be captured by the law, which bring different *concerns* within the scope of the law. What matters, therefore, is whether different conceptualisations of economic power are or would be caught by EU competition law. The EU's definition of dominance has, from the outset, represented an idiosyncratic take on power. The notion of market power most discussed in the last three decades is the ability to reduce output or sustain prices above competitive levels,[83] yet how closely this economic definition of market power is related to dominance as a legal concept is contested.[84] In addition to the open-endedness of the definition of dominance by the Courts, which is described in the next paragraphs, its usage by the Commission has varied over different periods, as is discussed in the subsequent sections.

The European Court of Justice provided EU competition law with its seminal definition of dominance in *United Brands*, describing it as a 'position of economic strength' which gives an undertaking the 'power to behave to an appreciable extent independently of its competitors, customers and ultimately of its consumers'. This position, according to the Court, enables the undertaking 'to prevent effective competition being maintained on the relevant market'.[85] The Court elaborated in *Hoffmann-La Roche* that a dominant position 'enables the undertaking which profits by it, if not to determine, at least to have an appreciable influence on the conditions under

80. For an argument that freedom does not fit within the jurisprudence, *see* Pinar Akman, *The Role of 'Freedom' in EU Competition Law*, 34(2) Legal Studies 183 https://doi.org/10.1111/lest.12003.
81. Stavros Makris, *A Smithian Political Economy Approach for the Competition Law of the 21st Century* [2024 working paper version, published version forthcoming in Modern Law Review] 37.
82. Petit, *supra* n. 75; Moritz Lorenz, *An Introduction to EU Competition Law* (Cambridge University Press 2013) 194; Roger van den Bergh, Peter Camesasca and Andra Giannaccari, Market Power, Market Definition and Entry Barriers' in Roger van den Bergh ed., *Comparative Competition Law and Economics* (Edward Elgar 2017) 125.
83. Petit, *supra* n. 75, Lorenz, *supra* n. 82; Van den Bergh, Camesasca and Giannaccari, *supra* n. 82; Luis Ortiz Blanco, *Market Power in EU Antitrust Law* (Bloomsbury Hart Publishing 2011).
84. Giorgio Monti, *The Concept of Dominance in Article 82*, 2 Special Issue European Competition Journal 31 (2006) https://doi.org/10.5235/ecj.v2n1s.31; Renato Nazzini, *The Foundations of European Union Competition Law: The Objective and Principles of Article 102* (Oxford University Press 2011) 327; Annelies Azzopardi, *'Dominant Position': A Term in Search of Meaning*, 8 ICC Global Antitrust Review 22; According to Ortiz Blanco, substantial market power and dominance can be equated (Ortiz Blanco, *supra* n. 83, 47).
85. Case 27/76, *United Brands v. Commission* EU:C:1978:22, para. 65.

which that competition will develop, and in any case to act largely in disregard of it so long as such conduct does not operate to its detriment'.[86] This 'independence' of competitors and customers is a curious element. It could overlap with power over price or output, and thus be consistent with the narrow economic interpretation of market power mentioned earlier. Yet, it is clearly broader language than merely pricing power and has been said to include 'commercial power', where an organisation has advantages compared to others on the market (including economic and strategic advantages and superior bargaining positions).[87]

The *United Brands* definition of dominance therefore leaves room for interpretation not only on the type of power it covers but also on the harm at its heart.[88] How dominance is understood should be closely related to the concerns which underpin the law. Arguably, an understanding of dominance as substantial market power could be linked to a concern with consumer welfare,[89] considering harm to parameters of competition relevant to consumers. It seems no coincidence that when the Commission modernised abuse of dominance in the early 2000s, introducing consumer harm as a ground for prioritising enforcement, this coincided with a refocus on substantial market power as a determinant for dominance, as discussed in the next section.[90] This can be contrasted, as Monti did in 2006, with a definition of dominance as economic strength or the ability to distort the market to the detriment of multiple economic actors (including but not limited to consumers). Such a definition appears more focused on the power to harm the competitive process and influence the conditions under which competition develops, to the detriment of many.[91] The focus on commercial power can also be understood from the perspective of the concern for economic freedom which has been part of EU competition policy from the outset.[92] Restrictions of freedom as a concept of harm can be found in the statements and decisions by the Commission before its more economic approach.[93] The Court at the time took a broad view too, less focused perhaps on economic freedom and more on competitive market structures and

86. Case 85/76, *Hoffmann-La Roche & Co AG v. Commission* EU:C:1979:36, para. 39.
87. Monti, *supra* n. 84, 31-33; Lorenz, *supra* n. 82, 194-195. Monti suggests a mix of market power and commercial power in the case law, referring to *United Brands* and *GE/Honeywell* as cases where dominance was commercial power.
88. Anne Witt, *The More Economic Approach to EU Antitrust Law* (Bloomsbury, Hart Publishing 2019) 219, criticised the dominance definition for being unclear on 'what type of harm is actually caused by an undertaking's ability to behave independently'.
89. Monti, *supra* n. 84, 38, 39-41; Van den Bergh, Camesasca and Giannaccari, *supra* n. 82, 125.
90. *See also* Witt, *supra* n. 88, 143-144, 146-147.
91. Monti, *supra* n. 84, 38; Nazzini, *supra* n. 84, 329. *See also TeliaSonera* where the Court seems to link its definition of dominance to its argument that more matters than direct harm to consumers: Case C-52/09, *Konkurrensverket v. TeliaSonera Sverige* ECLI:EU:C:2011:83, paras 23-24.
92. Monti, *supra* n. 84, 43; Van den Bergh, Camesasca and Giannaccari, *supra* n. 82, 125 footnote 2; Witt, *supra* n. 88, 89-102, 142 sets out the various objectives which could be found in secondary EU legislation as well as Commission documents before modernisation, which were varied and had to be understood against Arts 2 and 3 EEC. Her analysis points to various references to individual and commercial freedom (of opportunity) among various other goals.
93. Witt, *supra* n. 88, 142 refers to the Second Report on Competition Policy (1972) which explained that the Commission had attacked 'improper practices' under Art. 102 that had been designed to 'curtail the commercial freedom of dealers or to cut off supplies to a competitor'.

processes and merits-based competition, but still broadly aligned with the Commission's thinking.[94] Similarly, a focus on the power to exclude has been said to have roots in ordoliberal concepts about freedom and competition on the merits, since ordoliberals disapproved of prevention-competition whereby a company impedes the performance of others rather than improving its own performance.[95] The concern with the power to exclude can also be found in US antitrust, with its own particular context.[96]

The way dominance is understood reveals something about the goals and policy priorities within the scope of the law. These goals and priorities may change over time, and could (and should) be reflected in the way power and its exercise is interpreted. The next sections will reflect on the Commission's approach to power and harm in abuse of dominance in the 2000s, under its 'more economic approach'. This will be followed by a reflection on a possible rethinking in the 2024 draft Guidelines on exclusionary abuses.

4.2 Abuse of Dominance in the 2000s

The Commission's modernisation of competition law in the early 2000s (the so-called more economic approach) is believed to have altered its interpretation of the objectives of competition law, refocusing them from a myriad of values and concerns to a narrower focus on consumer welfare, understood as consumer harm and (to perhaps slightly less extent) efficiency.[97] Yet this restatement was more ambiguous under Article 102 than it was for Article 101. While the role of consumer welfare was made clear under Article 101, the Commission's final Guidance for Article 102 did not purport to be a statement of the law but merely on its enforcement priorities. Likely for that reason, the concepts of dominance and harm did not deviate wholly from the definitions in the jurisprudence of the EU Courts.

The initial preparatory study from the European Advisory Group on Competition Policy (EAGCP) proposed an understanding focused on effects on consumers, while DG Competition's Discussion Paper defined the objective of Article 102 as the protection of competition on the market as a means of enhancing consumer welfare and of ensuring an efficient allocation of resources.[98] When the 2009 Guidance was ultimately adopted, however, it did not explicitly pronounce itself on the objective of Article 102, merely listing benefits enforcement can bring. Instead, the Guidance

94. Witt, *supra* n. 88, 275-277; Case 85/76, *Hoffmann-La Roche & Co AG v. Commission* EU:C:1979:36.
95. Massimiliano Vatiero, *The Ordoliberal Notion of Market Power: An Institutionalist Reassessment*, 6(3) European Competition Journal 695 https://doi.org/10.5235/ecj.v6n3.689.
96. Monti, *supra* n. 84, 43-46; Lina Khan, *The End of Antitrust History Revisited*, 133 Harvard Law Review 1655 (2020); Charles A. Boston, *The Spirit Behind the Sherman Anti-Trust Law*, 21(5) The Yale Law Journal 341 (1912) https://doi.org/10.2307/784293; the Sherman Act was portrayed as the 'Magna Carta of free enterprise' in *United States v. Topco Assocs., Inc.*, 405 U.S. 596 (1972).
97. Witt, *supra* n. 88, 102-107.
98. Report by the EAGCP, *An Economic Approach to Article 82* (July 2005) 2; DG Competition, *Discussion Paper on the Application of Article 82 of the Treaty to Exclusionary Abuses* (December 2005) (hereafter 'Discussion Paper') para. 4.

reflected the priorities of the Commission when enforcing Article 102 against exclusionary conduct. Consumer welfare was not explicitly made into the main aim of enforcement, but brought in as a way of identifying when it would be beneficial for the Commission to intervene: the Commission would focus 'on those types of conduct that are most harmful to consumers'.[99] The Guidance still emphasised the need to protect the competitive process but used harm to consumers to determine when exclusion triggered the need for intervention. The Guidance put forward the idea that exclusion of competitors is an issue when it is not the result of competition on the merits, understood as the offer of better prices, quality, choice or innovation to consumers.[100] This focus only on the exclusion of those who compete on parameters relevant to consumers could be understood as replacing a broader concern with the commercial freedom of competitors for its own sake.

This concern for consumer welfare, broadly understood as including both final consumers and customers,[101] may have had an impact on the understanding of dominance in the Guidance. Before the early 2000s, the Commission had followed the Court's legal definition of dominance in *United Brands* - a definition which, as mentioned above, could be broader than market power defined around price or output. In its Discussion Paper, however, DG COMP explicitly interpreted dominance as substantial market power.[102] Its 'market power' would be measured not only around price and output, but also innovation, variety or quality of products, or other parameters of competition.[103] The Commission's Guidance on enforcement priorities also centred market power as an important element of dominance, explaining that independence is the result of an absence of effective competitive constraints and that this means an undertaking enjoys substantial market power.[104] While the Guidance defined market power as the capability of 'profitably increasing prices above the competitive level', it made it clear that 'increasing prices' is 'shorthand for the various ways in which the parameters of competition - such as prices, output, innovation, the variety or quality of goods or services - can be influenced to the advantage of the dominant undertaking and to the detriment of consumers'.[105] This shift away from the legal understanding of dominance in *United Brands/Hoffmann-La Roche* towards an emphasis on substantial market power[106] provided the Commission with 'a starting point of an attempt towards a more economic and effects-based approach towards dominance'.[107]

99. Communication from the Commission, *Guidance on the Commission's enforcement priorities in applying Article 82 of the EC Treaty to abusive exclusionary conduct by dominant undertakings*, OJ C 45, 24.2.2009 (hereafter 'Guidance') para. 5.
100. Guidance, *supra* n. 99, para. 6.
101. Pinar Akman, *'Consumer' Versus 'Customer': The Devil in the Detail*, 37(2) Journal of Law and Society 315 https://doi.org/10.1111/j.1467-6478.2010.00506.x.
102. Discussion Paper, *supra* n. 98, para. 23.
103. Discussion Paper, *supra* n. 98, para. 24.
104. Guidance, *supra* n. 99, para. 10.
105. Guidance, *supra* n. 99, para. 11.
106. Monti, *supra* n. 84, 2006 31-32.
107. Azzopardi, *supra* n. 84, 22.

The harm which Article 102 was supposed to address correspondingly narrowed. While harm to economic freedom, fairness, and equality of opportunities played a role before the more economic approach, the Commission's priorities seemed to shift towards consumer harm exclusively – at least as far as its Guidance and Discussion Paper had indicated. Its actual decisional practice after the adoption of the Guidance shows a muddier picture of the role of consumer harm: although consumer harm might guide the internal selection of cases to bring, its decisions do not consistently centre abuses which directly harm consumers. While the Commission added market power to the understanding of dominance and referred to consumer harm in its decisions in *Intel*[108] and *Telekomunikacja Polska*,[109] these decisions were less expansive on consumer harm than expected.[110] In general, the Commission's decisions seem to have been brief on consumer harm, at times assuming it as a consequence of exclusion.[111]

The Commission's attitude to consumer harm does not conflict with the jurisprudence. While the Court has gradually moved to an effects-based approach, it has not adopted the idea that it is necessary to establish harm to consumers from the exclusion of efficient undertakings to find an abuse.[112] Although it has moved towards accepting consumer welfare and efficiency as considerations in some cases, this has happened with varying levels of importance,[113] and been repudiated in other judgments. Indeed the Court of Justice held in *Servizio Elettrico Nazionale* that a dominant undertaking may try to defend its conduct by showing that the exclusion is 'counterbalanced or even outweighed by positive effects for consumers', but a competition authority does not have to show harm to consumers.[114] Although the Courts may have been influenced by the more economic approach in the 2009 Guidance Paper, the most appropriate portrayal of this evolution is one of adjustment within the traditional

108. Case COMP/C-3 /37.990, *Intel*, Commission Decision of 13 May 2009, paras 837-839.
109. Case COMP/39.525, *Telekomunikacja Polska*, Commission Decision of 22 June 2011, paras 640-641.
110. Heike Schweitzer and Simon de Ridder, *How to Fix a Failing Art. 102 TFEU: Substantive Interpretation, Evidentiary Requirements, and the Commission's Future Guidelines on Exclusionary Abuses*, 15(4) Journal of European Competition Law and Practice 226, footnote 26 https://doi.org/10.1093/jeclap/lpae033; Tristan Rohner, *Art. 102 AEUV und die Rolle der Ökonomie* (Nomos 2023) 22.
111. According to Rohner, *supra* n. 110, 220, with the exception of *Slovak Telekom*, but as he points out even in this case the assessment of harm to consumers was a response to an objection raised rather than an independent element of the case.
112. C-95/04 P, *British Airways* ECLI:EU:C:2007:166, para. 106; C-202/07 P, *France Télécom v. Commission* ECLI:EU:C:2009:214, para. 105; Case C-52/09, *Konkurrensverket v. TeliaSonera Sverige* ECLI:EU:C:2011:83, para. 24; Case C-553/12 P, *Commission v. DEI* ECLI:EU:C:2014:2083, paras 63-68. Statements indicating combinations in *European Superleague Company*, C-333/21, EU:C:2023:1011, para. 124; Case C-48/22 P, *Google LLC and Alphabet Inc. v. European Commission* ('*Google Shopping*') ECLI:EU:C:2024:726, para. 87; Case C-209/10, ECLI:EU:C:2012:172 *Post Danmark A/S v. Konkurrencerådet* paras 20-24.
113. *See* as illustration the difference between *Post Danmark I* (Case C-209/10, *Post Danmark I* EU:C:2012:172) and *Post Danmark II* (Case C-23/14, *Post Danmark II* EU:C:2015:651). The former focusing on consumer harm and as-efficient-competitors when establishing exclusionary abuse, and the latter referring again to the more traditional formulation of influencing the structure of the market.
114. Case C-377/20, *Servizio Elettrico Nazionale* paras ECLI:EU:C:2022:379 47-48.

framework, centred on a competitive process and effective markets, rather than a complete overhaul.

Nor has the Court unequivocally moved to market power based on price or output. Its record is mixed. In *AstraZeneca*, the General Court explicitly referred to findings of 'market power', defining it not only by giving the *United Brands* definition of independence but also by linking it to the ability, in particular, 'to maintain prices at a higher level while retaining a much higher market share than those of its competitors'.[115] The Court of Justice, on appeal, confirmed that the ability to maintain such high prices without losing market share was 'a relevant factor'.[116] However, in other cases, the Court retained the broad definition of dominance without reference to market power.[117]

Arguably, the Court linked its broader definition of dominance to objectives broader than consumer welfare in *France Télécom*. This can be deduced from the judgment when one considers the ground of appeal within which the Court defined dominance, which concerned the question of recoupment in a predatory pricing case. The Court did not agree that recoupment had to be shown, since practices are not abusive only if they cause direct harm to consumers but also if they have an impact on an effective competition structure.[118] It is in that context that the Court defined dominance and moreover linked it to the general Treaty objectives. It held that: 'according to settled case-law, Article 82 EC [now Article 102 TFEU] is an application of the general objective of European Community action laid down by Article 3(1)(g) EC, namely, the institution of a system ensuring that competition in the common market is not distorted. Thus, the dominant position referred to in Article 82 EC relates to a position of economic strength enjoyed by an undertaking which enables it to prevent effective competition being maintained on the relevant market by affording it the power to behave to an appreciable extent independently of its competitors, its customers and ultimately of the consumers'.[119] Thus, dominance is defined around independence and the ability to prevent effective competition, as in *Hoffmann-La Roche*, precisely because it is such power that may cause the harm envisaged by Article 3(1)(g) EC. If consumer welfare was the main goal, then dominance would be more narrowly defined around the ability to influence parameters of relevance to consumers, as captured by substantial market power (and recoupment may need to be shown, as well, as in *France Télécom*).

Overall, the Commission's attempt to centre market power and consumers under its 'more economic approach' has had mixed results in both its own decisional practice and the jurisprudence of the Courts. Now, the Commission embarks upon a more ambitious project: to adopt Guide*lines* on abuse of dominance.

115. Case T-321/05, *AstraZeneca* EU:T:2010:266, para. 267.
116. Case C-457/10 P, *AstraZeneca* EU:C:2012:770, para. 181.
117. Case C-52/09, *Konkurrensverket v. TeliaSonera Sverige* ECLI:EU:C:2011:83, para. 23.
118. Case C-202/07 P, *France Télécom v. Commission* ECLI:EU:C:2009:214, paras 103-107.
119. Case C-202/07 P, *France Télécom v. Commission* ECLI:EU:C:2009:214, para. 103. *See also* Case C-280/08 P, *Deutsche Telekom v. Commission* ECLI:EU:C:2010:603, para. 170.

4.3 The 2024 Review of Abuse of Dominance

The new Guidelines are portrayed as a statement of the law as it stands, bringing together the different strands of the jurisprudence in a coherent whole, providing guidance on the interpretation of the law which the Commission will follow. This wide-reaching project is nonetheless limited in substantive scope, in that the Guidelines are not portrayed as a change of direction in the goals pursued under Article 102. Instead, enforcement will be made 'workable'[120] and the procedural and evidentiary burdens on the Commission would be eased. Despite this seeming limited ambition, the Guidelines *can* be read as a rethinking of the concerns covered by Article 102, particularly as compared to the Guidance Paper. Makris has argued that the manner in which the Guidelines are pitched hides an apparent value disagreement, meant to de-emphasise the role of consumer welfare.[121] This has been vehemently criticised, not only by commentators who value the consumer welfare standard for its own sake but also by those worried that it is unclear what would replace it. Komninos passionately stated: 'While abandoning the general framework and guiding principles of the latter, the draft Guidelines offer in return no guiding principle at all. ... Contrary to the Guidance Paper, when reading the draft Guidelines, we do not really know what an exclusionary abuse is and, more importantly, why the law should prohibit such practices.'[122]

Whether or not one agrees with a change in direction, the reform the Commission is proposing with its new Guidelines is one worth unpacking. The Guidelines are put forward as founded on the case law of the Courts, and indeed they are. Yet it cannot be denied that they represent a shift in the thinking of the Commission, at least as compared to its thinking in the policy documents of the early 2000s. The new Guidelines, and particularly the policy brief adopted ahead of the guidelines, indicate some retreat from the focus on consumer harm and efficiency of the early more economic approach.

While the 2005 Discussion Paper stated that '[t]he essential objective of Article [102] when analysing exclusionary conduct is the protection of competition on the market as a means of enhancing consumer welfare and of ensuring an efficient allocation of resources',[123] the 2023 Policy Brief is explicit that protecting the competitive process means that consumers benefit, but that the 'enforcement of competition rules also contributes to achieving objectives that go beyond consumer welfare, at least when the latter is defined strictly in economic terms'. It refers to Vestager's speech which referred to EU competition policy pursuing 'multiple goals, such as fairness and level-playing field, market integration, preserving competitive processes, consumer welfare, efficiency, and innovation, and ultimately plurality and democracy.' The brief

120. Linsey McCallum et al., A *Dynamic and Workable Effects-Based Approach to Abuse of Dominance*, 1 Competition Policy Brief (March 2023) (hereafter 'Policy Brief').
121. Makris, *supra* n. 81, 36.
122. Assimakis Komninos, '*"J"accuse!': Four Deadly Sins of the Commission's Draft Guidelines on Exclusionary Abuses*, Network Law Review (2024), available at https://www.networklaw review.org/komninos-guidelines/.
123. Discussion Paper, *supra* n. 98, para. 4.

adds that the 'case law has also confirmed that competition law can achieve broader objectives, as ensuring consumer choice is a means to ultimately guarantee plurality in a democratic society'.[124] This is quite a broad statement of objectives. Some caution is in order, however, as this may not be a statement of the direct goals of competition law, but merely a statement of the benefits which could indirectly flow from effective enforcement of Article 102. The 2024 Draft Guidelines leave little doubt, though, that Article 102 addresses more harm than just that to consumers. It states that competition law 'pursues the protection of genuine, undistorted competition ("effective competition") in the internal market'. Effective competition achieves quite a few things, according to the draft Guidelines: not only does it drive 'market players to deliver the best products in terms of choice, quality and innovation, at the lowest prices for consumers' but it also 'ensures that markets remain open and dynamic, creating new opportunities for innovative players including small and medium sized enterprises ("SMEs") and start-ups to operate on a level playing field with other players. It also spurs innovation and ensures an efficient allocation of resources, thereby contributing to sustainable development and enabling strong and diversified supply chains, all of which contributes to the Union's resilience and long-term prosperity'.[125]

Harm to consumers nonetheless remains an important element of the enforcement of Article 102. This is understood broadly as a deterioration in a variety of parameters of competition relevant to consumers (including quality and innovation), aligned with the Commission's broad understanding even at the time of the more economic approach. It also adds consumer choice.[126] At the same time, the Guidelines emphasise that practices may harm consumers indirectly by undermining an effective structure of competition,[127] and going even further than that by referring to distortions of competition 'to the detriment of the public interest, other market players, and consumers.'[128] The priority of consumers in this list of concerns is unclear. It is also unclear to what extent this enumeration of various concerns is merely the result of the Commission's attempt to list all relevant expressions in the jurisprudence, or an attempt to state its own view that harm to other market players or to public interest can be issues independent of consumer harm.

What is clear is that the Commission, in line with the jurisprudence of the Court even after the Guidance, accepts that it is not necessary to show actual harm to consumers to establish an abuse. Whereas the Guidance focused on foreclosure as a result of which a dominant undertaking would be in a position to 'profitably increase prices to the detriment of consumers', the Commission amended the Guidance to remove this reference to the ability to profitably increase prices (or other parameters of competition). The Commission's Amending Communication and Policy Brief provide an explanation of this removal which focuses mostly on the unnecessary evidentiary

124. Policy Brief, *supra* n. 120,1.
125. Draft Guidelines, *supra* n. 1, para. 1.
126. Draft Guidelines, *supra* n. 1, para. 2.
127. Draft Guidelines, *supra* n. 1, para. 5.
128. Draft Guidelines, *supra* n. 1, para. 2.

burden that the original version entailed.[129] It does not link it explicitly to the rationale of Article 102 TFEU. Yet, there are two reasons why this change could signal more than merely an evidentiary change. First, when explaining the change, the Commission states that it aligns with the case law of the Court of Justice, which has dismissed this requirement in the context particularly of predatory pricing. It refers specifically to *France Télécom*.[130] As mentioned earlier in this chapter, in this case, the Court held that competition authorities do not need to show recoupment because abusive practices are not harmful solely due to direct consumer harm but also because they undermine an effective competition structure, reflecting the general objectives of EU competition law beyond consumer welfare. Second, and perhaps a confirmation of the first argument, the Commission changed more than the reference to the profitable increase of prices in this definition of foreclosure – it also replaced the 'hampering of competitors' with a broader 'adverse impact on an effective competitive structure'.

The amendment changes the definition of foreclosure from 'where effective access of actual or potential competitors to supplies or markets is hampered or eliminated as a result of the conduct of the dominant undertaking whereby the dominant undertaking is likely to be in a position to profitably increase prices to the detriment of consumers' to 'where the conduct of the dominant undertaking adversely impact an effective competitive structure thus allowing the dominant undertaking to negatively influence, to its own advantage and to the detriment of consumers, the various parameters of competition, such as price, production innovation, variety or quality of goods or services'.[131]

If the understanding of the concerns within the scope of Article 102 TFEU were to shift, it is not implausible that the Commission would redefine dominance to include broader notions of power. At first glance, the Draft Guidelines have not moved the needle much in the way they define dominance, yet there seems to be less emphasis on substantial market power as compared to the Guidance. The Draft Guidelines define dominance by reference to the broad *United Brands* definition rather than by reference to substantial market power.[132] Although there is no mention of market power in the paragraphs defining dominance, market power is mentioned when discussing market shares and barriers to expansion in the factors relevant to the assessment.[133] There is a reference to competitive constraints when discussing market definition.[134] The ability to influence parameters of competition is not mentioned when defining dominance, but does become relevant later on when discussing abuse, because the Guidelines discuss the concept of 'competition on the merits' as 'competition on the basis of performance' which 'in principle, relates to a competitive situation in which consumers benefit from

129. Policy Brief, *supra* n. 120, 4-5; Annex to Amending Communication para. 1 (Communication from the Commission, *Amendments to the Communication from the Commission Guidance on the Commission's enforcement priorities in applying Article 82 of the EC Treaty to abusive exclusionary conduct by dominant undertakings*, OJ C 116, 31.3.2023 (hereafter 'Amending Communication')).
130. Policy Brief, *supra* n. 120, 4-5.
131. Annex to Amending Communication, *supra* n. 129, para. 1.
132. Draft Guidelines, *supra* n. 1, paras 18 and 23.
133. Draft Guidelines, *supra* n. 1, para. 20, 26.
134. Draft Guidelines, *supra* n. 1, para. 20, footnote 32.

lower prices, better quality and a wider choice of new or improved goods or services.'[135] It seems to this author that what matters is the question whether the ability to influence parameters of competition is the kind of power the Commission is concerned about, exclusively, or whether there are broader notions of power that matter. This is intrinsically linked to the kind of harm Article 102 TFEU is supposed to address – a question which is not necessarily set in stone and involves (policy) choices. As mentioned earlier in the chapter, if commercial power or more broadly power over individual economic actors in weaker (bargaining) positions are concerns under Article 102, then that should have a bearing on the interpretation of dominance.

4.4 Looking Ahead

This may be the right time to reflect more closely on the types of (exercise of power) the EU wants to address under Article 102. Multiple scholars have suggested that abuse of dominance should consider broader societal goals. A few of them have related this to different types of power which could be covered by dominance,[136] including imbalances in bargaining, control over resources, or cross-market power or conglomerate advantages.[137]

Many accept that in modern times – and certainly since the 2000s – a dominant position can be equated with substantial market power. Ortiz Blanco has argued that the definition of dominance around independence is for all intents and purposes equivalent to the modern concept based on supra-competitive prices since '[i]n a market economy that focus on profit, independence can only lead to price increases and, at the same time, improvements in the results or the position of companies'.[138] Yet it would be an oversight not to point out the diversity of concerns in EU competition cases, covering not only price increases but also consumer choice, as well as the dependence and opportunities of trading partners. The capacity to control production may be a factor relevant to substantial market power,[139] and EU competition law does consider a broader list of parameters of competition as relevant to market power.[140] However, these economic definitions may still be more narrow than the concerns about the exploitation of customers or suppliers in weaker bargaining positions which are

135. Draft Guidelines, *supra* n. 1, para. 51.
136. Ioannis Lianos and Bruno Carballa-Smichowski, *A Coat of Many Colours: New Concepts and Metrics of Economic Power in Competition Law and Economics*, 18(4) Journal of Competition Law and Economics 795 https://doi.org/10.1093/joclec/nhac002; Ioannis Lianos, *Minding Competition in Complex Adaptive Social Systems: The Sociological Approach to Competition Law*, University College London Law Research Paper No. 19/2024, available at SSRN: https://ssrn.com/abstract=4851966; Gerbrandy and Phoa, *supra* n. 79, 212; Anna Gerbrandy, 'Revisiting the Concept of Power in the Digital Era', in Oles Andriychuk, ed., *Antitrust and the Bounds of Power: 25 Years On* (Bloomsbury, Hart Publishing 2023) 209.
137. These concepts are not entirely new. *See* Fishwick and Glais and Laurent, *supra* n. 50, referenced in Fishwick, *supra* n. 49.
138. Ortiz Blanco, *supra* n. 83, 47.
139. Ortiz Blanco, *supra* n. 83, 48.
140. Including in the Guidance, *supra* n. 99, para. 11.

more frequently coming to the fore in discourse and indeed enforcement of competition law.[141]

The role of dependence of trading partners in EU competition law is contentious. Ortiz Blanco describes dependence as at most 'an ancillary assessment criterion' which does not expand dominance beyond market power.[142] Indeed, the Court has not fully embraced attempts at establishing dominance merely based on the dependence of customers, while cautiously accepting its use as an additional factor.[143] However, there are two indications that – for better or for worse[144] – the weaker position of trading partners is a concern within the decisional practice. First, because markets have at times been defined narrowly to allow for a finding of dominance, in cases which appear to have dependence at their heart.[145] Second, because in recent cases against digital platforms, the unfair treatment of customers and users has played more significant roles in the theories of harm,[146] indicating an increased attention to the weaker position of those for whom the undertaking is an unavoidable partner. The Commission has held that exploitation of those in such a weaker position can be a concern independent of whether these unfair terms are strictly and exclusively the consequence of dominance or not.[147] Thus, even if dependence remains of concern only when it coincides with a dominant position, it is an exercise of power which matters.

141. E.g., European Commission decision in Case AT.40437 – *Apple – App Store Practices* (music streaming), Commission decision of 4 March 2024; Case C-252/21, *Meta Platforms, Inc. and Others v. Bundeskartellamt* ECLI:EU:C:2023:537.
142. Ortiz Blanco, *supra* n. 83, 65-67.
143. *ABG/Oil companies operating in the Netherlands* (IV/28.841) Commission Decision [1977] OJ L117/1, 9; Case 77/77, *Benzine en Petroleum Handelsmaatschappij BV and Others v. Commission* [1978] ECR 1513; Case 26/76, *Metro SB-Großmärkte GmbH & Co KG v. Commission* ECLI:EU:C:1977:167, paras 17-18 (*Metro I*); Case 75/84, *Metro SB-Großmärkte GmbH & Co KG v. Commission* ECLI:EU:C:1986:399, para. 86 (*Metro II*). *See* Brook and Eben, *supra* n. 25, 264-265 for a discussion.
144. Or Brook and Magali Eben, *Article 3 of Regulation 1/2003: A Historical and Empirical Account of an Unworkable Compromise,* 12(1) Journal of Antitrust Enforcement 45 (2024).
145. Cf. Case T-229/9 *Deutsche Bahn* ECLI:EU:T:1997:155 (1997) 57; Case IV/29.132, *Hugin/Lipton,* Commission decision of 8 December 1977; *British Leyland* (1982) and *Magill/TV Guide* (1988).
146. Magali Eben and Yingying (Jessie) Zhu, *Big Tech and Dominance: An Overview of EU and National Case Law* (Concurrences 2023).
147. Case AT.40437 – *Apple – App Store Practices* (music streaming), Commission decision of 4 March 2024, paras 538 and 545: 'It is precisely the position of economic strength which follows from a dominant position, and which makes the dominant undertaking an unavoidable trading partner that enables that undertaking to impose trading conditions on its trading partners. This "power" to impose conditions constitutes the specific link between the dominant position and the conduct in question, irrespectively of whether other non-dominant undertakings may use similar trading conditions.' ... 'In general, it would not be appropriate to adopt a restrictive reading of Article 102(a) of the Treaty excluding from its scope any trading condition imposed by a dominant company, even if unfair (such as the imposition of disproportionate exclusivity requirements extending far beyond the duration of a contractual commitment to provide certain services), simply because also non-dominant companies could (or do) request their trading partners to accept similar unfair conditions. Even if similar unfair conditions can be requested by non-dominant companies, they can still lead to an abuse if they are imposed by a dominant undertaking which has a special position of economic strength giving it the power to behave independently of its customers (for instance because it is an unavoidable trading partner), and therefore – according to the established case law – has a special responsibility under Article 102 of the Treaty.'

How much these expanded concepts of harm and power are meant to feed into the Commission's enforcement of abuse of dominance in the years to come is unclear. Indeed, the Guidelines on exclusionary abuses may leave room for interpretations of dominance and harm beyond price-based market power, but they do not adopt an explicit stance in that direction. Perhaps, as some have argued, this is a task better left for Guidance on *exploitative* abuse, although that does not currently seem on the cards. Although the focus is understandably on making the enforcement of the law currently less prone to under-enforcement, questions about power are important foundational questions for the future.

Filho referred to Karl Popper when he put forward that economic power is for competition law one of those concepts which are 'so fundamental and constitutive for a science that their definition is axiomatic'[148] – it is nearly pointless to attempt an incontrovertible definition, but rather what is necessary is to understand its manifestations, causes and effects.[149] That being said, where there is more than one type of economic power, it can be useful to distinguish them to at least assist in the crucial task of identifying their diverging manifestations, causes, and effects.

Competition law is in many ways an expression of what Amato saw as the dilemma of liberal democracy: to understand how power – both public and private – can be prevented from threatening freedom.[150] Although this provides us with an interesting starting point to consider competition law, it is too broad a statement to be useful without considering a particular competition law's content and context. The concerns surrounding power, and the additional goals competition policy may be called upon to achieve, are not set in stone.

EU competition policy still has, even after modernisation, a multitude of goals. Even if with a consumer welfare standard – broadly defined – efficiency may have become a relevant aim, it has not rendered other goals obsolete, such as economic freedom or market integration. Scholars have continued and will continue to consider forms of economic power distinct from (price-based) market power and the different concerns they bring.

Although we have had a period of attempted convergence on the narrative of competition law and the standards, principles, and methods used in competition law enforcement, this did not inevitably and endurably lead us to a point of universal convergence. Not only can goals change over time in the different jurisdictions but the use of the same terminology and – on the surface – methods also do not necessarily mean that authorities across the globe mean the same thing when they use these terms or intend the same outcomes through these methods or indeed use them in the same way. For (market) power and for market definition, this is important to bear in mind. Do we mean the same thing when we say '(exercise of) market power'? Did we intend to address the same concerns, when we use a HMT or SSNIP thought experiment? If the

148. Calixto Salomão Filho, *A Legal Theory of Economic Power: Implications for Social and Economic Development* (Edward Elgar 2011) 26.
149. Filho, *supra* n. 148, 26.
150. Amato, *supra* n. 78, 2.

concerns about the exercise of power diverge, it is not obvious that the same methodology to market definition is appropriate.

5 QUESTIONS FOR MARKET DEFINITION

Market definition is used by competition authorities as a framework within which to answer the factual and legal questions they need to resolve to arrive at a decision. The questions we try to solve through market definition may vary, particularly as theories of harm are based on diverging interpretations of injurious exercises of power. Power is more than just a metric to screen cases: since market power is an inherent element of the theory of harm in many cases, market power will still feature prominently. If there are different methods to establish market power as a metric, then market definition may not be needed for this particular purpose, but power remains implicit in the exercise. The questions we ask to establish the market may vary depending on the different ways market power can be used. Moreover, if different understandings of power are or become relevant to the theories of harm and objectives under Article 102 TFEU, market definition may require different approaches. Economists may have an important role to play in resolving this challenge, and developing appropriate methods, at least insofar as the concerns covered by the law can be externalised through econometric tools or thought exercises. Some US scholars have suggested developing different methods of market definition for different theories of harm,[151] but much more work remains to be done, particularly in the context of EU policy and priorities.

The Revised Market Definition Notice puts the purpose of market definition in the wider context of the identification of competition constraints, within which the assessment of market power is a notable (but not necessarily exclusive) aim.[152] It puts forward a notion of 'relative competitive strength' but clearly retains the emphasis on *market* power, stating that the 'Commission generally uses market definition where there is a need to assess the relative competitive strength of undertakings as part of the competitive assessment and, most notably, to assess whether an undertaking holds market power.'[153] This is a broader notion of market power than one solely focused on price or output since the Notice accepts a variety of parameters of competition.[154] This is not revolutionary, as the Commission has recognised for a while now that price is a shorthand for the various parameters of competition. Two aspects of this Notice are nonetheless significant. First, the Notice reflects a much wider range of considerations

151. *See, e.g.*, Sean Sullivan's work, *supra* n. 68. In a different context, *see* Robertson's argument on market characterisation (*supra* n. 5 & *supra* n. 13).
152. *See* Revised Notice, *supra* n. 1, paras 6-10, 22; Magali Eben, *The New Market Definition Notice: Embracing Change* (Kluwer Competition Law Blog, 27 February 2024), https://competitionlawblog.kluwercompetitionlaw.com/2024/02/28/the-new-market-definition-notice-embracing-change/; Magali Eben, *The Draft Revised Market Definition Notice: The European Commission Brings the Relevant Market Further into the 21st century* (Kluwer Competition Law Blog, 26 January 2023), https://competitionlawblog.kluwercompetitionlaw.com/2023/01/26/the-draft-revised-market-definition-notice-the-european-commission-brings-the-relevant-market-further-into-the-21st-century/.
153. Revised Notice, *supra* n. 1, para. 8.
154. Revised Notice, *supra* n. 1, footnote 14 and para. 15.

than in the past, including under 'quality' factors such as sustainability, privacy, and the image of security, as well as a broad understanding of innovation. Indeed, the Notice expressly links market definition to competition law's role in the tween green and digital transition, acknowledging that competition law can complement the Union's regulatory framework on environmental sustainability by considering sustainability as a factor of competition in the competitive assessment and in market definition.[155] There is a big question mark about what this means in practice, and how much it can be read as the inclusion of a broader set of policy goals and considerations where they can influence or be part of the parameters of competition. Second, in addition to its engagement with quality in various dimensions,[156] the Notice incorporates a tentative endorsement of a market definition *test* focused on quality.[157] The Notice accepts that there could be a conceptual framework to assess demand substitution based on quality, in the form of an SSNDQ test (small but significant non-transitory decrease in quality) but cautions that the quantitative application of such a test is challenging.[158]

The revised Notice is clear that market definition may vary across decisions because the relevant competitive constraints depend on the concerns in a specific case.[159] The Notice does not open up the debate on the different types of exercise of power and how this may impact approaches to market definition. This is unsurprising, given the aim of the Notice to provide guidance to increase clarity through updated guidance on market definition in light of past and current practice.[160] Its aim is not to open unsettled debates.

This does not mean the Notice does not provide some opportunity for reflection. The Revised Notice indicates an awareness that the theory of harm matters for the appropriateness of market definition methodologies. This comes out not so much as explicit acknowledgment, but as an implicit understanding, since the Notice discusses the SSNIP test and the cellophane fallacy.[161] In footnote 55 the Notice explains that, when the case requires assessing the current degree of dominance, there is a risk that the price is already at a supra-competitive level - so that the SSNIP test needs to be applied from a counterfactual price, or other evidence needs to be used to define the relevant market. However, if the focus of the case is on changes in market power, then the prevailing price is a good starting point for the SSNIP test. As the Notice states, 'market definition may not always lead to the same results in cases involving the assessment of a change in market power as in cases involving the assessment of

155. Revised Notice, *supra* n. 1, paras 3 and 15.
156. Paragraph 15 mentions: 'degree of innovation and its quality in various aspects - such as its sustainability, resource efficiency, durability, the value and variety of uses offered by the product, the possibility to integrate the product with other products, the image conveyed or the security and privacy protection afforded, as well as its availability, including in terms of lead-time, resilience of supply chains, reliability of supply and transport costs. The relative importance of these parameters for customers may change over time.'
157. Revised Notice, *supra* n. 1, para. 30 and footnote 54.
158. Revised Notice, *supra* n. 1, para. 54.
159. Revised Notice, *supra* n. 1, para. 18(c).
160. Revised Notice, *supra* n. 1, paras 3-5.
161. Revised Notice, *supra* n. 1, para. 30 and footnote 44.

existing market power'.[162] Although the Notice does not use the wording 'theories of harm' and merely limits itself to a discussion of the SSNIP test, this reflection tracks with the discussion in section 3 on the fact that the concerns which underpin a case could justify different approaches to market definition. The logic could be taken a step further, to ask whether market definition methodologies ought to be adapted, beyond the cellophane fallacy, if the law covers a more diverse range of concerns about the exercise of power.

The draft revised Notice had made a seemingly broader point in a footnote since it stated – before delving into the SSNIP test and the cellophane fallacy in a later footnote[163] – that though 'the outcome of market definition in a given case is usually unaffected by whether it takes place in the context of merger control or antitrust enforcement', market definition may actually 'lead to different results depending on the of analysis carried out', in particular, that the competitive constraints needing to be identified could differ depending on whether the focus is on changes in market power or on establishing market power relative to a competitive situation.[164] Stating this as a broader point first before reflecting on the SSNIP test could have evidenced an understanding that the point applies across different methodologies, not just the SSNIP test, but the revision in the final version of the revised Notice belies that impression.

As the Notice confirms, the SSNIP test is not obligatory, being only 'a conceptual framework' to interpret the available evidence[165] – it is possible, then, to imagine what other frameworks could be used. Imagining different approaches starts from a concretisation of the concerns which underpin the law, beyond the narrow concerns which underpin the hypothetical monopolist test. The revised Notice indicates some wider achievements which might flow from the enforcement of competition law, such as contributing to the green and digital transition and resilience of the single market.[166] The weight to give to this statement of (likely indirect) benefits seems rather light, however. Given the scope of the Notice as guidance on existing market definition practice, it is not here that the debate should start. Clarity is first needed on what concerns and power concepts will be in the scope of Article 102 TFEU in the years to come. Only then can there be a discussion on the right approaches to market definition. Indeed, market definition is not just an empirical exercise – it is a reflection of how competition law seeks to restrain economic power.

162. Revised Notice, *supra* n. 1, fn 55.
163. Draft Communication from the Commission, *Commission Notice on the Definition of the Relevant Market for the Purposes of Union Competition Law* (2022) (hereafter 'Draft Revised Notice'), footnotes 48 and 20.
164. Draft Revised Notice, *supra* n. 163, footnote 20.
165. Revised Notice, *supra* n. 1, para. 31.
166. Revised Notice, *supra* n. 1, para. 3.

CHAPTER 8

Market Definition in the Context of Article 102 TFEU: Reflections on Some (New) Challenges

Thomas Buettner[*]

1 INTRODUCTION

In February 2024, the Commission adopted a new notice on the definition of the relevant market (hereinafter 'market definition notice' or 'notice').[1] It was the first revision of the original market definition notice of 1997.[2]

Market definition is an important step in the assessment of many competition matters, including abuse of dominance cases and merger control. Market definition sets the scene for the competitive assessment and forms the basis for the calculation of market shares.

But much has changed over the more than twenty-five years during which the original notice was in force. The digital sector, in particular, has evolved dramatically during this time, raising new challenges regarding how markets should be defined. The Commission has also much more experience today on how to define markets in very innovative sectors. Moreover, the world is arguably more globalised today than it was at the end of the last century. In light of these and other developments, it was time to

* The views that are expressed in this article are those of the author and do not necessarily reflect the views of DG Competition or the European Commission. The author thanks his co-panellists and participants at the GCLC annual conference in March 2024 for interesting discussions and David Kovo for comments on a draft of this article. Any error or inconsistency remains the sole responsibility of the author.

1. Communication from the Commission – Commission Notice on the definition of the relevant market for the purposes of Union competition law, C/2023/6789, OJ C, C/2024/1645, 22.2.2024.
2. Communication from the Commission – Commission Notice on the definition of relevant market for the purposes of Community competition law, OJ C 372, 9.12.1997.

provide updated guidance on how the Commission will approach the definition of the relevant market for competition law enforcement.

This article will focus on challenges when defining markets in the context of cases under Article 102 TFEU.[3] To do so, we emphasise, first, that, as recognised in the new notice, the central purpose of market definition is to structure and facilitate the competitive assessment of the conduct or concentration under investigation in the specific case at hand. Market definition is only useful as a tool to the extent that it fulfils this role. This implies that market definition cannot be performed in the abstract. Instead, it needs to be tailored to the specific circumstances of the competitive assessment required in the case at hand.

We will then discuss in more detail some of the specific challenges that typically arise when defining markets in an Article 102 context, where the required assessment of dominance is about determining the level of existing market power by the undertaking concerned. In this context, we need to address the fact that when the starting point is a situation in which market power is already exercised to a substantial extent, substitution to alternative products is not the decisive criterion for market definition. This is exemplified by the well-known 'cellophane fallacy'.[4] But the cellophane fallacy is not just a technical issue that affects the application of the SSNIP test[5] in Article 102 cases. Its consequences are more far-reaching. Moreover, the theory of harm, or, in other words, the competitive concern under consideration can also have an effect on the definition of the relevant market.

Last, we touch upon market definition in digital markets or in the presence of innovation. Such markets often exhibit features that raise many complex issues. For this reason, it is not possible to provide very prescriptive guidance on how digital or innovative markets should be defined. Market definition that follows a rigid approach cannot do justice to this complexity. Instead, because of the complexity of such cases it is necessary to keep the central purpose of market definition in mind, i.e., that market definition is a tool to structure and facilitate the competitive assessment and that it is only useful if it performs that purpose.

2 THE PURPOSE OF MARKET DEFINITION

A useful starting point for the discussion is the role of market definition as described in the new notice. According to the notice, '[m]arket definition is a tool … to identify and

3. For an overview of the new market definition notice, *see, e.g.*, Atzeni, C. et al., *Recent Developments at DG Competition: 2023/2024*, Rev Ind Organ (2024). https://doi.org/10.1007/s11151-024-10001-1, s. 2.2.
4. The cellophane fallacy is named after the US Supreme Court's approach to market definition involving cellophane and other wrapping products (*United States v. E. I. du Pont de Nemours & Co.*, 351 U.S. 377 (1956)) which led the court to wrongly conclude, on the basis of a SSNIP test applied at the prevailing price, that the relevant market must be wider than the product of the dominant cellophane producer.
5. The SSNIP test, or hypothetical monopolist test, stipulates that a candidate set of products forms a relevant anti-trust market if a hypothetical monopolist over the set of candidate product finds it profitable to increase price by a small but significant non-transitory increase in prices (SSNIP).

define the boundaries of competition between undertakings. The main purpose of market definition is to identify in a systematic way the effective and immediate competitive constraints faced by the undertakings involved' (paragraph 6). Moreover, '[t]he Commission generally uses market definition where there is a need to assess the relative competitive strength of undertakings for the competitive assessment and, most notably, to assess whether an undertaking holds market power. Market definition is thus an intermediate tool to structure and facilitate the competitive assessment in appropriate cases' (paragraph 8).

These sentences contain two important messages. The first is that '[m]arket definition is an intermediate tool to structure and facilitate the competitive assessment' in the specific case at hand. While in case work often significant resources and a large part of the debate are spent on market definition, and while market definition and market shares are important for the assessment of dominance, market definition is not an end in itself. Moreover, it would be misguided to try to roll the entire competitive assessment into the definition of the relevant market, which, in most cases, consists of more than the calculation of market shares. It is hence important to keep in mind that market definition is only useful to the extent that it helps structure and facilitate the competitive assessment. Where this is not the case, or where one encounters diminishing returns, investigative efforts are better spent on other parts of the assessment than on market definition.

The second key message is that market definition, which is about identifying 'the competitive constraints faced by the undertakings involved', is very closely linked to the assessment of market power. Perhaps the most tangible consequence of defining 'boundaries of competition', i.e., from drawing bright lines of who or what is in or out of the relevant market, is that it allows us to compute market shares which are typically a first indicator of market power. In an Article 102 context, this implies that market definition is closely linked with the assessment of dominance.

A third central message, made later in the notice,[6] is that how market power and its effects need to be assessed very much depends on the specific context and can even depend on the specific conduct under investigation. This was already recognised in *United Brands* which stipulated that the relevant geographic market is the 'geographic area in which [...] the conditions of competition are sufficiently homogenous for the effect of the economic power of the undertaking concerned to be able to be evaluated'.[7] This is in line with the central point of this paper, that market definition is a tool to structure and facilitate the competitive assessment of the case at hand.

The interaction between market definition and the assessment of dominance on the one hand and its possible interdependence with the assessment of a specific conduct on the other raises particular challenges in Article 102 cases.

6. Market definition notice, para. 18(c).
7. Case C-27/76, *United Brands v. Commission*, 14.2.1978, ECLI:EU:C:1978:22, para. 11.

3 CHALLENGES OF MARKET DEFINITION IN ARTICLE 102 CASES

Despite the extensive guidance in the new notice, market definition is not a trivial exercise, especially in Article 102 cases.

A key challenge for market definition in Article 102 cases stems from the fact that the assessment of dominance amounts to assessing the level of existing market power of the undertaking concerned. This is in stark contrast to horizontal merger control where market definition typically needs to help structure and facilitate the assessment of how the transaction changes market power.[8] The consequence is that arguments about the competitive constraints faced by the undertaking concerned and hence the definition of the relevant market must be approached differently in an Article 102 case compared to a horizontal merger.

When the assessment relates to the level of existing market power of the (allegedly dominant) undertaking concerned, one has to take into account the fact that the undertaking concerned may have already exercised its market power to a substantial extent. Firms are expected to set prices and other competitive parameters to maximise profits. But when a firm does so, it will be constrained by substitution to alternative products or services, or by customers stopping purchasing the product or service altogether. Because if the firm was not constrained by such substitution, it could raise the price (or change other competitive parameters) to increase profits further. Even a monopolist will be constrained by such substitution when it charges the monopoly price.

This gives rise to the well-known cellophane fallacy which amounts to (wrongly) concluding that the market must be wider than the products of the undertaking in question because substitution to alternative products or services constrains that undertaking to profitably raise price. Instead, it is precisely because the firm exercises its dominance in a correctly defined relevant market that it will be constrained by substitution at the margin.

The cellophane fallacy is well-known, and its consequences are far-reaching. First, the cellophane fallacy implies that the relevant market for the purpose of assessing the dominance of an undertaking can be narrower than the relevant market when the same undertaking is involved in a horizontal merger. This is because the relevant question in the latter case is typically not about the level of market power but rather about how the elimination of the competitive constraint between the merging parties changes that market power.

Second, it is easy to overlook that the learnings from the cellophane fallacy apply very broadly. In particular, the cellophane fallacy is not just a mistake one must avoid when applying quantitative techniques for market definition, such as a quantification

8. As in Art. 102 cases, the assessment of non-horizontal mergers is often more focused on the level of existing market power of the merging parties in their respective activities. Moreover, some horizontal merger assessments may also require an assessment of dominance and existing market power, e.g., where the theory of harm relates to a strengthening of dominance. References to horizontal mergers in this paper should be understood to mean horizontal mergers where the theory of harm relates to non-coordinated effects resulting from the elimination of competition between the merging parties in the absence of pre-merger dominance.

of whether a hypothetical monopolist in the candidate market would find it profitable to implement a small but significant non-transitory increase in price. It equally applies to qualitative debates on constraints through substitution, including, for example, discussions on whether users of one (potentially dominant) platform or ecosystem might switch to alternative platforms if conditions on the first platforms worsened. If the first platform really is dominant, one has to address the question of whether such substitution, if established, is the result of the exercise of market power by the (potentially dominant) firm rather than evidence that that platform is constrained from exercising market power. Therefore, in the absence of convincing evidence that the existing parameters of competition do not already reflect the exercise of market power by the (potentially dominant) undertaking concerned, (long) discussions about constraints on that undertaking through substitution to alternatives are just not very useful. The existence of constraints from substitution at the margin cannot by itself disprove dominance or be used as evidence that the relevant market is defined too narrowly.

Hence, the challenges raised by cellophane fallacy issues are not a niche problem. Instead, they should be expected to arise generally when defining markets in Article 102 cases. But if substitution at the margin is typically not a decisive criterion for defining markets in Article 102 cases, what else can one look at? Unfortunately, there is no single clear recipe, and, in many cases, there will be an element of judgment involved.

From the point of view of economics, a standard indicator of market power, and hence for market definition and dominance in an Article 102 case, is the percentage markup of price over marginal cost – the so-called Lerner index. This is a direct indicator of pricing power, i.e., the ability of a firm to maintain a price above its marginal cost. When customers have close substitutes available under hypothetical 'competitive' prices, this substitution will constrain a firm's ability to raise its price above costs which will result in a low margin. Conversely, when substitution under unobserved competitive prices is weak, then a firm will be able to profitably raise its praise significantly above costs, resulting in high observed margins, before alternative products become an effective constraint. In this sense, looking at the percentage markup over marginal costs is an alternative and direct way to answer the question of whether the undertaking concerned has the market power to profitably raise the price by 5%-10% above the unobserved competitive price. In other words, margins can be thought of as a shortcut for performing an SSNIP-Test starting from the hypothetical competitive price which is an approach often proposed in response to the cellophane fallacy issues.

The percentage markup over marginal cost is hence an appealing concept to measure pricing power which will typically reflect the extent to which customers have access to products that are close substitutes to the products of the undertakings concerned. However, marginal costs are often difficult to measure. Moreover, in industries with high fixed or sunk costs, such as industries with significant investments in R&D, firms need to be able to recover these high fixed costs or sunk investments, at least in expected terms, through prices above marginal costs. This does not mean the Lerner index is not a useful indicator for 'ex-post' market power, i.e., to charge prices substantially above marginal costs. This may well be the relevant measure of market power in the context of the specific case. In other cases it may be more relevant to focus on '*ex-ante*' market power, i.e., rely on more readily available accounting measures, such as return on capital employed or earnings before interest and taxes, that take into account fixed or sunk costs. When such measures of *ex-ante* margins indicate high returns, one may also bypass this debate, because a firm that earns a return on capital that is substantially above market rates will typically have raised the price by much more than 5%-10% relative to the competitive price.

Other non-substitution-based indicators that can be relevant for market definition in an Article 102 context include barriers to entry or expansion. When entering an economic activity involves overcoming high barriers to entry, for example, as a result of high sunk costs of building infrastructure, entry poses a relatively weak threat to an incumbent in that activity. High barriers to entry are hence likely to provide the incumbent with significant market power even when there is some substitution to other technologies at the margin. Of course, this may be '*ex-post*' market power (once the incumbent has sunk the required costs) rather than '*ex-ante*' market power (prior to the investment). As for margins, the emphasis that can be placed on such measures therefore depends on the circumstances of the case. For example, when the entry barriers are the results of investments that were sunk a long time ago, or when the incumbent has inherited the infrastructure from previously state-owned enterprises, such entry barriers can play a greater role in market definition than in the very dynamic industries.

Apart from the challenges arising from the limitations of evidence on substitution in an Article 102 context, another key challenge is that the market power that needs to be assessed can also depend on the theory of harm,[9] i.e., the economic mechanism of how a particular conduct or concentration in question causes direct or indirect harm to the welfare of consumers. The most straightforward example for this is, as should be clear from the above, that the relevant market for the purposes of assessing a horizontal merger where the focus is on assessing the change in market power can be different from the relevant market for the purpose of assessing dominance in an Article 102 context in relation to the same economic activity by the same undertaking involved.

However, the dependence on the theory of harm can also lead to finding different relevant markets for different theories of harm under Article 102: Is the competitive concern that the undertaking concerned leverages its market power from one market or economic activity into another? Or is it that the firm will use its market power to exclude rivals from the same market? Is the concern that the conduct excludes a future competitor offering a close substitute? Or is it about excluding or marginalising actual competitors? Depending on the answers to these questions, and, more generally, on the specific theory of harm, the assessment of market power that is required may differ. The required approach to market definition and hence possibly the resulting relevant markets may then also depend on the theory of harm.

9. *See* para. 18(c) of the new market definition notice.

A specific example here is market definition for pharmaceuticals where the question that often arises is whether the relevant market consists of a single molecule by an originator firm that developed that molecule, or whether the relevant market should include different molecules or drugs in the same therapeutic class. It is common that originators compete with other originators offering drugs in a specific therapeutic class for new patients. But once a drug has been chosen for a specific patient, the patient may be very reluctant to change to alternative drugs which may be less effective. Existing patients of a drug may hence be locked in, giving the originator of the drug significant market power over patients using its drug. Molecules by originators are normally protected by patents. During their duration, patents shield originators from competition from generic copies of their molecule, which provide originators with '*ex-post*' market power over their molecule. And of course, such protection of '*ex-post*' market power is justified (for the duration of the patent) to provide originators with incentives to invest R&D into the development of new and improved drugs to the benefit of patients.

Now consider a situation where patients are matched with an appropriate drug while being treated in the hospital, and where they will then continue their treatment with the same drug upon leaving the hospital. A competitive concern in that context may be that an originator tries to exclude or marginalise drugs within the same therapeutic class by offering aggressive incentives or other benefits to hospitals or prescribing doctors. The competitive concern here is that such behaviour may distort the competition for new patients to the detriment of patients by excluding competitors from the same therapeutic class. In the context of such a theory of harm, it is relevant to assess whether the originator is dominant in the therapeutic class, i.e., whether it has sufficient market power to distort competition within the therapeutic class. The relevant market to structure and facilitate that assessment will most likely be the therapeutic class of the originator's drug.

Conversely, an originator may face a threat of entry by a generic copy of its molecule, for example, when the originator's patent nears expiry or when the validity of the patent is challenged. In that context, a concern may arise that the originator engages in conduct to deter or delay the entry of a perfect substitute to maintain its '*ex-post*' market power beyond patent protection. To structure and facilitate the assessment of such a concern, the appropriate relevant market most likely will be the molecule of the originator, not the entire therapeutic class.

Note that, despite the different outcomes of market definition in the two cases, the market power of the incumbent does not change. In both cases, the incumbent has *ex-post* market power over its molecule and may or may not have market power in the therapeutic class overall. While in the second case that market power over the molecule may be threatened by the prospect of entry, this threat of entry does not change the nature of the market power. Rather it is the difference in the theory of harm which requires an assessment of market power within the therapeutic class in the first case and market power over the molecule in the second. It is this difference in the theory of harm that makes it appropriate to find different relevant markets in the two cases.

Moreover, imagine a third scenario where the concern is that the originator leverages its *ex-post* market power over its base of existing patients into an adjacent market, for example, into a particular mode of administration that is specific to its drug. In such a scenario, it may also be relevant to assess the market power of the originator in a leveraging market that consists of the originator's molecule. So the theories of harm under which it may be appropriate to define the relevant market narrowly are not limited to concerns related to patent expiry.

4 CHALLENGES FOR MARKET DEFINITION IN DIGITAL AND INNOVATIVE SECTORS

The new market definition notice includes, for the first time, specific considerations for market definition in digital and innovative markets. These are treated in dedicated sections of the notice.[10]

The emergence or, at least, the increasing pervasiveness of digital markets in our daily lives has clearly been a key development over the quarter of a century since the original market definition notice, which has also brought new challenges for the enforcement of competition law.

For example, in the digital domain, one often must deal with multi-sided platforms or ecosystems. Multi-sided markets are characterised by indirect network effects where users on different sides of the platform may interact with one another and where participation on one side affects the value of the platform for users on the other side. Such effects may induce firms to offer services on one side of the platform for free (i.e., at a zero price) or even to pay users to join the platform (i.e., offer benefits or negative prices) with a view to monetising the platform by charging users on another side of the platform. The market power that a platform holds over users on one side often depends on whether users on the other side single-home or multi-home, i.e., whether such users frequent one or several platforms. A platform can be a gateway to single-homing users on one side which gives the platform market power over users on the other side.

Similarly, in the digital world, one often encounters situations where consumers choose between different ecosystems, i.e., between complex sets of related products that are often centred around a core product (such as an operating system, or a type of mobile phone, etc.).

Furthermore, in highly innovative industries competition often takes place in innovation spaces, i.e., in R&D efforts that may not, or at least not yet, be directed towards well-defined specific products.

All of this raises complex issues for assessing competitive concerns in such industries and with it for market definition. Should one define separate markets for each side of a multi-sided platform or an overall platform market? Should one define an overall ecosystem market in which firms compete in bundles of services, or a primary

10. Section 4.3 of the new notice discusses market definition in the presence of significant R&D, s. 4.4 market definition in the presence of multi-sided platforms, and s. 4.5 market definition in the presence of after-markets, bundles and (digital) ecosystems.

market for the core product with related products or services belonging to one or more separate aftermarkets? How can one define markets for products which have not yet been innovated?

The new market definition notice explains how the Commission has approached market definition in important cases in each of these categories over the last twenty-five years. That discussion illustrates that the approach to market definition is very much linked to the specific competitive concerns and circumstances of individual cases. This is perhaps even more so in digital and innovative sectors than in more traditional markets. Due to their dynamic nature, digital or innovative markets are, in many ways, moving targets.

This context makes it even more important not to lose sight of the key purpose of market definition, namely that market definition is a tool to structure and facilitate the competitive assessment. Therefore, the question that needs to be addressed in the competitive assessment should guide the appropriate approach to defining the relevant market.

For example, while the interaction between different sides of a multi-sided platform will always need to be accounted for, it may be more or less important in the context of the specific case. Moreover, the competitive concern under consideration may require a specific assessment of different effects on users on different sides of the market in one context, but not in another. So depending on the specific competitive concern, the assessment may be better structured by defining an overall platform market or by defining separate markets for different sides.

Overall, while it is not possible to give very prescriptive guidance on how to define markets in digital or innovative sectors, structuring and facilitating the competitive assessment in light of the specific competitive concern under consideration hence remains the key principle for market definition in digital and innovative sectors.

CHAPTER 9

The Importance of Defining the Relevant Market in Light of the Revised Market Definition Notice

Clara Chambrey

1 INTRODUCTION

The Commission's release of the revised Market Definition Notice (MDN) on 8 February 2024 was a long-anticipated moment in EU antitrust law.[1] This update, the first in twenty-seven years, underscores the importance of non-priced factors and the imperative to adapt market definition methodologies for digital economies. The advent of digital platforms introduced complexities that transcend traditional price-based analyses. By acknowledging the limitations of classic tools, the revised notice heralds a paradigm shift toward a more holistic understanding of market dynamics. Further, rather than a price-based conception of competition, the MDN introduces dynamic concepts of competition, with a particular focus on innovation.

The Notice doubled in size, since it encompasses a wider range of situations, and adapted itself to the changes which occurred over nearly thirty years. However, important questions remain: the 1997 Notice was criticised for not having anticipated new economies, and one might certainly address the same criticisms to the new notice, which actualises the market approach with the economies we know, only a few years too late. We can raise the same critiques that confronted its predecessor: is it not already too late for future practices?

Even more than the last, the 2024 Notice is heavily reliant on case law and does not project market definition to impending new markets. Is the Notice on the relevant

1. European Commission, *Commission Notice on the Definition of the Relevant Market for the Purposes of Union Competition Law*, Official Journal of the European Union, C/2024/1645 (2024), https://eur-lex.europa.eu/legal-content/EN/TXT/PDF/?uri=OJ:C_202401645.

market doomed to be a summary of evolutions that have already occurred, and limited to how the EU Courts resolved them? Is the EU relying solely on a regulatory approach to fix this intrinsic issue?

Viewed in this way, the Notice can be seen as an admission of the triviality of market definition. Some scholars have already expressed views on the futility of the market definition, advocating for its abandonment altogether.[2] Others support the thesis of a renewal of the concept of the market.[3]

From this turbulent debate arises the central question: market definition, *à quoi bon?*

2 THE IMPORTANCE OF MARKET DEFINITION IN A CONSTANTLY CHANGING WORLD

Essential to the enforcement of Article 102 TFEU is the definition of market boundaries, encompassing both product and geographic dimensions.[4] Market definition is essential for identifying dominant players and fostering competitive environments conducive to consumer welfare. Although market definition is just one step in the dominance analysis, it serves an important market power function by determining how wide or narrow the market is, and therefore how easy or difficult it is to establish dominance in the market.

2.1 The Rationale of Market Definition

Market definition is central in determining an abuse of dominant position. The legal definition of dominant position relates 'to a position of economic strength enjoyed by an undertaking which enables it to prevent effective competition being maintained on the relevant market by affording it the power to behave to an appreciable extent independently of its competitors, its customers and ultimately of the consumers'.[5] This 'economic strength' is the economic notion of 'market power'.

The *rationale* of the market definition is to enable inference about market power, which is, for some academics, its sole purpose.[6] However, this is not a settled debate as the antitrust market has been the object of different approaches, especially between

2. Richard S. Markovits, *On the Inevitable Arbitrariness of Market Definitions,* available at SSRN: https://ssrn.com/abstract=135991 (1998); Louis Kaplow, *Why (Ever) Define Markets?,* Harvard Law Review (2010) Forthcoming, Harvard Law and Economics Discussion Paper No. 666, Harvard Public Law Working Paper No. 11-08, Available at SSRN: https://ssrn.com/abstract=1750302.
3. Rupprecht Podszun, *The Arbitrariness of Market Definition and an Evolutionary Concept of Markets,* The Antitrust Bulletin 61(1) (2016), pp. 121-132; Magali Eben, *The Antitrust Market Does Not Exist: Pursuit of Objectivity in a Purposive Process,* Journal of Competition Law & Economics 17(3) (September 2021), pp. 586-619 https://doi.org/10.1093/joclec/nhab001.
4. Notice, s. 1.3.
5. Case 85/76, *Hoffman-La Roche & Co.AG v. Commission,* 13 February 1979, para. 38.
6. Massimo Motta stated that 'market definition is instrumental *only* to the assessment of market power' (own emphasis added) – Massimo Motta, *Competition Policy: Theory and Practice 102* (New York, USA, Cambridge University Press 2004).

American and European scholars.[7] According to Kaplow, defining, first, the market and then assessing market power is nonsensical, since a rigorous delimitation of the relevant market cannot be adopted without first assessing market power.[8]

For others, including D.F. Turner, the relevant market has a dual purpose: providing a 'rational economic basis for assessing the consequences of a particular kind of conduct', and then, as a market power indirect indicator.[9]

Some voices in Europe now advocate that, since the antitrust market does not exist in itself, the fiction of market enables us to understand economic interactions and serves as an analytical tool.[10] The relevant market might be defined to assess competitive constraints, to study the feasibility of the conduct or even the alleged conduct, or the alleged harm (regarding the theory of harm).[11] This 'purposive approach' must however be conducted in an objective manner, so that market definition can be used as a frame of reference.[12]

The European Commission, in its revised Notice, admits using market definition 'to assess the relative competitive strength of undertakings as part of the competitive assessment and, most notably, to assess whether an undertaking holds market power'.[13] Therefore, the Commission retained market power as its first indicator of competitive strength. However, perhaps under the impetus of scholarly debate about the *rationale* of market definition, and the development of case law, the Commission included a novel approach. Indeed, according to the Commission, as market definition 'seeks to identify the effective and immediate competitive constraints that are relevant for the competitive assessment of a specific conduct or concentration, the outcome of market definition can differ' depending on multiple factors such as which undertakings are involved, or the competitive concerns under consideration.[14] By adding this approach, the Commission acknowledged that market definition can vary regarding the type of market that is studied and the different concerns under analysis.

2.2 The Limits of Market Definition as a Legal Notion

Market Definition is not only a legal but also an economic notion. However, as the Commission underlines, 'the concept of relevant market in Union competition law is different from the use of the term 'market' in other contexts, in particular in business contexts'.[15]

7. Gregory J. Werden, *Why (Ever) Define Markets? An Answer to Professor Kaplow*, Antitrust Law Journal 78(3) (2013), p. 732. According to Werden, antitrust market definition is utile for 'the identification and delineation of the competitive process allegedly harmed'.
8. Louis Kaplow, *Market Definition and the Merger Guidelines*, Harvard Law and Economics Discussion Paper No. 695 (1 May 2011), pp. 107-125.
9. Donald F. Turner, *The Role of the '"Market"' Concept in Antitrust Law*, Antitrust Law Journal 49(3) (1980), pp. 1145-1147.
10. Eben, *supra* n. 3, pp. 586-619.
11. *Ibid.*
12. *Ibid.*
13. Notice, para. 8, emphasis added.
14. *Ibid.*, para. 18.
15. *Ibid.*, para. 19.

From an economist's perspective, market power can be determined through factors such as market shares, barriers to entry or the existence of countervailing power on the buyers' side. The analysis of these criteria does not require previously defining the relevant market, according to a part of the doctrine.[16] Moreover, economists have developed an effect-based approach, according to which the economic analysis of the effects of competition restrictions rendered the demonstration of the existence of a dominant position unnecessary.[17] In this sense, EU competition law and economic reality might face a (foreseen) divorce.[18]

Already in 1987, some authors pointed to the limits of market definition as:

> competition defines the market, **not vice versa**; [...] no market can contain competition among modern multi-product firms; [...] the market is a **still snapshot in frozen time**, unable to sense **change** or **innovation**; [...] the process of competition defies quantification; and hence [...] the concept of a finite, objectively defined market is an ever-receding mirage.[19]

The European competition policy was built on neoclassical economic models, which are 'essentially static'.[20] As regards Article 102 TFEU especially, this static vision could be seen as incapable of grasping innovation or technological progress, which are both central since they can capture the number of consumers on a market, the evolution of a market, the consumer trends, the number of firms, etc., and detect potential dominant position and abuses. However, as markets are constantly changing, often at a pace we cannot sense, it is necessary to have a static picture of a market to define it.[21] This approach is not opposed to the inclusion of dynamic elements of interpretation, as will be further developed in this chapter.

The *static-classic price* and *dynamic-innovation-based* approaches of competition are not true opposites, and one can complement the other. There is a difference in understanding the whole market as static, or to use a static picture when defining a market. The static methodology allows us to define a market at a specific time, which further allows us to be objective in this assessment.

Despite the numerous criticisms of the relevant market as a (quasi-) arbitrary economic notion, defining it is a necessary legal assessment and one that needs to be perfected.[22] The question of whether market definition is a perfect tool is indeed rarely,

16. Ariane Charpin, Gildas de Muizon, *Délimiter les marchés pertinents? Autant gratter une jambe de bois jusqu'à ce qu'elle saigne!*, Concurrences No. 2-2012, Market Definition: Is There a Need for New Guidance?, pp. 9-20.
17. EAGCP Report, *An Economic Approach to Article 82*, 2005.
18. Anne-Kathrin Kühnel-Fitchen, *The Software 'Market': Advocating an Alternative Approach to Competition Law Analysis under Article 102 TFEU* (Aberystwyth University 2016), p. 138.
19. Frederick M. Rowe, *Market as Mirage*, California Law Review 75 (1987), pp. 991-992 (emphasis added).
20. Simon Bishop and Mike Walker, *The Economics of EC Competition Law: Concepts, Application and Measurement* (Sweet & Maxwell 2010), para. 2-036.
21. Eben, *supra* n. 3, pp. 586-619.
22. Rupprecht Podszun, *The Arbitrariness of Market Definition and an Evolutionary Concept of Markets*, The Antitrust Bulletin 61(1) (2016), pp. 121-132.

if ever, answered in the affirmative.[23] Outside of competition law, the question of the relevant market is not tackled in economics and does not have 'a precise, well-defined answer', which proves its legal purpose.[24]

So far, its longevity demonstrates that no other tool can replace it as a part of a legal assessment. Market definition is now an instinctive reflex for competition authorities and lawyers, and still the best-suited tool for defining this 'space' of competition in which undertakings operate. Even though the Notice is a soft law instrument, which is not binding upon NCAs and institutions, it remains an essential step.

Nonetheless, and as the renewed Notice makes clear, the exercise of market definition has been challenged by emerging economies, especially digital systems.

2.3 Catching Up with the Digital Earthquake

The revised Notice includes digital markets, a move that was acclaimed by scholars and professionals alike. As traditional navigation instruments are 'flexible enough to ... be applied in the context of new market realities and, where necessary, adapted in the light of these realities',[25] including guidance about digital markets in this soft law tool seemed necessary.

The Notice even refers to ecosystems, a novelty that has not yet reached a consensus in competition law, since case law on the topic is still evolving.[26] The Notice limits itself to acknowledging that ecosystems 'can, in certain circumstances, be thought of as consisting of a primary core product and several secondary (digital) products whose consumption is connected to the core product' and/or the secondary products may be offered as a bundle, potentially producing aftermarkets.[27] Without truly giving guidance on the definition of the markets, for ecosystems, the Commission accepts the existence of those new systems and leaves room for further future consideration of their development.

In the case of multi-sided markets, the Market Definition Notice does not settle the debate about the number of markets to define. Contrary to the US Supreme Court,[28] the EU Court chose to define a market for each side of the product or service, while considering 'interactions between the two facets of a two-sided system' to assess

23. Duncan Cameron et al., *Good Riddance to Market Definition?*, The Antitrust Bulletin 57 (2012), pp. 719-746 https://doi.org/10.1177/0003603x1205700403.
24. Franklin M. Fischer, *Economic Analysis and 'Bright-Line' Tests*, Journal of Competition Law & Economics 4 (2008), §132 https://doi.org/10.1093/joclec/nhm023.
25. Thomas Kramler, *Adapting EU Competition Law to the Digital Economy*, The Evolution of Antitrust in the Digital Era 1 (2020), pp. 65-87 (at 87) (David Evans, Allan Fels & Catherine Tucker).
26. *See* Commission Decision of 25 September 2023 declaring a concentration incompatible with the internal market and the functioning of the EEA Agreement (Case M.10615 – *Booking Holdings/Etraveli Group*) (notified under document number C(2023) 6376).
27. Notice, para. 104.
28. United States Supreme Court: *Ohio v. American Express Co.*, 585 U.S. (2018).

whether a practice is harming competition.[29] This approach was employed for Article 101 TFEU. Within the framework of Article 102 TFEU, the most important case on this topic was the *Google Shopping* case.[30]

Alongside the revised Market Definition Notice, the Digital Markets Act (DMA) represents a landmark legislative effort to address the challenges of market definition in the digital era. By targeting 'gatekeepers' (firms holding a dominant position) managing digital platforms, the DMA seeks to safeguard competition and innovation in digital markets. However, its efficiency can be debated since its obligations apply objectively regardless of market definition or effect, without any prejudice to Article 102. This raises a paradoxical situation for digital markets. Under competition law provisions, among them, Article 102 TFEU, a dominant position in a relevant market should be proven, whereas under the DMA, the market definition is not needed.[31] This could be explained by the internal nature of this instrument, relying on a per se approach, where the formal market definition could be bypassed since the market structure in digital markets was the core motivation of the DMA (hence its name).[32]

This evolution illustrates the Commission's intention to find an alternative to market definition as a basis for identifying the market power of digital platforms. It remains to be seen whether, in the long run, this new direction will have an impact on classic antitrust market definition. That is how we might observe a resurgence of classic theories in doctrine, that can be applied to digital markets, such as Baumol's theory of contestable markets, which holds that markets served by a small number of competitors can be characterised by competitive equilibrium, and therefore desirable welfare can be the outcome, because of the existence of potential short-term entrants.[33] Likewise, according to Schumpeter, a few large firms may have a greater incentive to innovate, rather than small firms, and therefore the presence of those large firms holding market power would be beneficial for innovation.[34]

3 UPDATING ECONOMIC ANALYSIS TOOLS: THE IMPOSSIBLE COMPETITIVE 'PRICE'

As previously outlined, the Commission bases competition policy on a neoclassical price theory. However, with digital and zero-price markets, price is not always the focus for consumers, and therefore their welfare. The European understanding of consumer welfare is indeed not only based on price considerations but also on quality or innovation.

29. Case C-67/13P, *Groupement des cartes bancaires (CB) v. Commission*, paras 78-79, EU:C:2014:2204.
30. Case T-612/17, *Google and Alphabet v. Commission*, EU:T:2021:763.
31. On this point, the mandatory dimension of the definition of the relevant market, under Art. 102 TFEU, is further developed in this chapter.
32. Alexandre de Streel *et al.*, *Digital Markets Act: Making Economic Regulation of Platforms Fit for the Digital Age*, Centre on Regulation in Europe (CERRE) Report (December 2020), p. 34.
33. William J. Baumol, John C. Panzar and Robert D. Wilig, *Contestable Markets and the Theory of Industry Structure* (Harcourt College Pub 1982).
34. Joseph A. Schumpter, *Capitalism, Socialism, and Democracy* (Harper & Brothers 1942).

This paradigm raises the question of the competitive price level and its determination, and 'these questions are hard if not impossible to answer'.[35] In its renewed Notice, the Commission tackled the issues of the metrics and introduced a shift.

3.1 The Classic Metrics

3.1.1 The Fall Down of Market Shares

The role of market shares in the definition of the relevant market in the context of Article 102 TFEU has known some turbulence. Market shares and market power are indeed often referred to as two sides of the same coin. Contrary to a more 'classic' approach to competition law, the power to exclude competitors is not always associated with higher market share or profits.[36] Therefore, market shares and profits are not especially useful in indicating a strong market power.

The Notice relegates market shares to being just one of the tools to determine market power, rather than the main one, as 'market shares are not the sole indicator of an undertaking's strength in the market'.[37] Market shares have to be supported by other indicators.[38] This sits well with the presumption of dominance introduced by the case law.[39] This presumption can be reversed and does not determine, by itself, dominance. The Commission now has a wider margin of appreciation, which has also been extended to market share calculation. This, however, is a simple translation of the established case law.[40]

Market shares are useful for traditional economic business models relying on profits, but for others, market shares should be 'calculated using different plausible definitions of the relevant set of substitutes'.[41] Indeed, especially in digital markets and zero-price markets, market shares might be 'ephemeral', regarding the short innovation cycles.[42] When assessing market power, authorities need to consider that digital markets are fast-growing, highly concentrated, and will, often inevitably, lead to

35. Rafael Allendesalazar et al., *Oligopolies, Conscious Parallelism and Concertation*, in Claus-Dieter Ehlermann and Isabela Atanasiu (eds), European Competition Law Annual 2006: Enforcement of Prohibition of Cartels, Hart, pp. 119, 122, footnote 13.
36. GSMA, *Resetting Competition Policy Frameworks for the Digital Ecosystem*, 2016, https://www.gsma.com/solutions-and-impact/connectivity-for-good/public-policy/wp-content/uploads/2016/10/GSMA_Resetting-Competition_Report_Oct-2016_60pp_WEBv2.pdf, p. 25.
37. Notice, para. 106.
38. Draft Guidelines Art. 102 TFEU – 2024; Communication from the Commission – Guidance on the Commission's enforcement priorities in applying Article 82 of the EC Treaty to abusive exclusionary conduct by dominant undertakings [2009] OJ C 45/02, para. 15.
39. Case C-62/86 *AKZO v. Commission* [1991] EU:C:1991:286, para. 60, presumption of dominance when an undertaking owns 50% of the market shares.
40. Case T-584/19, *Thyssenkrupp AG v. Commission*, EU:T:2022:32, paras 74-78; and T-251/19, *Wieland-Werke AG v. Commission*, EU:T:2022:296, para. 38.
41. David S. Evans, *Multisided Platforms, Dynamic Competition, and the Assessment of Market Power for Internet-Based Firms* (2016) University of Chicago Coase-Sandor Institute for Law & Economics Research Paper No. 753.
42. Case T-79/12 *Cisco and Messagenet v. Commission* EU:T:2013:635, para. 69; *Apple/Shazam* (Case COMP/M.8788) Commission Decision of 6 September 2018, para. 162; *Facebook/WhatsApp* (Case COMP/M.7217) Commission Decision of 3 October 2014, para. 99.

margins, as innovation is costly. Those margins might, then, create dominant positions, and further abuses of dominant position. Nonetheless, market shares are still valuable, even for dynamic markets such as digital markets, and the Commission has already recognised its importance, particularly on stable dynamic digital markets.[43]

New indicators such as network externalities, use of data, and increasing returns to scale might be relevant indicators to assess market power, when defining digital market,[44] as the Commission underlines.[45]

3.1.2 The Quantitative Methodology

Non-price factors emerge as important determinants of market dynamics, necessitating a recalibration of analytical frameworks.

The traditional, price-focused antitrust tools for assessing dominance under Article 102 TFEU are challenged by the business models and features of digital platforms, such as the *SSNIP* (Small but Significant Non-transitory Increase in Price) test. Digital markets are indeed innovation-driven, and competitive pressure may not come merely from similar products. For non-priced products, the General Court stated that 'the SSNIP test may also prove unsuitable (...) where there are free goods or goods the cost of which is not borne by those determining the demand.'[46] Even before the digital revolution, the SSNIP test has been criticised for being based on the chimaera that consumers have perfect information on the market.[47] A perfect market is defined by 'perfect knowledge on the part of the traders', by which consumers will orient their consummation choices based on price, or quality.[48] In the revised Notice, the SSNIP test is indicated to serve as a mere 'conceptual framework'.[49] Although helpful, the hypothetical monopolist test, the SSNIP test, does not constitute a legal requirement for the Commission or national authorities in defining the relevant market.[50] This method is one of many, as the Commission can also rely on market research or an assessment of the points of view of consumers and competitors, without a 'rigid hierarchy between the different criteria available to the Commission'.[51]

Thus, the 'cellophane fallacy' showed that the SSNIP test analysis can lead to the detection of vast markets since the prices are (wrongly) inflated by a monopolistic price.[52] The Commission, in the Notice,[53] recalls that the SSNIP should be applied

43. Commission Decision, *Google Shopping* (Case AT.39740), 27 June 2017, para. 267.
44. Marc Bourreau and Alexandre de Streel, 'Digital Conglomerates and EU Competition Policy' (2019), https://ssrn.com/abstract=3350512.
45. Notice, para. 106.
46. Case T-699/14 *Topps Europe Ltd v. Commission*, EU:T:2017:2, para. 82. *See also*, Commission Decision, Case AT.39 740, *Google Search (Shopping)*, para. 245, 27 June 2017.
47. Josef Silhan, *The Concept of Relevant Market: Some Critical Remarks*, European Competition Law Review 33 (2012), p. 593.
48. G. Stigler, *The Theory of (Competitive) Price*, (Macmillan Publishers 1942), p. 82.
49. Notice, para. 31.
50. Case T-699/14 *Topps Europe Ltd v. Commission*, EU:T:2017:2, para. 82.
51. Case T-671/19 *Qualcomm v. Commission*, EU:T:2024:626, para. 233.
52. This 'cellophane fallacy' was named after the case *United States v. E.I. du Pont de Nemours & Co.* 351 U.S. 377 (1956).

carefully, as the Commission already stated in the *Slovak Telekom* case.[54] Nonetheless, the Notice refers to the possibility, 'in some cases', of applying an SSNIP test, to apply antitrust tools for ecosystems and multi-sided platforms, giving the Commission a broad margin of appreciation. The utilisation of the SSNIP test for zero-priced markets can be seen as incompatible with the commercial reality of multi-sided platforms.[55] This is where alternative methodologies can be used. Concerning quantitative factors, data has progressively become a useful indicator not only to detect market power but also to set market power. Indeed, data can provide information about market power, especially when focusing on how the provider is utilising the data, not its intrinsic value.[56] This methodology could help to detect market power.

Alternatively, the SSNIC test ('Small but Significant and Non-transitory Increase in Costs'), could be a suitable answer for the failure of classic tools.[57] This test, proposed by J. M. Newman, relies on the increase of costs for users, for example, in terms of attention and information, instead of the price.[58] Nonetheless, this test has been met with multiple difficulties, such as the capacity to evaluate those costs. How can we collect personal data concerning the attention of consumers, especially in the EU, where personal data is protected under the General Data Protection Regulation.[59] The test is, however, not cited by the Notice.

3.2 The Introduction of New Metrics and Dynamic Concepts of Competition

3.2.1 The Qualitative Methodology

First, the Commission has offered new possibilities, such as using the SSNDQ test ('Small but significant non-transitory decrease in quality') for zero-priced markets. The SSNDQ test is a consumer-based analysis, centred around the decrease in the quality of a product. This test, better suited to technological markets, differentiates itself from the SSNIP ('Small but significant non-transitory increase in price') test, which focuses on price. Those tools were rarely used by NCA. Recently, the Commission applied the

53. Notice, para. 30.
54. European Commission, AT.39523 *Slovak Telekom*, paras 158-171.
55. Daniel Mândrescu, *Chapter 3: Market Definition and Digital Platforms*, in Marc Wiggers et al. (eds), Digital Competition Law in Europe (Kluwer Law International 2023), pp. 37-76.
56. Inge Graef, *Market Definition and Market Power in Data: The Case of Online Platforms*, World Competition 38(4) (2015), p. 502 https://doi.org/10.54648/woco2015040.
57. Mandrescu, *The SSNIP Test and Zero-Pricing Strategies: Considerations for Online Platforms*, European Competition and Regulatory Law Review 2(4) (2018), p. 244.
58. John M. Newman, *Antitrust in Zero-Price Markets: Applications*, 94(29) (2016) Washington University Law Review 51; John M. Newman, *Antitrust in Zero-Price Markets: Foundations*, 164(149) (2015) University of Pennsylvania Law Review 150.
59. *See* Regulation (EU) 2016/679 of the European Parliament and of the Council of 27 April 2016 on the protection of natural persons with regard to the processing of personal data and on the free movement of such data, and repealing Directive 95/46/EC (General Data Protection Regulation), Art. 5.

SSNDQ test in the *Google Android* and *Google/Fitbit* cases.[60] However, the Commission did not develop its methodology, and which qualities of the product(s) were tested. As such, the OECD states that the usefulness of this SSNDQ test might be as a more conceptual concept than a preliminary step, applied by competition authorities.[61]

This scepticism can be explained due to the difficulty, in practice, of using the SSNDQ test. Especially for multi-sided platforms, the SSNDQ test could be used on one side of the platform, and not the other, and produce different results. Moreover, whereas the decrease in price can be opportunistic for consumers, and for firms, by attracting more consumers, the decrease in quality does not constitute a rational economic decision. Therefore, the SSNDQ might never be a plausible test in reality. The qualities that could be tested will 'need to be done on a case-by-case basis'.[62] The Notice, unfortunately, does not provide further guidance on a suitable methodology.

Then, the Notice opens the possibility of using other metrics as proofs, such as the number of (active) users, or website visits, streams to the platforms, time spent on the platform, and volume or value of transactions concluded on the platform, level of R&D, etc.[63] To simplify, any metrics 'used internally by market participants in their general course of business generally prove particularly relevant' can be presented by firms.[64]

Finally, the Notice highlights the role of multi-sided markets and network effects, where non-economic considerations such as digital inclusion or data interoperability may constitute barriers to substitution and switching costs.[65]

3.2.2 Future Markets and Innovation

The renewed Notice addresses the issue of a forward-looking market definition. The main concept is the one of 'sufficiently foreseeable changes' in demand, and competitive constraints.[66]

According to the Commission, the 'sufficient likelihood' that those changes will occur enables the Commission to take those elements into account when defining the market.[67]

This inclusion is a welcome one, as digital platforms are constantly evolving, and substitutes of products may overlap with the products in question. Moreover, consumer habits have put innovation at the heart of digital markets as new functionalities

60. European Commission, CaseAT.40099, *Google Android*, para. 267, 2018 and Case M.9660 – *GOOGLE/FITBIT*, para. 124, 2020, in a merger case.
61. OECD, 'Policy Roundtable: The Role and Measurement of Quality in Competition Analysis' (2013).
62. Mandrescu, *supra* n. 57, p. 254.
63. Notice, para. 108.
64. *Ibid.*
65. Notice, para. 57.
66. *Ibid.*, para. 8.
67. *Ibid.*, para. 21, whereas the draft required sufficient *probability*, or certainty (paras 16, 77).

or products may push a consumer to the 'new next thing'.[68] In this regard, the number of users can even be considered to identify possible substitutes, and principally, for digital platforms serving multiple functions, the potential substitutes need to be studied from a consumer perspective.[69] Therefore, detecting future markets in the market definition might be beneficial, particularly in markets prone to innovation.

In addition, the Notice dedicates a section to the relevance of research and development (R&D), especially regarding pipeline products.[70] During innovation cycles, the R&D process might result in different products, and not a specific one, creating difficulties in identifying the relevant market product.

Even though the product is not yet commercialised, firms must be transparent about the process, to allow the Commission to allocate a pipeline product to a relevant product market or define a new product market.

The Notice further mentions that the geographic market of those pipeline products 'can be broader than the relevant geographic market of commercialised products'.[71] Since the 1990s, the Commission considered, especially for pharmaceutical products, that the R&D for the relevant products should be considered, at the very least, on the EEA-wild markets, or global markets.[72] Interestingly, those views were not incorporated in the 1997 Notice, even though the Commission already tackled the future markets and R&D themes at that time. Once again, the Notice's revision is based on the Commission's practice used for merger cases, particularly in the pharmaceutical industry. The Commission indeed recognised 'innovation spaces' (not product markets), although they have not been detected outside of this pharmaceutical niche.[73]

Overall, the recognition of those innovation spaces, in the revised Notice, allows the authorities to detect boundaries, and encourage R&D even though innovation processes can be unpredictable and uncertain. This assessment allows NCAs to focus on innovation and therefore include dynamic elements in their analysis. Still, the use of concepts such as 'potential competition' or 'future markets' could be understood as a way of avoiding the development of an innovation-specific approach, which directly tackles innovation.[74]

68. David S. Evans, *Multisided Platforms, Dynamic Competition, and the Assessment of Market Power for Internet-Based Firms* (2016) University of Chicago Coase-Sandor Institute for Law & Economics Research Paper No. 753, 27.
69. T. Knapstad, *Digital Dominance: Assessing Market Definition and Market Power for Online Platforms under Article 102 TFEU*, European Competition Journal 20(2) (2023), pp. 412-436.
70. Notice, para. 92, footnote 125.
71. Notice, para. 92.
72. Commission decision of 17 July 1996 in Case M. 737 – *Ciba-Geigy/Sandoz*, para. 51; Commission decision of 28 January 2015, in Case M.7275 *Novartis/GSK Oncology Business*, para. 32; and M.7480 *Actavis/Allergan*, para. 17.
73. Commission Decision of 27 March 2017 declaring a concentration compatible with the internal market and the functioning of the EEA Agreement (Case M.7932 – *Dow/DuPont*), (notified under document C(2017) 1946).
74. Wolfgang Kerber, 'Towards a Dynamic Concept of Competition that Includes Innovation', OECD (8 June 2023).

Multiple voices in doctrine encourage the focus on capabilities and resources, as those elements can help to develop a framework for a dynamic approach to competition law.[75] By focusing on capabilities, the NCAs could then understand the capability of a firm to innovate. The capacity analyses could then serve to detect potential competition, future markets and innovation and better define the product market.

3.3 Balancing Economic and Non-economic Objectives

Non-economic factors, such as environmental sustainability and social objectives, have been explicitly addressed in the 2024 Market Definition Notice.[76] This paradigm shift reflects a growing recognition of the need to align competition law with broader EU policy goals, such as the Green Deal and digital transformation strategies. In this sense, the Notice aligns with the broader shift of the Competition policy, with competition law serving EU policy goals (e.g., the portfolio of Commissioner Ribera). The Notice outlines that consumer preferences, especially European consumers, are increasingly shaped by non-economic factors. Indeed, environmentally conscious consumers may prioritise sustainability over price.[77] Moreover, the Notice still suggests that competition authorities should consider such preferences when assessing product markets, particularly in sectors including energy, transport, and food, where sustainability plays a central role.[78]

4 FUTURE PERSPECTIVES

The Notice considers multiple new perspectives that its predecessor did not. However, there is still room for further questioning and development.

4.1 The Definition of the Relevant Market as a Compulsory Preliminary Step

Market definition is often the preliminary step to identify the existence of a dominant position. This legal assessment has its origins in the case law, especially the *Continental Can v. Commission* case, where the Court annulled the decision of the Commission on the basis of Article 102 TFEU, and the failure of the Commission to define the relevant market, making it necessary rather than optional.[79] The General Court once stated that 'the appropriate definition of the market in question is a <u>necessary</u>

75. *See,* for example, Wolfang Kerber and Simonetta Vezzoso, *Competition and Innovation: Incorporating a More Dynamic Perspective into Enforcement* (January 2025), http://dx.doi.org/10.2139/ssrn.5160223.
76. Notice, para. 3.
77. *Ibid.*, paras 15, 72.
78. *Ibid.*, para. 72; *See,* for example, case M.10047 *Schwarz Group/Suez Waste management companies*, paras 56-58, about environmental costs as one of the relevant factors when defining the geographic market.
79. Case 6/72, *Europemballage and Continental Can v. Commission*, EU:C:1973:22, para. 32.

precondition of any judgment concerning allegedly anti-competitive behaviour'.[80] Especially in the context of Article 102 TFEU, the General Court considered that the relevant market definition is a necessary condition since the abuse of a dominant position occurs in a market, which then, needs to be defined.[81]

Nonetheless, the Commission, in its Draft Guidelines on Article 102 TFEU, still referred to ECJ case law and retained this uncertainty about the compulsory requirement of the relevant market.[82] In the Notice, the Commission chose to maintain the market definition as a soft law tool for NCAs and affirmed that it 'is not a mandatory step in all assessments under Union competition law'.[83] To date, a majority of European countries refer to the market definition.[84]

Mario Monti, former Commissioner for competition declared that 'market definition is a cornerstone of competition policy, but not the entire building. Market definition is a tool for the competitive assessment, not a substitute for it. What is ultimately important is to understand the nature of the competitive situation facing the firms involved in a certain practice or in a proposed merger. The market definition is a first – and very important – step in the analysis'.[85] Perhaps not the entire building, but market definition is one of the foundations of competition policy and enforcement. Without defining a market in which competition infringements may occur, especially in the context of digital markets, prone to rapid changes, the national competition authorities could hardly justify the application of competition law provisions.

Recently, in the *Android Auto* case, the Court recalled that a precise definition of a downstream market, which is 'still developing or evolving rapidly', is not required since that market is only potential.[86] According to the Court, in a situation such as the refusal by an undertaking in a dominant position to ensure the interoperability of an application developed by a third-party undertaking with a digital platform owned by the undertaking in a dominant position, an NCA 'may limit itself to identifying the downstream market on which that refusal is likely to produce anticompetitive effects' when it is a potential market.[87] In that case, AG Medina noted the same finding, and added, considering the 2024 Notice, that it is sufficient, for the Authority, to establish 'that the conduct in question was capable of producing anticompetitive effects with regard to products or services which are in competition between them'.[88] Therefore, the Court ruled that it is sufficient to identify, and not define, a potential downstream

80. Joined cases T-68/89, T-77/89 and T-78/89, *Società Italiana Vetro SpA, Fabbrica Pisana SpA et PPG Vernante Pennitalia SpA v. Commission*, EU:T:1992:38, para. 159, emphasis added.
81. Case T-62/98, *Volkswagen v. Commission*, EU:T:2000:180, para. 230.
82. Draft Guidelines on Art. 102 TFEU, para. 20, stating that the market definition is 'in general necessary'.
83. Notice, para. 8.
84. We can count at least twenty-one countries, in alphabetical order Austria, Belgium, Bulgaria, Croatia, Cyprus, Czech Republic, Denmark, Estonia, Finland, Germany, Greece, Hungary, Latvia, Lithuania, Malta, Poland, Portugal, Romania, Slovakia, Slovenia, Spain.
85. Speech by Mario Monti, 'Market definition as a cornerstone of EU competition policy', 5 October 2001.
86. Case C-233/23, *Alphabet Inc. and Others*, EU:C:2025:110, paras 84-86.
87. *Ibid.*
88. Opinion of Advocate General Medina in Case C-233/23, *Alphabet Inc. and Others*, EU:C:2024:694, para. 88.

market if it can produce anticompetitive effects. This analysis sits well with the recent developments of a rather effect-based approach in enforcing Article 102 TFEU.

4.2 The Development of a Case-by-Case Analysis: Flexibility or Legal Certainty?

The notion of the relevant market has been developed in the case law. National competition authorities can (and often do) consider the developments led by the Court of Justice of the European Union, and the Commission since this authority is competent for the most important cases. Coherence is key to preserving the unity of the European market, and each authority needs to define the relevant market based on a common methodology. The revised Notice provides some guidance in the construction of a common framework, especially with regard to digital structures. However, the Notice leaves uncertainty, as it relies heavily on case law to justify the introduction of new concepts, which could lead to different practices from the NCAs.

The approach presently used by the Commission may harm legal certainty. For some, this may be a 'back to the future' moment, when the Commission, EU national Courts, and undertakings were complaining about the 'unpredictable nature of procedures'.[89] The renewed Notice relies on referring in the footnotes to case law, where its predecessor issued a conceptual framework. The paradigm shifted, and this casuistic approach is regrettable not only for firms but also for national competition authorities. This case-by-case analysis has proved controversial, since the Draft Guidelines on Article 102 TFEU recall that dominant undertakings have a 'special responsibility not to engage in conducts that impairs effective competition'.[90] Even though that affirmation has not yet been properly explained, this situation reflects the economic reality of markets, as some firms hold most market shares and are in a position of 'super-dominance'.[91] This concept has already emerged in case law.[92]

The balance between a holistic understanding of the notion of the market, a non-rigid methodology to define it and a case-by-case analysis is hard to reach. The evolution of the Notice based on case law enables an objective picture of the developments in antitrust over the last years. As has been advocated, markets have to be 'relied upon in the substantive analysis of conduct'.[93] The market definition methodology is intrinsically linked to economic evolution. Therefore, antitrust doctrines 'evolve as economic learning evolves, usually with a lag'.[94] This explains this persistent lack of ability to be *in advance* and to detect new practices or grasp them

89. Daniel Mandrescu, *Chapter 3: Market Definition and Digital Platforms*, in M. Wiggers *et al.* (eds), Digital Competition Law in Europe (Kluwer 2023), p. 41.
90. Draft Guidelines on Art. 102 TFEU, para. 44.
91. Alessia Sophia D'Amico and Baskaran Balasingham, *Super-Dominant and Super-Problematic? The Degree of Dominance in the Google Shopping Judgement*, European Competition Journal, 18(3) (5 September 2024), pp. 614-630.
92. Joined Cases C-395/96 P and C-396/96 P, *Compagnie Maritime Belge NV and Dafra-Lines v. Commission*, EU:C:2000:132, paras 182, 183.
93. Eben, *supra* n. 3; Knapstad, *supra* n. 69.
94. John E. Lopatka, *Market Definition?*, Review of Industrial Organization 39(1-2) (2011), p. 85.

when they are about to harm competition. The objective of the Notice is not to codify the case law but to provide guidance for firms. Nonetheless, the Commission, like firms, cannot predict those future economies.

4.3 The New Competition Tool

In 2024, the 'new competition tool' *(NCT)* was introduced in the *Draghi Report*, as a panacea aiming to face the structural lack of tools in some competition issues, although the scope of this NCT was not precisely defined. Mario Draghi asserted that considering the emergence of new technologies, the EU should innovate by 'revamping competition'.[95] Relying on an *ex ante* approach, the 'new competition tool' *(NCT)*, was first introduced by the Commission in 2020, in order to intervene to remedy structural market failures without finding an infringement of competition law.[96] Unfortunately, the Commission narrowed the NCT with the DMA, which is only applicable to the gatekeepers, and abandoned the concept as a 'stand-alone new tool'.[97]

In the Draghi Report, the scope of the NCT is limited to four areas: (1) markets with tacit collusion; (2) markets with a particular need for consumer protection; (3) markets with weak economic resilience; and (4) past enforcement action where data proves that the remedies are ineffective.[98]

As Jean Tirole, Nobel Prize winner in 2022, stated:

> what is needed is not a drastic change in antitrust law; indeed, the age-old statutes are worded in a broad enough manner that many of the behaviors we are concerned about are somehow already embodied in law. In contrast, the regulatory apparatus must be made more agile and in tune with evolving economic thinking in the digital age.[99]

The NCT can be opportunistic for the national regulators and may be an answer to the lack of flexibility and regulatory gaps. Indeed, the NCT would be used to tackle structural competition issues, while guaranteeing 'a measured and well calibrated intervention'.[100] This market design tool would allow for a better understanding of market dynamics and would contribute to avoiding type 1 errors and ensuring legal certainty.[101]

95. European Commission, *The Future of European Competitiveness*, Part A, September 2024, p. 67.
96. Proposal for a Regulation by the Council and the European Parliament introducing a new competition tool, 2 June 2020, https://eur-lex.europa.eu/legal-content/EN/ALL/?uri=PI_COM%3AAres%282020%292877634.
97. Francesco Ducci, *Gatekeepers and Platform Regulation: Is the EU Moving in the Right Direction?* (Sciences Po 2021).
98. European Commission, *The Future of European Competitiveness*, Part B, September 2024, p. 303.
99. Jean Tirole, *Competition and Industrial Policy in the 21st Century*, Oxford Open Economics, 3(1) (2024), pp. 983-1001 https://doi.org/10.1093/ooec/odad080, Quoted in the Draghi Report, p. 299.
100. Aurélien Boronat, *The New Competition Tool: A Market Design Tool for Pro-Competitive Industrial Policies in Europe?*, Journal of European Competition Law & Practice (2025), https://doi.org/10.1093/jeclap/lpaf014.
101. *Ibid.*

This tool is already applied by NCAs in the EU, and this number might grow over the years, raising the ultimate question of a potential unified EU NCT.[102] In the United Kingdom, the Competition Market Authority uses this tool to undertake market investigations where market features *may* distort competition and when the CMA can adopt market-wide remedies.[103] In Germany, the NCA can address remedies to 'undertakings whose conduct and their relevance for the market structure contributes significantly to the malfunctioning of competition'.[104]

Even though the NCT leaves behind doubts as to its realisation, this quest for a new tool, allowing the Commission to intervene without finding infringements on a certain market, outside of the DMA, underlines the urgent need for a better understanding of dynamic market structures.

5 CONCLUSION

Crucially, the revised Market Definition Notice confronts the challenges posed by digital platforms, and new economies more generally. It reflects and indeed heavily relies upon the developments of the case law and scholarly literature, while giving guidance on different approaches which can be applied to digital markets. The Notice marks a potential inclusion of a dynamic approach to competition law, focusing on innovation.

According to Commissioner Margrethe Vestager, the objective was to help firms evaluate their position in the market themselves, and therefore to assist them in complying with competition rules.[105] It remains to be seen whether this objective will be achieved.

In practice, the MDN's importance should not be overlooked, since this revised version mainly applies to digital firms, innovation-driven and non-priced markets. However, in a more abstract manner, the revised notice heralds a paradigm shift in competition policy and a novel understanding of the relevant market, as a market segment with its own competitive dynamic. More broadly, the Notice confirms that market definition is an essential concept and a source of legitimacy for the enforcement of EU law.

The evolution of the definition of relevant market is, now, definitively a policy choice, and competition law has been shaped by policy, as the Vestager mandate has highlighted. In this sense, the political approach precipitated a shift from competition law to competition policy, a 'politicisation' of competition.[106] The renewed Notice

102. So far Belgium, Bulgaria, Austria, Danmark, Romania, Lithuania, Iceland, Norway, Germany, Greece, and the UK have introduced an *ex ante* market investigation tool.
103. Under the UK Enterprise Act 2002.
104. Under the *Gesetz gegen Wettbewerbsbeschränkungen*, translation from Alessia D'Amico and Inge Graef, *Draghi's New Competition Tool Promises To Revamp Competition, but Comes With Challenges* (Promarket, 4 October 2024).
105. European Commission – Speech, Remarks by Executive Vice-President Vestager on the adoptions of a revised Market Definition Notice, Brussels, 8 February 2024.
106. A. Komninos and A. Palacios, *The 'End of Competition Law'?*, Competition Law International, 20(2) (December 2024).

reveals support for a holistic conception of antitrust, and a sincere attempt to reconcile competition law with the EU's broader objectives including the Green Deal, fostering innovation, and defence of the European market on an international level.

Part III Abuse and Legal Tests: Between Effectiveness and Legal Certainty

CHAPTER 10

The Role of Categories of Abuse under Article 102 TFEU and the Concept of 'Competition on the Merits'

Christian Ahlborn

1 INTRODUCTION

Categorisation has been an important tool for the application of the abuse control of dominant firms; indeed, categories have been hard-wired into Article 102 TFEU.

The categorisation of abuse reflects the influence of the Ordo-Liberal School during the early days of EU competition law, which distinguished conduct clearly into pro-competitive 'performance competition' and inherently harmful 'impediment competition'. The advent of the 'more economic' approach, which raised doubt about this neat dichotomy, led to a reduction of the significance of categories (as well as presumptions) at the expense of a more coherent, overarching analytical framework, as is evidenced in the 2008 Commission's Priorities Guidance (Priorities Guidance).[1]

The 2024 Draft Article 102 Guidelines (Draft Guidelines)[2] turn back the clock and mark a return to a stronger emphasis on categories and presumptions with the concept of 'competition on the merits' at the centre of its analytical framework.

Contrasting the approaches adopted by the Priorities Guidance and suggested by the Draft Guidelines, this chapter discusses the pros and cons of a more prominent role

1. Communication from the Commission (EU) Guidance on the Commission's enforcement priorities in applying Article 82 of the EC Treaty to abusive exclusionary conduct by dominant undertakings, C 45/7, 24.2.2009.
2. Communication from the Commission (EU) Draft Guidelines on the application of Article 102 of the Treaty on the Functioning of the European Union to abusive exclusionary conduct by dominant undertakings, 1.8.2024, paras 77-137.

of categories and presumptions. The chapter also considers the issues raised by using the concept of 'competition on the merits' as an operational tool.

2 THE ROLE OF CATEGORIES OF ABUSE UNDER ARTICLE 102

2.1 Categories of Abuse

2.1.1 Origin of Categories

Categories of abuse have been hardwired into Article 102 TFEU. Indeed, Article 102 TFEU itself lists examples of categories of conduct which may be abusive, including, among other things, discrimination ('applying dissimilar conditions to equivalent transactions with other trading parties, thereby placing them at a competitive disadvantage')[3] and tying ('making the conclusion of contracts subject to acceptance by the other parties of supplementary obligations which, by their nature or according to commercial usage have no connection with the subject of such contracts').[4]

The wording of Article 102 TFEU reflects the influence of the Freiburg Ordo-Liberal school during the early years of EU competition law. The Ordo-Liberals drew a clear line between performance competition (i.e., 'Leistungswettbewerb' which takes place in competitive markets) and impediment competition (i.e., 'Hindrungswettbewerb' which takes place in markets where competition has been weakened). They regarded certain types of unilateral behaviour, such as price discrimination, loyalty rebates and tying as clear examples of 'Hindrungswettbewerb' (impediment competition) with no redeeming features.

The view that certain categories of unilateral conduct are inherently harmful is reflected throughout the case law of the Court of Justice of the European Union (CJEU) with *Hoffman-La Roche* as one of the most prominent cases, distinguishing clearly between inherently pro-competitive conduct (volume rebates) and inherently anti-competitive conduct (loyalty rebates), with examples existing as late as 2003 (*Michelin II*)[5] and 2007 (*British Airways v. Commission*).[6]

Over time, it has been recognised that unilateral conduct could generally not be neatly classified into 'performance competition' and 'impediment competition'. For most types of conduct, the impact on competition is context-specific. Loyalty rebates, for example, were unlikely to lead to anti-competitive foreclosure effects where rival firms could compete for the entire demand of individual customers. Furthermore, it was also incorrect to assume that such conduct could only occur in markets where competition was weakened. Loyalty rebates may be motivated by pro-competitive motives and are persuasive in many competitive industries. As Spector rightly said:

3. Consolidated Version of the Treaty on the European Union and on the Functioning of the European Union, OJ C/326/49, 26.10.2012 ('TFEU'), Art. 102(c).
4. *Ibid.*, at (d).
5. Case T-203/01, *Manufacture française des pneumatiques Michelin v. Commission of the European Communities*, EU:T:2003:250, paras 242-244.
6. Case C-95/04 P, *British Airways plc v. Commission of the European Communities*, EU:C:2007:166, paras 143-145.

'nobody would claim that the coffee shop on the street corner offering a free espresso for every ten Euro of sales is doing so for sinister exclusionary motives'.[7]

2.1.2 *Classification of Categories*

Conduct potentially falling within the scope of Article 102 TFEU has been classified along a number of well-established dimensions.[8]

2.1.2.1 *Key Parameters*

First, abusive conduct has been divided into exclusionary conduct and exploitative conduct, depending on whether the conduct harms the competitive structure in the market, typically by excluding actual or potential competitors or whether conduct is aimed at exploiting market power to the detriment of customers, typically by extracting unfair benefits. The focus of this chapter (and the Draft Guidelines) is exclusively on exclusionary conduct.

Second, abusive conduct has been classified according to whether the conduct is price-based or non-price-based. Examples of price-based categories of abuse are predatory pricing, margin squeeze, exclusivity or loyalty discounts or bundled rebates. Examples of non-price-based categories of abuse are tying, exclusive dealing and refusal to deal. Certain price and non-price-based categories are closely related: for example, exclusive dealing and loyalty rebates, or tying and bundled rebates.

Third, abusive conduct can be categorised according to whether the impact on competition takes place in the market in which the firm is dominant ('in-market abuse') or whether the dominant firm leverages its dominance into related, whether in downstream or neighbouring markets ('leveraging abuses'). Examples of in-market abuses are predatory pricing and exclusive dealing; examples of leveraging abuses are tying and margin squeeze.

Fourth, practices differ depending on their motivation and, in particular, whether they are a plausible means to attain pro-competitive gains. The Courts have 'drawn a line between "naked" abuses - which serve no plausible purpose other than the restriction of competition - and conduct for which there is a potential pro-competitive justification'.[9]

Finally, commentators have also defined categories of abuses based on the 'nature of the remedy required to bring the infringement to an end', distinguishing between abuses where a 'reactive' remedy is sufficient (i.e., 'an obligation of a negative nature that is administered on a one-off basis', such as a cease and desist order) and a

7. David Spector, *Loyalty Rebates: An Assessment of Competition Concerns and a Proposed Structured Rule of Reason*, 1(2) Competition Policy International, 93 (2005).
8. Pablo Ibáñez Colomo, *What is an Abuse of a Dominant Position? Deconstructing the Prohibition and Categorizing* Practices, SSRN (11 June 2021), https://papers.ssrn.com/sol3/papers.cfm?abstract_id=3864292.
9. *Ibid.*, at 17.

'proactive' remedy (which 'relies on behavioural intervention' such as the imposition of a supply obligation).[10]

2.1.2.2 *Conduct Versus Impact*

Not all categories of abuse are created equal (and hence cannot be compared like for like). Certain categories of abuse are simply a description of a type of conduct: this, for example, is the case for exclusive dealing, or for conditional or bundles rebates. For those categories of abuse, a separate impact assessment is required (or an impact has to be presumed).

For other types of abuse, the category of abuse is not only a description of the conduct but also includes an in-built impact assessment. The most obvious example is predatory pricing. Here, the conduct description (low pricing) is combined with an 'as efficient competitor' test, i.e., the definition of predatory pricing includes a condition that the pricing of the dominant firm has been set below a benchmark of the firm's own cost such as average variable cost or average avoidable costs. The same applies in the case of margin squeeze with a negative margin. For other types of abuses, a weaker form of impact assessment has been included in the category definition. For example, the definition of 'tying', includes a 'separate product' requirement which ensures that certain conduct incapable of having an impact on the market is excluded.

Finally, certain categories of abuse do not involve any description of conduct at all but focus purely on the potential impact. This is the case, for example, for 'naked restrictions'. Here, any type of conduct is potentially caught (including the removal of tracks or making misleading statements), as long as there is no plausible purpose for that conduct other than the restriction of competition, in other words, any form of conduct which meets the 'no economic sense' test.

Figure 10.1 Scope of Certain Categories of Abuse Across Conduct and Impact

	Conduct	Impact	
Exclusivity obligations	✓		(Weak presumption)
Bundled rebates	✓		Effects
Predation	✓	✓	Presumption
Tying	✓	(✓)	(Weak presumption)/Effects
Naked restrictions		✓	Presumption

(shaded) = Scope of category

10. *Ibid.*, at 18.

2.2 Categories and Frameworks

The realisation that types of conduct are rarely inherently anti-competitive nor restricted to markets in which competition is weakened has led to a policy shift in Europe known as the 'more economic approach'. This includes a shift of focus from the role of categories to the creation of an analytical framework of general principles applicable across all categories.

This approach is reflected in the Priorities Guidance which is 'intended to provide greater clarity and predictability as regards the general framework of analysis which the Commission employs' in determining its enforcement priorities.[11] This overarching analytical framework included a clear policy objective, namely consumer welfare, which guided the Commission's enforcement efforts.[12] It set out the concept of 'anti-competitive foreclosure', guided by the 'as efficient competitor principle', i.e., that 'is not the purpose of Article 102 TFEU to ensure that competitors less efficient than an undertaking in ... [a dominant] a position should remain on the market'[13] and used the concept of the 'counterfactual' to ensure analytical rigour in its analysis.[14] Categories of abuse still play an important role in the Priorities Guidance but the focus is on the application of the general framework with related categories of abuse (such as exclusive purchasing and conditional rebates or tying and bundling) considered together. Presumptions play a small role in the Priorities Guidance, the underlying assumption being that most categories of abuse require a detailed assessment.[15]

The Draft Guidelines turn back the clock. While one has to be cautious in comparing guidance for enforcement priorities with guidelines which are intended to reflect the law as it stands, the difference in approach is nevertheless striking, particularly in light of the fact that the Priorities Guidance influenced the Court's case law in recent years.

The focus shifts back from the overarching analytical framework to individual categories of abuse. Key elements of the general framework set out in the Priorities Guidance are either de-emphasised or outright dismantled. The reference to anti-competitive foreclosure has disappeared and the role of both the 'as efficient competitor' principle and 'as efficient competitor' test is much reduced.[16] As Damien Neven points out: 'The [Draft Guidelines] weaken the discipline with respect to the definition of the counterfactual, suggesting that it may not be necessary when it is very difficult. And there is no longer reference to consumer harm, except as an overall objective of enforcement.'[17]

11. Priorities Guidance, para. 2.
12. *Ibid.*, at 5.
13. Case C-680/20, *Unilever Italia Mkt. Operations Srl*, EU:C:2023:33, para. 37.
14. Priorities Guidance, para. 21.
15. *Ibid.*, at 22: 'There may be circumstances where it is not necessary for the Commission to carry out a detailed assessment before concluding that the conduct in question is likely to result in consumer harm. If it appears that the conduct can only raise obstacles to competition and that it creates no efficiencies, its anti-competitive effect may be inferred.'
16. Damien J. Neven, *Competition on the Merits?*, EU Law Live (30 October 2024), p. 2, https://eulawlive.com/competition-corner/competition-on-the-merits-by-damien-j-neven/.
17. *Ibid.*

By contrast, the Draft Guidelines put a strong emphasis on 'categories of conduct' which are:

- Subject to 'specific legal tests', i.e., (1) exclusive dealing (which includes exclusivity rebates); (2) tying and pure bundling (mixed bundling); (3) refusal to supply; (4) predatory pricing; and (5) margin squeeze.[18]
- Not subject to 'specific legal tests', i.e., (1) conditional rebates (to the extent that they are not covered by exclusive dealing); (2) multi-product rebates or mixed bundling; (3) self-preferencing; and (4) access restrictions (to the extent that they do not amount to a refusal to supply).[19]

As a new 'general framework', i.e., 'general principles to determine if conduct by a dominant undertaking is liable to be abusive',[20] the Draft Guidelines put forward a two-step analysis which considers 'whether the conduct departs from competition on the merits' (step 1) and 'whether the conduct is capable of having exclusionary effects' (step 2). Again, this framework has a heavy focus on categorisation. We will review this analytical framework in more detail in section 4.3. Finally, the role of presumption takes centrestage within the Draft Guidelines, giving added significance to the categorisation.

2.3 Benefits and Costs of Categorisation

Far from being merely a remnant of a formalistic past, categories of abuse bring a number of tangible benefits to the enforcement of Article 102 TFEU. The benefits of categorisation, however, come at certain costs.

2.3.1 Predictability

The application of Article 102 TFEU is undeniably complex. A 'universal' abuse test (sometimes also referred to as 'unstructured rule of reason'), such as a 'consumer welfare' test is not easily administrable. The case-by-case balancing of the positive and negative dimensions of a practice is known to be a complex exercise that demands considerable resources and is exceedingly unlikely to assist courts and authorities in individual instances.[21]

Breaking down the concept of abuse into different categories of abuse and applying category-specific tests allows for the simplification of those rules in a way which enables the dominant firm to determine (at least directionally) which conduct is likely to contravene the abuse of dominance provisions.

18. Draft Guidelines, paras 77-137.
19. *Ibid.*, at 137-166.
20. *Ibid. See* s. 3.
21. Ibáñez Colomo, *supra* n. 8, at 9. Ibáñez Colomo also points out that some 'universal' tests, such as the 'no economic sense' test suffer from the fact that they do not have universal applicability.

Furthermore, certain categories of abuse reflect different competitive parameters of the unilateral conduct in question, which in turn may or may not allow the use of different tools. This is most noticeably the case in relation to price-based and non-price-based abuses. Exclusive dealings and loyalty rebates may have many similarities (in various dimensions of abuse classification) but loyalty rebates may lend themselves to the application of the 'as efficient competitor' test in a way in which exclusive dealings may not. The same logic applies to tying and bundled rebates.

While it is clear that the use of categories of abuse has significant advantages in terms of predictability over the enforcement of Article 102 TFEU through an unstructured rule of reason, the relative merit in terms of predictability is far less clear if we compare the use of categories of abuse with a weak overarching framework (as in the Draft Guidelines) with the use of categories of abuse with a strong overarching framework (as in the Priorities Guidance). While the former may allow for simpler rules for each of the underlying categories, this is likely to come at the price of greater uncertainty into which category a particular type of conduct will actually fall (for more on this point, *see* section 2.3).

2.3.2 *Enforcement Efficiency*

In addition, categories of abuse may help to make enforcement more efficient by calibrating the required evidential standard to the expected 'ex ante' harm of the types of conduct in question.

The CJEU has developed different evidential standards, depending on whether the type of conduct has no plausible purpose other than anti-competitive foreclosure (e.g., the removal of tracks to foreclose a rival – *Lithuanian Railways*),[22] whether the conduct could be either pro- or anti-competitive (as is the case in mixed bundling) or whether the conduct is presumptively lawful (refusing to grant access to an infrastructure which the dominant firm has developed for its own use, *Bronner*).[23] The role of presumptions and the related evidential standards will be discussed in more detail in section 3.2.

2.3.3 *Risk of Regulatory Arbitrage*

One potential downside of the categorisation of conduct is that categories may overlap or, in other words, the same type of conduct may fall into more than one abuse category.

Tying (i.e., making the sale of product B dependent on dominant product A) may, in certain circumstances, also be characterised as a refusal by a dominant firm to grant access to product A. A dominant firm's refusal to deal (reserving an infrastructure for its own use) is inherently discriminatory in nature, as the dominant firm favours itself over its competitors.

22. Case C-42/21 P, *Lietuvos geležinkeliai v. Commission*, EU:C:2023:12, paras 134-146.
23. Case C-7/97, *Oscar Bronner*, EU:C:1998:569, para. 47.

Conflicts in how to classify conduct potentially falling into more than one abuse category tend to be particularly acute when the categories in question are subject to different evidential standards. This in turn may give rise to a risk of 'regulatory arbitrage', i.e., where the competition authority in question (or claimants in court proceedings) will characterise the conduct in a way which attracts a lower evidential standard while the dominant firm will frame the unilateral behaviour such that it will attract a higher standard.

An example is the *Microsoft v. Commission* case. This case considered the question of whether Microsoft's inclusion of its Windows Media Player (WMP) into its Windows operating system which gave WMP a customer's reach not available to rival products amounted to an abuse of a dominant position. The European Commission framed the conduct as a tying abuse, forcing customers to take Microsoft's WMP when buying Windows (a category of conduct subject to an effects standard) while Microsoft characterised its behaviour as a refusal to grant rivals access to Windows as a distribution channel (refusal to supply being subject to the higher indispensability standard).[24] In *Google Shopping* the case turned on Google displaying the search results of its own shopping comparison site more prominently on its general search page while downgrading the results of rival shopping sites. The European Commission presented Google's conduct as discriminatory leveraging (subject to an effects standard) while Google took the view that it had refused rival shopping sites access to part of its 'infrastructure', such conduct being subject to the higher indispensability standard.[25]

Similar conflicts have also arisen at the other end of the evidential spectrum between conduct which could either be characterised as presumptively abusive or as subject to an effects standard. In *Unilever Italia,* Unilever was investigated by the Italian competition authority (AGCM), in relation to exclusivity obligations and loyalty rebates in the ice cream sector. The AGCM took the view that exclusivity obligations were a separate abuse from exclusivity rebates where the old case law of *Hoffman-La Roche* was still applicable (and which was hence presumptively unlawful) while Unilever argued that *Intel* applied to both pricing and non-pricing exclusivity (and was therefore subject, at least de facto, to an effects standard).[26]

2.3.4 *Risk of Inconsistencies Across Different Categories*

Even where conduct does not fall into overlapping categories of abuse and hence there is no risk of regulatory arbitrage as described in section 2.3.3, it is important to ensure overall consistency across different categories of abuse.

In other words, there needs to be not only a formal basis for delineating different categories of abuse from one another in a way which minimises overlap between those categories but also an economic basis for justifying differences in the substantive assessment, including differences in evidential standards. We will revisit this point in section 5 when considering the relationship between price-based and non-price-based

24. Case T-201/04, *Microsoft v. Commission*, EU:T:2007:289, paras 36-46.
25. Case C-48/22, *Google and Alphabet v. Commission*, EU:C:2024:726, paras 36 and 108.
26. Case C-680/20, *Unilever Italia Mkt. Operations Srl*, EU:C:2023:33, paras 5-7 and 14.

forms of exclusivity as well as the relationship between different categories of refusal to supply and self-preferencing and other forms of 'access limitation'.

2.3.5 *Risk of Insufficient Adaptation*

Where categories of abuse are subject to certain presumptions, it is important that these presumptions reflect the latest understanding of the nature and anti-competitive potential of a particular category of conduct.

The case law of the CJEU has reflected changing perceptions (and economic learning) of the likely harm (or indeed benefit) of certain forms of unilateral conduct, albeit, at times with significant time lags.

In the early days of EU competition law, coloured by the views of the ordo-liberal Freiburg School, loyalty rebates were seen as inherently anti-competitive and treated as presumptively abusive. Over time, it became clear that loyalty rebates are also pervasive in many industry sectors, including sectors in which there are no dominant firms. Several pro-competitive motives for loyalty rebates have been advanced, ranging from aligning the interests of manufacturers and distributors to risk allocation and solving hold-up problems.

It took more than a decade for these insights to translate into a change of presumptions for loyalty rebates. In 2017 (*Intel*), the CJEU 'clarified' the previous position of an irrebuttable presumption of harm set out in *Hoffmann-La Roche* to one which, at least de facto, seems to come close to the application of an effects standard.

A similar shift of presumptions can also be seen at the other end of the spectrum, where in relation to refusal to supply, the CJEU narrowed the scope of the presumption of legality set out in *Bronner*, by carving out scenarios where an obligation to deal could not harm firms' incentive to innovate.

3 CATEGORIES OF ABUSE AND THE ROLE OF PRESUMPTIONS

3.1 The Relationship Between Categories of Abuse and Presumptions

What brings the role of categories of abuse into sharp relief is the fact that different categories are subject to different presumptions (both of illegality and legality) and hence are subject to different evidential standards.

Presumptions play a significant role in EU competition law. The distinction between competition law offences where anti-competitive effects are presumed (object restrictions) and where they have to be established (effects restrictions) is reflected in the wording of Article 101 TFEU ('agreements ... which have as their object or effect the prevention, restriction or distortion of competition within the internal market')[27] and has long been established in CJEU case law.

27. TFEU, Art. 101.1.

While equivalent wording in Article 102 TFEU is absent, a similar dichotomy between object abuses (where anti-competitive effects are presumed) and effects abuses (where such effects need to be established) has developed over time.

3.2 The Role of Presumptions in the Draft Guidelines

Contrary to the Priorities Guidance which deals with the role of presumptions in a single paragraph,[28] the role of presumptions and their relationship with the different categories of abuse are central to the framework in the Draft Guidelines.[29]

The Draft Guidelines distinguish between two types of conduct, namely (1) 'conduct for which it is necessary to demonstrate a capability to produce exclusionary effects' which is defined as conduct where, for a finding of abuse, 'it is necessary to demonstrate on the basis of specific, tangible points of analysis and evidence, that such conduct is capable of having exclusionary effects' – conduct, which in the following shall be referred to as 'effects abuses';[30] and (2) 'conduct that is presumed to lead to exclusionary effects', i.e., so-called presumptive abuses. For presumptive abuses, 'once the factual existence of the relevant conduct is established ... its exclusionary effects can be presumed'.[31]

The Draft Guidelines divide presumptive abuses into two further categories: so-called naked restrictions which are defined as 'certain types of conduct by a dominant firm [which] have no economic interest for that undertaking, other than that of restricting competition'.[32] Examples listed in the Draft Guidelines are 'payments by the dominant undertaking to customers that are condition on the customers postponing or cancelling the launch of [competing] products'[33] (*Intel*)[34] or 'dominant undertakings actively dismantling an infrastructure used by a competitor'[35] (*Lithuanian Railways*).[36] The Draft Guidelines state that rebutting the presumptions for naked restrictions will be difficult and will only occur in very exceptional cases.

The other group of presumptive abuses covers types of conduct which are subject to legal tests where the CJEU has applied presumptions in the past, namely exclusive dealings, exclusivity rebates, predation, margin squeeze with negative spreads and certain forms of tying. According to the Draft Guidelines, these types of 'conduct [are] generally recognized as having a high potential to produce exclusionary effects'.[37] The Draft Guidelines are silent as to what is required to rebut the presumption of this second group of presumptive abuses.

28. Priorities Guidance, para. 22.
29. Draft Guidelines, *see* s. 3.3.1 'The evidentiary burden to demonstrate a conduct's capability to produce exclusionary effects.'
30. *Ibid.*, at 60(a).
31. *Ibid.*, at (b).
32. *Ibid.*, at (a).
33. *Ibid.*, at (c).
34. Case C-413/14 P, *Intel v. Commission*, EU:C:2017:632; Case T-201/04, *Microsoft v. Commission*, EU:T:2007:289, para. 96.
35. Draft Guidelines, para. 60(c).
36. Case C-42/21 P, *Lietuvos geležinkeliai v. Commission*, EU:C:2023:12, paras 83-84 and 89-91.
37. Draft Guidelines, para. 60(b).

3.3 Presumptions: Open Issues

3.3.1 Evidential Standards

As discussed in the preceding section, the Draft Guidelines set out two evidential standards according to which conduct will be assessed (three if the two groups of presumptive abuses are counted separately). Arguably, there is a further applicable standard of evidence which has not been mentioned in the Draft Guidelines, namely an evidential standard for presumptively lawful conduct, which covers certain forms of refusal to supply.[38]

Where a vertically integrated dominant firm refuses to grant a competitor access to facilities which it has developed for its own use, the CJEU has held that such a refusal can amount to an abuse of dominance only in exceptional circumstances. Here, for a finding of abuse, it is insufficient to demonstrate on the basis of specific, tangible points of analysis and evidence, that such conduct is capable of having exclusionary effects. Rather, the competition authority has to show that a facility to which access is refused is indispensable to carrying on the claimant's business, in as much as there is no actual or potential substitute in existence for that facility.[39] Furthermore, the refusal to deal must be likely to eliminate all competition in the relevant downstream market on the part of the person requesting the service.[40]

While the scope of the conduct subject to the indispensability standard has narrowed over time (most recently by the CJEU in *Android Auto*),[41] the indispensability standard nevertheless still applies to refusals to deal in relation to facilities which a dominant firm has developed for its own use.

Figure 10.2 Evidential Standards for Categories of Abuse

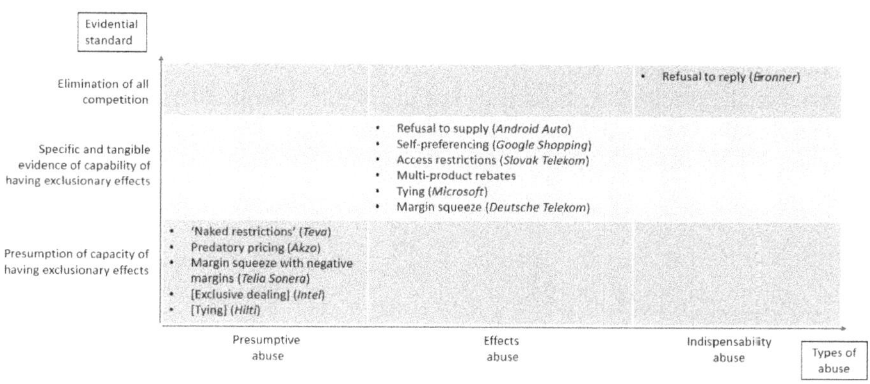

38. Case C-7/97, *Oscar Bronner*, EU:C:1998:569, paras 43-47.
39. *Ibid.*, at 45-46.
40. *Ibid.*, at 41.
41. Case C-233/23, *Alphabet (Google Android Auto)*, EU:C:2025:110, paras 36-47.

As we have discussed in this section and will expand further in section 5, the different evidential standards (i.e., presumptively unlawful, absence of presumptions and presumptively lawful), have caused (and no doubt will continue to cause) considerable frictions in the enforcement of Article 102 TFEU.

3.3.2 *Conduct Which Is Presumptively Abusive*

As mentioned above, the Draft Guidelines have identified two sets of categories which are subject to the presumptive standard (in other words, where it is sufficient to establish the factual existence of the relevant conduct in question).

3.3.2.1 *Naked Restrictions (As Object Abuses)*

The concept of 'naked restrictions' is a category of conduct which 'lacks redeeming virtues', in other words, conduct which can only be explained as a measure to foreclose competition, is uncontroversial and reflects a well-established line of cases including *Decca* (changes in transmission frequency to cause rival devices to malfunction),[42] *AstraZeneca* (providing misleading information to national patent offices with the aim of delaying rivals' entry)[43] and *Teva* (misuse of patent procedures and systematic disparagement campaign).[44]

As Ibáñez Colomo pointed out, the category of 'naked restrictions' is not only well-established but is also necessary to ensure consistency with the policy under Article 101 TFEU: 'If the behaviour under consideration is a restriction by object under Article 101 (1) TFEU, it stands to reason that it is also prohibited without the need to show effects under Article 102 TFEU.'[45] Ibáñez Colomo cites reverse payment settlements as an example of a 'by object' infringement scrutinised under both provisions.[46] FIFA's failure to ensure their authorisation rules for rival tournaments were transparent, objective and non-discriminatory is another example.[47]

While the existence of the category of 'naked restrictions' has been largely uncontroversial, its connotation has been controversial. Commentators have objected to the fact that the Draft Guidelines give a new name to a concept which has been well established by the CJEU under the heading of 'object abuse'. This new labelling

42. Commission Decision (EU) 89/113 of 21 December 1988 on IV/30.979 and 31.394 – *Decca Navigator System*, paras 97-103.
43. Case C-457/10 P, *AstraZeneca v. Commission*, EU:C:2012:770, paras 85-100.
44. Commission Decision (EU) of 31 October 2024 on AT.40588 – *Teva Copaxone* (notified under document C(2024) 7448), OJ C/2025/1680, paras 1014-1029.
45. Pablo Ibáñez Colomo, *On the Article 102 TFEU Guidelines (II): 'Naked Restrictions' (or 'By Object' Abuses)*, Chillin' Competition (19 November 2024), https://chillingcompetition.com/2024/11/19/on-the-article-102-tfeu-guidelines-ii-naked-restrictions-or-by-object-abuses/.
46. *Ibid.*
47. Case C-333/21, *European Superleague Company*, EU:C:2023:1011, para. 152.

obscures the natural link between similar concepts under Articles 101 and 102 TFEU but is also seen by some as an effort to expand the scope of presumptive abuses.[48]

3.3.2.2 Other Presumptive Abuses

According to the Draft Guidelines 'certain types of conduct are generally recognized as having a high potential to produce exclusionary effects' and 'accordingly they are subject to a presumption concerning their capability of producing exclusionary effects'.[49] Types of conduct which are subject to such a presumption include, according to the Draft Guidelines, '(1) exclusive supply or purchasing agreements; (2) rebates conditional upon exclusivity; (3) predatory pricing; (4) margin squeeze in the presence of negative spreads; and (5) certain forms of tying'.[50]

As discussed in section 3.2, these presumptive abuses fall into two very different camps. The description of predatory pricing and margin squeeze in the presence of negative spreads includes an implicit effects analysis in the form of an AEC test (e.g., pricing below AVC or similar cost benchmark). Where price-based conduct 'is capable of hampering competition from competitors which are considered to be as efficient as the dominant undertaking',[51] it is not surprising that such pricing is regarded as presumptively abusive.

The other three types of conduct (exclusive supply or purchasing agreements, rebates conditional upon exclusivity and certain forms of tying) are simply factual descriptions of relevant conduct to which the CJEU have in the past applied a presumption of illegality. However, the validity of these presumptions has increasingly been in doubt.

We will illustrate this point in relation to exclusive supply or purchasing agreements and rebates conditional upon exclusivity (but the arguments apply mutatis mutandis also to 'certain forms of tying'). First, the statement that exclusivity obligations and exclusivity rebates are generally recognised as having a high potential to produce exclusionary effects is not universally valid. The Priorities Guidance, for example, states: 'If competitors can compete on equal terms for each individual customer's entire demand, exclusive purchasing obligations are generally unlikely to hamper effective competition unless switching of customers is rendered difficult due to the duration of the exclusive purchasing obligation.'[52] This demonstrates that potential harm from exclusivity obligations is context-specific.

Second, even in circumstances where exclusivity obligations have a high potential to produce exclusionary effects, they may also have a significant potential for pro-competitive efficiencies, such as aligning the interests of producers with their distributors or addressing hold-up problems.

---

48. Assimakis Komninos, *'"J"accuse!' – Four Deadly Sins of the Commission's Draft Guidelines on Exclusionary Abuses*, Network Law Review (30 August 2024), https://www.networklawreview.org/komninos-guidelines.
49. Draft Guidelines, para. 60(b).
50. *Ibid.*
51. Priorities Guidance, para. 23.
52. *Ibid.*, at 36.

It is therefore not surprising that, for exclusivity clauses and exclusivity rebates, the European Court of Justice (ECJ) has moved away from the presumption *in Hoffmann-La Roche*. While it is technically correct that the ECJ in *Intel* has kept in place a presumption of illegality for exclusive dealing, the remaining presumption remains weak and can be rebutted by a dominant firm 'submits, during the administrative procedure, on the basis of supporting evidence, that its conduct was not capable of restricting competition and, in particular, of producing the alleged foreclosure effects'.[53] Given that a dominant firm will regularly contest the capability of its conduct to restrict competition, this raises the question of whether it would have been better for the Draft Guidelines to accept that exclusive dealing and tying should be best dealt with under an effects analysis.

3.3.3 Rebuttal of Presumptions

The Draft Guidelines give little to no guidance on what is needed to rebut the presumptions for various categories of presumptive abuses. In relation to 'naked restrictions' (or object abuses), they merely state that a rebuttal will only be possible in exceptional circumstances, while in relation to other presumptive abuses, the Draft Guidelines are entirely silent on this point.

There would be a clear benefit in having a coherent framework for the rebuttal of object infringements, first across Articles 101 and 102 TFEU and second across the different categories of presumptively abusive conduct. With respect to the former, the Court held in *European Superleague* that 'Articles 101 and 102 TFEU must be interpreted consistently.'[54] As mentioned earlier, it does not make sense from a policy perspective, to have a mismatch between the scope of restrictions which fall under an object restriction under Article 101 TFEU and the scope of unilateral conduct considered to be an object abuse under Article 102 TFEU. Furthermore, the application of Article 102 TFEU could benefit from the long-established case law of object restrictions under Article 101 TFEU.

And in the same way as there is a single test for object restrictions under Article 101 TFEU which will lead to different outcomes when applied to say cartels, RPM or cooperation agreements, a single similar test could be applied to 'naked restrictions' and other presumptive abuses.

The building blocks of such a test are set out in *Intel*, and reiterated in *Unilever Italia*, and have two alternative prongs: *first*, dominant firms could rebut the presumed capability of exclusionary effects by 'submitting that its conduct was not capable of restricting competition and, in particular, of producing the alleged foreclosure effects'.[55] According to the Court has to be done during the administrative procedure, on the basis of supporting evidence.

53. Case C-413/14 P, *Intel v. Commission*, EU:C:2017:632, para. 138.
54. Case C-333/21, *European Superleague Company*, EU:C:2023:1011, para. 186.
55. Case C-413/14 P, *Intel v. Commission*, EU:C:2017:632, para. 138.

Second, the competition authority is also required to assess, specifically, the ability of those clauses to restrict competition (rather than just relying on a presumption), where the dominant firm which is under suspicion, 'maintains that there are justifications for its conduct'.[56]

Applying these two prongs to the various categories of presumptive abuse, the results will reflect the type of conduct and the strength of the underlying presumption.

Given that naked restrictions comprise exclusively of types conduct by a dominant firm which, 'have no economic interest for that undertaking, other than that of restricting competition', it is not surprising that the Draft Guidelines conclude that the presumption can only be rebutted in 'very exceptional circumstances'.[57] Naked restrictions are by definition conduct for which the presumptions apply and have been identified on this basis (e.g., through the 'no economic sense' test).

Predatory pricing is pricing which has failed the inbuilt 'AEC' test. Pricing below average variable costs is presumed to be abusive on the basis, as the Court puts it, that such conduct makes no sense other than as a dominant firm's strategy of 'eliminating competitors so as to enable it subsequently to raise its prices by taking advantage of its monopolistic position'.[58] However, the presumption of competitive harm for predatory pricing is weaker than in the case of 'naked restrictions'. Contrary to the category of naked restrictions where the 'no economic sense' test has been applied directly (and found to be relevant), here the 'no economic sense' has merely been assumed on the basis of abstract considerations. There may be numerous individual circumstances where pricing below the relevant cost benchmark, such as average variable costs (AVC), may either not be harmful or exceptionally result in efficiencies.

As far as exclusive dealings and tying are concerned, we have shown in the previous section that a presumption that such conduct is inherently harmful is relatively weak, both in terms of capability to foreclose as well as in terms of any harm outweighing any efficiencies.

Finally, it is worth noting that rebutting the presumption does not exculpate the conduct of the dominant firm. It merely shifts the conduct from a presumptive abuse to an effects abuse where the Commission has to carry out a more detailed assessment.

4 THE CONCEPT OF 'COMPETITION (NOT) ON THE MERITS'

4.1 'Competition (Not) on the Merits' and 'Capacity to Foreclose'

The categories of abusive conduct and the role of presumptions are the building blocks for the Draft Guidelines' two-step analytical framework which combines the concept of 'competition on the merits' with the concept of 'capacity to have exclusionary effects' in order to identify when unilateral conduct is abusive under Article 102 TFEU.

56. Case C-680/20, *Unilever Italia Mkt. Operations Srl*, EU:C:2023:33, para. 53.
57. Draft Guidelines, para. 60(c).
58. Case C-62/86, *Akzo Chemie BV v. Commission*, EU:C:1991:286, para. 71.

The Draft Guidelines see the two steps as separate and independent: 'the assessment of whether the conduct departs from competition on the merits is conceptually different from the assessment of whether the conduct is capable of having exclusionary effects', although they acknowledge that 'certain factual elements may be relevant for the assessment of both'.[59]

4.2 'Competition on the Merits' and the 'Capability to Have Exclusionary Effects'

4.2.1 The Concept of 'Competition (Not) on the Merits'

'Competition on the merits' is defined in the Draft Guidelines as 'conduct within the scope of normal competition on the basis of the performance of economic operators and which in principle, relates to a competitive situation in which consumers benefit from lower prices'.[60]

The relatively straightforward definition of competition on the merits contrasts with a long and complex enumeration of 'conduct [that] departs from competition on the merits'.[61]

This includes, first, all types of conducts for which a specific legal test exists (such as predation or refusal to supply) and where such conduct 'satisf[ies] the applicable specific legal test'.[62] It further includes 'conduct that holds no economic interest for a dominant undertaking except that of restricting competition',[63] i.e., 'naked restrictions' as well as certain pricing practices (such as predatory pricing), which fail certain pricing tests. For further illustration, the Draft Guidelines also provide examples of conduct which in previous cases has been held to be abusive, such as 'prevent[ing] consumers from exercising their choice based on the merits of the products'[64] or 'biased or discriminatory treatment that favours itself over its competitors'.[65]

Finally, the Draft Guidelines point out that 'conduct that at first sight does not depart from competition on the merits (e.g., pricing above average total costs (ATC) and therefore does not normally infringe Article 102 TFEU may in specific circumstances, be found to depart from competition on the merits'[66] based on an analysis of certain legal and factual elements.

When all the examples set out in the Draft Guidelines are taken together, it becomes clear that 'competition not on the merits' amounts to any conduct which contravenes Article 102 TFEU.

59. Draft Guidelines, para. 46.
60. *Ibid.*, para. 51.
61. *Ibid.*, at 53-58.
62. *Ibid.*, at 53.
63. *Ibid.*, at 54.
64. *Ibid.*, at 55(a).
65. *Ibid.*, at (d).
66. *Ibid.*, at 57.

4.2.2 *The Concept of 'Capability to Have Exclusionary Effects'*

The concept of 'capability to have exclusionary effect' in the Draft Guidelines differs from the approach taken in the Priorities Guidance. The Priorities Guidance was explicit that its focus was on 'anti-competitive' foreclosure, i.e., when dominant firms 'impair effective competition by foreclosing their competitors in an anti-competitive way'[67] which in turn is linked to the concept of an as efficient competitor. By contrast, the Draft Guidelines merely refer to 'exclusionary effects'.

This has given rise to two alternative views: under one (wide) interpretation, the concept of 'capability to have exclusionary effects' in the Draft Guidelines should be interpreted as covering not only *anti-competitive* foreclosure but also exclusionary effects which result from *pro-competitive* actions, for example, harm to the competitive market structure as a result of introducing an innovative product. The concept of 'competition on the merits' can then be used as a criterion to distinguish between pro-competitive and anti-competitive foreclosure.

Under the alternative (narrow) interpretation, the Draft Guidelines do not make such a radical departure from the underlying framework of the Priorities Guidance. Rather, the 'capacity to have exclusionary effects' is still intended to cover only *anti-competitive* foreclosure. However, the omission of a reference to anticompetitive foreclosure could be a signal that, in future, the Commission will no longer be strictly guided by the 'as efficient' competitor principle and the Draft Guidelines have thus de facto lowered the bar to establishing an abuse.

The fact that reasonable people can take different views on such a fundamental point for the amendment of Article 102 TFEU is not a ringing endorsement of the quality of the guidance provided in the Draft Guidelines.

In the following section, we apply the narrow interpretation of capability to have exclusionary effects. We have done so, because we believe that: (1) such a radical shift (as the wide interpretation implies) would have been imposed more clearly; and (2) the concept of 'competition (not) on the merits' is not well suited to distinguishing between different possible effects abuses. However, we will come back to the implications of the wide interpretation at the end of this section.

4.3 The Two-Step Analytical Framework: Open Issues

The concept of 'competition on the merits' and the two-step framework in the Draft Guidelines raise a number of issues: First, the two-step framework appears to be internally inconsistent and there are doubts as to whether each of the two steps in the framework is indeed 'conceptually different' as postulated; furthermore, at least for effects abuses, the criterion of 'competition on the merits' does not seem to provide any additional clarity in determining whether conduct is abusive beyond what is gained by establishing that the conduct is capable of having exclusionary effects.

---

67. Priorities Guidance, para. 19.

4.3.1 *The Two-Step Framework Appears to Be Internally Inconsistent*

The two-step framework for the assessment of whether conduct amounts to an abuse under Article 102 TFEU raises questions about internal consistency within the Draft Guidelines. As mentioned above, the Draft Guidelines state that 'the assessment of whether conduct departs from competition on the merits is conceptually different from the assessment of whether the conduct is capable of having exclusionary effects'.[68]

At the same time, the Draft Guidelines also claim that: 'the concept of competition on the merits covers conduct within the scope of normal competition on the basis of the performance of economic operators, and which, in principle, relates to a competitive situation in which consumers benefit from lower, better quality and a wider choice of new or improved goods and services';[69] in other words, competition on the merits and a competitive situation resulting in positive outcomes for consumers are shown to be two sides of the same coin. It also suggests that competition not on the merits is linked to conduct where conduct is expected to lead to consumer harm, in the form of higher prices, lower quality or reduced choice.[70]

Luc Peeperkorn provides a simple way to test whether the two concepts of competition on the merits and capability to foreclose are indeed 'conceptually different' (in line with paragraph 46 of the Draft Guidelines) or are two sides of the same coin (in line with paragraph 51 of the Draft Guidelines).

The claim that the concepts of competition on the merits and capability to foreclose are conceptually different suggests, so Peeperkorn argues, that 'the Commission considers that it is not only theoretically possible but also practically relevant to distinguish', (1) competition on the merits which is capable of having exclusionary effects; (2) competition on the merits which is not capable of having exclusionary effects; (3) competition not on the merits which is capable of having exclusionary effects; and (4) competition not on the merits which is not capable of having exclusionary effects.[71]

68. Draft Guidelines, para. 45.
69. *Ibid.*, at 51.
70. As a matter of logic, the statement 'if A therefore B' allows the conclusions 'if Not B therefore Not A'.
71. Luc Peeperkorn, *The Draft Article 102 Guidelines: A Somewhat Confused Attempt to Partly Roll Back the Effects-based Approach of the Union Courts*, Kluwer Competition Law Blog (4 September 2024), https://competitionlawblog.kluwercompetitionlaw.com/2024/09/04/the-draft-article-102-guidelines-a-somewhat-confused-attempt-to-partly-roll-back-the-effects-based-approach-of-the-union-courts/.

Figure 10.3 Scenarios in the Two-Step Analysis (Narrow Interpretation)

Conduct \ Impact	Conduct capable of having exclusionary effects	Conduct not capable of having exclusionary effects
Competition on the merits	Not covered in the Draft Guidelines	Pro-competitive conduct (covered in the Draft Guidelines)
Competition not on the merits	Abuse (covered in the Draft Guidelines)	Not covered in the Draft Guidelines

Source: Based on Luc Peeperkorn, *The Draft Article 102 Guidelines: A Somewhat Confused Attempt to Partly Roll Back the Effects-based Approach of the Union Courts*, Kluwer Competition Law Blog (4 September 2024).

Peeperkorn points out that of these four possible scenarios only two scenarios have found their way into the Draft Guidelines: Scenario 2 (competition on the merits which is not capable of having exclusionary effect) is found in paragraph 52 of the Draft Guidelines and Scenario 3 (competition not on the merits which is capable of having exclusionary effects) is discussed at length in section 3.2.2 of the Draft Guidelines. However, 'no description is found of conduct that would fall in either [Scenario 1 or 4]. Not in Section 3 which presents general principles for determining whether conduct by a dominant undertaking is liable to be abusive and where the distinction and two-step tests are out forward, nor in Section 4, which sets out the principles for determining whether specific types of conduct are liable to be abusive'.[72]

This strongly suggests that the concepts of competition (not) on the merits and capability of having exclusionary effects, as set out in the Draft Guidelines, are not conceptually independent but directly related: competition not on the merits is conduct capable of having exclusionary effects while competition on the merits is conduct that leads to consumer benefits (and hence is not capable of having exclusionary effects).

4.3.2 The Concept of 'Competition (Not) on the Merits' Does Not Provide Any Added Guidance

In light of this direct relationship between competition on the merits and capability to have exclusionary effects, it is not surprising that the Draft Guidelines struggle to provide added guidance on the concept of competition (not) on the merits, beyond the fact that such conduct is capable of having exclusionary effects.

This is particularly obvious for certain categories of effects abuses, where 'it needs to be shown that the conduct departs from competition on the merits based on the specific circumstances of the case'.[73] Among the examples listed by Draft

72. *Ibid.*
73. Draft Guidelines, para. 55.

Guidelines of conduct which the Courts have held in the past to depart from competition on the merits are dominant firms 'prevent[ing]consumers from exercising their choice based on the merits of the products, including product quality'[74] (*Microsoft v. Commission*)[75] and 'conduct consist[ing] of, or enabl[ing] biased or discriminatory treatment that favours itself over its competition'[76] (*Servizio Elettrico Nazionale*).[77]

However, identical conduct can also amount to competition on the merits: smartphone producers integrate cameras into their product, thereby preventing customers from exercising their choice and the CJEU in *Google Shopping* explicitly stated that 'it cannot be considered that, as a general rule, a dominant undertaking which treats its own products or services more favourably than it treats those of its competitors is engaging in conduct which departs from competition on the merits irrespective of the circumstances of the case'.[78]

What distinguishes abusive from lawful tying and abusive from lawful self-preferencing is not the nature of the conduct but the context in which it takes place. The same conduct may be capable of having exclusionary effects in one context but not in another. Where it is established that a particular conduct has the capability of having an exclusionary effect in its given context, the nature of the conduct itself has no additional value in establishing an abuse.

The fact that context, not conduct, is the key determinant for establishing an abuse is acknowledged in the Draft Guidelines: 'Conduct that at first sight does not depart from competition on the merits (e.g., pricing above average total costs (ATC)) and therefore does not normally infringe Article 102 TFEU may, in specific circumstances, be found to depart from competition on the merits, based on an analysis of all legal and factual elements'.[79] For effect-based abuses, it is the capability of having exclusionary foreclosure which drives and determines what type of conduct amounts to an abuse.[80]

4.3.3 *An Alternative View of the Relationship Between 'Competition on the Merits' and 'Capability to Foreclose'*

Rather than treating competition on the merits and capability to have exclusionary effects as cumulative elements in a two-step test, there is support in the case law for treating the concepts as alternative tests for different types of abuses. The ECJ held in *Unilever Italy* that 'abuse of a dominant position could be established, inter alia, where the conduct complained of produced exclusionary effects in respect of competitors that

74. *Ibid.*, at 55(a).
75. Case T-201/04, *Microsoft v. Commission*, EU:T:2007:289, paras 1046-1047, 1057-1058 and 1069-1070.
76. Draft Guidelines, para. 55(d).
77. Case C-377/20, *Servizio Elettrico Nazionale*, EU:C:2022:379, paras 96-99.
78. Case C-48/22, *Google and Alphabet v. Commission*, EU:C:2024:726, para. 186.
79. Draft Guidelines, para. 57.
80. Case C-48/22, *Google and Alphabet v. Commission*, EU:C:2024:726, paras 168-172.

were as efficient as the perpetrator of that conduct in terms of cost structure, capacity to innovate, quality or where that conduct was based on the use of means other than those which come with the scope of "normal" competition, that is to say, competition on the merits'.[81] We deal with these two concepts below (in reverse order).

4.3.3.1 *Abuse (1): 'Conduct Based on the Use of Means Other Than Competition on the Merits'*

For presumptive abuses, the test under this proposed approach would be whether a conduct is 'competition not on the merits', i.e., whether the conduct falls into one of the categories which are presumed to be abusive.

Once it has been established that the conduct amounts to competition not on the merits, e.g., because it falls into the category of 'naked restriction' or, for example, constitutes predatory pricing, then the capability to foreclose is presumed and (unless the presumption is rebutted) does not have to be established.

In other words, presumptive abuses would be looked at through the lens of the 'competition on the merits', not through the lens of 'capability of having exclusionary effects'.

4.3.3.2 *Abuse (2): 'Conduct Produce[s] Exclusionary Effects in Respect of "As Efficient" Competitors'*

For effects abuses, the test for establishing an abuse would be the capability of having exclusionary effects which means having 'to demonstrate on the basis of specific, tangible points of analysis and evidence, that such conduct is capable of having exclusionary effects'.[82]

Once the capability to foreclose has been established, there would be no separate requirement to establish that the conduct is 'competition not on the merits'. The actual or potential anti-competitive effects in the given circumstances are what turns conduct (which in different circumstances may be competition on the merits) into an abuse under Article 102 TFEU.

As to the question of whether conduct amounting to an effects abuse should also be considered to be 'competition not on the merits', in our view, it would give clarity to limit that concept to presumptive abuses. However, it could also be extended to effects abuses in so much as once established that conduct is capable of having exclusionary effects, this would lead to an irrebuttable presumption that such conduct is not competition on the merits. However, this ultimately becomes a point of semantics.

---

81. Case C-680/20, *Unilever Italia Mkt. Operations Srl*, EU:C:2023:33, para. 39.
82. Draft Guidelines, para. 60(a).

4.4 Alternative Interpretation: Wide Interpretation of Capacity to Have Exclusionary Effects

This brings us back to the two potential interpretations of the concept 'capability to have exclusionary effects' set out in the Draft Guidelines (*see* section 4.2.2). Our analysis in the preceding section was predicated on the presumption that capacity to foreclose refers to anti-competitive foreclosure only.

The picture looks different on the basis of a wide interpretation of capacity to foreclose. Proponents of the wide concept of exclusionary effects include Schweitzer and de Ridder.[83] They point out that the Priorities Guidance has equated anti-competitive effects with a conduct's capability to foreclose AECs but take the view that the Union Courts' case law suggests a broader approach: in order to qualify as an abuse the relevant conduct must, first, have the (actual or potential) effect of hindering the maintenance of the degree of competition still existing in the market or the growth of that competition. However, a lessening of competition, namely a foreclosure of less efficient competitors may result from the very process of competition that competition law aims to protect.[84] As a result, Schweitzer and de Ridder see the need for a second criterion which 'distinguish[es] between pro-competitive and anti-competitive practices' and take the view that the concept of competition on the merits can play this role.[85]

Jorge Padilla comes to a similar position albeit from an economic perspective.[86] Padilla reviews the relevant facts and circumstances to be taken into account in assessing exclusionary effects in paragraph 70 of the Draft Guidelines (albeit taking a very different view of competition on the merits from Schweitzer and de Ridder) and concludes that factors listed in that paragraph '[are] consistent with both "mere" and "anti-competitive" foreclosure'.[87] As only anti-competitive foreclosure can amount to an abuse under Article 102 TFEU, Padilla argues that it is necessary to 'assess whether [conduct capable of having foreclosure effects] "impair[s]effective competition"'.[88] According to Padilla, 'only conduct that distorts the competitive process should be regarded as falling outside normal competition or competition on the merits'.[89] When is the competitive process distorted? Padilla's answer: when the conduct at issue cannot be profitably replicated by an 'as efficient competitor'.[90] So, the AEC principle

83. *See* Heike Schweitzer and Simon de Ridder, *How to Fix a Failing Art. 102 TFEU: Substantive Interpretation, Evidentiary Requirements, and the Commission's Future Guidelines on Exclusionary Abuses*, European Journal of International Law 222, 243 (2024) https://doi.org/10.1093/jeclap/lpae033.
84. *Ibid.*, p. 229.
85. *Ibid.*
86. *See* Jorge Padilla, *What Is an Exclusionary Abuse?* SSRN (3 January 2025), https://papers.ssrn.com/sol3/papers.cfm?abstract_id = 5006000.
87. *Ibid.*, at 12.
88. *Ibid.*
89. *Ibid.*, at 7.
90. *Ibid.*, at 4.

moves from being a factor in determining anti-competitive foreclosure to a factor in determining competition on the merits. On this basis, Padilla identifies four relevant scenarios in the context of the two-step abuse test with competition on the merits and capability to have exclusionary effects as the two parameters.

Figure 10.4 Scenarios in the Two-Step Analysis (Wide Interpretation)

Conduct \ Impact	Conduct capable of having exclusionary effects	Conduct not capable of having exclusionary effects
Competition on the merits	Pro-competitive conduct which leads to foreclosure	Pro-competitive conduct
Competition not on the merits	Abuse	Anti-competitive conduct which is not harmful

Dealing with the two scenarios which did not have any practical relevance in the world of the narrow interpretation of capability to foreclose, Padilla adds the following examples:

- For competition on the merits which is capable of having exclusionary effects, an example would be 'a situation where a dominant undertaking's investment in quality results in the marginalization or, even, the exit of competitors'.[91]
- For competition (not) on the merits not capable of having exclusionary effects, an example would be 'a scenario where a dominant company set prices-below costs for its "damaged goods" ... in order to clear its stocks of those products'.[92]

In terms of effects abuses, the outcome of Padilla's proposal would be virtually identical to the approach where the concept of capability to have exclusionary effects is defined as anti-competitive foreclosure within the meaning of the Priorities Guidance.[93] Where it differs is for the other types of abuses. Padilla uses as loadstar for 'competition on the merits' the replicability test (whether conduct is profitably replicable by an as-efficient competitor). This requires more from the test than it can perform. *First of all*, in the context of refusal to supply, conduct may fail the replicability test and the refusal may nevertheless be competition on the merits. *Second*, in relation to 'naked restrictions' only, the replicability test feels like forcing a square peg into a round hole. On balance, it seems easier to fix the problem where it arose, namely within the 'capability' concept.

91. *Ibid.*, at 5.
92. *Ibid.*
93. Priorities Guidance, para. 19.

5 THE NEED FOR CONSISTENCY ACROSS CATEGORIES

5.1 Consistency Across Different Evidential Standards

The focus so far has been on the classification of unilateral conduct into various categories of abuse, the use of presumptions and how categories and presumptions feed into the analytical framework of determining an abuse under Article 102 TFEU.

The various categories however are not independent from each other but are often closely related (such as bundled discount as the price-based equivalent to the non-priced-based tying category).

As mentioned in section 2.3.4, consistency is particularly important where related categories of abuse are subject to different evidential standards. As discussed in section 3.3, dividing lines between evidential standards arise at the intersection between presumptive abuses and effects abuses as well as at the intersection between effects abuses and indispensability abuses.

The Draft Guidelines are largely silent on this issue (as on many other aspects of a wider general framework, having removed or scaled back several of the key elements of the framework developed in the Priorities Guidance). However, the CJEU has dealt with such 'borderline' cases and its judgments provide some important insights.

5.2 Dividing Line Between Presumptive Abuses and Effects Abuses: *Unilever Italy*

5.2.1 Exclusive Rebates Versus Exclusivity Clauses

Pre-*Intel*, exclusivity rebates and exclusivity clauses were regarded as object abuses. In fact, under *Hoffmann-La Roche*, those types of conduct were subject to an irrebuttable presumption of harm. In *Intel*, a case concerning exclusivity rebates, the ECJ 'clarified' that position: while technically preserving the status of exclusivity rebates as a presumptive abuse, it imposed an obligation on the Commission to carry out a detailed market analysis where 'the undertaking concerned submits, during the administrative procedure, on the basis of supporting evidence, that its conduct was not capable of restricting competition and, in particular, of producing the alleged foreclosure effects'.[94] Given that dominant firms will regularly contest the fact that their conduct is capable of having exclusionary effects, for practical purposes, *Intel* may have turned exclusive rebates into an effects abuse.

The *Unilever Italy* case concerned an abuse investigation by the Italian competition authority, AGCM, in relation to, among other things, exclusivity clauses operated by distributors of Unilever's impulse ice cream business in Italy. During the administrative procedure, Unilever had submitted economic evidence, including an 'as

94. Case C-413/14 P, *Intel v. Commission*, EU:C:2017:632, para. 138.

efficient competitor test' claiming that its practices were not capable of having exclusionary effects.

The AGCM took the view that the Intel framework was limited to exclusivity rebates (i.e., pricing abuses). As Unilever's conduct primarily related to exclusivity clauses (i.e., non-pricing abuses), according to the AGCM, *Hoffmann-La Roche* continued to apply, and it was hence under no obligation to take into account the economic studies submitted by Unilever.[95] The ACGM concluded that Unilever Italy had abused its dominant position.

5.2.2 The Rationale for a Common Approach

This case was referred to the ECJ under Article 267 TFEU by the Italian Council of State. The ECJ's starting point was that there were two scenarios set out in *Intel* where a presumptive abuse required an effects analysis: *first*, where the dominant firm claimed (with evidence supporting its claim) that its conduct was not capable of producing exclusionary effects; and *second*, where a system of rebates, which, in principle, falls within the scope of the prohibition laid down in Article 102 TFEU, may be objectively justified.[96]

The Court held that those two scenarios were relevant for exclusivity clauses in the same way they were for exclusivity rebates. In relation to the first scenario (absence of capability), the Court stated that: 'although, by reason of their nature, exclusivity clauses give rise to legitimate concerns of competition, their ability to exclude competitors is not automatic',[97] citing the Commission's Priorities Guidance in support of its statement. In relation to the second scenario (objective justification), the Court held: 'since both rebates practices and exclusivity clauses are capable of being objectively justified or of having the disadvantages which they generate counterbalanced, or even outweighed, by advantages in terms of efficiency which also benefit the consumer, such a clarification must be understood as applying to both of those practices'.[98]

Therefore, rather than following the AGCM in using a purely formal distinction (price versus non-price abuse) for treating the two types of conduct differently, the Court looked at the underlying economic reality: neither exclusivity rebates nor exclusivity clauses were automatically capable of producing exclusionary effects (indeed in certain circumstances neither of them were even presumptively harmful); furthermore, exclusivity arrangements (whether price or non-price based) regularly have efficiency justifications. As a result, the same reasons that motivated the Court to apply the Intel framework to exclusive rebates were equally applicable to exclusivity clauses.

95. Case C-680/20, *Unilever Italia Mkt. Operations Srl*, EU:C:2023:33, paras 5-7.
96. *Ibid.*, at 47-50.
97. *Ibid.*, at 51.
98. *Ibid.*, at 50.

5.3 Dividing Line Between Effects Abuses and Indispensability Abuses: *Bronner, Google Shopping* and *Android Auto*

5.3.1 *Refusal to Supply Versus Similar Conduct*

In *Bronner*, the ECJ held that a 'refusal to supply' can amount to an abuse of dominance under Article 102 TFEU only in exceptional circumstances.

The case concerned Mediaprint, a large Austrian newspaper publisher which had developed a nationwide home delivery scheme to deliver newspapers to its subscribers at home. Oscar Bronner & Co was a publisher of a less widely read Austrian daily newspaper. Bronner sought to have its newspaper included in Mediaprint's home delivery scheme for a reasonable remuneration. Mediaprint refused Bronner access to its delivery scheme. In ruling on a request from the Austrian courts, the CJEU held that for a refusal to grant access to a facility (in this case, the home delivery scheme): (1) the facility must be 'indispensable to carry on the business [of the person claiming access], inasmuch as there is no actual or potential substitute in existence'; and (2) the refusal to grant access must be 'likely to eliminate all competition in the [downstream market in question] on the part of the person requesting access'.[99]

The ECJ has therefore imposed a significantly higher standard of demonstrating competitive harm than in regular effects abuse cases where it is sufficient to show that the conduct is capable of having exclusionary effects.

5.3.2 *The Rationale for a Different Approach*

This higher standard for demonstrating competitive harm was justified in *Bronner* by AG Jacob on two grounds (which were reiterated in subsequent judgments).

First, 'the right to choose one's trading partners and freely to dispose of one's property are generally recognised principles in the laws of Member States, in some cases with constitutional status. Incursions on those rights require justification'.[100]

Second, to protect dynamic competition and avoid harm to the incentive of firms to innovate. As AG Jacob put it:

> The justification in terms of competition policy for interfering with a dominant undertaking's freedom to contract often requires a careful balancing of conflicting considerations. In the long term it is generally pro-competitive and in the interest of consumers to allow a company to retain for its own use facilities which it has developed for the purpose of its business. For example, if access to a production, purchasing or distribution facility were allowed too easily there would be no incentive for a competitor to develop competing facilities. Thus while competition was increased in the short term it would be reduced in the long term. Moreover, the incentive for a dominant undertaking to invest in efficient facilities would be reduced if its competitors were, upon request, able to share the benefits. Thus the

99. Case C-7/97, *Oscar Bronner*, EU:C:1998:569, paras 41 and 38, respectively.
100. Opinion of AG Jacobs in Case C-7/97, *Oscar Bronner*, EU:C:1998:264, para. 56.

mere fact that by retaining a facility for its own use a dominant undertaking retains an advantage over a competitor cannot justify requiring access to it.[101]

5.3.3 *Early Deviations from* Bronner: Slovak Telecom *and* Lithuanian Railways

In the following years, the CJEU has reduced the scope of the indispensability abuse while maintaining the analytical framework set out by AG Jacobs in his Opinion (and the ECJ judgment) in *Bronner*.

The deviations from *Bronner* were justified at two levels: *first*, at a formal level, the ECJ set out why the case in question could be distinguished from a 'refusal to supply', e.g., because in a margin squeeze case, the dominant firm did not refuse to supply the goods and services (*Slovak Telekom*)[102] and *second*, because the destruction of infrastructure could not be equated to a refusal to supply on the basis that such a unilateral act deprives both the party requesting access and the dominant firm of the use of the infrastructure (*Lithuanian Railways*).[103]

Importantly, the ECJ then explained at a substantive level, why – in the specific circumstances of the case in question – the harmful impact on dynamic competition and the incentive to invest (either of the dominant firm or of its competitors) which had been the justification in *Bronner* for the higher evidential standard of harm could not be expected to arise here. Three scenarios have been identified by the Court in these cases.

The *first* scenario is where the dominant firm operates in a regulated sector (such as telecommunications) and as a result, it is subject to a regulatory obligation to grant access. In this scenario, there will be no harmful effect on dynamic competition as the obligation to supply already exists.

In the *second* scenario, the infrastructure has been financed and/or built by the state. While negative effects on the incentive to invest can be expected where the refusal of access relates to an 'infrastructure which the dominant firm owns and which it has developed for the needs of its own business by means of its own investment',[104] such effects are not obvious in a scenario where 'the infrastructure in question was financed by means not of the investments specific to the dominant undertaking, but by means of public funds and that undertaking is not the owner of that infrastructure'.[105]

The *third* scenario is where the refusal to grant access to infrastructure is not part of a normal business strategy but is a 'naked restriction' (or object abuse). The risk of a negative impact on an incentive to invest exists where a refusal to supply is aimed at ensuring that the dominant firm can reserve the use of the infrastructure for itself in pursuit of an immediate benefit. Such a risk cannot be assumed where the refusal to deal is part of an anti-competitive strategy, such as the destruction of infrastructure,

101. *Ibid.*, at 57.
102. *See* Case C-165/19 P, *Slovak Telekom v. Commission*, EU:C:2021:239, paras 49-61.
103. Case C-42/21 P, *Lietuvos geležinkeliai v. Commission*, EU:C:2023:12, paras 81-83.
104. *Ibid.*, para. 86.
105. *Ibid.*, para. 87.

such that 'the infrastructure inevitably becomes unusable by competitors but also by the dominant undertaking itself'.[106]

5.3.4 *Self-Preferencing:* Google Shopping

More recently, in *Google Shopping*, which dealt with 'self-preferencing', Google was held to have acted abusively through: (1) the more favourable positioning and display of its own specialised results within its general results pages than the positioning and display of results from competing comparison shopping services; and (2) the simultaneous demotion of results from competing comparison shopping services by the application of adjustment algorithms.

5.3.4.1 The General Court

In this case, the General Court (GC) distinguished between an explicit refusal to grant access to an input (refusal to supply) and practices which might, ultimately, at a formal level, result in an implicit refusal of access (including discriminatory practices). The GC held that 'not every issue of ... access ... necessarily means that the conditions set out in [*Bronner*] relating to the refusal to supply must be applied'.[107] Rather, the GC held that the case law for a refusal to supply and the conditions for such an abuse set out in *Bronner*, apply only where there is an 'express' request and refusal of access (i.e., the trigger for the relevant exclusionary effects 'lies principally in the refusal as such').[108]

However, in addition to the formalistic distinction between a 'refusal to supply' and 'self-preferencing', the GC also provided an economic underpinning for the different evidential standards of 'refusal to supply' and 'self-prefrencing'.

First, the GC highlighted the open nature of the infrastructure:

> The infrastructure at issue, namely Google's general results pages which generate traffic to other websites, including those of competing comparison shopping services, is, in principle, open, which distinguishes it from other infrastructures referred to in the case-law, consisting of tangible or intangible assets (press distribution systems or intellectual property rights, respectively) whose value depends on the proprietor's ability to retain exclusive use of them.[109]

This point echoed the openness of the infrastructure in *Slovak Telekom* albeit the origin of the openness was different (regulation versus market dynamics). However, the underlying topic is the same; the dominant firm is forced to operate an open infrastructure and the obligation to supply cannot necessarily be assumed to harm the incentive to innovate.

Second, the GC was of the view that such self-preferencing would not be rational unless the dominance and barriers to entry were such that no market entry within a

106. *Ibid.*, para. 83.
107. Case T-612/17, *Alphabet v. Commission* (*Google Shopping*), EU:T:2021:763, paras 230-232.
108. *Ibid.*
109. *Ibid.*, at 177.

sufficiently short period of time was possible in response to the limitation of internet users' choice.[110] Again, there is an echo from earlier case law, postulating that where the conduct is part of an anti-competitive strategy, imposing an obligation cannot be presumed to harm the incentive to innovate.

Interpreting the GC judgment in this way fits into a coherent framework for separating refusal to supply cases from other related conduct and builds on earlier case law, such as *Slovak Telekom* and *Lithuanian Railways*.

5.3.4.2 ECJ

On appeal to the ECJ, Google again argued that its conduct could not be abusive without the *Bronner* criteria being met, because, in Google's view, the Commission was essentially arguing that its conduct was a refusal to supply.

The ECJ also held that the *Bronner* criteria did not apply to this conduct, because the issue was not that Google was refusing competing comparison shopping services access to its general search services and to the general results pages, but instead that it made that access subject to discriminatory conditions: 'the disadvantage which results for comparison shopping services competing with Google from the combination of the two practices at issue ... concerns the conditions of access to Google's general results page, and not access to an allegedly separate infrastructure, consisting of boxes'.[111] The ECJ found that the boxes in which Google Shopping's results had been displayed did not constitute a separate 'facility' from Google's general results pages (noting that both the boxes and general search results were generated on the same results page).[112] Google's conduct could not be equated to a simple refusal to supply, since the competent competition authority or national court could not force the dominant undertaking to give access to its infrastructure, as that access has already been granted. It follows that any measures imposed would be less detrimental to the freedom of contract of the dominant undertaking and to its right to property than forcing it to give access to its infrastructure where it has reserved that infrastructure for the needs of its own business.[113]

Although the ECJ was clear that the *Bronner* test applies only to refusal to supply cases (and not to cases of discriminatory access), this largely seems to have turned on a rejection of the 'boxes' as separate infrastructure from the general search page (meaning that there had been no refusal of access to an essential facility) and the identification of the relevant conduct as a combination of practices which go beyond refusal.

This puts a lot of emphasis on the formal distinction between 'refusal to supply' and 'discriminatory access'. The judgment neither provides a clear methodology to identify the right scope of the relevant 'infrastructure' (or facility) for the application of the *Bronner* test. Nor does the ECJ link its conclusions to the underlying key rationale

110. *Ibid.*
111. Case C-48/22, *Google and Alphabet v. Commission*, EU:C:2024:726, para. 107.
112. *Ibid.*, at 105.
113. *Ibid.*, at 91.

for the higher indispensability standard in *Bronner*, i.e., the incentive to innovate and the impact on dynamic competition.

5.3.5 *Refusal to Grant Access to an Open Platform:* Android Auto

The most recent case narrowing the scope of the refusal to supply test in *Bronner* is *Android Auto*. There the ECJ held that the conditions in Bronner do not apply where the dominant firm 'has developed infrastructure not solely for the needs of its own business but with a view to enabling third-party undertakings to use that infrastructure'.[114]

The *Android Auto* case differs from previous cases which deviate from *Bronner* in that the Court accepts that the conduct in question is a refusal to supply. Instead, the Court relies on the framework developed in cases such as *Slovak Telekom* to explain why harm to the incentive to innovate would not arise in the circumstances of *Android Auto*. In the words of AG Medina:

> In order to determine whether the Bronner conditions apply to a case concerning a refusal to grant access, it is necessary to discern whether the infrastructure to which access is requested is to be consecrated to the dominant undertaking's own business and use and to be enjoyed exclusively by it, as a way of preserving the benefits of the investments made for the development of that infrastructure. By contrast, those conditions are not intended to apply where the infrastructure concerned is opened to other operators on the market, which, according to the Court, can result from the application of regulatory obligations, as was the case in the judgment in Slovak Telekom. Arguably, that must a fortiori be the case in respect of an infrastructure which is deliberately developed to be used by third-party operators.[115]

The reference to *Slovak Telekom* involves a big leap: in that case, the dominant firm was subject to a general obligation to deal which is very different to the situation in *Android Auto*, where Google had been willing to deal with certain types of customers but not others. This distinction is particularly important when considering the impact on firms' incentive to innovate.

Furthermore, it is not clear whether the *Bronner* refusal to supply test is now limited to cases where the interpretation in question is 'enjoyed exclusively by the [dominant firm]',[116] i.e., where access granted to a simple third-party would be sufficient to disapply *Bronner* or also where the 'infrastructure is [not] deliberately developed to be used by third-party operators'[117] which would give *Bronner* a wider application.

In this context, it is interesting that the infrastructure in *Bronner* itself was not 'enjoyed exclusively' by Mediaprint. Bronner had argued that Mediaprint was acting in a discriminatory fashion given it had granted a different third-party daily newspaper

114. Case C-233/23, *Alphabet (Google Android Auto)*, EU:C:2025:110, para. 44.
115. Opinion of AG Medina in Case C-233/23, *Alphabet (Google Android Auto)*, EU:C:2024:694, para. 35.
116. *Ibid.*
117. *Ibid.*

access to its home delivery service. Mediaprint had countered that making the system available to all Austrian newspaper publishers would exceed the natural capacity of its system and that the position of the third party to which it had granted access was not comparable to that of Bronner since the publisher of the former also entrusted Mediaprint with printing and distribution, including sale in kiosks, so that home-delivery network constituted only part of a package of services Mediaprint was providing. The Commission had noted that such conduct could amount to abusive discrimination but, on the facts, that was not the case, since discrimination was not at issue; the issue was Bronner gaining access in the first place, not the terms of access.[118] The ECJ did not engage with this issue.

The Court's reasoning here can be questioned. If the justification for the strict 'indispensability' requirement in *Bronner* is harm to the incentive to invest, then the question is whether the mere fact that the infrastructure is made available to some other third parties ensures that the incentive to invest is not harmed, such that dropping that 'indispensability' requirement makes sense. It is arguable that this is not necessarily the case, given that the dominant firm may well be willing to make the infrastructure available to some third parties but not others (e.g., those who would not be able to invest and with whom it does not compete downstream).

118. Case C-7/97, *Oscar Bronner*, EU:C:1998:569, para. 30.

CHAPTER 11

Refusal to Supply and the 'Essential Facilities' Doctrine from *Oscar Bronner* to *Google Shopping*: Independent Abuses, Variants and the Legal Test(s)

Georgia Theodorakopoulou[*]

1 INTRODUCTION

The recent cases before the European Courts have proven the non-exhaustive character of Article 102 of the Treaty on the Function of the European Union (TFEU). At the same time, they have triggered the debate on the boundaries of the traditional 'refusal to deal' abuse and relevance to date of the *Bronner* case law with a focus on the strict legal test it established, especially with regard to the criterion pertaining to the indispensability of input. The discussion is not irrelevant to the debate on the usefulness and practicability of structured legal tests[1] based on predetermined and clearly defined conditions and thus catered for specific categories of abuses. While it is commonly accepted that every legal system requires a certain degree of formalism, so that it can be administrable, the question remains on whether flexible tests, the conditions of which may be sometimes stretched or interpreted in a dynamic manner may be better suited in the realm of digital economy.

* The views expressed in this article are those of the author and do not necessarily represent the views of Grimaldi Alliance. The author had no involvement or personal interest in the cases discussed herein and has not received any funding or other support in the preparation of this article. All errors and omissions are of the author.

1. Pablo Ibáñez Colomo, *Structured Legal Tests, Effective Judicial Review and Missing the Trees for the Forest*, 13(7), Journal of European Competition Law & Practice, 461 (2022) https://doi.org/10.1093/jeclap/lpac057, last accessed on 23 July 2025.

At the same time, the long-awaited Draft Guidelines on exclusionary abuses that the European Commission (the 'Commission') issued some time ago have aimed once adopted to provide clearer guidance to market players and in particular undertakings in self-assessing compliance of their conduct with Article 102 TFEU by taking into account the evolution of the case law of the European Courts since the first 2008 Commission Guidance and thus to contribute to legal certainty. While it has been hoped that the Guidelines could indeed provide a *fil conducteur* on the assessment of conducts that have arisen in the digital era or that deviate from established abuses, the release of the Draft Guidelines has fallen short of the expectations in some instances.

The present article aims to focus on the evolution of 'refusal to supply' and the 'essential facilities' doctrine and discuss its usefulness to date and its potential development in the future. First, the emergence and establishment of the test in a traditional refusal to supply will be examined (section 2). Second, through a selective list of landmark cases, each of which has added value to the discussion on the boundaries of the *Oscar Bronner* test, the truths and myths of this case law will be attempted to be disentangled (section 3). Third, we will refer to Draft Guidelines and their contribution to the discussion around the novel and distinct from refusal to supply abuses and their classification in relation to their being subsumed under specific or non-specific legal tests (section 4). Finally, the conclusions will attempt to decode the discussion and foresee the future developments regarding the boundaries of 'refusal to deal' abuse (section 5).

2 OSCAR BRONNER: THE ESTABLISHMENT OF A STRICT LEGAL TEST IN THE SERVICE OF ARTICLE 102 TFEU

Although refusal to supply cases have been of the oldest caught by Article 102 TFEU, they have nonetheless always been complex to assess, as in their core substance lies the balancing of conflicting interests: on the one hand, the fundamental rights of the freedom of contract and the right to property that the dominant undertaking should legitimately enjoy and on the other hand, the objective of achieving the efficiencies stemming from competitive markets. This difficult balancing is behind the strict interpretation of the conditions comprising the legal test that the European Courts developed in the oldest cases relating to refusal to supply.

2.1 The First Case Law Asserting the Indispensability Condition

The well-entrenched legal test for refusal to supply is alternatively referred to as the 'Oscar Bronner' or 'Bronner' criteria owing to the most famous case[2] that established it or as the 'essential facilities doctrine', thus giving away, by means of its name, the most important feature of the assessment in the context of the test. Under the essential

2. Case C-7/97, *Oscar Bronner GmbH & Co. KG v. Mediaprint Zeitungs- und Zeitschriftenverlag GmbH & Co. KG, Mediaprint Zeitungsvertriebsgesellschaft mbH & Co. KG and Mediaprint Anzeigengesellschaft mbH & Co. KG* ('Oscar Bronner'), 26.11.1998, EU:C:1998:569.

facilities doctrine, a dominant company may be forced to grant rivals access to its infrastructure (in the upstream market) if the following strict conditions are met:[3]

- the refusal to grant access will likely eliminate all competition in another (the downstream) market;
- the infrastructure is indispensable for the requesting undertaking to compete in the downstream market and there are no actual or potential substitutes for it;[4]
- there is no objective justification for the refusal.

The existence of an objective justification is a question of fact to be established in the concrete circumstances of each case.[5] Both the Commission and the Union Courts have acknowledged that a dominant firm is entitled to refusal to supply, when it comes to protecting its legitimate commercial interests that could be otherwise put at risk when there is a disruption of production or shortage of stocks, for example, without prejudice to observing the principle of proportionality.[6]

It emerges from the above legal test and especially, the condition of indispensability, that the European Court of Justice (the 'Court of Justice') decided to resolve the complex weighting of contradictory interests by opting for a strict interpretation of the criterion of input indispensability. The threshold set for it to be satisfied is high, as it is not enough for the undertaking requesting access to show that the infrastructure is useful or convenient to have.[7] The infrastructure should be essential in the sense that there is no actual or potential substitute for it. As the Court of Justice specified in *Bronner*, the latter requirement is not met unless there are no other means available to competitors or there are technical, legal or economic hurdles making it impossible or unreasonably difficult for competitors to develop the facilities themselves.[8]

3. To these conditions, a fourth one is to be added, that of the prevention of the emergence of a new product, when the input is protected by intellectual property law or trade secrets.
4. The word 'indispensable' is the one that the Union Courts have tended to use, with reference to 'essential facilities' and inputs that are 'objectively necessary' being alternative expressions that may be used interchangeably for the purpose of this article. The Commission refers to the objective necessity of input when it comes to assessing a refusal to supply, *see* relevantly: Communication from the Commission – Guidance on the Commission's enforcement priorities in applying Article 82 of the EC Treaty to abusive exclusionary conduct by dominant undertakings, OJ C 45, 24.2.2009, paras 82-83.
5. Case T-201/04, *Microsoft Corp v. Commission*, 17.9.2007, EU:T:2007:289, paras 697-698.
6. Case 27/76, *United Brands Company and United Brands Continentaal BV v. Commission of the European Communities Chiquita Bananas (United Brands)*, 14.2.1978, EU:C:1978:22, para. 189; Guidance on the Commission's enforcement priorities, *supra* n. 4, paras 88-89. Richard Whish and David Bailey, *Competition Law* (10th ed., Oxford University Press 2021), at 744, where a series of examples if possible justifications from the case law are cited with the clarification that the dominant undertaking is required to show that its refusal is objectively necessary in the sense that it pursues a legitimate interest other than its own commercial advantage, and that it has behaved in a proportionate way.
7. It should be noted that the notion of *convenient facilities* was used to criticize the relaxation of the standards for holding refusals to deal abusive in the *Microsoft* case; *See* Richard Whish and David Bailey, *Competition Law* (10th ed., Oxford University Press 2021), at 739; Derek Ridyard, *Compulsory Access under EC Competition Law: A New Doctrine of 'Convenient Facilties' and the Case for Price Regulation*, 25 European Competition Law Review 669 (2004).
8. Case C-7/97, *Oscar Bronner*, paras 43, 44.

This intentionally narrow condition is based on a double rationale: from a *legal perspective*, the restriction of fundamental rights of the freedom of contract and the right to property[9] should be employed, only where no other solutions are available. In this regard, Advocate General (AG) Jacobs pointed out in his Opinion in *Oscar Bronner*[10] that the right to choose one's trading partners and freely dispose of one's property are generally recognized principles in the laws of Member States; from an *economic perspective*, if access to upstream or input infrastructure was to be granted too easily, then unavoidably we would end up in the paradoxical scenario where we would strive to maintain the dynamic efficiencies of competitive markets by securing the presence of other competitors than the dominant one, but the incentive of dominant competitors to invest and innovate would be devoid of reason and thus almost vanished in the long term as free-riders would find occasion to take advantage of investments made by other firms in the market. As AG Jacobs underpinned, 'in the long term it is generally pro-competitive and in the interest of consumers to allow a company to retain for its own use facilities which it has developed for the purpose of its business'.

It is widely supported that such strict interpretation is in line with the primary objective of Article 102 TFEU, which is to prevent the distortion of competition and not to protect the position of certain competitors on the market.[11] Remarkably, the Court concluded in the *Oscar Bronner* case that the legal test for refusal to supply was not satisfied and therefore that there was no abuse under Article 102 TFEU, as *first*, there were other *actual* means of distributing daily newspapers, namely shops, kiosks and distribution by post, even if less advantageous[12] and *second*, there could be potential means developed in the absence of technical, legal or economic obstacles.[13] Interestingly, *Oscar Bronner* clarified that the small size of a competitor could not constitute a valid reason for requesting and being granted access.[14]

9. Articles 16 and 17 of the Charter of Fundamental Rights of the EU, OJ [2007] C 303/17.
10. Opinion of Advocate General Jacobs in Case C-7/97, *Oscar Bronner*, 28.5.1998, EU:C:1998:264, para. 56.
11. Richard Whish and David Bailey, *Competition Law* (10th ed., Oxford University Press 2021), at 733.
12. Case C-7/97, *Oscar Bronner*, para. 43. The Court reiterated its position in Case C-418/01, *IMS Health*, 29.4.2004, EU:C:2004:257, para. 28, where it held that: 'in order to determine whether a product or service is indispensable for enabling an undertaking to carry on business in a particular market, it must be determined whether there are products or services which constitute alternative solutions, even if they are less advantageous, and whether there are technical, legal or economic obstacles capable of making it impossible or at least unreasonably difficult for any undertaking seeking to operate in the market to create, possibly in cooperation with other operators, the alternative products or services. [...]'.
13. Case C-7/97, *Oscar Bronner*, paras 44-46; *see also* Case C-418/01, *IMS Health*, 29.4.2004, EU:C:2004:257, para. 28: 'According to paragraph 46 of Bronner, in order to accept the existence of economic obstacles, it must be established, at the very least, that the creation of those products or services is not economically viable for production on a scale comparable to that of the undertaking which controls the existing product or service'.
14. Case C-7/97, *Oscar Bronner*, para. 45: 'in order to demonstrate that the creation of such a system is not a realistic potential alternative and that access to the existing system is therefore indispensable, it is not enough to argue that it is not economically viable by reason of the small circulation of the daily newspaper or newspapers to be distributed'.

The *Oscar Bronner* ruling also helped stress the *exceptional circumstances*[15] in the preceding *Magill* case that had first adopted the 'essential facilities' doctrine.[16] In that case, Magill wished to publish the listings of three television companies broadcasting in the UK and Ireland in the form of a single weekly publication as was the model in continental countries, at a time when this information was only available in daily newspapers and the three broadcasting companies enjoyed copyright protection for the daily TV listings, thus forcing Magill to require a licence. The Commission found that the broadcasting companies had abused their individual dominant positions by refusing to make their TV listings available to Magill and required that advance information be supplied in order to enable comprehensive weekly TV guides to be released. The Court of Justice upheld the ruling of the (then) Court of First Instance[17] that the three dominant companies relied on national copyright laws to refuse the sharing of the requested information. As a result, the Court of Justice ruled that Magill was prevented, without any objective justification, from accessing the downstream market for TV guides and offering a new product, for which there existed potential consumer demand.[18]

In the subsequent case of *IMS Health*, the scope of exceptional circumstances in which a competing undertaking could revendicate access to copyright licence was further clarified by the Court of Justice by means of the addition of an important condition.[19] According to the Court, in striking a fair balance between the need to protect the economic freedom of the owner of an intellectual property right and the protection of competition, the latter can prevail only where refusal to grant a licence prevents the development of the secondary market to the *detriment of consumers*.[20]

The *Bronner* criteria and the essential facilities doctrine were confirmed afterwards in an innovation-driven case of the General Court, the famous *Microsoft* case.[21] The General Court confirmed the correctness of the Commission's findings (by ruling that the Commission had not made a manifest error in its assessment) and upheld the latter's decision that Microsoft had abused its dominant position by refusing to supply interoperability information to its competitors.[22] This information was indispensable for competitors to develop server software that could interoperate with Microsoft's

15. *Ibid.*, para. 40.
16. Joined cases C-241/91 P and C-242/91 P, *Radio Telefis Eireann (RTE) and Independent Television Publications Ltd (ITP) v. Commission of the European Communities* (*'Magill'*), 6.4.1995, EU:C:1995:98.
17. T-69/89, etc., *RTE v. Commission* EU:T:1991:39.
18. *Ibid.*, paras 54-56.
19. Case C-418/01, *IMS Health GmbH & Co. OHG v. NDC Health GmbH & Co. KG*, 29.4.2004, EU:C:2004:257, para. 48.
20. *Ibid.*
21. Case T-201/04, *Microsoft Corp. v. Commission of the European Communities*, 17.9.2007, EU:T:2007:289, para. 421.
22. *Ibid.*, paras 381, 382 and 391 and para. 360 on the European Commission's argumentation that reads: 'The fact that the information at issue is indispensable if Microsoft's competitors are to be able to continue to represent a competitive constraint for Microsoft's products means that those competitors will be gradually eliminated from the market. That fact that their elimination is not yet complete does not show that the indispensability criterion is not fulfilled, since the essential thing is whether the information is indispensable in order to remain as a viable competitor on the market.'

Windows operating system.[23] Although the case pertained to the licensing of intellectual property rights, it reflected the balancing of interests found in cases of access to physical infrastructure.[24]

2.2 The Assimilation of the 'Essential Facilities' Doctrine in the Commission's Guidance

The Commission had elaborated on the requirement of indispensability in paragraph 83 of its Guidance on Article 102 Enforcement Priorities taking stock among others of the *Oscar Bronner* case. According to it, indispensability signifies the impossibility or at least the great difficulty for competitors from a technical, legal or economic perspective to duplicate the input infrastructure in the foreseeable future.[25] 'Duplication' thereunder is taken to mean the creation of an alternative source of efficient supply capable of allowing competitors to exert a competitive constraint on the dominant undertaking in the downstream market.[26] More specifically, duplication may be technically or physically impossible because of planning or environmental hurdles when it comes to large infrastructures, such as ports, airports or rail networks.[27] In what concerns impossibility from a legal perspective, this may consist in intellectual property rights held by the dominant undertaking and thus granting the undertaking the exclusive right to reproduce a work.[28] Last, the great difficulty or impossibility from an economic perspective may signify that the duplication of a second facility is not economically viable since the market is not large enough to sustain a second facility. This could also be the case of building a second airport in a specific geographic market.[29]

What renders the *Bronner* case a landmark jurisprudence is that it underpinned the significance of indispensability of input as the prerequisite to identify the practice of refusing to supply a competitor in the downstream market and thus set a high threshold for the competent competition authority to intervene in relevant cases. The level of flexibility of its boundaries however, has been at the centre of scrutiny in

23. Juliane Kokott and Mariya Serafimova, *Balancing Innovation and Competition in Dynamic Industries*, 24.1.2024, Owlit – Balancing Innovation and Competition in Dynamic Industries und Missbrauch einer marktbeherrschenden Stellung durch Lizenzverweigerung und Bündelung von Software-Produkten.
24. It should be noted that this case could have nonetheless been interpreted as a constructive refusal to deal, if the General Court was to endorse Microsoft's view that 'interoperability occurs along a continuum' and that 'it is not an absolute standard', as it was the degree of interoperability provided by Microsoft that was considered insufficient to enable effective competition. *See* Case T-201/04, *Microsoft Corp. v. Commission of the European Communities*, para. 119; *See* to this effect also, Niamh Dunne, *Dispensing with Indispensability*, 16(1), Journal of Competition Law & Economics (2020),74, 98 https://doi.org/10.1093/joclec/nhaa004, last accessed on 23 July 2025.
25. Guidance on the Commission's enforcement priorities, *supra* n. 4, para. 83.
26. Richard Whish and David Bailey, *Competition Law* (10th ed., Oxford University Press 2021), at 739.
27. *Ibid.*
28. Joined cases C-241/91 P and C-242/91 P, *Magill.*
29. Richard Whish and David Bailey, *Competition Law* (10th ed., Oxford University Press 2021), at 739 pointing out that this argument is relevant to the principle of the as-efficient competitor in non-pricing abuses.

subsequent cases where the refusal is not outright, but rather implicit or where there is no question of refusal to supply in the first place, as access is already granted by the dominant company either under a regulatory obligation not to refuse access to competitors in the downstream market or under the dominant's company business model, as will be discussed below.

3 ENDORSING OR REJECTING THE *OSCAR BRONNER* TEST? THE VARIANTS AND INDEPENDENT PRACTICES IN LATER CASES

The applicability (or not) of the Oscar Bronner test had been examined equally in cases that derogated from the concept of outright refusal to supply or to license but consisted in what the Commission called 'constructive refusal' in its Guidance Paper.[30]

More specifically, the Commission under section 'D. Refusal to Supply and margin Squeeze' of its Guidance Paper, subsumed under a common category (and thus, a common legal test) what it called the outright and the constructive refusal to supply. In the Commission's words, 'it is not necessary for there to be actual refusal on the part of a dominant undertaking; "constructive refusal" is sufficient'. The Guidance Paper further gave examples of what might amount to implicit or constructive refusal: the latter could take the form of unduly delaying or otherwise degrading the supply of the product or involve the imposition of unreasonable conditions in return for the supply.[31]

In this regard, the Commission overturned its approach in the Guidance Paper already with its Policy Brief of March 2023, when it first introduced the need for future Guidelines on Article 102 TFEU. While it underpinned that constructive refusals were viewed as similar to outright refusals, and the Guidance applied the same criteria to both types of abuses, it then stressed the need to distinguish situations of outright refusal to supply from situations where the dominant company makes access subject to unfair conditions, i.e., from constructive refusal to supply.[32] The Commission's approach was criticized in that this distinction was misleading in two respects: *first*, the Union Courts had not made any distinction between the 'outright' and the 'constructive' refusal to supply;[33] *second*, the discussion on indispensability lacks reason where the dominant undertaking is already subject to a regulatory obligation to grant access to its assets, in other words, it has no legal right to refuse access, but for example, it may offer access on unfair terms.[34]

30. Guidance on the Commission's enforcement priorities, *supra* n. 4, para. 79.
31. *Ibid.*
32. EC, Competition Policy Brief, *A Dynamic and Workable Effects-Based Approach to Abuse of Dominance*, Issue 1 (March 2023) at 7.
33. *See* to this effect: Assimakis Komninos, *Comments on* 'EC, Competition Policy Brief', *A Dynamic and Workable Effects-Based Approach to Abuse of Dominance*, Issue 1, March 2023; Alfonso Lamadrid, *Finding Consensus in Article 102 Cases (I): When Do the Bronner Conditions Apply?*, Chillin' Competition (21 February 2024), https://chillingcompetition.com/2024/02/, last accessed on 23 July 2025, where reference is made to the European Commission's rejoinder in Case T-851/14 *Slovak Telekom v. European Commission*.
34. Richard Whish and David Bailey, *Competition Law* (10th ed., Oxford University Press 2021), at 743.

3.1 The Case of *Slovak Telekom*: The Defiance of Oscar Bronner

The Court's ruling in *Slovak Telekom*[35] was instrumental in establishing this distinction from the *Oscar Bronner* case.[36] The case dealt with the refusal of Slovak Telekom, a subsidiary of Deutsche Telekom and the incumbent telecommunications operator in Slovakia, to provide rivals with *fair* access to its local loop network. The ruling had followed the Commission's decision in the case that focused not only on the margin squeeze strategy of the company but also equally on its non-price conducts, that were identified by the Commission as refusals to deal,[37] but could equally be labelled as 'margin squeeze by other means' according to Ibáñez Colomo.[38] These non-price strategies included the withholding of network information that alternative operators needed to compete and further entailed unjustifiably reducing the scope of the regulatory obligations borne by the dominant firm.[39] The practice under scrutiny was lying between a refusal to supply and a margin squeeze.[40] The Court clarified in *Slovak Telekom* that the seriousness of an infringement of Article 102 TFEU consisting in a refusal by a dominant undertaking to supply a product or service to other undertakings does not depend solely on its form, but is likely to depend on numerous factors independent of the explicit or implicit nature of that refusal.[41]

The legal question arising thus was whether the high threshold laid down by the Oscar Bronner criteria should be applicable in every refusal to supply or instead, there are circumstances providing for a derogation therefrom or for a different legal test.[42] What was made clear in the case is that the underlying regulatory context and the regulatory obligation borne by the incumbent firm to provide access to competitors rendered the scrutiny of a refusal to supply abuse pointless. The applicability of the *Bronner* criteria in such case is contingent on whether remedial intervention from a competition authority would impose on the dominant company a duty to deal and grant its competitors access to the infrastructure that it has developed for its own business.[43] As Ibáñez Colomo has underpinned, the scope of the *Bronner* criteria could

35. Case C-165/19 P, *Slovak Telekom, a.s. v. European Commission,* 25.3.2021, EU:C:2021:239.
36. Richard Whish and David Bailey, *Competition Law* (10th ed., Oxford University Press 2021), at 743.
37. *See* Commission Decision of 15 October 2014 in Case AT.39523 – Slovak Telekom, C(2014) 7465 final, at p. 113, 7.1'Legal framework for the assessment of abusive refusal to supply'.
38. Pablo Ibáñez Colomo, *The New EU Competition Law* (Bloomsbury Publishing 2023), at 168.
39. *See* Commission Decision of 15 October 2014 in Case AT.39523 – Slovak Telekom, at ss 7.6.2 and 7.6.3.
40. Pablo Ibáñez Colomo, *What Is an Abuse of a Dominant Position? Deconstructing the Prohibition and Categorizing Practices,* 82-100, 97 (Pinar Akman, Or Brook and Konstantinos Stylianou eds, Research Handbook on Abuse of Dominance and Monopolization, Edward Elgard Publishing 2023).
41. Case C-165/19 P, *Slovak Telekom, a.s. v. European Commission,* 25.3.2021, EU:C:2021:239, para. 133.
42. Ibáñez Colomo, *The New EU Competition Law, supra* n. 38, at p. 169.
43. Case C-165/19 P, *Slovak Telekom, a.s. v. European Commission,* 25.3.2021, EU:C:2021:239, para. 49: 'The application, to a particular case, of the conditions laid down by the Court of Justice in the judgment in Bronner, set out in paragraph 44 of the present judgment, and in particular the condition relating to the indispensability of the access to the dominant undertaking's infrastructure, allows the competent authority or national court to determine whether that

be defined in relation to the nature of a proactive remedial intervention, in the sense that where a remedy required to bring the infringement to an end would amount to mandating access and therefore would intrude with the firms' freedom of contract and their right to property, then indispensability should be part of the legal test.[44]

In the words of the Court of Justice, the *Oscar Bronner* case and the indispensability condition would be relevant where:

> a finding that a dominant undertaking abused its position due to a refusal to conclude a contract with a competitor has the consequence of forcing that undertaking to conclude a contract with that competitor.[45]

As will be outlined in section 3.3, this position was challenged in the context of the *Google Shopping* saga, where the Union Courts rejected any automatic link between the applicable legal test to an infringement and the remedies ordered for its termination.[46]

Further, the Court of Justice ruled in *Slovak Telekom* that:

> where a dominant undertaking gives access to its infrastructure but makes that access, provision of services or sale of products subject to unfair conditions, the conditions laid down by the Court of Justice in paragraph 41 of the judgment in Bronner do not apply.[47]

In such cases of underlying regulatory obligations, indispensability should not be part of the test to be met and competition authorities are discharged from any obligation to demonstrate that access is, in fact, indispensable for operating on a downstream market in order for the conduct to be abusive.[48] In this regard and in accordance with its case law, the Court of Justice also reminded us that for practices other than a refusal of access, the absence of indispensability is not in itself decisive for the purposes of examining potentially abusive conduct on the part of a dominant

undertaking has a genuinely tight grip on the market by virtue of that infrastructure. Thus, that undertaking may be forced to give a competitor access to an infrastructure that it has developed for the needs of its own business only where such access is indispensable to the business of such a competitor, namely where there is no actual or potential substitute for that infrastructure.'

44. Pablo Ibáñez Colomo, *Indispensability in Google Shopping: What the Court Did, and Did not, Address in Slovak Telekom*, Chillin' Competition (2 April 2021), https://chillingcompetition.com/2021/04/02/indispensability-in-google-shopping-what-the-court-did-and-did-not-address-in-slovak-telekom/, last accessed on 23 July 2025. This observation is consistent with the Courts' settled case law, also in Case C-165/19 P, *Slovak Telekom v. Commission*, para. 51, where the Court of Justice points to practices that 'cannot be equated to a simple refusal to allow a competitor access to the infrastructure, since the competent competition authority or national court will not have to force the dominant undertaking to give access to its infrastructure, as that access has already been granted'.
45. Case C-165/19 P, *Slovak Telekom*, para. 46.
46. *See* to this effect also, Niamh Dunne, *Dispensing with Indispensability*, 16(1), Journal of Competition Law & Economics (2020), 74, 111 https://doi.org/10.1093/joclec/nhaa004, last accessed on 23 July 2025.
47. Case C-165/19 P, *Slovak Telekom*, para. 50.
48. Richard Whish and David Bailey, *Competition Law* (10th ed., Oxford University Press 2021), at 743.

undertaking, where the conduct under scrutiny 'may be capable of having anti-competitive effects on the markets concerned'.[49]

Interestingly, in the amendments to the Guidance Paper that came out together with its Policy Brief and date from March 2023,[50] the Commission took out its prior reference to constructive refusal to supply as a variant to actual refusal to supply under paragraph 79 of the amended Guidance paper. The Commission split margin squeeze (which is a form of constructive refusal to supply)[51] from section 'D. Refusal to supply' and reallocated it to a separate section 'E', underlining that *margin squeeze is an independent form of abuse.*

3.2 *Lithuanian Railways*: An Underlying Legal Framework in a Paradoxical Practice

The applicability of the essential facilities doctrine and the boundaries of a practice identifying as refusal to supply was again tested in a paradoxical non-price practice that arose in the case of *Lithuanian Railways* (or alternatively '*Baltic Rail*').[52] The practice under scrutiny that has reasonably been cited as one of the most blatant abuses under Article 102 TFEU equivalent to a restriction by object,[53] entailed the decision of the Lithuanian railway company, namely Lietuvos geležinkeliai AB (LG), to dismantle 19 kilometres of its own railway tracks, rendering it unusable for both its own rail transport services and the services of its competitors. More specifically, LG suspended traffic on a 19-km section between Mažeikiai (Lithuania) and the border with Latvia, on account of a defect in the rail track on the short route to Latvia. While LG as the incumbent managing the railway infrastructure and providing transport services, undertook the complete removal of the track and its subsequent restoration in the short term, such restoration was not materialized and thus the lack thereof impeded the proper use of the contested part of the rail network overall.

49. *See* to this effect, C-52/09, *Konkurrensverket v. TeliaSonera Sverige AB*, 17.2.2011, EU:C:2011:83, para. 72 and Case C–165/19 P, *Slovak Telekom*, 25.3.021, EU:C:2021:239, para. 50.
50. Communication From the Commission – Amendments to the Communication from the Commission Guidance on the Commission's enforcement priorities in applying Article 82 of the EC Treaty to abusive exclusionary conduct by dominant undertakings, C/2023/1923 final OJ C 116, 31.3.2023.
51. Inge Graef, *The Future of Refusals to Deal and Margin Squeezes in the Face of Sector-Specific Regulation*, 162-181, 163 (Pinar Akman, Or Brook and Konstantinos Stylianou eds, Research Handbook on Abuse of Dominance and Monopolization, Edward Elgard Publishing 2023).
52. Commission Decision of 2 October 2017 in Case AT.39813, Baltic Rail; Case T-814/17, *Lietuvos geležinkeliai AB v. Commission*, 18.11.2020, EU:T:2020:545; Case C-42/21 P, *Lietuvos geležinkeliai v. Commission*, 12.1.2023, EU:C:2023:12.
53. Pablo Ibáñez Colomo, *GC Judgment in Case T–814/17, Lithuanian Railways: Part I: Object and Indispensability*, Chillin' Competition (1 December 2020), https://chillingcompetition.com/2020/12/01/gc-judgment-in-case-t%E2%80%91814-17-lithuanian-railways-part-i-object-and-indispensability/, last accessed on 23 July 2025.

Such practice could be seen as the non-price collateral of pricing below average variable costs,[54] as it comprised an unreasonable and profit-sacrificing conduct of the dominant undertaking.

In the words of the Court of Justice:

> destroying infrastructure entails sacrificing an asset, subject, where appropriate, to the costs associated with such destruction. As a result of the destruction, the infrastructure inevitably becomes unusable by competitors but also by the dominant undertaking itself.[55]

The central question in the General Court's assessment and, on appeal, in the Court of Justice's ruling, was whether such conduct constituted refusal to supply to which the Oscar Bronner criteria would be applicable. The Court of Justice assessed the conduct against the Oscar Bronner benchmark and demonstrated that none of its factual aspects could be related to the specific circumstances that pertain to this case law and the legal test applicable to it.[56] As the Court of Justice clarified that the Oscar Bronner case law implies 'maintaining infrastructure, the use of which the dominant undertaking reserves for itself in pursuit of an immediate benefit'[57] which was not the case at hand (but constituted rather the opposite), since access to that specific part of the network was blocked for all undertakings, including the dominant company, whereas potential competitors could still gain 'access, as appropriate, to that network by another route'.[58]

Further, the double rationale underlying the *Bronner* case was also rejected in the case of *Lithuanian Railways*, given that there was no investment incentive to protect since LG did not own and had not developed the infrastructure for the needs of its own business by means of its own investments, but only managed the infrastructure that was developed by means of public funds. The absence of private investment and of any entrepreneurial risk inherent in it thus rendered the application of the *Bronner* case groundless at hand.[59]

Most importantly, the underlying regulatory framework of the case differentiated it from a 'classic' refusal to access.[60] This is so in a case where an obligation to supply has already been imposed by a regulation to the dominant undertaking,[61] meaning that what may still make sense to examine under the scope of Article 102 TFEU is not an outright refusal, but the conditions of the mandated access that result from the

54. *See* to this effect Case C-62/86, *AKZO Chemie BV v. Commission of the European Communities*, 3.7.1991, EU:C:1991:286.
55. Case C-42/21 P, *Lietuvos geležinkeliai v. Commission*, para. 83.
56. *Ibid.*, paras 78-80.
57. *Ibid.*, paras 81-82.
58. *Ibid.*, para. 85.
59. *See also* Daniel Mandrescu, *The Essential Facility Doctrine and Google Android Auto Case C-233/23: The Good, the Bad and the Ugly*, Lexxion (8 January 2025), https://www.lexxion.eu/en/coreblogpost/the-essential-facility-doctrine-and-google-android-auto-case-c-233-23-the-good-the-bad-and-the-ugly/, last accessed on 23 July 2025.
60. Case C-42/21 P, *Lietuvos geležinkeliai v. Commission*, paras 88-89.
61. For a discussion on the historical context pertaining to the regulation of certain sectors, including transport and telecoms, *see* Richard Whish and David Bailey, *Competition Law* (10th ed., Oxford University Press 2021), at 734.

decision-making autonomy of the dominant company.[62] In this respect, the Court of Justice explicitly rejected LG's argument implying the indispensability condition should be part of the legal test to identify an abuse under Article 102 TFEU, since different legal criteria for undertakings in regulated sectors would impair legal certainty.[63] This is probably one of the most significant aspects of the ruling on appeal, that came to confirm the General Court's position which had not been received as completely uncontroversial.[64]

In the case of mandated access, the competition authority investigating an incumbent's conduct would need to identify whether a refusal to supply could result in anti-competitive foreclosure, without applying the stringent rules of the Oscar Bronner test, as the public authority imposing the access obligation would have already undertaken the necessary balancing of incentives in the incumbent's conduct 'between, on the one hand, the requirements of undistorted competition and, on the other hand, the freedom of contract and the right to property of the dominant undertaking'.[65]

In the most straightforward way, the General Court had rejected the applicability of the input indispensability as:

> such a requirement to protect the incentive of the undertaking in a dominant position to invest in the creation of essential facilities is not present where the applicable regulatory framework already imposes a duty to supply on the undertaking in a dominant position or where the dominant position which the undertaking has acquired on the market derives from a former State monopoly.[66]

In this respect, the Court of Justice confirmed that the General Court had rightfully upheld the Commission's finding that the removal of the track is to be identified as an *independent form of abuse* that had to be assessed under the general framework for abuse instead of the narrower essential facilities doctrine.[67]

At this point, reference to the Opinion of Advocate General Medina in the *LUKOIL Bulgaria and LUKOIL Neftohim Burgas* case is more than necessary for the diffusion of

62. Case C-42/21 P, *Lietuvos geležinkeliai v. Commission*, paras 86, 88.
63. *Ibid.*, para. 67, where LG as the appellant states: 'Next, ex post review under Article 102 TFEU and ex ante sector legislation serve different purposes. It would be contrary to the principle of legal certainty to make undertakings in regulated sectors subject to different legal criteria under Article 102 TFEU. [...]' and para. 88, where the Court states: 'While the existence of a regulatory obligation on the dominant undertaking to grant access to the infrastructure in question cannot relieve the Commission of the requirement to establish the existence of an "abuse" within the meaning of Article 102 TFEU, the fact remains that the imposition of such an obligation has the consequence that the dominant undertaking cannot actually refuse to give access to that infrastructure, without prejudice, as appropriate, to its decision-making autonomy in relation to the conditions for such access. [...]'.
64. Ibáñez Colomo, *GC Judgment in Case T–814/17, Lithuanian Railways: Part I: Object and Indispensability*, *supra* n. 53.
65. Guidance on the Commission's enforcement priorities, *supra* n. 4, para. 82; Richard Whish and David Bailey, *Competition Law* (10th ed., Oxford University Press 2021), at 733; European Commission, DG Competition discussion paper on the application of Article 82 of the Treaty to exclusionary abuses, December 2005, paras 234-236.
66. Case T-814/17, *Lietuvos geležinkeliai AB v. European Commission*, 18.11.2020, EU:T:2020:545, para. 91.
67. Case C-42/21 P, *Lietuvos geležinkeliai v. Commission*, paras 91-92.

any misunderstanding regarding facilities deriving from former State monopolies.[68] Among the other observations, the Advocate General pointed out that the *Bronner* legal test is not to be automatically cast aside when the infrastructure had previously been State-owned or had historically been State-built. Indeed, as the Advocate General stressed: 'Even where the essential facility has State-monopoly origins, the dominant undertaking may have made significant subsequent investments (maintenance, modernisation, capacity expansion, introduction of new products or services, and so forth) and/or have paid a fair price in the context of the privatisation.'[69] In this respect, the dominant undertaking acts as a reasonable market participant during the privatization or concession process and in the period thereafter and therefore, deserves the protection of its property rights and the freedom to contract. Consequently, the applicability of the *Bronner* test in such cases should not be mechanically defied.

3.3 The *Google Shopping* Saga: A Novel and Distinct Self-Preferencing Abuse?

The question on the scope of applicability of the *Oscar Bronner* test has been a central part of the realm of digital economy and specifically, in the long-lasting *Google Shopping* case, the latest chapter of which has come out with the ruling on appeal.[70] In its highly awaited judgment, the Court of Justice upheld the General Court's findings that the contested practices 'can be distinguished in their constituent elements from the refusal of access at issue in the case that gave rise to that judgment in Bronner and constitute an independent form of leveraging abuse'.[71]

The case pertained to the combination of two practices at issue: *first*, the more favourable positioning and display of Google's own specialized results in its general results pages than those of the results of competing comparison shopping services and, *second*, the simultaneous demotion, by adjustment algorithms, of results from competing comparison shopping services that amounted to the so-called self-preferencing practice.[72]

The General Court had initially held that the practice at stake should not amount to a refusal to supply requiring to comply with the essential facilities doctrine. Interestingly, the General Court had noticed that 'all or, at the very least, most practices capable of restricting or eliminating competition ("exclusionary practices") are liable to constitute implicit refusals to supply, since they tend to make access to a market more difficult'.[73] However, it took the position that were the *Oscar Bronner* criteria applicable

68. Opinion of Advocate General Medina in Case C-245/24, *LUKOIL Bulgaria EOOD, LUKOIL Neftohim Burgas AD v. Komisia za zashtita na konkurentsiata*, 10.7.2025, EU:C:2025:570, paras 47-61.
69. *Ibid.*, paras 71-72.
70. Case C-48/22 P, *Google and Alphabet v. Commission (Google Shopping)*, 10.9.2024, EU:C:2024:726.
71. *Ibid.*, paras 82 and 109.
72. *Ibid.*, para. 107.
73. Case T-612/17, *Google and Alphabet v. Commission (Google Shopping)*, 11.11.2021, EU:T:2021:763, para. 234 with reference to Advocate General Saugmandsgaard Øe in his Opinion in

at hand, then the letter and spirit of Article 102 TFEU would be discarded, as the scope of the latter article surpasses the restrictive interpretation of the 'indispensability' criterion of the *Oscar Bronner* test, as established by the case law.[74] It should not be discarded however, that the General Court had acknowledged that 'Google's general results page has characteristics akin to those of an essential facility [...], inasmuch as there is currently no actual or potential substitute available that would enable it to be replaced in an economically viable manner on the market [...].'[75] In this sense, the Court of Justice clarified on appeal that the case was indeed not unrelated to the issue of access, but the practice truly pertained to 'access to Google's general results pages under non-discriminatory conditions'.[76]

Therefore, it concluded that the practices fell short of satisfying the *Oscar Bronner* criteria, as they did not concern refusal of access of competing comparison shopping services (CSS) to boxes, but were differentiated in that they consisted in Google refusing *equal* access, i.e., access under non-discriminatory conditions, to its general results page, thereby putting at a disadvantage comparison shopping services competing with it.[77]

The practice had been labelled by the Commission as *self-preferencing*[78] and constituted an independent form of abuse that fell outside competition on the merits. The key observations of the General Court, as upheld by the Court of Justice that led to the infringement being considered 'independent' lied in *first*, the fact that the contested conduct did not follow an outright request and subsequent refusal and *second*, that the contested practice was not a 'passive' refusal either, but an 'active' preferential treatment.[79] This in turn triggered the debate as to its positioning next to traditional refusal to deal and constructive refusal to supply, the applicable legal test to it and the theory of harm.[80] The practice was established on a leveraging theory of harm,

Cases C-152/19 P and C-165/19 P, *Deutsche Telekom v. Commission* and *Slovak Telekom v. Commission*, 9.9.2020, EU:C:2020:678, paras 85-89.

74. Case T-612/17, *Google and Alphabet v. Commission (Google Shopping)*, para. 234.
75. *Ibid.*, para. 224 with Case T-201/04, *Microsoft v. Commission*, paras 208, 388, 390, 421 and 436.
76. Case C-48/22 P, *Google and Alphabet v. Commission (Google Shopping)*, para. 103.
77. *Ibid.*, para. 107. At this point, it is worth coming back to the Court's findings in Slovak Telekom, where it was underlined that: 'where a dominant undertaking gives access to its infrastructure but makes that access, provision of services or sale of products subject to unfair conditions, the conditions laid down by the Court of Justice in paragraph 41 of the judgment in Bronner do not apply. It is true that where access to such an infrastructure – or service or input – is indispensable in order to allow competitors of the dominant undertaking to operate profitably in a downstream market, this increases the likelihood that unfair practices on that market will have at least potentially anticompetitive effects and will constitute abuse within the meaning of Article 102 TFEU (see, to that effect, judgment of 14 October 2010, Deutsche Telekom v Commission, C-280/08 P, EU:C:2010:603, paragraph 234, and judgment in TeliaSonera, paragraphs 70 and 71). Nevertheless, as regards practices other than a refusal of access, the absence of such an indispensability is not in itself decisive for the purposes of the examination of potentially abusive practices on the part of a dominant undertaking (see, to that effect, the judgment in TeliaSonera, paragraph 72).'
78. Commission Decision in Case AT.39740, *Google Search (Shopping)* [2018] OJ C 9/11, para. 651.
79. *See also* for the second point Graef, *supra* n. 51, at p. 169.
80. Pablo Ibáñez Colomo, *Self-Preferencing: Yet Another Epithet in Need of Limiting Principles*, 43 World Competition 417 (2020) https://doi.org/10.54648/woco2020022, last accessed on 23 July 2025.

according to which the dominant undertaking at hand employed the contested practice in order to extend its position to a neighbouring but separate market by distorting competition.

The General Court and on appeal, the Court of Justice took stock of Google's business model in order to conclude that the contested practices were a form of unequal treatment under Article 102 TFEU, where Oscar Bronner does not apply.

Google's business model was based on offering a 'fundamentally open infrastructure designed to attract maximum number of internet users and to generate maximum volume of data traffic'.[81] In this respect, the case at hand was different from the famous *Microsoft* case of the General Court that was mentioned above, where the *Bronner* criteria were met, as in *Microsoft*, the contested infrastructure was not intended to be accessible to competing software developers back then. On the contrary, Google's business model signifies that Google has always granted competing CSS access to its general search result page to maximize positive network effects.

In addition, the Court of Justice had to resolve the notion of infrastructure in the case at hand, by discarding Google's argument that boxes[82] constitute a separate facility from Google's general results pages and to which access is denied for competing comparison shopping services.[83]

In this sense, the Court of Justice aligned with what had been first invoked in the Commission's decision against Google when the former concluded that the *Bronner* criteria are irrelevant in a situation where 'bringing to an end the infringement does not involve imposing a duty to transfer an asset or enter into agreements with persons with whom it has not chosen to contract'.[84]

This finding can also be supported by the nature of remedies imposed on Google following the Commission's decision and showcasing that the contested practices fall short of a refusal to supply, as the stakes consisted in Google ensuring that it would not treat competing comparison shopping services *less favourably* than its own comparison shopping service within its general results pages, but instead, it would be subject to the same processes and methods for positioning and display as third parties.[85] According to the Court, *any measure of implementation*[86] that could ensure the elimination of less favourable treatment could be effective in this respect.

Irrespective of the nature of the remedy finally imposed on Google, the case provoked the debate around the position that the imposition of a proactive remedy is

81. Opinion of Advocate General Kokott in Case C-48/22 P, *Google and Alphabet v. Commission (Google Shopping)*, 11.1.2024, EU:C:2024:14, para. 92.
82. Reference is made to 'Product OneBox', subsequently renamed 'Product Universal', by adding images.
83. Case C-48/22 P, *Google and Alphabet v. Commission (Google Shopping)*, paras 98, 105 and 107.
84. Commission Decision in Case AT.39740, *Google Search (Shopping)* [2018] OJ C 9/11, para. 651.
85. Case C-48/22 P, *Google and Alphabet v. Commission (Google Shopping)*, para. 98. *See also* Pablo Ibáñez Colomo, *Case C 48/22 P, Google Shopping: Great Cases Make … for Carefully Crafted Judgments*, Chillin' Competition, dated (16 September 2024), https://chillingcompetition.com/2024/09/16/case-c%E2%80%9148-22-p-google-shopping-great-cases-make-for-carefully-crafted-judgments/, last accessed on 23 July 2025.
86. Such measure would be less detrimental to Google's freedom of contract, given that Google already operated on an 'open' platform business model. *See* relevantly Case C-48/22 P, *Google and Alphabet v. Commission (Google Shopping)*, para. 112.

intrinsically related to a finding of indispensability, as was discussed in the case of *Slovak Telekom*. In this respect, Inge Graef has advanced that *Google Shopping* illustrated the complexities in designing an effective remedy that is hard to already conceive at the stage of the adoption of a competition decision (when legal benchmarks are tested and tests are employed) but becomes clearer at the actual stage of the implementation of the decision. In other words, arguing that where proactive remedies (namely structural remedies as well as behavioural remedies requiring a positive obligation and constant monitoring such as an access obligation) are implemented as best-suited solutions against an infringement should not lead – without much uncertainty – to the position that indispensability of input is a prerequisite part of the legal test against which the infringement was previously found by the competent authority.[87] As the General Court found in this regard, there 'can be no automatic link between the criteria for the legal classification of the abuse and the corrective measures enabling it to be remedied' and thus the applicability of the *Bronner* criteria should not depend on the measures ordered by the Commission to terminate an infringement.[88]

The contribution of the Google Shopping case has also been significant – *inter alia* – in the following way: the European Courts attempted to crystallize the dividing line between refusal to supply and other forms of leveraging abuses, including self-preferencing, under Article 102 TFEU, by establishing a form-based distinction between 'closed' and 'open' products on the basis of Google's business model.[89] In the case of 'closed' products, the dominant firm retains exclusive use of the product for the access of which there needs to be an express request followed by an outright refusal. On the contrary, in the case of 'open' products, i.e., the dominant firm is operating on an (inherently) open model providing its products or services to third parties as well as its own downstream service.[90] In the latter scenario, the condemned practice is not deriving from a refusal to supply but from 'an extrinsic practice' that 'deviate[s], by [its] very nature from competition on the merits' and could ultimately equate with an implicit refusal of access but remain an independent infringement nonetheless.[91] In the case of a self-preferencing abuse, the rationale is that the contested platform can never have expected an exclusive right of exploitation given its open nature. Hence, contrary to a forced obligation to provide access, a duty of equal access is less of a disincentive to invest.[92]

87. *See* relevantly Graef, *supra* n. 51, 162-181, 163, where it is stated that 'the distinction between proactive and reactive remedies is not always clear-cut so that it may not be capable of serving as a useful mechanism to determine whether the indispensability requirement needs to be applied'.
88. Case T-612/17, *Google and Alphabet v. Commission (Google Shopping)*, para. and Case C–48/22 P, *Google and Alphabet v. Commission (Google Shopping)*, para. 116.
89. Christian Ahlborn, Gerwin Van Gerven and William Leslie, *Bronner Revisited: Google Shopping and the Resurrection of Discrimination Under Article 102 TFEU*, 13(2), Journal of European Competition Law & Practice (11 March 2022) https://doi.org/10.1093/jeclap/lpac012, last accessed on 23 July 2025.
90. *Ibid.*
91. Case C–48/22 P, *Google and Alphabet v. Commission (Google Shopping)*, para. 82.
92. Ahlborn, Van Gerven and Leslie, *supra* n. 89.

Such distinction signifies a different requisite threshold of intervention for competition authorities, as it seems to point that in an 'open' business model, no refusal may be conceived to be compatible with the inherently open nature of a platform and therefore the *Bronner* case law remains inactive. This subsequently means that the competition authority benefits from a lower threshold of intervention, as it is discharged from the (burdensome) duty to prove that such platform is 'indispensable' for a competitor to be able to (profitably) operate in the downstream market. The authority's intervention only needs to focus on proving the anticompetitive effects of the practice to the detriment of consumers.

As will be discussed below, examining the openness of a platform through such binary approach may entail risks as to the application of the most suitable legal test and the bar of intervention by the competent authorities.

3.4 *Google Android Auto:* Towards a More Dynamic 'Essential Facilities' Doctrine?

The question of whether the *Oscar Bronner* test remains the appropriate benchmark in the context of the digital economy has been once again raised in the framework of a preliminary procedure initiated by the Italian Council of State (Consiglio di Stato) in the *Google Android Auto* case,[93] proving thus that the *Oscar Bronner* is not by default outdated. Similarly to the *Google Shopping* case, the *Google Android Auto* case has also triggered the debate as to the limits of the test depending on the nature of the facility contested, and more specifically the openness or not of the platform under scrutiny. It is worth noting that the Italian Court explicitly asked for guidance on the meaning of 'indispensability' and whether the indispensability criterion could also signify that 'access [is] indispensable for a more convenient use of the product or service offered by the undertaking requesting access'. Although the Court of Justice in its ruling decided to reformulate this question[94] and instead address the applicability of the Bronner doctrine in the particular case, it has indeed provided a new perspective on the future of the *Bronner* test in the context of digital platforms. The *Google Android Auto* case marks a valuable contribution to refining the relevance of the *Oscar Bronner* case law in the digital economy, although both the Court's and the Advocate General's reasoning regarding the nature of the contested facility and the platform's balancing of interests as well as the objective justification under Article 102 TFEU call for careful reading.

The section will proceed to a comparative analysis of the Opinion of the case that raised heated discussions with selected findings of the Court's ruling, which has largely confirmed the Opinion but further clarified some of the controversial points. The first

93. Case C-233/23, *Alphabet Inc., Google LLC, Google Italy Srl v. Autorità Garante della Concorrenza e del Mercato, joined parties: Enel X Italia Srl, Enel X Way Srl* ('*Alphabet and Others*'), 25.2.2025, EU:C:2025:110.

94. In doing so, the Court stated that the referring Court is uncertain whether 'there is no justification for disregarding or, at the very least, interpreting in a flexible manner the conditions set out, inter alia, in the judgment of 26 November 1998, Bronner'; C-233/23, *Alphabet and Others*, paras 33 and 35.

aspect lies in the categorization of the case as refusal in light of the *Oscar Bronner* doctrine, while the second pertains to crystallizing what objective justification for such refusal should mean.

In her not uncontroversially received Opinion in the case,[95] Advocate General Medina opined that Google's refusal to provide third parties with access to the Android Auto platform may constitute a separate abuse of dominance, striking down thus the applicability of the *Oscar Bronner* test. Before the request for a preliminary ruling from the Consiglio di Stato, Google had contested in an appeal before the Regional Administrative Court of Lazio its fine by the Italian Competition Authority (AGCM) under Article 102 TFEU for abusing its dominant position. According to the AGCM, Google's abuse consisted in its refusal to grant ENEL, an electric car charging services provider, access to its Android Auto product on the basis that the technical template required for enabling competing developers to create their own applications had not been yet developed by Google.[96] The AGCM had found that Google's Android Auto was the indispensable input for enabling app developers aimed at drivers to create their own products and therefore access the market.

In the context of examining the applicability of the *Oscar Bronner* and after having identified Android Auto's function as that of a platform.

AG Medina underlines that:

> Android Auto is deliberately open and has been conceived to be shared freely and to remain at the disposal of third parties, in line with Google's purpose to attract as many 'in-car apps' as possible so that car drivers benefit from as much assistance as possible while focusing on their driving.[97]

The observation seems to reiterate the Court of Justice's position in the *Google Shopping* case regarding the positive network effects triggered by Google's inherently open nature of its platform that were discussed above. On account of this observation, it could be argued that the open nature of the platform constitutes the pre-requisite for its viability and subsequently, that a refusal to grant access cannot have the purpose of reserving the facility (i.e., the Android Auto platform) for the dominant undertaking (i.e., Google).[98]

AG Medina explicitly reiterates that:

> the *Bronner* conditions apply only to cases where the infrastructure at issue has been developed for the needs of the dominant undertaking's own business and where that infrastructure is dedicated for its own use, to the exclusion of any other competitor in consistency with the Court's case law in *Slovak Telekom* and *Baltic Rail*.

95. Opinion of Advocate General Medina in Case C-233/23, *Alphabet Inc., Google LLC, Google Italy Srl v. Autorità Garante della Concorrenza e del Mercato, joined parties: Enel X Italia Srl, Enel X Way Srl* (*'Alphabet and Others'*), 5.9.2024, EU:C:2024:694.
96. After the matter came before the AGCM but before that authority adopted its decision, Google had nonetheless published a template for the design of experimental versions of electric vehicle charging apps interoperable with Android Auto; *see* Case C-233/23, *Alphabet and Others*, paras 12 and 62.
97. Opinion of Advocate General Medina in Case C-233/23, *Alphabet and Others*, paras 36 and 38.
98. *See also* Mandrescu, *supra* n. 59.

The Opinion seems, at first glance, to draw a clear-cut dichotomy between open and closed products (here platforms) in what concerns the applicability of the *Bronner* test. Nonetheless, an important detail, which is also crucial in the case at hand, should be placed in a (more) prominent position: there are varying degrees of platform openness.

AG Medina seems to acknowledge this nuanced interpretation, as:

> it could be argued that the absence of a specific template ensuring the interoperability of Android Auto with electric car charging apps, as is the case here, demonstrates Google's wish to reserve those services for itself.[99]

Still, the Advocate General concludes in this regard, that in the absence of a template for competitors, refusal could only be objectively justified if the development of such template is technically impossible or may adversely affect the platform's performance or contradict the platform's economic model or purpose.[100] In this point and in what concerns Android Auto, the scope of the target of third parties pursuant to Google's business model was that of car-related services, meaning that the platform was not to be regarded as overall open, but only to car-related apps.[101]

Consequently, a careful reading of the Opinion in *Auto Android* could unravel that the *Oscar Bronner* legal test could still be considered relevant to digital platforms of an open nature on account of their business model and functional purpose.

At the same time, the legal test to be applied should not be based on clear-cut dichotomies but should accommodate a more dynamic approach. A remedy that would impose on an – otherwise open – platform to actively develop a non-existing template, invest in technical and financial resources and in time in order to facilitate access to its competitors and improve interoperability with its competitors' products could imply an intervention in the platform's operating module and further an intervention in its contractual liberty.[102] Consequently, although the Opinion seems to favour the clear-cut approach to open platforms (and the resulting obligations for access to it), it still nuances this observation, as it underpins that what must be guaranteed above all is that:

> the application of Article 102 TFEU and the interoperability obligations that stem from it do not cause any disincentive in respect of the dominant undertaking as the initial developer and owner of the platform concerned.[103]

The Court of Justice has largely confirmed the findings of the Opinion in this respect. Most importantly, the answer of the Court to the question on the applicability

99. Opinion of Advocate General Medina in Case C-233/23, *Alphabet and Others*, para. 44.
100. *Ibid.*, para. 65. In this respect, it should be noted that the Opinion does not offer any further input of what an economic model or purpose may be.
101. Mandrescu, *supra* n. 59.
102. Opinion of Advocate General Medina in Case C-233/23, *Alphabet and Others*, para. 31; *See* relevantly, William Leslie, Eoin O' Reilly and Marilena Nteve, *Roadblocks: When Should the Essential Facilities Doctrine Apply in EU Competition Law?* (13 September 2024), https://techinsights.linklaters.com/post/102jj32/roadblocks-when-should-the-essential-facilities-doctrine-apply-in-eu-competitio, last accessed on 23 July 2025.
103. Opinion of Advocate General Medina in Case C-233/23, *Alphabet and Others*, para. 71.

of the *Bronner* case law implies that the boundaries of the traditional refusal to supply have now been stretched to accommodate refusals following outright requests to grant access to non-indispensable facilities. Although the Court has pondered the importance of contractual liberty of a dominant undertaking and the long-term chilling effects on innovation due to disincentives to invest,[104] it has concluded that on account of a dominant firm's open infrastructure:

> the fact of requiring the undertaking in a dominant position to provide access to that infrastructure to a third-party undertaking does not fundamentally alter the economic model which applied to the development of that infrastructure.[105]

The additional value in what concerns the future of *Oscar Bronner* more broadly, lies in that both the ruling and the Opinion attempt to outline a concrete framework of what constitutes a legitimate objective justification in refusal to grant access.[106] The framework that AG Medina proposed had been received not without criticism, as it could pose an overly high standard to the dominant undertaking to prove that its refusal to grant access on the basis of technical and financial hurdles derives from 'convincing evidence for calculating its costs'. Although the nature of calculations and evidence to be brought forward was not clarified, the Opinion opened up a new chapter in the interpretation and application in practice of the *Oscar Bronner* criteria. In this respect, the ruling in the case provided useful clarifications and better circumscribed the limits of 'objective justification' under Article 102 TFEU. The Court endorsed Google's argument and recognized concerns on the security or integrity of a platform as an objective justification for refusing any modification in the firm's business model or in ensuring interoperability with an app through the (proactive) design of a technical feature *ab initio*.[107] Nonetheless, it confirmed one of the most debated points of the Opinion that could be seen as not in absolute sync with its case law: unless security concerns are displayed and proven by the dominant firm, the latter is required to take proactive measures and enable interoperability with a third party requesting access, without prejudice to a disproportionate investment in time and resources from the dominant firm's part.[108] Most importantly, in the framework of these measures, the Court has identified that Article 102 TFEU does not preclude a contractual agreement between the dominant undertaking and the requesting firm that would aim to finance the development of the new feature that would ensure interoperability. However, the consistent position of the European Courts should not be overlooked: every obligation which Article 102 TFEU imposes on that undertaking to grant access or to supply to its competitors comes with an interference with its right to choose its trading partners and dispose of its property and must therefore be carefully weighed up and justified by the authorities mandating access. A different approach would imply a duty for the

104. C-233/23, *Alphabet and Others,* paras 41, 42.
105. *Ibid.*, paras 46, 52.
106. Opinion of Advocate General Medina in Case C-233/23, *Alphabet and Others,* para. 75.
107. C-233/23, *Alphabet and Others,* paras 73-74.
108. *Ibid.*, paras 75-81.

dominant undertaking to 'enter into agreements with persons with whom it has not chosen to contract'.[109]

4 THE DRAFT GUIDELINES ON ARTICLE 102 TFEU: BRINGING CLARITY OR BLURRING THE LINES?

The aspiration of the Commission to introduce Guidelines on exclusionary abuses had triggered vivid discussions on how this new tool could best add value to the state of the art of the Union Courts' case law and the Commission's decisional practice for Article 102 TFEU. On the one hand, it was acknowledged that the new Guidelines should be the soft tool that would crystallize the Commission's practice in line with the Union Courts' rulings in the multiple cases that followed the issuance of the Guidance Paper on Article 102 TFEU. On the other hand, it was equally supported that, for this tool to have added value, it would not be sufficient for the Commission to summarize the case law, as normally is the case when it issues Guidelines. Instead, the Commission would need to be future-proof on account of the accumulated experience of the flourishment of digital platforms and the conducts emerging therefrom. Therefore, the Commission would need to possibly flesh out new legal tests for assessing novel conducts of the past decade or even suggest a new methodology for assessing conducts that have not emerged yet but could be brought to the centre of attention of competition authorities in the future.[110] Most importantly, the Commission would need to justify its choices.

In this respect, although the release of the Draft Guidelines in the third quarter of 2024 conveys the Commission's plan for a more forward-looking approach to Article 102 TFEU that attempts to go beyond a mere summation of the case law and to extend the latter's current boundaries, this seems to have created paradoxically more uncertainty and unpredictability regarding the future of enforcement.[111] While the Commission introduces new forms of abuses on account of the Courts' rulings in recent years, such as that of *self-preferencing*, it moves away from the economic and effects-based approach adopted under the Guidance Paper on Enforcement Priorities and proceeds to a selective reading of the Courts' case law.[112]

Mario Draghi's report of September 2024 on the future of European competitiveness is highly critical of the Draft Guidelines underlining that 'excessive discretion on the finding of exclusionary abuses is left by the draft Guidelines on the enforcement of

---

109. *See* s. 3.3 and the discussion on *Google Shopping*.
110. Rupprecht Podszun, *Towards a Manageable Concept of Abuse of Dominance in the EU*, Foreword, No. 3 Concurrences (2023).
111. *See also* Luc Peeperkorn, *The Draft Article 102 Guidelines: A Somewhat Confused Attempt to Partly Roll Back the Effects-based Approach of the Union Courts*, Kluwer Competition Law Blog (4 September 2024), https://competitionlawblog.kluwercompetitionlaw.com/2024/09/04/the-draft-article-102-guidelines-a-somewhat-confused-attempt-to-partly-roll-back-the-effects-based-approach-of-the-union-courts/, last accessed on 23 July 2025.
112. Assimakis Komninos, *Op-Ed: The European Commission's Draft Guidelines on Exclusionary Abuses: A Very Selective Restatement of the Case Law*, EU Law Live (14 November 2024), https://eulawlive.com/competition-corner/op-ed-the-european-commissions-draft-guidelines-on-exclusionary-abuses-a-very-selective-restatement-of-the-case-law/, last accessed on 23 July 2025.

article 102 released in August 2024', whereas pointing out that the *speed* and *predictability* of decisions is what needs to be enhanced.[113] The most striking sign of formalism adopted in the Draft Guidelines is the introduction of presumptions put into force on account of the external and factual existence of the conduct under scrutiny that seek to tip the balance of the burden of proof away from the Commission, towards the allegedly dominant firm.[114] This categorization of practices and the application of different legal tests based on their formal characteristics could cause legal uncertainty, as it is not uncommon for practices to share common traits[115] or worse, that competition authorities frame similar practices in distinct ways to defuse strict legal tests. Additionally, the establishment of presumptions of exclusionary effects and therefore the shift in the allocation of the burden of proof towards the dominant companies is not to be met in the Union Courts' case law, especially when it comes to hard presumptions for finding infringements of Article 102 TFEU. On the contrary, what the Draft Guidelines have illustrated as presumptions of exclusionary effects are rules for the evidentiary standards that competition authorities need to meet to prove the likelihood of anticompetitive effects.[116]

In the context of this formalistic approach, they set out a two-stage test and distinguish between three categories of conducts. This two-stage test comprises first, whether the conduct under scrutiny departs from competition on the merits and second, whether the conduct is capable of having exclusionary effects.[117] The distinction of three categories is made on the basis of presumptions and comprises *first*, naked restrictions – equivalent to 'by object' abuses; *second*, conducts with a specific legal test and *third*, other conducts (without a specific test). The classification of the conducts discussed above ranging from a pure refusal to supply and margin squeeze to access restrictions and self-preferencing varies in the draft Guidelines and is not always without objection.[118]

The first category of 'naked restrictions' signifies conducts devoid of any economic rationale and departing from 'competition on the merits'. Therefore, they are presumed to lead to exclusionary effects by their very nature and it is highly unlikely that the dominant undertaking will prove that they are justified 'on the basis of an

113. The future of European competitiveness, Part B | In-depth analysis and recommendations (September 2024), https://commission.europa.eu/document/download/ec1409c1-d4b4-4882-8bdd-3519f86bbb92_en?filename=The%20future%20of%20European%20competitiveness_%20In-depth%20analysis%20and%20recommendations_0.pdf at p. 304 and footnote 9, last accessed on 23 July 2025.
114. Miroslava Marinova, *The European Commission's Draft Article 102 Guidelines under Fire: Examining the substance and the roots of the Criticism*, SSRN (15 January 2025), https://papers.ssrn.com/sol3/papers.cfm?abstract_id=5040143, last accessed on 23 July 2025; Komninos, *supra* n. 112.
115. Self-preferencing and tying is such an example.
116. Komninos, *supra* n. 112.
117. *Ibid.*, where it is supported that these two conditions should be considered one.
118. Pinar Akman, Chiara Fumagalli and Massimo Motta, *The European Commission's Draft Guidelines on Exclusionary Abuses: A Law and Economics Critique and Recommendations*, Journal of European Competition Law and Practice, SSRN (12 December 2024), https://papers.ssrn.com/sol3/papers.cfm?abstract_id=5027376, last accessed on 23 July 2025.

objective justification', save in exceptional circumstances.[119] The Commission subsumes the intentional dismantling of one's own infrastructure that is being used by a competitor under the category of 'naked restrictions' and explicitly cites the case of *Lithuanian Railways*.[120]

Refusal to supply and margin squeeze with negative spreads are identified in the Draft Guidelines as two of the five broad conducts for which the Commission fleshes out a specific legal test under the second category. In general, according to this category, if the examined conduct satisfies the prescribed test, then the conduct departs from competition on the merits and is presumed to have anticompetitive effects[121] according to paragraph 60(b) of the Draft Guidelines.[122] In what concerns the traditional refusal to supply, the Commission seems to go beyond the restrictive interpretation of what indispensable input is, by adopting a somewhat maximalist reading with no reference to case law.[123] According to it, a dominant undertaking may be forced to grant access to its input, when this is 'necessary for the requesting firm to remain viably on the market and exert an effective competitive constraint'.[124]

The third category dedicated to conducts without specific legal test comprises among others the novel category of *self-preferencing* and a distinct category of *access restrictions*. On the one hand, for the former category, the Draft Guidelines acknowledge that:

> it can be widespread in certain sectors of the economy and the question whether a given self-preferencing conduct contravenes Article 102 TFEU depends on an analysis of all relevant circumstances.

This last point unavoidably raises the question of determining the relevant factors so that the Guidelines truly serve the purpose for which they are drafted, namely to provide a framework to market actors particularly businesses and assist them in self-assessing their conduct. On the other hand, access restrictions, in the words of the Commission, refer to 'the imposition by a dominant undertaking of restrictions on access to an input that are different from a refusal to supply' when this input is 'not exclusively or mainly for its own use'.[125]

Regarding the new category of *self-preferencing*, the criticism of their illustration in the Draft Guidelines has focused mainly on a few points that showcase the Commission's selective application of the *Google Shopping* case law. The Draft Guidelines list three non-cumulative circumstances specific to self-preferencing abuses that are not in complete sync with the *Google Shopping*-based test.

---

119. Draft version of Communication from the Commission Guidelines on the application of Article 102 of the Treaty on the Functioning of the European Union to abusive exclusionary conduct by dominant undertakings ('Draft Guidelines') (2024), para. 60(c) 'Naked restrictions'.
120. *Ibid.*, and footnote 142; *see* relevantly Case C-42/21 P, *Lietuvos geležinkeliai v. Commission*, paras 83-84 and 89-91.
121. Draft Guidelines, paras 47 and 53.
122. *Ibid.*, para. 60(b) on 'Conduct that is presumed to lead to exclusionary effects'. A refusal to deal escapes this presumption however, according to para. 60(b) of the Draft Guidelines.
123. Komninos, *supra* n. 112.
124. Draft Guidelines, para. 101(iii).
125. *Ibid.*, para. 163 and footnote 340.

First, the preferential treatment takes place in a leveraging market that constitutes 'an important source of business' for competitors in the leveraged market and that they cannot effectively replace through other means. The Guidelines thus set a lower standard that facilitates the Commission's intervention, as focus should be on the traffic generated by Google's general search engine for comparison shopping services, meaning the traffic that is diverted because of the preferential treatment and not all the traffic on the market.[126] *Second*, the core issue of discrimination in preferential treatment is absent from the circumstances prescribing the practice of self-preferencing. The Draft Guidelines have failed to refer to the principle of discrimination which is not only embedded in Article 102(2)(c) TFEU but also confirmed by the Courts' case law. The Guidelines could have illustrated a discrimination requirement for the legal test of self-preferencing and further outline that in cases where 'the dominant undertaking may be discriminating between competitors and its own downstream operations under Article 102(c) TFEU' the application of the indispensability condition is ruled out.[127]

Third, the fact that preferential treatment is likely to influence the behaviour of users, irrespective of the intrinsic qualities of the leveraged product is interpreted in the Draft Guidelines as a non-cumulative and thus optional circumstance contrary to the *Google Shopping* case law.

To the second seemingly broad category of *access restrictions*, an effects-based approach is employed, while the *Bronner* case law and the indispensability condition are inapplicable. The Commission's illustration of practices subsumed under the 'access restrictions' category is not entirely consistent with the Union Courts' case law and will definitely continue to spark debates regarding recent or anticipated rulings, including the *Android Auto* case discussed above. On the one hand, faithful to the case law of *Slovak Telekom*, the Commission identifies a failure to comply with a regulatory obligation to grant access as an access restriction. On the other hand, however, it also lists disruption of supply along with a change in the dominant entity's business model as other examples of access restrictions.

The listings of these categories thereunder could be deemed as problematic: for disruption of supply, according to *Commercial Solvents*,[128] a stricter test than the one proposed in the Draft Guidelines is warranted, according to which the condition of elimination of all competition must still be met, even if indispensability needs not be proved. Additionally, the Commission's position that dominant companies may not cease supplying competitors in the downstream market or subsequently cease providing or restricting access to input that has been developed initially for the purpose of being shared widely is rather expansive and is not to be read without scepticism either. Such a negative duty on dominant companies to abstain from changing their business

126. Case C-48/22 P, *Google and Alphabet v. Commission (Google Shopping)*, para. 141.
127. Case T-612/17, *Google Shopping*, 10.11.2021, EU:T:2021:763, para. 239 citing also Advocate General Jacobs in his Opinion in Case C-7/97, *Bronner*, para. 54; Opinion of Advocate General Mazák in Case C-52/09, *TeliaSonera Sverige*, 17.2.2011, EU:C:2010:483, para. 32; Case T-228/97, *Irish Sugar v. Commission*, 7.10.1999, EU:T:1999:246, paras 166-167.
128. Joined cases 6 and 7-73, *Istituto Chemioterapico Italiano S.p.A. and Commercial Solvents Corporation v. Commission of the European Communities*, 6.3.1974, EU:C:1974:18.

model seems to overly impinge on their contractual liberty and right to property, although the Guidelines state in advance that the need to protect the undertaking's freedom of contract and incentives to invest does not apply here to the same extent as in a refusal to supply setting. This position could become even more questioned when examined opposite the recent ruling in the *Google Android Auto* case, where the Court adjudicated that Article 102 TFEU does not preclude a scenario where a dominant undertaking might be required to take proactive measures and facilitate access for a competitor by modifying its products or developing new ones.

Interestingly, delays in starting access negotiations and the signing of contracts to give access to third parties are also listed under such access restrictions. The practice outlined refers to existing supply of an input and not to input that does not yet exist.

As a last point on this category, it looks as if there is still room to crystallize the boundaries between *self-preferencing* and the category of *access restrictions*, as the Draft Guidelines do not provide sufficient justifications as to why the benchmark developed in the *Google Shopping* case should not be used to assess self-preferencing involving access restrictions, other than that remark that if self-preferencing is combined with other practices, the overall effects of the practices should be taken into account.[129] This could cause confusion as to which legal test is applicable when it comes to assessing a self-preferencing conduct that involves access restrictions or margin squeezes, e.g., the unfair positioning of products.[130]

The expansive approach to access restrictions set out in the Draft Guidelines starts from the point that the need to protect the undertaking's contractual freedom and incentives to invest does not apply to the same extent as in a refusal to supply setting. However, unless a careful balancing of interests is completed by the competent authority that investigates a potential infringement, it could raise significant implications for these freedoms that does not eventually preserve the objectives of Article 102 TFEU and could have adverse effects on competition in the long term.

The emergence of different layers of presumptions and tests calls for a clarification of their relationship on the part of the Commission.[131] As Akman, Fumagalli and Motta underline, the Guidelines should clarify the relationship between the operation of presumptions regarding the 'capability to produce exclusionary effects' when it comes to conducts with specific legal tests. In addition, the 'relevant circumstances' that determine the finding of specific abuses should be determined so that the competent authorities can verify the different conditions that need to be met for the conduct to be capable of producing anticompetitive effects and therefore to fit the theory of harm formulated. At least, in what concerns cases of non-outright refusals, including margin squeeze, access restrictions and self-preferencing, consistent treatment should be warranted. Overall, it is crucial that the different choices of the

129. Draft Guidelines, para. 162.
130. *See* to this effect, William Turtle, James Wells and Alice Steele, *Reflections on the Draft Article 102 Guidelines: Bringing Clarity or Creating Room to Manoeuvre?* (7 October 2024), https://www.slaughterandmay.com/insights/new-insights/reflections-on-the-draft-article-102-guidelines-bringing-clarity-or-creating-room-to-manoeuvre/, last accessed on 23 July 2025.
131. Akman, Fumagalli and Motta, *The European Commission's Draft Guidelines on Exclusionary Abuses: A Law and Economics Critique and Recommendations*, *supra* n. 118.

Commission are justified, so that conducts producing similar effects on the market are not treated differently.

5 CONCLUSIONS

The present contribution has intended to not only outline the evolution of the essential facilities doctrine as the applicable benchmark for refusal to supply abuses under Article 102 TFEU since its emergence in the *Magill* case and subsequent entrenchment in the *Oscar Bronner* case law but also discuss its relevance in today's novel practices in the digital economy. While the test initially set a high threshold for its conditions to be met – and particularly for that of the indispensability of input – rendering the *Bronner* case law applicable in exceptional circumstances, today there seems to emerge a (policy) need for a more nuanced interpretation.

The interpretation of the *Bronner* criteria has been contingent on the factual circumstances of the cases against which the test has been examined. In some cases, such as *Lithuanian Railways*, the non-applicability of the test derived naturally from the fact that a refusal to supply could not be conceived on account of the regulatory framework in which the contested practices occurred and which left no discretion to the firm, but to grant access in the first place. In this respect, the *external* boundaries of *Bronner* have been clear.

In what concerns the *internal* scope of the Bronner case law, the indispensability condition should not be construed in an overly narrow way that renders the 'essential facilities' doctrine inactive in practice. However, dispensing with indispensability would again stretch the boundaries of the test disproportionately, possibly leading to an excessive activity on the part of competition authorities and to false positives (Error I).

The most recent cases have brought forward some interesting points in the identification of the conduct and the reformulation of the *Oscar Bronner* test. The Court of Justice's preliminary ruling in the Italian *Google Android Auto* case has shown that an outright refusal to supply does not automatically render the *Bronner* legal test applicable, in the sense that refusal may be found without the need to meet the high threshold that the input to which access is requested is indispensable. This new development could find reason in the position that outright refusals to deal should not warrant a more demanding test than constructive or implicit refusals to deal.[132] This is in sync with the Union Courts' position that the seriousness of a refusal to supply does not depend on its external form. Further, in this respect, the external and formal characteristics of a conduct should not automatically lead to the application of a specific legal test. Such approach entails an important risk: competition authorities

132. Graef, *supra* n. 51, where the author mentions that this argument was brought by Slovak Telekom in the appeal before the General Court, in Case T-851/14, *Slovak Telekom*,13.12.2018, EU:T:2018:929, para. 130: 'In those circumstances, it is easier to prove a constructive refusal to supply access than an outright refusal, with the result that the more serious type of abuse would be treated less severely than the less serious abuse.'

could frame the targeted conducts in a way that would discharge them from the requirement to prove that a narrow legal test is satisfied.

The *Google Android Auto* case in addition to the *Google Shopping* case has also intensified the debate around the strict binary approach to 'closed' platforms where the *Bronner* case law still applies and 'open' platforms.

From an economics perspective, a solution would be to move from the 'essential facilities' doctrine to the 'crucial facilities' as in this way competition authorities would be discharged from trying to prove a condition that is to be narrowly interpreted and at the same time is not strictly necessary for a dominant undertaking to engage in vertical foreclosure having anticompetitive effects.[133] Such tailored approach has been advanced since the *Google Shopping* case, on account of the market conditions that comprised high market share, high barriers to entry in the form of network effects and the lack of multi-homing by consumers, rendering the dominant undertaking's product equal to this of an essential facility. In the presence of strong network effects, switching costs, and high barriers to entry, the lowering of the standards of intervention and the different weighting of the interests involved may be warranted.

In any event, tailoring the intervention standards for stimulating downstream competition should not lead to disincentivizing firms from investing in innovation at a long-term scale out of concern for their contractual freedom and right to property. This approach is one side of the coin; on the other side, the Digital Markets Act providing for data access and interoperability obligations might constitute a more appropriate framework for interoperability and platform access to digital ecosystems and (partly) answer the open questions.

133. Akman, Fumagalli and Motta, *The European Commission's Draft Guidelines on Exclusionary Abuses: A Law and Economics Critique and Recommendations*, *supra* n. 118.

CHAPTER 12

The Draft Article 102 Guidelines on Exclusionary Abuses: Background, Content and Outlook

Linsey McCallum & Massimiliano Max Kadar[*]

1 INTRODUCTION

On 27 March 2023, the European Commission (Commission) launched a new policy initiative in the area of abuse of dominance, namely the Guidelines on the application of Article 102 TFEU to abusive exclusionary conduct by dominant undertakings ('Guidelines on exclusionary abuses' or simply 'Guidelines').[1]

The launch of the initiative took place at the same time as the adoption of a Commission Communication (the 'Amending Communication') amending certain specific parts of the 2008 Guidance on enforcement priorities in applying Article 102 TFEU to exclusionary abuses (the 'Guidance Paper')[2] to bring them in line with the current Commission enforcement practice, pending the process leading to the adoption of the Guidelines on exclusionary abuses. The staff of the Commission's Directorate General for Competition (DG COMP) also published at the same time a policy brief

* All views expressed in this paper are strictly personal and should not be construed as reflecting the opinion of the European Commission. The authors would like to thank David Kovo and Pinelopi Stamou for their comments on a previous draft of the article, and Astrid Eriksson for the assistance with legal research. Any error or inconsistency remains the sole responsibility of the authors.

1. *See* European Commission press release of 27 March 2023, *Antitrust: Commission Announces Guidelines on Exclusionary Abuses and Amends Guidance on Enforcement Priorities*, IP/23/1911, https://ec.europa.eu/commission/presscorner/detail/en/ip_23_1911.
2. *See* Communication from the Commission – *Guidance on the Commission's enforcement priorities in applying Article 82 of the EC Treaty to abusive exclusionary conduct by dominant undertakings*, OJ (2009/C 45/02), 24.2.2009.

discussing the background of these initiatives and promoting the concept of a dynamic and workable effects-based approach to Article 102 TFEU (the '2023 Policy Brief').[3]

The Commission received forty-five submissions in response to the call for evidence announcing the launch of the Guidelines initiative. The initiative was broadly welcomed by stakeholders and many flagged the desirability of adopting Guidelines that would provide operational guidance on the application of Article 102 TFEU to exclusionary abuses, against the backdrop of a certain uncertainty on the current state of the law on abuse of dominance.

On 1 August 2024, the Commission published a draft of the Guidelines on exclusionary abuses for public consultation. The written phase of the public consultation closed on 31 October 2024, with the Commission receiving 117 submissions commenting on the text of the draft Guidelines. On 13 February 2025, the Commission hosted a stakeholder workshop that closed the public consultation.

This article will briefly outline the background to the Guidelines on exclusionary abuses, provide a concise description of the content of the draft Guidelines and set out some considerations on the next steps for the initiative, in light of a preliminary analysis of the outcome of the written public consultation and the case law developments that have intervened since the publication of the draft Guidelines.

2 BACKGROUND TO THE GUIDELINES INITIATIVE

The case law on Article 102 TFEU has evolved significantly in the past decades. At times, this evolution occurred incrementally. In other instances, the developments were more sudden, almost akin to a revolution.[4]

Naturally, the European Court of Justice (ECJ) and the General Court (together, the 'EU Courts') have been spearheading the advancements in case law, be it in the context of appeals of Commission decisions or preliminary ruling requests from the EU Member States' national courts. But the Commission also played its role in contributing to triggering, at least indirectly, the case law developments in the past fifteen years by means of advancements in its decisional practice and perhaps even more prominently, the adoption of the 2008 Guidance Paper.

The stated objective of the Guidance Paper was to mark a shift in the Commission's enforcement practice towards a 'more economic' or 'effects-based' approach to exclusionary abuses. These terms have been used to refer to an approach that focuses on the potential effects of a conduct, through the analysis of market dynamics, in line with mainstream economic thinking.[5] But the impact of the Guidance Paper went well

3. *See* Linsey McCallum et al., *A Dynamic and Workable Effects-Based Approach to Abuse of Dominance*, Publications Office of the European Union (2023), https://data.europa.eu/doi/10.2763/731952.
4. *See* Giorgio Monti and Ekaterina Rousseva, *The Special Responsibility of Dominant Undertakings*, in *Research Handbook on Abuse of Dominance and Monopolization* (Pinar Akman, Or Brook and Konstantinos Stylianou eds), Edward Elgar Publishing (2023) pp. 238-258.
5. *See* European Commissions press release of 3 December 2008, *Antitrust: Consumer Welfare at Heart of Commission Fight Against Abuses by Dominant Undertakings*, IP/08/1877, ec.europa.eu/commission/presscorner/detail/en/ip_08_1877.

beyond the Commission's enforcement priorities, given that the EU Courts took on board parts of the framework of assessment outlined in that document and incorporated them in their jurisprudence.[6] From this perspective, it can certainly be stated that the Guidance Paper was more than successful in its objective to 'contribute to the process of introducing a more economics based approach in European competition law enforcement'.[7]

At the same time, and while the historical importance of the Guidance Paper as a tool to steer enforcement towards a more economic approach cannot be overstated, one should also be mindful of the inherent limitations of that policy initiative and the context in which it was launched.

First, like the Discussion Paper before it,[8] the Guidance Paper outlined 'one possible methodology for the assessment of some of the most common abusive practices'.[9] In other words, the Guidance Paper reflected *one possible way* to incorporate an effects-based approach in the application of Article 102 TFEU but certainly not *the only way*. While in some areas the case law on Article 102 TFEU has converged with the Guidance Paper, in others it has not.[10] This is not because of alleged remnants of 'formalism' in the EU Courts' jurisprudence, but rather because there is a variety of possible ways to incorporate economic insight into the application of Article 102 TFEU.

Second, in order to formulate good law, considerations such as legal certainty and administrability also need to be taken into account and balanced against what may 'make sense' from a purely economic perspective. For example, while one may argue that there are no differences from an economic standpoint between 'outright' and 'constructive' refusal to supply, the EU Courts have made clear that the two conducts should be subject to different legal tests due to the fact that in the former scenario, the freedom of contract and the right to property of the dominant undertaking are relevant to setting a higher threshold of intervention.[11]

Third, the framework of analysis outlined in the Guidance Paper, while theoretically sound, was in some instances simply not sufficiently grounded on practical experience. For example, the price-cost 'as efficient competitor' test was presented in the Guidance Paper as the main tool to assess the exclusionary effects of conditional

6. *See*, for instance, Judgment of 27 March 2012, *Post Denmark*, Case C-209/10, EU:C:2012:172.
7. *See* the Frequently Asked Questions on *Antitrust: Guidance on Commission enforcement priorities in applying Article 82 to exclusionary conduct by dominant firms*, MEMO/08/761, ec.europa.eu /commission/presscorner/detail/en/memo_08_761.
8. *See* DG Competition discussion paper on the application of Art. 82 of the Treaty to exclusionary abuses, December 2005.
9. *See* European Commission press release of 19 December 2005, *Competition: Commission Publishes Discussion Paper on Abuse of Dominance*, IP/05/1626, ec.europa.eu/commission/press corner/detail/en/ip_05_1626.
10. *See* Communication from the Commission – *Amendments to the Communication from the Commission Guidance on the Commission's enforcement priorities in applying Article 82 of the EC Treaty to abusive exclusionary conduct by dominant undertakings*, C(2023) 1923 final, 27.3.2023.
11. Judgment of 25 March 2021, *Slovak Telekom, a.s. v. Commission*, Case C-165/19 P, EU:C: 2021:239, para. 46.

rebate schemes, despite the lack of decisional practice by the Commission in this area.[12]

Fourth, as in practically every other area of EU competition law, the Article 102 TFEU enforcement experience of DG COMP has evolved through the years. Since the adoption of the Guidance Paper, the Commission has adopted thirty-three decisions on exclusionary abuses. Some of these decisions have been upheld[13] before the EU Courts and some have been annulled,[14] with many valuable lessons coming from this growing body of case law. Even in the context of cases that have never been brought before the EU Courts, the Commission has accumulated significant experience in collecting and analysing evidence, shaping legal and economic theories of harm and assessing the likelihood that a convincing case can be built in the specific circumstances at hand. All in all, it is clear that the experience of DG COMP in running Article 102 TFEU investigations has significantly increased compared to the situation before the adoption of the Guidance Paper.

Fifth, the world of 2025 is quite different to the world of 2009. A growing body of evidence shows that the intensity of competition in the EU economy has decreased. Markets are more concentrated and profit mark-ups as an indicator of market power

12. At the time of adoption of the Guidance Paper, the Commission only had practical experience in the application of the price-cost test to predatory pricing (*see, e.g.*, Judgment of 3 July 1991, *AKZO v. Commission*, Case C-62/86, EU:C:1991:286; and Judgment of 14 November 1996, *Tetra Pak v. Commission*, Case C-33/94, EU:C:1996:436) and margin squeeze (*see, e.g.*, Judgment of 14 October 2010, *Deutsche Telecom v. Commission*, Case C-280/08 P, EU:C:2010:603; and Judgment of 19 December 2013, *Telefónica v. Commission*, Case C-274/12, EU:C:2013:852). The lack of prior experience with the price-cost test in the area of rebates before the adoption of the Guidance Paper is unfortunate. The enforcement experience of recent years has revealed that there are specific challenges that are related to the application of the price-cost test to retroactive rebates such as exclusivity rebates, notably as regards the calculation of the so-called contestable share and the high sensitivity of the test to small variations in the contestable share. In academic literature, *see* Giacomo Calzolari and Vincenzo Denicolò, *Loyalty Discounts and Price–Cost Tests*, International Journal of Industrial Organisation, Volume 73 (December 2020) https://doi.org/10.1016/j.ijindorg.2020.102589 ('Calzolari and Denicolò'): 'The discount-attribution test [i.e., the variant of the price-cost test that is applied to retroactive rebates] however raises the issue of the measurement of the share of contestable demand. In cases of bundled discounts, contestable demand is taken to be the demand for the tied products only. But in cases involving market-share discounts, contestable demand is conceptually more difficult to identify, and even more difficult to measure with any precision. […] What is perhaps most worrisome is the vagueness of the notion of contestability, which implies that the quantitative assessment of the share of contestable demand may be quite arbitrary.'
13. *See, e.g.*, Judgment of 25 March 2021, *Slovak Telekom, a.s. v. Commission*, Case C-165/19 P, EU:C:2021:239; Judgment of 12 January 2023, *Lietuvos geležinkeliai AB v. Commission*, Case C-42/21 P, EU:C:2023:12; Judgment of 10 September 2024, *Google and Alphabet v. Commission (Google Shopping)*, Case C-48/22 P, EU:C:2024:726; Judgment of 18 September 2024, *Qualcomm v. Commission (Qualcomm – Predation)*,Case T-671/19, EU:T:2024:626 (appeal is pending).
14. *See, e.g.*, Judgment of 24 of October 2024, *Commission v. Intel Corporation*, Case C-24/22 P, EU:C:2024:915; Judgments of 15 June 2022, *Qualcomm v. Commission (Qualcomm – Exclusivity payments)*, Case T-235/18, T:2022:358; Judgment of 25 October 2023, *Bulgarian Energy Holding EDA and Others v. Commission*, Case T-136/19, T:2023:669 (appeal is pending); Judgment of 18 September 2024, *Google and Alphabet v. Commission (Google AdSense for search)*, Case T-334/19, EU:T:2024:634 (appeal is pending).

have increased.[15] The digitisation of the EU economy and the central importance of the digital sector are likely to make it easier for dominant positions to become entrenched.[16] All of this calls for more vigilance by competition authorities and for an increased role for antitrust intervention. In other words, it is now more than ever important to ensure that an effects-based approach to Article 102 TFEU takes into account dynamic considerations and remains workable, so as to reduce the scope for false negatives and allow for effective enforcement of competition rules where appropriate.[17] And this is not only about economic welfare in the strict sense, as the broader positive impact of effective competition law enforcement on protecting the foundations of democratic states is gaining prominence in literature[18] and has been acknowledged in the EU Courts' case law.[19]

3 THE LAUNCH OF THE GUIDELINES INITIATIVE

The launch of the Guidelines on exclusionary abuses on 27 March 2023 has to be seen against the background outlined above and the significant body of case law and Commission practice that has developed after the adoption of the Guidance Paper.

Broadly speaking, the Guidelines have three intertwined objectives.

First, the Guidelines will fill the gap in the area of Article 102 TFEU by bringing it in line with other areas of competition enforcement, where experience has shown

15. *See* European Commission: Directorate-General for Competition, *Protecting Competition in a Changing World–Evidence on the Evolution of Competition in the EU During the Past 25 Years*, Publications Office of the European Union (2024), https://data.europa.eu/doi/10.2763/089949.
16. *See*, in that regard, European Commission: Directorate-General for Competition, Yves-Alexandre de Montjoye, Heike Schweitzer and Jacques Crémer, *Competition Policy for the Digital Era*, Publications Office (2019), https://data.europa.eu/doi/10.2763/407537, pp. 2-3: 'A consequence of these characteristics is the presence of strong "economies of scope," which favour the development of ecosystems and give incumbents a strong competitive advantage. Indeed, experience shows that large incumbent digital players are very difficult to dislodge, although there is little empirical evidence of the efficiency cost of this difficulty. From a competition policy point of view, there is also a reasonable concern that dominant digital firms have strong incentives to engage in anti-competitive behaviour. All these factors heavily influence the forms that competition takes in the digital economy; they require vigorous competition policy enforcement and justify adjustments to the way competition law is applied.'
17. *See* 2023 Policy Brief, pp. 2-4.
18. In 2024, the OECD has decided to dedicate a roundtable to the interactions between competition policy and democracy, *see* OECD Roundtables on Competition Policy Papers, *The interactions between competition and democracy*, No. 316, p. 3 'While competition policy may not need to be changed on account of democracy, the case that there are benefits to democracy from increased competition is an easy one to make. This provides another reason for robust and resourced competition policy to champion and preserve competition.' *See also, e.g.*, Eleanor M. Fox, *Antitrust and Democracy: How Markets Protect Democracy, Democracy Protects Markets, and Illiberal Politics Threatens to Hijack Both*, Legal Issues of Economic Integration, Volume 46, Issue 4 (2019) pp. 317-328 https://doi.org/10.54648/leie2019020; and Elias Deutscher, The Competition-Democracy Nexus Resurrected?: Four Precursors of a Competition-Democracy Nexus 4.0, Journal of Antitrust Enforcement, 2025, jnae053, https://doi.org/10.1093/jaenfo/jnae053.
19. *See, e.g.*, Judgment of 15 May 2022, *Servizio Elettrico Nazionale and Others*, Case C-377/20, EU:C:2022:379, para. 41; Judgment of 14 September 2022, *Google and Alphabet v. Commission (Google Android)*, Case T-604/18, EU:T:2022:541, para. 1028.

that guidelines are a suitable instrument to improve legal certainty and increase predictability. As indicated above, the Guidance Paper has certainly achieved its aim of fostering a move towards an effects-based approach to Article 102 TFEU. At the same time, the Guidance Paper's legal status has raised significant uncertainties in the past, including among academics[20] and in the context of litigation before the EU Courts.[21] But thanks to the developments in the state of the law on exclusionary abuses of dominance, it is now possible to replace mere guidance on enforcement priorities with substantive guidelines, thereby bringing Article 102 TFEU in line with other competition law instruments and solving the 'anomaly' that has characterised this provision until now. The Commission expects that this initiative will assist national courts and national competition authorities (NCAs) in the application of Article 102 TFEU,[22] which is particularly important in a context where approximately 85% of decisions enforcing Article 102 TFEU are adopted by NCAs[23] and where private enforcement at Member State level is on the rise.[24]

Second, being mindful of the complexity of the jurisprudence in this area and the fact that the case law has inevitably been developed incrementally,[25] the Guidelines on exclusionary abuses seek to provide operational guidance on the application of Article 102 TFEU to private undertakings. As far as potentially dominant undertakings are concerned, this is expected to increase compliance, with positive spillovers on market outcomes and the use of enforcement agencies' resources. As far as other stakeholders are concerned, this is aimed at facilitating the assessment and reporting of potentially abusive conduct, which would also have positive spillovers on enforcement action.

Third, the Guidelines seek to promote a workable effects-based approach to exclusionary abuses, meaning an approach that is not only firmly grounded in economic thinking but also enables an effective and timely enforcement of Article 102 TFEU. A lot of emphasis in the past fifteen years has been put on the importance of

20. *See* Liza Lovdahl Gormsen, *Why the European Commission's Enforcement Priorities on Article 82 EC Should Be Withdrawn,* The European Competition Law Review, Volume 31, Issue 2 (2010), pp. 45-51 and Pinar Akman, *The European Commission's Guidance on Article 102 TEFEU: From Inferno to Paradiso?,* The Modern Law Review, Volume 73, Issue 4 (2010), pp. 605-630 https://doi.org/10.1111/j.1468-2230.2010.00810.x.
21. *See, e.g.*, Judgment of 18 September 2024, *Qualcomm v. Commission (Qualcomm – Predation),* Case T-671/19, EU:T:2024:626, paras 523 and 605-622.
22. *See* Call for evidence for an initiative – *Guidelines on exclusionary abuses by dominant undertakings*, Ref. Ares(2023)2189183-27/03/2023, https://ec.europa.eu/info/law/better-regulation/have-your-say/initiatives/13796-EU-competition-law-guidelines-on-exclusionary-abuses-by-dominant-undertakings_en.
23. *See* Commission staff working document, *Evaluation of Regulation 1/2003 and 773/2004,* 5.9.2014, SWD(2024) 216 final, pp. 49 and 228.
24. The Superleague case represents a prominent example of recent standalone private enforcement in the area of exclusionary abuses, *see* Judgment of 21 December 2023, *European Superleague Company,* Case C-333/21, EU:C:2023:1011.
25. *See, e.g.*, replies to the call for evidence in relation to the Guidelines initiative, e.g., from Enel,https://ec.europa.eu/info/law/better-regulation/have-your-say/initiatives/13796-EU-competition-law-guidelines-on-exclusionary-abuses-by-dominant-undertakings/F3407268_en and the Finnish Competition and Consumer Authority: https://ec.europa.eu/info/law/better-regulation/have-your-say/initiatives/13796-EU-competition-law-guidelines-on-exclusionary-abuses-by-dominant-undertakings/F3406038_en.

ensuring that the enforcement of Article 102 TFEU does not lead to false positives.[26] These considerations remain valid and are certainly worth being kept in mind. At the same time, it has been observed that the increased centrality of an effects-based approach in the area of Article 102 TFEU has likely led to longer and more complex investigations, and ultimately to an increased risk of underenforcement,[27] which is an all the more relevant concern when considering the recent EU economic trends indicated in the section above. As an attempt to balance out the risks of false positives and false negatives in the current economic context, the Guidelines seek to interpret the case law of the EU Courts on the basis of the learnings gained from the Commission practice of the past decades, so as to ensure that an effects-based approach remains administrable and is not perceived as antithetic to a robust enforcement of Article 102 TFEU.

4 CONTENT OF THE DRAFT GUIDELINES ON EXCLUSIONARY ABUSES

The draft text of the Guidelines on exclusionary abuses that was published for public consultation on 1 August 2024 contains five sections: the introductory section 1 provides indications on the purpose, scope and structure of the Guidelines; section 2 describes the general principles applicable to the assessment of single-firm and collective dominance; section 3 describes the general legal test to assess whether conduct by dominant undertakings is liable to constitute an exclusionary abuse;[28] section 4 describes the principles to determine whether certain specific types of conduct by dominant undertakings are liable to be abusive; and section 5 describes the general principles applicable to the assessment of objective justifications and efficiencies. The specific content of these sections will be described in more detail in the remainder of this chapter, without any intent to be exhaustive and rather with a focus on the areas of the draft Guidelines that have emerged as attracting more attention during the public consultation.

26. *See* Damien Geradin and Stijn Huijts, *Abuse of Dominance: Has the Effect-Based Analysis Gone Too Far?* (21 July 2024), available at SSRN: https://ssrn.com/abstract=4900869; and Pablo Ibanez Colomo, *The (Second) Modernisation of Article 102 TFEU: Reconciling Effective Enforcement, Legal Certainty and Meaningful Judicial Review*, Journal of European Competition Law & Practice, Volume 14, Issue 8 (December 2023), pp. 608-623 https://doi.org/10.1093/jeclap/lpad064.

27. *See* Heike Schweitzer and Simon de Ridder, *How to Fix a Failing Art. 102 TFEU: Substantive Interpretation, Evidentiary Requirements, and the Commission's Future Guidelines on Exclusionary Abuses*, Journal of European Competition Law & Practice, Volume 15, Issue 4 (June 2024), pp. 222-243 https://doi.org/10.1093/jeclap/lpae033 ('Schweitzer and de Ridder'); Rupprecht Podszun and Tristan Rohner, *Making Article 102 TFEU Future-Proof: Learnings from the Past* (24 April 2023), available at SSRN: https://ssrn.com/abstract=4428170; Anne C. Witt, *Platform Regulation in Europe: Per Se Rules to the Rescue?*, Journal of Competition Law & Economics, Volume 18, Issue 3 (September 2022), pp. 670-708 https://doi.org/10.1093/joclec/nhac001.

28. The draft Guidelines use the expressions 'liable to be abusive' or 'liable to constitute an exclusionary abuse' in order to refer to conduct that departs from competition on the merits and it is capable of having exclusionary effects, irrespective of whether the conduct may be deemed, in a later step in the analysis, to be objectively justified or not (*see supra* n. 24 of the draft Guidelines).

Section 1: Introduction

The introductory section of the draft Guidelines contains important statements on principle concerning the objective of the document and its scope of application.

After a description of the general purpose of EU competition law and its importance as a tool to ensure that consumers obtain access to the best products in terms of price, choice, quality and innovation,[29] the draft Guidelines stress that Article 102 TFEU applies to all practices by dominant undertakings that may directly or indirectly harm the welfare of consumers.[30] In doing so, they endorse an interpretation of 'exclusionary effects' that encompasses any hindrance to actual or potential competitors' ability or incentive to exercise a competitive constraint on the dominant undertaking, such as the full-fledged exclusion or marginalisation of competitors, an increase in barriers to entry or expansion, the hampering or elimination of effective access to markets or to parts thereof or the imposition of constraints on the potential growth of competitors.[31] Importantly, they stress that not all exclusionary effects are liable to be in breach of Article 102 TFEU, but only those that result from 'recourse to means or resources different from those governing normal competition',[32] meaning competition on the merits.

The introductory section also contains important policy statements as regards the purpose of the Guidelines to enhance legal certainty in the context of decentralised enforcement of Article 102 TFEU and facilitate self-assessment,[33] as well as the importance of ensuring that Article 102 TFEU is applied vigorously and effectively.[34]

Finally, the introductory section briefly outlines the existing case law on the relationship between Article 102 TFEU and other regulations and areas of law.[35]

Section 2: General Principles Applicable to the Assessment of Dominance

Section 2 recalls that Article 102 TFEU does not prevent an undertaking from acquiring on its own merits, in particular on account of its skills and abilities, a dominant position in a given market. It only prohibits the abuse of such dominant position.[36] After having established general principles that are common to both types of dominance, section 2 deals sequentially with single-firm dominance and collective dominance.

As regards single-firm dominance, the draft Guidelines refer to the traditional building blocks that are relevant to the assessment, namely market shares,[37] barriers to expansion and entry[38] and countervailing buyer power.[39] Notably, the sub-section on barriers to expansion and entry includes a description of barriers that have been

29. *See* para. 1 of the draft Guidelines.
30. *See* paras 2 and 5 of the draft Guidelines.
31. *See* para. 6 of the draft Guidelines.
32. *Ibid.*
33. *See* para. 8 of the draft Guidelines.
34. *See* para. 4 of the draft Guidelines.
35. *See* para. 13 of the draft Guidelines.
36. *See* para. 17 of the draft Guidelines.
37. *See* sub-s. 2.2.1. *Market position of the undertaking concerned and of its competitors* of the draft Guidelines.
38. *See* sub-s. 2.2.2. *Barriers to expansion and entry* of the draft Guidelines.
39. *See* sub-s. 2.2.3. *Countervailing buyer power* of the draft Guidelines.

identified in recent Commission practice[40] and an explanation of the role of network effects in the assessment of dominance.[41]

As regards collective dominance, the draft Guidelines present the current state of the law in this area with regard to dominance achieved by means of: (i) economic links between undertakings in the form of contractual, structural or other links;[42] or (ii) tacit coordination between undertakings.[43]

Section 3: General Principles to Determine If Conduct by a Dominant Undertaking Is Liable to Be Abusive

Section 3 can be considered the 'core' section of the draft Guidelines. Given the complexity of the jurisprudence on the general legal standard that is applicable in cases of exclusionary abuses, this is the section where the interpretative work of the Commission was by necessity the most extensive. As a result, it is not surprising that the section has attracted the majority of the reactions by stakeholders in the context of the public consultation, as discussed in 5 below.

After recalling the dominant undertakings' special responsibility not to engage in conduct that impairs effective competition,[44] the draft Guidelines take the position that in order to determine whether conduct by dominant undertakings is liable to constitute an exclusionary abuse, it is generally necessary to establish whether the conduct departs from competition on the merits and whether the conduct is capable of having exclusionary effects. The draft Guidelines present these two prongs of the assessment as in principle cumulative, even if some EU Courts' judgments could be interpreted as the two being alternative.[45] At the same time, the draft Guidelines acknowledge that while the two limbs of the assessment are conceptually different, there are also some areas of overlap as certain factual elements may be relevant to the assessment of both.[46]

In presenting the notion of competition on the merits as a conceptually distinct one from the notion of exclusionary effects, the draft Guidelines acknowledge that not all forms of exclusion are caught by Article 102 TFEU and that in particular, Article 102 TFEU does not prohibit behaviour that is likely to benefit consumers in the form of lower prices, better quality and a wider choice of new or improved goods and services.[47] In this respect, the notion of competition on the merits plays in the draft Guidelines' architecture a function that is not dissimilar from that of the adjective 'anticompetitive' in the 'anticompetitive foreclosure' notion under the Guidance Paper.

The draft Guidelines seek to operationalise the approach of the jurisprudence to the notion of competition on the merits by providing guidance as to the types of

40. *See* para. 30 of the draft Guidelines.
41. *See* para. 31 of the draft Guidelines.
42. *See* para. 35 of the draft Guidelines.
43. *See* paras 36 to 42 of the draft Guidelines.
44. *See* para. 44 of the draft Guidelines.
45. *See* in particular Judgment of 19 January 2023, *Unilever Italia Mkt. Operations*, Case C-680/20, EU:C:2023:33, paras 39 and 41.
46. *See* para. 46 of the draft Guidelines.
47. *See* para. 51 of the draft Guidelines.

behaviour that can be considered departing from competition on the merits, essentially distinguishing between: (i) conduct that holds no economic interest for a dominant undertaking, except that of restricting competition (so-called naked restrictions), which is deemed 'by definition' to depart from competition on the merits;[48] (ii) conduct that is subject to the application of a specific legal test outlined by the EU Courts, which if fulfilled determines that the conduct departs from competition on the merits;[49] and (iii) other conduct, for which the specific circumstances of the case will need to be taken into account.[50] As regards this latter category, the draft Guidelines outline the circumstances that the EU Courts have considered relevant for the assessment, clarifying that this list should not be considered exhaustive.[51]

The draft Guidelines also explain that a price-cost test is required to establish whether the pricing behaviour of dominant undertakings departs from competition on the merits in the context of the predation and margin squeeze framework of analysis.[52] The draft Guidelines leave open the possibility to use a price-cost test as regards conditional rebates[53] and state that while in principle possible, the application of such test is generally inappropriate in the case of non-pricing practices.[54]

As regards the general framework for analysing a conduct's capability to produce exclusionary effects, the draft Guidelines seek to systematise the complex case law of the EU Courts on this topic by distinguishing between three types of behaviour: (a) conduct falling under the general rule for which it is necessary to demonstrate a capability to produce exclusionary effects;[55] (b) conduct that is generally recognised as having a high potential to produce exclusionary effects, which is subject to a 'soft' presumption concerning its capability to produce exclusionary effects;[56] and (c) conduct in relation to which there is no economic interest, other than that of restricting competition ('naked restrictions'), which is subject to a 'hard' presumption concerning its capability to produce exclusionary effects.[57]

This categorisation exercise reflects the basic idea that the likelihood that a conduct gives rise to exclusionary effects is higher in relation to certain types of behaviour than in relation to others. Importantly, both 'soft' and 'hard' presumptions described in the draft Guidelines are rebuttable, meaning that they are not 'per se' rules.[58] Unlike 'per se' rules, rebuttable presumptions are merely used to reverse the evidentiary burden of proof as regards the legal qualification of certain specific conduct. They are typically triggered once a party demonstrates to the requisite legal

48. *See* para. 54 of the draft Guidelines.
49. *See* para. 53 of the draft Guidelines.
50. *See* para. 55 of the draft Guidelines.
51. *Ibid.*
52. *See* paras 55(a) to (f) of the draft Guidelines.
53. This is the case in particular as regards rebates that are not conditional on exclusivity (*see* paras 143 and 144). As regards rebates that are conditional on exclusivity, the draft Guidelines is silent on the use of a price-cost test (*see* further below in 5).
54. *See* para. 56 of the draft Guidelines.
55. *See* para. 60(a) of the draft Guidelines.
56. *See* para. 60(b) of the draft Guidelines.
57. *See* para. 60(c) of the draft Guidelines.
58. Some commentators appear to have taken a different view and considered naked restrictions to amount to a form of irrebuttable presumption, meaning a 'per se' rules, *see* Juliane Kokott and

standard the existence of certain facts, e.g., the fact that an undertaking's market shares are above 50% (triggering a presumption of dominance) or that an undertaking has been pricing below cost (triggering a presumption of exclusionary effects).[59]

The use of presumptions, and in particular rebuttable presumptions, is entirely compatible with an effects-based approach to Article 102 TFEU as long as the presumptions are attributed to specific types of conduct in light of sound economic principles.[60] This is in line with a coherent interpretation of Articles 101 and 102 TFEU and notably with the assessment of certain conduct as anticompetitive 'by object' under Article 101 TFEU.[61] It is also in line with the legal tradition of the EU Member States in areas different from competition law, where presumptions are used in order to ensure an optimal allocation of the burden and standard of proof.[62]

Mariya Serafimova, Aktuelle Rechtsprechung der Unionsgerichte zum Missbrauchsverbot nach Art. 102 AEUV: hin zu einem Paradigmenwechsel?, in Wettbewerb auf digitalen Märkten, 323, p. 30.

59. *See* written contribution from the European Union submitted for Item 7 of the 144th OECD Competition Committee meeting on 5-6 December 2024, 'The Standard and the Burden of Proof in Competition Law Cases', DAF/COMP/WD(2024)57, available at https://one.oecd.org/document/DAF/COMP/WD(2024)57/en/pdf, para. 83.
60. *See* Massimo Motta and Chiara Fumagalli, *Economic Principles for the Enforcement of Abuse of Dominance Provisions*, Journal of Competition Law and Economics, Volume 20, Issue 1-2, pp. 85-107 (June 2024) https://doi.org/10.1093/joclec/nhae003 ('Motta and Fumagalli'), p. 2, 'Consistently with the objective of improving legal certainty, it is important to stress that an "effects-based" and "economic-sound" approach does not mean a "case-by-case" approach where each case is assessed in a completely different way, nor that each and every case should necessarily involve sophisticated quantitative evidence or bespoken economic theory models. We also note that in some quarters, the economic approach to abuse of dominance cases has been equated to using the (misleadingly named) "as-efficient competitor test". We strongly disagree: the now vast body of economic knowledge on exclusionary practices clearly indicates that price-cost tests are useful when dealing with certain practices, but irrelevant or misleading with others. Relatedly, certain practices, such as exclusive dealing and other practices that reference rivals, should simply be presumed to be anti-competitive. For other practices (e.g., predation, selective price cuts, quantity rebates), instead, the price-cost test is useful and its result should determine presumptions of harm or lawful behaviour.' *See also* Jorge Padilla, Salvatore Piccolo and Michael Gal, *Optimal Legal Rules for the Assessment of Unilateral Conduct by Dominant Firms* (3 February 2025), available at SSRN: https://ssrn.com/abstract=5126734 or http://dx.doi.org/10.2139/ssrn.5126734, 'We [...] endorse a preference for structured rules, unless irrebuttable presumptions are optimal: a rebuttable presumption of illegality, a rebuttable presumption of legality, and the structured rule of reason – which is associated to a neutral presumption. The choice of presumptions is then determined by the relative plausibility of the anti-competitive theory of harm and the pro-competitive justification for the conduct, and the relative costs of false positives and negatives.'
61. From a conceptual point of view the 'by object' category under Art. 101 TFEU and presumptions under Art. 102 TFEU respond to similar needs in terms of promoting administrability and legal certainty. However, under Art. 101 TFEU, the 'by object' characterisation makes the analysis of effects unnecessary, while under the framework of the draft Guidelines, it is left open for dominant firms to rebut even 'hard' presumptions. For this reason, the draft Guidelines did not include reference to 'by object' types of behaviour under Art. 102 TFEU.
62. Schweitzer and de Ridder, pp. 236 and following; David Bailey, *Presumptions in EU Competition Law,* Kölner Schrift zum Wirtschaftsrecht, Volume 1, Issue 3 (July 2010) https://doi.org/10.9785/ovs-kszw-2010-200; Cyril Ritter, *Presumptions in EU Competition Law,* Journal of Antitrust Enforcement, Volume 6, Issue 2 (August 2018), pp. 189-212, pp. 193-194 and 202 https://doi.org/10.1093/jaenfo/jny008.

The draft Guidelines acknowledge that any actual or potential exclusionary effects identified in the analysis need to be attributable to the conduct at issue. They also clarify that while conceptually the analysis of effects requires a comparison of the situation where the conduct was implemented with the situation absent the conduct, such comparison is generally carried out based on an analysis of the market after the implementation of the conduct.[63]

The draft Guidelines also include a detailed description of the elements that are typically considered relevant in order to assess the potential exclusionary effects of a conduct, namely the position of the dominant undertaking, the conditions of the relevant market, the position of the dominant undertaking's competitors, the extent of the allegedly abusive conduct, the position of the customers or input suppliers, the possible existence of evidence related to an exclusionary strategy or in relation to actual market developments.[64]

Finally, the draft Guidelines state that the assessment of whether a conduct is capable of having exclusionary effects does not require a demonstration that the actual or potential competitors that are affected by the conduct are as efficient as the dominant undertaking.[65] This is in line with the idea that the possible exclusion of as-efficient competitors, where relevant in the assessment,[66] only refers to *hypothetical* competitors and not to real-life competitors. Making use of the competitive parameter(s) of real-life competitors is likely to lead to reduced administrability, predictability and legal certainty and runs counter to the very rationale of the application of a price-cost test in the context of pricing abuses.[67]

Section 4: Principles for Determining Whether Specific Categories of Conduct Are Liable to Be Abusive

Section 4 presents the principles underlying the assessment of specific abuses, distinguishing between abuses for which the EU Courts have outlined specific legal tests that in practice incorporate the notions presented in section 3, and abuses for which no specific legal tests have been outlined but where some specific considerations are nonetheless warranted.

In the first category, the draft Guidelines present exclusive dealing, tying, refusal to supply, predatory pricing and margin squeeze. Specifically with regard to exclusive dealing, the draft Guidelines present this type of conduct as including both exclusivity

63. *See* paras 65 and 66 of the draft Guidelines.
64. *See* paras 70(a) to (g) of the draft Guidelines.
65. *See* para. 73 of the draft Guidelines.
66. A separate discussion concerns if and in which circumstances it should be considered in the assessment of exclusionary effects that the conduct is capable of excluding hypothetical as efficient competitors. *See* in this regard s. 5 below.
67. *See* Motta and Fumagalli, p. 4, 'It is also important to underline that price-cost tests should be carried out with measures of the dominant firm's costs, not of its rivals, whether as or less efficient. This is for at least two reasons: firstly, the price-cost test acts as a proxy for profit sacrifice by the dominant firm, and hence, the efficiency of the rivals is irrelevant; secondly, given that cost information is typically private information, using a measure of cost that the defendant does not know would undermine legal certainty.'

agreements and rebates conditional on a customer purchasing all or most of its requirements from a dominant firm ('exclusivity rebates'). In doing so, the draft Guidelines essentially replicate the choice of the Guidance Paper to make exclusivity rebates subject to the same treatment as exclusivity agreements, rather than to the same treatment as other types of conditional rebates.[68]

In the second category, the draft Guidelines present conditional rebates that are not subject to exclusivity conditions, multi-product rebates, self-preferencing and access restrictions different from refusal to supply.

Section 5: General Principles Applicable to the Assessment of Objective Justifications

Section 5 presents the general framework applicable to the assessment of objective justifications, including both so-called objective necessity defences and efficiency defences.

As regards objective necessity, the draft Guidelines state that such defence can be presented when the behaviour of a dominant undertaking is objectively necessary to achieve a certain aim that is linked to pursuing legitimate commercial considerations, technical justifications or public interest goals. The draft Guidelines state that in this context, it is up to the dominant firm to show that the conduct is both necessary and proportionate to reach these aims.[69]

As regards efficiencies, the draft Guidelines state that a dominant undertaking would need to demonstrate that the exclusionary effects resulting from its conduct are counterbalanced, or even outweighed, by advantages in efficiency that also benefit consumers. In more detail, it is up to the dominant firm to show: (a) that the efficiency gains likely to result from the conduct under consideration counteract any likely negative effects on competition and on the interests of consumers in the affected markets; (b) that those gains have been, or are likely to be, brought about as a result of the conduct; (c) that the conduct is necessary for the achievement of those efficiency gains; and (d) that the conduct does not eliminate effective competition, by removing all or most existing sources of actual or potential competition.[70]

---

68. It has been sometimes argued that under the Guidance Paper's assessment framework, exclusivity rebates should be subject to the application of a price-cost as-efficient competitor test. This may be due to the fact that the Commission made use of a price-cost test in the context of the *Intel* case, which was the first Commission decision on exclusivity rebates adopted after the publication of the Guidance Paper. However, the Guidance Paper does not contain any indication that a price-cost test should be applied to exclusivity rebates. The Paper considered exclusivity rebates as belonging to the broader 'exclusive dealing' category (*see* para. 34) and there is no reference to the price-cost test in the exclusive dealing section of the document. It is only in the section on conditional rebates that the use of the price-cost test is mentioned. This section does not include exclusivity rebates given that exclusivity is not mentioned among the elements that are relevant in the analysis of whether conditional rebates are likely to lead to foreclosure (namely, whether the rebates are incremental or retroactive and whether the rebates are based on standardised or individualised thresholds, *see* paras 40 and 45 of the Guidance Paper).
69. *See* para. 168 of the draft Guidelines.
70. *See* para. 169 of the draft Guidelines.

5 OUTLOOK ON THE WAY FORWARD

The draft Guidelines published on 1 August 2024 have been successful in triggering a wide debate on the relevant legal framework to apply Article 102 TFEU. In response to the consultation, the Commission received 117 written contributions commenting on the draft text. Furthermore, on 13 February 2025, the Commission hosted a stakeholder workshop to allow approximately 200 registered participants to express their views on the draft Guidelines.

The lively debate that has been generated by the public consultation confirms that there is significant interest among stakeholders in the application of Article 102 TFEU, even beyond the circles of so-called competition law experts.[71] By and large, it can be stated that the Guidelines initiative as such has been welcomed and that it is considered having the potential to improve the legal certainty and predictability of Article 102 TFEU enforcement both at the Union and national levels.

When it comes to the substance of the draft Guidelines, the public consultation shows that stakeholders' opinions are divided in many respects. While one should be mindful of not over-simplifying the feedback received, it can be stated that in general terms, academics, business associations and public authorities have mostly provided positive feedback and stressed the importance of ensuring a robust enforcement of abuse of dominance rules, while law firms, economic consultancies and large corporations have mostly provided critical feedback and warned against the risks of overenforcement.

The Commission is currently reflecting on the next steps in light of the outcome of the public consultation and it is clear that digesting all feedback that has been received will require time. In any event, it can be already stated at this stage that three topics that emerged during the public consultation will warrant future reflection: (i) the request for more clarity as regards the definition of the notion of competition on the merits, as well as the interaction and possible overlap between the two limbs of the general legal test presented in the draft Guidelines; (ii) the role of presumptions, which appear to be seen by most stakeholders as a possible way to streamline enforcement and provide increased legal certainty, but in relation to which there still seems to be limited consensus as regards the specific types of behaviours that are presumed to produce exclusionary effects; and (iii) the request for the Commission to provide more guidance on safe harbours for dominant firms and on how to raise an objective justification defence.

In the meantime, the EU Courts have issued five important judgments on exclusionary abuses of dominance. These are the ECJ judgments in *Google Shopping, Intel II* and *Android Auto* and the General Court judgments in *Google AdSense* and *Qualcomm predation*.[72] All of these rulings concern key parts of the framework to

71. By means of example, among the respondents to the public consultation feature the Bureau of European Consumer Organisations and the European Trade Union Confederation.
72. Judgments of 10 September 2024, *Google and Alphabet v. Commission (Google Shopping)*, Case C-48/22 P, EU:C:2024:726; Judgment of 24 of October 2024, *Commission v. Intel Corporation*, Case C-24/22 P, EU:C:2024:915; Judgment of 25 February 2025, *Google and Alphabet v. AGCM (Android Auto)*, Case C-233/23, EU:C:2025:110; Judgment of 18 September 2024, *Google and*

assess exclusionary abuses and their impact will need to be reflected upon thoroughly. Some preliminary considerations can nevertheless be advanced.

On the one hand, some parts of the judgments appear to confirm important elements of the draft Guidelines. A first example is provided by the approach taken by the ECJ as regards causality and counterfactual in the *Google Shopping* judgment. In essence, the ECJ confirms that in principle there is a need to establish a causal link between conduct and effects and that this can normally be done by examining market developments after the conduct was put in place.[73] A second example relates to the existence of presumptions of exclusionary effects in relation to certain behaviours by dominant undertakings. The *Qualcomm – Predation* judgment confirms the existence of a presumption in relation to predatory pricing[74] and the *Google AdSense* and *Intel II* judgments are at least consistent with the existence of a presumption in relation to exclusive dealing.[75] A third example is provided by the framework to assess specific forms of abuses as outlined in the draft Guidelines, which has been confirmed in essence by the ECJ, for instance, as regards self-preferencing[76] and the refusal to provide access to a platform that has been developed with a view to enabling third-parties to use it.[77]

On the other hand, other parts of the judgments warrant a reflection as to whether the framework of assessment outlined in the draft Guidelines can be maintained. Two examples are provided by the possible existence of a so-called as-efficient competitor principle and the application of the related price-cost as-efficient competitor test to exclusivity rebates.

First, while it is clear that the expression 'as efficient competitor principle' has become increasingly common, it is equally clear that this expression generates significant uncertainty, given that there is no consensus as to the content of such a 'principle'. Some see the 'as-efficient competitor principle' as the *descriptive* enunciation of the widely accepted notion that Article 102 TFEU does not seek to give

---

Alphabet v. Commission (Google AdSense for search), Case T-334/19, EU:T:2024:634 (Case C-826/24 P); Judgment of 18 September 2024, *Qualcomm v. Commission (Qualcomm – Predation)*, Case T-671/19, EU:T:2024:626.

73. Judgment of 10 September 2024, *Google and Alphabet v. Commission (Google Shopping)*, Case C-48/22 P, EU:C:2024:726 paras 224-225.
74. Judgment of 18 September 2024, *Qualcomm v. Commission (Qualcomm – Predation)*, Case T-671/19, EU:T:2024:626, para. 521.
75. Judgment of 18 September 2024, *Google and Alphabet v. Commission (Google AdSense for search)*, Case T-334/19, EU:T:2024:634, para. 385 (confirming that an effects analysis is necessary only 'where that undertaking disputes, during the procedure, the specific capacity of those clauses to exclude equally efficient competitors from the market, with supporting evidence'); Judgment of 24 October 2024,*Commission v. Intel Corporation*, Case C-240/22 P, EU:C:2024:915, para. 144 (confirming that an effects analysis is necessary 'only if that undertaking submits, during the administrative procedure, on the basis of supporting evidence, that its conduct was not capable of restricting competition'); *see also* Judgment of 26 January 2022 *Intel Corporation v. Commission*, Case T-286/09 RENV, EU:T:2022:19, para. 522 (in particular, the reference to the existence of a 'mere presumption' as regards exclusivity rebates, which the authors interpret as meaning a 'rebuttable presumption').
76. Judgment of 10 September 2024, *Google and Alphabet v. Commission (Google Shopping)*, Case C-48/22 P, EU:C:2024:726, paras 158-161; compare with Draft Guidelines, para. 161.
77. Judgment of 25 February 2025, *Google and Alphabet v. AGCM (Android Auto)*, Case C-233/23, EU:C:2025:110, para. 52; compare with Draft Guidelines, para. 166(d).

protection to inefficient competitors and to prevent their exit from the market.[78] Others argue that the 'as-efficient competitor principle' has in fact a *prescriptive* function in relation to the legal test to demonstrate the existence of an abuse.[79] This would imply that in order to show an infringement of Article 102 TFEU, it would as a rule be necessary to demonstrate that the conduct is capable of excluding as-efficient competitors, or (as an even more demanding variation) that the competitors that have been affected by the conduct are as-efficient as the dominant undertaking.

From the point of view of the authors, the view that there is a prescriptive 'as-efficient competitor principle' of general application appears to be based on a *non sequitur*: it is well acknowledged that Article 102 TFEU does not have the objective of protecting inefficient competitors. But this does not logically lead to the conclusion that Article 102 TFEU can only be applied when it is demonstrated that (hypothetical) as-efficient competitors are excluded by the conduct.[80] Moreover, a prescriptive as-efficient competitor principle of general application would likely lead to significant practical complications, notably in the absence of reliable ways to operationalise the notion of 'as-efficient' beyond pricing conduct in the strict sense.[81] This would likely increase the complexity of Article 102 TFEU enforcement and reduce its predictability.

78. *See, e.g.*, Giorgio Monti, Comments on *Guidelines on the Application of Article 102 of the Treaty on the Functioning of the European Union to abusive exclusionary conduct by dominant undertakings*, November 2024, available on DG COMP's website at https://competition-policy.ec.europa.eu/public-consultations/2024-article-102-guidelines_en, paras 41 and following: 'A principle is a general concept which provides a reason for a finding of abuse of dominance. In my view, the AEC principle does not exist. In spite of the ECJ's frequent references to a hypothetical as efficient rival, the Court has never explained it by reference to a principle, nor defined this principle. [...] At most, the AEC principle is sometimes useful, but it is not a necessary condition to find an abuse. I think this was also clear when looking at the 2009 Guidance Paper on predation (paras 68 and 69) where the document draws on economic literature to explain that below-cost pricing can be exclusionary without reference to the relative efficiency of the rival (e.g. predatory pricing by reputation excludes any new entrant, hypothetically as efficient or not).'
79. *See, e.g.*, Oxera Response to *the Public Consultation on the European Commission Draft Guidelines on Exclusionary Abuse under Article 102*, available on DG COMP's website at https://competition-policy.ec.europa.eu/public-consultations/2024-article-102-guidelines_en, pp. 69 and following, 'In recent judgments, Courts have established that for conduct to be liable to be abusive it should have the actual or potential effect of excluding equally efficient competing undertakings from the market or markets concerned, or hindering their growth on those markets. [...] Although historically the AEC principle grew from the specific price-cost test as set out in the Guidance Paper, the current case law as developed since has adopted the AEC principle more generally, independent of its test.'
80. The fact that A is not the objective of B does not mean that one needs to prove the non-existence of A as pre-condition to apply B.
81. This is recognised, e.g., in the Oxera Response to the public consultation on the draft Guidelines referred to in *supra* n. 76, 'First, conduct in the form of price competition (i.e. low pricing) is generally desirable from a competition policy perspective, whereas for non-pricing conduct such as exclusive dealing, refusal to supply, or other access restrictions this is not necessarily the case. Relatedly, the threat of being found to infringe Article 102 on the basis of an AEC test comes with a larger risk of chilling procompetitive behaviour in the context of pricing behaviour, as firms cannot avoid having to set at least a price. This is not the case in non-pricing conduct (e.g. because firms an simply abstain from requiring exclusivity or displaying competitor products less prominently). The risk of Type 1 errors is therefore higher in the case of pricing conduct. Second, pricing conduct comes with the general ability to robustly operationalise the AEC

Against this background, the draft Guidelines fully embrace the existence of a 'descriptive' as-efficient competitor principle and clearly refer to the relevant case law in the section on competition on the merits.[82] In addition, the draft Guidelines endorse a more 'prescriptive' dimension of the as-efficient competitor principle where such principle can play a meaningful role in the analysis because it can be operationalised, at least in theory, in a reliable and robust way. This is notably the case with regard to predation, margin squeeze and potentially non-exclusivity rebates, where the price-cost 'as-efficient competitor' test provides for an operational means to implement the principle.[83] The approach of the draft Guidelines is consistent with that under the Guidance Paper[84] and the recent case law of the EU Courts that referred to exclusionary effects in broader terms and not merely in terms of exclusion of as-efficient competitors.[85]

In line with the text of the draft Guidelines, the recent ECJ ruling in *Google Shopping* recognises that there is no general requirement to show that a conduct is capable of excluding a hypothetical as-efficient competitor as a precondition for any finding of abuse.[86] At the same time, the *Google Shopping* judgment appears to stress that there are circumstances where the finding that a conduct is capable of excluding a hypothetical as-efficient competitor is relevant 'as a rule'.[87] Given that this appears to suggest that the prescriptive scope of the so-called as-efficient competitor principle may be broader than envisaged in the draft Guidelines, a reflection in this regard will need to be undertaken.

Second, the draft Guidelines do not refer to the price-cost test as a tool to assess the exclusionary effects of exclusivity rebates. This is essentially for two reasons: first, economic literature suggests the likelihood of false negatives associated with the use of the price-cost test in the area of exclusivity rebates;[88] and second, the Commission's enforcement experience has shown that the tool has significant limitations in terms of

---

principle into a test, given that its constituent variables (effective price, cost) can generally be proxied well. In contrast, this is not (or at least not always) the case with non-pricing conduct.'

82. *See* para. 51 of the draft Guidelines.
83. As regards exclusivity rebates and the application of the price-cost test to them, *see* further below. In addition, the draft Guidelines also state outside of pricing behaviour that the lack of replicability of the conduct by an as-efficient competitor is one of the possible elements indicating that the conduct departs from competition on the merits, *see* para. 55(g) of the draft Guidelines.
84. The Guidance Paper did not contain reference to an 'as-efficient competitor principle' of general application. The Guidance Paper only referred to the use of the price-cost 'as-efficient competitor test' as regards pricing conduct.
85. *See, e.g.*, Judgment of 15 May 2022, *Servizio Elettrico Nazionale and Others*, Case C-377/20, EU:C:2022:379, para. 61.
86. Judgment of 10 September 2024, *Google and Alphabet v. Commission (Google Shopping)*, Case C-48/22 P, EU:C:2024:726, paras 263-264.
87. *Ibid.*, para. 165.
88. *See* Motta and Fumagalli, p. 3 '[exclusive dealing and rebates conditioned on buyers purchasing a large part of their needs from the dominant firm] do not necessarily require profit sacrifice on the side of the dominant firm and have a high anti-competitive potential. Accordingly, they should be treated as presumptively abusive, and the burden of proving otherwise should fall upon the dominant firm. For this category of cases, a price-cost test does not shed light on the lawfulness of the practice. Accordingly, if the defendant showed that it is setting prices above costs, this should not be treated as discharging its burden of proof'.

accuracy[89] and likelihood of delaying the proceedings.[90] These limitations mean that the costs associated with the use of the price-cost test in the specific case of exclusivity rebates would likely outweigh the benefits.[91] At the time of publishing the draft Guidelines, the *Intel I* judgment had not taken a position on this point and the *Intel II* case was still pending before the ECJ. The *Intel II* ruling could now be interpreted as suggesting that the price-cost test is 'as a rule' the tool used to assess the legality of all rebates, including exclusivity rebates.[92] A reflection will need to take place on whether this judgment needs to be read in the specific context of the case, where the Commission decision in itself dedicated approximately 150 pages to the price-cost test, or rather as outlining a rule of general application.

To conclude, the ongoing debate on the draft Guidelines has certainly shown that there is a plurality of views concerning the legal test of Article 102 TFEU and its practical implementation. Having promoted such an open debate is itself a success of the Guidelines initiative and additional reflections will certainly follow before the project is finalised. The Commission expects that once adopted, the Guidelines will enhance legal certainty and increase predictability in the application of Article 102 TFEU to exclusionary abuses, to the benefit of businesses and consumers alike. But of course, the Guidelines will not mark the end of the debate on the legal standard to enforce Article 102 as the definitive word on the interpretation of the law on abuse of dominance remains with the EU Courts.

89. As indicated in *supra* n. 12, when applied to retroactive rebates (including exclusivity rebates), the price-cost test is very sensitive to small variations in the so-called contestable share. The calculation of the contestable share is also in itself subject to significant conceptual and practical difficulties, and unlike other parameters in the test, it is not based on price and cost values of the dominant firm itself, *see, e.g.*, Calzolari and Denicolò: 'Actual volume and price are typically easy to observe. The dominant firm's cost must be estimated, but this poses the same problems as in standard predatory pricing tests. Over the years, antitrust authorities and the courts have come to cope with these problems. The estimation of the contestable demand, by contrast, is a very difficult problem that arises specifically when the [price-cost] test is applied [to retroactive rebates].'
90. It has been estimated on the basis of the proceedings in the Intel case that the use of the price-cost test in that case resulted in a delay of approximately two years (*see* Wouter P.J. Wils, *The Judgment of the EU General Court in Intel and the So-Called More Economic Approach to Abuse of Dominance*, World Competition: Law and Economics Review, Volume 37, Issue 4 (December 2014), p. 435). These figures are consistent with estimates from DG COMP based on the timeline of the Qualcomm predation case, according to which it emerges that it took three requests for information and fifteen months to collect the data to run the price-cost test before the Statement of Objections, and another two requests for information (among which one by decision, which was challenged before the EU courts) and sixteen months to collect the data after the Statement of Objections, leading to refinements in the test that were incorporated in a Supplementary Statement of Objections.
91. *See also* 2023 Policy Brief, p. 7. For the avoidance of doubt, these conclusions do not hold as regards predation and margin squeeze, where the use of the price-cost test would normally be necessary to reach a finding of infringement; and as regards non-exclusivity rebates, where the application of the test is as a rule informative from an economic perspective (*see* Motta and Fumagalli, p. 3, 'Price-cost tests are crucial evidence for the practices which likely include profit sacrifice, such as predation, selective price cuts and quantity rebates, i.e., all forms of discounts which do not reference rivals.').
92. Judgment of 24 October 2024, *Commission v. Intel Corporation*, Case C-240/22 P, EU:C:2024:915, paras 176 and 181.

CHAPTER 13

Some Recommendations for an Effects-Based Framework for the Enforcement of Article 102

Luc Peeperkorn[*]

1 INTRODUCTION

The title of the panel in which I participated was *Objectives of Article 102 and general framework of analysis*. As might be expected with such a title, a number of interrelated topics were discussed, in particular the role played by the 2008 Article 102 Guidance,[1] the consumer welfare objective and the (limited) role of wider societal goals, the importance of the As Efficient Competitor (AEC) principle and AEC test, the relevance of a by object category under Article 102 and the perceived practical difficulties of enforcement under the effects-based approach.[2]

In this contribution, I will discuss these topics in the light of the recent case law. The section on each topic concludes with one or more recommendations for the

* The opinions expressed are strictly personal. While I previously worked for the European Commission, nothing in this chapter represents the views of the European Commission, DG COMP or any other institution, entity, person, etc. I have no interests to declare except my own interest, as a European consumer, in a coherent and effective EU competition policy.
I would like to thank my fellow panellists and participants at the GCLC Annual Conference for the stimulating discussions and for their valuable comments. All errors and omissions are mine.

1. Guidance on the Commission's enforcement priorities in applying Article 82 of the EC Treaty to abusive exclusionary conduct by dominant undertakings (2008 Guidance), OJ C 45/7 of 24.2.2009.
2. In our panel, we also discussed the possibility that enforcement against exploitative abuses is becoming increasingly important. While I agree that intervention against exploitative abuse may indeed become more important in the enforcement of Art. 102, in view of entrenched dominant positions and quasi monopolies arising in the tech sector in particular, in this contribution I will only cover exclusionary abuses.

Commission's future Article 102 Guidelines. My aim is to contribute to the development of a coherent effects-based enforcement of the EU competition rules.

I originally intended to base this contribution on the draft Article 102 Guidelines (draft GL) that the Commission published for comments in the summer of 2024.[3] However, the draft GL offer very few useful elements for developing a coherent and effective effects-based policy. This contribution therefore refers only occasionally to the draft GL.

2 THE ROLE OF THE 2008 ARTICLE 102 GUIDANCE

The history of EU competition policy is the story of a gradual shift away from a focus on restrictions of the freedom of action of market participants, aimed at protecting the competitive process as such, to a focus on the effects of practices on the market, linked to a recognition that the goal should be the protection of consumer welfare.

This shift from a form-based and more legalistic approach, applied from the 1970s to the 1990s, to an effects-based and more economic approach, took place around the turn of the century, first in the new area of merger control and the application of Article 101 to supply and distribution agreements.[4] The effects-based approach was subsequently introduced for the application of Article 101 to other common types of agreements, in particular for horizontal cooperation agreements and technology transfer agreements. The shift came last to the application of Article 102, with the Commission's Microsoft decision of 2004[5] and the adoption of its Article 102 Guidance in 2008 (2008 Guidance).

In the 2008 Guidance, the Commission developed a full-blown effects-based approach for the enforcement of Article 102 against exclusionary conduct by dominant firms, including an efficiency defence aligned with Article 101(3). The Court of Justice (CoJ) essentially upheld this approach in its seminal *Post Danmark I* and *Intel* judgments and in subsequent judgments, such as *Post Danmark II, Slovak Telekom, SEN, Unilever Italia, European Superleague, Google Shopping* and the final *Commission v. Intel* judgment, it further refined the effects-based approach for the assessment of exclusionary conduct under Article 102.[6]

3. Draft Guidelines on the application of Article 102 of the Treaty on the Functioning of the European Union to abusive exclusionary conduct by dominant undertakings; found at https://competition-policy.ec.europa.eu/public-consultations/2024-article-102-guidelines_en (last accessed on 2 July 2025).
4. For a more extensive analysis of this shift from a form-based to an effects-based approach in EU competition policy, *see* Luc Peeperkorn, *The Effects-Based Approach: Still Just as Necessary for an Effective and Coherent EU Competition Policy*, Chapter 1 in *The Transformation of EU Competition Law: Next Generation Issues*, Adina Claici, Assimakis Komninos and Denis Waelbroeck (eds), Wolters Kluwer 2023.
5. Commission Decision 2007/53/EC of 24 March 2004, confirmed by the General Court in Case T-201/04 *Microsoft v. Commission* [2007] ECR II-3601.
6. Case C-209/10 *Post Danmark A/S v. Konkurrencerådet* (Post Denmark I), judgment of the CoJ (Grand Chamber) of 27 March 2012, ECLI:EU:C:2012:172; Case C-413/14 P *Intel v. Commission* (Intel), judgment of the CoJ (Grand Chamber) of 6 September 2017, ECLI:EU:C:2017:632; Case C-23/14 *Post Danmark A/S v. Konkurrencerådet* (Post Denmark II), judgment of the CoJ of 6 October 2015, ECLI:EU:C:2015:651; Case C-165/19 P *Slovak Telekom v. Commission* (Slovak

In view of the refinements to the effects-based approach made by the Court of Justice in the last fifteen years, the European Commission's initiative to issue guidelines on exclusionary abuses is both timely and welcome. What is however disappointing is that, instead of embracing the effects-based approach as confirmed and refined by the Court, the Commission seems mainly occupied with an unfortunate attempt to roll back that approach. Its draft GL, which displays a biased reading of the case law, is a prime example of the Commission's apparent ambition to roll back the effects-based approach.[7]

In fact, on several occasions since the adoption of the 2008 Guidance the Commission has proved unwilling to defend and apply its own Guidance. In the same vein, whereas the Union Courts have referred to the 2008 Guidance numerous times in their judgments, the Commission has avoided referring to it in its own decisions ever since 2009.

This unwillingness to fully apply or refer to the 2008 Guidance is also reflected in the Commission's description of the 2008 Guidance as *merely setting out the Commission's approach as to the choice of cases that it intends to pursue as a matter of priority*.[8] It is true that the title and initial paragraphs of the 2008 Guidance speak about a priority-setting document. However, it is also true that the 2008 Guidance was intended to set out enforcement principles for the assessment of exclusionary conduct by dominant companies.[9] In fact, there is nothing in the 2008 Guidance that can be used as a priority-setting instrument: no reference to a quick scan or anything similar that could help to select cases before investing resources in them to reach a final decision. In short, and despite its title, the 2008 Guidance was intended to provide guidance on how to assess exclusionary conduct.

Telekom), judgment of the CoJ of 25 March 2021, EU:C:2021:239; Case C-377/20 *Servizio Elettrico Nazionale v. Autorità Garante della Concorrenza e del Mercato* (SEN), judgment of the CoJ of 12 May 2022, ECLI:EU:C:2022:379; Case C–680/20 *Unilever Italia v. Autorità Garante della Concorrenza e del Mercato* (Unilever Italia), judgment of the CoJ of 19 January 2023, ECLI:EU:C:2023:33; Case C–333/21 *European Superleague Company v. Fédération internationale de football association* (European Superleague), judgment of the CoJ (Grand Chamber) of 21 December 2023, ECLI:EU:C:2023:1011; Case C–48/22 P *Google and Alphabet v. Commission* (Google Shopping), judgment of the CoJ (Grand Chamber) of 10 September 2024, ECLI:EU:C:2024:726; Case C–240/22 P *Commission v. Intel* (Commission v. Intel), judgment of the CoJ of 24 October 2024, ECLI:EU:C:2024:915.

7. Oxera's submission to the consultation provides a fair and extensive commentary on the draft GL: https://www.oxera.com/insights/reports/oxeras-response-to-the-public-consultation-on-the-article-102-draft-guidelines/ (last accessed on 2 July 2025). *See also* my submission https://www.linkedin.com/posts/luc-peeperkorn-0527b2aa_submission-regarding-the-draft-article-102-activity-7262111022948265984-sCJg?utm_source=share&utm_medium=member_desktop (last accessed on 2 July 2025).
8. *See*, for instance, the Commission's press release announcing the call for evidence for its future guidelines, its Communication amending the 2008 Guidance, as well as its Competition Policy Brief of March 2023, found at https://competition-policy.ec.europa.eu/antitrust-and-cartels/legislation/application-article-102-tfeu_en (last accessed on 2 July 2025).
9. *See also* §8 of the 2008 Guidance, which speaks of *the general enforcement principles* set out in the document.

Recommendation 1: It would be appropriate to use the 2008 Guidance as a starting point and basis for the future Article 102 Guidelines.[10] This is not to minimise the need to update the text in light of more recent case law, enforcement experience and market developments, but it would ensure that the many parts of the 2008 Guidance that set out a coherent policy, and which were already good law at the time, or have become so in the meantime, are retained in the new Guidelines. This applies in particular to the sections of the 2008 Guidance on market power and dominance, on the general test for anti-competitive foreclosure, on the application of the AEC principle to all price-based conduct, and to the sections on exclusive purchasing and rebates, tying and bundling and predatory pricing.

3 THE GOAL OF EU COMPETITION POLICY

That the goal of Article 101 is to protect competition for the benefit of the consumers of the products(s) in question can be easily deduced from the text of the Article itself. The second and third conditions of Article 101(3) make clear that as long as consumers benefit from a restriction of competition and the restriction is indispensable for producing the efficiencies responsible for the consumer benefit, an agreement that restricts competition is allowed. It is allowed even though the process of competition may be harmed and, for that matter, even if other Union objectives, such as employment or economic and social cohesion or balanced regional development, may be harmed. This also means that an agreement can only be prohibited under Article 101 in cases where the conditions of Article 101(3) are not fulfilled, that is where the restriction of competition harms the consumers of the product(s) in question and/or the agreement is not indispensable to obtain the efficiencies. This is also expressed in various Commission guidelines – *see* in particular the Article 101(3) Guidelines and the recently adopted Horizontal Cooperation Guidelines – and in the Commission's enforcement practice.[11]

That the four conditions of Article 101(3) are not only cumulative but also exhaustive, i.e., when the conditions are met, the exception is applicable and cannot be made dependent on any other condition, is neatly summarised in paragraph 42 of the Article 101(3) Guidelines: *Goals pursued by other Treaty provisions can be taken into account to the extent that they can be subsumed under the four conditions of Article*

10. The changes to the 2008 Guidance introduced by the Commission's Communication amending the 2008 Guidance are in large part superfluous and/or based on misunderstandings, and not useful and therefore better ignored. *See* my submission to the call for evidence referred to in footnote 7.
11. Guidelines on the application of Article 81(3) of the Treaty, OJ C 101/97, 27.4.2004, point 13 and Guidelines on the applicability of Article 101 of the Treaty on the Functioning of the European Union to horizontal co-operation agreements, OJ C 259, 21.7.2023, point 9. *See also* point 5 of the Guidelines on vertical restraints, OJ C 248, 30.6.2022 and point 5 of the Guidelines on the application of Article 101 of the Treaty on the Functioning of the European Union to technology transfer agreements, OJ C 89/3, 28.3.2014.

101(3). In other words, positive effects that contribute to other goals, for instance, positive environmental effects resulting from a potentially anti-competitive agreement between competitors, can only be taken into account under Article 101(3) to the extent that the positive effects benefit the relevant consumers.

That the goal of Article 102 is also to protect competition in the interest of consumers in the relevant market(s) is not only clear from the constant reminders from the Union Courts that the two Articles should *be interpreted and applied consistently* (*see*, for example, *European Superleague* §119) but also from explicit statements in recent case law relating exclusively to Article 102.

For instance, in *SEN* (§§44 and 46), the Court of Justice, referring to its *Post Denmark I* and *Intel* judgments among others, states that (underlining added): *Among these rules, the purpose of Article 102 TFEU more specifically is, according to settled case-law, to prevent conduct of a undertaking in a dominant position that has the effect, to the detriment of consumers, of hindering, through recourse to means or resources different from those governing normal competition, maintenance of the degree of competition existing in the market or the growth of that competition ... To that effect, as the Court has held, that provision seeks to sanction not only practices likely to cause direct harm to consumers but also those which cause them harm indirectly by undermining an effective structure of competition ... It follows that, as observed in essence by the Advocate General in point 100 of his Opinion, the well-being of both intermediary and final consumers must be regarded as the ultimate objective warranting the intervention of competition law in order to penalise abuse of a dominant position within the internal market or a substantial part of that market.* And in its *European Superleague* judgment (§124), referring among others to its *SEN* judgment (underlining added): .... *the purpose of that provision is to prevent competition from being restricted to the detriment of the public interest, individual undertakings and consumers, by sanctioning the conduct of undertakings in a dominant position that has the effect of hindering competition on the merits and is thus likely to cause direct harm to consumers, or which causes them harm indirectly by hindering or distorting that competition*.

It can thus be concluded that, as a matter of law, the Commission, the national competition authorities (NCAs) and national courts, when they apply EU competition law, are not free to replace the consumer welfare goal with a total welfare goal or to weigh the consumer welfare goal against other policy goals.[12] And it is thus justified and appropriate for the Commission and NCAs to focus in their cases on protecting competition and preventing the negative effects of market power in the interest of customers in the relevant market(s).

This is not to deny or ignore that the EU and the world face many other problems than the in-market effects of market power, most prominently the climate crisis, but

12. For a similar reasoning for the assessment of mergers, *see* Commission Decision in Case M.8084 – *Bayer/Monsanto* of 21.3.2018, paras 3010-3029, and Commissioner Vestager's response to petitions published in August 2017, https://ec.europa.eu/commission/presscorner/detail/en/IP_18_2282 (last accessed on 2 July 2025). Both texts make clear that non-competition concerns protected by other EU or national rules on human health, food safety, consumer protection and environmental and climate protection are of great importance but cannot provide the basis for a merger assessment.

also, for instance, security, poverty, unemployment, concerns about privacy in the digital world, the deplorable treatment of animals in factory farming, etc.

In view of these wider and often more important societal problems and a widespread dissatisfaction with the speed at which governments and intergovernmental organisations take action to address these problems, it is not surprising that there is a push to allow private firms to help solve these problems and for competition authorities and courts when dealing with competition cases, to focus not only on 'in-market' effects (negative and positive) but to also take into account wider societal interests, i.e., 'out-of-market' effects.

As explained above, however, there is limited scope under EU competition law to take other goals into account. Contrary to what some proponents of a society-wide balancing test argue, focussing only on in-market effects does not imply that EU competition policy fails to comply with the requirement, set out in Articles 7-13 of the Treaty on the Functioning of the European Union, to take into account the goals mentioned in Article 3 of the Treaty on European Union, including sustainable development. That requirement is respected by taking into account the negative and positive effects of conduct on other goals to the extent that those effects either harm or benefit consumers in the relevant market. It is only such in-market weighing of effects which can and should be done by EU competition policy.[13]

That there is only limited scope under EU competition law to take other policy goals into account is not only clear legally, from the text of Article 101 and the judgments of the Court of Justice, as explained above; but it is also appropriate and fortunate from an economic and effectiveness perspective.

It was Jan Tinbergen, the first Nobel Prize winner in economics, who demonstrated that it is optimal to have (at least) as many policy instruments as goals and to allocate one goal to each instrument.[14] The various goals can then be achieved by applying the appropriate mix of policy instruments, where necessary complemented by a hierarchy of instruments and goals.

Although this insight was developed some decades ago, it has not been superseded or lost any of its relevance, as demonstrated by Jean Tirole, another winner of the Nobel Prize in economics, in a recent article.[15] He warns convincingly about the many risks of widening agencies' missions to include climate change, inequality and other societal concerns ('mission creep'), using competition policy as an example. Among other risks, Tirole mentions the competition authority's lack of legitimacy to balance societal goals, its lack of capability to verify and weigh diverse claims and effects, the dispersion of responsibility and reduced accountability that results from requiring agencies to pursue multiple goals, as well as the increase in legal uncertainty for firms.

13. For some suggestions on how EU competition policy could improve this in-market assessment where sustainability agreements are concerned, *see* ss VIII and IX of Luc Peeperkorn, *Competition and Sustainability: What Can Competition Policy Do?*, Concurrences No. 4-2020.
14. On the virtues of having one goal per policy and having as many policies as goals: J. Tinbergen, *On the Theory of Economic Policy* (North Holland Publishing Company, 1952).
15. Jean Tirole, *Socially Responsible Agencies*, Competition Law & Policy Debate, 7(4), 2022 https://doi.org/10.4337/clpd.2022.04.05 (last accessed on 2 July 2025).

In other words, while efforts to integrate additional goals into EU competition policy and to incorporate a societal balancing exercise may be well-intentioned and may appear to offer a means to allow competition law to 'do more' and 'be part of the solution', in reality, they are likely to throw the baby out with the bath water. Attempting to assess conduct and agreements by reference to multiple goals, and to weigh up their effects across multiple groups and markets or for society at large would make the application of competition law more complex, more costly, slower and less certain.

A requirement to take out-of-market effects into account would undermine the predictability, rigour and uniformity of EU competition policy, not just because it is very difficult to weigh different interests and goals in a particular case, but also because of the large number of actors (Commission, NCAs, national courts, firms required to self-assess) and the very large number of agreements/mergers/conducts concerned. Weighing the pros and cons for one group, the consumers in the relevant market, can usually be done by asking those consumers which counterfactual they prefer. However, that type of survey would not be possible if different groups and interests were at stake; in that case, cumbersome quantification would be required. This loss of rigour and certainty might not be a problem for very big firms, with their armies of lawyers, economists and lobbyists, but it would harm the many smaller firms and, behind them, their customers and European consumers, all of whom depend on a rigorous competition policy for their protection. It would thus be a bad choice from an effective enforcement point of view.[16]

However, the choice between a test based only on in-market effects and one that also includes out-of-market effects is not merely a technical choice between different cost-benefit analyses and the impact on the effectiveness of enforcement.[17] The basic assumption underlying competition policy is that competition forces firms to listen to their customers and to make products that customers want, at the best possible price and quality. Without competition, or where competition is restricted, some firms will have a degree of market power, allowing them to increase their profits at the expense of their customers, by increasing the price and/or lowering the quality or innovativeness of their products. This means that, as a rule, competition authorities only need to intervene where competition is distorted by certain conduct or agreements between firms. As a result, competition policy enforcement can be limited to intervening on an ad-hoc/case-by-case basis.

However, a case-by-case approach is not suited to a scenario in which it is necessary to (also) take out-of-market effects into account, because in most cases such external effects will have no relation to the existence or use of market power. Instead, negative external effects will result from the legal production and consumption of certain products, and they may arise in both competitive markets and in less competitive ones.

---

16. Luc Peeperkorn, *Competition and Sustainability: What Can Competition Policy Do?*, Concurrences No. 4-2020, pp. 40-52, and a chapter about which test to apply in competition policy in the section *Agency Outlook: European Union*, in S. Holmes, D. Middelschulte and M. Snoep (eds), *Competition Law, Climate Change & Environmental Sustainability*, Concurrences, 2021.
17. The remainder of this section is in good part taken from Luc Peeperkorn, *Competition Policy Is Not a Stopgap!*, Journal of European Competition Law & Practice, 12(6), June 2021, pp. 415-418 https://doi.org/10.1093/jeclap/lpab039 (last accessed on 2 July 2025).

For instance, if a manufacturer changes its distribution system, this may have an effect not only on the attractiveness and availability of the products in question, but also on the transport needs of the firms involved and of their customers, and thereby on the external effects created by those transport needs. For example, if the new distributors are located further outside city centres, this may make it less costly to supply the distributors, but it may require customers to travel further. While the in-market price effects may be absent or *de minimis*, under a broad societal welfare test the out-of-market effects may bring the agreements within Article 101(1) and onto the radar of a competition authority.

In other words, in order to address these external effects, whether negative or positive, a competition authority will no longer be able to rely on ad hoc/case-by-case interventions, assuming that competition will lead to satisfactory outcomes in most markets. This is the reason why an out-of-market effects test is fundamentally at odds with the nature and purpose of competition policy. Net negative external effects may also arise in situations where the firms in question have no market power. The firms themselves, when they self-assess their conduct or agreements, and competition authorities and national courts, when they have to decide on the legality of the conduct or agreements, might often have to intervene in situations where the firms involved are incapable of harming their customers by increasing the price or reducing the quality of their products, i.e., where there are no negative in-market effects. In other words, competition policy would be turned into an ill-suited form of market regulation.

This far-reaching consequence has so far been conveniently ignored by the proponents of taking external effects into account, who instead focus on demands from industry to widen the efficiency defence under (EU) competition law and limit the discussion to horizontal agreements, i.e., to allow the negative in-market effects of cooperation between competitors to be compensated by positive out-of-market effects.[18] However, it should be obvious that if the positive external effects of an agreement or conduct are to be taken into account, then any negative external effects should also be taken into account. Not only because the same agreement or conduct may create both positive and negative external effects, on the same or different aspects of sustainability, for instance, but also because it would not make sense to ignore negative external effects if the aim is to apply a societal balancing test. Firms should therefore be careful what they wish for.

This is not to say that, by keeping markets competitive and focussing on its core goal, competition and competition policy cannot play a useful indirect role in helping to achieve other policy goals, including those related to sustainability, the creation of high-quality employment, protecting the security of supply, etc. For instance, as sufficiently demonstrated elsewhere, competition spurs innovation, and it is widely recognised that innovation is key to addressing the climate crisis. Competition also forces firms to use scarce resources efficiently and to listen to consumers when they

18. Except for Simon Holmes: while mainly speaking about using Art. 101(3) 'as a shield' for anti-competitive sustainability agreements, he also speaks of using Art. 101(1) 'as a sword', *Climate Change, Sustainability, and Competition Law*, Journal of Antitrust Enforcement, 8(2), July 2020, pp. 354-405 https://doi.org/10.1093/jaenfo/jnaa006 (last accessed on 2 July 2025).

demand more sustainable products. In other words, by protecting competition, competition policy will support climate policy (and other sustainability goals) indirectly. However, it can only fulfil this role if it is applied coherently and is not used as a stopgap or excuse when governments fail to regulate appropriately.

> **Recommendation 2**: It would be appropriate and desirable for the future Article 102 Guidelines to clearly state that the goal of Article 102 is to protect competition in the interest of consumers in the relevant market and that negative and positive effects on other EU policy goals will only be taken into account to the extent that they either harm or benefit consumers in the relevant market. Nonetheless, it could be added that other policy goals may be taken into account for the purpose of priority setting ('giving a higher priority to pursuing a milk cartel than a caviar cartel').
>
> **Recommendation 3**: In the unfortunate event that the Commission decides that EU competition policy should also pursue other policy goals, either in general or only in certain circumstances – such as the suggestion in the Draghi report to introduce an additional security and resilience test for four sectors[19] – it is recommended, in order to avoid blunting the competition instrument, that the future Article 102 Guidelines should make a clear analytical distinction and separation between the competition test and the additional test(s). In that context, it would also be advisable to grant DG Competition more independent decision-making powers, allowing it to take decisions based only on competition grounds, and to reserve to the College of Commissioners the power to (occasionally) overrule those decisions based on a balancing with other specific goals and interests.

4 THE ROLE OF THE AS EFFICIENT COMPETITOR PRINCIPLE AND TEST

The Court of Justice has more than fully incorporated the AEC principle and test set out in the 2008 Guidance. I say more than fully because the Court has not only confirmed the essential function of the AEC principle and test for all pricing conduct but has also stressed the importance of the AEC principle for non-pricing conduct. For non-pricing conduct, this goes beyond what the 2008 Guidance requires.

In various judgments since *Post Denmark I* the Union Courts not only emphasise that Article 102 is not there ... *to ensure that competitors less efficient than the dominant undertaking should remain on the market* ... and that ... *competition on the merits may lead to the departure from the market or the marginalisation of competitors which are less efficient and so less attractive to consumers from the point of view of, among other*

19. *The future of European competitiveness, Part B | In-depth analysis and recommendations*, s. 2, Ch. 4, September 2024.

things, price, output, choice, quality or innovation ..., but also that *consequently* ..., *in order to find, in a given case, that conduct must be categorised as 'abuse of a dominant position', it is necessary, as a rule, to demonstrate, through the use of methods other than those which are part of competition on the merits between undertakings, that that conduct has the actual or potential effect of restricting that competition by excluding equally efficient competing undertakings from the market or markets concerned or by hindering their growth on those markets.*[20]

Whatever one may think about the usefulness and practicality of applying the AEC principle to all types of conduct and not just pricing conduct, it is crystal clear that the Union Courts consider that Article 102 is not there to protect competitors, and certainly not less-efficient competitors, but to protect competition in the interest of consumers in the relevant market(s). The AEC principle is now part of the acquis of EU competition law, at least for the purpose of establishing the abuse of a dominant position.

This brings us to the question of what this means in practice for pricing conduct and for non-pricing conduct, respectively.

4.1 How to Apply the As-Efficient Competitor Principle and Test to Pricing Conduct

In cases concerning pricing conduct, the Court of Justice has basically recognised that: (1) price competition is essential to create benefits for consumers; (2) consumers should also be able to benefit from price competition by dominant firms; and (3) Article 102 is not there to provide a price umbrella for less efficient competitors.

For pricing conduct, the AEC principle translates into the AEC test, as clearly expressed by the Court of Justice in, for instance, *SEN* (§80): *Regarding pricing conduct, which includes loyalty rebates, low-pricing practices in the form of selective or predatory prices and margin-squeezing practices, it is clear from the case-law that those practices must be assessed, as a general rule, using the 'as-efficient competitor' test.*[21]

In other words, as a general rule, pricing that is not capable of foreclosing as efficient competitors is not abusive. Only pricing that is capable of excluding as efficient competitors may be abusive. Stated differently, below-cost pricing may be abusive, pricing above cost will normally not be abusive.

To be clear, the Court of Justice, while stressing the importance of the AEC test for pricing conduct in general, does not make the test obligatory (*see*, for instance, *SEN* §81-82). Sufficiently reliable data may be lacking, and the authority may use alternative means to apply the AEC principle to pricing conduct, but it should still show that the conduct is capable of excluding as-efficient competitors. Until now I have not seen credible alternatives to the AEC test. The *Qualcomm Exclusivity* case, which the

20. *Commission v. Intel*, §175-176, underlining added, referring to *European Superleague* (§§126, 127 and 129) and referring indirectly to, among others, *Post Denmark I*, *Intel* and *Servizio Elettrico Nazionale*.
21. *See also* §181 of *Commission v. Intel*.

Commission lost before the General Court (GC), shows that there are no easy alternatives (for more detail, *see* section 6 below).[22]

To assess whether its pricing is below cost, the dominant firm, as confirmed by the case law, can normally take its own costs as the benchmark.[23] This is obviously practical and helps to provide the necessary degree of legal certainty, given that a dominant firm may be held liable for its pricing conduct.

However, pricing above its actual costs does not provide an absolute safe harbour to a dominant firm. The Court of Justice gives competition authorities some leeway to intervene also in cases where a dominant firm prices above its actual costs.

In *SEN* the Court of Justice specifies that the dominant firm may have to compare its price not necessarily to its actual cost level, but to what its cost level would be if it were not benefitting from its dominant position, i.e., not benefitting from economies of scale and scope, network effects, etc. In §78 of *SEN*, the Court states that an abuse can also be found where a dominant firm engages in a pricing practice ... *that a hypothetical competitor – which, although it is as efficient, does not occupy a dominant position on the market in question – is unable to adopt, because that practice relies on the use of resources or means inherent to the holding of such a position.* This is an expansion of what was already foreseen in §24 of the 2008 Guidance. Where §24 speaks only about taking demand-related advantages, such as network effects, into account, the Court refers to all advantages linked to the dominant position.

This brings, for instance, *Post Denmark II* – in which Post Danmark held scale advantages over its competitors, due to its legal monopoly over part of the postal services market – back into the fold of the AEC test and principle. The CoJ observed that, because of Post Danmark's legal monopoly over part of the market, it was very difficult, if not impossible, for entrants to become as efficient, and that in such a situation there may be a good reason to intervene against the rebate scheme of a dominant firm, even though it cannot be shown that the effective price is below cost. However, this does require a finding that economies of scale are indeed an important feature of the market concerned and that the relevant competitors are currently below the minimum efficient scale. In addition, it would also be relevant to establish that the number of customers is high enough for there to be a coordination problem between them, making it unlikely or impossible for them to ensure a sufficient competitive supply of the input in question.

Even in such a scenario, applying a price-cost test using actual costs will still be useful: if the price is only marginally above cost, it is more likely that the pricing conduct is responsible, in combination with the deprivation of economies of scale, for anti-competitively foreclosing competitors, whereas such a conclusion may not be justified where the effective price is well above cost, in particular if the economies of scale are modest.

In addition to taking into account advantages linked to the dominant position, the Court of Justice also creates an opening to intervene against pricing above cost in cases

22. Case T-235/18 *Qualcomm v. Commission* (Qualcomm Exclusivity), judgment of the General Court of 15 June 2022, ECLI:EU:T:2022:358.
23. *See*, for instance, *Unilever Italia*, §56.

where the dominant firm's conduct forecloses potential competitors, i.e., where it hinders the entry into the market of new competitors. In *European Superleague*, the Court of Justice states (§131): *In addition, conduct may be categorised as 'abuse of a dominant position' not only where it has the actual or potential effect of restricting competition on the merits by excluding equally efficient competing undertakings from the market(s) concerned, but also where it has been proven to have the actual or potential effect – or even the object – of impeding potentially competing undertakings at an earlier stage, through the placing of obstacles to entry or the use of other blocking measures or other means different from those which govern competition on the merits, from even entering that or those market(s) and, in so doing, preventing the growth of competition therein to the detriment of consumers, by limiting production, product or alternative service development or innovation.*

This makes good sense from an economic point of view. Where the competitor of the dominant firm is not already established in the market but only a potential competitor or a recent entrant, it may not yet be able to make credible offers to customers. If customers fear that in due course the entrant may not be able to deliver, for instance, because it has not yet obtained sufficient demand to enter or stay in business, they could be persuaded to buy exclusively from the dominant firm, even though the price rebate offered in return for exclusivity is only minimal. The customer might do so in order to avoid the risk of not being able to fulfil all its requirements or the risk of being forced to purchase the remainder from the dominant firm at a higher, non-rebated price. For this fear to be realistic, there must be a coordination problem between the customers: the entrant's offer must lack credibility unless a certain number of customers have committed to purchase from it, and each customer must be too small for its individual demand, on its own, to make the entrant a credible supplier.[24]

In such a situation, an equally efficient entrant may be foreclosed, not because the dominant firm's effective price is so low as to make entry commercially unviable, but because customers are afraid to commit to buying from the entrant due to the risk of not being able to obtain (sufficient) supplies in the event that the entry does not materialise. While there is a pricing element, the foreclosure results from the inability of the entrant to make a credible offer and of individual customers to solicit a credible offer. In that case, it would not make sense to apply the AEC test. However, this does not seem to have been a common scenario in past Article 102 cases.

Finally, the possibility of finding an abuse could also be considered in cases where the dominant firm prices above cost but where the no-economic-sense test can be applied successfully. This test asks whether the dominant firm's conduct leads to avoidable losses or avoidable reductions in profit that only make commercial sense in view of the likely foreclosure effects. Avoidable losses imply pricing below cost and would not expand the possibilities of intervening above cost. However, taking into account reductions in profits that could have been avoided and which only make sense in view of the anti-competitive foreclosure, would make it possible to intervene also

24. *See* E. Elhauge and A. Wickelgren, *Robust Exclusion and Market Division Through Loyalty Discounts*, April 2014, paper presented at FTC/DOJ workshop on Conditional Pricing Practices, June 2014.

against pricing above cost. In *SEN* §77, there is a reference to the no-economic-sense test, indicating that such conduct is not competition on the merits.

It would however not be advisable to replace the AEC principle and test with the no-economic-sense test. That test is at best a possible useful extra. There are two good reasons for not applying the no-economic-sense test on its own, that test being essentially a 'sacrifice now and recoup later' test. The first is the practical difficulties associated with the test, which requires the authority or court to compare two hypothetical scenarios. Having to compare the profitability of the actual conduct as it would be without the resulting foreclosure effects with the profitability of alternative conducts that the dominant firm could have chosen to adopt, makes it not the most practical alternative. The second reason relates to the policy aim of preventing consumer harm. The focus of the AEC principle and AEC test is correctly on the potential loss of consumer welfare resulting from the foreclosure of efficient competitors, i.e., competitors that are able to compete head-on in terms of price and quality and thereby challenge the position of the dominant firm. In cases where that type of robust consumer harm is shown, it should not be possible to absolve the dominant firm's conduct by showing that the conduct did not entail a sacrifice but was the most profitable strategy even without the anti-competitive foreclosure effect.

4.2 How to Apply the As-Efficient Competitor Principle and Test to Non-pricing Conduct

Finally, what do the AEC principle and test mean for non-pricing conduct? As indicated by the case law cited at the beginning of this section, it is clear that the Court wants to apply the AEC principle also to non-pricing conduct. At the same time, it is accepted that the AEC test, which is a price-cost test, will generally not be useful or capable of application to non-pricing conduct.[25]

However, it is not very clear what the Court means when it speaks of applying the AEC principle to non-pricing conduct, beyond establishing likely anti-competitive foreclosure harming consumers. In principle, non-pricing conduct, such as exclusive purchasing obligations or tying or a refusal to deal, can foreclose both as- and more-efficient as well as less-efficient competitors. It therefore seems difficult to distinguish between non-pricing conduct that is only capable of foreclosing less-efficient competitors and conduct that is capable of foreclosing both as- and less-efficient competitors.

The replicability test proposed by Advocate General Rantos in his Opinion in the *SEN* case is useful, but different from the AEC principle.[26] It basically asks whether the conduct of the dominant firm can be replicated by non-dominant firms. Rantos states that, on the basis of the case law of the Court, exclusionary conduct of a dominant undertaking that can be replicated by equally efficient competitors does not constitute, in principle, conduct that may lead to anticompetitive foreclosure, and therefore

25. *See*, for instance, §57 of *Unilever Italia*, notwithstanding confusing language on the issue in §59.
26. Opinion of Advocate General Rantos, delivered on 9 December 2021 in case C-377/20, *Servizio Elettrico Nazionale*, ECLI:EU:C:2021:998, §§69-71.

cannot be abusive. It instead falls within the scope of competition on the merits. For instance, if also non-dominant firms can convince customers to agree to exclusive purchasing obligations because customers are willing and able to switch completely to an alternative supplier, there will be competition for the customer. In that case, it will at most be the duration of the obligations that raises concerns, not the exclusivity itself. Similarly, if also non-dominant firms can apply tying when selling different products, such tying cannot be abusive if undertaken by a dominant firm. In that case, competition will take place at the level of the tied bundle.

Recommendation 4: The future Article 102 Guidelines should recognise that the AEC principle is part of the assessment of abuse for all types of conduct and not just pricing conduct and that the Union Courts consider that Article 102 is not there to protect competitors, and certainly not less efficient competitors, but to protect competition in the interest of consumers in the relevant market(s).

Recommendation 5: The future Article 102 Guidelines should acknowledge that for all pricing conduct, including loyalty rebates, the AEC principle requires, as a general rule, the use of the AEC test.

Recommendation 6: It would be appropriate and useful for the future Article 102 Guidelines to describe clearly in which (exceptional) situations abuse may also be found where the dominant firm prices above its actual costs.

Recommendation 7: It would be appropriate and useful for the future Article 102 Guidelines to state clearly that the Commission interprets the Court's requirement to apply the AEC principle also to non-pricing conduct as a requirement to show likely anti-competitive foreclosure harming consumers.

5 PARALLELISM OF THE 'BY OBJECT' CONCEPT UNDER ARTICLES 101 AND 102

By applying and refining the effects-based approach adopted by the Commission in its 2008 Guidance, the Court of Justice has not only confirmed that approach; but it has also brought more consistency to the application of Articles 101 and 102.[27] Whether the exclusionary practice takes the form of an agreement or unilateral conduct, and whether it is assessed under Article 101 or 102, in both cases a prohibition can only follow, as a rule, if actual or potential anti-competitive effects are established. Further consistency was established when the Court of Justice confirmed, for the first time in *Post Denmark I*, that an efficiency defence is also available under Article 102. An escape from the prohibition of Article 102 is available if all the conditions for exemption are

27. On the need for and drive towards consistency between the application of Arts 101 and 102, *see*, for instance, Luc Peeperkorn, *Coherence in the Application of Articles 101 and 102: A Realistic Prospect or an Elusive Goal?* World Competition, 39(3) 2016, pp. 389-412 https://doi.org/10.54648/woco2016036 (last accessed on 2 July 2025).

fulfilled, and these conditions completely mirror the four conditions of Article 101(3), as was already suggested in the 2008 Guidance.

Until recently, it was not clear whether the Court of Justice would also confirm the existence of a distinction between 'by object' and 'by effect' infringements under Article 102, as we know it for Article 101 from the text of the Article itself. In the 2008 Guidance (point 22), the Commission already stated that, although, as a rule, conduct can only be found abusive once an anti-competitive effect has been established, in the case of conduct that can only raise obstacles to competition and which creates no efficiencies, its anti-competitive effect may be inferred. This 'by object' type of conduct came to be known in subsequent Commission decisions as 'naked restrictions', and the Union Courts appeared to recognise the distinction. For instance, when the Court of Justice annulled the first judgment of the General Court in *Intel*, it made the distinction and did not annul the part of the judgment concerning the naked restrictions in that case.

In its 2023 *European Superleague* and *ISU*[28] judgments, the Court of Justice developed a high degree if not full symmetry between the 'by object' approach under Articles 101 and 102. In those cases, the Court of Justice was asked to rule respectively on FIFA's and UEFA's conduct and agreements governing the prior authorisation of certain international football competitions and the participation therein of professional football clubs and players and on the ISU's prior authorisation and eligibility rules for organising and taking part in skating competitions.

The judgments make clear that also under Article 102, with regard to unilateral conduct, the distinction between 'by object' and 'by effect' applies, and that also under Article 102 the 'by object' category, while not an exception, should be defined in a strict way. The Court of Justice refers to conduct that infringes Article 102 *by its very existence* and *by its very nature.*[29] The Court indicates that conduct that is abusive by its very existence/nature must also be 'by object', if only because Articles 101 and 102 can apply simultaneously to the same conduct (as was the case in *European Superleague*) and the two Articles must (therefore) be interpreted consistently.[30] It is therefore not surprising that the Court seems to suggest that, also under Article 102, to find an abuse 'by object', it is necessary to look into the content, context and objectives of the conduct, i.e., the same three aspects that are well-established for finding a 'by object' restriction under Article 101.[31] Finally, the Court of Justice also makes clear that unilateral conduct and coordination that is found to be 'by object' under Article 102 and Article 101 respectively can only escape the prohibitions laid down in those Articles if all the conditions for exemption are fulfilled, and, as already stated, those conditions are, since *Post Denmark I*, exactly the same under both Articles.[32]

---

28. Case C-124/21 P *International Skating Union v. Commission* (ISU), judgment of the CoJ (Grand Chamber) of 21 December 2023, ECLI:EU:C:2023:1012.
29. Respectively *ISU* §127 and *European Superleague* §185. For instance, in *Post Denmark I* and *Intel* and *SEN* the CoJ already made clear that exclusive purchasing and loyalty rebates do not fall into the by object category.
30. *ISU* §128, *European Superleague* §186.
31. *ISU* §130.
32. Based on the Art. 101 case law, we know that there are two forms of objective justification. The first is the so-called necessity test (the *Wouters* route), as a result of which agreements can be considered to fall outside Art. 101(1). The second is the possibility of an individual exemption

European Superleague and *ISU* may therefore be seen as another step by the Court towards a consistent application of Articles 101 and 102, thereby following in the footsteps of *Post Denmark I* and *Intel*, which were also Grand Chamber judgments. It is also clear that the Court is not convinced by the argument that there is no place for a 'by object' category under Article 102, on the basis that, unlike Article 101, the text of the Treaty does not distinguish between conduct 'by effect' and 'by object'. This should not come as a surprise, as in *Post Denmark I* the Court already read an efficiency defence based on Article 101(3) into Article 102, although the text of Article 102 is silent on that issue also.[33]

Recommendation 8: It would be appropriate and useful for the future Article 102 Guidelines to reflect and support a consistent approach to the application of Articles 101 and 102 and, in particular, to incorporate the 'by object' concept and the distinction between conduct that is abusive 'by object' and conduct that is abusive 'by effect'.

Recommendation 9: It would be appropriate and useful for the future Article 102 Guidelines to characterise conduct falling within the 'by object' category as conduct that is devoid of the potential to create efficiencies, and to provide examples, also in order to limit the temptation for [other] enforcement authorities to define the 'by object' category too widely.

under Art. 101(3). In *European Superleague* (§§185-186), the CoJ has 'clarified' its previous case law by stating that the Wouters route is not available for practices classified as 'by object', no matter whether they are classified as such under Art. 101 or under Art. 102. *See* Luc Peeperkorn and Frank Wijckmans, 'By Object' or Not 'By Object': Issues Resolved?, E.C.L.R., 46(4) 2025.

33. For a view that there is no 'by object' category under Art. 102, *see* Pinar Akman, *A Critical Inquiry into 'Abuse' in EU Competition Law*, Oxford Journal of Legal Studies, 44(2), 2024, pp. 405-433, pp. 422-424 https://doi.org/10.1093/ojls/gqae008 (last accessed on 2 July 2025), in which the author refers to §435 of the General Court's judgment in Case T-612/17 *Google and Alphabet v. Commission*, EU:T:2021:763. However, that judgment precedes the judgments of the CoJ (Grand Chamber) in *European Superleague* and *ISU*. In addition, the author's reasoning (in footnote 104) that the Court could not have intended to refer in the *European Superleague* judgment to a 'by object' category of conduct under Art. 102, as this would conflict with the Court's reference in the same judgments to the possibility for the dominant undertaking to defend its conduct under the efficiency defence is based on a misunderstanding. Finding that a particular conduct or agreement is abusive or restrictive 'by object' simply means that the anti-competitive effects can be presumed. It does not exclude the possibility for the firms(s) in question to defend their conduct or agreement using the efficiency defence. If they substantiate that the conduct or agreement creates efficiencies and is indispensable to create those efficiencies and that the efficiencies benefit the consumers of the product(s) in question, it is for the competition authority or court to assess whether the pro-competitive effects and benefits for the consumers outweigh the anti-competitive effects. The authority will do this by verifying the pro-competitive effects and by substantiating the anti-competitive effects. In other words, the by object classification essentially inverts the order in which anti- and pro-competitive effects have to be shown by the two sides. *See* Luc Peeperkorn, *Defining 'by object' restrictions*, Concurrences No. 3-2015, pp. 40-50, point 12.

6 ENFORCEABILITY: IS THE BAR BECOMING TOO HIGH?

It is *bon ton* in some circles to attribute difficulties in enforcing the competition rules and Article 102 in particular to the effects-based approach.[34] It is argued that the effects-based approach, although in principle it leads to correct outcomes, is too cumbersome and resource-intensive, resulting in slower decision-making and greater legal uncertainty, whereas form-based rules are easier to apply and provide more certainty.

Concerns about the speed and effectiveness of Article 102 investigations are not unreasonable, in view of the average time of around four years to adopt Article 102 decisions. However, linking this to the effects-based approach is based on a misunderstanding consisting of comparing muddle with model, i.e., comparing the actual duration and complexity of cases under the current effects-based approach with the duration and simplicity that could theoretically be achieved under a different more form-based approach.

Experience of the form-based approach applied to vertical agreements between the 1970s and 1990s showed that, in practice, that approach led to a high level of legal uncertainty, as well as unjustified restrictions on the commercial freedom of firms. That experience is relevant for Article 102 because exclusionary conduct is in most cases vertical in nature: the exclusion generally takes the form of the dominant firm pushing its customers or suppliers not to do business with its competitors. Moreover, the average time taken by the Commission to adopt Article 102 decisions in the five-year period before the adoption of the 2008 Guidance was actually longer than the average time taken in the five-year period after the adoption of the effects-based approach.

The average time taken to adopt Article 102 decisions is indeed too long, but the cause is not the effects-based approach. In my experience, the effects-based approach, including the need to formulate a theory of harm, helps to focus and structure the investigation. The long duration of the investigation and decision-making process is explained by other factors. In particular, the often complex and non-public nature of unilateral conduct combined with the unwillingness of dominant firms to cooperate, and the increasing number of procedural safeguards of the parties' rights of defence required by the Union Courts. And last but not least, the decision-making process within the Commission involves multiple departments and checks and balances which create bottlenecks in the decision-making process.

In this context, it is also relevant that the judgments in the Article 102 cases that the Commission has lost on appeal do not indicate that those losses were the result of difficulties in applying the effects-based approach. Rather they resulted from obvious mistakes and a general unwillingness to properly apply the Commission's own 2008 Guidance and integrate the effects-based approach in the overall legal assessment.

34. *See*, for instance, Fernando Castillo de la Torre, *Is the Effects-Based Approach Too Cumbersome?*, Chapter 9 in *The Transformation of EU Competition Law: Next Generation Issues*, Adina Claici, Assimakis Komninos and Denis Waelbroeck (eds), Wolters Kluwer 2023.

For example, *Qualcomm Exclusivity* was lost because the Commission did not want to use the AEC test, i.e., did not want to apply a price-cost test in its decision. The Commission preferred to use other means to show why the rebates offered to Apple would lead to anti-competitive foreclosure on the market for LTE chipsets. After the General Court had indicated that such foreclosure was unlikely on the market of LTE chipsets in general, given that Apple did not have any alternative supplier to turn to for the specific LTE chipsets used in iPhones, which formed 90% of the total demand of Apple for LTE chipsets, the Commission realised it had missed a good opportunity to apply the AEC test. It could (and should) have argued that Apple's demand for chipsets for its iPhones was an uncontestable part of its demand and that the loss of rebates over this part and the remaining part of chipsets for tablets, in case Apple would switch supplier for the chipsets for tablets, meant that the effective price for the latter 10% of its (contestable) demand was very low and below cost. When the Commission brought this up and suggested applying such a price-cost test at the appeal hearing, the Court ruled that it was too late to bring new arguments.

The part of the *Google Android* decision relating to exclusivity rebates was lost not because of the difficulty of applying the AEC test but essentially because the Commission had not paid sufficient attention to the market coverage of the conduct, which was estimated by the General Court to have been between 0% and 5%.[35]

Lastly, in *Intel*, the Commission lost when the case came for the first time before the Court of Justice because it did not want to defend its effects-based approach but defended the case as a by object abuse. Later, when the General Court's judgment was annulled by the Court of Justice and the case was referred back to the General Court, the Commission lost again, basically because the General Court showed that the effects assessment had not been done properly: it again found a lack of attention to the market coverage rate and found that for certain periods prices had not been shown to be below the average avoidable cost (AAC) benchmark used by the Commission in its decision.[36]

That last defeat was particularly unfortunate: if the Commission had followed its own 2008 Guidance (in particular, §§43-44 thereof), it would have used the long-run average incremental cost or average total cost (LRAIC/ATC) as the upper-cost benchmark, which is about four times the AAC in that industry, which is characterised by heavy fixed investments. Using that benchmark, all pricing in all periods would have clearly been below cost and would have demonstrated that the conduct was capable of excluding as-efficient competitors. The AAC benchmark could still have been used in addition, to show that for most or certain periods Intel's pricing was even not rational but for the capability to foreclose. In other words, this case is a good example of what can go wrong if the authority is not willing to effectively integrate the effects-based approach in its legal assessment.

For the real antitrust aficionados: have a look at §1037 and footnote 1355 of the public version of the Commission decision. They indicate that the Commission saw the

35. Case T–604/18 *Google and Alphabet v. Commission* (*Google Android*), judgment of the General Court of 14 September 2022, ECLI:EU:T:2022:541.
36. Case T-286/09 RENV *Intel v. Commission* (Intel RENV), judgment of the General Court of 26 January 2022, ECLI:EU:T:2022:19.

option of using LRAIC as the cost benchmark, but did not make use of it: *In order to base its assessment on a conservative cost measure, that is to say a cost measure which is more favourable to Intel, the Commission for the purposes of the present procedure uses average avoidable costs (AAC) as a benchmark to assess the exclusionary effect of Intel's rebate schemes. ... Other cost benchmarks which also take into account fixed costs elements may be more appropriate. However because ability to foreclose as efficient competitors can in this instance be shown already using AAC, it is not necessary to further look into what the correct cost benchmark is for the case.*[37] This is what you get when the economists and lawyers working on a case do not talk to each other enough. Economists often prefer to use the AAC benchmark because pricing below AAC is not profit maximising, as it involves incurring avoidable losses, except if the conduct can foreclose competitors and the avoidable losses are a sacrifice that can be recouped later. However, from a legal point of view, in order to show that pricing is capable of excluding as-efficient competitors, it is sufficient to show that the price is below the higher benchmark of LRAIC/ATC. Being able to show that the price remained below AAC is just icing on the cake.

In conclusion, it is neither necessary nor useful to curtail the effects-based approach to improve the effectiveness of the enforcement of Article 102. Instead, the Commission can improve the effectiveness of its enforcement by improving how it integrates economic and legal aspects in its investigations and by reducing bottlenecks in its decision-making process.

In addition to the above, there is another thing that could be done to improve the effectiveness of the enforcement of Article 102, which relates to the distinction between direct and indirect exclusionary conduct and the practical problems of designing remedies in direct foreclosure cases.

Within the broad category of exclusionary conduct, it is useful to make a distinction between indirect (customer or input) foreclosure – where the dominant firm prevents or limits access by competitors to third-party upstream suppliers or downstream customers, for instance, by tying, bundling, predatory pricing, rebates, exclusive purchasing and exclusive sourcing – and direct input foreclosure – where the dominant firm refuses or obstructs (efficient) access by rivals to an input produced by the dominant firm or to an asset/facility owned by the dominant firm, and where the dominant firm is active both at the input level and, as a (potential) competitor, at the downstream level where the input is used.

In general, EU competition policy and the case law impose a more cautious approach for the finding of abuses consisting of direct foreclosure than for abuses consisting of indirect foreclosure. In particular, for cases involving a de novo refusal to supply, it is necessary to prove indispensability, that is, to establish that there are no actual or potential substitutes for the input/service/facility of the dominant undertaking (*see*

37. Commission Decision of 13 May 2009, COMP/37-990 Intel, available at https://ec.europa.eu/competition/antitrust/cases/dec_docs/37990/37990_3581_18.pdf (last accessed on 2 July 2025).

Oscar Bronner, Magill, IMS Health, Microsoft).[38] However, whereas the 2008 Guidance explicitly states that the stricter criteria for finding a direct foreclosure type abuse (should) apply equally to cases of de novo refusal to supply, termination of supply, constructive refusal and margin squeeze, more recent case law, in particular *TeliaSonera*[39] and *Slovak Telekom*, has made clear that the Union Courts distinguish between situations where a dominant firm refuses to start supplying a rival firm and situations where the two firms have an ongoing supply relationship, even though one of them may want to terminate the relationship, or the other may disagree with (some of) the conditions of supply (the latter type of situations hereafter referred to as 'termination of supply'). In the latter two judgments the Court held that, in cases of termination of supply, indispensability is an important factor, but that even where indispensability cannot be established, an abuse can still be found if there is an anti-competitive effect, namely the conduct is capable of excluding competitors that are at least as efficient as the dominant undertaking.

While the future Article 102 Guidelines should reflect the distinction made by the Union Courts between de novo refusal and termination of supply, it would also be useful to acknowledge in the Guidelines that there are two main reasons to be more cautious when intervening against direct foreclosure than against indirect foreclosure.

The first reason is linked to the potential negative effects of the intervention on the incentives to invest of the dominant firm and its competitors. The indispensability condition is intended to ensure that the dominant undertaking is not forced to share the benefits of its investments with its current or potential competitors and that those competitors do not rely on the dominant undertaking's investments but rather invest and innovate themselves, provided duplication of the input is feasible. Where possible, it is preferable to incentivise market operators to compete independently of each other, instead of creating a situation where competitors depend on each other for a particular input.

The second reason to be more cautious when intervening against direct foreclosure than against indirect foreclosure is that in direct foreclosure cases, the remedy will often be more intrusive and require monitoring and price setting by the authority. This means that the design of an effective remedy is generally difficult, as it is not easy to force a firm to effectively supply its competitors. If a dominant firm is forced to give access or not to limit access to its own input, this will often require the authority to determine the access conditions (price, quantity, etc.), and this often for prolonged periods and for various market scenarios. In general, it is considered that competition authorities and courts are not well placed to assume such a regulatory role and should do so only in exceptional circumstances.

38. Case 7/97 *Oscar Bronner v. Mediaprint Zeitungs- und Zeitschriftenverlag, Mediaprint Zeitungsvertriebsgesellschaft and Mediaprint Anzeigengesellschaft* [1998] ECR I-7791; Joined Cases C-241/91 P and C-242/91 *Radio Telefis Eireann (RTE) and Independent Television Publications (ITP) v. Commission (Magill)* [1995] ECR I-743; Case C-418/01 *IMS Health v. NDC Health* [2004] ECR I-5039; Case T-201/04 *Microsoft v. Commission* [2007] ECR II-3601.
39. Case C-52/09 *Konkurrensverket v. TeliaSonera Sverige AB*, judgment of the CoJ of 17 February 2011, ECR I527.

Conversely, in indirect foreclosure cases, the parties want to deal with each other, but the competition authority may object to aspects of the dominant firm's conduct that foreclose third parties (such as an exclusive purchasing requirement, tying or a certain type of rebate). As a remedy, it will be sufficient in most cases to adopt a cease-and-desist order, i.e., obliging the dominant firm not to impose a particular requirement on its customers or to stop applying a particular type of rebate. Once the remedy is in place, the dominant firm and its customers will continue to deal with each other, as that is what they wanted to do in the first place, and there will be no need for the authority to intervene in their future transactions.

For all termination of supply cases, the Commission and NCAs will have to decide, in the future Article 102 Guidelines and their enforcement, how to use the 'enforcement freedom' created by *TeliaSonera* and *Slovak Telekom*. Whether to simply apply the general test used for indirect foreclosure conduct, i.e., to find the termination abusive if it leads to anti-competitive foreclosure (foreclosure that is likely to harm consumers), or to introduce a new limiting principle, less stringent than the indispensability test.

While the choice of a limiting principle may have a limited practical impact on the assessment of traditional termination of supply cases in the telecoms sector, since in these cases a margin squeeze is generally applied by dominant firms that are already under a regulatory obligation to supply their (indispensable) input to competitors, this choice is important for the increasing number of complaints relating to termination of supply in digital markets.

It can be argued that the new termination of supply scenarios in (dynamic) digital markets differ on essential points from the more traditional essential facility cases, at least as regards the first reason for a higher intervention threshold. In digital markets, market power is often based on (in)direct network effects. Firms generally start with an open access strategy, granting equal and possibly free access to all parties that want to use their platform or service. However, once the platform or service has become unavoidable for a large share of users, the firm may change its strategy. It may exploit its market power by starting to price the access, possibly applying different rates for different users. In addition, the dominant firm may wish to enter other markets, in particular markets on which some of its customers/users are active. To facilitate such entry, the dominant firm may reduce access to its own platform/service for those users, while simultaneously entering the market(s) where the users are active.

It is obvious that in the above situation, there is no reason to fear that intervention, or applying a lower intervention threshold, could create a bias for the dominant firm not to supply in the first place. As indicated, in digital markets an open access strategy is commercially necessary at the start, when the market is new and developing, and market positions are still in a state of flux. This distinguishes these cases from the more traditional essential facility and IP cases, where the firm in question often does not intend to grant access when it undertakes the (sometimes very significant) investments that create the (natural) monopoly position.

More generally, it can be argued that if a dominant firm has found it to be in its interest to supply an input to one or more customers, this shows that it considered it efficient, at least at that point in time, to engage in such supply relationships. In other words, supplying had no negative effect on its incentives to invest. This and the fact that customers are likely to have made investments linked to these supply relationships mean that in such a scenario it may be less appropriate to impose the higher indispensability threshold for intervention.

However, it seems that the new termination of supply scenarios in digital markets do not differ substantially from the more traditional essential facility cases as regards the second reason for exercising caution. This is because the nature of the intervention and the remedy is and remains substantially different between indirect and direct foreclosure cases. It is no overstatement to say that also in termination of supply cases in digital markets there is a real risk that mandating competitive access is not easy to implement or to monitor. This suggests that it would be desirable to still have a limiting principle for termination of supply cases.

In addition to limiting the number of cases in which complex and time-consuming remedies have to be devised, a limiting principle would also help to ensure that competition authorities do not become a regulator that has to police the commercial relationships of many disgruntled competitors and their dominant supplier/buyer. Think of the dominant brewer which is also active in the pub market. The Commission and NCAs would be expected to deal with complaints by independent pubs about the pricing and delivery conditions of the dominant brewer's beer. Or the complaints of brand manufacturers that are not present or not satisfied with their position on the shelves relative to the position of the own brands of a dominant supermarket.

Avoiding this scenario by means of a limiting principle will not only increase the effectiveness of the enforcement policy; but it will also reduce the number of direct foreclosure cases in which complex remedies are necessary, thereby reducing overall the average time needed to take enforcement decisions.

Recommendation 10: To improve the speed and effectiveness of its enforcement in abuse of dominance cases, it would be useful for the Commission to reduce bottlenecks in its decision-making process and improve the way in which it integrates economic and legal aspects in its investigations (as is already customary in phase II merger cases).

Recommendation 11: It would be appropriate and useful for the future Article 102 Guidelines to introduce a limiting principle, less stringent than the indispensability test, for termination of supply cases, in order to avoid having to design complex remedies in too many cases.

CHAPTER 14

In Defence of Rebuttable Presumptions in Abuse of Dominance Cases

Jorge Padilla[*]

In this chapter, I rely on the decision-theoretic framework developed by Gal, Padilla and Piccolo (2025) to explain when the use of rebuttable presumptions, as opposed to irrebuttable presumptions or a case-by-case rule-of-reason standard (or balancing test), is justified as a matter of decision theory and economics. I then provide comments on the use of rebuttable presumptions in the Draft Guidelines.

1 INTRODUCTION

The European Commission ('Commission') published its long-awaited *Draft Guidelines on the Application of Article 102 TFEU to abusive exclusionary conduct by dominant undertakings* ('Draft Guidelines')[1] in August 2024. The Commission's consultation process has produced a considerable number of responses from practitioners, academics and industry.[2]

* This paper has not been commissioned or funded by any party, and no party had the right to review the paper prior to its circulation. I am solely compensated by Compass Lexecon, an economic consultancy. As a consultant, I have represented many companies involved in Art. 102 TFEU cases over the years, on both the complainant and defendant side. I hold no paid or unpaid position as officer, director, or board member of non-profit organizations or profit-making entities whose policy positions, goals, or financial interests relate to the article. The list of my clients in abusive of dominance cases, and other cases, can be found at https://www.compasslexecon.com/professionals/jorge-padilla. This paper does not necessarily represent the views of Compass Lexecon or its clients.

1. Draft Guidelines on the application of Art. 102 of the Treaty on the Functioning of the European Union to abusive exclusionary con-duct by dominant undertakings (2024), available at https://competition-policy.ec.europa.eu/public-consultations/2024-article-102-guidelines_en.
2. The non-confidential replies to the consultation can be found at https://competition-policy.ec.europa.eu/public-consultations/2024-article-102-guidelines_en#view-the-contributions.

The two issues that appear to have raised more controversy are: the notion of exclusionary abuse – in particular, the operational use of the concept of competition on the merits – and the reliance on rebuttable presumptions. This chapter focuses on the second issue.[3]

Under a rebuttable presumption of legality, a unilateral practice is presumed legal unless one or more well-defined, and empirically testable, conditions are met – i.e., the practice is considered pro-competitive but for exceptional circumstances. Instead, under a rebuttable presumption of illegality, a unilateral practice is presumed to be anti-competitive unless one or more well-defined, and empirically testable, conditions are met.

The Draft Guidelines rely on rebuttable presumptions in a way that has proved controversial. Specifically, *paragraph 60.b* of the Draft Guidelines states:

> Certain types of conduct are generally recognized as having a high potential to produce exclusionary effects. Accordingly, they are subject to a presumption concerning their capability of producing exclusionary effects. ... Once the factual existence of the relevant conduct is established, if need be under the conditions established in the specific legal test, its exclusionary effects can be presumed ...
>
> A dominant undertaking can seek to rebut the probative value of the presumption in the specific circumstances at hand by submitting, on the basis of supporting evidence, that the conduct is not capable of having exclusionary effects. ...
>
> A dominant undertaking may also seek to show that the conduct is justified on the basis of an objective justification. The fact that the conduct has a high potential to lead to exclusionary effects must be given due weight in the balancing exercise to be carried out in this context ... .

Some have argued that the Draft Guidelines err when claiming that the case law supports the legal presumptions it posits. For Assimakis Komninos, for example, 'the Commission's introduction of the "presumptions" approach is at variance with existing case law (with the possible exception of pricing below average variable cost in predation cases) and will not result in any practical consequences'.[4]

Others agree with the Commission's interpretation of the case law. For example, Pablo-Ibañez-Colomo considers the claim that 'some practices are abusive by their very nature (whether we call them "naked restrictions" or abuses by object) cannot be seriously disputed. It is an integral feature of the case law, and a useful one at that ... It is also difficult to dispute that the anticompetitive effects of some practices are presumed and thus that the creation of a specific category necessarily in relation to these practices is warranted'.[5]

---

3. For my views on the notion of exclusionary abuse in the Draft Guidelines, *see* Jorge Padilla, *What Is an Exclusionary Abuse?*, available at https://www.concurrences.com/en/review/issues/no-4-2024/on-topic/the-new-eu-commission-competition-policy. An earlier version can be found at https://papers.ssrn.com/sol3/papers.cfm?abstract_id=5006000.
4. Assimakis Komninos, '"J"Accuse!: Four Deadly Sins of the Commission's Draft Guidelines on Exclusionary Abuses', *Network Law Review*, 2024, available at https://www.networklawreview.org/komninos-guidelines/.
5. Pablo Ibañez-Colomo opines. *See* Pablo Ibañez-Colomo, 'On the Article 102 TFEU Guidelines (I): The Three Categories of Practices Make Sense, but a Fourth Is Missing', *Chillin'Competition*,

The criticisms are not only coming from legal practitioners and scholars but some economists also have raised objections to the extensive use of rebuttable presumptions in the Draft Guidelines.

Frontier Economics, for example, opines that 'for conducts where no established and practicable economic test exist to show that the conduct "pursues no economic objective other than eliminating its competitors", presumptions are not effective and may even present a chilling effect on competition'.[6]

RBB-Economics in turn states, 'in most cases, we believe that the competitive effects of any given conduct depend too greatly on the specific circumstances, such that it is not possible to determine reliably whether the dominant firm's conduct has resulted in anti-competitive foreclosure without developing a clear theory of harm that is substantiated persuasively by the facts of the case. This applies to all conduct–including the list of behaviours that the Commission identifies as presumptively harmful'.[7] They conclude that 'enforcement based on rebuttable presumptions therefore goes against the primary objective of intervention to deliver competitive outcomes'.[8]

Last but not least, Akman, Fumagalli and Motta, while 'generally sympathetic to the establishment of well-crafted rebuttable presumptions' note that some of the presumptions in the Draft Guidelines 'are not grounded in economics'.[9] In particular, they complain about the lack of clarity regarding whether the presumptions established in the Draft Guidelines really are rebuttable presumptions, as the standard of proof for rebutting the presumption of capability to produce exclusionary effects is not properly specified.

In what follows, I do not discuss whether the Draft Guidelines are faithfully aligned with the case law that they purport to summarize, as that is not my area of expertise. Instead, I rely on the decision-theoretic framework[10] developed by Gal,

2024, available at https://chillingcompetition.com/2024/11/12/on-the-article-102-tfeu-guidelines-i-the-three-categories-of-practices-make-sense-but-a-fourth-is-missing/.

6. Frontier Economics, 'European Commission's Consultation on the Draft Guidelines on the Application of Article 102 TFEU Response of Frontier Economics', p. 6. *See supra* n. 2.
7. RBB-Economics 'The EC's Draft Guidelines on the application of Article 102 TFEU Response by RBB Economics to the EC consultation', p. 8. *See supra* n. 2.
8. *Ibid.*
9. Pinar Akman, Chiara Fumagalli and Massimo Motta, 'Submission to the Consultation on the Draft Guidelines on Exclusionary Abuses', pp. 5-7. *See supra* n. 2.
10. As stated by Steve Salop, 'Decision theory provides a formal methodology for rational decision-making when information is imperfect. This methodology can be described as a rational process in which a decision-maker begins with some initial, rationally-based beliefs about the possible effects of a decision. As a formal matter, those initial beliefs can be seen as a set of probabilities of potential alternative outcomes. The decision-maker bases the initial beliefs on prior knowledge and then gathers additional information to refine and improve upon those initial beliefs in order to "update" the presumption to create revised beliefs.' Steven C. Salop, 'An Enquiry Meet for the Case: Decision Theory, Presumptions, and Evidentiary Burdens in Formulating Antitrust Legal Standards', 2017, available at https://ssrn.com/abstract=3068157. *See also* Richard A. Posner, Economic Analysis of the Law: 9th Edition, *Aspen Casebook Series*, 2014, Ch. 22; Richard A. Posner, 'An Economic Approach to Legal Procedure and Judicial Administration', *Journal Legal Studies*, 2, 1973, p. 399 https://doi.org/10.1086/467503; Frank H. Easterbrook, 'The Limits of Antitrust', *Texas Law Review*, 63(1), 1984, pp. 1-40; C. Frederick Beckner III and Steven C. Salop, 'Decision Theory and Antitrust Rules', *Antitrust Law Journal*, 67, 1999, p. 41; Keith N. Hylton and Michael Salinger, 'Tying Law and Policy: A Decision-Theoretic Approach',

Padilla and Piccolo (2025) to explain when the use of rebuttable presumptions, as opposed to irrebuttable presumptions or a case-by-case rule-of-reason standard (or balancing test), is justified as a matter of decision theory and economics.[11] But before doing so, I will discuss the nature and scope of the legal rules commonly used in competition law.

2 LEGAL RULES IN COMPETITION LAW

Legal rules assist agencies and courts – the regulatory decision makers – to distinguish anti-competitive from pro-competitive conduct. Legal rules establish a correspondence between, on the one hand, the conduct under scrutiny and the legal and economic context in which the conduct takes place and, on the other hand, the permissible or impermissible categorization of the conduct.

As Sir John Vickers states:

> There must be rules of law in this area of competition policy, not least for reasons of predictability and accountability. So the issue is not rules versus discretion, but how well the rules are grounded in economics.[12]

2.1 Rules Versus Discretion

Legal rules, whether rebuttable presumptions or rule of reason (i.e., balancing) tests, are *structured* – i.e., they specify the placement and possible shifts in the burden of proof between agencies (or claimants) and defendants.

The rule of reason first places the burden of proof to show anti-competitive effects on the agency. The burden of proof to demonstrate that there are offsetting efficiencies is then shifted to the defendant, while the burden of performing the balancing anti- and pro-competitive effects is typically allocated to the agency.

Under a rebuttable presumption of illegality (respectively, legality), whereas it is incumbent on the agency (respectively, the defendant) to establish that the conditions giving rise to the presumption are satisfied, the burden of proof in relation to the rebuttal falls on the defendant (respectively, the agency).

Structured legal rules 'contribute to the administrability and predictability of the system'[13] and, while their implementation may not lead to the correct decision in each particular case, they may help to deter more effectively and efficiently 'anti-competitive

---

Antitrust Law Journal, 69, 2001, p. 469; and Jorge Padilla, 'Decision Theory and Legal Process in EU Competition Law', in Kris Dekeyser et al. (eds) *Regulation 1/2003 and EU Antitrust Enforcement: A Systematic Guide*. (Kluwer L. Int. 2022), Ch. 24, available at https://ssrn.com/abstract=3859937.

11. Michal Gal, Jorge Padilla and Salvatore Piccolo, 'Optimal Legal Rules for the Assessment of Unilateral Conduct by Dominant Firms', 2025, available at [TBC].
12. John Vickers, 'Abuse of Market Power', *Economic Journal*, 2005, p. 244 https://doi.org/10.1111/j.1468-0297.2005.01004.x.
13. Pablo Ibáñez Colomo, 'Form and Substance in EU Competition Law', *World Competition*, 2023, pp. 401- 428 https://doi.org/10.54648/woco2023024.

behaviour throughout the economy given all the relevant costs, benefits and uncertainties associated with diagnoses and remedies'.[14]

2.2 Effect-Based Rules

That a (structured) legal rule eliminates discretion on a case-by-case basis does not imply that it is formalistic, or not *effects-based*. A legal rule based not solely on the form of the conduct, but reflecting the economic context when designing and implementing the rule should be treated as effects-based if it is properly grounded in economics.

The rule of reason is commonly considered an effects-based standard. A rebuttable presumption of illegality (legality) is also effects-based if a successful rebuttal requires proving to the requisite standard that the case-specific information contradicts the presumption.

Rebuttable presumptions are generally not formalistic, since the rebuttal typically involves an assessment of the likely effects of the conduct and, possibly, of its potential efficiencies, based on the specific facts of the case at hand. Only 'irrebuttable' presumptions – i.e., per se rules – are unambiguously formalistic.

However, that does not mean that irrebuttable presumptions are necessarily not grounded in economics. They are justified as a matter of economics if they reflect economic theory and evidence showing that the impugned conduct is bound to produce anti-competitive effects (presumption of illegality) or pro-competitive effects (presumption of legality).

2.3 A Workable Effects-Based Approach

Schweitzer and de Ridder (2024) are right when saying that the enforcement of a dynamic and workable effects-based approach to the assessment of abuses of dominance requires redefining and specifying the preconditions under which anti-competitive effects can be initially inferred or even presumed, what kind of evidence must be produced to counter the inference or presumption, and what additional evidence may then revive the case.[15]

That is, a workable effects-based approach must rely, to the extent possible, on 'simplifying rules that implicate an inference of anti-competitive effects', which are however 'differentiated and sensitive to context within a structured proceeding in which the burden to produce evidence and the burden of proof shift to and fro'.

14. Paul L. Joskow, 'Transaction Cost Economics, Antitrust Rules and Remedies', *Journal of Law, Economics, and Organization*, 2002, p. 99 https://doi.org/10.1093/jleo/18.1.95.
15. Heike Schweitzer and Simon de Ridder, 'How to Fix a Failing Art. 102 TFEU: Substantive Interpretation, Evidentiary Requirements, and the Commission's Future Guidelines on Exclusionary Abuses', *Journal of European Competition Law & Practice*, 2024, at p. 228, available at https://academic.oup.com/jeclap/article/15/4/222/7690940, https://doi.org/10.1093/jeclap/lpae033.

2.4 Optimally Simple Legal Rules

Those simplifying rules must be as simple as they can be while being properly grounded in economics and evidence, but not simpler. Irrebuttable presumptions are simpler than rebuttable presumptions, which in turn are simpler rules than the rule of reason.

Simple legal rules are attractive for at least two reasons. First, the direct cost of enforcing simpler legal rules is lower. The enforcement of rebuttable presumptions involves the cost of gathering and assessing case-specific, economic and non-economic evidence at the rebuttal stage; a cost that is saved when using an irrebuttable presumption. Secondly, simple legal rules arguably are easier to comply with, increasing legal certainty and minimizing compliance risks.

However, simple legal rules are too simple when they are likely to cause too many decision errors: Type 1 (false positive) errors, where permissible conduct is incorrectly condemned, and Type 2 (false negative) errors, where impermissible conduct is incorrectly permitted. Such errors are likely to result in a welfare loss for consumers, which must be taken into account together with the cost of enforcement and compliance.

In short, a legal rule is *optimally simple* when it minimizes the expected consumer welfare costs of decision errors, including the information and enforcement costs required to reduce errors.

Finally, nothing prevents these optimally simple rules from relying on the categorization of conduct, since such categorization 'is not inherently form-based or effects-based'.[16] What is important is that the rules applied to different categories of conduct are consistent, so that they reflect the same error cost and enforcement cost minimization principles. This ensures the internal consistency of the law, and eliminates the incentives to (mis)-categorize the impugned conduct as a matter of fact and economics in order to benefit from a more favourable legal test.

3 OPTIMAL LEGAL RULES IN ABUSE OF DOMINANCE CASES

In this section, I describe the analytical framework and results of Gal, Padilla and Piccolo (2025). They apply basic principles in decision theory to characterize optimal legal rules for the assessment of the unilateral conduct of dominant firms in abuse of dominance cases.

An optimal legal rule in their framework maximizes long-term consumer welfare, taking into account: (a) the risk and cost of both Type 1 (false positive) errors and Type 2 (false negative) errors;[17] and (b) the costs of applying those legal rules in practice –

16. Ibáñez Colomo, *supra* n. 13.
17. Decision errors are caused because decisions are typically made with imperfect information, and obtaining all relevant information is expensive, time-consuming, or simply impossible. These costs should include not only the current consumer welfare costs of an incorrect finding but also the costs of chilling or promoting pro-competitive conduct in the future. They are estimated using the empirical evidence and theoretical learnings from the academic literature, as well as

including the costs of gathering and analysing the conduct-specific evidence available when the rules are laid out, and the case-specific evidence that may eventually be used to implement such rules (e.g., to rebut a presumption of illegality).

They consider three different rules: a *presumption of illegality*, a *presumption of legality*, and the *structured rule of reason* – which is associated with a neutral presumption.[18]

The choice among presumptions – i.e., legal rules – is determined by, on the one hand, the *relative plausibility* of the anti-competitive theory of harm – the plaintiff's narrative – and the pro-competitive justification for the conduct – the defendant's narrative; and, on the other hand, the relative costs of the Type 1 and Type 2 errors, and the relative information costs for reducing each type of error.

The relative costs of the Type 1 and Type 2 errors define the *persuasion threshold* used to assess the relative plausibility of the competing narratives. The relative costs of implementing the rules determine whether the optimal rule involves a rebuttable or irrebuttable presumption.

They find that for any given conduct the optimal legal rule is:

- a presumption of illegality, when the anti-competitive theory of harm associated with the conduct is sufficiently more plausible than the pro-competitive justification, given precedent and state-of-the-art economic theory and evidence;
- a presumption of legality, when the pro-competitive justification is sufficiently more plausible than the anti-competitive theory of harm; and
- no presumption (or a neutral presumption), when both the pro-competitive justification and the anti-competitive theory of harm are similarly plausible.

As regards the rebuttable or irrebuttable character of the optimal presumptions above, the authors conclude that:

- collecting and analysing the information necessary for rebutting a presumption and differentiating a specific case from the typical one, is costly;
- presumptions should optimally be *irrebuttable* when the cost of gathering and assessing the case-specific evidence that could be used to rebut the presumption exceeds the expected costs of false positive errors (for a presumption of illegality) or false negative errors (for a presumption of legality);

post-mortem analysis from previous cases, and – for false positives – should also reflect the penalties and remedies that will likely be imposed in case of an infringement decision.

18. A neutral presumption in the sense above need not be 'neutral' in practice, if plaintiffs or defendants have relatively more resources. These asymmetries may provide an additional justification for the use of presumptions. Hovenkamp and Salop argue that if it is relatively less difficult for one of the parties to obtain the additional evidence, or to obtain the additional evidence, or if that party (e.g., the defendant) has higher stakes, its relatively higher incentive to produce favourable evidence might skew the outcome away from the merits to the advantage of that litigant. Erik Hovenkamp and Steven C. Salop, 'Litigation with Inalienable Judgments', *Journal of Legal Studies*, 52, 2023, pp. 1-50 https://doi.org/10.1086/721979.

- when the costs of collecting and analysing case-specific information are lower than the expected costs of making a wrong decision in a specific case, the presumptions identified above should be rebuttable.

Finally, as regards the standard of proof for a successful rebuttal, they find that:

- successfully rebutting a presumption of illegality ought to require showing that the pro-competitive justification fits those case-specific facts better than a sound anti-competitive theory of harm;[19]
- the standard of proof for a successful rebuttal depends on the strength of the presumption as well as, once more, the relative costs of the Type 1 and Type 2 errors:
  - When the expected costs of Type 1 and Type 2 errors are identical, the optimal standard of proof is the *preponderance of evidence standard*.[20]
  - Otherwise, when one error is more costly and likely than the other, the right standard of proof would be closer to the *clear and convincing evidence standard* (applied in civil and administrative cases in common law countries)[21] or the *intimate conviction standard* (applied by EU courts).[22]

4 COMMENTS ON THE DRAFT GUIDELINES

In this section, I rely on the lessons from the previous section to provide comments on the use of rebuttable presumptions in the Draft Guidelines.

4.1 Rebuttable Presumptions in the Draft Guidelines

As stated in the Introduction, *paragraph 60.b* of the Draft Guidelines certain conduct is presumed to lead to exclusionary effects. This rebuttable presumption applies to: (i) exclusive supply or purchasing agreements; (ii) rebates conditional upon exclusivity;

19. We are not considering here an intermediate scenario in which the gathering and assessing the case-specific evidence that could be used to rebut the presumption are neither too high to justify the adoption of an irrebuttable presumption, nor too low to allow for an evidence intensive rebuttal exercise. In that intermediate scenario, the optimal legal rule make take the form of a 'quick look' rule, whereby the presumption is rebutted only if the rebuttal is justified on the basis of a quick-look to the available evidence.
20. *See* Cornell Law School, Preponderance of evidence https://www.law.cornell.edu/wex/preponderance_of_the_evidence#: ~ :text = Preponderance%20refers%20to%20the%20evidentiary,likely%20true%20than%20not%20true.
21. *Ibid.*
22. *See* Eric Gippini-Fournier, 'The Elusive Standard of Proof in EU Competition Cases', *World Competition*, 33(2), 2010, pp.187-207 https://doi.org/10.54648/woco2010017; Per Hellström, 'A Uniform Standard of Proof in EU Competition Proceedings', in *European Competition Law Annual 2009, Evaluation of Evidence and its Judicial Review in Competition Cases* (Hart Publishing, July 2011), available at SSRN: https://ssrn.com/abstract=2147705; Fernando Castillo de la Torre and Eric Gippini-Fournier, *Evidence, Proof and Judicial Review in EU Competition Law*, 2nd ed., Edward Elgar Publishing Ltd. 2023; and Adriani Kalintiri, *Evidence Standards in EU Competition Enforcement*, Hart Publishing, 2019.

(iii) predatory pricing; (iv) margin squeeze in the presence of negative spreads; and (v) certain forms of tying.

Take, for example, the case of exclusive dealing. *Paragraph 82* states that exclusive dealing is presumed to be capable of having exclusionary effects. This presumption is justified because '[e]xclusive dealing by a dominant firm has a high potential to produce exclusionary effects as it is likely to deprive or restrict the customer's or seller's choice of possible sources of supply or demand'. *Paragraph 83* clarifies that such a presumption can be rebutted.

Is the presumption of illegality justified? Answering this question requires assessing whether the presumption of illegality is properly grounded in economics, so that the anti-competitive theory of harm associated with exclusive dealing is sufficiently more plausible than the pro-competitive justification, given state-of-the-art economic theory and evidence.

Exclusive dealing arrangements may involve a buyer committing to purchasing exclusively from a dominant supplier, or a supplier agreeing to sell exclusively to a particular distributor. This is distinct from exclusivity rebates, which are discounts offered to buyers conditional on sourcing all or most of their requirements from a specific supplier without an explicit commitment from the buyer.

Exclusive dealing alters the competitive dynamics of a market by restricting the ability of firms to transact with alternative partners. Exclusive contracts serve different economic purposes depending on market conditions, firm incentives, and the presence (or absence) of market power. Economic theory[23] and empirical research show that these agreements can have both pro-competitive and anti-competitive effects. The economic analysis of exclusive dealing is crucial for distinguishing between conduct that enhances efficiency and innovation, from that which leads to market foreclosure and harms consumer welfare.

Exclusive dealing can serve as an efficiency-enhancing contractual mechanism. *First*, firms frequently invest in assets that are specific to a trading relationship, such as specialized equipment, training programs, or branding efforts. Without exclusivity, there is a risk that opportunistic behaviour (e.g., free-riding) will undermine such investments. Exclusive dealing contracts provide certainty, encouraging firms to undertake these investments, thereby promoting efficiency and innovation.

23. In a seminal paper, Bernheim and Whinston analyse a broad class of models to identify scenarios where exclusive dealing can have anticompetitive consequences, particularly in non-coincident markets – markets other than those where exclusive dealing is practiced. For example, a manufacturer might use exclusive contracts to foreclose competitors from essential distribution channels, thereby hindering their ability to compete effectively. This foreclosure can lead to reduced competition and potential harm to consumer welfare. They also explore situations where exclusive dealing can enhance efficiency. In markets where common representation leads to incentive conflicts – such as when a retailer's efforts to promote one product diminish its efforts to promote another – exclusive dealing can mitigate these conflicts. By aligning the incentives of retailers and manufacturers, exclusive contracts can lead to more efficient outcomes and improved service for consumers. Bernheim and Whinston's analysis underscores the complexity of exclusive dealing arrangements. Their findings suggest that the impact of exclusive dealing on market competition and efficiency is highly context-dependent. *See* B. Douglas Bernheim and Michael D. Whinston, 'Exclusive Dealing', *Journal of Political Economy*, 106(1), 1998, pp. 64-103 https://doi.org/10.1086/250003.

Second, exclusive dealing may simplify contractual arrangements by reducing the need for constant renegotiation. By stabilizing supply and demand relationships, these agreements can lower transaction costs and facilitate long-term planning.

Third, retailers or distributors may invest in promoting a supplier's products, but if competitors can benefit from this investment without incurring the costs (e.g., by selling cheaper substitutes after demand has been created), firms may underinvest in promotion and marketing. Exclusive dealing ensures that the firm making the investments is the one capturing the benefits of promotion.

Fourth, in industries where product quality is critical, exclusive dealing can help suppliers maintain control over distribution and service levels. This is particularly relevant in sectors, such as luxury goods, pharmaceuticals, and franchising, where brand reputation and customer experience are key drivers of demand.

While the abovementioned efficiency rationales suggest that exclusive dealing can be beneficial, it may also be a tool that firms can use to foreclose rivals and restrict competition.[24] *First*, if a firm ties up a substantial share of distribution or input sources through exclusive contracts, rivals may be unable to reach the necessary scale to compete effectively. This can lead to inefficient market outcomes where high-quality, lower-cost competitors are excluded.[25]

Second, exclusive dealing can force competitors to rely on alternative (and often more expensive) supply or distribution channels. When a firm locks up key customers or suppliers, rivals must either pay a premium to access the remaining portion of the market or exit altogether.

Third, in some cases, exclusive dealing can act as a mechanism to sustain anti-competitive collusion. By controlling distribution, firms may reduce price competition and allocate market shares more predictably, reducing competitive pressure.

24. Exclusive dealing can also be rivalry-enhancing. For example, Calzolari and Denicolò find that, under conditions of incomplete information about demand. while firms have unilateral incentives to employ these contractual arrangements to better extract buyers' informational rents, exclusive contracts tend to intensify competition. *See* Guglielmo Calzolari and Vicenzo Denicolò, 'Competition with Exclusive Contracts and Market Share Discounts', *American Economic Review*, 103(6), 2013, pp. 2384-2411 https://doi.org/10.1257/aer.103.6.2384. *See also* Benjamin Klein and Kevin M. Murphy, 'Exclusive Dealing Intensifies Competition for Distribution', *Antitrust Law Journal*, 75(2), 2008, pp. 433-466. The authors show that exclusive contracts for retail distribution can enhance competition among manufacturers when competitive retailers have installed bases of loyal customers. Zenger notes that the pro-competitive outcomes suggested by Klein and Murphy are contingent upon specific market conditions, such as the nature of competition among manufacturers and the structure of distribution networks. Without these conditions, exclusive dealing could potentially have neutral or even adverse effects on competition. Hans Zegner, 'When Does Exclusive Dealing Intensify Competition for Distribution? Comment on Klein and Murphy', *Antitrust Law Journal*, 77(1), 2010, pp. 205-2011.
25. Historically, the Chicago School posited that exclusive dealing could not be anti-competitive, arguing that any attempt by an incumbent to deter entry through such contracts would necessitate compensating buyers to an extent that would render the strategy unprofitable. Fumagalli, Motta, and Calcagno challenge this view by showing that when an incumbent secures exclusive contracts with a sufficient number of buyers, it can effectively foreclose the market to potential entrants, especially if these entrants require a minimum efficient scale to operate profitably. *See* Chiara Fumagalli, Massimo Motta, and Claudio Calcagno, *Exclusionary Practices: The Economics of Monopolization and Abuse of Dominance*, Cambridge University Press, 2018, Chapter 3.

Finally, when used by an already dominant firm, exclusive dealing can prevent new entrants from gaining a foothold in the market. If potential entrants cannot access distribution or input sources at a reasonable scale, they may be deterred from entering altogether, leading to long-term market inefficiencies.

The empirical literature on exclusive dealing suggests that the impact of exclusive dealing is highly context-dependent.[26] Research on exclusive supply agreements in the beverage and consumer goods industries has found that, on the one hand, exclusive contracts can lead to lower prices and higher promotional investments in some cases, but, on the other hand, they are associated with reduced entry and competition in others. In the pharmaceutical sector, exclusive contracts between drug manufacturers and insurers (or pharmacy benefit managers) have been shown to limit generic competition, delaying market entry and leading to higher drug prices. However, they can also reduce transaction costs and ensure more efficient supply chain management. Finally, in high-tech markets, exclusive dealing has been used both as a pro-competitive tool (e.g., ensuring stability in R&D partnerships) and as an exclusionary tactic (e.g., locking up key software applications to limit platform competition).

In short, the economics of exclusive dealing reveals a fundamental tension: while such agreements can enhance efficiency, investment, and competition in many cases, they also have the potential to entrench dominance and restrict market access.

In the context of the models developed by Gal, Padilla and Piccolo (2025), the *plausibility ratio* – i.e., the relative plausibility of the theory of harm and the pro-competitive justification – is likely to be close to one. That is, the anti-competitive theory of harm associated with the conduct (i.e., exclusive dealing) is in principle as plausible as the pro-competitive justification. It follows that the presumption of illegality in the Draft Guidelines can be regarded as properly grounded in economics only if the expected cost of the Type 2 error exceeds the expected cost of the Type 1 error in exclusive dealing cases. In that case, the plausibility ratio – equal to one – would exceed the *persuasion ratio*, which is given by the ratio of the expected cost of the Type 1 error and the expected cost of the Type 2 error – smaller than one. I do not believe the economic literature is sufficiently informative in that regard.

The practical significance of this conclusion is, however, limited since the presumption in the Draft Guidelines is rebuttable and, therefore, its appropriateness ultimately depends on the validity of the factors identified for a successful rebuttal in *paragraph 83* of the Draft Guidelines.

This paragraph states that if the dominant undertaking submits evidence that the conduct is not capable of producing exclusionary effects, the Commission will assess

26. *See*, for example, Jan B. Heide, Shantanu Dutta and Mark Bergen, 'Exclusive Dealing and Business Efficiency: Evidence from Industry Practice' *Journal of Law and Economics*, 41(2), 1998, pp. 387-408 https://doi.org/10.1086/467394; Tim R. Sass, 'The Competitive Effects of Exclusive Dealing: Evidence from the U.S. Beer Industry', *International Journal of Industrial Organization*, 23(3), 2005, pp. 203-225 https://doi.org/10.1016/j.ijindorg.2005.01.006; Chia-Wen Chen and Shiou Shieh, 'Does Exclusive Dealing Matter? Evidence from Distribution Contract Changes in the U.S. Beer Industry', *Journal of Industrial Economics*, 64(3), 2016, 411-435 https://doi.org/10.1111/joie.12108; and Hiroshi Kitamura, Noriaki Matsushima and Misato Sato, 'Defending Home Against Giants: Exclusive Dealing as a Survival Strategy', *Journal of Industrial Economics*, 71(2), 2023, pp. 441-463.

such evidence by considering: (a) the extent of the undertaking's dominant position on the relevant market and, in particular, whether the dominant undertaking may be an unavoidable trading partner for a given share of the demand; (b) the share of the market that is affected by the conduct; (c) the conditions and arrangements of the exclusivity conditions, such as their duration or whether the agreement directly or indirectly references volumes purchased from competitors; and (d) the possible existence of a strategy aimed at excluding actual or potential competitors of the dominant firm.[27]

That is, if the defendant proves that, in the context of the case at hand, the pro-competitive justification is not just plausible but probable, then the Commission must prove that its theory of harm is not only plausible but also more probable than the pro-competitive justification. If conditions (a) to (d) are satisfied, then it is clear that the theory of harm is consistent with the facts of the case at hand, and the likelihood and magnitude of the anti-competitive effects are sufficient to offset the efficiencies adduced.

Condition (d) is of particular importance. As a matter of economics, it is important to be able to show that the alleged foreclosure strategy is *rational* – i.e., that the dominant firm has both the incentive and ability to foreclose its rivals. If that is not the case, then either the dominant firm is acting irrationally, which is of course no excuse but, being hard to presume, needs to be established; or the true motivation for the impugned conduct is efficiency.

Note also that when (a) to (d) above hold, the likelihood and cost of a Type 2 error is increased. So, if the Commission is able to prove (a) to (d), it is both increasing the relative plausibility of the theory of harm and reducing the threshold of persuasion required for that theory to be accepted.

It is for these reasons that I consider the rebuttable presumption of illegality for exclusive dealing justified as a matter of economics and decision theory.

4.2 Irrebuttable Presumptions in the Draft Guidelines

Paragraph 60.c of the Draft Guidelines covers the so-called naked restrictions – i.e., conducts which, because they have no economic interest other than that of restricting competition, can be presumed capable of having exclusionary effects.

---

27. Note that in markets where buyers compete downstream, the incentives to accept exclusive deals can differ significantly. In such competitive downstream markets, a buyer that rejects an exclusive deal can gain a competitive advantage by sourcing from a more efficient entrant, thereby increasing its market share at the expense of rivals who have accepted exclusivity. This dynamic can make it more challenging for an incumbent to maintain exclusivity across the market. *See* Chiara Fumagalli and Massimo Motta, 'Exclusive Dealing and Entry when Buyers Compete', *American Economic Review*, 96(3), 2006, pp. 785-795 https://doi.org/10.1257/aer.96.3.785. On the contrary, when firms set prices above marginal costs, exclusive dealing can be directly profitable and anticompetitive, provided the dominant firm has a competitive advantage. The dominant firm benefits immediately from a boost in demand when buyers enter into exclusive contracts, rather than relying on future gains or advantages in adjacent markets. *See* Guglielmo Calzolari, Vicenzo Denicolò and Pier Carlo Zanchettin, 'The Demand-Boost Theory of Exclusive Dealing', *RAND Journal of Economics*, 51(3), 2020, pp. 713-738 https://doi.org/10.1111/1756-2171.12338.

The Draft Guidelines identify the following examples of naked restrictions: (i) payments by the dominant undertaking to customers that are conditional on the customers postponing or cancelling the launch of products that are based on products offered by competitors; (ii) the dominant undertaking agreeing with its distributors that they will swap a competing product with its own under the threat of withdrawing discounts benefiting the distributors; or (iii) the dominant undertaking actively dismantling an infrastructure used by a competitor.

The Draft Guidelines finally explain that, while these presumptions can in principle be objectively justified, the likelihood of success is so limited that they can be treated as de facto 'irrebuttable'.

According to Gal. Padilla and Piccolo, presumptions of illegality should be *irrebuttable* when the costs of gathering and assessing the case-specific evidence that could be used to rebut the presumption exceed the expected costs of false positive errors. I understand that the conducts regarded as naked restrictions in the Draft Guidelines are such that the expected cost of a false positive or Type 1 error is very small since they are unlikely to be pro-competitive. So, it does not matter whether they are more or less likely to cause anti-competitive effects; their net effects on the structure of competition and on consumer welfare are bound to be negative. The costs of assessing the likelihood and magnitude of those effects to balance them with an unlikely pro-competitive rationale will necessarily exceed the expected cost of a false positive.

It is for these reasons that I consider the use of naked restrictions and their (quasi)-irrebuttable character justified as a matter of economics and decision theory.

5 CONCLUDING REMARKS

In this chapter, I have critically reviewed the use of presumptions in the European Commission's Draft Guidelines using the decision-theoretic framework developed by Gal, Padilla and Piccolo (2025).

In particular, I have applied that framework to assess whether the rebuttable presumption of illegality posited for exclusive dealing cases is well supported in economics and decision theory. I concluded that the case for a presumption of illegality is weak, and it would perhaps be better to postulate a presumption of neutrality. However, because the presumption is rebuttable and the evidence required to assess the merits of the rebuttal is well-grounded in economics the legal rule specified in the Draft Guidelines is justified as a matter of economics and decision theory.

I have not applied this framework to other categories of abuse for which the Draft Guidelines also specify rebuttable presumptions of illegality – rebates conditional upon exclusivity, predatory pricing, margin squeeze in the presence of negative spreads, and certain forms of tying. This may be an interesting exercise for further research.

CHAPTER 15

Balancing the Scales in the Face of Lower Thresholds of Intervention under Article 102 TFEU

Álvaro Salgado Carranza[*]

1 INTRODUCTION

On 25 February 2025, the CJEU ruled in the preliminary ruling on *Google Android Auto*. The CJEU stated that '*in order to find, in a given case, that conduct must be categorised as "abuse of a dominant position" within the meaning of Article 102 TFEU, it is necessary, as a rule, to demonstrate, through the use of methods other than those which are part of competition on the merits between undertakings, that that conduct has the actual or potential effect of restricting that competition by excluding equally efficient competing undertakings from the market or markets concerned, or by hindering their growth on those markets, although the latter may be either the dominated markets or related or neighbouring markets, where that conduct is liable to produce its actual or potential effects (judgment of 10 September 2024, Google and Alphabet v Commission (Google Shopping), C-48/22 P, EU:C:2024:726, paragraph 165 and the case-law cited)* (emphasis added)'.[1]

There are two elements in the above therefore constitutive of abuse. First, the idea of artificial conduct ('bad conduct', if we used the US terminology) as deviation from competition on the merits. Second, the conduct may provoke the exit from the market of current or future competition, be that in a dominated market or in an adjacent one. It is these two elements of the notion of effects which are of interest to the

* Personal views, not representing the views of the firm the author works for.

1. *See* C-233/23, *Google Android Auto*, EU:C:2025:110, para. 54.

discussion below: the idea of 'hindering growth' and the idea of 'non dominated markets' being affected.

In the meantime, in August 2024 the Commission published the 'Draft Guidelines on the application of Article 102 of the Treaty on the Functioning of the European Union to abusive exclusionary conduct by dominant undertakings' ('DG'). The Commission proposed a two-stage test to determine whether a conduct is liable under Article 102 TFEU because of producing an anticompetitive exclusionary effect. The two-pronged test aims to determine whether a conduct departs from the (in)famous concept of 'competition on the merits'; and second, whether such conduct is capable or not of having an exclusionary effect.

Consequently, the DG differentiate between:

(i) *conduct which has no economic rationale for an undertaking unless that of restricting competition* – such behaviour is not competitive on the merits and will likely exclude competitors from the market;[2]
(ii) conduct for which the DG elaborate a *specific legal test* to determine whether it is not competing on the merits and is thus presumed to be capable of producing exclusionary effects (hence putting the burden on the undertaking to rebut the presumption by demonstrating that no such effects have taken place); and
(iii) conduct for which *no specific legal test* is provided, but for which still the Commission sets our factors to be assessed when analysing whether the conduct is liable under Article 102 TFEU. The latter covers conditional rebates that are not subject to exclusive purchase or supply requirements, multi-product rebates, self-preferencing and access restrictions.

The DG seem to favour precedent over case-specific economic analysis of the dominant undertaking's conduct. In an attempt to bring further legal certainty and clarity to the Commission's enforcement efforts, the DG risk however becoming an overly formalistic instrument which, much like the infamous *Microsoft* decision, serves the market with a detached approach to everyday business. The categorisation of practices into three categories, based on the presumption of anticompetitive abuse and the burden of proof to rebut the presumption, would not be necessarily unwelcome if accompanied by an overarching analytical framework of exclusionary abuse capable of bringing a coherent approach to anticompetitive conduct, be it collusive or unilateral. This is, however, not present.

Furthermore, the DG indicate that it is not necessary for the purpose of demonstrating that a conduct is capable of having exclusionary effects to prove that 'the actual or potential competitors that are affected by the conduct are as efficient as the

2. The Draft Guidelines provide a few examples of such conduct, including: (i) payments by a dominant undertaking to customers that are conditional on the customer's postponing or cancelling the launch of products that are based on products offered by the dominant undertaking's competitors; (ii) a dominant undertaking agreeing with its distributors that they will swap a competing product with its own under the threat of withdrawing discounts benefiting the distributors; and (iii) a dominant undertaking actively dismantling an infrastructure used by a competitor.

dominant undertaking'.[3] In addition, the Commission accepts that conduct liable under Article 102 TFEU could be producing exclusionary effects on dominated and non-dominated markets, with the substantive legal standard being the same for both instances. The Commission qualifies the latter approach by establishing that the affected non-dominated market be 'related to' the dominated market.[4]

The present article will explore the above suggestions, trying to understand if it would be possible for the Commission to engage in two novel approaches to the assessment of abuse under Article 102 TFEU. Be it either by accepting harm to less efficient competitors as a conduct liable under the current EU competition law framework, or by establishing that abusive conduct can also take place in non-dominated markets, the Draft Guidelines would be moving away from a 'free competition' paradigm and onto a 'fair competition' state-of-mind. Free competition speaks to the ordoliberal roots of EU competition rules, a market correction toolkit to ensure that market power is not unduly exploited by successful, dominant firms in already weakened markets. The ordoliberal stance, preoccupied with the competitive structure (i.e., with the competition itself and not with specific competitors) is built off an artificial/natural divide – the competition authority should not be replacing the business rationale with its own, and let the Schumpeterian destructive nature of 'business as usual' ensure competition is healthy in the markets. Only when this Hobbesian 'natural state' of affairs were corrupted by an unduly Leviathan should the authority intervene. 'Fair competition', however, would be open to protecting minorities in the market and weak operators who need affirmative action on the side of the public authority to maintain their presence in the market. This redistributive approach to the value chain sees the Commission's enforcement efforts as not only market corrections but also a tool for shaping markets and redistributing value along the different undertakings in pursuit of a series of objectives (from resilience to sustainability). The recent Clean Industrial Deal defended by the Commission seems to be embracing the latter approach, at least in the world of merger control, when indicating that the future revision of the Horizontal Merger Guidelines will aim to '*ensure that the impact of mergers on the affordability of sustainable products and on clean innovation or on creating efficiencies that bring sustainable benefits, <u>but also on innovation resilience, and the investment intensity of competition in certain strategic sectors are better integrated in the competition analysis</u>*' (emphasis added).[5] Economic efficiency may not be the rule of thumb in the Commission's competition analysis any longer.

The recent resurrection of fairness in the debate around competition law with the upsurge of critics of the Chicago school overseas has called on antitrust to undertake a series of objectives distant from the efficiency and consumer welfare standard that has characterised competition law since Bork's time. These critics see antitrust law as a proper instrument to regulate private market power and as such to aid public policy in

3. *See* Draft Guidelines, para. 73.
4. *See* Draft Guidelines, para. 68.
5. *See* European Commission 'Communication from the Commission to the European Parliament, the Council, the European Economic and Social Committee and the Committee of the Regions', 'The Clean Industrial Deal: A joint roadmap for competitiveness and decarbonisation', COM(2025) 85 final.

obtaining a series of public interest objectives that settle far from the restricted scope of price-based effects. Other authors, however, have already indicated that this definition of fairness is inadequate in the EU context, and have instead argued for a conception of fairness as 'correct behaviour on the market'.[6] These authors suggest that competition law be tasked with 'guaranteeing equality of opportunities among market participants',[7] which ultimately hinges on the (in)famous concept of 'special responsibility' of the dominant firm.

This article suggests that the transition from free to fair competition enforcement under Article 102 TFEU could take either of two (to this author's) imaginable routes. The first would be to upheave precedent and legal standard, and further the already existing divide between pricing and non-pricing conduct. As will be explored further below, out of the Draft Guidelines three categories, two of which clearly relate to pricing strategies (with the exception of *Lithuanian Railways*-style behaviour) whereas the grey area of conduct for which it is necessary to demonstrate a capability to produce exclusionary effects is kept as an experimental space. The lack of a unified theory of exclusionary abuse risks keeping provinces of conduct apart and artificially constructing dissimilar legal standards for, e.g., price-based constructive refusals to supply (i.e., margin squeezes) and non-price-based constructive refusals to supply (i.e., self-preferencing). This approach particularly risks upheaving the 'as efficient competitor' principle, which the Commission seems to accept for price-based conduct, but whose application for non-pricing-based conduct is not so clear in the Draft Guidelines.

The second approach aims to redefine the concept of dominance. The Draft Guidelines dedicate entire sections to the definition of individual and collective dominance. However, and as indicated above, the reference to abuse in (related to, or leveraged) non-dominated markets opens the door to incorporating a new family of practices into the Commission's enforcement toolkit: abuses of superior bargaining position.

This article suggests that the Commission refrain from entering into either of the above enterprises. *First,* because efforts should be taken to formulate an overarching analytical framework for exclusionary abuses, not to further atomise the legal standard. Rather, long-term competition could be factored into the assessment of 'as efficient competitors', mirroring the approach undertaken in neighbouring areas of law, like merger control. *Second,* because to extend the scope of abuse beyond dominant position and into the world of superior bargaining position would risk an overlap with coexisting rules on the matter enacted at the national level. Rather, the revised Market Definition Notice may prove the proper instrument to clearly define markets in their product, geographical and temporal dimensions, enabling a more accurate and surgical labelling of an undertaking as 'dominant'. In addition, for all practices escaping the scope of the Article 102 TFEU rule, Article 3 of Regulation 1/2003

6. *See* Pera, A. (2022). *Fairness, Competition on the Merits and Article 102.* European Competition Journal, 18(2), 232 https://doi.org/10.1080/17441056.2022.2056347.
7. *See* Pera, A. (2022). *Fairness, Competition on the merits and Article 102.* European Competition Journal, 18(2), 232 https://doi.org/10.1080/17441056.2022.2056347.

(also soon to be revised) offers the necessary scope of action to national authorities enforcing concomitant objectives to EU competition law.

2 'ABUSE' OF DOMINANT POSITION

Is there such a thing as a 'killer abuse'? The last years have been full of talk about 'killer acquisitions' and their purported pernicious effects on the market's competition and innovation rates. If powerful firms buy potential rivals before they can become entrenched enough to challenge them, there could be important new products and firms getting lost in a not-so-natural selection process. Does money buy happiness? Maybe not, but it does give peace of mind. And, if there is something that kills competition, it is comfort.

However, the idea of a killer abuse seemed foreign. At least until the recent case law insists on the idea that a dominant firm's conduct could be sanctioned if it has the potential of hindering the growth of competition in a market – does this not amount in essence to protecting less efficient competitors in the hopes that they will become as efficient competitors in due term?

The Draft Guidelines classify conduct into:

(i) naked restrictions (including pay-for-delay or threats to dismantle the competitors' supply chain) for which there can be no other economic interest other than attempting to restrict competition, only accepting an alternative rationale in 'exceptional cases';[8]

(ii) conduct (including exclusive dealing, conditional rebates hinged on exclusivity, refusal to supply, predatory pricing, margin squeezes or certain forms of tying) which is presumed to be highly likely to produce exclusionary effects. The Commission provides specific legal tests for each of these sub-categories which, if fulfilled, lays the burden of rebutting proof on the undertaking; and

(iii) any other conduct which will not enjoy a precedent-based specific legal test and which should be analysed under the general legal principles set out by the Draft Guidelines. The burden of proof rests with the Commission to prove that the conduct *'departs from competition on the merits and is capable of having exclusionary effects'*.[9] Practices which could be assessed under this framework may include conditional rebates that are not subject to exclusive purchase or supply requirements, multi-product rebates, self-preferencing and access restrictions.

As explained above, the latter category is elusive as to whether the 'as efficient competitor' principle and the requirement of dominance remain the applicable standard. The threshold for evidence does not require the Commission to demonstrate that

8. *See* Draft Guidelines, para. 60.c).
9. *See* Draft Guidelines, para. 142.

the conduct affected 'actual or potential competitors (...) as efficient as the dominant undertaking' nor that the 'conduct is enabled by the dominant position'.[10]

The two-stage test reflects the two-pronged concept of abuse of dominance, which is based on the artificiality of the exit of competitors from the market. As such, the Draft Guidelines requires first that a conduct is demonstrated not to be competitive on the merits, and then that it is capable of producing exclusionary effects.

As regards whether conduct is competitive on the merits, categories (i) and (ii) above enjoy the Commission's specific legal tests to determine whether they are. Any other conduct analysable under category (iii), however, would have to assess: whether the consumer's freedom of choice is curtailed, whether the undertaking has abused a regulatory instrument or procedure to the detriment of the authority or its competitors, whether there is a cross-violation with other areas of law, whether there has been discriminatory behaviour against competitors, whether an undertaking decides to shift previous market practice without a reasonable explanation to it, and whether a 'hypothetical competitor as efficient as the dominant undertaking would be unable to adopt the same conduct, notably because that conduct relies on the use of resources or means inherent to the holding of the dominant position, particularly to leverage or strengthen that position in the same or another market'.[11]

As regards the capability of provoking exclusionary effects, the CJEU's ruling in *Servizio Elettrico Nazionale*, indicated that the importance of assessing whether there is a 'material or rational impossibility' for a hypothetical as-efficient competitor to replicate the conduct 'is clear from the case-law on practices both related and unrelated to prices'.[12]

Competition on the merits is a complex legal standard to build. The Draft Guidelines provide overlapping assessments of conduct which is not competitive on the merits and conduct which is capable of producing exclusionary effects. AG Rantos in his Opinion in *Servizio Elettrico Nazionale* advocated this overlap, stating that demonstrating that a conduct is competitive on the merits and assessing its restrictive effects should not be a separate exercise.[13]

Alternative categorisations have been proposed, including differentiating: (i) naked restrictions which are inherently against competition on the merits and hence abusive; (ii) conduct which, by its very nature, is an expression of competition on the merits and as such incapable of having actual or potential effects on competition; (iii) conduct that is presumptively abusive and thus at odds with competition on the merits; and (iv) case-by-case assessments.[14]

The continuum above would be more at ease with a unified theory of exclusionary abuse such as the proposed 'relative efficiency criterion', which would retain the two-state test adopted by the Commission in the DG. First, and as far as 'competition

10. *See* Draft Guidelines, paras 72-73.
11. *See* Draft Guidelines, para. 55.
12. *See* C-377/20, *Servizio Elettrico Nazionale SpA and Others*, EU:C:2022:379, para. 79.
13. *See ibid.*, para. 43.
14. *See* Ibañez Colomo, P., 'On the Article 102 TFEU Guidelines (V): competition on the merits as an irritant', published on 10 January 2025 (link available https://chillingcompetition.com/2025/01/10/on-the-article-102-tfeu-guidelines-v-competition-on-the-merits-as-an-irritant/).

on the merits' is concerned, an advantage rendered available to a dominant undertaking would be economically sound when it stems from conduct 'specifically designed to foreclose equally efficient competitors or that equally efficient competitors cannot use to derive a comparable advantage'. Second, effects would take place when an 'equally efficient competitor cannot offset by other means' the exclusionary strategy of the dominant undertaking. Much aligned with the case law on free movement of goods, the whole ordeal is subject to rebuttal by the dominant undertaking, which could then try to provide an alternative explanation for the exit of the equally efficient competitor, hence doing away with the causality element of the assessment; or provide an objective justification; or demonstrate that the assessment of the competition authority were failed.[15] This unifying theory of exclusionary abuse is built on the back *of Servizio Elettrico Nazionale*, read as a formalisation of an efficiency-based criterion for the assessment of exclusionary abuses.

The first interesting aspect of the unitary theory is that it renders the ambiguous term of competition on the merits to an operational nature. As such, the efficiency-based criterion accepts the lawful weakening of competition in an already weakly competitive market (due to the existence of a dominant undertaking) when less efficient competitors are ousted from the market. This would be the result of competition on the merits which would 'lead to the departure from the market or the marginalisation of competitors that are less efficient and so less attractive to consumers from the point of view of, among other things, price, choice, quality or innovation'.[16] That is, according to the proponents of the unitary exclusionary abuse theory, the natural state of affairs in a Darwinian natural selection state of affairs. And thus the only unnatural behaviour, that deviates from the competitive merits logic of natural selection, would be that which ousted equally efficient competitors.[17] Thus, causality would be investigated to ascertain whether an equally efficient competitor engaging in the same behaviour as the dominant undertaking[18] would have been able to obtain a similarly advantageous position in the market.[19] The same tenet would however remain: less efficient competitors are not the appropriate comparator since any exit from the market would be linked not to the conduct, but to their own lower efficiency.

This unitary theory of exclusionary abuse hinges on *Servizio Elettrico Nazionale*'s advocacy of the 'as efficient competitor principle' ('AEC principle'). The AEC principle aims to ensure that there is, conceivably, an intelligible, exclusive causal relationship between the allegedly abusive conduct and its effects. Therefore, for less efficient

15. *See* Solano Díaz, P. (2024). *Quantum Antitrust–A Unified Exclusionary Abuse Theory*. IIC-International Review of Intellectual Property and Competition Law, 55(4), 591-592 https://doi.org/10.1007/s40319-024-01454-8.
16. *See* C-209/10 *Post Danmark*, EU:C:2012:172, para. 22.
17. *See* Solano Díaz, P. (2024). *Quantum Antitrust–A Unified Exclusionary Abuse Theory*. IIC-International Review of Intellectual Property and Competition Law, 55(4), 566 https://doi.org/10.1007/s40319-024-01454-8.
18. Solano Díaz refers back to the *Astrazeneca* cases, but the recent *Teva* decision analysing disparaging practices would also serve as an illustrative instance.
19. *See* Solano Díaz, P. (2024). *Quantum Antitrust–A Unified Exclusionary Abuse Theory*. IIC-International Review of Intellectual Property and Competition Law, 55(4), 567 https://doi.org/10.1007/s40319-024-01454-8.

competitors, since the simplest explanation for their exit would be their own underperformance, then no exclusive causal relationship can be imagined. Article 102 TFEU's ordoliberal nature would therefore shy away from protecting competitors themselves and only care about the overarching competitive structure of the market. *Servizio Elettrico Nazionale* was supposed to have enshrined this, a case about a non-pricing conduct clearly embracing the as efficient competitor principle in their assessment.

The Draft Guidelines seem to have maintained a normative continuance with the 2008 Guidance as far as their definition of competition on the merits is concerned ('Article 102 TFEU does not preclude the departure from the market or the marginalisation, as a result of competition on the merits, of competitors that are less efficient than the dominant undertaking and so less attractive to consumers from the point of view of, among other things, price, choice, quality or innovation').[20] However, the analysis of potential anticompetitive effects for category (ii)-conduct and the general principles to be considered when assessing category (iii)-conduct seem to undermine the idea of normative continuity. Examples include:

(i) Regarding conditional rebates, the Draft Guidelines indicate that when the inducements made by the dominant undertaking were not monetary, or there exist high barriers to new entrants in the market, then '*even a less efficient competitor may also exert a genuine constraint on the dominant undertaking*' (emphasis added).
(ii) Regarding self-preferencing practices, the Draft Guidelines list the following factors to be assessed:[21]
    (a) that the preferential treatment takes place on a leveraging market that constitutes *'an important source of business'* for competitors in the leveraged market that they cannot effectively replace through other means;
    (b) that the preferential treatment is *likely to influence the behaviour of users*, irrespective of the intrinsic qualities of the leveraged product; and
    (c) that the self-preferencing is *likely to be contrary to the firm's* 'business rationale' in the leveraging market.
(iii) Regarding access restrictions, the Draft Guidelines list access restrictions which could prove abusive 'even if the input at stake is not indispensable, as the need to protect the undertaking's freedom of contract and incentives to invest does not apply to the same extent as in a refusal to supply setting. However, the importance of the input for the access seeker will increase the likelihood that access restrictions will lead to exclusionary effects'.[22] Examples of access restrictions liable to be abusive under Article 102 TFEU include: (i) where the commercial practices of the dominant undertaking may lead to the **disruption of supply** of existing customers; (ii) where the

20. *See* Draft Guidelines, para. 51.
21. *See* Draft Guidelines, para. 161.
22. *See* Draft Guidelines, para. 166.

dominant undertaking fails to comply with a regulatory obligation to give access; (iii) where the dominant undertaking degrades or delays the existing supply of an input by imposing *unfair access conditions*; and (iv) where the dominant undertaking develops an input for the declared purpose of sharing it widely with third parties but later does not provide or restricts access.[23]

The Draft Guidelines generally define anticompetitive effects as '*any hindrance to actual or potential competitors' ability or incentive to exercise a competitive constraint on the dominant undertaking, such as the full-fledged exclusion or marginalisation of competitors, an increase in barriers to entry or expansion, the hampering or elimination of effective access to markets or to parts thereof or the imposition of constraints on the potential growth of competitors*' (emphasis added).[24]

This definition, coupled with the examples provided above, is a broad one and may include any competitive barrier which an undertaking may (lawfully) deploy to compete against its rivals in the market. However, such a conception would amount to completely conflating the two-pronged test (meaning that any conduct deemed by a regulator not to be competitive on the merits due to moral or policy reasons would amount to anticompetitive foreclosure) and accepting that there are abuses 'by object' (the feared object box now being part of the assessment of abuse). Furthermore, the Draft Guidelines' definition brings the link between dominance and conduct above very close to the line beyond which all conduct engaged by the dominant firm would be liable to constitute abuse (is the 'special responsibility of the dominant firm' a backdoor for object-box type of abuses?). That, or we forego the objectiveness of the notion and engage in an intentionality assessment, studying the behaviour of the dominant undertaking to understand if they intended, or not, to foreclose their rivals from the market. To make abuse a subjective, instead of an objective notion, would however place a burdensome discovery effort on both the enforcement agencies and on the investigated undertaking.

The Draft Guidelines endorse *Servizio Elettrico Nazionale's* statement that Article 102 TFEU aims to sanction not only practices likely to cause direct harm to consumers but also those which cause them harm indirectly by undermining an effective structure of competition.[25] Likewise, and in line with the over-encompassing 'any hindrance' concept used by the Draft Guidelines, *Servizio Elettrico Nazionale* indicated that Article 102 TFEU will sanction 'any practice capable of adversely affecting, by way of resources other than those which govern normal competition, an effective competition structure. (...) [penalizing conduct which had the] effect of hindering the maintenance of the degree of competition still existing in the market or the **growth of that competition**'. Unlike the 2008 Guidance which spoke also of 'pro-competitive foreclosure',[26] the Draft Guidelines only engage in discussion about the broader idea of 'exclusionary effects'. This differentiation was also endorsed by *Servizio Elettrico Nazionale*'s rule that 'not every exclusionary effect is necessarily detrimental to

23. *See* Draft Guidelines, para. 166.
24. *See* Draft Guidelines, para. 6.
25. *See* C-377/20, *Servizio Elettrico Nazionale SpA and Others*, EU:C:2022:379, para. 44.
26. *See* 2008 Guidance Paper, point 19.

competition (...) [as it could lead to] the departure from the market or the marginalization of competitors that are less efficient'. The Commission could have legitimately endorsed the CJEU's ruling, and yet it did not.

Efficiency is predicated on the basis of cost structures, quality, or capacity to innovate. The operationalisation of the assessment of the AEC principle, however, could prove difficult in some of the markets that Draft Guidelines aim to address. When undertakings offer a product whose uniqueness or position in the value chain makes it hard to replicate it could prove unfeasible for a competitor, actual or potential, to fabricate the same product with a comparable cost structure.[27] This is of particular relevance to non-pricing practices, which albeit included in *Servizio Elettrico Nazionale*'s endorsement of the AEC principle, rely largely on the indispensability case law of the essential facilities doctrine as a guiding standard. And *Bronner* is, as *Android Auto* has demonstrated, no longer a 'safe harbour'.

There are instances where the AEC principle applied to pricing conduct through the as efficient competitor test may deliver underenforcement. For instance:[28]

(i) Due to asymmetry of information, competitors to the dominant firm can be hindered by buyer discoordination – for instance, when faced with exclusivity rebates and in the context of a low-transparency level market, customers will not be willing to renounce an exclusivity deal without knowing if the other customers will also close a deal with the competitors to the dominant firm (a classic example of a prisoners' dilemma).
(ii) When the competitors could technically have the ability to address the whole contestable share of the dominant undertaking, but a system of, e.g., retroactive rebates or discounts to loyalty buyers (which could, in principle, be considered pro-competitive) makes it so that the rival firms lose the incentive to address all of the contestable shares of the dominant undertaking.

As regards non-pricing conduct, there is uncertainty about how to apply the AEC principle. Yet again in *Google Shopping*, the CJEU has insisted that the objective of Article 102 TFEU is 'not to ensure that competitors less efficient than the dominant undertaking remain on the market'[29] even if finding abuse is 'not subject to proof that the conduct concerned is capable of excluding an as-efficient competitor'.[30]

The Policy Brief accompanying the revisions to the 2008 Guidance published in 2023 included an express acceptance of the Commission to the difficulty of operationalising the AEC principle in the context of non-pricing conduct: '[t]he Union Courts

27. *See* Neven, D.J. (2023). *The As-Efficient Competitor Test and Principle. What Role in the Proposed Guidelines?*. Journal of European Competition Law & Practice, 14(8), 565-581 https://doi.org/10.1093/jeclap/lpad063.
28. *See* Neven, D.J. (2023). *The As-Efficient Competitor Test and Principle. What Role in the Proposed Guidelines?*. Journal of European Competition Law & Practice, 14(8), 578-580 https://doi.org/10.1093/jeclap/lpad063.
29. *See* C-48/22 P, *Google LLC and Alphabet Inc. v. Commission (Google Shopping)*, EU:C:2024:726, para. 263.
30. *Ibid.*, para. 264.

have also recognised first, that the notion of "as-efficient" has to be interpreted in a broad sense, and second, that, in certain instances, genuine competition may also come from undertakings that are less efficient than the dominant firm [...] That may be the case in particular in markets where the emergence of as-efficient competitors may not be possible because of the "structure of the market" or where the relevant market is protected by significant barriers'. Digital markets were, of course, the subject of an example, signalling how economies of scale and scope imply that 'market challengers may not be expected to be able to achieve the same or even a similar cost structure as the incumbent', thus 'mandating evidence of foreclosure of as-efficient competitors in these scenarios would likely lead to under-enforcement'.

The key could be of a temporal nature. As such, in *European Superleague*, the CJEU argued that 'conduct may be categorised as "abuse of a dominant position" not only where it has the actual or potential effect of restricting competition on the merits by excluding equally efficient competing undertakings from the market(s) concerned, but also where it has been proven to have the actual or potential effect – or even the object – of impeding potentially competing undertakings at an earlier stage, through the placing of obstacles to entry or the use of other blocking measures or other means different from those which govern competition on the merits, from even entering that or those market(s) and, in so doing, preventing the growth of competition therein to the detriment of consumers, by limiting production, product or alternative service development or innovation'.[31]

Android Auto may have reconciled the two families of anticompetitive behaviour, unilateral and collusive, by concluding that certain unilateral behaviour reveals in and of itself a sufficient degree of harm as to be considered an abuse by object. Causation by law rebuttable by an alternative explanation for the practice is therefore the formalistic replacement of the assessment of all circumstances enshrined in the case law of the CJEU.[32] Exclusionary abuse only results when from the assessment of the nature and effects of a unilateral practice (which is normally prone to competition, unlike concerted practices) it can be ruled out that a hypothetically as efficient competitor would be able to obtain the same benefit from the same conduct, or would be able to offset the advantage gained by the dominant undertaking.[33] 'Killer abuses', mirroring the theory of harm enshrined in killer acquisitions in the merger control context, are advocated by the CJEU in the judgment, also building on the rulings in *European Superleague* and *Google Shopping* – this is, conduct preventing currently less efficient competitors from becoming hypothetically equally efficient competitors.[34]

There is no such thing as an 'object box' in the context of Article 102 TFEU, much like there is no longer such an element of formalistic assessment under Article 101 TFEU, and so the business rationale (all circumstances assessment) of the undertaking needs to be analysed to understand if a conduct is artificial or not. However, the CJEU's

31. *See* C-333/21, *European Superleague Company*, EU:C:2023:1011, para. 131.
32. *See* Solano Díaz, *Android Auto* (C-233/23): Beyond stating the obvious? (link available https://www.competitionactually.com/abuse-dominant-position-article-102/android-auto-c-233-23-beyond-stating-the-obvious/#more-256).
33. *See ibid.*
34. *See ibid.*

willingness to recognise abuses by object by insisting on the idea that the sole capability to foreclose is enough to prove potential effects further collapses the analysis of artificiality in the two prongs of the test. The CJEU insists that there could be conduct so irrational or deviated from the business rationale that there can only be a restrictive objective logic inferred.[35] This would circumvent the need to engage in 'complex counterfactual analysis where the theory of harm is the elimination of competitors before they grow equally efficient ("killer abuse")'.[36] The Commission further deals with this idea of potential competition in the ruling, when stating: 'In applying Article 102 TFEU, a precise definition of the product market and the geographic market is not necessarily required to identify the downstream market. In certain circumstances, it is sufficient that a potential or even hypothetical market can be identified (judgment of 29 April 2004, IMS Health, C-418/01, EU:C:2004:257, paragraph 44). Where the downstream market concerned is still developing or is evolving rapidly and, therefore, its scope is not fully defined on the date on which the undertaking in a dominant position implements the allegedly abusive conduct, it is sufficient for the competition authority to identify that market, even if it is only a potential market. That authority must then, taking account of the characteristics and the potential scope of that market, demonstrate that that conduct is capable of having anticompetitive effects on that same market, even if only potential competition exists on that market between the products or services of the undertaking in a dominant position and – in the case of conduct consisting of that dominant undertaking refusing the interoperability, as requested by a third-party undertaking, with a digital platform owned by the undertaking in a dominant position – the products or services of the undertaking requesting that interoperability.'[37]

Consistently, the Commission insisted in its Policy Brief to the application of Article 102 TFEU to digital markets that markets characterised by network effects require an *effective and swift enforcement* to intervene before an entrenched market position is created. Some authors already mull over the idea of reducing the threshold of intervention from the 'as efficient competitor' to the 'potentially as efficient competitor' principle. However, this would in turn require raising the evidentiary threshold so that the burden of proof, then necessarily with the Commission, entailed an assessment of all circumstances and market realities which was contestable by the investigated undertaking. This would contradict the current approach in the Draft Guidelines, which exempt the Commission from having to show actual harm, harm to consumers, nor even an economic assessment of the consequences of the conduct on the 'potentially as efficient competitors'. Although the humour is for a more formalistic Guideline, reducing the threshold of intervention would necessarily require the Commission to once again adopt a pure economics-based approach to the assessment of harm.

35. *Ibid. See also* C–233/23, *Google Android Auto*, EU:C:2025:110, paras 55-58.
36. *See* Solano Díaz, *Android Auto* (C-233/23): Beyond stating the obvious? (link available https://www.competitionactually.com/abuse-dominant-position-article-102/android-auto-c-233-23-beyond-stating-the-obvious/#more-256).
37. *See* C–233/23, *Google Android Auto*, EU:C:2025:110, para. 85.

As explained above, the Commission's decisional practice has not shied away from restricting fundamental freedoms to deal with dominant undertakings under exceptional circumstances. However, this doctrine has been slowly expanding, coming to render outdated the established understanding that if a dominant undertaking lacked capacity to meet its competitors' requests, then no refusal, British-style or not, could concur. A recent decision from the Commission, whose legal certainty remains untested since the investigation was closed with commitments, *ENI*, suggests that dominant undertakings do not only have a duty to deal in the present but also to make sure that they will be able to deal in the future.

Strategic underinvestment would constitute an abuse of dominant position in those circumstances where a dominant firm would have decided not to invest sufficiently in the expansion of their infrastructure *despite having sufficient predicting capacity to know* that there would be a higher long-term demand than the one currently being supplied. The firm would therefore have acted irrationally (foregoing future profit) for the purpose of limiting the number of competitors in the future market. In *ENI*, the Commission indicated that the dominant undertaking controlled access to indispensable infrastructures for the import of gas into Italy. The Commission found abuse from a traditional perspective (i.e., because the undertaking would have hoarded capacity or only provided it under disadvantageous conditions) but it expanded the notion of abuse to encompass not only past or current economically irrational behaviour but also future (i.e., foregoing a highly likely profit upstream to ensure less competition and hence potentially lower profits downstream).

In line with the Draft Guidelines' suggestion that not only 'as efficient' competitors should be guaranteed protection from anticompetitive strategies, *ENI*'s strategic underinvestment rationale suggests that dominant undertakings not only have a duty to refrain from acting anticompetitively but also to act 'pro-competitively'. Hence, a refusal to deal would be analysed not only on the basis of current competitors who, if given the chance, would be able to enter the market and increase competition. Dominant undertakings are tasked with the private regulatory power of shaping market conditions to invite future competitors (who likely are currently not as efficient or capable as them) to enter the future and enact competitive pressure. Although it has disappeared from the wording of the Draft Guidelines, we would do well to remember that the ordoliberal nature of Article 102 TFEU entails that foreclosure can be pro-competitive – by allowing for underperforming operators to exit the market, we allow for competition to grow, increasing the return to investment and the addressable market share for all well-performing operators. Any abuse of dominance predicated on the basis of harm to less efficient competitors, as potentially efficient as they could be, should be measured against the efficiencies that this conduct can bring to the market. A recent example in the merger control province is that of the *Vodafone/Three* joint venture. An agreement where the CMA found 'particularly significant' competition concerns was cleared on the basis of countervailing efficiencies outweighing adverse impact on competition.[38] One of these, namely a commitment to investment in the

38. *See* CMA, 'Summary of final report', *Vodafone/Three* paras 4-5 (link available https://assets.publishing.service.gov.uk/media/675146fe9ef923a1bbc97b18/Summary_of_final_report_3.pdf).

network programme of the UK, would 'result in a significant improvement in the quality of the Merged Entity's mobile network, boosting competition between MNOs in the long term and benefiting millions of consumers and businesses'.[39] It is this long-term perspective to competition which should be observed as well in any non-standardised, particularly non-pricing conduct under Article 102 TFEU, which could find trouble in assessing the efficiency of competitors. And it would align with precedent, in particular with the expanded doctrine of essential facilities.

Additionally, the rationale behind the purported abuse of less efficient competitors or hindering of competition growth could more easily be linked to the extractive logic of exploitative abuse. The exit of a less efficient competitor from the market does not, in principle, engender a market failure - its exit, as explained above, will improve allocative efficiency of investment, resources and return between the remaining competitors. The logical place for less efficient competitors is as a factor in the assessment of 'all the relevant factual circumstances'[40] as per *Intel*.[41] However, here is an alternative path, even if it is beyond the scope of this article to explore the possibility of the Commission to undertake exploitative abuse investigations. If anything, a suggestion about the possibility of mirroring the assessment under the merger control test, where a 'significant impediment to effective competition' can be found either through the elaboration of a theory of harm based on exclusionary or extractive practices (i.e., either because the merged entity forecloses access to competitors to important market bottlenecks, or because the competitors will not be able to exert sufficient countervailing power against the merged entity's anticompetitive tactics after the transaction).[42] Yet, even this avenue would bring us back to the same closing statement: process makes substance, and if the Commission aims to expand the scope for sanction then there needs to be an expanded scope for defence available to undertakings.

The relative efficiency criterion unifying theory would allow for a single plausibility standard, subject to rebuttal, following the stead of merger control proceedings, to be the standard of quality of evidence required to demonstrate abuse.[43] The enforcement authorities would thus be required to prove the plausibility that the conduct rendered competition artificial (either because it completely ignored the business' rationale or because as-efficient competitors were ousted from the market due to the impossibility of replicating a similar advantage). In situations where from the aforementioned the room for alternative explanation is brittle, then it would fall

39. *See* CMA, 'Summary of final report', *Vodafone/Three* para. 8 (link available https://assets.publishing.service.gov.uk/media/675146fe9ef923a1bbc97b18/Summary_of_final_report_3.pdf).
40. *See* Solano Díaz, '*Dear Santa, I'd like to ask a consistent framework for Article 102 TFEU*' (link available https://www.competitionactually.com/abuse-dominant-position-article-102/dear-santa-id-like-to-ask-a-consistent-framework-for-article-102-tfeu/).
41. *See* C-413/14 *Intel Corp. v. Commission*, EU:C:2017:632, paras 138-141; C-240/22 P *Commission v. Intel Corp.*, EU:C:2024:915, paras 179-180.
42. *See* Solano Díaz, '*Dear Santa, I'd like to ask a consistent framework for Article 102 TFEU*' (link available https://www.competitionactually.com/abuse-dominant-position-article-102/dear-santa-id-like-to-ask-a-consistent-framework-for-article-102-tfeu/).
43. *See ibid.*

upon the undertaking to 'build one alternative assessment which competition authorities are compelled to analyse in detail'. Rather than engage in hypothetical counterfactuals devised by the competition authorities, it is the undertaking which demonstrates that its conduct: (i) were objectively justified; or (ii) is the source of (long-term, trickle-down) procompetitive effects.[44]

In conclusion, if the Commission's enforcement continues addressing markets where it is difficult to operationalise the 'as efficient competitor' principle in quantitative terms, then the resulting lower threshold of intervention must be coupled with a higher evidentiary threshold and concomitant assessment of 'all circumstances', including, despite the traditional reluctance, efficiency claims presented by the dominant undertaking.

3 ABUSE OF 'DOMINANT POSITION'

Fair competition, and its subsequent intervention below the current thresholds applicable to free competition, could also be attained by broadening the scope of application of Article 102 TFEU not on the basis of offence (abuse) but the offender (dominant undertaking).

The Draft Guidelines provide a series of general principles to assess dominance. Dominance is understood as the capacity of an undertaking to behave up to 'an appreciable extent' independently from its competitors as regards its market strategy without fearing 'suffering detrimental effects from such behaviour'.[45] Only once dominance has been established is Article 102 TFEU applicable.[46] The Draft Guidelines dedicate a section to understanding the yet largely uncharted territory of collective dominance, but most relevantly they list a (non-exhaustive) series of factors which may prove the existence of a dominant position. These are namely:

(i) *The market position of the undertaking concerned and of its competitors.* The most important proxy for this dimension is market shares, which are 'in themselves, save in exceptional circumstances, evidence of the existence of a dominant position'.[47] Article 102 TFEU's legal tenet implies the existence of a dominant position which enables the dominant undertaking to engage in artificial behaviour. However, the Draft Guidelines' concept of dominance undermines this requirement by presuming dominance above 50% market share and establishing a very low 10% market share safe harbour. 'Dominance may also be found in cases where an undertaking has a market share below 50%. (...) Market shares below 10 % exclude the existence of a dominant market position save in exceptional circumstances.'[48] The approach largely broadens the 2008 Guidance which considered dominance unlikely to exist below the 40% market share. As such, the Commission is

44. *See ibid.*
45. *See* Draft Guidelines, para. 19.
46. *See* Draft Guidelines, para. 21.
47. *See* Draft Guidelines, para. 26.
48. *See* Draft Guidelines, para. 26.

not only expanding the range of conducts which may attract 102 TFEU liability but also how many undertakings may be found liable for it. It is disputable how much competitive value shall be restored to the competitive structure when correcting the behaviour of an undertaking that has no real capacity to independently shape the market with its behaviour. The Draft Guidelines accept that market shares must, in any case, be 'interpreted in light of the relevant market conditions, the dynamics of the market and the extent to which products are differentiated'.[49]

(ii) *Barriers to expansion and entry*. The lack of these will limit the ability of any undertaking to behave independently, at the risk of making the market more attractive for new entrants. The Draft Guidelines list a series of factors which could lead to the enactment of barriers: tariffs, licences, statutory monopolies, IP rights, economies of scale or scope, network effects, vertical integration and self-preferential access, access to critical input, customer inertia, reputation, data-driven advantages, first mover advantage... The Draft Guidelines single out platform markets as victims of network effects due to the switching costs experienced by users and the limited multi-homing.[50]

(iii) *Countervailing buyer power.*

Market power, and its utmost manifestation as monopoly power, are generally associated with high market shares. As an operational tool, high market shares are a proxy of a firm's strong market power. Critics, however, argue that they are a picture of static market power which sidelines other elements of the analysis, such as product differentiation, asymmetric information and client-specific investments.[51] The decision of the Commission to expand the range of market shares likely to be found as an expression of dominance and leaving behind the 40% presumption that existed previously signals a willingness to explore other sources of market power.

These sources of market power are dealt at the national level through the framework of economic dependence. Economic freedom is an expression of contractual relationships allowing market participants to behave free of any restrictions enacted thanks to the market power of other participants. Abuse of dominance needs to be found in a relevant market and will analyse the economic weight of the firm in that delimited space. Relative dominance explores the economic power that market participants may enact vis-a-vis other market operators due to the superior bargaining position it enjoys.[52] The advantageous leverage enjoyed by a firm, however, could well be the product of an effective 'competition on the merits'. The potential departure from the 'as efficient competitor' principle, as explained above, could be a welcoming stance to the analysis of new conducts. As much as an uneven market power can affect the

49. *See* Draft Guidelines, para. 28.
50. *See* Draft Guidelines, paras 29-32.
51. *See* Këllezi, P. (2008). *Abuse Below the Threshold of Dominance? Market Power, Market Dominance, and Abuse of Economic Dependence: In Abuse of Dominant Position: New Interpretation, New Enforcement Mechanisms?* (pp. 55-88). Springer Berlin Heidelberg, p. 60.
52. *See* ICN, 'Report on Abuse of Superior Bargaining Position' (2008) available at: https://www.internationalcompetitionnetwork.org/wp-content/uploads/2019/11/SP_ASBP2008.pdf.

economic freedom of only one undertaking, a systematic approach followed by an undertaking enjoying access to, e.g., a key input for the industry, could result in an aggregated network of contracts eventually affecting the structure of the market.[53]

Market power can be understood as power over price, meaning that a firm will be able to raise price above the cost of production. Deadweight loss occurs as a result, proving the economic inefficiency that stems from market power. There are however instances of non-market power. This is the case of price increases resulting from shifts in demand and supply curves, profits, or bargaining power. Regarding the latter, economists consider that an excessive 'price' paid to a seller is merely a transfer of resources, with 'no consequential or moral reason to deem increases in sellers' utility less socially worthy compared to increases in buyers' utility'. Superior bargaining power rises from 'information asymmetries, incomplete contracts, risk aversion, transaction costs, or asset specific investments', and all these 'market imperfections', while not market power, can also determine outcomes like 'holdup, consumer exploitation, lock-in and economic dependence'.[54]

In a perfectly competitive market, superior bargaining power can remain, and 'changing what the market can bear is not a market problem'.[55] EU competition law is a system of 'market power containment',[56] yet there is a widespread reluctance to use the term. Whether this is a reflection of the ordoliberal essence of Article 102 TFEU (concerned with market position, not power, and the protection of the competitive structure, not criminalising dominance but only its abuse) or of the instrumentalisation of EU antitrust as a tool for regional economic integration, the truth is that there is a pro-concentration philosophy under the tenets of EU competition law.[57] EU law should be inherently neutral toward the formation of monopoly power (the Draft Guidelines indicate that 'Article 102 TFEU does not prevent an undertaking from acquiring on its own merits, in particular on account of its skills and abilities, a dominant position on a given market').[58] This is in line with precedent from the courts, with the CJEU having safeguarded the formation of market power from attack (to that effect, the CJEU insisted in *Volkswagen* that Article 102 TFEU is applicable 'at the time of abuse').[59] There is a tacit understanding that EU law will not assess whether there is a pro-competitive origin to market power, be it from internal growth, merger policy or State-granted privileges. The lack of structural remedies implying divestment and reduction in the market share of a dominant undertaking as a result of abuse liability speaks as well to this idea: it is not a weakened competition that concerns Article 102 TFEU, but the artificial abuse (as per the definition given to this artificiality in section

53. *See* Bakhoum, M. (2018). *Abuse Without Dominance in Competition Law: Abuse of Economic Dependence and Its Interface with Abuse of Dominance. In Abusive Practices in Competition Law* (pp. 157-184). Edward Elgar Publishing, p. 11.
54. *See* Petit, N. (2022). Understanding Market Power. Robert Schuman Centre for Advanced Studies Research Paper No. RSC_14, pp. 14-16.
55. *See ibid.*, p. 16.
56. *See ibid.*, p. 22.
57. *See ibid.*, p. 234.
58. *See* Draft Guidelines, para. 17.
59. *See* T-62/98 *Volkswagen AG v. Commission*, EU:T:2000:180, para. 230.

2 of such weakened competition to further entrench a dominant position.[60] This is a slightly different approach to the one embraced by US antitrust law, which targets monopoly power through a 'bad conduct' lens. Bad conduct is that which 'deviates from normality'.[61] In *Grinnell*, the Supreme Court defined it as the 'willful acquisition or maintenance of that power as distinguished from growth or development as a consequence of a superior product. business acumen, or historic accident'.[62] There is a deliberate, willing conduct (not negligence or accident) to monopolise, distinct from the intent to engage in a conduct.[63] As Petit coins, under the US lens, bad conduct implies not an exercise of monopoly power (or dominant position in the EU terminology) but of oppression: 'a firm will be deemed to pursue an anticompetitive end when it chooses oppressive behaviour over efficiency'.[64]

This is not, in principle, the province of EU competition law. As explained above, our ordoliberal, objective notion of abuse of dominance does not concern the creation of market power, but only the abuse of an already existing monopoly power. Yet, let me bring attention to the careful wording of the Draft Guidelines: 'Article 102 TFEU does not prevent an undertaking from acquiring **on its own merits, in particular on account of its skills and abilities**, a dominant position on a given market.'[65] One can draw a quick parallel between this definition and that of *Grinnell*.

As Petit observes, the removal of causality between dominance and conduct, and the focus on the causality between dominance and effects broadens the scope of application from conduct which is enabled by the existence of a dominant position to any conduct engaged by a dominant firm which results in anticompetitive foreclosure (even if it takes place in a leveraged market).[66] In the Draft Guidelines, the Commission accepts that conduct liable under Article 102 TFEU could be producing exclusionary effects on dominated and non-dominated markets, with the substantive legal standard being the same for both instances. The Commission qualifies the latter approach by establishing that the affected non-dominated market be 'related to' the dominated market.[67] Furthermore, the ruling of the CJEU in *Generics*, where a dominant position was presumed, may have weakened the idea that liability can only be attracted at the time of abuse, and not when a dominant position has already disappeared and there is an attempt either to regain it or acquire it.

Uneven trading terms and unequal bargaining power are, in principle, not the province of competition law but that of contract or consumer law, on the basis that the freedom of market participants to contract as they wish is to be respected as long as these interactions do not further weaken competition in an already weakly competitive

60. *See* Petit, N. (2022). Understanding Market Power. Robert Schuman Centre for Advanced Studies Research Paper No. RSC_14, p. 30.
61. *See ibid.*, p. 27.
62. *See United States v. Grinnell Corp.* 384 U.S. 571 (1966).
63. *See* Petit, N. (2022). Understanding Market Power. Robert Schuman Centre for Advanced Studies Research Paper No. RSC_14, p. 28.
64. *See ibid.*, p. 28.
65. *See* Draft Guidelines, para. 17.
66. *See* Petit, N. (2022). Understanding Market Power. Robert Schuman Centre for Advanced Studies Research Paper No. RSC_14, p. 42.
67. *See* Draft Guidelines, para. 68.

market. 'Competition law is not concerned with ensuring formal economic equality between market participants, [but with] keeping the market open and competitive and protecting all market participants' opportunities to compete, regardless of their market power.'[68] Economic dependence or superior bargaining power provisions, however, are designed to protect the weaker part in a trading relationship. This is in principle opposite to the spirit of Article 102 TFEU, which is not to protect competitors but to protect the competitive structure itself. However, there are imaginable situations where an undertaking were not yet dominant in the relevant market, but it were relatively dominant vis-à-vis its trading partners because it, for example, has a data-driven advantage or access to a critical raw material, to use the terms of the Draft Guidelines in its general principles of assessment of dominance. The relatively dominant undertaking could then use these unique capabilities to leverage the relative dominance as a means to obtain dominance in the relevant market. The question we could then pose is whether this would constitute 'an undertaking (...) acquiring on its own merits, in particular on account of its skills and abilities, a dominant position on a given market'.[69] If we approach the Draft Guidelines from a holistic, coherent perspective, then the same definition given to competition on the merits for the purpose of ascertaining whether competition was natural or artificial in the context of abuse post-dominance should then apply to the pre-dominance window.

To this purpose, the Draft Guidelines provide a series of factors to assess:

- whether consumer's freedom of choice is curtailed;
- whether the undertaking has abused a regulatory instrument or procedure to the detriment of the authority or its competitors;
- whether there is a cross-violation with other areas of law;
- whether there has been discriminatory behaviour against competitors;
- whether an undertaking decides to shift previous market practice without a reasonable explanation for it; and
- whether a 'hypothetical competitor as efficient as the dominant undertaking would be unable to adopt the same conduct, notably because that conduct relies on the use of resources or means inherent to the holding of the dominant position, particularly to leverage or strengthen that position in the same or another market'.[70]

It is, therefore, conceivable to extend the scope of application of Article 102 TFEU so that it covers not only conduct 'at the time of abuse' but also the means employed to obtain that competitive advantage and market dominance. Would this not derail the very essence of the provision in the EU context, which is not to criminalise market power but its abuse, and only to sanction the abusive marginal weakening of an already weakly competitive market? Or is it possible that an aggregated network of

68. *See* Bakhoum, M. (2018). *Abuse Without Dominance in Competition Law: Abuse of Economic Dependence and Its Interface with Abuse of Dominance. In Abusive Practices in Competition Law* (pp. 157-184). Edward Elgar Publishing, p. 4.
69. *See* Draft Guidelines, para. 17.
70. *See* Draft Guidelines, para. 55.

unevenly negotiated contracts could change the structure of the market to the point where market access is restricted for the weakest links and thereby free competition is constrained?

Although there are no provisions to this effect in the EU and US antitrust laws, examples of rules dealing with abuse of relative dominance (i.e., 'the impossibility or costs of a trading partner to shift to another trading partner') arise at the national level.[71] The existence of an alternative supply chain is one of the four criteria used by the French competition authority to assess the existence of economic dependence, and it has also been adopted by the German laws (section 20 of the German Act Against Restriction of Competition qualifies it as 'sufficient and reasonable possibilities'). Economic dependence, unlike market power, is not predicated on the size or strength of a particular market, but on the possibility of a trading partner to find a suitable alternative within a reasonable effort. As Barkhoum indicates, the concern in these provisions is that of keeping a competitive market open, allowing for firms to, indeed, compete on the merits of their products and prevent 'lock-in' effects from materialising:

(i) *In Germany*, the German Act Against Restriction of Competition analyses the bilateral relations between undertakings under section 20, with a restricted scope that only grants protection against discriminatory practices to small and medium enterprises. The strength of a brand, long-standing relationships and the share of business dedicated to a particular trading partner, shortage, buying or technical dependence are all manifestations of economic dependence covered by the provision. However, as the German Federal Court held in *Rosignol*,[72] these provisions may only have an effect when the enterprise 'does not hold a market-dominating position'. There is then a clear attempt at delineating different scopes of action for provisions covering abuse of dominance and abuses of economic dependence.

(ii) *In France*, Article L 420-2 of the Commercial Code states that '[a]*lso prohibited, <u>whenever it is susceptible to affect the functioning or structure of competition</u>, is the abusive exploitation, by a company or group of companies, of the condition of economic dependence in which a customer company or supplier finds itself vis-à-vis such company*' (emphasis added). The analysis will be circumscribed to the trading relationship between the undertakings and evaluate brand strength, the importance of a supplier's input into the final product price, and the difficulty of finding alternative trading partners. The boundaries between abuse of economic dependence and abuse of dominance are blurred, however, with abuse of economic dependence being found alongside abuse of dominance in cases such as *Cannes Palm Beach*,

71. *See* Bakhoum, M. (2018). *Abuse Without Dominance in Competition Law: Abuse of Economic Dependence and Its Interface with Abuse of Dominance. In Abusive Practices in Competition Law* (pp. 157-184). Edward Elgar Publishing, p. 11, fn. 39.

72. *See* Këllezi, P. (2008). *Abuse Below the Threshold of Dominance? Market Power, Market Dominance, and Abuse of Economic Dependence. In Abuse of Dominant Position: New Interpretation, New Enforcement Mechanisms*? (pp. 55-88). Springer Berlin Heidelberg, fn. 42.

Filmdis and *Reims Bio.*[73] Yet, the authors consider that whereas in analysing a dominant position the authority will focus on market shares and economic weight, in finding abuse of economic dependence the focus will lie on analysing the existence of alternative trading partners. The provisions are, therefore, not coextensive.

(iii) **In Italy**, antitrust authorities have been reluctant to introduce economic dependence in the province of antitrust law and it has been introduced as Article 9 of the Italian Law on Industrial Subcontracting, also with a focus on alternative trading partners tackling discriminatory and explcitative practices. However, the national authority warned of the risk of conflating economic efficiency (the protected province of antitrust) with market equity aimed at protecting weaker parties. The Italian competition authority preferred to nuance the approach to abuse of dominance to consider the effect that contractual relationships could have in the definition of the relevant market.[74]

Policing economic dependency and superior bargaining powers could amount to the aforementioned Rousseaunian intervention in the Hobbesian natural jungle. Yet proponents of the idea put forward a compelling argument, namely that the unstrained competitive process which Article 102 TFEU aims to protect is also curtailed when market operators do not operate freely in the market dynamics. The protection of free participation clashes thence with the protection of unfettered competition, and this interaction between the objective and subjective dimensions of freedom is summarised as a 'freedom paradox'.[75]

Provisions restraining abuse of economic dependence need not be a backdoor protection for inefficient competitors, but rather protecting weaker (not necessarily less efficient) firms – seeing as there can be no free competition to protect if no competitors remain.[76] To prevent abuse of economic dependence does not entail protecting profits or ensuring survival, but rather ensuring that the *means* to compete on the merits against rival (non-)dominant undertakings remain. Potentially, it could even be coherent with the EU approach to competition law, which does not hinge on consumer harm but is amenable to consider all kinds of market harm,[77] including the possibility of curtailed freedom to participate for final consumers, intermediate consumers, producers and suppliers.[78] This 'producer welfare' approach could be reconciled with

73. *See ibid.*, p. 65.
74. *See ibid.*, pp. 68-69.
75. *See* Bakhoum, M. (2018). *Abuse Without Dominance in Competition Law: Abuse of Economic Dependence and Its Interface with Abuse of Dominance. In Abusive Practices in Competition Law* (pp. 157-184). Edward Elgar Publishing, p. 21. *See also* Fikentscher, W., Hacker, P. and Podszun, R., *Fair Economy: Crises. Culture, Competition and the Role of Law*, pp. 50-51.
76. *See* Bakhoum, M. (2018). *Abuse Without Dominance in Competition Law: Abuse of Economic Dependence and Its Interface with Abuse of Dominance. In Abusive Practices in Competition Law* (pp. 157-184). Edward Elgar Publishing, pp. 22-23.
77. *See ibid.*, p. 27.
78. *See ibid.*, p. 28.

the increasing concern about growth and resilience that the Commission has been recently advocating.

However, as much as protecting the freedom of participants in the competitive process is compatible with the objectives of Article 102 TFEU, it is arguably not the province of this provision to engage in these deliberations. Two pathways are available.

First, to incorporate abuse of economic dependence provisions into the scope of Article 102 TFEU. If a potentially abusive conduct escapes the grasp of national authorities, then the 'bad conduct' which allowed a firm to obtain market power in the first place should be assessed under the general principles for assessment of whether a conduct is competitive on the merits or not, specifically whether there has been cross-violation of other areas of law. Furthermore, sector-specific regulation at the EU level should provide a comprehensive, common standard to understand whether behaviour constitutes 'bad conduct' or not (because, for instance, in the digital markets, a non-dominant undertaking engages in the type of conduct which would be prohibited for a designated gatekeeper). There is however an intentionality element to the concept of 'bad conduct' which is not present in the objective notion of abuse of dominance. It would require applying two different legal standards to one potentially single, continuous infringement: abuse as a subjective notion (with the consequential discovery procedure and assessment of internal documents) before the time of dominance; and abuse as an objective notion, concerned with effects and results, after the time of dominance. It is possible that any direct intervention of EU law into matters concerned with restrictions on the economic freedom to participate and access the market faced by individual undertakings should be the province of the provisions on fundamental freedoms, particularly freedom of movement of goods and services, as well as freedom of establishment, be it through indirect effect or through the invocability of horizontal direct effect when available. Furthermore, we could consider the possibility of exploitative abuse, and the incorporation of an anti-extractive logic to Article 102 TFEU. As indicated above, it is beyond the scope of this article to analyse all the implications of this extended scope. Suffice it to say, there is potential merit to the idea of mirroring the standard of 'significant impediment to effective competition' and its multiple limbs of exclusionary and exploitative theories of harm, as long as this is coupled with an expanded procedural scope for defence and a more detailed consideration of the resulting efficiencies of any foreclosing strategy deployed by an undertaking.

In any event, if we still want to consider an available avenue to consider these activities in the assessment of Article 102 TFEU, then I suggest the proper instrument to use would be the Market Definition Notice ('MDN').[79]

Market definition is the keystone of antitrust analysis, allowing to both establish formal liability requirements and assess the anticompetitive effects of the investigated conducts, and conducing either to excessively narrow markets with the resulting

79. *See* European Commission 'Commission Notice on the definition of the relevant market for the purposes of Union competition law', C/2024/1645.

overenforcement, or overestimations of competition resulting in underenforcement in excessively broad markets.[80]

The issue at stake here is the similarity of conditions of competition between different trading partners, i.e., discrimination between (intermediate) customers. As explained above, it is conduct which deviates from normality that constitutes 'bad conduct'.[81] The revised Notice has broadened the application of the criterion of discrimination between different groups of customers, now applying it both for product and geographic market definition.[82]

This is a deviation from previous practice and from the hypothetical monopolist test ('HMT')-based framework and focuses on the homogeneity of the conditions of competition ('HCC') in a certain market. In the HMT framework, demand-side substitutability remains the most important competitive constraint on undertakings – it is however this very same market power which is encroached upon by a superior bargaining position in an economic dependence framework. A profit sacrifice test is the underlying rationale under the SSNIP test which guides the HMT framework, and it contrasts with the HCC framework insofar as the latter focuses on assessing markets with sufficiently similar competitive conditions which differ sufficiently from the ones afforded to other customer groups.[83] Some of the criteria used by the Commission in an HCC context are the position in the market of the supplier and its rivals, customer inertia, tariffs and other barriers to supply across areas.[84] The Notice stresses the importance of finding customers who are similarly affected by the conditions of competition in a certain market. For discrimination to be possible, the Notice identifies several conditions, such as the capacity to discriminate between customers, the customers' incapacity to inter-trade their purchases, and that discrimination is non-transitory.[85] If all of these are fulfilled, then a narrower segment of the market can be identified.[86]

Narrower markets may arise under the HCC framework than under the HMT if there are strong group-specific differences which do not necessarily reflect supply-demand substitution.[87] The application of the HCC framework would shift again the focus on the subsequent competitive assessment.[88] It would not do good to forget that products and companies not operating on a defined relevant market may still impose competitive constraints on the investigated undertaking,[89] even if there is a *décalage*

80. *See* Galli, N. and Parcu, P.L. (2024). *Market Definition and Multi-Sided Markets: A Primer on the 2024 EU Market Definition Notice*, p. 11.
81. *See* Petit, N. (2022). Understanding Market Power. Robert Schuman Centre for Advanced Studies Research Paper No. RSC_14, p. 27.
82. *See* Galli, N. & Parcu, P. L. (2024). *Market Definition and Multi-Sided Markets: A Primer on the 2024 EU Market Definition Notice*, p. 3.
83. *See* Barros, L. *et al.* (2024). *Market Definition under the EC Market Definition Notice: Substitutability Versus Homogeneous Conditions of Competition.* Available at SSRN 5017843. p. 8.
84. *See* MDN, paras 38 and 39.
85. *See* MDN, para. 88.
86. *See* MDN, para. 89.
87. *See* Barros, L. et al. (2024). *Market Definition under the EC Market Definition Notice: Substitutability Versus Homogeneous Conditions of Competition.* Available at SSRN 5017843., p. 11.
88. *See ibid.*, p. 21.
89. *See ibid.*, p. 22.

which leaves them outside the narrower market definition. A shift from in-market constraints under the HMT framework to out-of-market constraints under the HCC framework would increase the importance of proof of potential anticompetitive effects in the competitive analysis carried out by the Commission. The HCC framework focuses on customer behaviour, whereas the HMT framework rests on identifying the competitors.

This Copernican turn in focus would have necessary practical implications, however. As explained above regarding a potential lower threshold of intervention by considering harm to potentially as efficient competitors instead of only as efficient competitors, a broader use of the HCC framework for product market definition (something that the Notice does not develop in detail) would raise the evidentiary threshold expected from the Commission when proving any anticompetitive effects. This calls, yet again, for a quick abandonment of the purported formalistic approach to assessing abuse under Article 102 TFEU and a quick return to the valued economics-based approach.

It can be argued, in any event, that any and all matters connected to economic dependence should remain the province of Member States' law seems therefore the most attractive avenue. Many of the areas affected by these provisions pertain to the dimension of private law, which remains a largely uncharted province for EU law.

In the German Competition Authority's *Facebook* decision, the *Solange* spirit proved itself alive as far as the decentralised enforcement of Articles 101 and 102 TFEU is concerned ('the concept of protection developed by German case law on the general clause of Section 19(1) GWB, (...), has so far found no equivalent in European case law or application practice'). In principle, the conflict rule established in Article 3 of Regulation 1/2003 allows Member States to unconditionally impose stricter rules on unilateral conduct than those prohibited under Article 102 TFEU even if the conduct itself could also be captured under the EU provision.[90] Furthermore, Member States can concomitantly apply national laws pursuing objectives predominantly different from those enshrined in Articles 101 and 102 TFEU insofar as these are subject to the general principles of EU law.

Following *Tele2Polska*, there is a CJEU-condoned asymmetry of powers between the Commission and national competition authorities as regards the enforcement of Articles 101 and 102 TFEU. Dual federalism sleeps at the core of Regulation 1/2003: there must be cooperation between entities with exclusive competence spheres. Nonetheless, under Article 102 TFEU national competition authorities can operate as agents of the Commission when applying EU competition law. As such, Article 3 of Regulation 1/2003 imposes an obligation on national competition authorities to apply EU rules to those cases under their oversight which present interstate trade elements. National laws, however, can go beyond the current reading of Article 102 TFEU at the EU level in order to sanction conduct which may have been cleared by the Commission.

National authorities are bound in their interpretation of the law to the letter of EU secondary legislation, the CJEU case law or decisions by the Commission, insofar as

90. *See* Mota Delgado, M. and Petit, N. (2023). *Article 3 of Regulation 1/2003 and the Doctrine of Pre-emption*. Available at https://papers.ssrn.com/sol3/papers.cfm?abstract_id=4325094.

national agents (which include both courts and NCAs) can come to independent conclusions but always applying criteria set out by the CJEU. Under no circumstance may the application of national rules jeopardise the effective application and enforcement of EU antitrust rules.

However, this rule of pre-emption contained in Article 3 of Regulation 1/2003 allows enforcement autonomy to the national agents when the law has not been pre-empted and there are no (quasi)exhaustive criteria of procedural or substantive nature. Their capacity to shape antitrust spirits can only be pre-empted by any future interpretation delivered by an EU agent.

It is true, nonetheless, that recent CJEU rulings have raised concerns about the endangering of *ne bis in idem* under the decentralised system of antitrust enforcement. The incoming reformed Regulation 1/2003 is the adequate place to introduce specific conflict rule-interpretation pre-emption rules. When the EU agents have delivered formal substantive or procedural boundaries (including for that purpose Article 10 of Regulation 1's decisions of inapplicability), national agents may not go beyond. In the absence of such, we welcome cases such as Germany's *Facebook*. First, because it will allow the CJEU to admit preliminary rulings requests from national courts acting on behalf of national authorities' investigations stretching the limits of EU antitrust. What was once a concern about data privacy's interaction with competition is today part of the digital single market toolkit control under the DMA and DSA. And in the forum of ECN + , informal guidance, which may not pre-empt national action, can deliver in the form of Joint Statements and Commission Communications signals to the market as to the objectives and goals of EU antitrust. In a multilevel, experimentalist system of governance of antitrust such as the EU's, determining the appropriate aggregator technology is never easy. And yet, this may be the most appropriate system of enforcement and coupling of any rules dealing with the abuse of superior bargaining position and economic dependence which could end up sanctioned under that ambiguous tenet of the Draft Guidelines: 'an undertaking (...) acquiring <u>on its own merits, in particular on account of its skills and abilities</u>, a dominant position on a given market'.[91] If we want competition on the merits between undertakings, we might as well request cooperation on the merits from the enforcement agencies.

4 CONCLUSIONS

Is Article 102 TFEU a market correcting, or a market shaping tool? The debate we all thought closed (with regulatory tools like the DMA taking the role of shaping the markets and EU competition law remaining as a tool for marginal behaviours) is not conclusive. The question held in the original drafting remains – is this an anti-exclusionary tool or does it have an anti-extractive limb to it as well?

This is not an isolated request for Article 102 TFEU – if killer acquisitions, sustainable efficiencies to prima facie anticompetitive agreements and excessive fees charged by an App Store have anything in common, it is that they all remain branches

91. *See* Draft Guidelines, para. 17.

to a tree of yet unclear nature. EU competition law at large faces increasing external pressure to advocate its political nature and aid Europe in a daunting challenge – a growth and autonomy agenda.

Ironically enough, the claims for 'fair competition' to substitute the ordoliberal structure of our competition rules may prove counterproductive. EU competition law, through Articles 101 and 102 TFEU alongside merger control, is inherently *pro-competitive*. To posit these market correcting tools as pathways to shape markets would be to abandon the 'relative efficiency criterion' that underlies the current application of rules in the EU.

On the one hand, if the Commission persists in the path toward an objectification of abuse, as *Android Auto* showcased, then the devil should be in the details – there must be two sides to the table, after all. For conduct such that no 'abuse by object' could be established, then the standard of proof for the Commission should be heightened. The current framework whereby there is no need to demonstrate actual harm to the competitive structure and causation by law is sufficient needs should be replaced by a reinforced economics-based approach. For conduct such that an 'abuse by object' could be inferred, there should be a more structured dialogue between the Commission and undertakings to understand how this behaviour could have trickle-down procompetitive effects. Furthermore, if abuse is eventually found, the current framework for remedies is deficient – off with it, and let us welcome the proposals for a more dynamic dialogue between authorities and undertakings.[92]

On the other hand, if the Commission persists in seeking dominance where only superior bargaining power lies, this should be done not by superfluous assessments of the relative market, but by detailed incorporation of the HCC test into the product market definition, emulative of its geographic counterpart application. In any event, we should trust the four-layered system of EU competition enforcement and use the incoming revision of Regulation 1/2003 to establish clearer rules for pre-emption between national and central authorities to police concomitant objectives of rules ensuring market openness, freedom and participation.

It is perhaps at the level of the national jurisdiction where best fits an extractive logic behind abuse below dominance or abuse of hypothetical as efficient competitors. This is because: (i) of the possibility to lawfully pursue concomitant objectives to Article 102 TFEU in lawsuits which are built under this tenet's criteria; and (ii) the single market imperative which guides the ordoliberal, or structuralist, nature of Article 102 TFEU. An anti-extractive limb to Article 102 TFEU shares the logic of justifications for free movement restrictions enacted by Member States, more so than the market access logic behind free movement provisions.

92. *See*, to this effect, Ibáñez Colomo, P. (2025). *Remedies in EU Antitrust Law*. Journal of Competition Law & Economics, 21(2), 137-162, https://doi.org/10.1093/joclec/nhae022.

Part IV Epilogue

Article 102 TFEU: When Do You Know Whether You Comply or Not?

Philip Lowe

When I went back in September 2002 to DG Competition to be Director General for Competition in the European Commission, there were many ongoing cases which more than occupied my available working hours as well as those of my colleagues. Beyond mergers, perhaps the most challenging one was created by the complaints of a number of high-tech companies against the practices of Microsoft, in particular on issues of interoperability with the Windows operating system and of tying and bundling applications with Windows. By the time I became involved in the Microsoft case in 2003, the Commission had already issued two statements of objections against Microsoft but it was not until after a third statement of objections which was issued in August 2003, that we felt sufficiently confident that our concerns about Microsoft's abuse of its dominant position could be defended successfully in court.

Under the guidance of the then Competition Commissioner Mario Monti, we intensified discussions with Microsoft towards the end of 2003 and at the beginning of 2004 to see whether the case could be resolved by an agreed settlement or whether it would be necessary for the Commission to take a formal decision against Microsoft. A settlement would have had the advantage of more immediate compliance with the agreed terms but a decision against the company would obviously establish an important legal precedent which would potentially encourage dominant companies to pay serious attention to the responsibility on them to behave in compliance with Article 102 of the EU Treaty. After all what case law existed then with respect to Article 102 at least reminded dominant companies that they had a special responsibility to avoid abusive conduct which would harm competition, competitors and consumers.

As is now well-known, the discussions with Microsoft at the time were inconclusive and the Commission took the first of a number of decisions against Microsoft in March 2004.

In hindsight, I do not lose any sleep on the justification for that decision.

I did however lose some sleep about the wider question as to whether a company such as Microsoft could have predicted that its behaviour was anti-competitive and what were the potential consequences of non-compliance. Few competition law enforcers had any concern about the capacity of a global hi-tech company to pay a large fine. A fine as a percentage of turnover was reasonable and companies such as these could easily pay them. But the reputational damage to firms which were the subject of antitrust decisions was arguably more important. So too are the private damage actions which could follow from the decision of antitrust authorities. They could potentially have a substantial impact on shareholder value. So is it not reasonable for firms to demand a minimum amount of predictable rule on how Article 102 will be applied?

You could of course argue that knowing when you are compliant with the relatively abstract provisions of Article 102 (*see* the text box) is a difficult task. I asked AI Chat GBT to comment and its answer was fairly predictable: 'Compliance with article 102 requires ongoing diligence and proactive management of competitive practice', which I think basically means that any dominant firm can muddle through, prolong the debate with competition authorities, make some limited concessions and hopefully avoid any major decisions against it.

After all, both firms and competition authorities can agree for different reasons that every case has specific facts and needs to be assessed on its merits. For competition authorities, this means they have the freedom to attack any conduct which they like. For firms, it means that they can endlessly dance around the playground in the hope that they will never be caught. Or at least they will delay investigations and make any solution proposed by a competition authority for rapidly changing markets look as if it is tackling yesterday's problem with a now irrelevant solution.

My intuition, then in 2004 and still today, is that leaving firms without clear guidance as to whether their conduct may be anticompetitive or not is on the one hand bad for them – no predictability or certainty with respect to many practices- and bad for competition law enforcement – no deterrence effect against clearly anti-competitive conducts and no possibility for competition authorities to concentrate their scarce resources on difficult and problematic cases.

So on the one hand from the point of view of due process and fairness to firms targeted by Article 102 enforcement and on the other hand from the point of view of the effectiveness of that enforcement, allowing 102 enforcement to proceed without any guidance on the principles and priorities behind it was in my view problematic. For these reasons, I and a number of like-minded colleagues in DG Competition launched the idea of guidelines on the application of Article 102.

It was of course immediately opposed within and outside the Commission as an attempt to limit the discretion of the Commission to go after the cases it wanted to. Guidelines obviously bind the Commission but do not bind courts or defending or intervening parties. Some also said that it weakened competition law enforcement overall. They believed that a competition authority should not provide any serious element of predictability. It should be able, like a cat hiding in a bush in the garden, to leap out and catch wrongdoers unawares.

In my view, this approach ignores in particular the fundamental realities of effective and efficient law enforcement. The deterrence effect of making it clear to companies that there are conducts to be avoided (in a red zone) in general far outweighs the risk that by creating a green zone of conducts, an authority would let through conducts which are at the margin of being anti-competitive. At the same time, conducts which are more difficult to assess from a competition point of view and can with sufficient resources be investigated rigorously in the public interest and also with full respect for the interests and rights of defending companies and of complainants.

However, there is a parallel balance to be achieved between giving greater predictability to companies while at the same time ensuring that most conducts which are anticompetitive are proscribed (avoiding so-called Type 2 error) and that most conducts which are neutral or procompetitive are allowed through (avoiding Type 1 error).

This task is not easy, as evidenced by the debates which have followed the adoption of the Guidance Paper in Enforcement Priorities under Article 102 and the recent publication by the Commission of Draft Guidelines for the enforcement of Article 102. The interpretation of the provisions of Article 102, particularly on specific commercial practices, cannot result in black or white judgments. Within any published Guidelines, there can be several shades of grey: burden of proof on the parties to prove there is no harm to competition, rebuttable presumptions, safe harbours and so on. Case law is also necessarily case-specific and it is rare for judges to draft judgment as if they were guidelines. But in an administrative system, the responsibility for providing guidance surely lies with the administrative authority and not simply on the guidance provided by court judgments.

The issue of the workability of Article 102 enforcement is also relevant here. It would for example be inefficient and ineffective to expect competition authorities to carry the burden of investigation of cases where there is sufficient historical evidence to suggest that anti-competitive behaviour can be presumed without much difficulty. For these cases, the burden of fact and argument to be provided by the competition law enforcer should be much lighter.

However, absent somebody of *ex-ante* rules and/or guidance based on past cases and empirical evidence, both defending companies and competition authorities will in my view be on the high seas. And for competition authorities, this means they will not be able to establish any meaningful priorities in enforcement in a situation where they will continue to have limited resources to investigate cases. For companies, this implies accepting AI Chat GBT's conclusion which I repeat: 'Compliance with article 102 requires ongoing diligence and proactive management of competitive practices'. Guidelines make that task much easier.

www.ingramcontent.com/pod-product-compliance
Lightning Source LLC
Chambersburg PA
CBHW070251260926
51849CB00001BA/142
9789403506999